Adolescents' DEVELOPMENT *and* &DUCATION

A Janus Knot

Edited by

RALPH L. MOSHER
Boston University

McCutchan Publishing Corporation
2526 Grove Street
Berkeley, California 94704

ISBN 0-8211-1253-8
Library of Congress Catalog Card Number 78-62642

Cover illustration and design by Catherine Conner, Griffin Graphics
Typesetting composition by TypArt in AlphaSette English

To Robin Mosher, who taught me more about adolescence than I wanted to know, particularly that nothing requires a parent to be so unfailingly adult.

To Dick and Sandy Krasker, who let me write at the "White House" (down Maine, that is).

To Pat Fox, whose rigor and excellence as editor contributed so substantially to this book.

Contributors

Donald H. Blocher, Professor of Education, Department of Counseling, Psychology and Student Development, State University of New York, Albany

John M. Broughton, Assistant Professor of Psychology and Education, Teachers College, Columbia University

Charles Bujold, Professor of Psychology and Education, Department of Counseling and Guidance, Laval University

Everett Dulit, Clinical Associate Professor, Cornell Medical College, and Director, Adolescent Psychiatry, New York Hospital-Cornell Medical Center-Westchester Division

Henry Dupont, Visiting Professor of Elementary and Secondary Education, Department of Elementary and Secondary Education, University of Wisconsin, Eau Claire

Robert F. Durham, Assistant Director, Pine Canyon Boys' Ranch, a home for troubled adolescents, Tooele, Utah

David Elkind, Professor of Psychology, University of Rochester

V. Lois Erickson, Assistant Professor, Department of Psychoeducational Studies, University of Minnesota

Erik H. Erikson, Professor of Human Development, Emeritus, Harvard University

Carol Gilligan, Assistant Professor of Education, Graduate School of Education, Harvard University

Marilyn A. Johnston, open classroom teacher, Dillworth Elementary School, Salt Lake City, Utah

Lawrence Kohlberg, Professor of Education and Social Psychology, Harvard University

Thomas J. Ladenburg, history teacher, Brookline High School, Brookline, Massachusetts

Anton E. Lawson, Assistant Professor of Science Education, Department of Physics, Arizona State University, Tempe

Jane Loevinger, Professor of Psychology, Washington University

Rochelle S. Mayer, Research Associate, Baker Street College, New York

Fred M. Newmann, Professor of Curriculum and Instruction, Department of Curriculum and Instruction, University of Wisconsin

Michael J. Parsons, Associate Professor, Division of Cultural Foundations of Education, University of Utah

R. S. Peters, Professor of Philosophy of Education, Institute of Education, University of London

John W. Renner, Professor of Science Education, College of Education, University of Oklahoma

Seymour B. Sarason, Professor of Psychology, Yale University

Peter Scharf, Assistant Professor, Department of Social Ecology, University of California, Irvine

Robert L. Selman, Lecturer on Education, Graduate School of Education, Harvard University

Norman A. Sprinthall, Professor of Educational Psychology, Department of Psychoeducational Studies, University of Minnesota

Sheila F. Stanley, psychologist, Central New Hampshire Community Mental Health Services, Concord

Paul J. Sullivan, Director, Ethical Quest in a Democratic Society Project, Tacoma Public Schools, Tacoma, Washington

Thomas C. Wilson, Director, Student Development Center, Loyola Marymount University, Los Angeles

Contents

Introduction

A colleague, not knowing of my editorship of this work, remarked recently: "Why would anyone write another book on adolescence?" An answer to that question may be the best introduction to this book. Publishers' market surveys (a process no writer questions) indicate a significant potential audience for new material on adolescents, their development and education. This is, presumably, related to the fact that the baby boom of the late 1950's and early 1960's is now at flood tide in American high schools and homes. While understanding and dealing with the largest number of teenagers we will have in this society in the next twenty-five years is an eminently practical motivation, I believe that schoolmen's interest runs deeper than this. My view is that profound new bodies of knowledge about adolescents and their education recently have appeared and that many educators are aware of their existence if not their content and implications for schooling. One of the most important reasons for publishing this book, in fact, is to present a summary of current developmental knowledge of adolescents and how they grow as well as describe and analyze some of the new educational programs intended to stimulate their all-around growth. Such a book does not exist and can be justified as timely for psychologists and educators.

Coming of Age in America

What is this new knowledge about adolescents and their education? Let me illustrate by reference to that holiest of holies in the mission of the high school—teaching youths to think. Harvard University awarded Jean Piaget an honorary doctorate in 1936. But it is only in the last five to ten years in this country that the major implications for education of the accumulating knowledge about how and under what conditions human

1

beings develop cognitively has begun to register on school people. One might take as an example early adolescence, when change is so significant that it can be compared to the child's acquisition of language. And anyone who has observed that earlier change knows how profoundly learning to talk alters the child's relationship with his world and the way people respond to him.

I am referring, of course, to the shift from what Piaget calls concrete operations—thinking that is anchored in and limited by reality as the child experiences it—to "formal operations" or abstract thinking—thinking that builds on thinking. Let me illustrate the problems of communication between people living in these two different cognitive worlds. The channel selection dial on the family TV set broke recently. I solved the problem rather cleverly by substituting the UHF dial for the regular one. This meant, however, that selection of channels depended either on being able to substitute, mentally, low numbers for high numbers or on a procedure of "seek and ye shall find." My eight-year-old daughter was watching "ZOOM" (which in my area appears on Channel 2). At the end of the program I asked her to turn the dial to Channel 4 so that I might watch the evening news. Note my unexpressed solution: two turns to the left. Pammy made several abortive attempts to find the channel by turning the dial. Note her problem: what and where is Channel 4? Observing her inability to find the channel, I said, probably somewhat impatiently, "Pammy, where is Channel 4?" Immediately she picked up the broken channel dial, carried it to where I was sitting, pointed to the number 4 on it, and said, conclusively, "Here it is, daddy."

The intellectual capacity to deal with abstract hypotheses, relationships, theories, symbols, ideals, problems, and reasoning—things that never were and never will be concrete—is critically essential to success in much of the secondary school program. And yet, until recently, we have not been aware of or sensitive to this development in adolescence. (One of the many unfortunate educational consequences of IQ testing has been the idea that a student's intellectual ability was a constant; either he was bright or dull, and that was that. The concept of mental age, which was closer to the "reality" of cognitive development as now understood, never received the attention it should have.) We have created and taught curricula that flew in the face of the fact that many kids (like Pammy) are simply unready or unable to deal with an implicit intellectual demand. Several of the innovative and imaginative curricula of the 1960's may have foundered here. Nor have we attempted to establish whether our ways of educating adolescents in fact contribute anything to this critical increment in human intelligence. Indeed, I suspect a careful study using Piagetian developmental measures of the traditional subject areas in the high school in terms of success in teaching students to think would produce explosive findings. (See Ladenburg's discussion of this issue in Chapter 9.) My hunch is that we teach teenagers new content but not new ways of thinking; we teach them answers, which are conventional, sophisticated, or useful, rather than how to think about and act on problems. The essential point is that developmental psychology calls into question the cognitive fit of much of our present curricular material and pedagogy as these relate to adolescents, while at the same time establishing that this is a prime time for education. The issues in this paradox are: When does the individual adolescent make this transition to rational and abstract thought? What kinds of intellectual and educational experiences contribute to this development? What are the implications for present or alternate education programs if the bottle for any given class of adolescents can be half full and half empty cognitively? Dulit (see Chapter 1) estimates that only one-third to one-half of American adolescents and adults achieve fully this capacity for formal thought.

A further illustration that current developmental knowledge of children and adolescents and how they grow has profound implications for their education is to be found in Kohlberg's research on moral development. Most people who write about adolescents, for example, refer to the idealism of this age group. Adolescents have to make difficult personal decisions as to what is right and what is wrong. Their moral concern and sensibility easily may be subverted into rigid political ideology, into new and exotic moralities or religions, or into despair. Underlying all of this is a concern to make moral and ethical sense of their world. Ritual disagreements with authorities (for example, parents or teachers) and an idolatry of unconventional flora (for example, grass) and fauna (What adult can dig Elton John's costumes?) mask a profound adolescent movement toward the social and moral conventions of family, church, and state. Indeed, if adolescence goes according to the developmental script, it is a rehearsal and perfecting of the lines, roles, norms, and rules of being adult. In a social sense, adolescence means giving up an exclusive selfishness, a hedonism, and an instrumental use of others. The perspective that replaces this "Me Firstism" is a gradually enlarging recognition of the rights and feelings of other people—typically friends and family—that can also encompass a genuine concern, too, for others in the family of man. How else can one explain the idealism of twenty-five-mile walkathons for victims of muscular dystrophy or fasts for African famine relief?

Because of Kohlberg's major theoretical contributions, we have a relatively clear blueprint for this aspect of human development: the characteristics of moral reasoning in childhood and adolescence, its progression, and some, at least, of the experiences critical to its stimulation. A précis of Kohlberg's Stage 2 moral reasoning or that of Stage 3 would be premature here; it appears in Chapter 2. And yet these stages are powerful characterizations or metaphors for preadolescence and adolescence. The knowledge that systematic discussion of moral dilemmas, learning to understand the thinking and feeling of other people, action on behalf of social and moral goals, and experiences in democratic rule making and in creating fairer institutions can stimulate development from Stage 2 to Stage 3 is both less gratuitous to the reader and what we should expect from developmental education. Indeed, knowledge specific enough to order these experiences and others to stimulate consecutive development is an aim and criterion of developmental education. Part II of the book returns to this challenge. The general point is that developmental psychology, in Kohlberg's work, has established with considerable validity and exactness "what [moral] tendencies are especially seeking expression at a particular time." The evidence of developmental psychology also is that the child, and especially the adolescent, is less likely to develop any more sophisticated ethical position as an adult if his natural efforts to create a personal moral philosophy are unsupported by systematic moral education. Thus, adolescence is established by developmental psychology as a prime time for values or ethical education of a nonindoctrinative character—something eschewed by American public schools for forty years.

The world of work also affects adolescents, with the degree depending upon social class. Work may be nothing more than a part-time job at MacDonalds as a way to achieve some financial independence of one's family. The minimum wage is, of course, an index of becoming one's own person. Work also can be an imminent issue for students going into the armed services or into apprentice training at the end of high school. For many adolescents, those who are college bound, the issue is more what college than what job. For them, career decisions are deferred until the end of college or perhaps longer. But work, as one more attribute of what it is to be adult, impinges on the adolescent.

It is almost a cliché in the discussion of adolescence to talk about this period in terms of the formation of identity. Erik Erikson's belief that the central problem the teenager faces is to define himself—to decide who he is and will become—has probably been the most influential theory of American adolescence in the past twenty-five years. It and a recent statement by Erikson on the ideologies that will compete for young people's identities in 2000 are included in Chapter 4. The position is, essentially, that adolescents are struggling to form more comprehensive answers to the question: "Who am I?" Their new intellectual capabilities are applied to (indeed, permit) that question. Ethically they are trying to answer it; this is also true in the development of new competencies and in the context of their relationship with peers. One of the theses of this book, particularly Part II, is that because this question is a central one, developmentally, it must also be a basic focus of education.

The most contemporary and comprehensive theory of ego development is that advanced by Jane Loevinger (see Chapter 3). Her descriptions of ego stages tell us much about the person's character development, his social "style," what he thinks about most, and how his mind works. For example, many adolescents are at the conformist stage of ego development. They conform to external rules and express shame or guilt for breaking rules. In the social sphere they are concerned to belong and evidence a superficial niceness to friends. They are consciously pre-occupied with their appearance, with social acceptance by peers, and with what adults consider "banal" feelings and behavior (such as endless telephone discussions concerning friends of both sexes and buying and listening to rock music). The conformist tends, conceptually, to simplifications. He uses many stereotypes about adolescents different than himself ("He hangs around with rich snobs from Chestnut Hill." "They're jocks; they only drink milk.") and clichés ("That's cool." "Shine her on."). The essential point here is that Loevinger's data are especially rich in describing, empirically, a wide and central strand of the teenager's development: his ego and character.

What is often not said about adolescents is that they can be remarkably competent. Some adolescents can learn to teach or counsel other people as effectively as graduate students or practicing professionals. They can carry out sophisticated programs of social research and action. They learned to fly military aircraft and helicopters in Vietnam. They can produce musicals, conduct complicated scientific experiments, and write subtle poetry. Extensive opportunities to do these things are essential if adolescents are to develop into competent adults. There is much psychological and educational evidence to support this. Adolescents need opportunities to take active social roles, to have significant and systematic responsibility for analysis and action on real problems, and to be held accountable.

In summary, physical development is completed in adolescence. Although it is typical for the adolescent to be uncomfortable or self-conscious about his or her body, it is adult. And its most interesting parts achieve sexual maturity. Adult intellectual capacity is being reached. Though much knowledge and most wisdom lie ahead, the kind of thinking that will characterize adult life is already operating. Idealism is strong. Direct family influence wanes and is supplanted by that of contemporaries. Economic independence from the family increasingly is possible, as are many adult competencies. The rites of passage to adulthood (a driver's license, leaving school, legal drinking, voting) are available or within view. And it behooves all adults in sensitive roles relative to that coming of age—teachers, counselors, and parents—to know all they can about, and to care redemptively for, the generation most closely following them.

Development as the Aim of Education

A second general assumption underlies this book and has to do with so simple a question as the purpose of education. That purpose is the stimulation of individual development. The education of adolescents must stimulate cognitive or intellectual growth, moral sensibilities and reasoning, social skills, vocational competencies, aesthetic development, and physical maturation. The basic idea is that education should discern and provide those systematic experiences or stimuli that give the individual the greatest opportunity to develop or grow in interaction with his environment.

This is a conception of education as old or as "progressive" as John Dewey: "Only knowledge of the order and connection of the stages in the development of the psychical functions can insure the full maturing of the psychical powers. Education is the work of supplying the conditions which will enable the psychical functions, as they successively arise, to mature and pass into higher functions in the freest and fullest manner . . . ."[1] Dewey's view that the aim of education is human development is analyzed at length in Chapter 8. Kohlberg and Mayer have recently restated it (also in Chapter 8):

The . . . stream of educational ideology which is still best termed "progressive," following Dewey . . . holds that education should nourish the child's natural inter-action with a developing society or environment . . . development [is] a progression through invariant ordered sequential stages. The educational goal is the eventual attainment of a higher level or stage of development in adulthood, not merely the healthy functioning of the child at a present level . . . this aim requires an educational environment that actively stimulates development through the presentation of resolvable but genuine problems or conflicts. For progressives, the organizing and developing force in the child's experience is the child's active thinking, and thinking is stimulated by the problematic, by cognitive conflict. Educative experience makes the child think—think in ways which organize both cognition and emotion . . . the acquisition of "knowledge" is *an active change in patterns of thinking* brought about by experiential problem-solving situations.[2]

What educators now have available to them is an extraordinary amount of psychological knowledge about human development that was not "known" to Dewey. Morris Cogan used to say that the problem with educational psychology was not how little we knew about the learner and the processes of teaching or learning but how little *use* we made in teaching of what we knew. The central thesis of this book is that this steadily increasing body of knowledge about the stage, sequence, and causes of individual development tied to Dewey's philosophical case for development as the aim of education can lead to a renewed emphasis on and greater effectiveness for developmental education in this country.

But why argue for a neoprogressivism? A personal reminiscence may provide part of the answer. My first teaching experience was twenty years ago in a small town in Nova Scotia. I was asked to tutor an attractive eighth-grade girl in Canadian history. I coached her energetically, seriously, and unquestioningly on the residual powers clause of the British North America Act and similar mysteries. That was my thing, I knew it, and Canadian history had, I am sure, the support of the community. Gayle dutifully tried to learn, but she was distracted. Part of her distraction was explained by what I learned several months later—she was pregnant. My academic singularity in the face of her crisis and need as a person has been a source of much reflection in the intervening years. In a larger sense, I was confronting an old educational conundrum: that whole adolescents sat in my high school classrooms. For example, Boyd, older than the others, embarrassed to be in the tenth grade, a gifted hockey player, terribly willing and decent, but confused and dull in the subjects that were my specialty; Linda, very quiet, bright, conscientious, and plain; Donald, handsome, hard working, ambitious to go to college but very average. All my students, as people, had gifts and promise; all, as humans, were flawed. Perhaps their youth and mine prevented both of us from a full recognition of what that meant. But certainly my commitment to teach them the things I had learned in college—history, economics, geography—which their parents paid me to teach and on which an educational establishment (or "Regents") examined them stringently, and our social roles as "teacher" and "student" blinded me to the broader compass of the things *they* were concerned to learn and become.

Another part of the case for developmental education stems from the disillusion of a counseling psychologist, which is, actually, a long and a short way from teaching constitutional history to Gayle to thousands of hours of counseling Harvard graduate students and American high school students. Suffice to say that I, like many others, succumbed to the romantic, client-centered belief that the way truly to help is to listen, support, and clarify the confusion and pain that mark most young people's coming of age. Certainly the focus on the personal, social, and career dilemmas faced by young people seemed valid. And it *was* possible to be of help by listening and supporting empathically. The vicarious participation in other people's private lives was undoubtedly part of the fascination, as was becoming expert at a craft—counseling. But the myth that counseling or therapy was some kind of model or ideal for education (Carl Rogers on one end of a log) simply could not be sustained. The connotation that such problems and adolescents are better understood in terms of "mental health" rather than development, the reluctance of counselors to challenge their clients intellectually or ethically, the scent of pathology about the whole therapy-counseling enterprise, always troubled me. The evidence as to the lack of training[3] and effect[4] of school counselors, added to the patent injustice of providing special services to only one out of five high school students who have a right to them, became irrefutable.

Lawrence Cremin has observed that the guidance counselor is the most characteristic child of the progressive movement in American education.[5] But what happens to disillusioned counselors? For me, the answer is to go back to the underlying ideals and assumptions of progressivism: helping the individual develop to the fullest his mind, body, character, person, career, arts, and societies is the most valid objective of education in a democracy. Such neoprogressivism can be built, as noted before, on a much deeper psychological knowledge of what contributes to human growth in these areas. It will require educational programs—the provision of systematic opportunities for the adolescent to study and act on a wide range of personal and social problems—that go substantially beyond, but need not reject, constitutional law or empathy as means to human development.

Educating the Whole Child

Personal anecdotes do not constitute my entire case that the individual's development and his education must be conceived holistically. It has already been established that a concern with complete human development is a heritage of the progressive education movement. Dewey gave the idea of stimulating rationality, character, and social responsibility respectability in American education, even though it was ultimately misapplied and ridiculed as "so little for the mind." Certainly to argue the case for progressivism is hardly to argue something new or radical although it may be misinterpreted as arguing something permissive or soft.

A second argument is made powerfully, if metaphorically, by the song "Tradition" from *Fiddler on the Roof.* Education has always arrogated to itself the stimulation of intellect, of teaching people to think. The degree of success, as noted earlier, is another matter. While the personal development of students has been honored more by pious commencement rhetoric than by actual schooling, it has been at least a secondary concern behind some curricula in English and social studies, or it reflects the private guilt of committed teachers and counselors. It is one reason for many alternative schools.

Willy Loman in *Death of a Salesman* is asked by a son if he did not get lonely during all his years on the road. He replies: "Lonely? Loneliness goes with the territory." In an analogous sense educators profoundly, if unintentionally, affect the identities, the values, the personal esteem of students through the hidden curriculum of schools. Affecting the whole human being inexorably goes with the territory of formal education. Further, it is perfectly obvious that people grow and live in three dimensions. Adolescents do not go to school, or live outside it, simply from the neck up. To conceive of education on one dimension only—mind (or affect, or character)—is myopic, neglecting the way people grow and live. It is arguing the obvious to say that we have to put mind-body and mind-other dualisms aside.

Finally, and by definition, people whose development and education are whole will be socially more responsible and competent. While it may be committing the naturalistic fallacy, any careful analysis of the "higher" stages of ego, moral, or social development indicates that an enlarged social perspective and responsibility, acceptance of social convention and law, an effort to consider others' rights and to be fair, and individuation responsive to principle are at the heart of the individual's development.

A holistic conception of education for human development, then, guards against idolatry of intellect, joy, the sensate, morality, political action, or any singular conception of what about human beings is of most worth. Educational dualisms, whether they be mind-body, mind-affect, or another, become pointless. The answer to each aspect of growth is yes. Morally, how can educators deny each individual the right to maximum growth? It is clear that the position commits the naturalistic fallacy; let us hope it gets away with it. What *is* in the process of human development—an interrelated progression along major dimensions of human thinking and behavior—should be reflected in a comprehensive set of educational experiences to support and stimulate cognition, morality, emotions, ego, social life, career, the aesthetic, and the physical. Seeing human development in its whole potential and sequence guards against educational support for unbridled individualism—the "do your own thing" Stage 4½ ethic, the bourgeois liberalism against which Chairman Mao and those of us who care about this society and the individual's contribution to it inveigh. "The method of correction is primarily to strengthen education so as to rectify individualism ideologically . . . . In our educational work we must explain that in its social origin individualism is a reflection within the Party of petit-bourgeois and bourgeois ideas."[6] The aim of enhancing all-around and optimal human growth may also guard against the other half of that dualism: educating people solely to be conventional.

Profound and recurring questions about the size, curricular priorities, and adverse effects on students' development of the American high school are also a part of the case for developmental education. Sprinthall and I present this critique in Chapter 8. The analysis will be briefly reviewed here. Our view is that schools, either city, suburban, or rural, have tended to define their role as the transmitters of academic ideas and skills. Recent efforts at reform have been directed toward revitalizing the existing academic curriculum and its teaching. Little intellectual energy or funding has been directed toward reformulating education—developing essentially new curricula and new forms of educating adolescents. In most schools and in most eras the personal side of education has had a lower priority than the academic. There has always been extensive rhetoric about individual growth, but, in fact, personal or psychological development was largely the result of random and inimical forces in the school. It is obvious that poor black and white children have indelibly learned to regard themselves with self-contempt as a result of schooling.[7]

The real question is how well the American high school is achieving either the academic or personal and social development of its students. Passow[8] recently summarized both the indictment and proposals for change in our high schools. I am aware that criticism is easy while constructive reformulation of education is complex, hard work. Nor do I have a temperamental need to change institutions that are working; indeed, I think we do so at great cost. But, if educators cannot point with certainty to significant benefits that the high school provides its students, and, if the human costs appear to be negative for many poor black and white teenagers, then the profession is between the proverbial rock and a hard place.

Thus, we return to the summary case for developmental education. It derives from a distinctively American conception and belief that the education of the person must be whole: it must stimulate cognitive or intellectual growth, moral reasoning and action, emotional growth, social skills, vocational competencies, aesthetic development, and a sound body. The basic purpose of education is overall ego or personal development within a democratic society. The explicit assumption is that all people are equal before the law and have a moral right to an education that will fully develop their potential. Only such an education is truly democratic.

The traditional academic curriculum, by contrast, is elitist and may very well be hollow at the core of its proudest claim—that it teaches adolescents to think. The argument is not that the traditional system be eliminated. To the extent that the academic disciplines can be demonstrated or used to stimulate human rationality, morality, and social consciousness, they have a significant place in developmental education. I suspect that if adolescents can study psychology by doing psychology or history by experiencing the process of research—piecing together clues and inferences about the problematic in America's history or taking the role of actual historical figures—then it may be possible to have both the discipline and development. Ladenburg and Renner and Lawson argue this position persuasively in Chapter 9. That a fundamental educational concern with adolescent development will go beyond reformulated curriculum and teaching of the disciplines becomes clear in Part II of the book. This part describes substantial educational experiences for teenagers in school governance, social service and political action in the community, women's development, and joint efforts with parents to modify the structure of justice in the family. An education for all-around adolescent growth will be far more involved with learning environments and resources outside the school than is the present curriculum. But the case for or against the old regime is not the concern of this book.

Notes

1. J. Dewey and J. McLellan, "The Psychology of Number," in *John Dewey on Education: Selected Writings,* ed. R. Archambault (New York: Random House, 1964), 207.

2. L. Kohlberg and R. Mayer, "Development as the Aim of Education," *Harvard Educational Review*, 42 (November 1972), 454-455.

3. D. J. Armor, *The American School Counselor: A Case Study in the Sociology of Professions* (New York: Russell Sage Foundation, 1969).

4. T. Volsky *et al., The Outcomes of Counseling and Psychotherapy* (Minneapolis: University of Minnesota Press, 1965); A. E. Bergin, "The Evaluation of Therapeutic Outcomes," in *Handbook of Psychotherapy and Behavior Change*, ed. *id.* and S. L. Garfield (New York: John Wiley, 1971).

5. Lawrence Cremin, "The Progressive Heritage of the Guidance Movement," in *Guidance: An Examination*, ed. R. Mosher *et al.* (New York: Harcourt, Brace and World, 1965).

6. Mao Tse-tung, *Five Articles* (Peking: Foreign Language Press, 1972), 46.

7. James S. Coleman, *The Adolescent Society* (New York: Free Press, 1961); Jonathan Kozal, *Death at an Early Age* (Boston: Houghton Mifflin, 1967).

8. A. Harry Passow, "The Future of the High School," *Teachers College Record*, 79 (September 1977), 15-31.

I
Adolescent Development

The purpose of Part I is to introduce modern psychological theories or conceptions of human development, particularly as they describe the interrelated components of adolescent growth: intellectual, moral, ego, identity, vocational, and aesthetic. The chapters in this part follow that order of presentation without implying that any strand of development is more defining of, or critically valued in, human beings. If pressed for priorities, I probably would emphasize intellect and character; the average teenager might say that formation of identity and social or sexual development are most compelling; the reader may have yet another perspective on what is of most worth in human beings or teenagers. The objective of Part I is to acknowledge and honor, if not describe, *all* facets of human growth. It is the basic ideological premise of the book that we need psychology to comprehend and education to support the many pathways along which adolescents are coming of age. That they do so asymmetrically (of which their physical development can be a classic example) should not obscure the wholeness and the complexity that they are trying to actualize. Indeed, complex integrative understanding (and educational practice) is especially necessary for those who would help because the adolescent is struggling with an analogous, elusive task—individuation—of understanding who he is in the new complexity of his life. Neither the compartmentalized nature of the book nor deletions of topics resulting from space limitations should obscure for the reader the need to understand integratively, and educate for, whole adolescents.

The impossibility of telling the whole story of adolescent growth in Part I is evident. Readers will not find any extensive discussion of physical growth, the emergence of political beliefs and ideology, religious thought, social cognition in general, the psychopathology of adolescence—the delinquency, rage, suicide, or the more endemic pain and confusion that

15

so preempt the analysis of this stage in many theories and texts. The experience of adolescence among minority groups in America and an examination of adolescence as a stage in the human life cycle similarly are integral to any genuinely holistic understanding of this time of life. There are reasons, of course, why all these topics are not covered: space limitations; the fact that some at least, of these matters, are the standard fare of many texts on adolescence while modern developmental theories are not; and the objective of bringing together in one book both theory and education for adolescent development.

From another point of view, we simply do not know the whole story of adolescent development. In an epistemological sense, that will always be true. Many analysts of adolescence are satisfied with the explanation of this time of life as Oedipus revisited and with Anna Freud's view that all teenagers are crazy at times. About the only thing adults can do is wait out the period. The developmental psychologists included in this book might be more prone to argue that they know too little as yet about adolescence, that what they know is certainly insufficient to plan educational programs based on their knowledge.

In this regard, Piaget's investigation of how thinking and logic evolve, Kohlberg's studies of moral development, Loevinger's research on the ego, Selman's studies of social cognition, and Erikson's clinical investigation of the formation of identity are relatively advanced. Certainly the glass of what we know about these dimensions of adolescent development is at least half full. Conversely, the glass of what we know about affective, vocational, and aesthetic development is at least half empty. Dupont's chapter on affective development, Bujold's conception of vocation, and Parsons' studies of developmental stages in the aesthetic judgment of children and adolescents are not included, however, simply for symmetry. They are, rather, in Part I because of their theoretical promise and their power to reorient for education these critical dimensions of teenage development. Lewin has said that there is nothing so practical as a good theory. We might add that there is nothing so generative for theory as good practice. Another aim of the book is to fuel that interaction.

Thus, Part I is written for serious students of psychology, but it is also for teachers, counselors, administrators, and graduate students in education who are prepared to roll up their sleeves and do some careful reading in order to understand and use the material professionally.

Papers critical of the developmental theories and their application to education are also included. It is my belief that these theories have a philosophical and intellectual weight that can stand up to hard questions. In my own introductory commentaries on each theory I attempt to balance description and critical analysis.

1
Some Preliminary Thinking about Teenage Thinking

The book begins with several excerpts on the nature of adolescent thinking, as developmental psychology and, more particularly, Piaget describe it. In one sense this is a rather conservative, undramatic place to begin a discussion of teenage development. Adolescent dating practices, sexual behavior, use of drugs, or California beach-bum hedonism would be more colorful and attention-getting topics. This book quite unashamedly will focus on the more enduring changes in adolescence that underlie (and may be obscured by) the topical content of teenage existence (rock music and concerts, parties, sports, and so on).

A profound change in human thinking is now in progress. Further, schools, whatever else they may attempt to do, believe that they should teach children to think. And so do I. Indeed, I feel that a unique task of formal education is to provide the conditions that will stimulate in children or adolescents the next higher stage of thinking, more specifically, to assist in the emergence of abstract, reflective thought in adolescence. I suspect that any effective teacher, when asked about his objectives, will say unequivocally that he is trying to help students think more deeply, critically, or comprehensively about, say, American history, modern literature, marine biology, or the distributive principle. Why these objectives do not always materialize in practice is, in part, what these excerpts are about.

Thus, it seems appropriate in a book designed for teachers, administrators, and educators to begin here—with thinking, or cognition, and what modern psychology is saying about its characteristics and development in adolescence. As noted in the Introduction, adolescence is the time when the human capacity for thinking can mature fully. What now becomes feasible for many teenagers is abstraction: to think about the possible and the many things that might be, could be, and should be in their physical, social, and personal worlds. Reality—the concrete things that are, that can be seen, manipulated, and clarified, which bound and preoccupy younger children's thinking (remember Pammy and Channel 4)—begins to shift to the background. What moves to the forefront is a way of thinking and knowing that Piaget calls "formal operations," that is, thinking that builds on thinking, that can conceive of all the logical possibilities in a problem. The adolescent at this stage can think about thoughts, words, ideas, concepts, and hypotheses, and he can do so concerning a wide range of phenomena, from the physical world to real and ideal concepts of himself.

A brief overview of formal operations may be pertinent here although it is the purpose of the contributions by Dulit, Elkind, and Broughton to do this much more fully. Formal operations is the last stage of intellectual development in Piaget's theory; he believed it to be typically attained by all adolescents between the ages of eleven and fifteen. Dulit, Elkind, and others have established that this is not so for American teenagers. Flavell has described formal operations as characterizing human beings "at their cognitive best."[1] Broughton's critique questions whether this way of thinking is either a crowning achievement or the final stage in intellectual development. But what is unique is the emergence of a more comprehensive, logically exhaustive, systematic, and abstract way of thinking that is demonstrated by the manner in which adolescents cope with scientific problems in general and in particular how they reason about events they observe. At this stage of development the person can make hypotheses, arrive at logical deductions, and experimentally verify what he or someone else asserts. He makes logical propositions or statements. The essence of formal thinking is to understand a problem in terms of its full logical complexity, to consider all the possible values of all the possible variables in the problem. In so doing, four ways of thinking are used implicitly: Identity, Negation, Reciprocity, and Correlativity. A concrete illustration of these processes is helpful: "if putting weight onto one side of a previously balanced scale is the initial operation [Identity] then Negation would be directly removing that weight, Reciprocity would be either shifting the pan or adding weight on the other side to restore the balance, and Correlativity would be the operation undoing that reciprocal change thereby leading to the same effect as was created by the initial operation (with which it thus 'correlates')."[2]

Flavell offers another level of description of formal operations as: first, dealing with the real versus the possible, where what actually happens is seen as only one of several hypothetical possibilities; second, relying on hypotheses and the logic of deduction to determine what is real and what is possible; third, being, above all propositional and combinatorial thinking—thinking that systematically considers each variable in a problem as well as all possible combinations thereof. Concerning any developmental theory it is necessary to ask: what is the theory's view of the highest or most mature stage of the particular human competence being analyzed, and from what sample of people were the data collected? It is quite clear that for Piaget the scientific method is central to, indeed the model of, all mature thinking. The tasks used to describe the stage and to test for formal operations, when observed or tried, really resemble high school physics problems. Broughton says: "The root metaphor grounding Piaget's theory is that of the developing child as a little scientist, where 'scientist' is given the very restricted interpretation of 'rule-guided methodologist.'"[3] And he questions, appropriately, whether that kind of thinking is what "Piagetian pedagogy" wants to educate for. But that is to run ahead of our story.

Further, it is interesting that when Dulit first found discrepancies in Piaget's data he thought they might possibly be attributable to real differences in cognitive development between Swiss and American adolescents. The actual differences (100 percent of the Swiss adolescents were at the stage of formal operations while only half of the American teenagers were) had, however, to do with the samples of teenagers being studied in Geneva and in New York.

A first concern of this section is to have the reader grasp what Piaget means by concrete and formal operations, the two stages of intellectual development particularly pertinent to those who teach adolescents. It is my belief that teenagers' ability to think abstractly or formally has much to do with their capacity genuinely to understand what we try to teach them in high school and, in particular, the failure of much abstract curricula and teaching. Elkind laments how much developmental psychology still has to learn about teenage thinking. And these excerpts do not tell us much about what to *do* for adolescents who do not think like scientists. Ashton's cross-cultural summary of the effects of schooling on logical thinking[4] contends that there is some—which is encouraging. There is, however, far too little information on how education can assist the emergence of abstract, reflective thought in adolescence. In my view, some of the most important educational research and development to be done in the next decade will address this kind of issue at the intersection of developmental psychology and education.

It is clear that there are problems involved in stimulating this stage. How to do so, quite apart from whether we should, is largely unstudied.

Puzzling sex differences exist with regard to abstract thinking, as Piaget describes it. Girls do less formal thinking than boys. And that seems suspect. Is it that they apply complex thought to the social and emotional realm, not to the scientific? (Gilligan,[5] for example, believes that women develop a mature morality based on responsibility and caring, not justice, as universal principles. She further criticizes the sexist bias of Kohlberg's research.)

It is clear also that the model of Piaget's formal operations is scientific thought and of a dated, hypothetical-deductive type. That scientific thought is man's "crowning achievement of intellectual development" might be questioned by someone listening to a Beethoven symphony or reading the American Constitution. And there is Broughton's telling point that the intellectual essence of adolescence is as an epistemological stage, when to know oneself becomes the most crucial cognitive process. ". . . there are certain phenomena of adolescence, especially the emergence of self-consciousness or reflection, that Piaget's notion of formal operations cannot explain."[6]

It is also the case that no one challenges the connection between formal operations and performance in mathematics, the sciences, and other aspects of the high school curriculum requiring abstract thinking. Dulit "commonly" found students who did not use fully formal operations and yet "ranked at the top of their class in a difficult and selective school."[7] School achievement results from perspiration as well as inspiration. It is obvious that we need to know much more about the reciprocation between formal operations and formal education. Ashton indicates that schooling contributes to the emergence of formal operations because, among other things, of its emphasis on symbolic thinking. Thus it is important for adolescents to talk about objects without the objects' being present, to discuss ideas about other ideas (for example, the value to a person of being able to think abstractly), and to transfer learning from one task to another. She also says that the use of concrete manipulative materials is crucial to the development of logical operations (that is, representational thought depends upon using our senses and our hands, upon concrete activity). It is perhaps not surprising that poor schooling can have a detrimental effect on cognitive development; Ashton's most critical general point is that schooling—educational experiences, curricula, and teaching—must be related to the student's developmental level if cognitive development is to be enhanced.[8]

Part II of the book returns to the fundamental, enduring challenge for education: to stimulate human rationality, however psychology understands it. Meanwhile, knowledge of the ways adolescents think and know is critical to teaching them in the here and now.

Notes

1. J. H. Flavell, *Developmental Psychology of Jean Piaget* (Princeton, N.J.: D. Van Nostrand, 1963), 87.

2. Everett Dulit, "Adolescent Thinking a la Piaget: The Formal Stage," *Journal of Youth and Adolescence*, 1 (No. 4, 1972), 285.

3. John Broughton, "'Beyond Formal Operations': Theoretical Thought in Adolescence," *Teachers College Record*, 79 (September 1977), 91.

4. Patricia T. Ashton, "Cross-Cultural Piagetian Research: An Experimental Perspective," *Harvard Educational Review*, 45 (November 1975), 475-506.

5. Carol Gilligan, "In a Different Voice: Women's Conception of the Self and of Morality," *ibid.*, 47 (November 1977).

6. Broughton, "'Beyond Formal Operations,'" 94.

7. Dulit, "Adolescent Thinking a la Piaget," 299.

8. Ashton, "Cross-Cultural Piagetian Research," 495.

Adolescent Thinking a la Piaget:
The Formal Stage

Everett Dulit

Introduction

Piaget introduces his concept of the formal stage for the first time and most fully in *The Growth of Logical Thinking from Childhood to Adolescence*, published in English by Basic Books in 1958. The formal stage is the final and highest stage in the sequence of stages described and defined by Piaget in what he calls "genetic epistemology," his systematic conception of the development of intelligence from childhood through adolescence.

This paper reports a replication of some selected parts of that work, with gifted and average adolescents, leading to results which mostly support but which significantly qualify some of the central themes of the Piaget-Inhelder point of view. This paper begins with a brief exposition of the formal stage set against the background of the concrete stage which

Reprinted from *Journal of Youth and Adolescence*, 1 (No. 4, 1972), 281-301, © Plenum Publishing Corporation. This work has been supported by NIMH Research Career Development Award K3-MH-I8, 701. The author wishes to thank Dr. S. Escalona and Professors Piaget and Inhelder for their help and support.

it follows, then reports the experiments and the results, and concludes with a discussion of findings and implications and with some reformulations.

Piaget's genetic epistemology distinguishes four main stages: (1) *the sensorimotor stage*, in the first two years of life; (2) *the egocentric or "pre-operational" stage* (sometimes treated merely as a transitional stage), roughly covering the years two through five; (3) *the concrete stage* of middle childhood, with gradual onset over the years five through eight, gradually giving way in preadolescence and early adolescence to (4) *the formal stage*, characteristic of the years from middle adolescence onward, including adulthood.

The focus in genetic epistemology is on cognition (problem solving, directed thinking) and not on thinking more broadly defined to include motivations, affects, or fantasy. Furthermore, the emphasis throughout is on the study of relatively universal features of cognitive development, with little systematic attention given to the matter of "individual differences"; they are recognized but treated as relatively peripheral matters. Each stage reflects what is essentially an optimal trend within its associated age range.

The Concrete Stage

Thinking in the concrete stage is limited primarily (almost exclusively) to thinking about *things*. (By contrast, in the formal stage thinking is about words, ideas, concepts, hypotheses, propositions, and so forth, in addition to being about things. In this respect, as is generally the case, the formal stage subsumes the concrete stage hierarchically as a part of itself rather than replacing it altogether.) The fundamental "building blocks" of the concrete stage are the Logic of Class and the Logic of Relations.

The *Logic of Class* refers to the child's capacity to handle problems of classification. The child decides whether something is or is not a member of a given class. (The class boundaries are treated as "given." Thinking at this stage is about things, and the class boundaries are, by and large, *not* treated as "things".)

The *Logic of Relations* refers to the child's capacity to relate things of differing size within the context of graded and ordered series. The child can take things of varying sizes and place them in size place, relating any one to any other one within the context of the series. Furthermore, the child can set one series into correspondence with another series by means of "one to one correspondence," which is a major first step toward the mastery of cause and effect relationships.

The operations of this stage, like all others, function generally outside of awareness. In that sense, they are more commonly latent rather than manifest, although they can be made manifest to some degree under circumstances that call for it.

By and large, the concrete-stage child is limited to thinking about actual concrete situations and things as they are presented to him in the real world. (Fantasy and reverie are for these purposes "something else"; the focus here is on cognition, on thinking as directed problem solving.) To be sure, there is some limited capacity in the concrete stage to think about some abstractions (such as "redness," for example), but the degree is sufficiently limited and the "abstractions" are usually sufficiently close to concrete and perceptual realities as to warrant the generalization that thought about abstractions does not come until the formal stage. (One could point in passing to a relation here with the Vigotsky-type tests of "concrete thinking" in schizophrenia and organic mental syndrome, where the thinking of the patient, like that of the concrete-stage child, is much more "bound" to "the thing itself," as compared with the thinking of the normal adult, who is capable of shifting much more flexibly among different ways of categorizing the very same "things.")

The Formal Stage

The distinguishing characteristics of the formal stage are suggested by the three names that are used interchangeably for this stage: "formal," "propositional," "abstract." "Formal" emphasizes that what "counts" is form and not content, as in formal logic where the focus is on the formal relations between the propositions or as in mathematics where an equation represents a formal relation among the symbols that is essentially independent of the particular realities they represent. "Propositional" emphasizes that, as in formal logic, thinking is cast in terms of "propositions," statements, hypotheses. "Abstract" emphasizes that thinking here is no longer bound by "the thing itself" but deals with attributes abstracted from the thing itself; formal-stage thinking deals with words, thoughts, propositions, concepts, hypotheses, ideas, ideologies, as well as with "things" themselves.

Perhaps the single most important hallmark of the formal stage, according to Piaget, is the reversal of the relation between concrete *reality (actuality)* and *possibility*. In the concrete stage, *actuality* is in the foreground. In the formal stage, the relation is reversed and *possibility* comes to the foreground. New possibilities can be derived and are derived from recombinations of the variables inherent in the problem, without regard to whether they were ever previously actualized or experienced. That is perhaps the most crucial new development of the formal stage. What counts in the formal stage is what "could be" and not merely what "is" or "was." Formal-stage thinking is cast in terms of the *full range of possibilities* inherent in the problem or situation at hand. All combinations of all possible values of all the relevant variables are given equal weight in formal-stage thought without regard to whether they are actualized or not. In the actual experiments, the subject commonly "turns away" (sometimes literally) from the setup on the table to deal in thought with some relevant subset of the full matrix of possibilities inherent in the problem and then "turns back" to the actualized situation at hand, which is in that sense treated as "merely the interesting special case at hand."

The fundamental theoretical "building blocks" of the formal stage are the Combinatorial System (sometimes also called the Structured Whole) and the INRC Group of Operations. They are conceptualized as the theoretical foundations of the formal stage, analogous to the Logic of Class and the Logic of Relations for the concrete stage.

The *Combinatorial System* refers to the complete and ordered (organized) matrix of all possible combinations of all possible values of all possible variables inherent in a problem. It can be visualized as an *n*-dimensional matrix, like the girder framework of a building in three dimensions, with each intersection representing some particular combination of values of the variables. (The Combinatorial System is described here in terms of a *matrix*, which implies variables that take on discrete values. The model can be generalized to cover continuous variables, but for Piaget's purposes the discrete form is most appropriate since application here is primarily to propositions which have only two discrete values, true or false. In principle, one could extend the model to cover "probabilistic logic" with its continuously variable degree of "truth.")

The *INRC Group* is the set of four logical operations that together with the Combinatorial System constitutes the theoretical foundations of the formal stage. The four operations are Identity, Negation, Reciprocity, and Correlativity, each represented by its initial in INRC. They are the operations by means of which one "gets around" within the Combinatorial Matrix, transforming one combination into another and grouping combinations into logically significant groupings. They are a "complete set" (in mathematical terms a Kleinian Viergruppe); that is, they are all the operators necessary and sufficient to do the job. They have the special relation of "going with" the Combinatorial System, like the relation that the four arithmetical operations (addition, subtraction, multiplication, division) have with the complete system represented by all the arithmetical numbers. They "go together."

The INRC Group can be rigorously defined in terms of mathematical logic, but will be defined here in terms of a concrete example; what is lost in rigor hopefully will be more than made up for in accessibility. *Identity* refers to some initial given operation. *Negation* is a simple direct undoing of that operation. *Reciprocity* is undoing the *effect* of the initial operation by changing some other variable in the system. *Correlativity* refers to negation of the reciprocal change, completing the set. As illustration, if putting weight onto one side of a previously balanced scale is the initial operation, then Negation would be directly removing that weight, Reciprocity would be either shifting the pan or adding weight on the other side to restore the balance, and Correlativity would be the operation undoing that reciprocal change thereby leading to the same effect as was created by the initial operation (with which it thus "correlates").

It should be emphasized that the essential new acquisition in the formal stage, in these terms, is the appearance for the first time, in the context of the INRC Group, of a fully developed form of Reciprocity in an integrated functional relation with Negation. Negation itself is well developed by the end of the concrete stage; well-developed Reciprocity working "easily and interchangeably" with Negation appears in the formal stage.

The Combinatorial System can be illustrated particularly well by utilizing an example which has special theoretical and practical importance: the sixteen-element matrix formed by two propositions and their negatives. This matrix is the prototype of the Combinatorial System because it is the smallest such matrix one can construct, having only two variables (propositions), each variable having only two values (true or false). Because so much of formal-stage reasoning is concerned with trying to relate just two variables ("all other things being held constant"), this sixteen-element matrix is also the particular Combinatorial System that recurs most frequently in Piaget's logical analysis of the interview data.

Let P and Q stand for two propositions (statements, hypotheses, assertions). Let $\bar{P}$ and $\bar{Q}$ stand for their negatives. In other words, P stands for "P is true" or "P is present," whereas $\bar{P}$ stands for "P is false" or "P is not present."

The whole Combinatorial Matrix, arrived at by forming all possible combinations of P, $\bar{P}$, Q, and $\bar{Q}$, would look like the following:

$$PQ \quad P\bar{Q} \quad \bar{P}Q \quad \bar{P}\bar{Q}$$

PQ and $P\bar{Q}$ PQ and $\bar{P}Q$ PQ and $\bar{P}\bar{Q}$ $P\bar{Q}$ and $\bar{P}Q$ $P\bar{Q}$ and $\bar{P}\bar{Q}$ $\bar{P}Q$ and $\bar{P}\bar{Q}$

PQ and $P\bar{Q}$ and $\bar{P}Q$ PQ and $P\bar{Q}$ and $\bar{P}\bar{Q}$ PQ and $\bar{P}Q$ and $\bar{P}\bar{Q}$ $P\bar{Q}$ and $\bar{P}Q$ and $\bar{P}\bar{Q}$

$$PQ \text{ and } P\bar{Q} \text{ and } \bar{P}Q \text{ and } \bar{P}\bar{Q}$$

Zero

Expressing the same things in numbers, where 1, 2, 3, and 4 stand for the first four combinations, it looks like

$$1 \quad 2 \quad 3 \quad 4$$
$$12 \quad 13 \quad 14 \quad 23 \quad 24 \quad 34$$
$$123 \quad 124 \quad 134 \quad 234$$
$$1234$$
$$0$$

Each of the foregoing represents some particular logical relation between two hypotheses, each of which has a name as follows:

1. PQ	Conjunction
2. $P\bar{Q}$	Nonimplication of Q by P
3. $\bar{P}Q$	Nonimplication of P by Q
4. $P\bar{Q}$	Conjunctive Negation
5. PQ and $P\bar{Q}$	Affirmation of P
6. PQ and $\bar{P}Q$	Affirmation of Q
7. PQ and $\bar{P}\bar{Q}$	Equivalence
8. $P\bar{Q}$ and $\bar{P}Q$	Reciprocal Exclusion
9. $P\bar{Q}$ and $\bar{P}\bar{Q}$	Negation of Q
10. $\bar{P}Q$ and $\bar{P}\bar{Q}$	Negation of P
11. PQ and $P\bar{Q}$ and $\bar{P}Q$	Dysjunction
12. PQ and $P\bar{Q}$ and $\bar{P}\bar{Q}$	Reciprocal Implication (Q implies P)
13. PQ and $\bar{P}Q$ and $\bar{P}\bar{Q}$	Implication (P implies Q)
14. $P\bar{Q}$ and $\bar{P}Q$ and $\bar{P}\bar{Q}$	Incompatibility (inverse of 1)
15. PQ and $P\bar{Q}$ and $\bar{P}Q$ and $\bar{P}\bar{Q}$	Complete Affirmation
16. 0	Negation

Note that the four pairs given in the first line of the Combinatorial Matrix are routinely generated by subjects in the concrete stage. (For example, a concrete-stage child can routinely generate the four possibilities red long, red short, black long, black short from red or black "times" long or short.) But when dealing with hypotheses, the formal-stage subject goes *beyond* that to generate the *further* combinations, each of which has some logical significance and some potentially necessary role to play in thinking. Here we see illustrated quite explicitly in the matrix itself how the formal stage includes the concrete stage as a part of itself.

Let us look at some of the combinations more closely to illustrate the role they might play when the matrix is used as part of logical thinking: (a) The double combination PQ and $\bar{P}\bar{Q}$ corresponds to equivalence or mutual implication. In other words, they go together or not at all. (b) The double combination formed by $P\bar{Q}$ and $\bar{P}Q$ corresponds to reciprocal exclusion. In other words, if one is true the other is false. If one is present the other is absent. (c) The triple combination of PQ and $\bar{P}Q$ and $\bar{P}\bar{Q}$ corresponds to the logical implication of Q by P. We can have both present, or neither present, or Q present for some other reason than P. But to say that P implies Q, there must be *no* instance of $P\bar{Q}$. Where the concrete-stage subject might conclude that "*P* implies *Q*" from merely noting many cases of *PQ*, the formal-stage subject would have a sharp eye out for instances of *PQ̄* and would require that there be instances of *everything except PQ̄*.

How does the formal-stage subject use the Combinatorial System and the INRC Group? By feeding data from an "experiment" into it and by reading logical conclusions and guidelines out of it. Combinations within the matrix are guided by the "incoming data" (which combinations do or do not occur in reality? which propositions are true and which are false?), and in turn the grouping guides the search for further data (which facts do I need to decide between these various hypotheses?). Not all of the potentially available matrix need be involved at any one time; only some parts of it may "light up" as relevant and needed. It is this process of working implicitly with combinations within the matrix that is conceptualized as the basis of formal thought.

Note that the Combinatorial System and INRC Group are not expected to be manifest and explicit in the interview material. They are inferred (induced) from the subject's capacity to seek for and to operate with those combinations which are necessary and sufficient to enable him to test hypotheses and to solve problems at the formal level. Thus, in general, they are conceptualized as latent rather than manifest, implicit rather than explicit.

As previously noted, in the concrete stage Actuality dominates while Possibility is limited to little more than reevocation of previous actualities. In the formal stage, Possibility comes to the fore and Actuality becomes "just one of the many possibilities" all of which are generated by the thought process itself rather than from reevocation of previous experience. Clearly that provides a cognitive base for the characteristic full flowering in adolescence of an intense commitment to systems of thought and especially to "those things which could be but are not." The valedictory address would be a classic example.

Proportionality is emphasized here because it is central to the Rings Experiment, which is one of those[1] replicated here. The capacity to handle problems requiring an operational grasp of the concept of Proportionality makes its appearance in the formal stage. Piaget derives this from the INRC Group via the concept of "logical proportions."[2] For a less rigorous argument, note that the numerator and denominator in a ratio (that is, a proportion) bear a *reciprocal* relation to one another (one can compensate for increase in one by increase in the other). Reciprocity is a characteristic acquisition of the formal stage. Note also that comparing two ratios (which is fundamental in using ratios for problem solving) amounts to setting up a relation between relations. Insofar as the concrete stage tends to be restricted to thinking about "things," one would expect that operations involving a "relation between relations" would have to await the formal stage.

Summary of the Distinctions
between Concrete- and Formal-Stage Function

The *concrete stage* roughly spans the years of latency, seven to eleven. Concrete thinking is restricted, by and large, to thought about things. The logical foundations of the concrete stage are the Logic of Class (in or out, a member or not a member of a given class) and the Logic of Relations (bigger or smaller, size place). Some central features of the concrete stage, which are treated as derivatives of the Logic of Class and Relations, are Seriation (the capacity to form ordered series) and Correspondence (the capacity to relate two ordered series by means of one to one correspondence). The latter can serve as a means for relating two variables ("the bigger it is, the heavier it is"), which is a precursor of more complex cause and effect relations. Multiple variables at this stage are characteristically handled by means of Logical Multiplication. For the particularly important example of two variables and their negatives, this gives only the four pairs PQ, $P\bar{Q}$, $\bar{P}Q$, $\bar{P}\bar{Q}$. The dominant form of reversibility at this stage is Negation. Quantitative operations are largely restricted to addition and subtraction.

The *formal stage* has its onset in early adolescence and is regarded as characteristic of the years from middle adolescence on through adulthood, being the "final equilibrium" in cognitive development as formulated by Piaget. The terms "abstract" or "propositional" are also used for the formal stage. Formal-stage thinking is not only about things, but it goes beyond that to be thought about thoughts, including words, ideas, concepts, hypotheses, and, particularly important from the logical point of view, propositions. In general, the formal stage bears a hierarchical relation to the concrete stage, subsuming concrete-stage function as a part of itself rather than simply replacing it. The logical foundations of the formal stage are the Combinatorial System (also referred to as the Structured Whole) and the INRC Group of Operations. The Combinatorial System is the matrix of all possible combinations of all possible values of all possible variables inherent in the problem. The INRC Group of Operations includes the two different forms of reversibility, Negation and Reciprocity, which are integrated for the first time into one system of logical operations. Negation has already been a characteristic of the concrete stage. The new acquisition is Reciprocity in an integrated working relation with Negation. Some central features of the formal stage which are regarded as derivatives of the Combinatorial System and the INRC Group are the capacity to operate with Proportions and access to the schema All Things Held Constant Except the Variable in Question. One also notes for the first time access to the classical operations of formal deductive and inductive logic (for example, implication, exclusion, equivalence, dysjunction). Multiple variables at this stage are composed by means of the Combinatorial System. For the particularly important case of two variables and their negatives, this gives the matrix of sixteen elements. That matrix includes as a part of itself the four pairs given by the concrete-stage operation of Logical Multiplication. Each of the sixteen combinations corresponds to some particular logical relation between the two variables (propositions) involved. Quantitative operations include multiplication and division, along with addition and subtraction. At another level of description, one notes a reversal of the relation between actuality and possibility. The full range of possibility inherent in a problem comes to the fore and is generated by the thought process itself, while actuality comes to be treated as "just one of the many possibilities."

The Experiments

The Choice of Experiments

The *Growth of Logical Thinking* reports a total of fifteen experiments. Of those, the two experiments that were chosen for replication and further study were

1. The Rings Experiment:[3] This experiment seemed to have the advantage of being directly related to the concept of *Proportionality*, which is identified as an acquisition of the formal stage and as a direct derivative of the formal INRC operations.

2. The Liquids Experiment:[4] This experiment is directly related to the concept of the *Combinatorial System*, which, along with the INRC operations, is fundamental to Piaget's conception of the formal stage.

Both experiments seemed free of technical difficulties with the apparatus, unlike some of the others.

The Rings Experiment

Piaget describes this experiment as follows: "Rings of varying diameters are placed between a light source and a screen. The size of their shadows is directly proportional to the diameters and inversely proportional to the distance between them and the light source. Specifically, we ask the subject to find two shadows which cover each other exactly, using two unequal sizes. To do so, he need only place the larger one further from the light, in proportion to its size, and there will be compensation between distances and diameters."

Of the relation between this particular experiment and the theory of the formal stage, he says: "the present research raises a question about the formal operational schema relative to proportionality . . . . the proportions we shall study in connection with the projection of shadows are of an essentially geometrical nature." . . .

The Liquids Experiment

Piaget describes the rationale for including this experiment as follows: "One may wonder what would happen if we posed a problem that involved combinations directly . . . . The best technique with regard to this matter is to ask subjects to combine chemical substances among themselves." The experiment is intended to elicit quite directly the subject's capacity for generating a complete Combinatorial System.

The apparatus consists of five large bottles, each filled to the same level with fluids that all look like plain water. The bottles are distinguished only by the large numbers, 1 through 5, with which each is labeled. On the table are a number of empty glasses. The experimenter shows the subject a glass full of yellow-colored fluid (or actually prepares it while the subject is present but not looking) and says: "I made this colored fluid from the fluids in those bottles. I didn't use anything else. Do you think you could do the same thing? How would you go about trying?"

The correct combinations are 245 and 1245. Note especially that *no* mere pair will suffice .[5] . . .

The Subject Groups

1. Average Younger Adolescent Group: Age fourteen. Randomly selected from a large junior high school in a suburban community. Students who were doing failing work in science and math were excluded, to avoid subjects who might be regarded as particularly impaired.

2. Average Older Adolescent Group: Ages sixteen, seventeen. Randomly selected from a large high school in a suburban community. Science and math failures also excluded.

3. Gifted Older Adolescent Group: Ages sixteen, seventeen. Selected from a high school where the entire student population is highly selected for very superior academic aptitude and performance, especially in the sciences. (This special school draws from a very large metropolitan area. Only very superior students generally apply. There is a competitive entrance exam, and only a fraction of the applicants are accepted. The average IQ is reported to be in the 130 to 140 range.) Some of the early subjects in this group were randomly selected from within the school, but most of the subjects in our group were even more highly selected, being those students with the highest academic ratings in the senior class. The random group was small and the differences between the two subgroups were not great, so the two groups were combined for this report.

4. Average Adult Group: Ages ranged from twenty to fifty-five. What was intended here was simply a "spot check" to test the expectation, based on results with the older adolescents, that it would not be difficult to find "normal adults" who fail to function at the fully formal level. Only

a very rough criterion of "normal" was used; individuals were chosen who functioned well at some "middle level" occupation and who seemed to be of average intelligence or better. The occupations and approximate ages were two secretaries (twenty, twenty-five), two laboratory research assistants (twenty-five, thirty), two businessmen (forty-five, fifty-five), two business administrators (thirty, thirty-five), two housewives (forty-five, fifty-five), one school teacher (forty), one plumber (forty-five).

Data Collection and Scoring

While the interview was in progress, an assistant recorded the interview material on a sheet which listed an extensive set of criteria and relevant observables for each experiment, the criteria being drawn directly from the Piaget-Inhelder text. Immediately following the interview, this was reviewed by the interviewer, who then added a brief "ad lib" paragraph setting down immediate impressions, including highlights, idiosyncracies, and an immediate judgment as to cognitive level. Subsequently, these sheets were reviewed, particular points being checked against tape recordings which were made of each interview. Then all data for each subject were reviewed, and a final determination of cognitive level was made on the basis of the criteria given below.

The criterion for "full formal function" (Piaget's Stage 3) on the Rings Experiment was the capacity to place two rings properly (including at least one of the odd-size rings), to make some verbal statement equivalent to the proportionality principle, and to be able to show some understanding of the connection between the principle and the correct placement. We scored some few subjects 3A (*almost* full formal function) who failed to get final correct placement but seemed on the verge of it (for example, seeming to make some "careless mistake" in placement and never recouping it but making a correct statement of the Proportionality principle).

The criterion for "full formal function" (Stage 3) on the Liquids Experiment was the capacity to generate *all* the combinations by *any* systematic procedure. Duplications and going back to fill in were allowed. A few subjects seemed to have the idea but missed a few combinations (for example, they might leave out one pair and one trio, seemingly "carelessly"). They were scored as 3A (almost full formal function) if they missed no more than *one* combination in any group (pairs, trios, quartets).

The Major Findings Summarized

1. No subject in the youngest (fourteen-year-old) group functioned at the fully formal level on *both* problems (Tables 1-1 and 1-2). (In the Liquids Experiment, two out of twenty-one subjects did function at the fully formal level.)

Table 1-1
Summary of data

		Rings Experiment		Liquids Experiment	
		Formal level	Not formal level	Formal level	Not formal level
Average younger	Boys	0	10	0	10
adolescent	Girls	0	11	2	9
($N = 21$)	Total	0	21	2	19
Average older	Boys	11	8	4	13
adolescent	Girls	3	18	2	17
($N = 40$, rings;	Total	14	26	6	30
$N = 36$, liquids)					
Gifted older	Boys	12	5	12	4
adolescent	Girls	1	5	1	4
($N = 23$, rings;	Total	13	10	13	8
$N = 21$, liquids)					
Average adult	Men	3	3	2	4
($N = 12$)	Women	1	5	1	5
	Total	4	8	3	9

Table 1-2

Percentage of subjects who functioned at
the fully formal level[a]

	Rings Experiment	Liquids Experiment
Average younger adolescent	0	10
Average older adolescent	35	17
Gifted older adolescent	57	62
Average adult	33	25

[a] Percentages in this table are based on numbers
from Table 1-1.

2. The most representative figure for the average older adolescent and adult groups would appear to be something like *one-quarter to one-third functioning at the fully formal level* (Tables 1-1 and 1-2). (Note that these figures are themselves averages of the distinctly different results for boys and girls, for which see Table 1-4 and item 5 . . . .)

3. Roughly 60 percent of the gifted group functioned at the fully formal level. For boys in the group, the percentage of fully formal was 75 percent, the highest percentage in these study groups.

4. Note that including the "almost formal" subjects with fully formal subjects (in Piagetian terminology: including 3A with 3) leads to no significant change in the broad outline of the results, there being only a modest rise of only some of the percentages (Table 1-3).

5. Boys functioned at the fully formal level significantly more frequently than did girls (Table 1-4). For the three older groups (where the numbers seem large enough to support the generalization), the percentages for boys were from two to four times as great as those for girls.

6. On the Liquids Experiment, it was most unusual for a subject to go on spontaneously once he had hit upon a successful combination (that is, once he had hit 245, which is usually achieved before 1245). That runs somewhat counter to the claim made by Piaget that the formal-stage subject is "not satisfied with a single solution to the problem, does not stop there but looks for others," in a search through *all* the possible combinations. In this study, subjects almost always stopped when they hit on a correct combination and gave every indication that they felt that they were "through." We found it necessary, after a while, to wonder aloud whether there might not be "any other possibilities," after which they usually started up again and generated all the additional combinations they could think of.

Table 1-3
Percentages of formal level obtained using "relaxed criteria"

	Rings Experiment		Liquids Experiment	
	Standard criteria	Relaxed criteria	Standard criteria	Relaxed criteria
Average younger adolescent	0	0	10	19
Average older adolescent	35	50	17	28
Gifted older adolescent	57	65	62	62
Adult	33	33	25	25

Table 1-4

Percentages of fully formal level, boys and girls compared

	Rings Experiment			Liquids Experiment		
	Boys	Girls	Ratio	Boys	Girls	Ratio
Average younger adolescent	0	0	—	0	18	—
Average older adolescent	58	14	4	23	10	2
Gifted older adolescent	71	17	4	75	20	4
Adult	50	17	3	33	17	2

7. On the Rings Experiment, we noted the schema we dubbed "Equal to or Twice," which refers to the subject's almost automatic readiness to try a distance which is equal to (or, next best, twice as great as) some other distance which "looks important." The most common example occurred when subjects had to place a third ring after two rings were already correctly placed. The single most common response at that point in the experiment was to try the same spacing again (without regard to the size of the rings) and if that didn't work to say "Maybe twice as far?" Other forms occurred of a similar "pull" toward thinking in terms of distances that are "equal or twice" some prominent or presumably significant distance. The schema seems of importance because (a) it is so common, (b) it seems intermediate between concrete (addition) and formal (the simplest ratio: two to one), (c) it seems to serve as a stepping-stone from concrete to formal for some subjects, (d) it is neither specifically identified nor discussed by Piaget and Inhelder in this context (although one *could* relate it to their more general concept of "absolute distances"), (e) it may contribute to an apparent difference in results between the Geneva study and this one, since subjects *can* correctly place the regular series of rings used in the Piaget-Inhelder study on the basis of this simpler principle *without* really being in the formal stage.

Conclusions and Discussions

1. Fully developed formal-stage thinking seems to be far from commonplace or routine among normal adolescents and adults. Using the definitions and criteria for the formal stage as given by Piaget and Inhelder in *The Growth of Logical Thinking*, the publication in which they first define and describe the formal stage within the context of their systematic

conception of the development of intelligence, we find formal-stage thinking to be fully developed in only a modest proportion of the population and only very partially developed in most. In our group of average older adolescents, only 20 to 35 percent functioned at a fully formal level. The same modest percentages applied to our "spot check" of a small group of average adults.

To get consistently higher percentages, it is necessary to turn to increasingly select groups. The highest percentage in this study was 75 percent functioning at the fully formal level in a group of scientifically gifted older adolescent boys. (To get higher percentages would require either even more highly select groups or criteria *appreciably* relaxed *below* the standards implied by the Piaget-Inhelder definition of the stage.)

2. In this respect, the formal stage appears to differ appreciably and significantly from the earlier Piagetian stages. Full development appears to be very much the rule at the earlier stages, but it appears to be the exception at this stage. Failure to develop fully at the earlier stages seems highly correlated with major psychopathology or with major cultural difference.[6] Not so for the formal stage, where failure to develop fully appears commonplace among normal adolescents and adults.

3. These results appear to be in conflict with the Piaget-Inhelder publications on the formal stage. Their report leaves the firm impression that formal-stage thinking is the rule in adolescence, since all adolescent protocols included in their report are at the fully formal level and because throughout the book they link "formal stage" with "adolescence." However, a closer look reveals that the difference is more appearance than reality. Nowhere in their book do they make any *explicit* claim that *all* (or even most) adolescents actually do function at the fully formal level, nor do they make any explicit claim that they are reporting *all* cases tested. Personal communication with Dr. Inhelder confirms that *indeed not all cases were reported*. Their orientation was to describe and to formulate for the first time the characteristics of the formal stage. There was no intention to speak to the question of "frequency" or "incidence." Protocols were used simply as illustrations. Adolescents who failed to function at the formal stage were simply not reported. Thus there is no real conflict between the results of this study and the essentials of their basic contribution.

However, their presentation *is* seriously misleading on the matter of "frequency," which may be of peripheral concern within the context of genetic epistemology but is of central import in other contexts, such as in clinical work or in educational psychology. Their presentation *leaves the impression* that full formal-stage thinking is the rule in adolescence. This study shows that it is not.[7]

4. This study makes fully developed formal-stage thinking appear to stand somewhere between the more nearly universal developmental acquisitions (walking, talking, the early Piagetian stages) and the relatively rare special "talents" (highly developed musical, mathematical, graphic, mechanical capacities). It seems neither so common as the former nor so exceptional as the latter, but somewhere in between.

5. Since formal-stage functioning does *not* appear to be commonplace among normal adolescents, formal-stage thinking is not "characteristic" or "typical" of adolescence in all senses. Adolescence does indeed seem to be the *characteristic age of onset*. Latent formal patterns *may* even impart a characteristic "formal flavor" to adolescent thought in some cases despite the fact that adolescents may lack access to formal patterns adequate to the task of problem solving. But formal-stage thinking does *not* appear to be "characteristic" of adolescence in the sense of being routine, expected, or highly likely. By contrast, the earlier Piagetian stages *are* characteristic or typical at their age ranges in *all* the usual senses of those words. Thus for adolescents the formal stage is more of a *characteristic potentiality* only sometimes becoming an actuality: an intriguing echo of a central feature of the stage itself.

6. The data suggest an overall formulation something like the following: Up through early adolescence, it appears that the development of intelligence can be characterized fairly well as a sequence of stages — sensorimotor, egocentric, concrete—through which virtually every child passes. The model would be that of a single path. Everyone in the "normal population" goes down that path, with only some modest variations in pace and emphasis. Although that model may exclude some refinements, as a first approximation it seems to serve very well to cover the facts.

But from early adolescence onward, that kind of a model will no longer serve at all, *even as a first approximation*. From that age onward, there is no longer any single path down which nearly everyone goes. Even to begin to cover the facts, one must introduce into the model at least some such concept as "dropout rate" or "branching into parallel tracks." One main track would be the formal stage, but only some modest proportion of the normal population would proceed down that royal road to full formal function. Other tracks would represent the development of alternative patterns of thought, those alternative patterns (see below) involving only partial or minimal development of the capacity for formal-stage thought as defined by Piaget.

Such a formulation would be consistent with other work in the study of intelligence (intelligence testing) which shows that a single measure of general intelligence (IQ, G factor) is most serviceable through childhood because in that age range the intercorrelation among the various subtests is high. But by adolescence that *single* measure of intelligence becomes increasingly and seriously inadequate because of decreasing intercorrelation among the various subtests. In other words, there is increasing "specialization" or "branching," with some components of functioning intelligence developing rather independently of others. Full formal-stage functioning can be viewed as one of those components, albeit a centrally significant one.

To treat formal-stage functioning as one among alternatives is not to put it on a par with the alternatives. It seems clear that the formal stage is a natural, logical, and "optimal" extension of the earlier cognitive stages to the next higher and most general logical level. Piaget even more strongly gives the formal stage a very special status, identifying it as the "final equilibrium" beyond which there is no other. The essence of Piaget's exposition on this point is that the logical character of the formal stage, *as theoretically defined*, is complete and general (those words being rather specifically defined within the context of mathematical logic) in such a way as to make it the "highest stage" by definition. I have the impression that his analysis does not do justice to meaningful variations *within* the formal stage as it occurs "in nature," all of which are treated together within one overarching definition of the formal stage as a ne plus ultra. While the Piagetian formulation may indeed point to a meaningful quasi-mathematical *theoretical reality*, it gives too little attention to variations *within* the formal stage as a *functioning psychological reality* (let alone to the fact that *most* people don't even seem to make it fully into that stage at all).

7. As for the alternative "tracks" associated with partial or minimal development of the capacity for formal-stage thinking, I think we saw two of them in our study: (a) Among the groups from the high school for academically superior students, it was common to find subjects who failed to function at a fully formal level but who tried instead to match the problem at hand to some repertoire of "standard problems with their standard solutions." We called them "standard method" types. On a scale of cognitive development, clearly such an approach is inferior to fully developed formal-stage thought. It lacks the power of formal-stage thought for the solution of *new* problems. But from an adaptive point of view such a method of problem solving may serve quite well in "everyday life" if the repertoire of standard methods is at all adequate to the range of problems encountered and if there is adequate "skill" in matching the problems with the methods. Judging from the fact that many of these students ranked at the top of their class in a difficult and selective school, it seems to have served them well enough, judged by that standard in that particular "average expectable environment." (b) Less frequent, and occurring more

commonly among subjects in our "average high school," we saw individuals whom we dubbed as "inspirational." They would leap at a solution, or, to put it differently, answers just seemed to leap into their minds. Usually they could say very little by way of explanation. Sometimes they were right. (If so, we scored them as formal, since the Piagetian criteria do not require awareness of the underlying formal mechanisms.) But more commonly they were only right in part and were unable to come up with an adequate solution to the problem. These seemed to be young people who had career ambitions in the arts or letters, who had occasional and partial access to their capacity for formal thought in "inspirational leaps," but who tended to be relatively less successful than the "standard method" subjects at this kind of problem solving, judging from their school performance and their performance in this study. They were probably cultivating other aspects of themselves.

These two types fit nicely with the formulations of Liam Hudson in his book *Contrary Imaginations*.[8] Hudson identifies two rather different cognitive styles among bright adolescents which he labels "convergent" (focusing down on one right answer) and "divergent" (freely generating a rich variety of answers). Our standard method type adolescents do seem aptly identified as convergers and our inspirational types as divergers. Using that terminology, optimal formal-stage function might be identified with some optimal balance ("equilibrium") between divergence and convergence, especially since Piaget quite explicitly identifies the Combinatorial Matrix as having the virtue of being the framework within which one can *both* focus down on one crucial combination and/or freely generate all possible relevant combinations. The subjects in our study who did function at the fully formal stage, however, did, in their handling of the problems, seem to manifest a more convergent style (like those only partially formal subjects we dubbed the "standard method" types). They may have been influenced in that direction by the nature of the problems, which tend to call for "a right answer." Or it may well be that the concept of the formal stage itself is much more appropriate and useful as a model for convergent styles of thought, as compared with divergent styles to which it may apply technically but without being a good model for capturing "naturally" crucial features of that style.

8. It seems reasonable to speculate that one reason for the relatively modest incidence of fully developed formal-stage functioning in the normal population, especially by comparison with the earlier stages, is that there is less of a "demand" for it. It is probably correct that the "average expectable environment" for most normal individuals does not make much demand for full formal function. By contrast, the "demand" for concrete-level functioning (conservation of number, conservation of mass

and volume, serial ordering, correspondence) is very considerable in modern society, even in "everyday life." Piagetian studies of primitive or agrarian societies have shown that in such societies even adults may not function at the concrete level,[9] which would tend to support speculation about some connection between the "demand function" of the society and the degree to which the potential for each stage is actualized. One could draw a parallel here to the "emergence" of childhood as a stage of life in medieval times[10] and to the emergence of "adolescence" and "youth"[11] as increasingly well-defined developmental stages in more "advanced" industrialized affluent societies. The nearly universal "emergence" of the concrete stage in societies like our own and the *still only partial* emergence of the formal stage is a parallel phenomenon on the cognitive level.

9. The markedly greater percentage of boys in our fully formal samples is noteworthy, but this study throws no light whatsoever on reasons for the difference; therefore, beyond recording the fact, it seems appropriate to add nothing but that the finding is consistent with a similar sex difference noted in virtually all studies of abstract thinking (particularly on mathematical and "scientific" forms) in adolescence. If one accepts the finding (and it seems solid enough), then clearly the next questions are what are the complex interactions here of nature and nurture, of biological givens, of culture-based child-rearing practices, of educational practices, and of psychosexual developmental patterns and influences? On those questions this study throws no light whatsoever.

10. In summary, then, fully developed formal-stage thinking appears to be a kind of "cognitive maturity." It integrates all that has gone before. It is far from being commonplace among adolescents or adults. In that sense, it is more ideal than typical, more potential than actual. It has important quantitative aspects, varying degrees of access for a given individual being common and partial degrees of access being more common in the normal population than either full or zero access. Like most other aspects of psychological maturity, it is a potentiality only partially attained by most and fully attained only by some.

Notes

1. J. Piaget and B. Inhelder, *The Growth of Logical Thinking from Childhood to Adolescence* (New York: Basic Books, 1958), Chapter 13.

2. See *ibid.*, 314.

3. *Ibid.*, Chapter 13.

4. *Ibid.*, Chapter 17.

5. The bottles actually contain (1) plain water, (2) dilute sulfuric acid, (3)

sodium thiosulfate solution, (4) hydrogen peroxide, (5) potassium iodine. The peroxide will oxidize the iodine in the presence of acid, releasing iodine, which colors the solution. Thus at least 245 are required. Adding 1 (water) makes no change, 3 excludes the color, the reducing agent functioning as a bleach. *Thus, of all the combinations possible with the five bottles, only 245 and 1245 will give the color reaction.* Any reasonable quantities will suffice, and subjects are so informed if they begin to become concerned about quantitative variations.

6. J. Bruner, *Studies in Cognitive Growth* (New York: John Wiley, 1966), Chapters 11, 12, and 13.

7. Before having the information noted above, that not all cases are reported in the Piaget-Inhelder book, it occurred to me and others that the apparent disparity of results might represent a cross-cultural difference. That interpretation seemed from the outset highly unlikely, since it seemed hard to believe (chauvinism aside) that an *unselected* Swiss group would function at *100 percent* and a *highly select* American group (scientifically gifted, or intellectually oriented, the best from a large metropolitan area) would function at *75 percent or less.* But with the information that not all cases are reported we have neither the need nor support for any cross-cultural hypotheses.

8. L. Hudson, *Contrary Imaginations* (New York: Schocken Books, 1966).

9. See Bruner, *Studies in Cognitive Growth.*

10. See P. Aries, *Centuries of Childhood* (New York: Vintage Books, 1965).

11. See K. Keniston, "A New Stage of Life," *American Scholar*, 39 (Autumn 1970), 631-654.

Recent Research on
Cognitive Development
in Adolescence

David Elkind

Studies of cognitive development in adolescence have generally comprised only a small fraction of the total number of studies of mental growth. G. Stanley Hall[1] complained of this situation almost three-quarters of a century ago, and he would be equally chagrined if he looked at the research literature today. The reasons for the relative dearth of studies on adolescent thinking are multiple and intricate. One of the most important

Reprinted from *Adolescence in the Life Cycle: Psychological Change and the Social Context*, ed. S. E. Dragastin and G. H. Elder, Jr. (New York: Halsted Press, 1975), © Hemisphere Publishing Corporation.

of these is the diversity and the complexity of adolescent thinking, which requires equally complex and diverse methods of investigation. We have only just begun to develop methods for exploring the manner in which adolescents think. Another reason for the paucity of studies in this area is that adolescents are, generally, less accessible and are likely to be less cooperative than children.

Despite these and other difficulties in investigating adolescent thought, research continues to be done in this area, but it is centered around only a few problems. One of these problems has to do with moral judgment and behavior, another with the generality of formal operations in adolescence, still another deals with the self-concept in adolescence, and a fourth is concerned with conceptual orientation shifts, the ease with which children and adolescents shift from one level of cognitive functioning to another. A final problem, not limited to adolescent cognition, has to do with ethnic differences in cognitive ability. No effort will be made in this paper to survey every study done on each of these issues. Rather, some representative recent studies will be reviewed to illustrate the problems, the methods of investigation, and some characteristic findings . . . .

Generality of Formal Operations in Adolescence

Some years ago, as part of a series of replication studies of Piaget's research, I came across a surprising finding. While my results[2] supported those of Piaget with respect to the ages at which mass and weight were conserved, they did not support Piaget's finding that the conservation of volume is attained by 75 percent of eleven- to twelve-year-old children. In my study, only 27 percent of the eleven- to twelve-year-old youngsters gave evidence of an abstract conception of volume. This failure to confirm Piaget's age for the attainment of the volume conception in elementary school children led to a second replication[3] using junior and senior high school students, ages twelve to eighteen. Results showed that of the 469 students tested, 87 percent had demonstrated conservation of mass and weight, but only 47 percent demonstrated conservation of volume. In a third replication,[4] with 240 college students, comparable results were obtained. While 92 percent of the college students demonstrated the conservation of mass and weight, only 58 percent gave evidence of volume conservation. It was also found that among the junior and senior high school students, as well as among the college students, significantly more men than women gave evidence of volume conservation.

My reading of these findings at that time was that while all adolescents of average intellectual ability probably attain formal operations, they do not apply them equally to all aspects of reality. In adolescence, girls for social role reasons, are more likely to apply their formal operational thinking to interpersonal matters than to matters of science. The absence of volume conservation in some adolescents and particularly among women was seen as a matter of differential application of mental abilities and not as evidence for the absence of formal operational thinking. Piaget[5] has made the same argument in his recent discussion of intellectual evolution from adolescence to adulthood.

Other investigators, however, doubt that most individuals attain formal operations in the sense described by Inhelder and Piaget.[6] Bynum, Thomas, and Weitz,[7] for example, question the Inhelder and Piaget assumption that formal operational thinkers use all sixteen binary operations of truth-functional logic in solving problems. In their investigation, they found evidence for only eight of the sixteen operations described by Inhelder and Piaget. In addition, they believe the Inhelder-Piaget logical analysis of the multiple variable, tasks, and of adolescents' responses to them, to be faulty in its demonstration that subjects used all sixteen binary operations.

Other studies report findings comparable to those that I obtained in the Piaget replication studies. Hobbs[8] tested 906 young people in grades seven through twelve with weight and volume tasks at several difficulty levels. Ninety-six percent of the subjects conserved weight when the task involved recognizing that a ball of clay remained the same in weight when rolled into a sausage. While 40 to 50 percent of the boys demonstrated volume conservation, only 20 to 30 percent of the young women did so. For both men and women and for both mass and volume, conservation was more difficult when the transformation involved a change of state (for example, solid to liquid) than when it involved only a change in form.

Similar findings were reported by Tomlinson-Keasey,[9] who tested three groups of females, whose ages were eleven, nineteen, and fifty-four years, respectively. She examined them on Piaget's pendulum balance and flexibility problems. Thirty-two percent of the eleven-year-olds, 67 percent of the nineteen-year-olds, and 57 percent of the fifty-four-year-olds were at the formal level of thinking. Attainment of the highest level of formal operational thinking was rare at all age levels.

Working with minimally educated adults, Graves[10] used the group testing procedures I had employed in my studies. The subjects in her study were 120 adults (black and white) who were enrolled in night school basic education classes. Graves observed that 78 percent of her subjects attained the conservation of mass, and 67 percent conserved weight, but only 24 percent conserved volume. These figures are lower than those I obtained with college students and may reflect cultural and IQ differences. It would be wrong, however, to infer from these findings that the subjects who failed the volume conservation task were deficient in formal operations. What needs to be done is to test such subjects in tasks that require formal operations, but that are in their particular domain of expertise.

A somewhat different approach to the problem of the universality of formal operations was taken by Siegler, Liebert, and Liebert,[11] who trained preadolescents to solve the Piagetian pendulum problem. The training involved presenting young people with a conceptual framework for approaching the problem and with analogous problems. The unaided ten- and eleven-year-old children did not solve the pendulum problem, but they were able to solve it after training. As in all training studies, this one raises as many questions as it answers. The crucial question is: Does training affect competence, or does it merely alter performance? Unfortunately, this training study, like so many others, provides no information on whether the effects demonstrate improved performance or enhanced ability.

In general the work on the universality of formal operations remains an open question. Piaget's suggestion[12] that people be tested in formal operations in their area of specialization seems reasonable in principle but difficult to achieve in practice. How does a salesman, a shoe clerk, or a carpenter use formal operations? To be sure some areas of specialization may require formal operational thinking, but not all occupations do. Devising tests of formal operations for specific fields is a difficult task but one that has to be attempted if the question of the generality or universality of formal operations is to be answered.

Adolescent Self-Concept

The domain of cognitive psychology is ill defined at best and particularly so where the self-concept is concerned. To the extent that the self-concept is considered a concept, it clearly falls within the domain of cognitive psychology. As soon as the self-concept is considered an affective schema whose measurement reveals facets of personality, the boundaries between the affective and the cognitive domains become more blurred. Many of the studies of self-concept reside in the never-never land between the cognitive and the affective domains. . . . a few studies of adolescent self-concept will be described here.

Some of the most extensive work on adolescent self-concept has been done in Europe and is reported in two recent books. In *Le moi et l'autre dans la conscience de l'adolescent*, Rodriguez Tomé[13] presents a theoretically oriented questionnaire study of adolescents' conceptions of themselves and others. Tomé distinguished three dimensions of adolescent self-conceptions: egotism (for example, the tendency to feel superior); self-control (for example, the ability to solve problems without help); and sociability (for example, confidence). Tomé found that these three factors were statistically almost completely independent of one another.

Tomé distinguished between the individual's self-image proper and his social self-image. Subjects were asked to describe themselves as they saw themselves (self-image proper) and as they thought other people saw them (social self-image). The same three factors of personality appeared in both descriptions and were as uncorrelated for descriptions of the self-image proper as they were for the social self-image. There was almost no change with age for boys (from twelve to eighteen years) and girls (from twelve to twenty-one years) in the relative weights that were given to egotism, self-control, and sociability. At all age levels, adolescents ranked themselves highest on sociability and lowest on egotism.

Tomé also compared the adolescent's self-image with the images his parents held of him. He found that parents generally regarded their offspring as more egotistical and less self-controlled than did the adolescent himself. Parents and their offspring did agree on the adolescent's sociability. Mothers and fathers were in good agreement as to their appraisal of their adolescent children. Tomé also had each adolescent judge himself as he thought his parents would judge him and had the parents judge the adolescent as they thought the adolescent would judge himself. The adolescents were closer to the mark than were the parents. It appeared that the adolescents had a better picture of what the parents thought of them than the parents had of what the adolescents thought of themselves.

In another comprehensive study, Gérard Lutte[14] looked at the evolution of the ego ideal in children between the ages of ten and eleven and sixteen and seventeen in several different countries. It is not possible to summarize all the findings, but some of the most striking results can be reported. First, the ego ideal does not develop in the same manner in different cultures. In America, the ego ideal is first the parent, but this changes in adolescence. In Germany and Portugal, however, parents remain an important ego ideal from age ten through age seventeen. Likewise, the model for the ego ideal is different for boys than it is for girls between the ages of ten and thirteen. For the girl, the model is often a friend, whereas for the boy it is more likely to be a celebrity. Lutte argues that it is hard to defend the position that the ego ideal evolves in regular stages because it is affected by so many different variables.

Among the factors that affect the adolescent's self-concept is his social class. Lutte found that adolescents from both the middle class and the working class aspired to better occupational and financial positions in life. But the adolescents of low socioeconomic status aspired too high

and placed between their dreams and reality obstacles difficult to sur-
mount given their station and the society in which they lived. Middle-class
adolescents were more realistic about their limitations and gave more
weight to such factors as intelligence and willpower in attaining success.
This finding among European young people replicates comparable findings among American adolescents.

Several other recent studies of adolescent self-concept will illustrate
the nature of work in this area. In a factor analytic study of developmental
trends in self-concept, Monge[15] found that semantic differential factors
remained constant among young people in grades six through twelve. This
consistency of self-evaluation was greater for boys than it was for girls.
There were some exceptions. Boys, but not girls, showed an increase in
both achievement and leadership. For both sexes, congeniality and sociability increased after grade ten. Both boys and girls scored lower on adjustment with increasing age, and this was particularly true for girls. Both
boys and girls scored higher on scales of masculinity with increasing age.

In a somewhat different type of study, Sinha[16] looked at the readiness
of adolescents to reveal themselves on a "self-disclosure inventory." Her
subjects were 250 adolescent girls living in an urban area of India. Sinha
found that the readiness of adolescents to reveal themselves declined with
increasing age. Social environment also affects self-esteem in systematic
ways. A study of adolescents raised on a kibbutz suggested that such young
people were more social and had higher self-esteem (at least among boys)
than did children who were raised on moshavim.[17]

While the studies of adolescent self-concept are of interest from a
descriptive point of view, they lack theoretical direction and coherence.
The one exception is the study by Tomé,[18] but the theory employed in
that study was more sociological then developmental. In particular, the
role of cognitive development in the elaboration of the self-concept during
adolescence needs to be articulated and explored systematically. The
formal operations described by Piaget make it possible for the young
person to see himself from the perspective of others, and this must have
a significant impact upon the self. Moreover, the ability to think about
thinking allows the adolescent to discover the privateness of his thoughts
and the social isolation of his reflective self. How the adolescent handles
these new discoveries and the changes in his body and in his social relations has yet to be explored in a systematic way . . . .

Ethnic Differences in Cognitive Development

One of the issues that has received considerable public as well as professional airing in recent years concerns ethnic differences in IQ. Much

of the discussion was generated by Jensen's article[19] in which he suggested that compensatory education failed because the children it served were not really capable of profiting from the extra educational push. On the basis of a vast marshaling of research studies, Jensen concluded that blacks differed significantly from whites in IQ and were better at associative learning while whites were better at abstract thinking.

Jensen's work has been criticized from many points of view.[20] Anthropologists and biologists have pointed out that racial differences are hard to establish. Because of intermarriage, the gene pools of blacks and whites in America are, at most, only several generations apart. Developmental psychologists point out that the difference in associative versus abstract thinking is developmental rather than genetic. Black children may simply attain abstract thinking at a later age than the relatively young black and white children studied by Jensen. And, finally, statisticians point out that, in any case, the ethnic differences are only relative. Even if one accepts the overall statistical difference as valid, intelligence is still distributed according to a bell-shaped curve for both blacks and whites. Accordingly, 50 percent of the blacks are still brighter than 33 percent of the whites.

One of the questions raised by Jensen's paper and the subsequent discussion concerning it relates to the intellectual ability of black adolescents. To what extent, one might ask, are such adolescents deficient in abstract thinking, and to what extent, if any, can this deficiency be attributed to genetic factors? It was to this issue that a recent paper[21] was addressed. It built upon my more than ten years of work with delinquent adolescents. The aim of the paper was to demonstrate that intelligence test scores of low-income adolescents are meaningless when they are interpreted independently of the sociocultural context in which they are obtained.

Basically, in clinical practice, one can observe two types of low-income adolescents who score low on intelligence tests but who give other indications of average intellectual development. These types of adolescents are not limited to delinquents and are to be found among low-income blacks (and whites) who never come to the attention of the authorities. In the absence of a clinical evaluation of their test performances, however, their obtained test scores are apt to be grossly misleading.

One type of low-income adolescent who scores low in IQ tests might be called "prematurely structured." Such young people have, from an early age, had to cope with some rather harsh realities. They have had to care for themselves and their siblings (and sometimes for their parents) and to forage for food and clothing. They had little time for play, and their cognitive skills were developed in the service of survival. To adults they seem crafty, shrewd, and worldly wise beyond their years. But this premature structuring of their practical intelligence is purchased at the price of the development of abstract intelligence. There is nothing genetic about the intellectual limitations of these young people; rather, the limitations are quite adaptive given the circumstances of their existence.

Another type of low-income adolescent develops his abstract intelligence but in directions not measured by standard intelligence tests. Such adolescents often model their behavior after successful adults in their society. By the age of thirteen or fourteen they may have several girls working for them, may be pushing dope, and may also be involved in robbery and extortion. They know how to stay out of trouble with the law, how to con the "Johns" and other "dudes," and how to dominate women and other men. They have a rich vocabulary of words and phrases that one would never find in Webster's dictionary and an array of interpersonal skills and talents that would be the pride of any used-car salesman. These young people have shown an *alternative elaboration* of their intellectual abilities that is never assessed by standard intelligence tests.

These clinical observations, or so it seems to me, point up still another danger of using intelligence test data to make inferences about genetics and heredity. Mental tests assume that mental development follows a path common to all individuals. But that is simply not the case, and there are exceptional patterns of development that are occasioned by sociocultural factors. The work of Cole, Gay, Glick, and Sharp[22] gives further evidence of the influence of these sociocultural factors on intellectual development and test performances. Such a vast conceptual gulf exists between the level of gene complexes and the level of psychological test performance that any inferences made from one to the other must be regarded as highly conjectural.

Notes

1. G. S. Hall, *Adolescence: Its Psychology and Its Relations to Physiology, Anthropology, Sociology, Sex, Crime, Religion and Education*, Volume 1 (New York: Appleton, 1904).

2. D. Elkind, "Children's Discovery of the Conservation of Mass, Weight and Volume," *Journal of Genetic Psychology*, 98 (June 1961), 219-227.

3. *Id.*, "Quantity Conceptions in Junior and Senior High School Students," *Child Development*, 32 (No. 3, 1961), 551-560.

4. *Id.*, "Quantity Conceptions in College Students," *Journal of Social Psychology*, 57 (August 1962), 459-465.

5. J. Piaget, "Intellectual Evolution from Adolescence to Adulthood," *Human Development*, 15 (No. 1, 1972), 1-12.

6. B. Inhelder and J. Piaget, *The Growth of Logical Thinking from Childhood to Adolescence* (New York: Basic Books, 1958).

7. T. W. Bynum, J. A. Thomas, and L. J. Weitz, "Truth Functional Logic in Formal Operational Thinking: Inhelder's and Piaget's Evidence," *Developmental Psychology*, 7 (No. 2, 1972), 129-132.

8. E. D. Hobbs, "Adolescents' Concepts of Physical Quantity," *ibid.*, 9 (No. 3, 1973), 431.

9. C. Tomlinson-Keasey, "Formal Operations in Females from Eleven to Fifty-four Years of Age," *ibid.*, 6 (No. 2, 1972), 364.

10. A. J. Graves, "Attainment of Mass, Weight and Volume in Minimally Educated Adults," *ibid.*, 7 (No. 2, 1972), 223.

11. R. S. Siegler, E. E. Liebert, and R. M. Liebert, "Inhelder and Piaget's Pendulum Problem: Teaching Preadolescents to Act as Scientists," *ibid.*, 9 (No. 1, 1973), 97-101.

12. Piaget, "Intellectual Evolution from Adolescence to Adulthood," 1-12.

13. H. R. Tomé, *Le moi et l'autre dans la conscience de l'adolescent* (Paris: Delachaux & Niestle, 1972).

14. G. Lutte, *Le moi idéal de l'adolescent* (Brussels: Dessart, 1971).

15. R. H. Monge, "Developmental Trends in Factors of Adolescent Self-Concept," *Developmental Psychology*, 8 (No. 3, 1973), 382-393.

16. V. Sinha, "Age Differences in Self-Disclosure," *ibid.*, 7 (No. 3, 1972), 257-258.

17. B. H. Long, E. H. Henderson, and L. Platt, "Self-Other Orientations of Israeli Adolescents Reared in Kibbutzim and Moshavim," *ibid.*, 8 (No. 2, 1973), 300-308.

18. Tomé, *Le moi et l'autre dans la conscience de l'adolescent.*

19. A. R. Jensen, "How Much Can We Boost IQ and Scholastic Achievement?" *Harvard Educational Review*, 39 (No. 1, 1969), 1-123.

20. "How Much Can We Boost IQ and Scholastic Achievement? A Discussion," ed. D. R. Moore, *ibid.*, 273-356.

21. D. Elkind, "Borderline Retardation in Low and Middle Income Adolescents," in *Theories of Cognitive Development*, ed. R. M. Allen, A. D. Artazzo, and R. P. Toister (Coral Gables, Fla.: University of Miami Press, 1973).

22. M. Cole *et al.*, *The Cultural Context of Learning and Thinking* (New York: Basic Books, 1971).

The Limits of Formal Thought

John M. Broughton

The Appeal of Piaget's Theory

Under the influence of Dewey, Piaget, and, more recently, Kohlberg, development has increasingly come to be seen as the aim of education.[1] According to this view, the psychology of knowledge provides the only adequate theory and practice for pedagogy. Piaget has tied developmental psychology into a larger whole of "genetic epistemology," which also includes intellectual history, culminating in modern scientific thought as the climax of human intelligence.[2] For Piaget, as for Dewey, instrumental technical rationality is the greatest achievement of human development and holds the greatest promise for the future of human culture. More than this, it defines the very nature of life itself. Piaget's theory offers, therefore, a vision of individual and cultural progress, an image of rational man, and a developmental psychology of some philosophical sophistication, all of which are prolifically substantiated by empirical evidence. The comprehensive and scholarly quality of Piaget's eclecticism has powerfully legitimated the idea of a developmental education, as can be seen from the burgeoning literature on Piagetian pedagogy.[3] This, in turn, fuels the expanding market in neo-Piagetian and anti-Piagetian theory, to the delight and frustration of the psychology consumer.

In the professional appropriation of Piagetian theory, the stage of "formal operations" has received relatively little serious attention. Only one of Piaget's books, of which he was not even the primary author, considered systematically the emergence of adolescent intelligence.[4] It would be difficult, however, to overestimate the significance of the final stage in a developmental theory. It is not just a matter of characterizing the nature of adolescents' thinking in order to determine how best to teach them. A final stage defines and epitomizes the totality of development. It describes the domain, gives it unity, and establishes the fact that successive stages represent progress. It also characterizes the adult person and provides criteria for evaluating when someone becomes mature.

Thanks to Marta Zahaykevich and Howard Gadlin for their close reading and constructive suggestions. Augusto Blasi and the late Klaus Riegel have had a considerable influence on my thinking about formal thought in general, which should be acknowledged. A debt of gratitude is also owed to all those students at Teachers College and Wayne State University who have contributed in both formal and informal ways to the gradual emergence of these ideas.

Following is an examination of the way in which formal operations combines logic and scientific method. Criticism will focus on the incoherence of the latter and the irrelevance of the former. Beyond these weaknesses, the image of adults crystallized in formal operations is itself a particular social and historical product, limited in both truth and value by its narrow emphasis on technical skill.

Why "Formal Operations"?

Piaget often describes the final stage in the development of intelligence in terms of the "lattice structure" of mature formal logic, or the "INRC groups" of transformations constituting that structure. The book by Inhelder and Piaget reveals, however, that the empirical procedures used to tap formal thought comprise tasks whose solution requires the application of scientific method: the formulation and controlled experimental testing of hypotheses. The logic of abstract thought provides, on the one hand, a deductive system for interrelating hypothetical possibilities and, on the other hand, a normative system for regulating the process by which hypotheses are inductively confirmed.

Why has Piaget's theory evolved in such a way that logic and scientific method are made the essential part of knowledge and the highest expression of its development? Why did he resolve "to have confidence only in experimentation or calculation (biometrical or logical)"?[6] The answer is to be found in Piaget's commitment to the positivistic tradition of analytic philosophy called "logical empiricism."[7] This Anglo-Saxon school of philosophy maintains that experience is the only means of knowing the world and that science offers the only guarantee of true knowledge. The central concern is to consolidate a "Unified Science," and the most appropriate model for unifying different scientific disciplines is seen as the method used in the mathematical and natural sciences. This method democratically ensures that knowledge reflects consensual experience, accessible to all, an agreement best expressed in a purified language. Thus, "philosophy must start with exact logical analysis of the language in which scientific questions are formulated"[8] and should prescribe a manner in which scientific theories can be translated into consistent, logical formalizations. Logic itself does not yield knowledge. Rather, propositions are to be given consideration on the basis of their verifiability and then confirmed by a rigorous method of testing. In this way, logical empiricism attempts to heal the historical breach between the rational and the empirical, the world of rules and the world of causes.

Piaget terms his overall project "genetic epistemology." His developmental theory appears to have a much narrower purview, however, dealing specifically with the development of scientific knowledge.[9] This narrowing of focus exactly parallels the philosophical shift brought about by logical empiricism, in which questions of epistemology were progressively confined to matters of the philosophy of science. More than this, science was narrowly and ahistorically viewed as nothing more than a hypothetico-deductive system linked to observational procedures. It should be admitted that at its basis the logical empiricist perspective did well to emphasize the methodological self-awareness of the active knower. This resulted, however, in restricting the scope of epistemology to the matter of confirming hypotheses through evidence, that is, constructing an inductive method. Correspondingly, at Piaget's formal stage the problem is to integrate deduction and induction. Formal logic and scientific method are combined at this stage to explain the "interaction of deductions with the data of experience."[10] This interaction is accomplished by the hypothesis-testing activities of the formal thinker, activities that attempt verification while also refining the hypotheses themselves. In serving this double function, Piaget's formal operations structure heals the breach between the "context of justification" and the "context of discovery." His final stage, therefore, thoroughly reflects the logical empiricist model of science, much as his attempt at logical formalization of the stages reflects the logical empiricist ideal for a fully developed scientific theory.

Formal Operations and the Nature of Science

Genetic epistemology is distinguished by its claim that the norm of individual cognitive development is determined by the intellectual development of the human species occurring in the history of science.[11] Even within the narrow definition of knowledge as science, therefore, formal operations stands or falls with formal logic and scientific method. The strength of a genetic epistemological theory is also its liability because it must reflect advances in our understanding and philosophic justification of science as well as advances in our scientific, psychological understanding of intelligence.

It is unfortunate for Piagetians that recent philosophy of science has exposed basic inadequacies in the experimental hypothetico-deductive model of scientific investigation.[12] Confirming or refuting hypotheses through testing predictions, devising "crucial tests" for competing theories, segregating what is observed from what is theory, limiting "evidence" to observable facts, and using experiment unidirectionally to evaluate theory (excluding its reverse) are all key components of scientific method according to the hypothetico-deductive model. Yet each of these components has been seriously questioned by modern philosophy of science. Much of the critique has been grounded in advances in our understanding of the history of science, particularly through what Feyerabend calls "anthropological" insights into scientific discovery and explanation. While the logical empiricist model stipulates that true scientific theories require a firm axiomatic base and a logically consistent formalization, "there exist legitimate scientific statements which violate simple logical rules," and "there does not exist a single science or other form of life that is useful, progressive, as well as in agreement with logical demands." In a similar way, the inductive model of scientific method as hypothesis testing is a reconstruction after the fact of "normal science." It is a routine system-maintenance activity occurring within a strictly delimited community. It cannot account for either how scientific discovery and explanation actually proceed or how they should proceed. "The principles of precision, consistency, experimental falsification, crucial tests, respect for facts etc., practised with determination, would bring science to a standstill."[13]

The distant, regulative attitude of logical empiricism toward the process of inquiry and its prestige as a rigorous arbiter of method now appear as liabilities symptomatic of a fundamental misconception of science and of epistemology in general. Thus, the particular end point that Piaget proposes for intellectual development fails to account for the structure of knowledge, either in the form of mature intelligence or of modern science.

It may be asked whether an alternative and more adequate theory of scientific inquiry would also provide a model to help explain mature intelligence. This seems unlikely for a number of reasons. First, it is by no means agreed that knowledge is the core of intelligence. Second, even if it were the core, the "scientistic" claim that scientific knowledge is the only true knowledge could not hold water, since science itself depends upon extrascientific and prescientific forms of understanding. Third, epistemology is not reducible to the philosophy of science. Fourth, the methods and deterministic assumptions of the natural sciences are inadequate to encompass the social or cultural sciences, a point to be elaborated below. Thus, not only the hypothetico-deductive model of scientific discovery and explanation but also the most general presuppositions comprising the program of logical empiricism (scientism, determinism, and so on) are found inadequate by multiple philosophic criteria.

The Relation of Logic to Psychology

The lattice structure and INRC groups constituting formal operations are derived from a particular theory of mathematical logic, which has been critically examined by experts in symbolic logic.[14] It is possible, however, to ask some general questions about the nature of symbolic logic and its appropriateness as a model for mature intelligence without going into these detailed problems. This is especially fitting since Piaget's theory attempts primarily to establish an original position on the relation of logic to psychology.

Piaget sees logic as a normative question of foundations, of deductively discovering and expressing in rule systems the conditions under which reasoning can be accepted as formally valid. He has been accused of "logicism," of contending that thought mirrors logic. He has, however, explicitly rejected this position. He argues (as did Baldwin before him) that logic is not prior to experience, but, rather, is constructed by each individual through reflection upon his own actions.[15]

One can, nevertheless, raise the objection that what is attempted in using logic as a model for cognition is an unwarranted "cognitive monopoly." Is thinking really unified in the way that the absolute unity of a formal logical system suggests? Arendt, for example, has recently reminded us of the validity of Kant's distinction between "knowing" and "thinking," the former concerned with matters of truth, the latter with meaning.[16] In general, even if there were a unity to cognition, there is reason to question whether either thinking or knowing could be adequately or exhaustively characterized as a process guided by logical or axiomatic systems of rules.[17]

The use of formal logic as a model of thought has also been criticized on the grounds of its formal nature. For example, James Mark Baldwin, the founder of genetic epistemology, has said that formal logic is "the Logician's Logic: it is certainly not the psychologist's logic—that is, not the science of the actual thought process as the psychologist finds it—nor is it the logic of the knower himself in the process of acquiring and utilizing knowledge."[18] Thus, Baldwin is objecting to the transfer of certain assumptions of formal logic into the psychological domain. The first assumption is that there are elements that have "algebraic" meanings that are so fixed and exact that they do not change at all in the course of thinking; being defined as entirely abstract, these elements carry no "surplus meaning." The second assumption is that formal logic should be construed as the "Laws of Thought" representing absolute requirements for any cognitive experience.

In relation to such objections, it is helpful to see the *structuralist* nature of what Piaget is doing. Modern structuralism suggests that what underlies intelligent performance is an abstract "competence." This is a universal code, such as the lattice structure of formal operations, or the "grammar" of transformational linguists. A code is typically made up of a set of discrete elements such as Piaget's operations or binary propositions. Such an abstract competence calls for some kind of combinatorial system which can permute the various elements of the code in different arrays.[19] These finite systems are "closed," in the sense that relations between the elements are internal to the system. The code or system is self-sufficient, and has no relations with external realities. As a result, cognition, language, and so forth are no longer seen as "forms of life," but as relatively isolated and autonomous networks of inner relationships.

In the case of formal operations the symbolic group logic of interiorized actions could be characterized as such a closed system. It is important, however, to approach Piaget's theory whole and to see that, like the logical empiricists, he adds to an abstract deductive logic a dynamic inductive system of inquiry—a scientific method guided by the logical component, which, in turn, is concretely realized by that method. While Baldwin is correct in saying that there is no sphere of actual experience that lies inside the assumptions, and, from Piaget's point of view, the words of his forebear merely serve to underscore the fact that formal thinking, like science, combines deduction and induction—justification and discovery— through wedding an axiomatics of reason to an experimental science. Piaget maintains this merger precisely because logic's "own purity is merely a limit which is never completely attained."[20] The laws of thought delimit the ideal characteristics of our human understanding. They reflect lawlike tendencies in rational thought, not generalizations about empirical regularities. Logical principles are not "applied" in everyday activity. Rather, for Piaget, actions are organized according to a set of rules arising from the actions themselves. Intelligence is incapable of spontaneously applying axioms (like the principle of noncontradiction), since these axioms codify theoretical patterns formulated after the construction of thought; they do not describe the continuously creative and constructive process of thinking itself. Logic is less a mechanism for generating or comprehending thought than it is a rule book for reference and for legitimation where instances of dubious logic—self's or other's—are under examination. In the final analysis, "it is only in the outcome of actual experience and through a reflective interpretation of it, that we become aware of the logical categories and practical imperatives by which we conduct our lives. The separation of form and matter is simply an artifice; such and such form is form only as there is such and such content which is so formed."[21]

Formal Operations and Concrete Practice

While Piaget's use of symbolic logic as a psychological model is narrow, it is not incoherent. In formal operations, however, a broad structural

understanding of reasoning is obtained at the risk of losing a detailed explanation of the actual process of thinking.[22] The role of concrete practice
is unimportant in Piaget's theory. The testing of hypotheses is a relatively
weak way of describing either thinking or action. The situations amenable
to such a form of understanding appear to be limited, for example, to
problem solving in which the framework of a problem is already set ex-
trinsically. These situations are clearest in closed systems of mechanical
equilibriums, such as swinging pendulums and rolling balls.

Finally, the hypothesis-testing perspective is not only unneccessary
but is also inappropriate for sociopsychological situations. This is the case
because nonphysical systems do not necessarily have properties of equilibrium, and because, in the sociopsychological world, some types of possibility have their origin in will, imagination, creativity, or discourse,
rather than being already given or derived from logical permutations of
givens.[23] In general, one can, in the sociological and psychological realms,
isolate variables and carry out controlled experiments with them only to
a limited extent and primarily under artificial conditions created by a
wrenching out of context. Such wrenching, accompanied by the manipulation of sociopsychological variables, often results in immorality[24] or
alienation; thus, consistent formal operational conduct in day-to-day life,
besides encouraging pedantry, would considerably resemble psychopathology.

The extension of formal operations to explain the mature personality,[25] which is attempted by Inhelder and Piaget, must, therefore, be
viewed with considerable skepticism. In the same way that human beings
are not primarily concerned with logical consistency, they are also not
solely or even primarily motivated by a theoretic interest in experimentally
formulating true laws. Formal operations as an ideal norm for life would
exclude other significant kinds of rational interest, such as in developing
conceptual understanding, seeing things differently, revising and restructuring beliefs and goals, and constructing a deeper social and historical
meaning in the world or in one's own life. Thus, while logic explains and
safeguards certain universal and necessary implications in thought, one
must not reify them, since "universality and necessity, so far from being
presuppositions of reality in all its aspects, are merely ideals arising in the
operation of partial and restricted processes of cognition."[26]

Technical and Cultural Understanding

Piaget's genetic epistemology promises a general curricular orientation
based on the idea that common logical structures underlie different
disciplines.[27] But can this promise be fulfilled? Piaget echoes the

conception of knowledge of the deductive and natural sciences. While sharing the genetic aspirations of Hegel, Piaget departs from the Hegelian contention that philosophical knowledge must encompass the totality of cultural forms. Logic and methodological rules do not themselves have meaning. Given the way that Piaget characterizes intelligence, it can only be described structurally. Logical forms cannot be subjected to an *interpretation*, but cultural symbolic forms (for example, religious, aesthetic, and mythical) can and should be. Thus, only the cultural sciences require an investigation into the "consciousness of symbols"[28] and presume a human being able to make such interpretations, rather than one primarily operative on the basis of logical principles which, in turn, regulate a quest for control over cause-effect relationships.

While these two kinds of abilities, interpretive and logical, are by no means incompatible in principle, Piaget's exclusion of the former from his final stage means that the interpretive and expressive relations of individuals to themselves, each other, and society suffer one of the three following fates: they remain recondite; they are dismissed as parts or extensions of logical cognition; or they are pejoratively labeled as "regressions" to the symbolic and intuitive preoperational stage.[29] If some conceptual means of distinguishing the two modes of consciousness is not made available, then the individual's ability to differentiate the peculiarly scientific aspects of experience from religious-aesthetic-mythical ones remains inexplicable. The unity of scientific knowing thereby collapses, and the understanding of the logical structure to the natural world threatens always to be pervaded by unidentifiable "symbolic" meanings.

Piaget's Theory and the Image of Man as Formal Operator

While one can supplement Piaget's model of scientific intelligence with one of moral judgment (borrowed from his earlier work[30]), he presents an image of the adult as an analytic theorist and a disinterested observer of a given and accepted reality. Though this person's practical activities may take others' perspectives into account, the activities are still technical applications of theoretical knowledge. The world has a structure independent of the knower, and that world can be neither judged nor changed. One can become conscious of self only by separating self from world and developing a recursive form of logic and an experimental method for manipulating given variables. The attainment of this enlightened self-consciousness, and the end of idealistic adolescence, is (as in Erikson's theory) signaled by the demise of utopian visions and the acceptance of an assigned role within the division of labor prescribed within current technological society.[31]

The technical way in which this individual operates precludes his having a historical dimension. How the thought structures actually developed within the individual's biography is erased from consciousness. Logic and method have no memory, and the fact that one has developed is forgotten in the very process of developmental restructuring. There is also a parallel social and political amnesia. In the Piagetian perspective the social or cultural construction of forms as a historical process is dismissed because the activities of the individual and the logical principles interiorized by him represent eternal verities. Activities are directed by a "closed" code that nullifies cooperation and discourse as the major means of man's social development. Logic aspires to an individuality, objectivity, and reversibility that have difficulty in accommodating the collective, man-made, and irreversible nature of historical transformations. Yet the very separation of form from content and the notion of abstract cognition that are presupposed in this individual constructivism are themselves historical results of capitalist modes of commodity production and division of labor in urban commercial cultures.[32] "With the advent of wage-labor, production as well as exchange acquired abstract value, and the purely formal language of mathematics (the language of commercial transactions) became the expression of the social relations of production as well as those of the marketplace."[33]

Formal operations as a mode of consciousness must be seen, as must logical empiricism, as specific content within the historical structure of social reality. Self-consciousness cannot be severed from the understanding and criticism of social and political conditions, and these activities, in turn, constitute concrete human existence. By providing the sociohistorical context for formal operations one does not destroy it as a scientifically validated construct.[34] When alternatives to capitalism are envisioned, however, one can no longer contend that those forms of cognition which were made possible by the transactional system of capitalism consist of absolute, necessary, and universal principles of thought. It is not that the cognitive stage of formal operations has no validity. To show the specific historical and social conditions of society under which formal thought arose, and to demonstrate its primary function in regulating the abstract exchange of labor for wages, is not to argue that formal operational cognition is an empirical illusion. Then formal operations is in fact very real. Whether or not Piaget's structural description of thought is the precisely correct one, the fact remains that, from adolescence on, a good proportion of us do indeed reason formally. Formal thought may even be present in most cultures, at least the urban commercial ones.

In the above sense, formal operations is a partially true construct. With increased critical insight into the history and nature of social reality, we can place formal thinking in a much broader context. Throughout this analysis we have tried to demarcate a limited sphere for formal operations. If it were considered a comprehensive description of adolescent and adult rationality and personality, formal operations would appear less like a scientifically validated psychological construct and more like a caricature of the oppressive social realities that have given rise to it—the monopoly of technological interests, precise and efficient production and control, and the idolization of science as the instrument of those interests. The extent to which the stage of formal operations pervades areas of reason and conduct beyond its appropriate domain is a sign that it describes modern ideology in which technical logic and methods engulf the practical, moral, and political spheres. If this is the case, and it can be demonstrated scientifically that formal operations is, in fact, a general stage of personal and social development, or at least the primary basis of that development, then we are in a peculiar position. Instead of seeing formal operations as the climax of "natural development," we would be forced to interpret it as the culmination of a destructive socialization that alienates our thinking and our being. Much as authority announces itself as "logic," alienation and ideology disguise themselves as "development"[35] and thereby legitimate themselves as the goals of child rearing and education.[36]

If we admit the above, then we should not discount Piaget as obsolete and go shopping for an alternative theoretical basis for adolescent instruction. To do that would be to conform to the expected pattern of consumer behavior when faced with a discredited commodity. Rather, we should question the "naturalness" of development in general and consider the possibility of *compensatory* education. Such a "pedagogy of the oppressed" would offer to present and future adolescents a resocialization designed to offset through critical awareness and practice the alienation of reason so deeply invading their own psyches. Such compensatory education could also serve to defend these young people against the further penetration of ideology which takes place through the instrument of the modern cognitive psychology of adolescence.

Notes

1. L. Kohlberg and R. Mayer, "Development as the Aim of Education," *Harvard Educational Review*, 42 (November 1972), 449-496.

2. H. Bruber and J. Voneche, *The Essential Piaget* (New York: Basic Books, 1977).

3. I. J. Athey and D. C. Rubadeau, *Educational Implications of Piaget's Theory* (Waltham, Mass.: Ginn-Blaisdell, 1970).

4. B. Inhelder and J. Piaget, *The Growth of Logical Thinking from Childhood to Adolescence* (New York: Basic Books, 1958); see also J. Piaget, "Intellectual Evolution from Adolescence to Adulthood," *Human Development*, 15 (No. 1, 1972), 1-12.

5. J. M. Broughton and M. K. Zahaykevich, "Personality and Ideology in Ego Development," in *La dialectique d'aujourd'hui*, ed. V. Trinh van Thao (Paris: Anthropos, forthcoming).

6. W. E. Beth and J. Piaget, *Mathematical Epistemology and Psychology* (Dordrecht, Holland: D. Reidel, 1966), 131.

7. G. Radnitzky, *Contemporary Schools of Metascience* (Göteborg, Sweden: Akademiforlaget, 1968), in T. W. Adorno *et al., The Positivist Dispute in German Sociology* (New York: Harper and Row, 1976).

8. L. Kolakowski, *Positivist Philosophy* (Harmondsworth, Eng.: Penguin Books, 1972), 203.

9. J. M. Broughton, "Beyond Formal Operations," *Teachers College Record*, 79 (September 1977), 1, 87-97.

10. J. Piaget, *To Understand Is to Invent* (Harmondsworth, Eng.: Penguin Books, 1976), 21.

11. M. Wartofsky, "From Praxis to Logos," in *Cognitive Development and Genetic Epistemology,* ed. T. Mischel (New York: Academic Press, 1971).

12. For an account of the traditional model, see R. Braithwaite, *Scientific Explanation* (Cambridge, Eng.: Cambridge University Press, 1953).

13. P. Feyerabend, *Against Method* (London: New Left Books, 1975), 258-260.

14. See Broughton, "Beyond Formal Operations," 90. On Piaget's mathematico-logical model, see J. Piaget, *Psychology of Intelligence* (London: Routledge and Kegan Paul, 1950).

15. Beth and Piaget, *Mathematical Epistemology and Psychology.* Piaget's position is anticipated in J. M. Baldwin, *Genetic Theory of Reality* (New York: G. P. Putnam, 1915), e.g., 220-221, and throughout *id., Thought and Things*, Volumes 1-3 (London: Swann Sonnenschein, 1906-1911). The accusation of logicism is leveled, for example, by P. Wason, in *Piaget and Knowing*, ed. B. Geber (London: Routledge and Kegan Paul, 1977).

16. H. Arendt, *The Life of the Mind*, Volume 1, *Thinking* (New York: Littlefield, Adams, 1977).

17. The general notion that human behavior is essentially guided by rules encounters profound problems. See J. D. Ingleby, "New Paradigms for Old," *Radical Philosophy* (No. 6, 1973), 42-45; M. Merleau-Ponty, *Structure of Behavior* (Boston: Beacon Press, 1963).

18. Throughout Baldwin, *Thought and Things*, Volume 1.

19. P. Ricoeur, *Interpretation Theory: Discourse and the Surplus of Meaning* (Fort Worth: Texas Christian University Press, 1976).

20. Piaget, *Psychology of Intelligence,* 28.

21. Baldwin, *Genetic Theory of Reality,* 186; cf. E. V. Sullivan, *Kohlberg's Structuralism: A Critical Appraisal* (Toronto: Ontario Institute for Studies in Education, 1977).

22. M. Berkowitz, J. C. Gibbs, and J. M. Broughton, "Structure and Process: An Inquiry into the "What" and "How" of Moral Judgement Development," in *Proceedings of the 7th Annual Meeting of Society for Piaget and the Helping Professions* (Los Angeles: University of Southern California, forthcoming). The relation between structural developmentalism and sociolinguistics is best explicated by J. Habermas in two articles: "Moral Development and Ego Identity," *Telos,* 24 (Summer 1975), 41-55, and "Toward a Theory of Communicative Competence," in *Recent Sociology #2,* ed. H. P. Dreitzel (New York: Macmillan, 1970).

24. One could cite here the ethical infringements implicit in E. J. Webb *et al., Unobtrusive Measures: Nonreactive Research in the Social Sciences* (Chicago: Rand McNally, 1966).

25. Cf. A. Blasi, "Concepts of Development in Personality Theory," in J. Loevinger, *Development: Conceptions and Theories* (San Francisco: Jossey-Bass, 1976).

26. Baldwin, *Genetic Theory of Reality,* 223; see also J. Glick, "Functional and Structural Aspects of Rationality," paper presented to the Jean Piaget Society, Philadelphia, May 21, 1977; and J. Smedslund, "Piaget's Psychology in Practice," *British Journal of Educational Psychology,* 47 (Part 1, 1977), 1-6.

27. J. Piaget, *Science of Education and the Psychology of the Child* (New York: Viking Press, 1970); C. T. Swensen, "An Epistemology and the Curriculum," doctoral dissertation, Teachers College, Columbia University, 1974.

28. E. Cassirer, *The Logic of Humanities* (New Haven, Conn.: Yale University Press, 1967), 174; E. Oestereicher, "Praxis: The Dialectical Sources of Knowledge," *Dialectical Anthropology,* 1 (No. 3, 1976), 225-238.

29. In regard to the third fate, see S. Buck-Morss, "Piaget, Adorno and the Possibilities of Dialectical Operations," *Stony Brook Studies in Philosophy,* 4 (in press).

30. J. Piaget, *The Moral Judgement of the Child* (London: Routledge and Kegan Paul, 1932).

31. Inhelder and Piaget, *The Growth of Logical Thinking from Childhood to Adolescence*; J. M. Broughton, "The Development of Natural Epistemology in the Years 10-26," doctoral dissertation, Graduate School of Education, Harvard University, 1974.

32. G. Lukacs, *History and Class Consciousness* (Cambridge, Mass.: M.I.T. Press, 1971); Oestereicher, "Praxis"; S. Buck-Morss, "Socio-Economic Bias in Piaget's Theory and Its Implications for the Cross-Culture Controversy," *Human Development,* 18 (No. 1-2, 1975), 35-49.

33. Buck-Morss, "Piaget, Adorno and the Possibilities of Dialectical Operations," 2-3.

34. J. M. Broughton, review of J. Gabel, *False Consciousness, Telos,* 29 (Fall 1976), 223-238; J. M. Broughton, "Dialectics and Moral Development Ideology," in *Readings in Moral Education,* ed. P. Scharf (Minneapolis: Winston Press, 1978).

35. R. Jacoby, *Social Amnesia* (Boston: Beacon Press, 1975).

36. H. Gadlin, "Scars and Emblems: Paradoxes of American Family Life," *Journal of Social History* (in press).

2

"Who Is the Fairest of Them All?"

We turn now to moral development in adolescence even though no compelling developmental logic dictates that character should be discussed next. Dewey saw rationality and character as the absolute keystones of education and presumably of human personality. For him, the aim of education is growth or development, both intellectual and moral. Ethical and psychological principles can aid the school "in the greatest of all constructions—the building of a free and powerful character."[1] In significant degree that is a bias (possibly old-fashioned) of this book, although the central thesis is that both psychology and education must lead to *whole* people. Rationality, character, ego, social contribution, the aesthetic, a sound body, emotion, work, and soul are integral parts of human being and potential—the ninefold helix that is everyone's birthright. Of these, ego development, or the meaning the individual makes of himself and his life, may be the most central and comprehensive strand. Moral development is discussed next because it has a long tradition in education; because it is closely tied in modern developmental psychology to cognitive growth; because adults clamor for it in their children, even if the latter do not; and because much is known about it.

The excerpts here focus essentially on Kohlberg's research on the psychology of moral development. In his article he acknowledges the substantial antecedents to his own study in Dewey's theoretical speculations about ethics and in Piaget's epistemological research. Those antecedents strengthen Kohlberg's position, but it should be acknowledged that Kohlberg has not, in R. S. Peters' terms, "told the whole story." Peters is critical of Kohlberg for asserting that a morality of justice (in contrast to a morality of utilitarianism, or virtue, or integrity, or courage) is "the true one."[2] Aron points out that Kohlberg's morality deals only with questions of right and wrong—one's obligations—and not with issues of what is good or bad—one's virtues.[3]

In another sense, Kohlberg needs little formal introduction in this book. His article presented here is terse but clear. In my Introduction I briefly comment on his work and its significance. In Part II many of the programs in developmental education refer to his theoretical influence. Only the essentials of the theory need be reviewed.

Morality as Reasoning and as Development

Kohlberg says that the heart (perhaps one should say the "head") of morality in human beings is their reasoning: how they decide what they ought to do, what is right and wrong, what their obligations and rights are. After studying the way people judge these matters, he has concluded that their moral reasoning develops in a predictable sequence. Not only does their reasoning about issues of right and wrong become, with experience, more complex, but it also becomes more subject to the application of principle in deciding; that is, it becomes more moral. Kohlberg has found, empirically, that moral reasoning progresses through six stages, each with distinctive rules or criteria for deciding right from wrong. Each stage is a kind of self-contained moral code, philosophy, or point of view. Our moral reasoning typically reflects one predominant stage; we always have access to the "lower" stages through which we have passed; we cannot jump, leave out, or easily learn any stage. In part this is because a stage is a complex "structure" of thought about right and wrong, a schema of rules, criteria, justifications, and understandings of which we are not especially conscious, and which changes slowly. Further, this structure is distinct from the *content* of our moral thinking, which may be about sex, cheating on income tax, breaking traffic rules, punishing children, or practicing a particular religion.

Thinking is not, of course, all there is to morality, even in the common-sense understanding of that term. One may know what the right thing to do is and not do it. Circumstances (Is a police car enforcing the fifty-five-mile limit on the highway?) and willpower, determination, courage, and strength to do the right thing are part of moral behavior. Kohlberg acknowledges this. He does not (usually) claim that his theory explains more than our thinking about what is right and wrong. He does say that moral reasoning is the single most influential factor yet discovered in moral behavior and that "persons at a higher level of moral development not only reason better, but they act in accordance with their judgements."[4] He says, further, that reasoning is the only distinctive moral factor in moral behavior. (Conventional moral thinkers with strong willpower are less likely to cheat, while preconventional moral thinkers with strong will-power are more likely to cheat.) When we understand more exactly the relationship between knowing what is right and doing what is right, be-tween having the capacity for moral judgment and being moral, Kohlberg's ultimate contribution to our understanding of people's character will be clearer. And Kohlberg himself, as noted above, is edging toward the posi-tion that what is distinctively moral about our behavior is the ethical reasoning that accompanies it. Where an understanding of human beings is concerned, we always deal with incomplete theory. It is not cynical to say that understanding moral reasoning, as Kohlberg enables us to do, is substantially better than nothing.

A Theory for Practice

I can attest from considerable experience that children and adoles-cents do think in ways consistent with Kohlberg's stages. Indeed, it was hearing high school students and my own children talk this way that con-vinced me that Kohlberg had not arbitrarily created these stages. Compre-hending the stages and the concerns, the justifications and criteria about right and wrong, and the unique way of thinking that characterizes each of them can help teachers and administrators understand teenagers (to say nothing of colleagues), even if they have no interest in systematic moral education per se.

One of the principal applications of developmental theory is illustrated here. To understand formal operations, Kohlberg's Stage 3 and Loevinger's 3-4 Stage (see Chapter 3), is to know some of what to expect from adoles-cents and the "naturalness" of it; to have a lens through which to compre-hend diversity, progress, and potential in teenagers; and, it is to be hoped, to do so without categorizing or labeling them. Aron[5] is properly con-cerned that teachers not label students (as, for example, "a Stage 2") nor that they adopt a part of morality as if it were the whole. But educators must have something between IQ or SAT scores on the one hand (Thorn-dike rampant on a field of California achievement tests) and, on the other, the humanists' passionate desire to eliminate all systems that categorize people and thus reduce the uniqueness and richness of the human per-sonality to commonalities. Stage theories offer rich, multiple perspectives of the adolescent to those trying both to understand and to enhance his growth.

Further, education has an important role to play in Kohlberg's theory of moral development. It says that human character can be stimulated by certain kinds of systematic experiences. Discussing moral dilemmas in class, helping other people, and participating in social action, as well as making real moral choices within the classroom or the family, all seem to produce moral growth in children. In a larger sense, Kohlberg points to something Dewey recognized: the powerful effects on our development of the social environments, such as schools and families, in which we live and learn. That does not make the educator's job any easier, incidentally, if one of the tasks facing him is so modest a one as democratizing the school. Finally, Kohlberg's research offers a way, albeit a cumbersome one of uncertain reliability, to measure the effects of what we do, educationally, on our children's moral stature.

What Are the Paradoxes?

Those who know Kohlberg's theory and its educational applications most intimately are perhaps in the strongest position to know where the problems lie. I mention five of them here. First, the relationship between moral judgment and moral action is uncertain. There is encouraging evidence that people do what they think is right. One study, for example, demonstrated that only 20 percent of students showing some principled thinking cheated compared to 55 percent of conventional and 70 percent of preconventional students.[6] But the correlation between judgment and action is far from absolute and, theoretically, as mentioned earlier, should be. And there are few studies of that relationship. This lack of information may ultimately limit the power of programs of moral education that focus solely on developing the ability to reason. The alternative—to know what virtue or behavior is moral and how most effectively to inculcate it—is an exceedingly thorny matter. Peters[7] suggests that we teach a good-boy-good-girl morality to children. Such a morality involves concern for others, the value of being truthful and fair, and the need to follow rules such as not stealing and to keep promises. We must do these things, however, in a way that does not stunt the child's later capacity to take a more autonomous view toward them. We also turn to Peters to introduce the second problem concerning Kohlberg's theory: "He [Kohlberg] suffers from the rather touching belief that a Kantian type of morality, represented in modern times most notably by Hare and Rawls, is the only one . . . ."[8] Stage 6 in particular seems both empirically shaky—since it is so rarely found—and philosophically vulnerable.[9] The third problem with Kohlberg's theory is that it may generate a reductionism, what Moore has termed "a creeping moral developmentalism."[10] There is a danger in reducing, as Kohlberg does, civic education to political education to moral education since both political reasoning and political action derive from underlying patterns of moral reasoning. In a similar way it is also clear that democratic classrooms and democratic schools may have effects and certainly purposes that go substantially beyond the stimulation of students' moral development. And yet they may be seen as less important than gains in moral reasoning. A fourth and related problem is that there is a de facto blindness in much of Kohlberg's theory to strands of human development other than the moral. Obsessions with justice are noble, but they are nonetheless obsessions. The fifth problem concerning Kohlberg's theory is discussed by Gilligan.[11] She criticizes the sexist bias in his research and in his conception of morality. Women are not deficient (arrested Stage 3's) or deviant in development, she believes. Rather, women have a distinctive voice, one that speaks to the concepts of nonviolence, responsibility to others, and caring or love as central principles in human morality.

Though I have strongly criticized Kohlberg's theory of moral development, I must conclude this introduction by saying that, after Piaget, Kohlberg has produced the most seminal of the developmental psychologies for education. It is perhaps for its heuristic value—in showing the remarkable richness and power of developmental psychology to generate educational hypotheses, programs, and outcomes—that Kohlberg's theory should be celebrated. Certainly it has been generative. And so has Kohlberg. He is not afraid to enter the arena; nor is he disdainful of doing so. Indeed, he has advanced his ideas for education arm in arm with educators and prison officials. Here is no armchair empiricist. Finally, there is in Kohlberg's work what Rest has termed "the venerable lineage (Dewey-Piaget-Kohlberg . . .)", "the intellectual heft" of these ideas, and "the promise of initiating something more than a superficial, piecemeal, short-lived fad."[12] Powerful ideas, after all, are the only ones worth holding to.

Notes

1. J. Dewey and J. McClellan, "The Psychology of Number," in *John Dewey on Education*, ed. R. Archambault (New York: Random House, 1964), 198.

2. Richard S. Peters, "Why Doesn't Lawrence Kohlberg Do His Homework?" *Phi Delta Kappan*, 56 (June 1975), 678.

3. Israela E. Aron, "Moral Philosophy and Moral Education: A Critique of Kohlberg's Theory," *School Review*, 85 (February 1977), 197-217.

4. L. Kohlberg and E. Turiel, "Moral Development and Moral Education," in *Psychology and Educational Practice*, ed. G. Lesser (Chicago: Scott, Foresman, 1971), 414.

5. Aron, "Moral Philosophy and Moral Education."

6. Kohlberg and Turiel, "Moral Development and Moral Education," 458.

7. Peters, "Why Doesn't Lawrence Kohlberg Do His Homework?"

8. *Ibid.*, 678.

9. Aron, "Moral Philosophy and Moral Education"; John C. Gibbs, "Kohlberg's Stages of Moral Judgment: A Constructive Critique," *Harvard Educational Review*, 47 (February 1977), 43-61.

10. David Moore, personal communication with the author.

11. Carol Gilligan, "In a Different Voice: Women's Conception of the Self and Morality," *Harvard Educational Review*, 47 (November 1977), 481-517.

12. James Rest, "Developmental Psychology as a Guide to Value Education: A Review of 'Kohlbergian' Programs," *Review of Educational Research*, 44 (No. 2, 1974), 241.

The Adolescent as a Philosopher: The Discovery of the Self in a Postconventional World

Lawrence Kohlberg
Carol Gilligan

Those whose exterior semblance doth belie
Thy Soul's immensity;
Thou best Philosopher . . .

Thou little child, yet glorious in the might
Of heaven-born freedom on thy Being's height,
Why with such earnest pains dost though provoke,
The years to bring the inevitable yoke?
Thus blindly with thy blessedness at strife?
Full soon thy Soul shall have her earthly freight,
And customs lie upon thee with a weight
Heavy as frost, and deep almost as life!

The thought of our past years in me doth breed
Perpetual benediction; not indeed
For that which is most worthy to be blest;
Delight and liberty, the simple creed of childhood . . .

Reprinted from *Daedalus,* 100 (Fall 1971), 1051-1086.

> But for those obstinate questionings
> Of sense and outward things,
> Fallings from us, vanishings;
> Moving about in worlds not realized,
> High instincts before which our mortal Nature
> Did tremble like a guilty thing surprised:
>
> Wordsworth, *Intimations of Immortality*

The central themes of this essay are first, the definition of adolescence as a universal stage of development; second, the way in which the universal features of adolescence seem to be acquiring unique colorings in the present era in America; and third, the implications of these changes for education.

Adolescence as a Role Transition and as a Stage of Development

In turn-of-the-century America, G. Stanley Hall launched developmental psychology with his discussion of adolescence as a stage of development. For the next fifty years, however, most American educators and psychologists tended to think about adolescence not as a stage but as a period in life, "the teens." The teenager was viewed as half-child, half-grown-up, with a half-serious peer "culture" or "youth culture" of his own. Textbook after textbook on adolescence was written telling in statistical detail the sort of information which could be gathered from reading *Seventeen* or Harold Teen.

Even with the textbook description of the teenager, one could surmise that the central phenomenon of adolescence is the discovery of the self as something unique, uncertain, and questioning in its position in life. The discovery of the body and its sexual drive, and self-conscious uncertainty about that body, is one stock theme of adolescent psychology. The romantic concerns and hopes for the self's future has always been another element of the stock description of the adolescent. The third stock theme implied by the discovery of the self is the need for independence, for self-determination and choice, as opposed to acceptance of adult direction and control. The fourth stock theme implied by the adolescent discovery of self is adolescent egocentrism and hedonism, the adolescent focus upon events as they bear upon his self-image and as they lead to immediate experiences. (While the child is egocentric and hedonistic, he is not subjective; he focuses upon events, not upon his subjective experience of the events, as what is important.)

While the discovery of the self in the senses just listed has been a stock theme in American discussion of adolescence, it has been subordinated to another theme, the theme of adolescence as a marginal role between being a child and being grown-up. The adolescent sense of self, with its multiple possibilities, its uncertainties, and its self-consciousness, has been viewed as the result of a social position in which one is seen and sees oneself, sometimes as adult, sometimes as child. In the marginal role view, the adolescent's need for independence and fantasies of the future are seen as the desire to "be grown-up," his conflicts and instabilities are seen as the conflict between the desire to be grown-up and a role and personality not yet consistent with being grown-up.

This social role view of adolescence, the adolescent as teenager, places the instability of the adolescent self against the background of a stable society. Against the background of the moods and tantrums and dreams of the American teenager lay an unquestioned acknowledgment of the stability and reality of the social order the adolescent was to enter. Underneath the hedonism and rebellion of the teenager lay the conformist. Harold Teen and Andy Hardy's first law was conformity to the norms of the peer group. Beneath this conformity to the peer group, however, was the teenager's recognition that when the chips were down about your future you listened to dear old Dad. An extreme example in reality of the American image of the teenager as cutting up while basically conforming is a group of California suburban high school seniors of the late 1950's. This group celebrated graduation by a summer of well-planned robberies. Their one concern while they engaged in their delinquent activities was that if they were detected, they would not get into the college of their choice.

Conformity to the peer culture, then, was the first theme of the American treatment of the adolescent in the 1950's, of August Hollingshead's *Elmtown's Youth*, James Coleman's *Adolescent Society*, Albert K. Cohen's *Delinquent Boys*. The second theme was that this peer culture was itself determined by the realities of adult social class and mobility in which the peer culture was embedded. Whether grind, jock, or hood, glamour girl, sex kitten, or Plain Jane, the teenager's discovery of self led to the enactment of the stock roles of the adolescent culture. At a different level than the sociology of the teenager, American literature also presented adolescence as accepting unquestioningly the reality of adult society. Adolescence was presented as an imaginative expansion of the innocence of childhood facing the sordid but unquestionable reality of adult life. From *Huckleberry Finn* to *Catcher in the Rye*, the true American adolescent brought the child's innocence to a new awareness of adult reality, leading to a vision of the phoniness and corruption of the adult world, which was, however, unquestioned in its reality. Sherwood Anderson's story of the fourteen-year-old finding his father figure with a prostitute is titled "I Want to Know Why." While the American adolescent might be shocked by the sordid elements of adult life and might "want to know why" there was no question that he would eventually enter and accept "adult reality." Even when he wanted to know why, the American adolescent seldom questioned the American assumptions of progress and upward mobility, the assumption that society was moving ahead. Rather, he questioned the wisdom of his parents because they were old-fashioned. This questioning was itself an expression of faith in the adult society of the future. The adolescent's sense of the superiority of his values to those of his parents was an expression of the adolescent's belief in a greater closeness to the adult society of the future than his parents had; it was a faith in progress.

Today, we are aware of the possibility of a deeper questioning by the adolescent than was true at earlier times. Our image of the adolescent must accommodate to the phenomena of the counterculture, of the hippie and the revolutionary who does not believe in progress and upward mobility. Both the hippie and the New Left reject not only the *content* of adult society but its *forms*. The new radical refuses to organize as his revolutionary predecessors of the 1930's did. Unlike the revolutionary of the 1930's, he does not want to be a grown-up, to really transform and govern the adult society of the future. And beneath a questioning of social *forms* is a questioning of social *functions*. The current radical rejection of adult society seems to be the rejection of any adult society whatever, if an adult society means one including institutions of work, family, law, and government. Radicals have always questioned the social *forms* of authority, of competitive achievement, and of the nuclear privatistic family and have dreamed of a more egalitarian and communal society. The essential realities of the social *functions* of work, child rearing, and of an organized social order were never questioned, however. Since Paul Goodman's *Growing Up Absurd*, we have been aware that the reality of work and making a living has come into question. Now the new ethics of population control and the women's liberation movement leads to the questioning of the supreme reality of adulthood, being a parent and having children. Finally, the reality of social order is in question. When current adolescents talk of revolution, they do not seem to mean merely that adult society is evil and is resistant to rational change. More deeply, they seem to be saying that there is no real social order to destroy anyway. Social order is a myth or illusion in the adult's mind and revolution is not the destruction of an order, whether good or bad. On the optimistic side this is the message of Charles Reich's "revolution in consciousness," the idea that the young can transform society without entering or dealing with it. On the pessimistic side, the popular versions of the counterculture reiterate the theme of *Easy Rider*, the theme that the adult culture is hostile and absurd, that it does not want you to join it but that it envies you and will destroy you in the end no matter what you do.

To summarize, all accounts of adolescence stress both the sense of questioning and the parallel discovery or search for a new self of the adolescent. Usually this questioning and search for self have been seen as the product of the adolescent's marginal role between childhood and adulthood. Usually, too, it has been assumed that there are underlying givens beneath the questioning, that whatever uncertainties the adolescent has, he wants to be a grown-up. Recent experience makes real for Americans the much deeper forms of questioning which may characterize adolescence, one which is not merely a matter of roles. The potential for a deeper questioning by the adolescent is implied by the identity conflict central to Erik Erikson's psychohistorical stage theory of adolescence. It is the philosophic doubting about truth, goodness, and reality implied by J. Piaget's epistemological stage theory of adolescence. It is the doubting represented by Dostoevsky's adolescents, not Mark Twain's. Deeper doubting is still a rare phenomenon, for adolescents. Beneath most hippie exteriors is an interior more like Harold Teen than Hamlet or Raskolnikov. But theoretical understanding of adolescence as a stage must stress its ideal type potential, not its "average" manifestations.

The importance of taking adolescent questioning seriously is not only important for psychological theory, it is also central to a successful resolution of the current problems of the American high school. For education, the problem of meaning just raised is the problem of whether the high school has meaning to the adolescent. We said that American psychology placed the adolescent discovery of the self against a stable but progressive social order. It saw the discovery of self within a desire to be "grown-up," however confused or vague this image of the grown-up was. The high school had a double meaning to the adolescent from this point of view. First, it was the locus of the peer culture in which he found his immediate identity, whether as grind, jock, or hood. Second, on the academic side, it was a point of connection to a place in the adult world. In most high schools these meanings still remain and the questioning of the reality of adulthood is not that deep. In others, however, it is a serious problem and high school is essentially a meaningless place. Before we can solve the problem of the felt meaninglessness of the high school, a clearer view of adolescent questioning is required. For this, we must turn to stage theory of the Erikson and Piaget variety.

The Meaning of the Stage Concept—
Illustrated from the Preschool Years

To understand the universal meanings of adolescence as a stage and its implications for education, it will help to examine briefly an earlier stage and its implications for education, one more thoroughly understood than the stage of adolescence. Almost all cultures implicitly recognize two great stages or transformations in development. Adolescence, the second transformation, traditionally terminated compulsory schooling. The first transformation occurring from five to seven years of age initiated compulsory schooling.[1] This five-to-seven shift is termed the "onset of the latency period" by Freudian theory, the onset of concrete logical thought by Piaget. As embodied in educational thought, the Freudian interpretation of the five-to-seven shift implied letting the child grow, letting him work through his fantasies until he had repressed his sexual instincts and was ready to turn his energies into formal learning. This Freudian interpretation of the preschool stage suffered both from lack of confirmation by empirical research and from irrelevance to the intellectual development and everyday behavior with which the schools were concerned. When the Great Society decided to do something for the disadvantaged child, the Freudian "let him work through his Oedipus complex" implications of the five-to-seven shift were dismissed as a luxury for the wealthy. Programs of preschool intellectual stimulation and academic schooling were initiated, with the expectation of long-range effects on intelligence and achievement. These programs failed to fulfill their initial hope of changing general intellectual maturity or long-range achievement.[2]

One reason they failed was because they confused specific teaching and learning with the development of new levels of thinking truly indicative of cognitive maturity. The evidence of limitations of these early education programs, together with growing positive research evidence of the existence of cognitive stages, convinced early educators of the reality of the stage transformation at the age five to seven. The stage transformation of the period five to seven is now conceived in quite a different way than in the vogue of Freudian education. In the Freudian view, the preschooler was in a stage of domination of thought by sexual and aggressive fantasies. The new stage which succeeded this was defined negatively as latency, rather than positively. Under the influence of Piaget, more recent thinking sees the preschool child's fantasy as only one aspect of the preschooler's pattern of prelogical thought. In the prelogical stage, subjective appearance is not fully distinguished from "reality"; the permanent identities of things are not differentiated from their momentary transformations.

In the prelogical stage view, the preschool child's special fantasy is not the expression of an instinct later repressed but of a cognitive level of thought. The decline of fantasy in the years five to seven, longitudinally documented by R. Scheffler,[3] is not a repression; it is closely related to the positive development of concrete logical patterns of thought.

The child's changed orientation to reality in the five-to-seven period is part of the development of concrete logical operations then. During this period the child develops the operations of categorical classifications, of serial ordering, addition, subtraction, and inversion of classes and relations. This development occurs in the absence of schooling in African and Taiwanese villagers in much the same way that it occurs in the American suburban child.[4]

As a concrete example, Piaget and the writers have asked children if they had had a bad dream and if they were frightened when they woke up from their bad dream.[5] Susie, aged four, said she dreamt about a giant and answered, "Yes, I was scared, my tummy was shaking and I cried and told my mommy about the giant." Asked, "Was it a real giant or was it just pretend? Did the giant just seem to be there, or was it really there?" she answered, "It was really there but it left when I woke up. I saw its footprint on the floor."

According to Piaget, Susie's response is not to be dismissed as the product of a wild imagination, but represents the young child's general failure to differentiate subjective from objective components of his experience. Children go through a regular series of steps in their understanding of dreams as subjective phenomena. The first step, achieved before five by most American middle-class children, is the recognition that dreams are not real events. The next step, achieved soon thereafter, is the realization that dreams cannot be seen by others. The third step is the notion that dreams are internal (but still material) events.

By the ages six to eight children are clearly aware that dreams are thoughts caused by themselves. To say such cognitive changes define stages implies the following things:

1. That young children's responses represent not mere ignorance or error, but rather a spontaneous manner of thinking about the world that is qualitatively different from the way we adults think and yet has a structure of its own.

2. The notion of different developmental structures of thought implies consistency of level of response from task to task. If a child's response represents a general structure rather than a specific learning, then the child should demonstrate the same relative structural levels in a variety of tasks.

3. The concept of stage implies an invariance of sequence in development, a regularity of stepwise progression regardless of cultural teaching

or circumstance. Cultural teaching and experience can speed up or slow down development, but it cannot change its order or sequence.

The concept of stage, then, imples that both the youngest children's conceptions of the dream as real and the school age children's view of the dream as subjective are their own; they are products of the general state of the child's cognitive development, rather than the learning of adult teachings.

Cross-cultural studies indicate the universality of the basic sequence of development of thinking about the dream, even where adult beliefs about the meaning and significance of dreams are somewhat different from our own.[6] While the stage of concrete operations is culturally universal and in a sense natural, this does not mean it is either innate or that it is inevitable and will develop regardless of environmental stimulation. In the United States, the doctrine of stages was assumed for sometime to mean that children's behavior unfolded through a series of age-specific patterns, and that these patterns and their order were wired into the organism. This indeed was the view of Gesell and Freud, and Americans misunderstood Piaget as maintaining the same thing. The implications of the Gesellian and Freudian theory for early education were clear; early teaching and stimulation would do no good since we must wait for the unfolding of the behavior, or at least the unfolding of the readiness to learn it.

In contrast, Piaget used the existence of stages to argue that basic cognitive structures are not wired in, but are general forms of equilibrium resulting from the interaction between organism and environment. If children have their own logic, adult logic or mental structure cannot be derived from innate neurological patterning because such patterning should hold also in childhood. (It is hardly plausible to view a succession of logics as an evolutionary and functional program of innate wiring.) At the same time, however, Piaget argued that stages indicate that mental structure is not merely a reflection of external physical realities or of cultural concepts of different complexities. The structure of the child's concepts in Piaget's view is not only less complex than the adult's, it is also different. The child's thought is not just a simplified version of the adult's.

Stages, or mental structures, then, are not wired into the organism though they depend upon inborn organizing tendencies. Stages are not direct reflections of the child's culture and external world, though they depend upon experience for their formation. Stages are rather the products of interactional experience between the child and the world, experience which leads to a restructuring of the child's own organization rather than to the direct imposition of the culture's pattern upon the child. While hereditary components of IQ, of the child's rate of information processing

have some influence on the rate at which the child moves through invariant cognitive sequences, experiential factors heavily influence the
rate of cognitive-structural development.[7] The kind of experience which
stimulates cognitive stage development is, however, very different from the
direct academic teaching of information and skills which is the focus of
ordinary schooling. Programs of early education which take account of
cognitive stages, then, look neither like the permissive "let them grow"
nursery school pattern nor like the early teaching programs popular in
the 1960's. They are a new form now coming into being.[8]

Cognitive Stages in Adolescence

The older children get, the more difficult it is to distinguish universal
stage changes from sociocultural transitions in development. We said that
the core phenomenon of adolescence as a stage was the discovery of the
subjective self and subjective experience and a parallel questioning of
adult cultural reality. The manifestations of this discovery, however, are
heavily colored not only by historical and cultural variations, but also by
previous patterns of life history of the child.

In our first section, we discussed one manifestation of the discovery of
the self, the discovery of the body and its sexual drives. In part this is, of
course, a biological universal, the physical growth spurt marking adolescent puberty and an accompanying qualitatively new sex drive. If there is
anything which can be safely said about what is new in the minds of adolescents, it is that they, like their elders, have sex on their minds. These
changes, of course, have been the focus of Freudian thinking about adolescence as a stage. If anything, however, Freudian thinking has under-
estimated the novel elements of sexual experience in adolescence. For
the Freudian, early adolescent sexuality is the reawakening of early childhood sexuality previously latent, with a consequent resurrection of Oedipal
feeling. Although it is true that adolescent sexuality bears the stamp of
earlier experience, it is not the resurrection of earlier sexual feelings.
Adolescent sexual drive is a qualitatively new phenomenon.[9]

While sexual drives are awakened at puberty, there are vast individual
and cultural variations in the extent to which they determine the adolescent's behavior and experience. Sexuality is a central concern for the self
of some fourteen-year-olds; it is something deferred to the future for
others. What is common for all, however, is an intensified emotionality
whether experienced as sexual or not. This emotionality, too, is now experienced as a part of the self rather than as a correlate of objective events
in the world. C. Ellinwood studied the age development of the verbal
experiencing and expression of emotion in projective tests and in free

self-descriptions. She found that prior to adolescence (aged twelve or so), emotions were experienced as objective concomitants of activities and objects. The child experienced anger because events or persons were bad; he experienced affection because persons were good or giving; he felt excitement because activities were exciting or fun. At adolescence, however, emotions are experienced as the result of states of the self rather than as the direct correlate of external events.[10]

The difference may perhaps be clarified by reference to middle-class drug experiences. Occasionally, a psychological preadolescent may take drugs, as he may drink beer or sneak cigarettes. When he does this, he does this as an activity of an exciting forbidden and grown-up variety. For the adolescent drug taker, drugs represent rather a vehicle to certain subjective moods, feelings, and sensations. In many cases, the drug experience is a vehicle for overcoming depression, felt as an inner subjective mood. In any case, drug taking is not an activity with an objective quality; it is a mode of activating subjective inner feelings and states. The same is true of such activities as intensive listening to music, an activity characteristically first engaged in at early adolescence (ages eleven to fourteen). The rock, folk-rock, and blues music so popular with adolescents is explicitly a presentation of subjective mood and is listened to in that spirit.

Associated with the discovery of subjective feelings and moods is the discovery of ambivalence and conflicts of feeling. If feelings are objective correlates of external good and bad events, there can be little tolerance and acceptance of feeling hate and love for the same person, of enjoying sadness and feeling sad about pleasure. Ellinwood's study documents that adolescents are consciously expressing such ambivalence, which is of course the stock-in-trade of the blues and folk-rock music beamed to them.

We have spoken of the adolescent discovery of subjective moods and feelings as linked to puberty. More basically, it is linked to the universal cognitive stages of Piaget. We have said that the post-age-twelve or so transition is defined by Piaget as the transition to *abstract, reflective* thought. More exactly, it is the transition from logical inference as a set of *concrete operations* to logical inference as a set of *formal operations* or "operations upon operations." "Operations upon operations" imply that the adolescent can classify classification, that he can combine combinations, that he can relate relationships. It implies that he can think about thought, and create thought systems or "hypothetico-deductive" theories. This involves the logical construction of all possibilities—that is, the awareness of the observed as only a subset of what may be logically possible. In related fashion, it implies the hypothetico-deductive attitude, the notion that a belief or proposition is not an immediate truth but a hypothesis whose truth value consists in the truth of the concrete propositions derivable from it.

An example of the shift from concrete to formal operations may be taken from the work of E. A. Peel.[11] Peel asked children what they thought about the following event: "Only brave pilots are allowed to fly over high mountains. A fighter pilot flying over the Alps collided with an aeriel cable-way, and cut a main cable causing some cars to fall to the glacier below. Several people were killed." A child at the concrete-operational level answered: "I think that the pilot was not very good at flying. He would have been better off if he went on fighting." A formal-operational child responded: "He was either not informed of the mountain railway on his route or he was flying too low also his flying compass may have been affected by something before or after take-off this setting him off course causing collision with the cable."

The concrete-operational child assumes that if there was a collision the pilot was a bad pilot; the formal-operational child considers all the possibilities that might have caused the collision. The concrete-operational child adopts the hypothesis that seems most probable or likely to him. The formal-operational child constructs all possibilities and checks them out one by one.

As a second example, we may cite one of Piaget's tasks, systematically replicated by D. Kuhn, J. Langer, and L. Kohlberg.[12] The child is shown a pendulum whose length may vary as well as the number of weights attached. The child is asked to discover or explain what determines the speed of movement (or "period") of the pendulum. Only the formal-operational child will "isolate variables," that is, vary length holding weight constant, and so forth, and arrive at the correct solution (for example, that period is determined by length). Success at the task is unrelated to relevant verbal knowledge about science or physics, but is a function of logical level.

In fact the passage from concrete to formal operations is not an all or none phenomenon. There are one or two substages of formal operations prior to the full awareness of all possibilities just described. These substages are described in Table 2-1, which presents an overview of the Piaget cognitive stages. For simplifying purposes, we may say that for middle-class Americans, one stage of formal operations is reached at age ten to thirteen, while the consideration of all possibilities is reached around fifteen to sixteen. At the first formal-operational stage, children became capable of reversing relationships and ordering relationships one at a time or in chains, but not of abstract consideration of all possibilities. (They are capable of "forming the inverse of the reciprocal," in Piaget's terminology; but not of combining all relationships.) A social thinking example of failure to reverse relationships is shown in concrete-operational children's responses to the question: "What does the Golden Rule tell you to do if

Table 2-1

Piaget's eras and stages of logical and cognitive development

---

Era I (age 0-2) The era of sensorimotor intelligence

Stage 1. Reflex action.

Stage 2. Coordination of reflexes and sensorimotor repetition (primary circular reaction).

Stage 3. Activities to make interesting events in the environment reappear (secondary circular reaction).

Stage 4. Means-ends behavior and search for absent objects.

Stage 5. Experimental search for new means (tertiary circular reaction).

Stage 6. Use of imagery in insightful invention of new means and in recall of absent objects and events.

Era II (age 2-5) Symbolic, intuitive, or prelogical thought

Inference is carried on through images and symbols which do not maintain logical relations or invariances with one another. "Magical thinking" in the sense of (a) confusion of apparent or imagined events with real events and objects and (b) confusion of perceptual appearances of qualitative and quantitative change with actual change.

Era III (ages 6-10) Concrete-operational thought

Inferences carried on through system of classes, relations, and quantities maintaining logically invariant properties and which *refer to concrete objects*. These include such logical processes as (a) inclusion of lower-order classes in higher-order classes; (b) transitive seriation (recognition that if $a > b$ and $b > c$, then $a > c$); (c) logical addition and multiplication of classes and quantities; (d) conservation of number, class membership, length, and mass under apparent change.

Substage 1. Formation of stable categorical classes.

Substage 2. Formation of quantitative and numerical relations of invariance.

Era IV (age 11 to adulthood) Formal-operational thought

Inferences through logical operations upon propositions or "operations upon operations." Reasoning about reasoning. Construction of systems of all possible relations or implications. Hypothetico-deductive isolation of variables and testing of hypotheses.

Substage 1. Formation of the inverse of the reciprocal. Capacity to form negative classes (for example, the class of all not-crows) and to see relations as simultaneously reciprocal (for example, to understand that liquid in a U-shaped tube holds an equal level because of counterbalanced pressures).

Substage 2. Capacity to order triads of propositions or relations (for example, to understand that if Bob is taller than Joe and Joe is shorter than Dick, then Joe is the shortest of the three).

Substage 3. True formal thought. Construction of all possible combinations of relations, systematic isolation of variables, and deductive hypothesis testing.

---

someone comes up on the street and hits you?" The typical answer is
"hit him back, do unto others as they do unto you." The painful process
of the transitional formal-operational child in response to the question is
given by the following response: "Well for the Golden Rule you have to
like dream that your mind leaves your body and goes into the other person,
then it comes back into you and you see it like he does and you act like
the way you saw it from there."[13]

We have described Piaget's stage of formal operations as a logical
stage. What is of special importance for understanding adolescents,
however, is not the logic of formal operations, but its epistemology, its
conception of truth and reality. In the previous section we said that the
child's attainment of concrete operations at age six to seven led to the
differentiation of subjective and objective, appearance and reality. The
differentiation at this level was one in which reality was equated with the
physical and the external. We cited the child's concept of the dream, in
which the unreality of the dream was equivalent to its definition as an
inner mental event with no physical external correlate. The subjective
and the mental are to the concrete-operational child equated with fantasies, with unrealistic replicas of external physical events. The development of formal operations leads, however, to a new view of the external
and the physical. The external and the physical are only one set of many
possibilities of a subjective experience. The external is no longer the real,
"the objective," and the internal the "unreal." The internal may be real
and the external unreal. At its extreme, adolescent thought entertains
solipsism or at least the Cartesian cogito, the notion that the only thing
real is the self. I asked a fifteen-year-old girl: "What is the most real thing
to you?" Her unhesitating reply was "myself."

The lines from Wordsworth introducing this essay represent his own
adolescent experience described by him as follows: "I was often unable to
think of external things as having external existence, and I communed
with all that I saw as something not apart from, but inherent in, my own
material nature. Many times while going to school have I grasped at a
wall or tree to recall myself from this abyss of idealism to the reality. At
this time I was afraid of such processes."[14]

Wordsworth's adolescent solipsism was linked to his awakened poetic
sense, to his experience of nature, and to his transcendental religiosity.
It seems that for all adolescents the discovery of the subjective is a condition for aesthetic feeling in the adult sense, for the experience of nature as
a contemplative experience, and for religiosity of a mystical varity. It is
probably the condition for adolescent romantic love as well. This whole
constellation of experiences is called romantic because it is centered on a
celebration of the self's experience as the self enters into union with the

self's counterpart outside. The common view of romanticism as adolescent, then, is correct in defining the origins of romanticism in the birth of the subjective self in adolescence.

If the discovery of subjective experience and the transcendental self is one side of the new differentiation of subjective and objective made by the adolescent, the clouding and questioning of the validity of society's truths and its rightness is the other. To consider this side of adolescence we must turn from cognitive to moral stages.

Before we turn to adolescent moral thought we need to note a real difference between the development of concrete operations and the development of formal operations. There are two facts which distinguish the adolescent revolution in logical and epistemological thinking from the five-to-seven revolution in thinking. The first is that the adolescent revolution is extremely variable as to time. The second is that for many people it never occurs at all. With regard to concrete operations, some children attain clear capacity for logical reasoning at five, some at eight or nine. But all children ultimately display some clear capacity for concrete-logical reasoning.[15] This is not true for formal-operational reasoning. As an example, the percentage of 235 persons at various ages showing clear formal-operational reasoning at the pendulum task is as follows:

Age ten to fifteen: 45 percent

Age sixteen to twenty: 53 percent

Age twenty-one to thirty: 65 percent

Age forty-five to fifty: 57 percent.[16]

The subjects studied were lower-middle and upper-middle-class California parents (age forty-five to fifty) and their children (age ten to thirty). The figures indicate that it is not until age twenty-one to thirty that a clear majority (65 percent) attain formal reasoning by this criterion. They suggest that there is no further development of formal reasoning after age thirty. This means that almost 50 percent of American adults never reach adolescence in the cognitive sense. The figures should not be taken with too great seriousness, since various tasks requiring formal operations are of somewhat varying difficulty. In the study cited another problem, a "correlation problem," was used which was passed by even fewer members of the adult population. It is possible that easier tasks could be devised which would lead to more people displaying formal reasoning. The point, however, is that a large proportion of Americans never develop the capacity for abstract thought. Most who do, develop it in earlier adolescence (age eleven to fifteen), but some do not reach full formal reasoning until the twenties. We should note, too, that rate of attainment of formal operations is not simply a function of IQ: the correlations between Piaget and IQ measures are in the 50's. Finally, in simpler cultures—for example, villages in Turkey—full formal operations never seem to be reached at all (though it is reached by urbanized educated Turks).

The high variability in age of attainment of formal operations, then, indicates that we cannot equate a cognitive stage with a definite age period. Puberty, the attainment of formal operations, and the transition from childhood to adult status are all components of adolescence variable in time and in their relations to one another.

Moral Stages in Adolescence and Their Relation to Cognitive Stages

Joseph Adelson [*Daedalus*, 100 (Fall 1971)] documents the way in which the adolescent's thinking about political society is transformed by the advent of formal-operational thought. To understand the adolescent's social thinking, however, we need to be aware not only of logical stages but also of stages of moral judgment. In our research, we have found six definite and universal stages of development in moral thought. In our longitudinal study of seventy-six American boys from preadolescence, youths were presented with hypothetical moral dilemmas, all deliberately philosophical, some of them found in medieval works of casuistry.

On the basis of their reasoning about these dilemmas at a given age, each boy's stage of moral thought could be determined for each of twelve basic moral concepts, values, or issues. The six stages of moral thought are divided into three major levels, the *preconventional*, the *conventional*, and the *postconventional* or autonomous.

While the preconventional child is often "well-behaved" and is responsive to cultural labels of good and bad, he interprets these labels in terms of their physical consequences (punishment, reward, exchange of favors) or in terms of the physical power of those who enunciate the rules and labels of good and bad. This level is usually occupied in the middle class by children aged four to ten.

The second or conventional level usually becomes dominant in preadolescence. Maintaining the expectation and rules of the individual's family, group, or nation is perceived as valuable in its own right. There is concern not only with conforming to the individual's social order, but also in maintaining, supporting, and justifying this order.

The postconventional level is first evident in adolescence and is characterized by a major thrust toward autonomous moral principles which have validity and application apart from authority of the groups or persons who hold them and apart from the individual's identification with those persons or groups.

Within each of these three levels there are two discernible stages. At the preconventional level we have: Stage 1: Orientation toward punishment

and unquestioning deference to superior power. The physical consequences of action regardless of their human meaning or value determine
its goodness or badness. Stage 2: Right action consists of that which
instrumentally satisfies one's own needs and occasionally the needs of
others. Human relations are viewed in terms like those of the marketplace. Elements of fairness, reciprocity, and equal sharing are present,
but they are always interpreted in a physical, pragmatic way. Reciprocity
is a matter of "you scratch my back and I'll scratch yours," not of loyalty,
gratitude, or justice.

At the conventional level we have: Stage 3: Good-boy-good-girl orientation. Good behavior is that which pleases or helps others and is approved
by them. There is much conformity to stereotypical images of what is
majority or "natural" behavior. Behavior is often judged by intention—
"he means well" becomes important for the first time and is overused. One
seeks approval by being "nice." Stage 4: Orientation toward authority,
fixed rules, and the maintenance of the social order. Right behavior consists of doing one's duty, showing respect for authority, and maintaining
the given social order for its own sake. One earns respect by performing
dutifully.

At the postconventional level we have: Stage 5A: A social contract
orientation, generally with legalistic and utilitarian overtones. Right action
tends to be defined in terms of general rights and in terms of standards
which have been critically examined and agreed upon by the whole society.
There is a clear awareness of the relativism of personal values and opinions and a corresponding emphasis upon procedural rules for reaching
consensus. Aside from what is constitutionally agreed upon, right or wrong
is a matter of personal values and opinion. The result is an emphasis upon
the legal point of view, but with an emphasis upon the possibility of changing law in terms of rational considerations of social utility, rather than
freezing it in the terms of Stage 4, law and order. Outside the legal realm,
free agreement and contract are the binding elements of obligation. This
is the official morality of American government, and finds its ground in
the thought of the writers of the Constitution. Stage 5B: Orientation to
internal decisions of conscience but without clear rational or universal
principles. Stage 6: Orientation toward ethical principles appealing to
logical comprehensiveness, universality, and consistency. These principles
are abstract and ethical (the Golden Rule, the categorical imperative);
they are not concrete moral rules like the Ten Commandments. Instead,
they are universal principles of justice, of the reciprocity and equality of
human rights, and of respect for the dignity of human beings as individual
persons.

These stages are defined by twelve basic issues of moral judgment.

On one such issue, Conscience, Motive Given for Rule Obedience or Moral Action, the six stages look like this:

1. Obey rules to avoid punishment.
2. Conform to obtain rewards, have favors returned, and so on.
3. Conform to avoid disapproval, dislike by others.
4. Conform to avoid censure by legitimate authorities and resultant guilt.

5A. Conform to maintain the respect of the impartial spectator judging in terms of community welfare.

5B. Conform to avoid self-condemnation.

In another of these moral issues, the value of human life, the six stages can be defined thus:

1. The value of a human life is confused with the value of physical objects and is based on the social status or physical attributes of its possessor.
2. The value of a human life is seen as instrumental to the satisfaction of the needs of its possessor or of other persons.
3. The value of a human life is based on the empathy and affection of family members and others toward its possessor.
4. Life is conceived as sacred in terms of its place in a categorical moral or religious order of rights and duties.
5. Life is valued both in terms of its relation to community welfare and in terms of being a universal human right.
6. Belief in the sacredness of human life as representing a universal human value of respect for the individual.

We call our types "stages" because they seem to represent an invariant developmental sequence. True stages come one at a time and always in the same order.

All movement is forward in sequence and does not skip steps. Children may move through these stages at varying speeds, of course, and may be found half in and half out of a particular stage. An individual may stop at any given stage and at any age, but if he continues to move, he must move in accord with these steps. Moral reasoning of the conventional or Stage 3-4 kind never occurs before the preconventional Stage 1 and Stage 2 thought has taken place. No adult in Stage 4 has gone through Stage 6, but all Stage 6 adults have gone at least through 4.

While the evidence is not complete, our study strongly suggests that moral change fits the stage pattern just described. Figures 2-1 and 2-2 indicate the cultural universality of the sequence of stages which we found. Figure 2-1 presents the age trends for middle-class urban boys in the United States, Taiwan, and Mexico. At age ten in each country, the order of use of each stage is the same as the order of its difficulty or maturity. In the

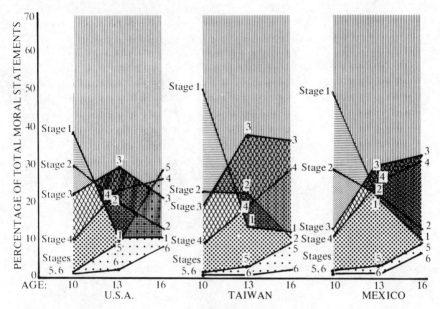

Figure 2-1

Moral development among middle-class urban boys
in the U.S., Taiwan, and Mexico

(At age 10, the stages are used according to difficulty. At age 13, Stage 3 is most used by all three groups. At age 16, U.S. boys have reversed the order of age 10 stages [with the exception of 6]. In Taiwan and Mexico, conventional [3-4] stages prevail at age 16, with Stage 5 also little used.)

United States, by age sixteen the order is the reverse, from the highest to the lowest, except that Stage 6 is still little used. The results in Mexico and Taiwan are the same, except that development is a little slower. The most conspicuous feature is that at the age of sixteen, Stage 5 thinking is much more salient in the United States than in Mexico or Taiwan. Nevertheless, it is present in the other countries, so we know that this is not purely an American democratic construct.

Why should there be such a universal invariant sequence of development? In answering this question, we need first to analyze these developing social concepts in terms of their internal logical structure. At each stage, the same basic moral concept or aspect is defined, but at each higher stage this definition is more differentiated, more integrated and more general or universal. When one's concept of human life moves from Stage 1 to Stage 2 the value of life becomes more differentiated from the value of property, more integrated (the value of life enters an organizational

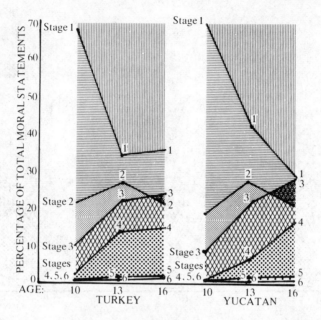

Figure 2-2

**Moral development among boys in two isolated villages,
one in Turkey, the other in Yucatan,
showing similar patterns to those in Figure 2-1**

(There is no reversal of order, and preconventional [1-2] thought does not gain a clear
ascendancy over conventional stages at age 16.)

hierarchy where it is "higher" than property so that one steals property
in order to save life) and more universalized (the life of any sentient being
is valuable regardless of status or property). The same advance is true
at each stage in the hierarchy. Each step of development, then, is a better
cognitive organization than the one before it, one which takes account of
everything present in the previous stage, but making new distinctions and
organizing them into a more comprehensive or more equilibrated structure.

What is the relation of moral stage development in adolescence to
cognitive stage development? In Piaget's and our view, both types of
thought and types of valuing (or of feeling) are schemata which develop
a set of general structural characteristics representing successive forms
of psychological equilibrium. The equilibrium of affective and interpersonal schemata, justice or fairness, involves many of the same basic
structural features as the equilibrium of cognitive schemata logicality.
Justice (portrayed as balancing the scales) is a form of equilibrium

between conflicting interpersonal claims, so that "in contrast to a given rule imposed upon the child from outside, the rule of justice is an imminent condition of social relationships or a law governing their equilibrium."[17]

What is being asserted, then, is not that moral judgment stages are cognitive—they are not the mere application of logic to moral problems—but that the existence of moral stages implies that normal development has a basic cognitive-structural component.

The Piagetian rationale just advanced suggests that cognitive maturity is a necessary, but not a sufficient condition for moral judgment maturity. While formal operations may be necessary for principled morality, one may be a theoretical physicist and yet not make moral judgments at the principled level.

As noted in the previous section, Kuhn, Langer, and Kohlberg found that 60 percent of persons over sixteen had attained formal operational thinking (by their particular measures). Only 10 percent of subjects over sixteen showed clear principled (Stages 5 and 6) thinking, but all these 10 percent were capable of formal-operational logical thought. More generally, there is a point-to-point correspondence between Piaget's logical and [Kohlberg's] moral judgment stages, as indicated in Table 2-2. The relation is that attainment of the logical stage is a necessary but not sufficient condition for attainment of the moral stage. As we shall note in the next section, the fact that many adolescents have formal logical capacities without yet having developed the corresponding degree of moral judgment maturity is a particularly important background factor in some of the current dilemmas of adolescents.

Adolescent Questioning and the Problem of Relativity of Truth and Value

The cornerstone of a Piagetian interpretation of adolescence is the dramatic shift in cognition from concrete to formal operations by which old conceptions of the world are restructured in terms of a new philosophy. Piaget defined the preschool child as a philosopher, revolutionizing child psychology by demonstrating that the child at each stage of development actively organizes his experience and makes sense of the physical and social world with which he interacts in terms of the classical categories and questions of philosophers concerning space, time, causality, reality, and so on. It is, however, only in adolescence that the child becomes a philosopher in the formal or traditional sense. This emergence of philosophic questioning has been studied most carefully in the moral realm.

The transition from preconventional to conventional morality generally

Table 2-2

Relations between Piaget's logical stages and Kohlberg's moral stages

(All relations are that attainment of the logical stages is necessary, but not sufficient, for attainment of the moral stage.)

Logical stage	Moral stage
Symbolic, intuitive thought	*Stage O:* The good is what I want and like
Concrete operations, Substage 1	*Stage 1:* Punishment-obedience orientation
Categorical classification	
Concrete operations, Substage 2	*Stage 2:* Instrumental hedonism and concrete reciprocity
Reversible concrete thought	
Formal operations, Substage 1	*Stage 3:* Orientation to interpersonal relations of mutuality
Relations involving the inverse of	
the reciprocal	
Formal operations, Substage 2	*Stage 4:* Maintenance of social order, fixed rules, and authority
Formal operations, Substage 3	*Stage 5A:* Social contract, utilitarian law-making perspective
	Stage 5B: Higher law and conscience orientation
	Stage 6: Universal ethical principle orientation

occurs during the late elementary school years. The shift in adolescence from concrete to formal operations, the ability now to see the given as only a subset of the possible and to spin out the alternatives, constitutes the necessary precondition for the transition from conventional to principled moral reasoning. It is in adolescence, then, that the child has the cognitive capability for moving from a conventional to a postconventional, reflective, or philosophic view of values and society.

The rejection of conventional moral reasoning begins with the perception of relativism, the awareness that any given society's definition of right and wrong, however legitimate, is only one among many, both in fact and theory. To clarify the issue of moral relativism as perceived by an adolescent, we will consider some adolescent responses to the following dilemma:

In Europe, a woman was near death from a very bad disease, a special kind of cancer. There was one drug that the doctors thought might save her. It was a form of radium that a druggist in the same town had recently discovered. The drug was expensive to make, but the druggist was charging ten times what the drug cost him to make. He paid $200 for the radium and charged $2,000 for a small dose of the drug. The sick woman's husband, Heinz, went to everyone he knew to borrow the money, but he could only get together about $1,000 which was half of what it cost. He told the druggist that his wife was dying, and asked him to sell it cheaper or let him pay later. But the druggist said, "No, I discovered the drug and I'm going to make money from it." Heinz got desperate and broke into the man's store to steal the drug for his wife.

Should the husband have done that? Was it right or wrong? Bob, a junior in a liberal private high school, says:

There's a million ways to look at it. Heinz had a moral decision to make. Was it worse to steal or let his wife die? In my mind I can either condemn him or condone him. In this case I think it was fine. But possibly the druggist was working on a capitalist morality of supply and demand.

I went on to ask Bob, "Would it be wrong if he did not steal it?

It depends on how he is oriented morally. If he thinks it's worse to steal than to let his wife die, then it would be wrong what he did. It's all relative, what I would do is steal the drug. I can't say that's right or wrong or that it's what everyone should do.

Bob started the interview by wondering if he could answer because he "questioned the whole terminology, the whole moral bag." He goes on:

But then I'm also an incredible moralist, a real puritan in some sense and moods. My moral judgment and the way I perceive things morally changes very much when my mood changes. When I'm in a cynical mood, I take a cynical view of morals, but still whether I like it or not, I'm terribly moral in the way I look at things. But I'm not too comfortable with it.

Here are some other juniors from an upper-middle-class public high school:

Dan: Immoral is strictly a relative term which can be applied to almost any thought on a particular subject . . . if you have a man and a woman in bed, that is immoral as opposed to if you were a Roman a few thousand years ago and you were used to orgies all the time, that would not be immoral. Things vary so when you call something immoral, it's relative to that society at that time and it varies frequently. [Are there any circumstances in which wrong in some abstract moral sense would be applicable?] Well, in that sense, the only thing I could find wrong would be when you were hurting somebody against their will.
Elliot: I think one individual's set of moral values is as good as the next individual's . . . . I think you have a right to believe in what you believe in, but I don't think you have a right to enforce it on other people.

88 **Adolescent Development**

John: I don't think anybody should be swayed by the dictates of society. It's probably very much up to the individual all the time and there's no general principle except when the views of society seem to conflict with your views and your opportunities at the moment and it seems that the views of society don't really have any basis as being right and in that case, most people, I think, would tend to say forget it and I'll do what I want.

The high school students just quoted are, from the point of view of moral stage theory, in a transitional zone. They understand and can use conventional moral thinking, but view it as arbitrary and relative. They do not yet have any clear understanding of, or commitment to, moral principles which are universal, which have a claim to some nonrelative validity. Insofar as they see any "principles" as nonrelative, it is the principle of "do your own thing, and let others do theirs." This "principle" has a close resemblance to the "principles" characteristic of younger children's Stage 2 instrumental egoistic thinking. The following examples of a ten-year-old naive egoist and a college student transition relativistic response are more clearly of this instrumental egoistic form.

Jimmy (American city, age 10): It depends on how much he loved his wife. He should if he does. [If he doesn't love her much?] If he wanted her to die, I don't think he should. [Would it be right to steal?] In a way it's right because he knew his wife would die if he didn't and it would be right to save her. [Does the druggist have the right to charge that much if no law?] Yes, it's his drug, look at all he's got invested in it. [Should the judge punish?] He should put him in jail for stealing and he should put the druggist in because he charged so much and the drug didn't work.

Roger (Berkeley Free Speech Movement student, age 20): He was a victim of circumstances and can only be judged by other men whose varying value and interest frameworks produce subjective decisions which are neither permanent nor absolute. The same is true of the druggist. I'd do it. As far as duty, a husband's duty is up to the husband to decide, and anybody can judge him, and he can judge anybody's judgment. If he values her life over the consequences of theft, he should do it. [Did the druggist have a right?] One can talk about rights until doomsday and never say anything. Does the lion have a right to the zebra's life when he starves? When he wants sport? Or when he will take it at will? Does he consider rights? Is man so different? [Should he be punished by the judge?] All this could be avoided if the people would organize a planned economy. I think the judge should let him go, but if he does, it will provide less incentive for the poorer people to organize.

Relativity, Moral Stages, and Ego Identity

We first came across extreme relativist responses in some of our longitudinal subjects shortly after college entrance in the early 1960's.[18] At

that time, we interpreted their responses as a regression to Stage 2 thinking. Fifteen percent of our college-bound male students who were a mixture of conventional (Stage 4) and social compact-legalist (Stage 5) thought
at the end of high school, "retrogressed" to an apparent Stage 2 instrum-
entalist pattern in college.

In terms of behavior, everyone of our retrogressed subjects had high
moral character ratings in high school, as defined by both teachers and
peers. In college at least half had engaged in anticonventional acts of a
more or less delinquent sort. As an example a Stage 2 Nietzchean had
been the most respected high school student council president in years.
In his college sophomore interview, however, he told how two days before
he had stolen a gold watch from a friend at work. He had done so, he said,
because his friend was just too good, too Christ-like, too trusting, and he
wanted to teach him what the world was like. He felt no guilt about the
stealing, he said, but he did feel frustrated. His act had failed, he said,
because his trusting friend insisted he lost or mislaid the watch and simply
refused to believe it had been stolen.

The forces of development which led our 20 percent from upstanding
conventional morality to Raskolnikov moral defiance eventually set them
all to right. Every single one of our "retrogressors" had returned to a Stage
5 morality by age twenty-five, with more Stage 5 social contract principle,
less Stage 4 or convention, than in high school. All, too, were conventionally moral in behavior, at least as far as we can observe them. In sum, this
20 percent was among the highest group at high school, was the lowest in
college, and again among the highest at twenty-five.

In other words, moral relativism and nihilism, no matter how extensive,
seemed to be a transitional attitude in the movement from conventional
to principled morality.

Cognitive Moral Stages and Ego Identity

In considering further the meaning of relativism in adolescence, it is
helpful to relate logical and moral stages to Erikson's stages of ego identity.
Logical and moral stages are structures of thought through which the
child moves sequentially. Erikson's stages are rather segments of the life
histories of individuals; they define the central concerns of persons in a
developmental period. An adolescent does not know or care that he is
moving from concrete to formal thought; he knows and cares that he is
having an Erikson "identity crisis."

Cognitive-developmental stages are stages of structure, not of content.
The stages tell us *how* the child thinks concerning good and bad, truth,
love, sex, and so forth. They do not tell us *what* he thinks about, whether
he is preoccupied with morality or sex or achievement. They do not tell

us what is on the adolescent's mind, but only how he thinks about what is on his mind. The dramatic changes in adolescence are not changes in structure, but changes in content. The adolescent need not know or care he is going from conventional to principled moral thinking, but he does know and care that sex is on his mind. In this sense cognitive structural stages may be contrasted with both psychosexual and Eriksonian stages.[19]

When we turn to Erikson's ego stages, we are partly dealing with a logical sequence as in logical and moral stages. Within Erikson's stages is the logical necessity that every later disposition presupposes each prior disposition, that each is a differentiation of prior dispositions. Erikson's ego stage centers around a series of forms of self-esteem (or their inverse, negative self-esteem). The first polarity trust-mistrust is one in which self and other are not differentiated. Trust is a positive feeling about self and other; mistrust is a negative feeling. The next polarity, autonomy versus shame, involves the self-other differentiation. Autonomy is a trust in the self (as opposed to the other); shame is a depreciation of self in the eyes of another whose status remains intact. Shame, however, is itself a failure to differentiate what one is from what one is in the eyes of the other, a differentiation implied in the sense of guilt. Similarly, initiative (I can be like him, it's all right to be or do it) is a differentiation from autonomy (I can do it). Such sequential progressive differentiations in self-esteem are involved throughout the Erikson stages. While there is an inherent logical (as opposed to biological) sequence to the Erikson ego stages, they are not hierarchical in the way cognitive stages are. Resolutions of identity problems are not also resolutions of trust or initiative problems, that is, each of the earlier problems and dispositions persists rather than being integrated into or being hierarchically dominated by the next. As a result, when we turn to Erikson's stages as defining focal concerns, we have a stage scheme which is so multidimensional as to resist empirical proof in the sense in which Piagetian stages may be proved. Ultimately the Erikson stages are "ideal-typical" in Weber's sense. They are not universal abstractions from data, but purifications and exaggerations of typical life histories. They do not predict regularities in the data; they aid in establishing historical connections in case histories. As Erikson uses his stage schema, it helps to suggest historical connections in a particular life, like Luther's. The truth of the stage schema is not in question; the truth of particular historical connections is. The stage schema helps select and illuminate these historical connections. In this sense, the stage of identity formation is not a step in an abstract but observable universal sequence, but is an ideal-typical characterization for a concrete historical period of adolescence.

As such, it need not have any exact logical relation to logical and moral stages, as they must to one another. While Erikson's stages cannot be defined, measured, or logically handled in the same sense as cognitive-developmental stages, suggestive empirical relations between ego identity terms and moral stages are found.

M. H. Podd[20] gave an ego identity interview to 134 male college juniors and seniors as well as the moral judgment interview. Following J. E. Marcia,[21] the identity interview covered occupational choice, religious beliefs, and political ideology. "Crisis" and "commitment" are assessed in each of these areas and serve to define each identity status. When an individual undergoes active consideration of alternative goals and values he is said to have experienced a "crisis." "Commitment" is the extent to which an individual has invested himself in his choices. The identity statuses operationally defined are: (1) identity achievement—has gone through a crisis and is committed; (2) moratorium—is in crisis with vague commitments; (3) foreclosure—has experienced no crisis, but is committed to goals and values of parents or significant others; (4) identity diffusion—has no commitment regardless of crisis.

Subjects in the Podd study could be grouped into three major groups, the conventional (Stages 3 and 4), the principled (Stages 5 and 6), and the transitional. The transitional subjects could in turn be divided into two groups, those who were a combination of conventional and principled thinking and the extreme relativists who rejected conventional thought and used more instrumental egoistic ("Stage 2") modes. Two-thirds of the principled subjects had an "identity achievement" status. So too did about 40 percent of the conventional subjects, the remainder being mainly in "identity foreclosure" (a status missing among the principled). None of the morally transitional subjects had an identity achievement status, and very few had foreclosed identity questioning.

Essentially, then, morally transitional subjects were in transition with regard to identity issues as well as moral issues. Stated slightly differently, to have questioned conventional morality you must have questioned your identity as well, though you may continue to hold a conventional moral position after having done so.

The impact of the Podd study is that the relativistic questioning of conventional morality and conventional reality associated with logical and moral stage development is also central to the adolescent's identity concerns. As a corollary, morally conventional subjects have a considerable likelihood of never having an identity crisis or an identity questioning at all. Erikson's picture of an adolescent stage of identity crisis and its resolutions, then, is a picture dependent upon attainment of formal logical thought and of questioning of conventional morality. It fits best, then, the picture of adolescence in the developmentally elite and needs further elaboration for other adolescents . . . .

Implications for Education

The extreme relativism of a considerable portion of high school adolescents provides both a threat to current educational practice and a potentiality for a new focus of education.

We said earlier that the five-to-seven shift has been traditionally represented in education by the beginning of formal schooling. The traditional educational embodiment of the adolescent shift has been a different one, that of a two-track educational system dividing adolescents into two groups, an elite capable of abstract thought and hence of profiting from a liberal education and the masses who are not. At first, this division was made between the wealthy and those who went to work. As public high schools developed, the tracking system instead became that of an academic school or lycée leading to the university and a vocational school. The clearest formulation of this two-track system as based on the dawn of abstract thought was found in the British 11+ system. Based on his score on an intelligence test given at the dawn of adolescence, a child was assigned to either a grammar (academic) or a modern (vocational-commercial) high school.

The aristocratic tracking system just described rested on the assumption that the capacity for abstract thought is all or none, that it appears at a fixed age, and that it is hereditarily limited to an elite group in the population. The evidence on formal operational thought does not support these assumptions. However, when democratic secondary education ignored the existence of the adolescent cognitive shift and individual differences in their attainment, real difficulties emerged. Most recently this [ignoring] occurred in the wave of high school curriculum reform of the late 1950's and early 1960's in America, the "new math," the "new science," and the "new social studies." These curricula reforms were guided by the notion that more intellectual content could be put into high school and that this content should not be factual content and rote skills, but the basic pattern of thinking of the academic disciplines of mathematics, physics, or social science. The focus was to be upon understanding the basic logical assumptions and structure of the discipline and the use of these assumptions in reflective or critical thinking and problem solving. Clearly the new curricula assumed formal-operational thought, rather than attempting to develop it. Partly as a result of this [oversight], some of the most enlightened proponents of the new curricula became discouraged as they saw only a sub-group of the high school population engaging with it. The solution we have proposed is that the new curricula be reformulated as tools for developing principled logical and moral thought rather than presupposing it.[22]

Experimental work by our colleagues and ourselves[23] has shown that even crude efforts based on such objectives are challenging and are successful in inducing considerable upward stage movement in thought. Hopefully, our efforts are the beginning of reformulating the "new" high school science, mathematics, social studies, and literature as approaches using "disciplines" as vehicles for the stimulation of the development of thought, rather than making young Ph.D.'s.

The difficulties and failures of the new curricula and of the general movement to democratize higher learning or liberal education, then, is not due to hereditary differences in capacity used to justify the two-track system. They represent, instead, the failure of secondary education to take developmental psychology seriously. When stage development is taken seriously by educators as an aim, real developmental change can occur through education.

In saying this, we return to the thought of John Dewey which is at the heart of a democratic educational philosophy. According to Dewey, education was the stimulation of development through stages by providing opportunities for active thought and active organization of experience.

The only solid ground of assurance that the educator is not setting up impossible artificial aims, that he is not using ineffective and perverting methods, is a clear and definite knowledge of the normal end and focus of mental action. Only knowledge of the order and connection of the stages in the development of the psychical functions can, negatively, guard against those evils, or positively, insure the full maturation and free, yet, orderly, exercises of the physical powers. Education is precisely the work of supplying the conditions which will enable the psychical functions, as they successively arise, to mature and pass into higher functions in the freest and fullest manner. This result can be secured only by a knowledge of the process of development, that is only by a knowledge of "psychology."[24]

Besides a clear focus on development, an aspect of Dewey's educational thought which needs revival is that school experience must be and represent real life experience in stimulating development. American education in the twentieth century was shaped by the victory of Thorndike over Dewey. Achievement rather than development has been its aim. But now the achieving society, the achieving individual, and even the achievement tests are seriously questioned, by adults and adolescents alike. If development rather than achievement is to be the aim of education, such development must be meaningful or real to the adolescent himself. In this sense education must be sensed by the adolescent as aiding him in his search for identity, and it must deal with life. Neither a concern with self or with life are concerns opposed to intellectuality or intellectual development. The opposition of "intellect" and "life" is itself a reflection of the two-track system in which a long period of academic education provided a moratorium for leisurely self-crystallization of an adult role identity by the elite while the masses were to acquire an early adult vocational identity, either through going to work or through commitment to a vocation in a vocational high school.

Our discussion of adolescent relativism and identity diffusion suggests that the two tracks are both breaking down and fusing. Vocational goals are evaded by relativism and counterculture questioning as are deferred goals of intellectual development. An identity crisis and questioning are no longer the prerogative of the elite, and they now occur earlier and without the background of logical and moral development they previously entailed. If the high school is to have meaning it must take account of this, which means it must take account of the adolescent's current notion of himself and his identity. Like most psychologists, most adolescents think the self has little to do with intellectual or moral development. The relativistic adolescent is content to answer "myself" to questions as to the source and basis of value and meaning. Like most psychologists he tends to equate the content of self-development with the ego, with self-awareness, with identity. The other pole of ego or self-development, however, is that of new awareness of the world and values; it is the awareness of new meanings in life.

We discussed the moral strand of ego development, which is clearly philosophical. We have also noted aesthetic, religious, metaphysical, and epistemological concepts and values born in adolescence. One side of ego development is the structure of the self-concept and the other side is the individual's concept of the true, the good, the beautiful, and the real. If education is to promote self-development, ego development must be seen as one side of an education whose other side consists of the arts and sciences as philosophically conceived. We have pointed to the need for defining the aims of teaching the arts and sciences in developmental terms. In this sense one basic aim of teaching high school science and mathematics is to stimulate the stage of principled or formal-operational logical thought, of high school social studies, the stimulation of principled moral judgment. A basic aim of teaching literature is the development of a stage or level of aesthetic comprehension, expression, judgment. Behind all of these developmental goals lie moral and philosophic dimensions of the meaning of life, which the adolescent currently questions and the school needs to confront. The adolescent is a philosopher by nature, and if not by nature, by countercultural pressure. The high school must have, and represent, a philosophy if it is to be meaningful to the adolescent. If the high school is to offer some purposes and meanings which can stand up to relativistic questioning, it must learn philosophy.

Notes

1. S. H. White, "Some General Outlines of the Matrix of Developmental Changes between Five to Seven Years," *Bulletin of the Orton Society*, 20 (No. 41, 1970), 41-57.

2. L. Kohlberg, "Early Education: A Cognitive-Developmental Approach," *Child Development,* 39 (December 1968), 1013-1062; A. R. Jensen, "How Much Can We Boost I.Q. and Scholastic Achievement?" *Harvard Educational Review,* 39 (No. 1, 1969), 1-123.

3. R. Scheffler, "The Development of Children's Orientations to Fantasy in the Years 5 to 7," doctoral dissertation, Harvard University, 1971.

4. L. Kohlberg, "Moral Education in the School," *School Review*, 74 (No. 1, 1966), 1-30; *id.*, "Early Education."

5. *Id.*, "Moral Education in the School."

6. *Ibid.*

7. Cognitive stage maturity is different from IQ, a separate factor, though the two are correlated. (See L. Kohlberg and R. DeVries, "Relations between Piaget and Psychometric Assessments of Intelligence," in *The Natural Curriculum*, ed. C. Lavatelli [Urbana: University of Illinois Press, 1971].) General impoverishment of organized physical and social stimulation leads to retardation in stage development. Culturally disadvantaged children tend to be somewhat retarded compared to middle-class children with the same IQ's in concrete-operational logic. Experimental intervention can to some extent accelerate cognitive development if it is based on providing experiences of cognitive conflict which stimulate the child to reorganize or rethink his patterns of cognitive ordering.

8. Kohlberg, "Early Education."

9. *Id.*, "Moral Education in the School."

10. C. Ellinwood, "Structural Development in the Expression of Emotion by Children," doctoral dissertation, University of Chicago, 1969.

11. E. A. Peel, *The Psychological Basis of Education*, 2d ed. (Edinburgh and London: Oliver and Boyd, 1967).

12. D. Kuhn, J. Langer, and L. Kohlberg, "The Development of Formal-Operational Thought," unpublished paper, 1971.

13. Another example of transitional stage response is success on the question: "Joe is shorter than Bob, Joe is taller than Alex, who is the tallest?" The transitional child can solve this by the required reversing of relations and serial ordering of them, but will fail the pendulum task.

14. Wordsworth's note to ode on *Intimations of Immortality,* quoted in Lionel Trilling, *The Liberal Imagination* (New York: Viking Press, 1941).

15. Kohlberg, "Moral Education in the School."

16. Taken from Kuhn, Langer, and Kohlberg, "The Development of Formal-Operational Thought."

17. J. Piaget, *The Moral Judgment of the Child* (Glencoe, Ill.: Free Press, 1948 [originally published in 1932]).

18. L. Kohlberg and R. Kramer, "Continuities and Discontinuities in Childhood and Adult Moral Development," *Human Development*, 12 (1969), 93-120.

19. J. Loevinger, "The Meaning and Measurement of Ego Development," *American Psychologist*, 21 (No. 3, 1966), 195-206.

20. M. H. Podd, "The Relationship between Ego Identity Status and Two Measures of Morality: An Empirical Investigation of Two Developmental Concepts," doctoral dissertation, State University of New York at Buffalo, 1970.

21. J. E. Marcia, "Development and Validation of Ego Identity Status," *Journal of Personality and Social Psychology*, 3 (No. 5, 1966), 551-558.

22. L. Kohlberg and A. Lockwood, "Cognitive-Developmental Psychology and Political Education: Progress in the Sixties," speech for Social Science Consortium Convention, Boulder, Colorado, 1970; L. Kohlberg and E. Turiel, "Moral Development and Moral Education," in *Psychology and Educational Practice,* ed. G. S. Lesser (Glenview, Ill.: Scott, Foresman, 1971).

23. L. Kohlberg and M. Blatt, "The Effects of Classroom Discussion on Level of Moral Judgment," in *Recent Research in Moral Development*, ed. Kohlberg and Turiel.

24. J. Dewey, *On Education: Selected Writing*, ed. R. D. Archambault (New York: Modern Library, republished 1964).

Form and Content in Moral Education

R. S. Peters

... In considering questions about moral development the work of Jean Piaget and his follower, Lawrence Kohlberg, are of particular relevance. For they are concerned with the development of a rational form of morality and Kohlberg particularly has views about the development of its form as distinct from the learning of its content. I shall not be concerned with the niceties of differences between these two psychologists—only with the general outline of the theory adopted by both.

Kohlberg broke down Piaget's three stages into six and also did some cross-cultural studies to support the main thesis that, though the content of morality varies from culture to culture, there is an invariant order in the development of its form. Children pass from an egocentric stage, at which they see rules as injunctions to be complied with in order to avoid punishment or to obtain rewards, to a stage of what Kohlberg calls "good-boy morality," at which they see rules as there, as part of the order of the world, which are linked with praise and shame, approval and disapproval in their minds. Their morality at this stage is a conventional or

Reprinted from R. S. Peters, *Authority, Responsibility and Education* (London: George Allen and Unwin, 1959).

traditional one. Rules are regarded as fixed entities emanating from the gang, or from authority figures such as parents. It is only when they pass to the third stage, that of autonomy, that they question the validity of rules. They begin to appreciate that they could be otherwise. They see their necessity for social life and can imagine what it would be like if they were not observed. They are capable of putting themselves in other people's shoes. The morality of consent and reciprocity begins to take the place of the morality of convention and constraint.

All sorts of qualifications are made, of course, to this simple picture. Being at a particular stage is not an all-or-nothing affair, only a matter of the predominating view of rules. Individuals differ in the rate at which they pass through these stages and so do cultures. In some cultures, too, there is very little development beyond the second stage and individuals within a culture, where there is such development, may get stuck at earlier stages. All this can be admitted and is admitted. But the general picture still stands.

What is the explanation of this cultural invariance? Both Piaget and Kohlberg strongly resist, for a variety of reasons, the suggestion that it comes about through the explicit instruction of adults. Their view is that there are a limited number of possible ways in which rules can be conceived and that these form a hierarchical order, logically speaking. One could not, for instance, have an autonomous or rational form of morality in which one adopts certain rules for oneself unless one had been through a stage at which one knew what it is to follow a rule. So the third stage presupposes the second. What then determines the transition from one stage to another, supposing that the stages must occur in a certain order? The answer is that children gradually come to see things differently as a result of social interaction. This process can be aided by "cognitive stimulation," but children cannot be explicitly taught to see rules differently any more than, in the scientific sphere, they can be taught to appreciate a principle like that of the conservation of volume. Given appropriate experiences the penny gradually drops. The content of particular rules can, however, be explicitly taught. Just as, once a child has, by this dawning process, got the concept of a thing he can be taught to recognize countless particular things, so also once he is at the second stage, for instance, he can be taught a great number of rules by instruction backed up by praise or approval for conformity. The content of morality, therefore, can be taught; but its form develops.

What is to be made of this very exciting account of moral development which seems so pertinent because of its emphasis on the distinction between form and content in the sphere of learning? In my view it can only be accepted with certain major qualifications. Let me discuss first the thesis about the development of the form of morality. I will then pass to that about the learning of its content.

The first point to make, surely, is that a very restricted view is taken of teaching which is more or less equated with pinning children down and telling them things. This is contrasted with cognitive stimulation exemplified, in Kohlberg's view, by Socrates leading the slave in the *Meno* to grasp geometrical truths by a sustained process of cross-questioning. But surely Socrates was teaching the slave all right even though he was not telling him anything in any explicit way. For to teach is to bring someone to learn something by indicating in some way what has to be learned in a manner that is adapted to his level of understanding. This can be done without any explicit telling. Indeed the Socratic type of teaching method is much favored in the primary schools for the learning of mathematics and many other things.

Secondly, "cognitive stimulation" must include much more indirect influences than this structured type of probing; for Kohlberg notes that there is much more of such stimulation in some types of home than in others and that this is why some children advance so much more quickly in their moral understanding. This stimulation must include the example set by adults and older children and methods of child raising, as well as the amount of discussion and cross-questioning that goes on. It also includes the type of language that is used, which may be more or less abstract and hence more or less conducive to the development of reasoning. There is ample evidence from sociological and anthropological studies to confirm the importance of these more all-pervasive influences on the development of reasoning. So "cognitive stimulation" must be extended to cover all these social influences, many of which could be legitimately thought of as forms of teaching.

Thirdly, this account of moral development is explicitly put forward only as an account of the development of moral judgment. But there is a danger of this very cognitive account of moral development being equated with the whole story. And this would be very misleading. Consider, for instance, the development of the reasoning of the autonomous person. If his reasoning is going to influence his behavior he has to be able to grasp that, for instance, the effect on other people is a relevant consideration in reflecting on the ethics of keeping a promise. But he may be capable of seeing that other people may be inconvenienced but he may not care overmuch about their predicament. How do children come to care? Does it not start very early on and is it not, in part, due to the attitudes of parents from whom it is "caught"? Piaget only shows that, in their very early years, children cannot perform the cognitive feat of connecting something like harm to others with questions about the rightness of rules. But there is no reason why sympathy for others should not be strongly felt before such reasoning develops. And there must be some early sensitization of this sort for concern for others to function later as a principle which influences action in a rational morality. But there is no developmental account of the genesis of sympathy in the Piaget-Kohlberg scheme. At least, therefore, their account needs supplementation in relation to the motivational and affective aspects of morality. For, as has been argued since Socrates, there is a close connection between moral judgment and action. A satisfactory account of the development of the form of rational morality must not only study the development of the ability to reason; it must also pay attention to early sensitization to features such as the suffering of others which later are to function as principles that make reasons relevant. And this account must cover their potentiality for influencing behavior.

With these reservations, however, there is much to be said for the Piaget-Kohlberg type of emphasis with regard to the factors which affect the development of the rational form of morality. Indirect influences and stimulation are probably more relevant than explicit instruction.

What, then, is to be said about the learning of the content of morality? Piaget and Kohlberg have little to say about this because they think it unimportant. Kohlberg, for instance, tends to make rather derisive remarks about the "bag of virtues" conception of morality. He is impressed by evidence which he thinks, however correctly, shows that such disconnected habits are situation specific and of little importance in the development of moral character.

There are reasons, however, for suggesting that more attention should be paid to this aspect of morality. To start with, children and unreflective people have to live with others. And without a few essential virtues in their bag, they are likely to be a social menace. Hobbes once made the remark that a sobering feature of the human condition is that even a small child can kill a man when he is asleep. Also, if I am robbed in the street, my interest in whether the thief is at Stage 1, 2, or 3, in the way in which he views the operation, is a trifle academic; the point is that he has relieved me of my wallet and I am lying in the gutter, dimly struggling back to consciousness. Also, as has already been pointed out, children have to pass through the second "good-boy" stage of morality before they can emerge to autonomy. They have to learn from the inside, as it were, that a rule is a rule. And they learn this, presumably, by generalizing their experience of picking up some particular "bag of virtues." It may also be the case, too, that there may be ways of teaching them rules which fix them at this stage or which even hinder them from entering it. It could be that permissive parents are so anxious for their children to become autonomous that they expect them to pass from early egocentricity to autonomy without going through the rather conventional, authority-ridden, second stage. So they shrink from anything that smacks of instruction on their part or from acting as models for their children.

Suppose that the case for providing children with some "bag of virtues" in their early years could be made out along these lines. Two questions then arise. Firstly, what are these virtues to be? Secondly, how are they to be taught? The answer to the first question is obvious enough if the structure of morality previously set out is accepted. These virtues will either be those such as concern for others, truth telling, and fairness which later, when the autonomous stage is attained, will function as fundamental principles. Or they will be rules such as not stealing and the keeping of promises which can be defended by reference to fundamental principles as being indispensable for social life under almost any conceivable social conditions. If, because of the influence of early learning, children do develop rather an inflexible attitude to such rules, at least they will have such an attitude to rules that are likely to be apposite in any form of social life that they are likely to encounter in a time of social change.

But how is such a content of rules to be taught? Surely in any way that helps them to learn rules which does not stunt their capacity to develop a more autonomous attitude to them. When children are at or near the autonomous stage obviously discussion, persuasion, learning "for themselves" in practical situations with adults and peers, taking part in group activities such as games and drama productions, all help to stimulate development, to encourage seeing the other person's point of view, and so on. But what about the earlier stages before these more rational types of technique are meaningful to children? There will have to be a certain amount of instruction as well as models provided by parents and older children of such rules being followed; for most of them presuppose the grasp of complicated social arrangements. It would be impossible, for instance, for a child to understand what it is not to steal unless he is instructed in concepts to do with property, the difference between borrowing, being given something, and just taking it.

But such instruction and example will probably not be sufficient. For although it is often claimed that, at this stage, children enjoy conforming to rules in the way in which they enjoy keeping to the rules in games, the fact is that there would be no point in having such rules unless there existed in human nature some contrary tendency to do what the rule forbids. Some counterinclinations have therefore to be brought into play to strengthen any tendency that exists to conform to the rule. The obvious counterinclinations are those connected with rewards and punishments, praise and blame, approval and disapproval. These are the usual rudders that steer children into the channels of rule conformity.

Psychologists of the Skinnerian school have much to say at this point about the options that are open to parents and teachers. They claim that positive "reinforcements," such as rewards, praise, and approval, are much more conducive to learning than negative "reinforcements." There is a mass of evidence, too, to suggest that parental warmth is much more conducive to moral development than any kind of rejecting attitude. It could well be, too, that many of the cases, studied by psychologists of the Freudian school, of people who became fixated at this stage with extreme irrational feelings of guilt and unworthiness about their conduct, are the victims of punitive and rejecting parental techniques. Evidence suggests that if children are to develop sensibly to an autonomous form of morality they require a consistent pattern of rules in their early years, backed up by approval for conformity. Development is likely to be stunted either by inconsistency in relation to what is expected or by no determinate expectations; for the anxiety occasioned by such conflict or anomie is not conducive to learning. Also under such conditions the child has little basis for predictability in his social environment which is necessary for the development of planning and reasoning generally. Alternatively development can be stunted by the use of punitive, rejecting techniques. These create anxiety which hinders learning and also undermine the development of self-confidence and trust.

It might be thought that this type of teaching smacks of secondhandedness and a lack of authenticity. Children, it might be objected, are being lured into conformity without appreciating the proper reasons for it. This is a poor preparation for an authentic rational form of life. But the question has to be faced: what else is practicable? If children in their early years cannot acquire rules because they see the proper point of them and if, for the reasons explained, they have to start off with some "bag of virtues," it is difficult to see what other alternatives are open. If they can think in no other way about rules at this early stage, it is difficult to make the charge of inauthenticity stick. For there exists no possibility of authenticity. Also for some virtues, such as fairness or concern for others, it is difficult to see what further reasons *could* be given. For sensitivity to them is a precondition of there being reasons. For it is principles such as these which determine relevance in morals.

Something, however, can be said to rebut any charge of indoctrination which might be leveled against this mixture of instruction and positive "reinforcement." Indoctrination can be distinguished as a special type of instruction that can be employed at this stage. It consists in getting children to accept a *fixed* body of rules in such a way that they are incapacitated from adopting a critical or autonomous attitude toward them. Various techniques can be used which permanently fixate people in a "good-boy" type of morality. They are thus led permanently to associate such a fixed body of rules with loyalty to their group or with obedience to some authority figure whose disapproval they dare not incur. The shaming techniques of the traditional English public school or of a communist collective are an example of this. But the public schools did at least encourage prefects to develop toward a more autonomous form of morality. Their practices encouraged a Stage 3 morality for the few and Stage 2 for the many. But not all instruction need take this indoctrinating form. Indeed, it must not take this form if development toward a rational type of morality is to take place. Thus the uneasiness felt by parents and teachers about indoctrinating children . . . can perhaps be dispelled by explaining in this way what is specific to it as a teaching technique.

The distinction between the form and content of morality has been shown to be extremely relevant to the question, "How is morality to be taught?" as well as to questions about the structure of what is to be taught. For the crucial problem of methods in early moral education can be stated in this way: given that it is thought desirable that children should develop an autonomous form of morality, and given that, if Piaget and Kohlberg are right, they cannot, in their early years, learn in a way that presupposes such a form, how can a basic content for morality be provided that gives them a firm basis for moral behavior without impeding the development of a rational form for it? What nonrational methods of teaching aid, or at least do not impede, the development of rationality? This is the basic problem of early moral education.

It is to this more specific problem that sensitive parents and teachers should address themselves instead of withdrawing from the scene for fear of indoctrination. For by withdrawing and by refusing to act as models and instructors they are equally in danger of preventing the development toward autonomy that they so much desire. In moral education the method is not quite the message; for a rational morality has to evolve out of conventional mores. Socratic techniques of discussion and persuasion are the ideal. But Socrates operated on the dubious wisdom enshrined in traditions and authorities. Without these he would have had nothing to be critical about. But these traditions themselves were passed on by less rational techniques. Children were "brought up" by their parents. But the problem is to ensure an early upbringing unlike that of Alcibiades, which nullified the later efforts even of a gifted educator such as Socrates.

3

Ego and Character:
Shoveling Smoke

Loevinger's Theory of Ego Development

Senator Howard Baker, at the time of the televised Watergate hearings, quoted Justice Brandeis as saying that "Lawyers spend their professional lives shoveling smoke." The reader may conclude from the following articles that psychologists studying human characteristics as complex as the "ego and character," "what the person thinks of as his self," or "the meaning the person makes of his life" face similar occupational hazards. There is a quality of elusiveness, abstraction, and complexity in Loevinger's discussion of the ego and its development. The logic of Piaget's description of cognitive development and Kohlberg's singular focus on the adolescent's moral reasoning are missing. Loevinger's study deals with human personality and being. Ego and character are abstractions that describe people's intrinsic properties and processes of which they are not conscious. Thus, because of their very nature, there is about them a certain elusiveness in understanding and description. But in a book whose central thesis is the need for both a psychology and an education for all-around human development it is hard to quarrel with the broad aim of Loevinger's study. One is reminded of the admiring comment made about the charge of the Light Brigade: "C'est magnifique, mais ce n'est pas la guerre."

What part of the person is Loevinger describing? In commonsense terms, it is the self, one's personality, what a person would reply if asked who he is or how he sees himself. Indeed, it may be a useful exercise for the reader at this point to answer the preceding question as candidly as possible in order to establish a reference point for the readings that follow.

At first thought one's ego may seem as wraithlike as conscience. Loevinger argues, however, that the ego is a much more powerful and stable characteristic than we realize. She explains the ego in psychological

103

language as a set of implicit understandings we have (what we *think*) about ourselves and our lives. People have ideas, judgments, rules, and a more or less organized point of view concerning themselves and their lives; in that structure of meaning is the most essential defining process of the individual. One can describe the core of the person by determining what those ideas are and the way they are organized. Further, these ideas and meanings evolve and progress with experience. Though most of us reach a stable ego stage and remain there (the Self-Aware Level or the Transition from Conformist to Conscientious Stage "is probably the modal level for adults in our society"), evolution is nonetheless important. Loevinger, with the other theorists already discussed, believes that the way the person thinks about himself and his life progresses through ego stages that are predictable, logical, and sequential. This is not to say that there is nothing new under the sun, for each stage is "new" to the individual. There is empirical evidence, however, that people have common meanings and priorities about life.

Loevinger's descriptions of ego stages tell us about the person's character development, his social style, what he thinks about most, and how his mind works. We may seem to ourselves and others to be very different over time because of changes in these facets of our personality. And in a real sense we are. But there is an inner logic to the ego stages and their progression that produces both a consistence and a commonality with many other people at the same stage of development. In this sense Loevinger's stages also describe personality types, such as the wary, self-protective adolescent who cheats on an examination or the businessman who installs a defective swimming pool. Here Loevinger is saying that human beings are much more alike than they are different, or at least that there are sufficient commonalities to merit our careful study.

In summary, Loevinger argues that ego is the keystone of our personality and that its purpose is to synthesize experience and give meaning and purpose to our lives; that ego is active thinking about the core issues of the human personality—the self and morality; that ego is structural—an evolving intellectual framework of rules, criteria, and schemata about life; that ego develops through identifiable stages and related personality types that can be described in detail; and that ego has common roots in all people and grows in interaction with other individuals.

The conception of ego development as a sequence of *stages* that also constitutes a set of personality *types* is necessarily an *abstraction*. The fundamental characteristics of the ego are that it is a *process*, a *structure*, *social* in origin, functioning as a *whole*, and guided by *purpose* and *meaning*. Development implies *structural change* but the mechanistic philosophy of some structuralists forecloses our topic of study . . . . We acknowledge both *consciousness* and the possibility of freedom and the validity of the *dynamic unconscious*; so the ego is not the same as the whole personality. It is close to what the person thinks of as his self.[1]

Where There Is Smoke Is There Fire?

Do these ego stages affect our behavior or attitudes? Do they do more than provide us with a way to describe a person's self and character? Loevinger's theory does not assume or predict any relationship between ego development and overt behavior. "But there may be patterns of behavior—'helping behavior,' 'responsibility-taking,' 'conformity' which are congruent with and predictable from the individual's ego level."[2] The research findings on this issue are not conclusive. Some studies indicate correlations between ego stage and social behavior and attitude. For example, Frank and Quinlan[3] found delinquent adolescent girls to be at lower levels of ego development (specifically the Impulsive Stage) than nondelinquent girls of the same age and ethnic background. Girls at the lower stages of ego development (Impulsive and Delta) engaged in significantly more acts of street fighting, homosexuality, and running away than the adolescents from all other stages. Blasi found a significant relationship between ego development in sixth-grade children and the way in which they accept responsibility.[4] Hoppe discovered that adolescent boys within the conformist range of the ego development stages showed a high degree of conforming behaviors—in ratings by their peers, in an experimental test, and in records of school discipline.[5]

Studies of college students show striking differences among those at different stages of ego development in how they "react and adjust to non-academic college life, dormitory living and special programs the college offers." For example, postconformist students were most involved in extracurricular activities (26 percent) while preconformist students were least involved (0 percent). By contrast, 45 percent of the preconformists were placed on disciplinary probation, while none of the postconformists were.[6] Erickson studied the relationship between ego development and the attitudes of women toward their rights and roles. High school sophomores were her subjects, and she found that their attitudes toward women's roles and rights change with increasing ego development. Thus, postconformist students view what women should do and be entitled to in terms of greater equality and complexity.

And so it seems that where there is psychological smoke there is also fire. The predictive relationship between ego stage or personality type and social behavior and attitudes is incompletely known. This is the "newest" of the developmental theories so far discussed; its use by researchers is highly contemporary. Loevinger would not see her ego stages as rising or falling, in any sense, on whether they explain behavior. But practitioners—teachers and counselors—look for such ties. And if there are correlations between ego stages and such nonacademic factors as discipline and participation in extracurricular activities, they may have an added incentive to take seriously the ego stages and education to stimulate ego development.

Some further comments on the utility of ego development theory for teachers and counselors may be appropriate. One point worth noting is that Loevinger did not make armchair observations concerning ego stages or personality types. She arrived at her results by testing thousands of Americans. As a matter of fact, none of the other developmental theories discussed in this book has as solid an empirical base, and, incidentally, its data on women's development are especially rich.

Counselors will probably be sympathetic to Loevinger's effort to study and understand adolescents as completely or holistically as possible. "Self," "ego," and the meaning and purpose the adolescent is trying to give his life are central concerns of counseling. That may be less true of teachers, whose main function is to increase the student's cognitive knowledge in a particular subject. But I suspect that most teachers recognize that students, too, have a hidden curriculum (their personal lives) and that many want to help their students grow personally. Certainly this book is committed to that objective of education. Thus, portraits of personality—broadly describing self, character, intellectual style, and the types of adolescent and young adult thinking that teachers may encounter— should be helpful. Ego stages describe some of what to expect of adolescents; they imply also that there is a reasonable chance teenagers "are growing out of it." It may be an unfortunate (or Freudian) analogy, but if one knows the stages of an illness from onset to recovery, the condition, while acute, is much more tolerable. And there are times for parents and teachers (perhaps for teenagers, too) when Anna Freud's stark belief that adolescents are all crazy at some point and that adults can only wait for the fever to break has a compelling validity.

Beyond presenting knowledge concerning the characteristic behavior of students, it is a tenet of this book that education can and should help people grow. Loevinger is not optimistic about this: "Nothing in the theory justifies the hope that changes can be wrought in short time by brief laboratory, classroom or even life experiences."[7] The evidence in Part II of this book indicates, however, that high school education and teaching can significantly stimulate adolescents' ego development. Further, Loevinger offers a manageable instrument to measure such growth. It is not an instrument that teachers can score without training, but it is certainly one they can administer and have scored for them.

Criticisms of Loevinger

We have talked about the problem of elusiveness and abstraction in Loevinger's theory—that we see the ego through a glass darkly. A practical alternative is to concentrate on understanding the stages; for high school teachers this means reading carefully the descriptions of them. There is also the problem of whether the higher ego stages are preferable—for people or societies. The commonsense answer is "yes" because a little ego or character limits the person in a complex world. Loevinger, however, offers no philosophical examination or justification for the desirability of the higher stages. She says the stages are not her biases or catechism for how personal development should proceed. Her descriptions of stages and personality types, after all, follow human nature as she has found it expressed in thousands of lives. But it could be easy here to accept the psychologists' fallacy of assuming that because the Conscientious Stage is psychologically and morally more complex than the Self-Protective Stage it is better. Senility and death follow Loevinger's Integrated Stage, but are they better? That issue (of taking a single leap from the human "is" to the "ought to be") bears more heavily on educators, who want to stimulate ego development, than on Loevinger, who wants only to describe it. Part II will return to this issue.

It is also important to note that development is not as rigid as one might assume. Most of us, when we think carefully and honestly about who we are, will find ourselves or our students in several of Loevinger's stages at the same or different times. "What is more likely . . . is different levels in different specific circumstances, such as sex life versus work, or relations with men versus relations with women, or relations with bosses and relations with employees . . . . Regressions under stress probably take place with respect to all facets . . . . Classifying a person at a given stage means, approximately, that this is the highest level at which he is capable of functioning consistently."[8] Probably the complexity and the flexibility of ego stages constitute what life must be. Blasi and Loevinger see consciousness and freedom as critical elements in developing unity and autonomy in our personalities.[9] They are concerned that ego stages not become so rigid as to be antihumanistic or to negate the individual personality. People are more than the sum of their stages; the ego actively constructs itself. If the material in Part II is valid, education may help people transcend the stage at which they find themselves. In so doing, education will contribute to progress in some of the most basic facets of the human personality.

The Core of Human Intelligence

No review of contemporary developmental research pertinent to education would be complete without Selman's study of social reasoning and judgment. The subject is how we think about social reality: ourselves and others, friends, family, peers, groups, institutions. It has been suggested several times in Part I that an enlargement of the individual's social perspective and responsibility is a core index of his development, a benchmark both in the psychologist's description of what is and the philosopher's conceptions of what ought to be. Many of the educational programs discussed in Part II have as an important objective this shift from "me first" to "we." Selman's research has focused on developmental levels in the child's understanding of his social perspective and that of other people, "a process G. H. Mead . . . claimed to be the core of human intelligence."[10] Empathy, the ability to understand the thinking and feeling of another person, to put oneself in another's position, to see oneself as others do are rough synonyms for the social cognition that interests Selman. He considers such social reasoning to have the same deep structural properties as Piaget's logical-mathematical stages, and yet at the same time it is a qualitatively distinct way of thinking about social, in contrast to physical, reality. In this respect his claim for its significance in human development is little different from that of Mead.

Selman says that the way in which children think about social phenomena grows through an invariant sequence of stages, and he outlines the characteristics of these stages. Such developing patterns of reasoning are the child's way of actively constructing her social world rather than being conditioned by it. And they are energized by the experience of social problems ("My parents want me to play with Elizabeth, but I want to play with Jane.") plus the opportunity to consider alternative ways of thinking that are more advanced than her own. In the same way that a concept such as IQ does not tell us much about what characterizes a bright or a dull mind at work, "Perspective-taking levels are skeletal structures [the how] of social reasoning in search of some content to which they can be applied (for example, contents such as social problem solving, communication skills, interpersonal relations, moral reasoning, and so forth)."[11] Selman is describing a basic cognitive capability that is applied to such social and moral problems.

What is equally important, Selman shows us schematically how mathematical-scientific logic as described by Piaget and moral judgment and social thinking relate to one another. The educator may question whether this theoretical trip is necessary, but, in a book describing the psychological complexity and integration of human growth, it is an appropriate expedition. The model is, in general, of hierarchical and prerequisite interaction. Scientific logic and social perspective taking are deep structures or forms of thought; social and moral reasoning are significant "content areas" for applying perspective taking; social conceptions of others— peers, groups, and institutions—are nearest the surface of our thinking.

This model leads Selman to provide certain advice for those who want to educate for social reasoning or social behavior. He believes it will be easier to stimulate change in social or moral reasoning than in the underlying structures of logical thinking and perspective taking. Initial educational research[12] tends to bear him out. All this implies that "intervention research should aim to stimulate development of the more basic abilities through the 'relatively more content related' areas of reasoning."[13] In the case of *The Godfather*, for example, it is more productive to talk about the moral issues involved in the attempt to assassinate the Godfather and in Michael's revenge killings than to focus on those acts from the perspective of Michael, the corrupt police captain, the rival Capo, or Don Corleone himself.

A further implication concerns the complex tie between social reasoning and social behavior and what that suggests about the different purposes and effects of social education. For example, children who lag far behind peers in their social cognitive stage have difficulty relating to these peers. Here we should teach interpersonal skills and behavior rather than social and moral reasoning for its own sake. Average social reasoning is necessary, but it is not sufficient for adequate relationships with peers. Social education with normal children does, however, strengthen the deeper structures of perspective taking and lay the groundwork for movement to the next higher stage. Nor is teaching children to reason about social relations enough. "Raising the level of social cognition does not guarantee concomitant change in behavior." The preoccupation with enhanced reasoning and its uncertain effect on behavior (whether academic, moral, or social) is a recurrent and basic criticism of cognitive developmental theories. Selman makes the interesting suggestion that children may behave themselves into higher stages of social reasoning and that psychologists and teachers should cooperate to create education that regards social reasoning and social relations as a two-way street. Selman's own efforts to produce curriculum materials that do that are commercially available as *First Things: Social Reasoning* and *First Things: Values*.

Notes

1. Jane Loevinger, *Ego Development: Conceptions and Theories* (San Francisco: Jossey-Bass, 1976), 67.

2. N. Cox, "Prior Help, Ego Development and Helping Behavior," *Child Development*, 45 (No. 3, 1974), 594-603; A. Blasi, "A Developmental Approach to Responsibility Training," doctoral dissertation, Washington University, 1972; C. Hoppe, "Ego Development and Conformity Behavior," doctoral dissertation, Washington University, 1972; Stuart T. Hauser, "Loevinger's Model and Measure of Ego Development: A Critical Review," *Psychological Bulletin*, 83 (No. 5, 1976), 928-955.

3. S. Frank and D. Quinlan, "Ego Development and Female Delinquency," *Journal of Abnormal Psychology*, 85 (October 1976), 505-510, cited in Hauser, "Loevinger's Model and Measure of Ego Development."

4. Blasi, "A Developmental Approach to Responsibility Training."

5. Hoppe, "Ego Development and Conformity Behavior."

6. N. Goldberger, "Developmental Stage and the Early College Student," in progress report, evaluation project, Simon's Rock Early College, Great Barrington, Massachusetts, 1975, cited in Hauser, "Loevinger's Model and Measure of Ego Development."

7. Loevinger, *Ego Development*, 426.

8. *Ibid.*, 200.

9. Blasi, "A Developmental Approach to Responsibility Training"; Loevinger, *Ego Development*.

10. Robert L. Selman, "A Structural-Developmental Model of Social Cognition; Implications for Intervention Research," *Counseling Psychologist*, 6 (No. 4, 1977), 3.

11. *Ibid.*

12. Diana Paolitto, "Role-Taking Opportunities for Early Adolescents: A Program in Moral Education," doctoral dissertation, Boston University, 1975.

13. Selman, "A Structural-Developmental Model of Social Cognition," 5.

Stages of Ego Development

Jane Loevinger

Ego development is at once a developmental sequence and a dimension of individual differences in any age cohort, but this description does not suffice as a definition, for mental age can also be described so. In lieu of a logical definition, this chapter will present impressionistic descriptions of the stages, pieced together from many sources. . . .

The question most often asked—What age does each stage correspond to?—I shall not answer. For one thing, there are two different answers,

Reprinted from Jane Loevinger, *Ego Development: Conceptions and Theories* (San Francisco: Jossey-Bass, 1976), 13-28.

since the average stage for a given age is not the same as the average age for a given stage. More importantly, to describe the progress of average children would be to slip back into a classical child psychology study of socialization. That would defeat the purpose [here]. In principle, I seek to describe every stage in a way that applies to a wide range of ages (granted, of course, that the earliest stages are rare after childhood and that the highest stages are impossible in childhood and rare even in adolescence). What I seek to describe is what persons of each stage have in common, whatever their age. This attempt requires excluding age-specific contingencies (such as, "This behavior pattern indicates Stage X if the subject is a small child, but not if he is over fifteen").

In describing the stages abstractly with minimal reference to age-specific elements such as entering school, puberty, courtship, marriage, and so on, a series of questions is opened up: What is the earliest possible age for transition to a given stage? The latest possible age? The optimal age? What conditions other than age are necessary for a given transition to take place? What conditions are favorable, though not necessary? What conditions inhibit or prohibit a given transition? Only a conception that is, in the first instance, independent of age permits asking such questions, which are more meaningful than the question of average ages.

A word about terminology: these stages should be referred to by name or by code symbol, not by a number. Several authors have numbered their stages. That practice invariably leads either to a terminological impasse when further stages are identified or to cutting off new insights arbitrarily. The conception presented here has grown during our research from a four-point to a ten-point scale, and I do not foreclose further evolution. Only confusion can result from referring to the "third stage," for example. That could mean any of several stages, since the first stage can be counted as one, as two, or not counted at all, since it does not enter our research. Moreover, what we call a *transition* someone else might call a *stage*. Even if such difficulties were arbitrarily resolved by a fixed numbering scheme [here], others might assign a different numbering scheme to our stages.

While referring to stages by name avoids the difficulties of numbering them, it has its own hazards. Because I dislike neologisms, I have taken as the name for each stage a term from common speech, the name of some broad human function or characteristic. No such function arises all at once in one stage and perishes in the passage to the next. Impulsiveness, self-protection, conformity, and so on are terms that apply more or less to everyone. People differ with respect to such characteristics; those differences are related to but not identical with differences in ego level. Though stage names suggest characteristics that are usually at a maximum at that stage, nothing less than the total pattern defines a stage. An attempt to reason about ego development by a rigid interpretation of stage names can lead to disastrous errors. There is no substitute for grasping what Polanyi has called the "tacit component."[1] While the tacit component cannot, by definition, be made fully explicit, and the possibilities for misunderstanding can therefore never be eliminated, progress lies in making as much explicit as possible.

[Here,] capital letters will be used to distinguish the names of stages and types of people who can be classed in those stages. Where the same words are used for general human characteristics, whether of people at the corresponding stage or of people at other stages, lowercase letters will be used. (Arbitrary code symbols used in our research laboratory are given following the stage names in the next section.)

Descriptions of Stages

Presocial Stage (I-1). The baby at birth cannot be said to have an ego. His first task is to learn to differentiate himself from his surroundings, which becomes the "construction of reality," the realization that there is a stable world of objects. Aspects of the process have been referred to as achievement of *object constancy* and of *conservation of objects*. In the process, the baby constructs a self differentiated from the outer world. The child who remains at the stage where self is undifferentiated from the world of inanimate objects long past its appropriate time is referred to as *autistic*.

Symbiotic Stage (I-1). Even after he has a grasp of the stability of the world of objects, the baby retains a symbiotic relation with his mother or whoever plays that part in his life.[2] The process of differentiating self from nonself is significantly advanced as the baby emerges from that symbiosis. Language plays a large part in consolidating the baby's sense of being a separate person. Partly for that reason, the remnants of the Presocial and Symbiotic stages do not appear to be accessible by means of language in later life, as remnants of all later stages are.

Impulsive Stage (I-2). The child's own impulses help him to affirm his separate identity. The emphatic "No!" and the later "Do it by self" are evidences. The child's impulses are curbed at first by constraint, later also by immediate rewards and punishments. Punishment is perceived as retaliatory or as immanent in things. The child's need for other people is strong but demanding and dependent; others are seen and valued in terms of what they can give him. He tends to class people as good or bad, not as a truly moral judgment but as a value judgment. Good and bad at times are confounded with "nice-to-me" versus "mean-to-me" or even with clean and pure versus dirty and nasty, reminiscent of what Ferenczi called "sphincter morality."[3] The child is preoccupied with bodily impulses, particularly (age-appropriate) sexual and aggressive ones. Emotions may be intense, but they are almost physiological. The vocabulary of older children of this stage to describe their emotions is limited to terms like *mad, upset, sick, high, turned on,* and *hot.*

The child's orientation at this stage is almost exclusively to the present rather than to past or future. Although he may, if he is sufficiently intelligent, understand physical causation, he lacks a sense of psychological causation. Motive, cause, and logical justification are confounded.

A child who remains too long at the Impulsive Stage may be called *uncontrollable* or *incorrigible.* He himself is likely to see his troubles as located in a place rather than in a situation, much less in himself; thus he will often run away or run home. Superstitious ideas are probably common.

Self-Protective Stage (Delta Δ). The first step toward self-control of impulses is taken when the child learns to anticipate immediate, short-term rewards and punishments. Controls are at first fragile, and there is a corresponding vulnerability and guardedness, hence we term the stage Self-Protective. The child at this stage understands that there are rules, something not at all clear to the Impulsive child. His main rule is, however, "Don't get caught." While he uses rules for his own satisfaction and advantage, that is a step forward from the external constraint necessary to contain the impulsiveness of the previous stage.

The Self-Protective person has the notion of blame, but he externalizes it to other people or to circumstances. Somebody "gets into trouble" because he runs around with "the wrong people." Self-criticism is not characteristic. If he acknowledges responsibility for doing wrong, he is likely to blame it on some part of himself for which he disclaims responsibility, "my eyes" or "my figure." This tendency may help explain the imaginary companion some children have. Getting caught defines an action as wrong.

The small child's pleasure in rituals is an aspect of this stage. An older child or adult who remains here may become opportunistic, deceptive, and preoccupied with control and advantage in his relations with other people. For such a person, life is a zero-sum game; what one person gains, someone else has to lose. There is a more or less opportunistic hedonism. Work is perceived as onerous. The good life is the easy life with lots of money and nice things.

Conformist Stage (I-3). A momentous step is taken when the child starts to identify his own welfare with that of the group, usually his family for the small child and the peer group for an older child. In order for this step to take place or to be consolidated, there must be a strong element of trust. The child who feels that he lives among enemies lacks that trust. He may not become Conformist, taking instead the malignant version of the Self-Protective course, that is, opportunism, exploitativeness, deception, and ridicule of others. Perhaps that is one route to a more or less permanent "identification with the aggressor."[4]

The Conformist obeys the rules just because they are the group-accepted rules, not primarily because he fears punishment. Disapproval is a potent sanction for him. His moral code defines actions as right or wrong according to compliance with rules rather than according to consequences, which are crucial at higher stages. Conformists do not distinguish obligatory rules from norms of conduct, as we see when they condemn unusual dress or hairstyles as immoral or as signs of immorality.

In addition to *being* conformist and to *approving* of conformity, the person at this stage tends to *perceive* himself and others as conforming to socially approved norms. While he observes group differences, he is insensitive to individual differences. The groups are defined in terms of obvious external characteristics, beginning with sex, age, race, nationality, and the like. Within groups so defined, he sees everyone as being pretty much alike, or at least he thinks they ought to be. Psychometricians call this phenomenon *social desirability*: people are what they ought to be, which is whatever is socially approved. The Conformist's views of people and of situations involving people are conceptually simple, admitting few contingencies or exceptions.

While the Conformist likes and trusts other people within his own group, he may define that group narrowly and reject any or all out-groups. He is particularly prone to stereotyped conception of sex roles; usually those will be conventional ones, but the same kind of rigid adherence to stereotyped norms can occur in unconventional groups. Conformity and conventionality are not the same. Outwardly conventional people can occur at any ego level except the lowest ones, just as outwardly unconventional people can be strict conformists in terms of the norms of their own group.

The Conformist values niceness, helpfulness, and cooperation with others, as compared to the more competitive orientation of the Self-Protective person. However, he sees behavior in terms of its externals rather than in terms of feelings, in contrast to persons at higher levels. Inner life he sees in banal terms such as *happy, sad, glad, joy, sorrow,* and *love and understanding.* He is given to clichés, particularly moralistic ones. His concern for the externals of life takes the form of interest in appearance, in social acceptance and reputation, and in material things. Belonging makes him feel secure.

Self-Aware Level: Transition from Conformist to Conscientious Stage

(I-3/4). The transition from the Conformist to the Conscientious Stage is the easiest transition to study, since it is probably the modal level for adults in our society. Leaving open the question of whether this is a stage in itself or a transition between stages or whether there is no real difference between those two possibilities, we shall refer to it as a *level* rather than as a *stage.* Many characteristics of the Conformist Stage hold also for the transitional level; it can be called the Conscientious-Conformist Level. It is transitional only in a theoretical sense, for it appears to be a stable position in mature life.

Two salient differences from the Conformist Stage are an increase in self-awareness and the appreciation of multiple possibilities in situations. A factor in moving out of the Conformist Stage is awareness of oneself as not always living up to the idealized portrait set by social norms. The growing awareness of inner life is, however, still couched in banalities, often in terms of vague "feelings." Typically the feelings have some reference to the relation of the individual to other persons or to the group, such as *lonely, embarrassed, homesick, self-confident,* and most often, *self-conscious.* Consciousness of self is a prerequisite to the replacement of group standards by self-evaluated ones, characteristic of the next stage.

Where the Conformist lives in a conceptually simple world with the same thing right always and for everyone, the person in the Self-Aware Level sees alternatives. Exceptions and contingencies are allowed for, though still in terms of stereotypic and demographic categories like age, sex, marital status, and race, rather than in terms of individual differences in traits and needs. Perception of alternatives and exceptions paves the way for the true conceptual complexity of the next stage. For example, at this level a person might say that people should not have children unless they are married, or unless they are old enough. At the next stage, they are more likely to say unless they really want children, or unless the parents really love each other.

While the Conformist hardly perceives individual differences in traits, and the person at the Conscientious Stage may command a fairly elaborate catalogue of traits, in the transitional level one typically finds a kind of pseudotrait conception. Pseudotraits partake of the nature of moods, norms, or virtues, such as those mentioned in the Boy Scout oath. Norms are the most interesting, since they reveal the transitional nature of these conceptions, midway between the group stereotypes of the Conformist and the appreciation for individual differences at higher levels.

A trait adjective common at this level, at least among women, is "feminine." Different people cherish different connotations to the term: passive, seductive, manipulative, intraceptive, narcissistic, aesthetic, and many others. Those alternatives are closer to being true trait terms, and they are concepts more characteristic of the next higher, or Conscientious, stage.

Conscientious Stage (I-4). Precisely where one first finds signs of conscience depends on what is called *conscience*. A child at the Impulsive Stage does more labeling of people as *good* and *bad* than do those at higher stages, but the connotations are not clearly moral. The notion of blame is evident at the Self-Protective Stage, but rarely does the person blame himself. Occasionally one will find total self-rejection at the lowest levels, but without a corresponding sense of responsibility for actions or their consequences. (Self-rejection may occur in depressed persons of any level; what is characteristic for low ego levels appears to be similar reactions without the overall depression.) A Conformist feels guilty if he breaks the rules; moreover, he classes actions, not just people, as right and wrong. Although self-criticism is not characteristic for the Conformist, one could say he has a conscience because he has guilt feelings. At the Conscientious Stage, the major elements of an adult conscience are present. They include long-term, self-evaluated goals and ideals, differentiated self-criticism, and a sense of responsibility. Only a few persons as young as thirteen or fourteen years reach this stage.

The internalization of rules is completed at the Conscientious Stage. Where the Self-Protective person obeys rules in order to avoid getting into trouble and the Conformist obeys rules because the group sanctions them, the Conscientious person evaluates and chooses the rules for himself. He may even feel compelled to break the law on account of his own code, a fact recognized in the status of the "conscientious objector." Thus rules are no longer absolutes, the same for everyone all the time; rather, exceptions and contingencies are recognized. A person at this stage is less likely than the Conformist to feel guilty for having broken a rule, but more likely to feel guilty if what he does hurts another person, even though it may conform to the rules.

At this stage a person is his brother's keeper; he feels responsible for other people, at times to the extent of feeling obliged to shape another's life or to prevent him from making errors. Along with the concepts of responsibility and obligations go the correlative concepts of privileges, rights, and fairness. All of them imply a sense of choice rather than being a pawn of fate. The Conscientious person sees himself as the origin of his own destiny.

He aspires to achievement, *ad astra per aspera*, in contrast to the feeling at lower stages that work is intrinsically onerous, but he may object to some work as being routine, boring, or trivial. Achievement for him is measured primarily by his own standards, rather than mainly by recognition or by competitive advantage, as at lower levels.

An aspect of the characteristic conceptual complexity is that distinctions are made between, say, moral standards and social manners or between moral and aesthetic standards. Things are not just classes as "right" and "wrong." A Conscientious person thinks in terms of polarities, but more complex and differentiated ones: trivial versus important, love versus lust, dependent versus independent, inner life versus outward appearances.

A rich and differentiated inner life characterizes the Conscientious person. He experiences in himself and observes in others a variety of cognitively shaded emotions. Behavior is seen not just in terms of actions but in terms of patterns, hence of traits and motives. His descriptions of himself and others are more vivid and realistic than those of persons at lower levels. With the deepened understanding of other people's viewpoints, mutuality in interpersonal relations becomes possible. The ability to see matters from other people's view is a connecting link between his deeper interpersonal relations and his more mature conscience. Contributing to a more mature conscience are the longer time perspective and the tendency to look at things in a broader social context; these characteristics are even more salient at higher stages.

Individualistic Level: Transition from Conscientious to Autonomous Stages (I-4/5). The transition from the Conscientious to the Autonomous Stage is marked by a heightened sense of individuality and a concern for emotional dependence. The problem of dependence and independence is a recurrent one throughout development. What characterizes this level is the awareness that it is an emotional rather than a purely pragmatic problem, that one can remain emotionally dependent on others even when no longer physically or financially dependent. To proceed beyond the Conscientious Stage a person must become more tolerant of himself and of others. This toleration grows out of the recognition of individual differences and of complexities of circumstances at the Conscientious Stage. The next step, not only to accept but to cherish individuality, marks the Autonomous Stage.

Relations with other people, which become more intensive as the person grows from the Conformist to the Conscientious Stage, are now seen as partly antagonistic to the striving for achievement and the sometimes excessive moralism and responsibility for self and others at the Conscientious Stage. Moralism begins to be replaced by an awareness of inner conflict. At this level, however, the conflict, for example, over marriage versus career for a woman, is likely to be seen as only partly internal. If only society or one's husband were more helpful and accommodating, there need be no conflict. That conflict is part of the human condition is not recognized until the Autonomous Stage. Increased ability to tolerate paradox and contradiction leads to greater conceptual complexity, shown by awareness of the discrepancies between inner reality and outward appearances, between psychological and physiological responses, between process and outcome. Psychological causality and psychological development, which are notions that do not occur spontaneously below the Conscientious Stage, are natural modes of thought to persons in the Individualistic Level.

Autonomous Stage (I-5). A distinctive mark of the Autonomous Stage is the capacity to acknowledge and to cope with inner conflict, that is, conflicting needs, conflicting duties, and the conflict between needs and duties. Probably the Autonomous person does not have more conflict than others; rather he has the courage (and whatever other qualities it takes) to acknowledge and deal with conflict rather than ignoring it or projecting it onto the environment. Where the Conscientious person tends to construe the world in terms of polar opposites, the Autonomous person partly transcends those polarities, seeing reality as complex and multifaceted. He is able to unite and integrate ideas that appear as incompatible alternatives to those at lower stages; there is a high toleration for ambiguity.[5] Conceptual complexity is an outstanding sign of both the Autonomous and the Integrated stages.

The Autonomous Stage is so named partly because the person at that point recognizes other people's need for autonomy, partly because it is marked by some freeing of the person from oppressive demands of conscience in the preceding stage. A crucial instance can be the willingness to let one's children make their own mistakes. The autonomous person, however, typically recognizes the limitations to autonomy, that emotional interdependence is inevitable. He will often cherish personal ties as among his most precious values.

Where the Conscientious person is aware of others as having motives, the Autonomous person sees himself and others as having motives that have developed as a result of past experiences. The interest in development thus represents a further complication of psychological causation. Self-fulfillment becomes a frequent goal, partly supplanting achievement. Many persons have some conception of role or office at this stage, recognizing that they function differently in different roles or that different offices have different requirements. The person at this stage expresses his feelings vividly and convincingly, including sensual experiences, poignant sorrows, and existential humor, the humor intrinsic to the paradoxes of life. Sexual relations are enjoyed, or sometimes just accepted, as a physical experience in the context of a mutual relation. The Autonomous person takes a broad view of his life as a whole. He aspires to be realistic and objective about himself and others. He holds to broad, abstract social ideals, such as justice.

Integrated Stage (I-6). We call the highest stage Integrated, implying some transcending of the conflicts of the Autonomous Stage. It is the hardest stage to describe for several reasons. Because it is rare, one is hard put to find instances to study. Moreover, the psychologist trying to study this stage must acknowledge his own limitations as a potential hindrance to comprehension. The higher the stage studied, the more it is likely to exceed his own and thus to stretch his capacity. For the most part, the description of the Autonomous Stage holds also for the Integrated Stage. A new element is consolidation of a sense of identity. Probably the best description of this stage is that of Maslow's Self-Actualizing person . . . .[6]

To telescope the whole sequence of ego development in terms of describing the lowest and highest levels is to miss the spirit of the exposition. Growth does not proceed by a straight line from one low level to another higher level. There are many way stations, and they are all important as stages of life and as illuminations of the conception. In some sense, moreover, there is no highest stage but only an opening to new possibilities.

Conclusions

What changes during the course of ego development is a complexly interwoven fabric of impulse control, character, interpersonal relations, conscious preoccupations, and cognitive complexity, among other things. Table 3-1 presents a somewhat arbitrary condensation of the preceding discussion. To interpret it as indicating four separate dimensions of ego development is a mistake. There is just one dimension. The four descriptive columns display four facets of a single coherent process. Such, at least, is the conception intended. Other authors have depicted essentially the same dimension with major stress on one or another facet. . . . Most have also implicated other facets in their exposition, but details differ. One might ask, why not get together and agree on a definition of ego development? Authors cannot be forced to adjudicate their differences, nor would a concept arrived at by committee be superior or more true to nature. Frequently it is suggested that differences would be settled by empirical research. To some extent this research is taking place, despite many methodological difficulties. What has not been done, what perhaps cannot be done, and what may not even be meaningful is what is most often suggested: to measure separately the four facets displayed in Table 3-1 and then correlate them, to prove that they are indeed aspects of a single process. . . .

Discussion of facets reveals one reason this dimension should be called *ego development* rather than *moral development, development of cognitive complexity*, or *development of capacity for interpersonal relations.*

Table 3-1

Some milestones of ego development

Stage	Code	Impulse control, character development	Interpersonal style	Conscious preoccupations	Cognitive style
Presocial Symbiotic	I-1		Autistic Symbiotic	Self *vs.* nonself	
Impulsive	I-2	Impulsive, fear of retaliation	Receiving, dependent, exploitative	Bodily feelings, expecially sexual and aggressive	Stereotyping, conceptual confusion
Self-Protective	Δ	Fear of being caught, externalizing blame, opportunistic	Wary, manipulative, exploitative	Self-protection, trouble, wishes, things, advantage, control	
Conformist	I-3	Conformity to external rules, shame, guilt for breaking rules	Belonging, superficial niceness	Appearance, social acceptability, banal feelings, behavior	Conceptual simplicity, stereotypes, clichés
Conscientious-Conformist	I-3/4	Differentiation of norms, goals	Aware of self in relation to group, helping	Adjustment, problems, reasons, opportunities (vague)	Multiplicity
Conscientious	I-4	Self-evaluated standards, self-criticism, guilt for consequences, long-term goals and ideals	Intensive, responsible, mutual, concern for communication	Differentiated feelings, motives for behavior, self-respect, achievements, traits, expression	Conceptual complexity, idea of patterning
Individualistic	I-4/5	*Add:* Respect for individuality	*Add:* Dependence as an emotional problem	*Add:* Development, social problems, differentiation of inner life from outer	*Add:* Distinction of process and outcome

				Increased conceptual complexity, complex patterns, toleration for ambiguity, broad scope, objectivity
Autonomous	I-5	*Add:* Coping with conflicting inner needs, toleration	*Add:* Respect for autonomy, interdependence	Vividly conveyed feelings, intergration of physiological and psychological causation of behavior, role conception, self-fulfillment, self in social context
Integrated	I-6	*Add:* Reconciling inner conflicts, renunciation of unattainable	*Add:* Cherishing of individuality	*Add:* Identity

Note: "*Add*" means in addition to the description applying to the previous level.

All of those are involved. Nothing less than the ego encompasses so wide a scope.

Some critics assert that the description of stages of ego development is so ordered as to be a rationalization of society's scheme of values. That criticism does not hold. All societies are built on conformity and value conformity in the individual; perhaps that is how it must be. Persons driven to nonconformity by conscience are punished as harshly or more harshly by society as those incapable of conformity because of uncontrolled impulsiveness or those who choose nonconformity out of opportunism and self-interest. All nations appear to operate at the Self-Protective level. International relations are conducted as a zero-sum game, and perhaps no regime could survive that did not operate on that principle.

Another criticism is that the stages of ego development are ordered in accord with increasing approval by the writer. The answer to this charge will become evident gradually. There is, for one thing, substantial agreement among authors. Moreover, there are other lines of evidence to support the ordering. While I alone have written this [piece], the ordering of stages has come from work that has been intimately collaborative.[7] Ruthless mutual criticism by persons of diverse backgrounds and dispositions, many of them skilled clinicians, has helped to divest the conception of personal idiosyncrasies. Kohlberg[8] has answered at length a similar criticism of his work.

Some persons believe that society ought to favor arrangements that will lead more people to stages above Conformity. Society, they may propose, should reward the Conscientious and Autonomous persons as it now rewards the Conformist and often the opportunist. But that proposal is, or leads to, paradox. For the essence of the Conscientious Stage is to be at least partially liberated from socially imposed rewards and punishments. How can one manipulate rewards so as to free a person from responding to them and being shaped by them? That, indeed, is the question a parent or teacher faces who aspires to encourage moral development. How people liberate themselves from the dominion of external rewards and punishments is a central mystery of human development and one of the lures that leads us to our subject matter.

While the criticisms that the sequence of stages merely encodes either my own values or those of society will not hold, two questions lie behind those criticisms. What determines the direction of growth? And how do we discover the sequence? . . .

Notes

1. M. Polanyi, *Personal Knowledge* (Chicago: University of Chicago Press, 1958); *id.*, *The Tacit Dimension* (Garden City, N.Y.: Doubleday, 1966).

2. M. S. Mahler, *On Human Symbiosis and the Vicissitudes of Individuation*, Volume 1, *Infantile Psychosis* (New York: International Universities Press, 1968).

3. S. Ferenczi, "Psycho-Analysis of Sexual Habits," *International Journal of Psycho-Analysis*, 6 (No. 4, 1925), 372-404.

4. A. Freud, *The Ego and the Mechanisms of Defence* (New York: International Universities Press, 1946 [originally published in 1936]).

5. E. Frenkel-Brunswick, "Intolerance of Ambiguity as an Emotional and Perceptual Personality Variable," *Journal of Personality*, 18 (September-June 1949), 108-143.

6. A. H. Maslow, *Motivation and Personality* (New York: Harper and Row, 1954); *id.*, *Toward a Psychology of Being* (New York: D. Van Nostrand, 1962).

7. J. Loevinger and R. Wessler, *Measuring Ego Development I: Construction and Use of a Sentence Completion Test* (San Francisco: Jossey-Bass, 1970).

8. L. Kohlberg, "From Is to Ought: How to Commit the Naturalistic Fallacy and Get Away with It in the Study of Moral Development," in *Cognitive Development and Epistemology*, ed. T. Mischel (New York: Academic Press, 1971).

A Structural-Developmental Model of Social Cognition: Implications for Intervention Research

Robert L. Selman

Basic Assumptions in the Structural Approach to Social-Cognitive Research

Although the renewed study of social cognition is a relatively recent addition to the field of developmental research, it has already begun to have an impact on the thinking of educators and interventionists. It is my impression that such interest has generated some misunderstandings of

Reprinted, by permission, from *The Counseling Psychologist*, 6 (No. 4, 1977), 3-6 © 1977. Paper presented at the Convention of the American Psychological Association, Chicago, 1975. Symposium: Developmental Counseling Psychology: Early Childhood and Primary Years. A Structural Developmental Model of Social Cognition; Implications for Intervention Research.

the claims for intervention and education that can be made from a structural-developmental approach. Proponents, psychologists and educators alike, interpret the evidence for invariant stage sequences in social cognition as a call for the immediate elevation of all humanity to the next higher stage. Opponents point to psychological phenomena to which the developmental approaches do not directly speak, and because the structural or cognitive-developmental model does not explain everything, they assume it really cannot explain anything.

It is my intention to present a model of social cognition which might help to clarify what the structural-developmental approach does imply for social intervention research and application, and what it does not. This approach is primarily concerned with social reasoning and judgment; with how children reason about social phenomena, not just what they reason. The how of social reasoning is called *structure*, what is reasoned about, *content*—thus, the term structural-developmental stresses the how, that is, stresses the developing process of social reasoning.

The basic assumption of this approach is that social reasoning develops through an invariant sequence of stages; each stage is qualitatively distinct from the previous stage, but hierarchically related to the prior stage insofar as it is based upon the reorganization of the ideas or concepts of the prior stage into more adequate and inclusive concepts and ideas. In addition, this approach seeks a clarification of the developmental relations among various domains of reasoning; reasoning about logico-mathematical experiences, about the experience of the physical world, as well as about the experience of the social domain. Research in each of these areas has generated stage descriptions and it is one aim of this approach to search for structural similarities across domains. By "structural similarity" I simply mean that certain patterns of thinking appear to be common across the disparate "content" areas.

This structural assumption generates a basic developmental question. If a child is functioning at a certain stage in one domain, what can this tell us about his or her stage of reasoning in the next? Does stage theory imply strict uniformity of thought about all reality at a given point in development? Recent research as well as common sense do not lead us to this expectation. Psychologically speaking, a child's stage performance at any given time is as much a function of what he or she is reasoning about (the content) as of his or her basic level of structural capability. Conceptually (or logically), however, there do appear to be important similarities as well as differences in stages across various domains. It is the nature of these similarities and differences which has a direct bearing on education. To concretely discuss this issue I will briefly describe our own structural-developmental approach to social development, and then draw implications for education from some of our recent research of the social and physical-cognitive development of normal and disturbed children.

Our own research has focused on developmental levels in the child's form of understanding of the relation of his or her social perspective to the social perspective of other, a process G. H. Mead[1] claimed to be the core of human intelligence. Using both social games and social and moral dilemmas, we have developed procedures to infer the developmental progress of this social perspective-taking process. Between early childhood and preadolescence, we have identified four such levels,[2] which are briefly described as follows:

At the egocentric level (0), although the child can separate the attitudes or viewpoints of self and other (you like carrots, I do not), he or she assumes unreflectively that in similar contexts, others will feel or act as he or she would in that situation. At Level 1, the subjective level, there comes a clear recognition that the self's perspective is separate from other's and is thus unique; other's subjectivity, his or her thoughts, feelings, and intentions, are distinct from those of the self. At Level 2, the self-reflective level, the child becomes aware that the perspectives of self and other are seen to exist in a state of reciprocal influence—the child recognizes that his or her own subjective judgments are open to the scrutiny and evaluation of others, and his or her conception of other persons is reconstructed to fit the new realization that others can view the self as a subject. At Level 3, the third person perspective level, the preadolescent is able to hypothetically step outside of the dyadic relation and becomes aware from this third person view that persons can simultaneously be aware of each other's subjectivity—of each other's mutuality. Higher levels may occur in adolescence and adulthood.

Although we believe the levels of social perspective-taking described represent real developmental processes, it is obvious as well that they are also formalistic, that is, they lack psychological content. The very fact that it may be easy to recognize the logic behind the claim of universality of the developmental *sequence* of social perspective-taking levels also accounts for the constraints on their implications for social-psychological development. This is a very real problem, particularly for intervention or clinical practice. If social-cognitive descriptions are too structural, they present a universal but very skeletal description of social development, one not particularly descriptive of or applicable to the individual child. On the other hand, if stage descriptions are too broadly based on content, they may paint rich pictures of some but not all children. Perspective-taking levels are skeletal structures of social reasoning in search of some content to which they can be applied (for example, contents such as social problem solving, communication skills, interpersonal relations, moral reasoning, and so forth). In the real world these "content" domains intersect with one another; for theoretical purposes however, it is useful to explore the role of perspective-taking in each area separately and each in relation to the other. And although we claim the order of emergence of the perspective-taking levels is invariant, it appears that the age of functional emergence of a given level will vary to a certain degree as a function of the content within which it is applied, the mode of assessment (for example, real or hypothetical situations), or the context (for example, under stress, under group pressure, and so forth).

In our current work we are examining the role of perspective-taking in the context of reasoning about various types of interpersonal relationships, such as peer relations, parent-child relations, group relations, and so on,[3] as well as in moral reasoning.[4] Our basic working hypothesis is that, logically or conceptually, each level of perspective-taking is necessary but not sufficient for each structurally parallel stage of interpersonal (or moral) reasoning. We believe that a stage of interpersonal (or moral) reasoning logically implies a specific level of perspective-taking but that a specific level of perspective-taking does not necessarily imply the structurally parallel interpersonal (or moral) stage, that is, the child may use a perspective-taking level in one area but not see or seek to use it in another.

To exemplify and concretize this point, I will draw upon some evidence from our descriptive research into the development of stages of interpersonal role relationships, in this case the structure of developing friendship concepts. To study this area of social development in childhood and preadolescence we present children with commonplace and familiar interpersonal dilemmas depicted on audiovisual filmstrips of eight to ten minutes duration. Each dilemma is oriented toward issues revolving around a particular type of role relationship—peers, siblings, groups, parent-child, and so forth. For example, in one dilemma, a young girl, Kathy, has been asked by a new girl in town, Jeanette, to go to the circus with her the next afternoon. Unfortunately this conflicts with a long-standing date with a longtime friend, Debbie, to play in the park. To complicate matters, Debbie, the old friend, does not like Jeanette, the new girl. Following the presentation of the dilemma, we ask questions to which the child, in responding, must apply his or her friendship concepts. For example, we are interested in conceptions of how friendships are formed, how they are maintained, and what factors cause the breakup of friendships. We find that each level of perspective-taking, as a structural process, helps us to understand each of the stages in developing conceptions of interpersonal role relationships such as peer friendships.

At Level 1 perspective-taking, although the child can construct a picture of self and other as unique subjects, he or she does not view the reciprocity of persons as a concern for each other's particular view. Hence, at Stage 1 of interpersonal concept, he or she sees friendship predominantly from the perspective of only one of the parties, not both. Relations are based more on whether the actions of one party please the person whose perspective the child is taking, rather than focusing on the underlying intentions. According to the child reasoning at Stage 1, if Kathy's act of going to the circus with Jeanette is viewed with displeasure by Debbie, this is sufficient to end the friendship.

At Level 2 perspective-taking we note an awareness of the reciprocity of subjective viewpoints—an awareness that other's perspective is inclusive of the self's. At Stage 2, interpersonal relationships are still determined by the particular social event, rather than the social act being based on the strength of the relationship. However, there is now an awareness of the need to consider both parties' perspectives in a reciprocal trade-off. If she cares about keeping Debbie's friendship, Kathy has to weigh both how she will feel and how Debbie will feel. If either party is unhappy with an event, the friendship is over. Fortunately, friendships can be reconstituted at Stage 2 as quickly as they are dissolved; friendships are seen as relatively specific to the immediate context or situation.

At Stage 3 of interpersonal relation concepts, the relationship (friendship) determines the act and not the reverse as at the previous stage. Friendship is seen as based on mutuality or common interest built up over time, not simply the reciprocity of the here and now as at Stage 2. There is a shift from friendship as cooperation for self-interest to collaboration for mutual interest. Level 3 perspective-taking involves the ability to stand outside of the dyad and view it as a mutually interacting system. Our claim is that the third person perspective is a basic understanding which underlies this particular restructuring of friendship concepts.

Psychologically, the claim that a given level of perspective-taking (A) is necessary but not sufficient for a parallel interpersonal stage (B) means that there can exist in reality only three of four theoretically possible relations between the two. At any given stage there can be subjects without the given level for either perspective-taking or interpersonal reasoning ($\overline{A} \bullet \overline{B}$); there can be subjects with that structure for both perspective-taking and interpersonal reasoning ($A \bullet B$); or there can be subjects with the perspective-taking level but not the interpersonal level ($A \bullet \overline{B}$). But the model claims there can be no subject at a given interpersonal stage who does not also have the parallel perspective-taking level ($\overline{A} \bullet B$); hence logical implication.

It must be stressed that logical implication is not the same as psychological causation. A given level of perspective-taking does not cause an interpersonal stage, but is merely prerequisite to it. In practice, this logically prerequisite perspective-taking level may be only requisite, that is, it may develop synchronously as a function of the same conditions that stimulate development in interpersonal reasoning. To reiterate, we are claiming that a level of perspective-taking is logically a deeper structure which underlies the more surface structure of interpersonal or moral stages; it may develop before or with interpersonal or moral reasoning but it cannot develop after. Psychologically, however, the relation may be better described as a feedback system in which interpersonal experience stimulates interpersonal reasoning which in turn stimulates and is itself stimulated by the restructuring of perspective-taking levels.

A Hierarchical Model of Social Cognition

This model can be expanded to consider the place of perspective-taking in relation on the one hand to logico-mathematical stages as described by Piaget[5], and on the other to social or moral reasoning stages as described by structural-developmental researchers. Figure 3-1 presents a model of the hierarchical relation among the domains of social and physical cognition. Keeping in mind that this model represents a logical, not a psychological, hierarchy, there are two points which can be made. First, the terms structure and content as we defined them earlier are relative terms. Each perspective-taking level is a content in relation to each of the general (more formal) Piagetian stages, but a structure in relation to (more content-based) interpersonal and moral stages. Interpersonal and moral stages in turn are the content of perspective-taking levels but the structures of more differentiated concepts at the third order of analysis. In other words, interpersonal and moral stages are more content based than perspective-taking which in turn is more content bound than general formalistic Piagetian logico-mathematical stages. It is in this sense that we speak of structures as being relatively deep or surface.

Second, according to this model, whereas both physical and social cognition have basic logico-mathematical structures, for example, reciprocity, negation, inversion, and so forth, one domain is not reducible to the other. In other words, this model implies that the logical structures are not necessarily developed in one area (the physical) and applied to the other (the social). More likely is that they are developed independently in each domain or that there is interplay in the development of the structures between domains. While most researchers have found that logical structures first appear in the physical and later in the social domain, it is conceivable that under certain circumstances, the opposite might obtain. Logical operations might appear to develop earlier when dealing with

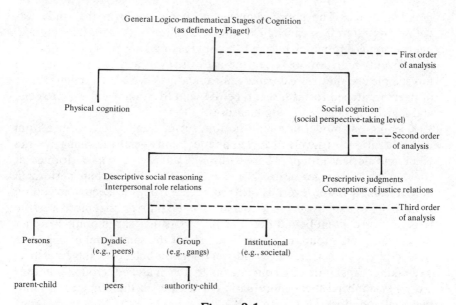

Figure 3-1

Relations among domains of physical and social cognition

(Reprinted from R. L. Selman, "Toward a Structural-Developmental Analysis of Interpersonal Relationship Concepts: Research with Normal and Disturbed Preadolescent Boys," in *X Annual Minnesota Symposium on Child Psychology*, ed. A. Pick [Minneapolis: University of Minnesota Press, 1976], 175.)

physical objects than with human subjects because of the greater practice with objects, the less emotional arousal involved in dealing with objects, or the greater consistency of the object world, not to mention the possibility of methodological artifacts. There may be less difficulty in the structuralization of the content of the physical domain. However, certain cases can be imagined in which the operation is developed in social interactions earlier than in physical: for example, where emotional arousal is great in the physical domain (repeated learning failures in school), in groups or cultures where social interaction is heavily stressed and there is little opportunity for practice with physical objects, or in specific cases of deprivation or manipulation with regard to the physical environment.

There are two related sets of implications of this model for intervention, implications which not only come from the theoretical model but also receive some support from a recently completed comparative study of logico-physical, perspective-taking, interpersonal, and moral reasoning in matched samples of socially well-adjusted and poorly adjusted preadolescents.[6] The poorly adjusted or *clinic group* in the study was defined by referral to special classes for children with both learning and interpersonal difficulties but with no obvious or known organic difficulties. Twenty-four boys between the ages of seven and twelve comprised this sample and they were compared to a relatively well-functioning sample of peers (matched for age, sex, race, IQ, and SES) on a battery of social and logico-physical reasoning measures.

Keeping our model in mind, the first set of implications comes from our comparison of levels of logico-physical and social reasoning for the clinic and normal group. Whereas the well-adjusted group performed at roughly parallel stages across the domains, the clinic group performed at increasingly lower levels as one progressed from the deeper structural concepts (logico-physical and perspective-taking) to the more surface structure or content-bound domains (interpersonal and moral). In other words, the clinic group, in general, had about the same level of cognitive (logico-physical) performance and were slightly behind in their perspective-taking capabilities in comparison to the matched group, but they were not applying these more basic capabilities in the domains of interpersonal and moral reasoning.

Unfortunately, many proponents of the structural-developmental approach have interpreted this type of data, combined with the necessary but not sufficient model, as indicating that if a child does not give evidence of a prerequisite level on the deeper structures (logico-mathematical or perspective-taking), intervention aimed at the more surface structures of interpersonal or moral stage will be a waste of time. This misconclusion arises from the confusion of logical necessity and psychological causality.

Perspective-taking does not develop magically in a vacuum devoid of social experience. As we stressed previously, parallel levels of perspective-taking and interpersonal reasoning *can* develop synchronously ($\underline{A} \cdot \underline{B}$, $A \cdot \overline{B}$, $\overline{A} \cdot \overline{B}$), and in reality it is likely that it is through interpersonal and/or moral experiences that the development of the deeper structural domain of perspective-taking is stimulated. In other words, one implication is that intervention research should aim to stimulate development of the more basic abilities through the "relatively more content related" areas of reasoning. Certainly this is an interesting hypothesis and one open to research.

Confidence that such intervention is worthwhile also requires some assurance of a relation between developing conceptions of social relationships to actual social relations. The second implication is derived from an examination of patterns of social reasoning within the clinical sample in the study to which we referred.[7] We found here that although as a group the clinical population was functioning at lower levels of interpersonal and moral reasoning than their peers, this was not true of every child in this group. The data show that whereas the matched sample of normal children did normally or better on the social cognitive measures, disturbed children did everywhere from very poorly to very well. Some very interpersonally disturbed children did very well on all of our interpersonal and moral concept measures.

However, if a child was at an extremely low level of interpersonal reasoning, chances were extremely high that he or she would be a child in the clinic group. It appears then that children with average or adequate level of social cognition for their age may act maturely or immaturely; we cannot reliably predict which. However, children who do lag far behind their peers in the social cognitive stage also appear to have difficulty relating to peers. The second implication, then, is that average or adequate interpersonal or social cognitive reasoning is necessary but not sufficient for adequate interpersonal relating. This does not mean that low levels of interpersonal conception *cause* poor social behavior, but that they are closely associated with behavioral difficulties in a way that is different from the relation of average or adequate social reasoning to social relations, that is, extremely low levels of social reasoning may have a certain limiting effect on maturity of social behavior.

In sum, the implications of these findings in conjunction with the model we have put forth are as follows: 1) It is probably easier to educationally stimulate change in the more content-bound domains such as interpersonal or moral reasoning than in the relatively deeper structural domains of logical and perspective-taking. 2) For normal children who function adequately, social cognitive education may have the effect of strengthening the deeper structures (perspective-taking) through stimulation of a wide range of skills which are based on this process and in so doing, prepare the groundwork of general structural movement to the next stage. However, for children who lag behind in domains such as interpersonal or moral reasoning, but who have adequate perspective-taking abilities intervention may be construed as the application of perspective-taking to these more specific skills. 3) Finally, even if social-cognitive training is important, it is not everything; although it is a critical step, raising the level of social cognition does not guarantee concomitant change in behavior. For we know from our research that even when interpersonal reasoning is at age normative levels, interpersonal relating may still be immature. In fact, in its strictest interpretation, this model implies that by generally improving the *structure* of interpersonal behavior one is likely to improve reasoning, rather than the reverse. Intervention research carefully designed to feed back into theory is the most appropriate way to clarify not only the relations among social and physical cognitive domains, but also between social reasoning and social relations.

Notes

1. G. H. Mead, *Mind, Self and Society* (Chicago: University of Chicago Press, 1934).

2. R. L. Selman and D. A. Byrne, "A Structural-Developmental Analysis of Levels of Role-Taking in Middle Childhood," *Child Development*, 45 (No. 3, 1974), 803-806; R. L. Selman, "The Development of Social-Cognitive Understanding: A Guide to Educational and Clinical Practice," in *Morality: Theory, Research and Intervention*, ed. T. Lickona (New York: Holt, Rinehart and Winston, 1976).

3. R. L. Selman, "Toward a Structural-Developmental Analysis of Interpersonal Relationship Concepts: Research with Normal and Disturbed Preadolescent Boys," in *X Annual Minnesota Symposium on Child Psychology*, ed. A. Pick (Minneapolis: University of Minnesota Press, 1976).

4. Selman, "The Development of Social-Cognitive Understanding."

5. J. Piaget and B. Inhelder, *The Psychology of the Child* (New York: Basic Books, 1969).

6. Selman, "Toward a Structural-Developmental Analysis of Interpersonal Relationship Concepts."

7. *Ibid.*

4

Erik Erikson: The Man Who Gave Adolescents an Identity Crisis

The primary purpose of Part I is to review contemporary developmental theories of adolescence. Piaget, Kohlberg, and Loevinger are given special emphasis. Their research on cognitive development, moral reasoning, and the self is highly pertinent to a fuller understanding of adolescence. Further, it is not comprehensively represented in most contemporary psychological reviews; nor, in my opinion, is it understood by a majority of educators. On the more abstract level, these theories share certain commonalities that make their study of human development exemplary. First, their approach is empirical and scientific—to find order, laws, or a plan in complex aspects of man's growth and behavior. The theories, which are based in data, are scientific explanations of the development of thought, morality, and the self. Piaget is the least empirical and closest to the methodology of the European ethologists; Loevinger has accumulated very extensive data to deduce her stages of ego development. Further, these modern developmentalists find and describe common characteristics—stages—in the lives and growth of individuals. The sequence in which we experience these developments is invariant for all of us although few complete the entire passage. Stages are found in the way we think about the abstract logical or applied problems we encounter, in the way we decide right from wrong, and in the meaning we make of ourselves and our social world. Another commonality of these theories is that they focus on development in *human thinking* across a broad array of concerns (that is, they are cognitive-developmental theories in part or in whole). All postulate that development occurs as a result of interaction between an inquiring person and a problem, that social experience stimulates or retards growth, and that people grow toward greater intellectual, moral, and social complexity.

In light of the above, why include two excerpts by Erik Erikson, one

133

written just after World War II and the other addressed to the Commission on the Year 2000, which are not cognitive developmental in their conception of adolescence and youth? One reason is that adolescence is not solely a state of mind. Or, if it is, its equilibrium is subject to strong and various perturbations—the buffeting, even anarchy, of sexual drives and of such powerful emotions as anger, lust, intolerance, a need to be free, and anxiety about the future. The emotional volatility of adolescents is well chronicled and stereotyped, and educators and parents attempt to deal with it in the most effective way possible. And yet this emotional, existential intensity of adolescence is not captured in the otherwise extremely valuable descriptions of formal operations, Stage 3, or even Loevinger's Self-Protective Stage. Erikson does focus on the emotions, the ambivalence of a time when "deep down you are not quite sure that you are a man (or a woman), that you will ever grow together again and be attractive, that you will be able to master your drives, that you really know who you are . . . that you know what you want to be, that you know what you look like to others, and that you will know how to make the right decisions without, once for all, committing yourself to the wrong friend, sexual partner, leader, or career."[1]

Erikson writes as a psychoanalyst from his experience with adolescent patients. Much of his early professional concern was with the question of whether someone is healthy or disturbed and, if the latter, how to cure him. That does not lead one directly to a theory for the prevention of such disturbances, which Erikson admits, nor to the empirical study of normal adolescents and their growth, which is the domain of the developmentalist. But Erikson, in addition to being a compassionate therapist, is interested in the growth of the healthy personality, the emotional crises in that process, and their treatment. He would argue that disturbance or crisis is not a phenomenon separate from development—that is, its dark or alien side. It is, rather, dialectical to growth and conflict resolution, especially in adolescence.

Further, Erikson believes that adults, parents, psychologists, and teachers have much to do with the perturbations or crises of adolescent growth.

Youth after youth, bewildered by some assumed role, a role forced on him by the inexorable standardization of American adolescence, runs away in one form or another: leaving schools and jobs, staying out all night, or withdrawing into bizarre and inaccessible moods. Once "delinquent," his greatest need and often his only salvation is the refusal on the part of older friends, advisers, and judiciary personnel to type him further by pat diagnoses and social judgments which ignore the special dynamic conditions of adolescence. For if diagnosed and treated correctly, seemingly psychotic and criminal incidents do not in adolescence have the same fatal significance which they have at other ages. Yet many a youth, finding that the authorities expect him to be "a bum," "a queer," or off the beam, perversely obliges by becoming just that.[2]

Here the themes of compassion for the young and of adolescents' resilience or potential to overcome are clear.

In the first excerpt that follows, "Growth and Crises of the Healthy Personality," Erikson presents a classical conception of development. This conception has profoundly influenced American thinking about adolescence in the generation since its publication. (Again, his comments in the second article that "The actions of young people are always in part and by necessity reactions to the stereotypes held up to them by their elders"[3] are full of double entendre. Thus, it is Erikson who has given American teenagers an identity crisis.) His conception of development has several elements.

First, Erikson's conception intentionally combined ideas from psychoanalysis (for example, that adults carry unresolved childhood conflicts in the recesses of their personality) with the then (1950) emerging study of child and adolescent development. He defines the stages of ego development as a series of tasks facing the individual (for example, the adolescent defining who he is), each of which results in a crisis (such as the adolescent conflict between identity and identity diffusion).

Second, Erikson's stages are inclusive or generic: they attempt to characterize and describe the central issue facing the person during a particular period in his life. They are not broken down, psychologically, as in the case of Loevinger although Erikson recognizes that the healthy personality develops gradually "in many complicated steps."[4] Here the existential metaphors of the clinician take the place of the detailed descriptive data of the developmentalist.

Third, Erikson's stages are more broadly conceived and rooted in feelings, in the preconscious, and in what troubles or produces conflict for the adolescent than is true for the cognitive-developmental stages of reason, morality, and ego. It is the case, however, that while the teenager is not conscious of using abstract thought or a good-boy-good-girl morality, he is painfully aware that he is having an identity crisis.

Fourth, Erikson's stages are related to age; they are triggered by the calendar and "inner laws of development." They are an inevitable part of our lives, and all of us must make the passage. "Each [developmental task] comes to its ascendance, meets its crisis, and finds its lasting solution . . . *toward the end of the stages.* . . ."[5] Here there is no need for education to stimulate development or prevent fixation. Development will happen. Though Erikson recognizes the need for therapy, for understanding and compassion, he says little about prevention. This conception of developmental stage is, of course, substantially different from that of the cognitive developmentalists, who contend that the individual may and does become fixed in his growth, with higher stages remaining forever latent for him.

Fifth, Erikson is describing the unconscious side of adolescent development or, stated more accurately, the interrelationship between adolescent thinking about objective problems, morality, work, and self and the impelling, noncognitive demands of one's body, genitals, and feelings. That these many strands of the developmental helix interact dynamically and holistically is evident in the disequilibrium of adolescents' lives. For example, Loevinger feels that the Conscientious Stage of ego development is typically not achieved until young adulthood. Erikson interprets conscientiousness, however, as "the inner residue in the adult of his past inequality to his parent"—as an unconscious, cruel need to justify himself to his parent. No theorist except Erikson has discussed the effect of the unconscious drama on the developmental stages. For example, Erikson explains many of the adolescent behaviors described by Kohlberg as Stage 3 or by Loevinger as Conformist as an unconscious defense: "they [adolescents] become remarkably clannish, intolerant, and cruel in their exclusion of others who are 'different,' in skin color or cultural background, in tastes and gifts, and often in entirely petty aspects of dress and gesture arbitrarily selected as *the* signs of an in-grouper or out-grouper. It is important to understand . . . such intolerance as the necessary *defense against a sense of identity diffusion*, which is unavoidable at . . . [this] time of life . . . ."[6] What Erikson contributes is not so much the new barbarian character of this stage but the unconscious and emotional part of its explanation.

Part II extends this point a bit further by presenting the work of Newmann and Mosher, who describe efforts to educate adolescents to be democratic by having them govern their own schools and participate in social and political action in their communities. Erikson predicts unconscious resistance and unreadiness on the part of many adolescents. American democracy poses special problems to adolescent identity formation;—"it insists on *self-made identities* ready to grasp many chances and ready to adjust . . . . Our democracy . . . must present the adolescent with ideals which can be shared by youths of many backgrounds and which emphasize autonomy in the form of independence and initiative in the form of enterprise."[7] Erikson contends that this effort goes against the natural tendency for adolescents, as a defense against identity diffusion, to stereotype "themselves, their ideals, and their enemies . . . ." Thus, "simple and cruel totalitarian doctrines" have appeal to the young. Young people can "find convincing and satisfactory identities in the simple totalitarian doctrines of race, class, or nation."[8]

In the second excerpt, "Memorandum on Youth," Erikson is writing as a visionary whose qualifications rest on a distinguished lifelong study of the dialectic between the rational and irrational forces (including societal and ideological pressures) in the lives of the young. His view to the year 2000 is unromantic, indeed somewhat chilling, provocative for adults in regard to the myths they perpetuate about themselves and their children, and, most of all, compassionate for youth.

It is not surprising, perhaps, that Erikson is concerned primarily with the ideological forces that will shape the identity of adolescents and youth in the future. Individuation, becoming one's own man or woman, is the central developmental task. Erikson sees the struggle for the minds and identities of young people to be between two ideologies. In the first, the ideology of technology and science, youth *"become* what they *do* . . . the food harvested, the goods produced, the money made, the ideas substantiated or the technological problems solved."[9] In the second, the humanist, universalist ideology, man is the measure, and the search is not for the technically possible but "for the criteria for the optimal and the ethically permissible"; the ideology is characterized by humanitarian activism to assist the underprivileged everywhere and "an insistence on the widest range of human possibilities—beyond the technological."[10] It is my hope that the reader will see a parallel between Erikson's universalist ideology and the philosophy of this book.

Erikson makes a strong ethical appeal and offers hope in his "Memorandum": "we . . . can orient ourselves and offer orientation only by recognizing and cultivating an age-specific *ethical* capacity in *older* youth . . . ." He urges his generation to help youth develop "ethical, affirmative, resacralizing rules of conduct"[11]rather than to stereotype them as *anti-institutional, hedonistic, desacralizing"*[12] and in that process drive them further into a new barbarism.

Finally, Erikson foresees a change in the generational process itself, an increasing awareness that older and younger generations share a common fate; that aging itself will be a different experience; that life stages will be further subdivided, with the relative waning of parents and tradition and the emergence of the "not-too-young specialist" as the new arbiters (here I must note that Erikson has more confidence in "the best and the brightest" than I do); that new roles for both sexes will emerge at all stages of life. And so we end with a wise clinician's view of where individual and societal development is heading, a view that is especially penetrating in its characterization of technological and humanist youth and moving in its compassion for young people and their generation.

Notes

1. Erik Erikson, "Growth and Crises of the Healthy Personality," in *Identity and the Life Cycle* (New York: International Universities Press, 1959), 93. Published by *Psychological Issues*, 1 (No. 1, 1959).

2. *Ibid.*, 91-92.

3. Erik Erikson, "Memorandum on Youth," *Daedalus*, 96 (Summer 1967), 860.

4. *Id.*, "Growth and Crises of the Healthy Personality," 51.

5. *Ibid.*, 53.

6. *Ibid.*, 92.

7. *Ibid.*, 93.

8. *Ibid.*, 92.

9. Erikson, "Memorandum on Youth," 864.

10. *Ibid.*, 866.

11. *Ibid.*, 869.

12. *Ibid.*, 869.

Growth and Crises of the Healthy Personality

Erik H. Erikson

The Fact-finding Committee of the White House Conference on Childhood and Youth has asked me to repeat here in greater detail a few ideas set forth in another context.[1] There the matter of the healthy personality emerges, as if accidentally, from a variety of clinical and anthropological considerations. Here it is to become the central theme.

An expert, it is said, can separate fact from theory, and knowledge from opinion. It is his jog to know the available techniques by which statements in his field can be verified. If, in this paper, I were to restrict myself to what is, in this sense, *known* about the "healthy personality," I would lead the reader and myself into a very honorable but very uninspiring

Selections are reprinted from "Growth and Crises of the Healthy Personality," from *Identity and the Life Cycle*, Selected Papers, by Erik H. Erikson, published by *Psychological Issues*, 1 (No. 1, 1959), with the permission of W. W. Norton & Company, Inc. Copyright © 1959 by International Universities Press, Inc. The original version of this paper appeared in *Symposium on the Healthy Personality*, Supplement II, *Problems of Infancy and Childhood, Transactions of Fourth Conference, March, 1950*, ed. M. J. E. Senn (New York: Josiah Macy, Jr., Foundation, 1950).

austerity. In the matter of man's relation to himself and to others, methodological problems are not such as to be either instructive or suggestive in a short treatise.

On the other hand, if I were to write this paper in order to give another introduction to the theory of Freudian psychoanalysis, I would hardly contribute much to an understanding of the healthy personality. For the psychoanalyst knows very much more about the dynamics and cure of the disturbances which he treats daily than about the prevention of such disturbances.

I will, however, start out from Freud's far-reaching discovery that neurotic conflict is not very different in content from the conflicts which every child must live through in his childhood, and that every adult carries these conflicts with him in the recesses of his personality. I shall take account of this fact by stating for each childhood stage what these critical psychological conflicts are. For man, to remain psychologically alive, must resolve these conflicts unceasingly, even as his body must unceasingly combat the encroachment of physical decomposition. However, since I cannot accept the conclusion that just to be alive, or not to be sick, means to be healthy, I must have recourse to a few concepts which are not part of the official terminology of my field. Being interested also in cultural anthropology, I shall try to describe those elements of a really healthy personality which—so it seems to me—are most noticeably absent or defective in neurotic patients and which are most obviously present in the kind of man that educational and cultural systems seem to be striving, each in its own way, to create, to support, and to maintain.

I shall present human growth from the point of view of the conflicts, inner and outer, which the healthy personality weathers, emerging and re-emerging with an increased sense of inner unity, with an increase of good judgment, and an increase in the capacity to do well, according to the standards of those who are significant to him. The use of the words "to do well," of course, points up the whole question of cultural relativity. For example, those who are significant to a man may think he is doing well when he "does some good"; or when he "does well" in the sense of acquiring possessions; or when he is doing well in the sense of learning new skills or new ways of understanding or mastering reality; or when he is not much more than just getting along.

Formulations of what constitutes a healthy personality in an adult are presented in other parts of the Fact-finding Committee's work. If I may take up only one, namely, Marie Jahoda's definition,[2] according to which a healthy personality *actively masters his environment*, shows a certain *unity of personality*, and is able to *perceive the world and himself correctly*, it is clear that all of these criteria are relative to the child's cognitive and social development. In fact, we may say that childhood is defined by their initial absence and by their gradual development in many complicated steps. I consider it my task to approach this question from the genetic point of view: How does a healthy personality grow or, as it were, accrue from the successive stages of increasing capacity to master life's outer and inner dangers—with some vital enthusiasm to spare?

On Health and Growth

Whenever we try to understand growth, it is well to remember the *epigenetic principle* which is derived from the growth of organisms *in utero*. Somewhat generalized, this principle states that anything that grows has a *ground plan*, and that out of this ground plan the *parts* arise, each part having its *time* of special ascendancy, until all parts have arisen to form a *functioning whole*. At birth the baby leaves the chemical exchange of the womb for the social exchange system of his society, where his gradually increasing capacities meet the opportunities and limitations of his culture. How the maturing organism continues to unfold, not by developing new organs, but by a prescribed sequence of locomotor, sensory, and social capacities, is described in the child-development literature. Psychoanalysis has given us an understanding of the more idiosyncratic experiences and especially the inner conflicts, which constitute the manner in which an individual becomes a distinct personality. But here, too, it is important to realize that in the sequence of his most personal experiences the healthy child, given a reasonable amount of guidance, can be trusted to obey inner laws of development, laws which create a *succession of potentialities for significant interaction* with those who tend him. While such interaction varies from culture to culture, it must remain within the *proper rate and the proper sequence* which govern the *growth of a personality* as well as that of an organism. Personality can be said to develop according to steps predetermined in the human organism's readiness to be driven toward, to be aware of, and to interact with, a widening social radius, beginning with the dim image of a mother and ending with mankind, or at any rate that segment of mankind which "counts" in the particular individual's life.

It is for this reason that, in the presentation of stages in the development of the personality, we employ an *epigenetic diagram* analogous to one previously employed for an analysis of Freud's psychosexual stages.[3] It is, in fact, the purpose of this presentation to bridge the theory of infantile sexuality (without repeating it here in detail), and our knowledge of the child's physical and social growth within his family and the social structure. An epigenetic diagram [appears in Figure 4-1].

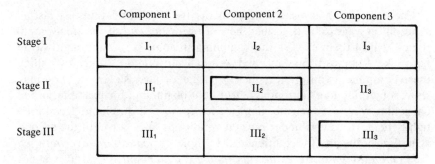

	Component 1	Component 2	Component 3
Stage I	I_1	I_2	I_3
Stage II	II_1	II_2	II_3
Stage III	III_1	III_2	III_3

Figure 4-1
An epigenetic diagram

The double-lined squares signify both a sequence of stages (I to III) and a gradual development of component parts; in other words, the diagram formalizes a *progression through time of a differentiation of parts.* This indicates (1) that each item of the healthy personality to be discussed is *systematically related to all others,* and that they all depend on the *proper development in the proper sequence of each item;* and (2) that each item *exists in some form before "its" decisive and critical time* normally arrives.

If I say, for example, that a *sense of basic trust* is the first component of mental health to develop in life, a *sense of autonomous will* the second, and a *sense of initiative* the third, the purpose of the diagram may become clearer . . . . [See Figure 4-2.]

This diagrammatic statement, in turn, is meant to express a number of fundamental relations that exist among the three components, as well as a few fundamental facts for each.

First Stage (about first year)	BASIC TRUST	Earlier form of AUTONOMY	Earlier form of INITIATIVE
Second Stage (about second and third years)	Later form of BASIC TRUST	AUTONOMY	Earlier form of INITIATIVE
Third Stage (about fourth and fifth years)	Later form of BASIC TRUST	Later form of AUTONOMY	INITIATIVE

Figure 4-2
Diagrammatic statement of components of mental health

Each comes to its ascendance, meets its crisis, and finds its lasting solution (in ways to be described here) *toward the end of the stages* mentioned. All of them exist in the beginning in some form, although we do not make a point of this fact, and we shall not confuse things by calling these components different names at earlier or later stages. A baby may show something like "autonomy" from the beginning, for example, in the particular way in which he angrily tries to wriggle his hand free when tightly held. However, under normal conditions, it is not until the second year that he begins to experience the whole *critical alternative between being an autonomous creature and being a dependent one*; and it is not until then that he is ready for a *decisive encounter* with his environment, an environment which, in turn, feels called upon to convey to him its *particular ideas and concepts of autonomy and coercion* in ways decisively contributing to the character, the efficiency, and the health of his personality in his culture.

It is this *encounter*, together with the resulting crisis, which is to be described for each stage. Each stage becomes a *crisis* because incipient growth and awareness in a significant part-function go together with a shift in instinctual energy and yet cause specific vulnerability in that part. One of the most difficult questions to decide, therefore, is whether or not a child at a given stage is weak or strong. Perhaps it would be best to say that he is always vulnerable in some respects and completely oblivious and insensitive in others, but that at the same time he is unbelievably persistent in the same respects in which he is vulnerable. It must be added that the smallest baby's weakness gives him power; out of his very dependence and weakness he makes signs to which his environment (if it is guided well by a responsiveness based both on instinctive and traditional patterns) is peculiarly sensitive. A baby's presence exerts a consistent and persistent domination over the outer and inner lives of every member of a household. Because these members must reorient themselves to accommodate his presence, they must also grow as individuals and as a group. It is as true to say that babies control and bring up their families as it is to say the converse. A family can bring up a baby only by being brought up by him. His growth consists of a series of challenges to them to serve his newly developing potentialities for social interaction.

Each successive step, then, is a potential crisis because of a radical *change in perspective*. There is, at the beginning of life, the most radical change of all: from intrauterine to extrauterine life. But in postnatal existence, too, such radical adjustments of perspective as lying relaxed, sitting firmly, and running fast must all be accomplished in their own good time. With them, the interpersonal perspective, too, changes rapidly and often radically, as is testified by the proximity in time of such

opposites as "not letting mother out of sight" and "wanting to be independent." Thus, *different capacities use different opportunities* to become full-grown components of the ever-new configuration that is the
growing personality . . . .

Identity versus Identity Diffusion

I

With the establishment of a good relationship to the world of skills
and to those who teach and share the new skills, childhood proper comes
to an end. Youth begins. But in puberty and adolescence all sameness
and continuities relied on earlier are questioned again because of a rapidity
of body growth which equals that of early childhood and because of the
entirely new addition of physical genital maturity. The growing and developing young people, faced with this physiological revolution within
them, are now primarily concerned with attempts at consolidating their
social roles. They are sometimes morbidly, often curiously, preoccupied
with what they appear to be in the eyes of others as compared with what
they feel they are and with the question of how to connect the earlier
cultivated roles and skills with the ideal prototypes of the day. In their
search for a new sense of continuity and sameness, some adolescents have
to refight many of the crises of earlier years, and they are never ready to
install lasting idols and ideals as guardians of a final identity.

The integration now taking place in the form of the ego identity is
more than the sum of the childhood identifications. It is the inner capital
accrued from all those experiences of each successive stage, when successful identification led to a successful alignment of the individual's *basic
drives* with his *endowment* and his *opportunities*. In psychoanalysis we
ascribe such successful alignments to "ego synthesis"; I have tried to demonstrate that the ego values accrued in childhood culminate in what I
have called *a sense of ego identity*. The sense of ego identity, then, is the
accrued confidence that one's ability to maintain inner sameness and
continuity (one's ego in the psychological sense) is matched by the sameness and continuity of one's meaning for others. Thus, self-esteem, confirmed at the end of each major crisis, grows to be a conviction that one
is learning effective steps toward a tangible future, that one is developing
a defined personality within a social reality which one understands. The
growing child must, at every step, derive a vitalizing sense of reality from
the awareness that his individual way of mastering experience is a successful variant of the way other people around him master experience and
recognize such mastery.

In this, children cannot be fooled by empty praise and condescending encouragement. They may have to accept artificial bolstering of their self-esteem in lieu of something better, but what I call their accruing ego identity gains real strength only from wholehearted and consistent recognition of real accomplishment, that is, achievement that has meaning in their culture. On the other hand, should a child feel that the environment tries to deprive him too radically of all the forms of expression which permit him to develop and to integrate the next step in his ego identity, he will resist with the astonishing strength encountered in animals who are suddenly forced to defend their lives. Indeed, in the social jungle of human existence, there is no feeling of being alive without a sense of ego identity. To understand this would be to understand the trouble of adolescents better, especially the trouble of all those who cannot just be "nice" boys and girls, but are desperately seeking for a satisfactory sense of belonging, be it in cliques and gangs here in our country or in inspiring mass movements in others.

Ego identity, then, develops out of a gradual integration of all identifications, but here, if anywhere, the whole has a different quality than the sum of its parts. Under favorable circumstances children have the nucleus of a separate identity in early life; often they must defend it against any pressure which would make them overidentify with one of their parents. This is difficult to learn from patients, because the neurotic ego has, by definition, fallen prey to overidentification and to faulty identifications with disturbed parents, a circumstance which isolated the small individual both from his budding identity and from his milieu. But we can study it profitably in the children of minority-group Americans who, having successfully graduated from a marked and well-guided stage of autonomy, enter the most decisive stage of American childhood: that of initiative and industry.

Minority groups of a lesser degree of Americanization (Negroes, Indians, Mexicans, and certain European groups) often are privileged in the enjoyment of a more sensual early childhood. Their crises come when their parents and teachers, losing trust in themselves and using sudden correctives in order to approach the vague but pervasive Anglo-Saxon ideal, create violent discontinuities; or where, indeed, the children themselves learn to disavow their sensual and overprotective mothers as temptations and a hindrance to the formation of a more American personality.

On the whole, it can be said that American schools successfully meet the challenge of training children of play-school age and of the elementary grades in a spirit of self-reliance and enterprise. Children of these ages seem remarkably free of prejudice and apprehension, preoccupied as they still are with growing and learning and with the new pleasures of association outside their families. This, to forestall the sense of individual inferiority, must lead to a hope for "industrial association," for equality with all those who apply themselves wholeheartedly to the same skills and adventures in learning. Many individual successes, on the other hand, only expose the now overly encouraged children of mixed backgrounds and somewhat deviant endowments to the shock of American adolescence: the standardization of individuality and the intolerance of "differences."

The emerging ego identity, then, bridges the early childhood stages, when the body and the parent images were given their specific meanings, and the later stages, when a variety of social roles becomes available and increasingly coercive. A lasting ego identity cannot begin to exist without the trust of the first oral stage; it cannot be completed without a promise of fulfillment which from the dominant image of adulthood reaches down into the baby's beginnings and which creates at every step an accruing sense of ego strength.

II

The danger of this stage is *identity diffusion*; as Biff puts it in Arthur Miller's *Death of a Salesman*, "I just can't take hold, Mom, I can't take hold of some kind of a life." Where such a dilemma is based on a strong previous doubt of one's ethnic and sexual identity, delinquent and outright psychotic incidents are not uncommon. Youth after youth, bewildered by some assumed role, a role forced on him by the inexorable standardization of American adolescence, runs away in one form or another: leaving schools and jobs, staying out all night, or withdrawing into bizarre and inaccessible moods. Once "delinquent," his greatest need and often his only salvation is the refusal on the part of older friends, advisers, and judiciary personnel to type him further by pat diagnoses and social judgments which ignore the special dynamic conditions of adolescence. For if diagnosed and treated correctly, seemingly psychotic and criminal incidents do not in adolescence have the same fatal significance which they have at other ages. Yet many a youth, finding that the authorities expect him to be "a bum," or "a queer," or "off the beam," perversely obliges by becoming just that.

In general it is primarily the inability to settle on an occupational identity which disturbs young people. To keep themselves together they temporarily overidentify, to the point of apparent complete loss of identity, with the heroes of cliques and crowds. On the other hand, they become remarkably clannish, intolerant, and cruel in their exclusion of others who are "different," in skin color or cultural background, in tastes and gifts, and often in entirely petty aspects of dress and gesture arbitrarily selected as *the* signs of an in-grouper or out-grouper. It is important to understand (which does not mean condone or participate in) such intolerance as the necessary *defense against a sense of identity diffusion*, which is unavoidable at a time of life when the body changes its proportions radically, when genital maturity floods body and imagination with all manners of drives, when intimacy with the other sex approaches and is, on occasion, forced on the youngster, and when life lies before one with a variety of conflicting possibilities and choices. Adolescents help one another temporarily through such discomfort by forming cliques and by stereotyping themselves, their ideals, and their enemies.

It is important to understand this because it makes clear the appeal which simple and cruel totalitarian doctrines have on the minds of the youth of such countries and classes as have lost or are losing their group identities (feudal, agrarian, national, and so forth) in these times of world-wide industrialization, emancipation, and wider intercommunication. The dynamic quality of the tempestuous adolescences lived through in patriarchal and agrarian countries (countries which face the most radical changes in political structure and in economy) explains the fact that their young people find convincing and satisfactory identities in the simple totalitarian doctrines of race, class, or nation. Even though we may be forced to win wars against their leaders, we still are faced with the job of winning the peace with these grim youths by convincingly demonstrating to them (by giving it) a democratic identity which can be strong and yet tolerant, judicious and still determined.

But it is increasingly important to understand this also in order to treat the intolerances of our adolescents at home with understanding and guidance rather than with verbal stereotypes or prohibitions. It is difficult to be tolerant if deep down you are not quite sure that you are a man (or a woman), that you will ever grow together again and be attractive, that you will be able to master your drives, that you really know who you are,[4] that you know what you want to be, that you know what you look like to others, and that you will know how to make the right decisions without, once for all, committing yourself to the wrong friend, sexual partner, leader, or career.

Democracy in a country like America poses special problems in that it insists on *self-made identities* ready to grasp many chances and ready to adjust to changing necessities of booms and busts, of peace and war, of migration and determined sedentary life. Our democracy, furthermore, must present the adolescent with ideals which can be shared by youths of many backgrounds and which emphasize autonomy in the form of independence and initiative in the form of enterprise. These promises, in turn, are not easy to fulfill in increasingly complex and centralized systems of economic and political organization, systems which, if geared to war, must automatically neglect the "self-made" identities of millions of individuals and put them where they are most needed. This is hard on many young Americans because their whole upbringing, and therefore the development of a healthy personality, depends on a certain degree of *choice,* a certain hope for an individual *chance,* and a certain conviction in freedom of *self-determination.*

We are speaking here not only of high privileges and lofty ideals but also of psychological necessities. Psychologically speaking, a gradually accruing ego identity is the only safeguard against the *anarchy of drives* as well as the *autocracy of conscience,* that is, the cruel overconscientiousness which is the inner residue in the adult of his past inequality in regard to his parent. Any loss of a sense of identity exposes the individual to his own childhood conflicts—as could be observed, for example, in the neuroses of World War II among men and women who could not stand the general dislocation of their careers or a variety of other special pressures of war. Our adversaries, it seems, understand this. Their psychological warfare consists in the determined continuation of general conditions which permit them to indoctrinate mankind within their orbit with the simple and yet for them undoubtedly effective identities of class warfare and nationalism, while they know that the psychology, as well as the economy, of free enterprise and of self-determination is stretched to the breaking point under the conditions of long-drawn-out cold and luke-warm war. It is clear, therefore, that we must bend every effort to present our young men and women with the tangible and trustworthy promise of opportunities for a rededication to the life for which the country's history, as well as their own childhood, has prepared them. Among the tasks of national defense, this one must not be forgotten.

I have referred to the relationship of the problem of trust to matters of adult faith; to that of the problem of autonomy to matters of adult independence in work and citizenship. I have pointed to the connection between a sense of initiative and the kind of enterprise sanctioned in the economic system, and between the sense of industry and a culture's technology. In searching for the social values which guide identity, one confronts the problem of aristocracy, in its widest possible sense which connotes the conviction that the best people rule and that that rule develops the best in people. In order not to become cynically or apathetically lost, young people in search of an identity must somewhere be able to convince themselves that those who succeed thereby shoulder the obligation of being the best, that is, of personifying the nation's ideals. In this country, as in any other, we have those successful types who become the cynical representatives of the "inside track," the "bosses" of impersonal machinery. In a culture once pervaded with the value of the self-made man, a

special danger ensues from the idea of a synthetic personality: as if you
are what you can appear to be, or as if you are what you can buy. This
can be counteracted only by a system of education that transmits values
and goals which determinedly aspire beyond mere "functioning" and
"making the grade."

Three Stages of Adulthood

Intimacy and Distantiation versus Self-Absorption

When childhood and youth come to an end, life, so the saying goes,
begins: by which we mean work or study for a specified career, sociability with the other sex, and in time, marriage and a family of one's own.
But it is only after a reasonable sense of identity has been established that
real *intimacy* with the other sex (or, for that matter, with any other person
or even with oneself) is possible. Sexual intimacy is only part of what I
have in mind, for it is obvious that sexual intimacies do not always wait
for the ability to develop a true and mutual psychological intimacy with
another person. The youth who is not sure of his identity shies away from
interpersonal intimacy; but the surer he becomes of himself, the more he
seeks it in the form of friendship, combat, leadership, love, and inspiration. There is a kind of adolescent attachment between boy and girl which
is often mistaken either for mere sexual attraction or for love. Except
where the mores demand heterosexual behavior, such attachment is often
devoted to an attempt at arriving at a definition of one's identity by talking things over endlessly, by confessing what one feels like and what the
other seems like, and by discussing plans, wishes, and expectations. Where
a youth does not accomplish such intimate relation with others—and, I
would add, with his own inner resources—in late adolescence or early
adulthood, he may either isolate himself and find, at best, highly stereotyped and formal interpersonal relations (formal in the sense of lacking
in spontaneity, warmth, and real exchange of fellowship), or he must seek
them in repeated attempts and repeated failures. Unfortunately, many
young people marry under such circumstances, hoping to find themselves
in finding one another; but, alas, the early obligation to act in a defined
way, as mates and as parents, disturbs them in the completion of this work
on themselves. Obviously, a change of mate is rarely the answer, but
rather some wisely guided insight into the fact that the condition of a
true twoness is that one must first become oneself.

The counterpart of intimacy is *distantiation:* the readiness to repudiate,
to isolate, and, if necessary, to destroy those forces and people whose
essence seems dangerous to one's own. This more mature and more efficient repudiation (it is utilized and exploited in politics and in war) is

an outgrowth of the blinder prejudices which during the struggle for an identity differentiate sharply and cruelly between the familiar and the foreign. At first, intimate, competitive, and combative relations are experienced with and against the selfsame people. Gradually, a polarization occurs along the lines of the competitive encounter, the sexual embrace, and various forms of incisive combat.

Freud was once asked what he thought a normal person should be able to do well. The questioner probably expected a complicated, a "deep" answer. But Freud simply said, *"Lieben und arbeiten"* ("to love and to work"). It pays to ponder on this simple formula; it gets deeper as you think about it. For when Freud said "love," he meant the expansiveness of generosity as well as genital love; when he said love *and* work, he meant a general work productiveness which would not preoccupy the individual to the extent that his right or capacity to be a sexual and a loving being would be lost.

Psychoanalysis has emphasized *genitality* as one of the chief signs of a healthy personality. Genitality is the potential capacity to develop orgastic potency in relation to a loved partner of the opposite sex. Orgastic potency here means not the discharge of sex products in the sense of Kinsey's "outlets" but heterosexual mutuality, with full genital sensitivity and with an overall discharge of tension from the whole body. This is a rather concrete way of saying something about a process which we really do not understand. But the idea clearly is that the experience of the climactic mutuality of orgasm provides a supreme example of the mutual regulation of complicated patterns and in some way appeases the potential rages caused by the daily evidence of the oppositeness of male and female, of fact and fancy, of love and hate, of work and play. Satisfactory sex relations make sex less obsessive and sadistic control superfluous. But here the prescription of psychiatry faces overwhelming inner prejudices and situational limitations in parts of the population whose sense of identity is based on the complete subordination of sexuality and, indeed, sensuality to a life of toil, duty, and worship. Here only gradual frank discussion can clarify the respective dangers of traditional rigidity and abrupt or merely superficial change . . . .

Notes

1. E. H. Erikson, *Childhood and Society* (New York: W. W. Norton, 1950).

2. M. Jahoda, "Toward a Social Psychology of Mental Health," in *Symposium on the Healthy Personality*, Supplement II, *Problems of Infancy and Childhood, Transactions of Fourth Conference, March, 1950*, ed. M. J. E. Senn (New York: Josiah Macy, Jr., Foundation, 1950).

3. See Part I of Erikson, *Childhood and Society.*

4. On the wall of a cowboys' bar in the wide-open West hangs a saying: "I ain't what I ought to be, I ain't what I'm going to be, but I ain't what I was."

Memorandum on Youth

Erik H. Erikson

I

In responding to the inquiry of the Commission on the Year 2000, I will take the liberty of quoting the statements put to me in order to reflect on some of the stereotyped thinking about youth that has become representative of us, the older generation. This, it seems to me, is prognostically as important as the behavior of the young people themselves; for youth is, after all, a *generational phenomenon*, even though its problems are now treated as those of an outlandish tribe descended on us from Mars. The actions of young people are always in part and by necessity reactions to the stereotypes held up to them by their elders. To understand this becomes especially important in our time when the so-called communications media, far from merely mediating, interpose themselves between the generations as manufacturers of stereotypes, often forcing youth to live out the caricatures of the images that at first they had only "projected" in experimental fashion. Much will depend on what we do about this. In spite of our pretensions of being able to study the youth of today with the eyes of detached naturalists, we are helping to make youth in the year 2000 what it will be by the kinds of questions we now ask. So I will point out the ideological beams in our eyes as I attempt to put into words what I see ahead. I will begin with questions that are diagnostic and then proceed to those that are more prognostic in character.

I would assume that adolescents today and tomorrow are struggling to define new models of conduct which are relevant to their lives.

Young people of a questioning bent have always done this. But more than any young generation before and with less reliance on a meaningful choice of traditional world images, the youth of today is forced to ask

Reprinted from *Daedalus*, 96 (Summer 1967), 860-870.

what is *universally relevant* in human life in this technological age at this junction of history. Even some of the most faddish, neurotic, delinquent preoccupation with "their" lives is a symptom of this fact.

Yet, this is within the context of two culture factors which seem to be extraordinary in the history of moral temper. One is the skepticism of all authority, the refusal to define natural authority (perhaps even that of paternal authority), and a cast of mind which is essentially anti-institutional and even antinomian.

I do not believe that even in the minority of youths to whom this statement is at all applicable there is a skepticism of *all* authority. There is an abiding mistrust of people who act authoritatively without authentic authority or refuse to assume the authority that is theirs by right and necessity. Paternal authority? Oh, yes—pompous fathers have been exposed everywhere by the world wars and the revolutions. It is interesting, though, that the word *paternal* is used rather than *parental*, for authority, while less paternal, may not slip altogether from the parent generation, insofar as a better balance of maternal and paternal authority may evolve from a changing position of women. As a teacher, I am more impressed with our varying incapacity to own up to the almost oppressive authority we really do have in the minds of the young than in the alleged skepticism of *all* authority in the young. Their *skepticism*, even in its most cynical and violent forms, often seems to express a good sense for what true authority is, or should be, or yet could be. If they "refuse to define natural authority"—are they not right if they indicate by all the overt, mocking, and challenging kinds of "alienation" that it is up to *us* to help them define it, or rather redefine it, since we have undermined it—and feel mighty guilty?

As to the essentially anti-institutional cast of mind, one must ask what alternative is here rejected. It appears that the majority of young people are, in fact, all too needy for, trusting in, and conforming to present institutions, organizations, parties, industrial complexes, supermachineries— and this because true personal authority is waning. Even the anti-institutional minority (whom we know better and who are apt to know our writings) seem to me to plead with existing institutions for permission to rebel— just as in private they often seem to plead with their parents to love them doubly for rejecting them. And are they not remarkably eager for old and new uniforms (a kind of uniformity of nonconformity), for public rituals, and for a collective style of individual isolation? Within this minority, however, as well as in the majority, there are great numbers who are deeply interested in and responsive to a more concerted critique of institutions from a newer and more adequate ethical point of view than we can offer them.

The second factor is an extraordinary hedonism—using the word in the broadest sense—in that there is a desacralization of life and an attitude that all experience is permissible and even desirable.

Again, the word *hedonism* illustrates the way in which we use outdated terms for entirely new phenomena. Although many young people entertain a greater variety of sensual and sexual experiences than their parents did, I see in their pleasure seeking relatively little relaxed joy and often compulsive and addictive search for *relevant* experience. And here we should admit that our generation and our heritage made "all" experience relative by opening it to ruthless inquiry and by assuming that one could pursue radical enlightenment without changing radically or, indeed, changing the coming generations radically. The young have no choice but to experiment with what is left of the "enlightened," "analyzed," and standardized world that we have bequeathed to them. Yet their search is not for all-permissibility, but for new logical and ethical boundaries. Now only direct experience can offer correctives that our traditional mixture of radical enlightenment and middle-class moralism has failed to provide. I suspect that "hedonistic" perversity will soon lose much of its attractiveness in deed and in print when the available inventory has been experimented with and found only moderately satisfying, once it is permitted. New boundaries will then emerge from new ways of finding out what really counts, for there are much latent affirmation and much overt solidarity in all this search. All you have to do is to see some of these nihilists with babies, and you are less sure of what one of the statements as yet to be quoted terms the "Hegelian certainty" that the next generation will be even more alienated.

As for the desacralization of life by the young, it must be obvious that our generation desacralized their lives by (to mention only the intellectual side) naive scientism, thoughtless skepticism, dilettante political opposition, and irresponsible technical expansion. I find, in fact, more of a search for resacralization in the younger than in the older generation.

At the same time society imposes new forms of specialization, of extended training, of new hierarchies and organizations. Thus, one finds an unprecedented divorce between the culture and the society. And, from all indications, such a separation will increase.

Here, much depends on what one means by the word *imposes*. As I have already indicated, in much of youth new hierarchies and organizations are accepted and welcome. We are apt to forget that young people (if not burdened with their parents' conflicts) have no reason to feel that radical change as such is an imposition. The unprecedented divorce we perceive is between *our* traditional culture (Or shall I spell it *Kultur*?) and the tasks of *their* society. A new generation growing up with technological and scientific progress may well experience technology and its new modes of thought as the link between a new culture and new forms of society.

In this respect, assuming this hypothesis is true, the greatest strains will be on the youth. This particular generation, like its predecessors, may come back to some form of accommodation with the society as it grows older and accepts positions within the society. But the experiences also leave a "cultural deposit" which is cumulative consciousness and—to this extent I am a Hegelian—is irreversible, and the next generation therefore starts from a more advanced position of alienation and detachment.

Does it make sense that a generation involved in such unprecedented change should "come back to some form of accommodation with the society"? This was the fate of certain rebels and romantics in the past; but there may soon be no predictable society to "come back to," even if coming back were a viable term or image in the minds of youth. Rather, I would expect the majority to be only too willing to overaccommodate to the exploiters of change, and the minority we speak of to feel cast off until their function becomes clearer—with whatever help we can give.

II

Having somewhat summarily disavowed the statements formulated by others, I would now like to ask a question more in line with my own thinking, and thereby not necessarily more free from stereotype: Where *are* some of the principal contemporary sources of identity strength? This question leads us from diagnosis to prognosis, for to me a sense of identity (and here the widest connotation of the term will do) includes a sense of anticipated future. The traditional sources of identity strength—economic, racial, national, religious, occupational—are all in the process of allying themselves with a new world image in which the vision of an anticipated future and, in fact, of a future in a permanent state of planning will take over much of the power of tradition. If I call such sources of identity strength *ideological*, I am using the word again most generally to denote a system of ideas providing a convincing world image. Such a system each new generation needs—so much so that it cannot wait for it to be tested in advance. I will call the two principal ideological orientations basic to future identities the *technological* and the *humanist* orientations, and I will assume that even the great politico-economic alternatives will be subordinated to them.

I will assume, then, that especially in this country, but increasingly also abroad, masses of young people feel attuned, both by giftedness and by opportunity, to the technological and scientific promises of indefinite progress; and that these promises, if sustained by schooling, imply a new ideological world image and a new kind of identity for many. As in every past technology and each historical period, there are vast numbers of individuals who can combine the dominant techniques of mastery and domination with their identity development, and *become* what they *do*. They can settle on that *cultural consolidation* that follows shifts in technology and secures what mutual verification and what transitory familiarity lie in doing things together and in doing them right—a rightness proved by the bountiful response of "nature," whether in the form of the prey bagged, the food harvested, the goods produced, the money made, the ideas substantiated, or the technological problems solved.

Each such consolidation, of course, also makes for new kinds of entrenched privileges, enforced sacrifices, institutionalized inequalities, and built-in contradictions that become glaringly obvious to outsiders— those who lack the appropriate gifts and opportunities or have a surplus of not quite appropriate talents. Yet it would be intellectual vindictiveness to overlook the sense of embeddedness and natural flux that each age provides in the midst of the artifacts of organization; how it helps to bring to ascendance some particular type of man and style of perfection; how it permits those thus consolidated to limit their horizon effectively so as *not* to see what might destroy their newly won unity with time and space or expose them to the fear of death—and of killing. Such a consolidation along technological and scientific lines is, I submit, now taking place. Those young people who feel at home in it can, in fact, go along with their parents and teachers—not too respectfully, to be sure—in a kind of *fraternal identification*, because parents and children can jointly leave it to technology and science to provide a self-perpetuating and self-accelerating way of life. No need is felt to limit expansionist ideals so long as certain old-fashioned rationalizations continue to provide the hope (a hope that has long been an intrinsic part of an American ideology) that in regard to any possible built-in evil in the very nature of superorganizations, appropriate brakes, corrections, and amendments will be invented in the nick of time and without any undue investment of strenuously new principles. While they "work" these supermachineries, organizations, and associations provide a sufficiently adjustable identity for all those who feel actively engaged in and by them.

All of us sense the danger of overaccommodation in this, as in any other consolidation of a new world image, and maybe the danger *is* greater today. It is the danger that a willful and playful testing of the now limitless range of the technically possible will replace the search for the criteria for the optimal and the ethically permissible, which includes what can be given on from generation to generation. This can only cause subliminal panic, especially where the old decencies will prove glaringly inadequate, and where the threat or the mere possibility of overkill can be denied only with increasing mental strain—a strain, incidentally, which will match the sexual repression of the passing era in unconscious pathogenic power.

It is against this danger, I think, that the nonaccommodators put their very existence "on the line," often in a thoroughly confounding way because the manifestations of alienation and commitment are sometimes indistinguishable. The insistence on the question "to be or not to be" always looks gratuitously strange to the consolidated. If the question of being oneself and of dying one's own death in a world of overkill seems to appear in a more confused and confusing form, it is the ruthless heritage of radical enlightenment that forces some intelligent young people into a seemingly cynical pride, demanding that they be human without illusion, naked without narcissism, loving without idealization, ethical without moral passion, restless without being classifiably neurotic, and political without lying: truly a utopia to end all utopias. What should we call this youth? *Humanist* would seem right if by this we mean a recovery, with new implications, of man as the measure, a man far grimmer and with much less temptation to congratulate himself on his exalted position in the universe, a self-congratulation that has in the past always encouraged more cruel and more thoughtless consolidations. The new humanism ranges from an *existential* insistence that every man *is* an island unto himself to a new kind of humaneness that is more than compassion for stray animals and savages, and a decidedly *humanitarian* activism ready to meet concrete dangers and hardships in the service of assisting the underprivileged anywhere. Maybe *universalist* would cover all this better, if we mean by it an insistence on the widest range of human possibilities— beyond the technological.

But whatever you call it, the universalist orientation, no less than the technological one, is a *cluster* of ideas, images, and aspirations, of hopes, fears, and hates; otherwise, neither could lay claim to the identity development of the young. *Somewhat* like the "hawks" and the "doves," the technologists and the universalists seem almost to belong to different species, living in separate ecologies. "Technological" youth, for example, expects the dominant forces in foreign as well as in domestic matters to work themselves out into some new form of balance of power (Or is it an old-fashioned balance of entirely new powers?). It is willing, for the sake of such an expectation, to do a reasonable amount of killing—and of dying. "Humanist" youth, on the other hand, not only opposes unlimited mechanization and regimentation, but also cultivates a sensitive awareness of the humanness of any individual in gunsight range. The two orientations must obviously oppose and repel each other totally; the acceptance of even a part of one could cause an ideological slide in the whole configuration of images and, it follows, in the kind of courage to be—and to die. These two views, therefore, face each other as if the other were *the* enemy, although he may be brother or friend—and, indeed, oneself at a different stage of one's own life, or even in a different mood of the same stage.

Each side, of course, is overly aware of the dangers inherent in the other. In fact, it makes out of the other, in my jargon, a negative identity. I have sketched the danger felt to exist in the technological orientation. On the "humanist" side, there is the danger of a starry-eyed faith in the certainty that if you "mean it," you can move quite monolithic mountains, and of a subsequent total inertia when the mountain moves only a bit at a time or slides right back. This segment of youth lacks as yet the leadership that would replace the loss of revolutionary tradition, or any other tradition of discipline. Then there is the danger of a retreat into all kinds of "beat" snobbishness or into parallel private worlds, each with its own artificially expanded consciousness.

III

As one is apt to do in arguing over diagnosis, I have now overdrawn two "ideal" syndromes so as to consider the prognosis suggested in a further question presented to me:

Is it possible that the fabric of traditional authority has been torn so severely in the last decades that the reestablishment of certain earlier forms of convention is all but unlikely?

I have already indicated that I would answer this question in the affirmative; I would not expect a future accommodation to be characterized by a "coming back" either to conventions or to old-fashioned movements. Has not every major era in history been characterized by a division into a new class of *power-specialists* (who "know what they are doing") and an intense new group of *universalists* (who "mean what they are saying")? And do not these two poles determine an era's character? The specialists ruthlessly test the limits of power, while the universalists always in remembering man's soul also remember the "poor"—those cut off from the resources of power. What is as yet dormant in that third group, the truly underprivileged, is hard to say, especially if an all-colored anticolonial solidarity that would include our Negro youth should emerge. But it would seem probable that all new revolutionary identities will be drawn into the struggle of the two ideological orientations sketched here, and that nothing could preclude a fruitful polarity between these two orientations—provided we survive.

But is not the fact that we are still here already a result of the polarization I have spoken of? If our supertechnicians had not been able to put warning signals and brakes into the very machinery of armament, certainly our universalists would not have known how to save or how to govern the world. It also seems reasonable to assume that without the apocalyptic warnings of the universalists, the new technocrats might not have been shocked into restraining the power they wield.

What speaks for a fruitful polarization is the probability that a new generation growing up with and in technological and scientific progress as a matter of course will be forced by the daily confrontation with unheard-of practical and theoretical possibilities to entertain radically new modes of thought that may suggest daring innovations in both culture and society. "Humanist" youth, in turn, will find some accommodation with the machine age in which they, of course, already participate in their daily needs and habits. Thus, each group may reach in the other what imagination, sensitivity, or commitment may be ready for activation. I do not mean, however, even to wish that the clarity of opposition of the technological and the humanist identity be blurred, for dynamic interplay needs clear poles.

What, finally, is apt to bring youth of different persuasions together is a change in the generational process itself—an awareness that they share a common fate. Already today the mere division into an older—parent—generation and a younger—adolescing—one is becoming superannuated. Technological change makes it impossible for any traditional way of being older (an age difference suggested by the questions quoted) ever to become again so institutionalized that the younger generation could "accommodate" to it or, indeed, resist it in good-old revolutionary fashion. Aging, it is already widely noted, will be (or already is) a quite different experience for those who find themselves rather early occupationally outdated and for those who may have something more lasting to offer. By the same token, young adulthood will be divided into older and younger young adults. The not-too-young and not-too-old specialist will probably move into the position of principal arbiter, that is, for the limited period of the ascendance of his specialty. His power, in many ways, will replace the sanction of tradition or, indeed, of parents. But the "younger generation," too, will be (or already is) divided more clearly into the older- and the younger-young generation, where the older young will have to take over (and are eager to take over) much of the direction of the conduct of the younger young. Thus, the relative waning of the parents and the emergence of the young adult specialist as the permanent and permanently changing authority are bringing about a shift by which older youth will have to take increasing responsibility for the conduct of younger youth—and older people for the orientation of the specialists and of older youth. By the same token, future religious ethics would be grounded less in the emotions and the imagery of infantile guilt than in that of mutual responsibility in the fleeting present.

In such change we on our part can orient ourselves and offer orientation only by recognizing and cultivating an age-specific *ethical* capacity in *older* youth, for there are age-specific factors that speak for a differentiation between morality and ethics. The child's conscience tends to be impressed with a moralism which says "no" without giving reasons; in this sense, the infantile superego has become a danger to human survival, for suppression in childhood leads to the exploitation of others in adulthood, and moralistic self-denial ends up in the wish to annihilate others. There is also an age-specific ethical capacity in older youth that we should learn to foster. That we, instead, consistently neglect this ethical potential and, in fact, deny it with the moralistic reaction that we traditionally employ toward and against youth (*anti-institutional, hedonistic, desacralizing*) is probably resented much more by young people than our dutiful attempts to keep them in order by prohibition. At any rate, the ethical questions of the future will be less determined by the influence of the older generation on the younger one than by the interplay of subdivisions in a life scheme in which the whole life span is extended; in which the life stages will be further subdivided; in which new roles for both sexes will emerge in all life stages; and in which a certain margin of free choice and individualized identity will come to be considered the reward for technical inventiveness. In the next decade, youth will force us to help them to develop ethical, affirmative, resacralizing rules of conduct that remain flexibly adjustable to the promises and the dangers of worldwide technology and communication. These developments, of course, include two "things"— one gigantic, one tiny—the irreversible presence of which will have to find acknowledgement in daily life: the bomb and the loop. They together will call for everyday decisions involving the sanctity of life and death. Once man has decided not to kill needlessly and not to give birth carelessly, he must try to establish what capacity for living, and for letting live, each generation owes to every child planned to be born—anywhere.

One can, I guess, undertake to predict only on the basis of one of two premises: either one expects that things will be as bad as they always have been, only worse; or one visualizes what one is willing to take a chance on at the risk of being irrelevant. As I implied at the beginning, a committee that wants to foretell the future may have to take a chance with itself by asking what its combined wisdom and talent would wish might be done with what seems to be given.

5

No Hard Feelings

Missing pieces in a puzzle, book, or our understanding of human development are a source of frustration, but are a special pleasure when found. In discussing the limits of psychological knowledge that constrain education I have questioned elsewhere: "What theory of emotional or aesthetic development is adequate to the developmental educator?"[1] Henry Dupont's "Affective Development: Stage and Sequence" is such a missing link. Drawing on Piaget's writing on the nature of affect, its development, and its relation to cognition, Dupont has created an impressive hypothetical model of affective development.

Dupont suggests that affect, which he variously defines as our emotions, feelings, values, motives, and self-image, is "invested" or structured differently as the person develops. For example, affect is focused on authority and on dependent relationships with parents early in life; on one's peers in middle childhood and in early adolescence; and on ideals, values, and life plans in later adolescence. He says that the way we understand and focus our feelings and values develops in sequential stages. Our cognitive growth on the one hand and our emotional and social experiences on the other—not age—cause this growth to occur. People may become fixated at lower stages, which Dupont sees as seriously dysfunctional to the individual and to society. "Human empathic sensibilities are being dulled, or never fully developed, while many never grow beyond the simplest concern for self-protection and self-aggrandizement. At the same time, man's intellectual expansion continues at an ever more rapid pace, unchecked and untouched by his affective faculties."[2] But, because the model is an interactive one (that is, our affective development depends on the quality of our social and emotional experience), there is hope, and there is also a central role for the education of affect at all stages.

Dupont, following Piaget, points out that we think about and define

160

our emotions cognitively. Thus, we are conscious of and use language to make such statements as: "I am angry." The point is that even emotions, the most elementary form of affect, do not exist in a pure state. And, similarly, thinking does not exist independently of affect. Affective development, then, is an integral part of general mental development, and the way we understand our feelings, values, and motives evidences all the characteristics of cognitive developmental stages. We have already emphasized that affect is learned or develops primarily through our experience and interaction with others, such as parents and peers. Affective stages are also structural; they are ways of thinking, feeling, and valuing that can be generalized in many specific contexts. Further, affective stages are sequential; emotions, feelings, and values develop in an invariant order in every person. Dupont points to the great importance this has for the educator who wants to support or stimulate affective development: "Do we know what cognitive, moral and affective structures are needed to be effective citizens in a democracy? And, further, what learnings are prerequisite to the necessary structures?"[3]

Dupont offers what is, at this time, primarily a conceptual, rather than an empirical, model of affective development. Six affective stages are described: egocentric-impersonal, heteronomous, interpersonal, psychological-personal, autonomous, integritous. Dupont reports "research data . . . that essentially validate stages 1-4, and we have seen behavior that suggests that stages 5-7 are meaningful ways of conceptualizing affective development."[4] His concept of affective development is closely tied logically to the work of Kohlberg, Loevinger, Elkind, and other cognitive developmental theorists. His description of the stages of affective development is closely related to the analogous stages of cognitive, moral, and ego development. Thus, the piece is an excellent illustration of how development is a helix and should be discussed as such. It is intended to describe the psychological nature of affective development. The model is of great heuristic value for psychological research on feelings, values, and motives and how they evolve. Its data base is promising and confirming but limited. Nor is there a philosophical analysis or justification that the "higher" stages of affective development are better for individuals or society. This point is important both theoretically and practically because the model has already generated impressive curricula to stimulate affective stage development and a sophisticated measure.[5]

Because of space limitations, it is possible to publish only part of Dupont's article. A detailed description of the psychological-personal stage, which he suggests will characterize most adolescents, is, however, included. It would be unfortunate if the reader perceived Dupont as a theory builder only. This theory originated in Dupont's work in affective education and his recognition of the critical need for theory to order practice. Thus, it illustrates knowledge from practice. At the same time, Dupont's affective education curricula are among the most extensively tested developmental education programs presently available. They are published as *Toward Affective Development—1* (for children eight to twelve years of age) and *Transition* (for students twelve to fifteen years of age) and will be particularly valuable to teachers or counselors who want classroom programs and practices to accompany their theory.

Notes

1. Ralph L. Mosher, "Education for Human Development," in *Humanistic Education: Visions and Realities*, ed. R. H. Weller (Berkeley, Calif.: McCutchan Publishing Corp., 1977), 172.

2. Henry Dupont, "Affective Development: Stage and Sequence," in *Adolescents' Development and Education: A Janus Knot,* ed. Ralph L. Mosher (Berkeley, Calif.: McCutchan Publishing Corp., 1979), Chapter 5.

3. Henry Dupont, "Affective Development: Stage and Sequence, A Piagetian Interpretation," unpublished paper, University of Wisconsin—Eau Claire, 1976, 42.

4. *Id.*, "Toward Affective Development: Theory, Program Development and Learner Verification," unpublished paper, University of Wisconsin—Eau Claire, 1976, 4; see also *id.*, "Affective Development: A Piagetian Model," in *Proceedings of Eighth Annual Interdisciplinary International Conference: "Piagetian Theory and the Helping Professions"* (Los Angeles: University of Southern California, forthcoming).

5. *Id.*, O. Gardner, and D. Brody, *Toward Affective Development* (Circle Pines, Minn.: American Guidance Service, 1974); H. Dupont and C. Dupont, *Transition* (Circle Pines, Minn.: American Guidance Service, 1978); H. Dupont, "Assessing Affective Development: Test Manual," unpublished paper, University of Wisconsin—Eau Claire, 1976.

Affective Development: Stage and Sequence

Henry Dupont

In 1960 the philosopher-logician Bertrand Russell made a frightening prediction: "Will and feeling should keep pace with thought if man as a whole is to grow as his knowledge grows. If this cannot be achieved—if, while knowledge becomes cosmic, will and feeling remain parochial— there will be a lack of harmony producing a kind of madness of which the effects cannot but be disastrous."[1] Certainly in the first half of the 1970's we have seen many signs of this prophecy's becoming a reality. In all aspects of our society the symptoms of a general breakdown of traditional values can be observed. From corrupt politicians and inhuman barbarity on the battlefield to rising crime and divorce rates, the evidence mounts. Humane empathic sensibilities are being dulled, or never fully developed, while many never grow beyond the simplest concern for self-protection and self-aggrandizement. At the same time, man's intellectual expansion continues at an ever more rapid pace, unchecked and untouched by his affective faculties.

In the tradition of the American public school, the development of affectivity—feelings, values, motives—has been regarded as the responsibility of other elements of society, such as the home, church, national leaders, and the example and precept of the upright and moral citizens children saw around them. Today, these facets of the child's environment have an increasingly more tenuous and diffuse hold on his attention and loyalty.

A close examination of the significant social factors outside of school that stimulate a child's affective development might reveal that the child devotes an inordinate amount of his attention to the commercial media (from the nightly news, through various "action" programs of violence and corruption, to the multitude of advertisements subtly and effectively creating values, expectations, motivations, and self-images within the child). Role models for the child are likely to come from his peer group, older adolescents, or stars in the world of entertainment. Where then but the school is the child to receive guidance in the development of concern for other humans? Who but educators will help him to develop humane values? How else will he acquire a viable ethics that takes others into account?

The author wishes to thank John LeCapitaine of Boston University for his assistance in the collection and analysis of the data, John Mardis, Consultant, Area Education Agency-7, Chronically Disruptive Program, Waterloo, Iowa, for his assistance in the preparation of this paper, and Christine Dupont for editing and typing the manuscript.

The realm of affectivity is too important to leave to unscrupulous or unstructured, subliminal influences. Education must become as intentional in guiding affective development as in teaching the principles of algebra. Especially in light of the traumatic events and tremendous social changes that have occurred recently in our society, educators and counselors are increasingly prepared to accept this responsibility. Educators are confronted with the challenge of providing a prominent place in their curricula for programs that will promote the affective growth of their clients.

Only in recent years have psychologists and educators begun to concern themselves with this aspect of human development as a focus for building curricula. Why was affective development as an aim of education neglected for so long? In part this neglect was caused by a feeling that anything outside the intellectual sphere was not the business of the schools. Another roadblock continues to be the "value-neutral" stance taken by many educators. They feel that to promote affective growth actively, or to deal in any way with issues charged with significant affective investment on the part of students, is to impose their values or the values of the most vociferous or prestigious students on the members of their class. A full discussion of the illogic of this position can be found in an article by Kohlberg and Mayer.[2] A small portion of their argument is paraphrased below.

Since affect is intimately involved in everything people do, and since their values largely determine the kinds of activities and relationships that occur in classrooms, it is impossible for teachers to be value-neutral. Teachers who attempt to maintain this stance merely end up giving time and importance to trivial or localized issues. A value-neutral education cannot avoid being dull and is probably irrelevant to the interests and concerns of students.

The major impediment to affective programs has been the conceptual problems that have plagued the field for so many years, one aspect of which has been the tendency to confuse "the emotions" with affectivity. This has not been a productive approach because of the complex and intimate relations between affectivity and cognition, ego functioning, sexuality, and moral reasoning. Affectivity comprises values, feelings, and motives as well as emotions. Perhaps an even greater difficulty with this approach has been the lack of any adequate theoretical construct of the development or maturation of the emotions from which educators could generate objectives and build curricula. Indeed, the dearth of viable theoretical models of affectivity and affective development has prevented until recent years any serious work on curriculum development in this field.

An extensive review of research, curriculum developments, and theories of psychological and emotional (affective) development was made in an effort to find a rationale and guidelines for a program to stimulate affective development in some deliberate, systematic way. Of the many interesting theories that were examined, Piaget's theory of mental development, in which affective development is linked to cognitive development on the one hand and social development on the other, provided the most meaningful framework and concepts.

Later work by other theorists, notably that of Kohlberg[3] and Kohlberg and Turiel[4] in moral development, Loevinger[5] in ego development, and Mosher,[6] Sprinthall,[7] and Mosher and Sprinthall[8] in psychological education, added much to the elaboration of a model of affective development and its relationship to other facets of mental development.

What follows, then, is an attempt to construct a theory of affective development, based on the theory of Piaget, and drawing on the work of Kohlberg, Turiel, Loevinger, Mosher, Sprinthall, and to some extent Erikson[9] and Kagan.[10] I propose to shift the emphasis from the emotions to affect, to define affective development, and to outline a theory of affective development suitable for present educational goals and curriculum building. I will show that the stages of affective development occur in a natural sequence, as do those of cognitive, moral, and ego development. As Piaget pointed out, however, the way affect develops may differ significantly from the way cognition develops. I intend to describe these differences as well as to show how affective development is related to cognitive, moral, and ego development. Finally, I will review the implications of this theory of affective development for education.

Piaget's Major Concepts

While Piaget's work has contributed in large part to increased worldwide interest in developmental psychology, his ideas and observations concerning the affective transformations that accompany various stages of cognitive development have been almost totally neglected in American psychology. His thoughts about the relationships between affective and cognitive development are, however, extremely cogent and provide the basis for further development in the construction and elaboration of a theory of affective development.

In a number of books and papers, Piaget[11] and Piaget and Inhelder[12] describe how mental development takes place as the individual makes ever more differentiated and complex adaptations to his physical and human environment. These adaptations, called periods, stages of equilibrium, or simply stages, are an outcome of the interaction between the individual and his environment. Piaget employs the concepts of assimilation and accommodation to explain change and development. The child's earliest interactions are mediated by reflexes that become schemata of reactions as the organism matures and the interactions become more complex. At any one point, the child reacts to new experiences with the schemata he has at hand; that is, he attempts to assimilate new experiences through the template, so to speak, of the schemata he already has. When he discovers, however, that the schema (or the template) he is imposing on this new experience does not quite fit, he experiences disequilibrium and modifies the schema (or template) to fit the new experience. This is called accommodation (the modification of major ways of experiencing the physical or social world). The major accommodations or qualitative changes made to the physical and social world that result in extended periods of equilibrium (all templates fit) are called stages of development.

In Piaget's theory, these accommodations have both cognitive and affective aspects, and one of the most interesting facets of Piaget's thought is his continual effort to reconcile these two dimensions of development. The parallel transformations of affectivity and intelligence move through four major stages: first, the stage of egocentric-impersonal affectivity; second, the stage of heteronomous affectivity and sensorimotor intelligence; third, the stage of interpersonal affectivity and concrete operations; and fourth, the stage of autonomous affectivity and formal operations. Between the first and second stages there is a transitional period during which affect, objects, and relationships become represented in thought, and these representations become internalized. These four stages of parallel developments are shown in Table 5-1.

At the egocentric-impersonal stage, affect is undifferentiated and essentially unstructured as children are aware of only their own sensations and actions.

At the heteronomous stage, affect is influenced primarily by the dynamics of the authority-dependence relationships with the significant adults in the child's life. This stage typically lasts through the sensorimotor and representational stages of cognitive development.

Table 5-1
Parallel stages of cognitive and affective development

Typical age period	Cognitive stage	Affective stage
0 - 2	Sensorimotor	Egocentric-impersonal
2 - 7	Representational	Heteronomous
7 - 12	Concrete operations	Interpersonal
12 - 15	Formal operations	Autonomous

The interpersonal-affective stage is characterized by major investment of affect in the child's peers and his interrelations with them. Although the child is still involved in heteronomous relationships with adults, a new stage of affective development has been reached. The child's dependence and the adults' authority are still significant but, from an affective standpoint, the important facet of the child's environment is his peer group. The stage of interpersonal affectivity is associated with the concrete operations stage of cognitive development.

When the autonomous stage is reached, affect begins to be increasingly invested in ideals, values, and life plans. Again, authority figures and peers have not lost their affective importance, but, in the transformation to the autonomous stage, they no longer hold the preeminent position they occupied in the earlier stages.

In his earlier writings, Piaget seemed to focus almost exclusively on the parallel irreducible nature of the affective and the cognitive. In his more recent work, however, he makes several important observations on the interaction of cognition and affect:

There are no acts of intelligence, even of practical intelligence, without interest at the point of departure and affective regulation during the entire course of action, without joy at success, or sorrow at failure . . . . Just as there is no purely cognitive state, there is no purely affective state, no matter how elementary it may be. A state of emotion, for example—and emotion is one of the most elementary forms of affect—supposes a discrimination and, therefore, a cognitive element.[13]

According to Piaget, then, affect and its transformation play a vital role in the development and function of intelligence, just as cognition plays a vital role in the structuring of affective processes. Although I recognize the interdependence of affectivity and cognition, and, in turn, their close relationship to ego and moral development, in order to develop an integrated theory of affective development, I will treat affectivity and its development as a separate and distinct entity. As the theory is elaborated, however, I will show how affective development is related to other facets of mental development.

Outline of a Theory of Affective Development

Several definitions and assumptions are fundamental to my theory:

1. Affect refers to a reflexive arousal accompanied by physiological changes and a tendency toward action.

2. Affective development pertains to age-related developmental trends in the differentiation and integration of affective responses and the stimuli that elicit them. Affective development, then, implies a structural or

organizational component and (directional) structural transformations in affective responses. As so conceived, the structural development of affect has basic dimensions in common with the structural development of cognition.[14]

3. Affectivity concerns changes or alterations of affect.

4. It is assumed that all thought and actions are accompanied by some modulation of affect.

5. It is further assumed that the transformations of affect to which Piaget calls our attention are developmental stages and, as such, provide the basis for a theory of affective development that is predictive as well as descriptive.

6. Affective development is best thought of as occurring in six stages. These stages and their major characteristics are shown in Table 5-2.

Empirical Vignette

Believing that these six stages of affective development were essentially convincing, I sought ways of identifying their manifestations in the behavior of children. I also wanted some way of verifying that the stages were sequential and were related to age.

Piaget reminds us that the "emotions" are only one manifestation of affect. I decided, however, that a study of the structured changes occurring in a selected sample of emotions over an appropriate range of ages might

Table 5-2
Six stages of affective development

Affective stage	Major referent	Cognitive style
Egocentric-impersonal	Impersonal (undifferentiated) world	Impulse dominant
Heteronomous	Significant adults	Thought action bound
Interpersonal	Peers	Thought concrete, but can be used to make comparisons and differentiations
Psychological-personal	Abstract psychological concepts, ideals, and values	Thought reflective and analytic
Autonomous	Self and others as autonomous entities	Thought reflective and analytic
Integritous	Wholeness and integrity of self and others	Thought reflective and analytic

help me understand how affect is structured by cognitive processes and how the structure changes with age. Data were collected from children and youth at five, ten, and fifteen years of age. Ten boys and ten girls at each of these three age levels were asked to describe the context within which a sample of ten emotions would probably occur. These data show very clearly that the stimuli that arouse affect change with age and that between the ages of five and fifteen there is a marked increase in the number of psychological constructs employed in the representation and integration of affectivity.

In this study, each child's description of what happened for each of the ten emotions was scored as heteronomous, interpersonal, or psychological-personal. Comparisons among several scorers indicated that the scoring procedure was objective. The percentage of heteronomous (H), interpersonal (I), and psychological-personal (P) responses given by the students is shown in Table 5-3.

The data included in Table 5-3 confirm Piaget's observations on the transformations of affect that occur as the child develops physically and his social interactions with his environment change. Thus, the child's affectivity seems to be centered in his relationships with adults until about age five and become centered in his relationships with his peers around age eight or nine. Affectivity becomes increasingly mediated by abstract concepts so that by age fifteen more than half of the child's emotional interactions with his environment are influenced by abstract concepts. I am convinced that interests, motives, and values, each of which includes affect structured by cognitive processes, have similar stage developmental characteristics.

The obvious conclusion is that the child should be provided with adequate experience with warm, appreciative adults and later with a representative group of peers. In addition, these findings support the conclusion that we should begin to facilitate the child's efforts to relate to

Table 5-3

Number of responses in each category at each age level

Age	H	Percentage	I	Percentage	P	Percentage	Totals
5	102	.61	60	.36	6	.04	168
10	66	.36	91	.50	24	.13	181
15	33	.17	63	.32	98	.51	194
TOTALS	201		214		128		

his world through abstract concepts and values in the upper elementary grades and certainly in the early secondary grades. This conclusion follows from the notion that in developmental education we should build the curriculum around those things the child is ready to learn. The fact that some students are using psychological concepts and constructs by ten years of age suggests that many children may be ready for experiences that foster movement to this stage of affective development. Further studies of affective development as described and defined here are obviously needed and may add considerably to our understanding of this, until now, conceptually unstructured dimension of human development.

Description of the Stages

A brief review of the stages of affective development was presented earlier. In the material that follows, each stage is described and discussed in detail. It should be clear to the thoughtful reader that the cross-sectional data I have collected confirm only the heteronomous, interpersonal, and psychological-personal stages. My conception of the egocentric-impersonal stage is based almost entirely on observations and extrapolations from the work of others. The autonomous and integritous stages should also be seen for what they are: hypotheses based on clinical experience and the work of others. There is, obviously, great need for additional research to clarify and confirm or to reject the efficacy of these stages.

The Egocentric-Impersonal Stage

This first stage in a child's affective development, like those that follow, is far from static. The child undergoes tremendous physiological growth, and, in response, his social environment changes significantly. A newborn child does not differentiate between the self and the human and physical environment. "Insofar as the self remains undifferentiated, and thus unconscious of itself, all affectivity is centered on the child's own body and action."[15]

At this level, affect is associated with the alternations of tension and relaxation that become differentiated in the child's global activity. The affective element in tension and relaxation is related to the search for and movement toward agreeable stimuli and the effort to avoid disagreeable stimuli. Contentment and discomfort or pain are perhaps the only affective states at this point. Before age four, many children, even those with well-developed verbal skills, do not relate their fluctuating affective states to their interactions with other persons. They relate their feelings to the weather, the absence of tension, or to not being sick.

The Heteronomous Stage

Affective development begins when both cognition and affect are no longer centered on the self. With the differentiation of the external world from the self, the child acquires those cognitive structures that provide for the objectification of reality. The first such structure is the development of relations with other objects. Several theorists believe that the transferral of affect to the mothering figure is the preliminary step in recognizing objects external to the self. According to Piaget, the creation of the object and the investment of affect in it occur at the same time with neither preceding the other. For most children, actions that are easily classified as giving affection are observable before the end of the first year. These actions are usually concerned with attachment and withdrawal and interest and avoidance.

At this first level, before the child recognizes the permanence of objects, affect is stimulated only in the presence of an object or person. This level is marked by the acquisition of prehension and the beginnings of mobility. The child's newly found skills and awareness of his external environment are accompanied by intense interest in exploring this new world and mastering new motor skills.

Before the child is two years of age, those patterns of affect termed the primary emotions—anger, fear, happiness or delight, and sadness—become evident. During these first two years, affect is related to survival and tends to be an inseparable component of self-protective, self-enhancing behavior.

When the child is about a year and a half, he becomes actively involved in learning names for things. This development of language and the representational process has great significance for all development that follows. It lays the foundation for a continuous process of learning to represent affect, including static, dynamic, real, and imagined affect, for the rest of his life. During the previous stage of development, all of which takes place before language development, other persons arouse affect only as they are physically present. With representation, the physical presence of other persons is no longer necessary, and the basis for more or less permanent feelings for these persons is established. This same phenomenon can also occur with respect to situations and objects. Their representation in thought, together with the arousal usually associated with them, become habits of thought and feeling that have a life span of their own, independent of the physical presence of the situation or object.

Throughout this age period, which is marked by the increasing representation of the child's human and physical environment in thought, the child's social world is dominated by adults. He does not yet fully understand that others have a perspective different from his own. Real understanding and communication with peers are yet to be achieved.

The affectivity that is labeled and represented in thought consists of the heteronomous affects that are involved in the child's continued submissive status. The names for the basic feelings—fear, anger, happiness or delight, and sadness—are learned during this period. The names for the affectivity associated with the more complex social relationships of late childhood are learned later (after about age seven) as they are experienced, symbolized, and represented in thought. Affectivity and learning to represent affectivity in thought are contingent upon social activity (experience), social exchange (communication), and self-regulation. In this instance, self-regulation involves changes in thought and feeling that the child makes to improve mutual understanding, communication, and cooperation in shared social activities. Adults usually supervise activity at this level.

Symbolic play begins to appear after the acquisition of language. Piaget believes such play to have considerable importance in the child's assimilation and accommodation to his environment and thus to his increasingly differentiated and sophisticated understanding of his world. Even a casual observation of this kind of play shows the great part affect has in a young child's learning process.

This period of the child's affective development coincides with the stage of ego development Loevinger[16] calls Impulsive. The child does not initially recognize abstractions such as rules. Gradually, however, through experience, he begins to classify actions. Bad actions result in punishment, and good ones are rewarded. A wide range of actions are neutral in terms of punishment and reward, but, in their own right, have an affective value for the child. It is obvious that the adults who care for the child play a major role in establishing the good-bad parameters of affect associated with the child's actions.

Because the child's impulses are poorly controlled, or not controlled at all, he is subject to the control and guidance of others. Erikson[17] identifies this stage as particularly important to the future mental health of the child. As the child learns to exercise choice, and experiences the urge to discriminate and manipulate his physical and human environment, the parents' control of his impulses can set the stage for the development of appropriate or excessive self-control.

Around the age of four, the child enters a phase of the heteronomous stage recognized by many observers: he starts to assert himself strongly in his social milieu, usually by attempting to become increasingly independent of his parents. Having experienced a sense of trust and security and having internalized the idea of his parents' continuing presence, the child no longer needs or desires to have parental control. He wants to "do it myself." The child frequently engages in a power struggle within the family situation as he attempts to dominate his environment. Although he is still dependent, he resents his submissive status. An increased awareness and understanding of rules or codes of behavior is shown by the child's attempts to "get away with" behavior that runs counter to the rules. Where this is not possible, the child is often able to control his impulses until a more opportune moment.

Loevinger[18] characterizes this period as the Opportunistic Stage of ego development, in which the child is consciously preoccupied with his relative standing to significant others on a dominance-dependence scale. On his scale of ascendant motives, Kagan[19] views the period in essentially the same terms as Loevinger. In Kohlberg's hierarchy of moral development,[20] this period probably marks the transition from Stage 1—an orientation toward punishment and obedience—to Stage 2—instrumental relativism.

Although affectivity is still largely invested in the child's relations with adults, the first signs of peer sociability are evident at the end of this stage of development. As yet the child is not truly playing with other children; he is merely playing in their presence. This social activity gradually becomes a more important part of his life. During the years he attends school, peers become increasingly the focus of the child's activity, and his affectivity reflects this change in relationships.

The Interpersonal Stage

A number of processes influence the child's shift from the stage of heteronomous affect to the interpersonal stage in which affectivity is focused upon relations with peers. It is not clear which of these processes is ascendant, or if they operate in a simultaneous fashion, none taking precedence over the others.

An obvious effect is the change in the child's social status owing to physical maturation, mastery of speech, the physical manipulation of the important aspects of his environment, his increased mobility, and his increasing independence from the need for parental care. Because he has accommodated himself (though in an expedient way) to the prevalent rules governing his particular milieu, because he no longer requires constant supervision for his own protection, and because he is able to do for himself in most situations, he and his age-mates are left to themselves more often and thus have the opportunity to acquire those skills of sociability requisite to the attainment of the interpersonal stage of affective development.

At age six, the child, in Western society at least, is plunged into school. While school life is in some respects even more rigidly structured by adults than home life and requires the child to remain in a heteronomous position much of the day, it also institutionalizes a peer subculture. The child is forced to develop significant affects in his peer relationships as a matter of social survival.

An important change in the child's psychosexual development also occurs during this transitional phase. Prior to the age of six, the child is normally caught up in various intense sexual conflicts and processes of adjustment in which such feelings as genital inadequacy and identification with and rivalry with the parent of the same sex occupy much of the child's subconscious energies. These processes focus the child's affect upon his parents in as strong, if less overt, a way as the parents' efforts to bring up the child.

According to Erikson[21] and others, it is the child's resolution of the Oedipal conflict that releases him into the extrafamilial world and allows him to focus his attention on other aspects of existence, including his peers. This resolution is accompanied (followed) by a general inhibition of sexuality, which implies a lessening of the parental attraction and enables the child to become further involved in the relative sexual neutrality of his peer group.

A factor of great importance to the transition to interpersonal affectivity accompanies the entry into the concrete operations phase of cognitive development: according to Piaget, at about age seven the child becomes capable of cooperation because he no longer confuses his own point of view with that of others. There is evidence that many children do not develop this social perspective until much later, at ten to twelve years of age.[22] These exceptions do not, however, detract from the essential soundness of Piaget's ideas concerning cognitive development.

It is quite clear that role-taking skill—the ability to experience other points of view—is absolutely essential to the development of interpersonal affects. The embryo of role taking is the child's ability to recognize that others do not have the same viewpoint and do not experience and interpret reality as he does. The skill becomes fully developed when, much later, one is able to experience reality vicariously, with attendant affects, as a peer would. When the individual is able to encounter the world imaginatively in the same way as another individual, he lays the foundation for mutual respect, for the tendency to yield his own desire to a stronger need, and for the interest in knowing what others think about him.

Prior to this acquisition of other-centered frames of reference, the child's actions and affect are centered on his own ego. Piaget explains that this occurs because of adult constraint and exercise of authority: "it is because the child cannot establish a genuinely mutual contact with the adult that he remains shut up in his own ego."[23] Childhood egocentricity, then, is the natural consequence of the heteronomous relationship. The adult's constraints on the child take the form of rules of behavior that resemble divine revelation. But, lacking the ability to reflect on his own actions from an external point of view, the child confuses intention and practice and is not aware of the extent to which his actions fail to correspond to the rule. Since all children of this age are egocentric, true cooperation with peers is impossible. They do, however, enjoy playing together, gaining "a diffused feeling of collective participation"[24] without any of the substance of cooperation.

As mentioned earlier, around the age of four, the child begins to spend more and more time with his age-mates, and, at age five or six, he enters the new and demanding social environment of school. Perhaps because of the tensions and conflicts of adjusting one's own desires and intentions to the opposite desires of one's peers, the child acquires at this point not only the ability to recognize other points of view, but the capability of at least rudimentary reflection. Such reflection is essentially discussion with oneself, and it culminates in thoughts that express intentions. The child can think in concrete terms of the future consequences of actions and is able to take the points of view of others into account in his thinking. Concomitantly, he begins to invest in his peers the affect formerly reserved for adults. Attempts at cooperation lead to a coordination of points of view and the development of reciprocity, which assure both individual autonomy and group cohesion.

Whereas respect in the younger child is reserved for adults, with increasing age the child develops respect for his peers. Mutual respect arises when two individuals attribute to each other equivalent personal interests and feelings. One child frequently feels superior to another child in some respects and equal to him in others. But, when children interact repeatedly, a sense of equality and mutual respect usually develops. The child's behavior is guided at an earlier age by his feelings of obedience; it has an external referent. With mutual respect comes mutual agreement as a guide for interpersonal feelings and behavior. Mutual respect gradually becomes differentiated from unilateral respect and leads to a new structuring of interpersonal feelings and actions. Cooperation and mutual respect become a higher form of equilibrium than obedience and submission to adults and unilateral respect for them.

As may be expected, children move into the interpersonal stage of affective development gradually. Mutual respect takes time and experience to acquire. We can understand the changing dynamics of the interpersonal stage by examining the concomitant progress taking place in moral and ego development. The child enters into peer relations from a period that was structured both affectively and socially by heteronomous relationships with adults. The child has learned to act expediently and opportunely within this structure, and his behavior is organized into patterns of either achieving or submitting to dominance and control. Loevinger[25] characterizes this stage of ego development as being exploitative and manipulative. The child brings these tendencies with him into his relations with peers. To the extent that the ends of the group are the desired ends of the child, no modifications are necessary, but when the ends of individuals within the group differ, accommodation must be found. Initially for most children, for a longer period for some, expedience will eventually demand reciprocity. According to Kohlberg,[26] the period from age four to ten is when children are typically at the second stage of preconventional moral development. At this stage, one's moral concerns still center on the satisfaction of personal needs, and occasionally those of one's peers. Reciprocity and equal sharing are present, but are used pragmatically for the immediate advantage of the individual.

As may be inferred from the description of moral and ego developmental stages associated with this period, the heteronomous affects previously accorded adults have not yet disappeared. For another, the child has, to some extent, come under the authority of older children and more dominant peers. Indeed, one of the characteristics of emotionally disturbed children is that they have not developed any of the feelings of mutual respect and reciprocity necessary to enter into the interpersonal affective stage. For most children, however, these heteronomous relations are gradually replaced by interpersonal affects invested in the peer group.

The culmination of this process is the entry into what Loevinger[27] calls the Conformist Stage. Here genuine interpersonal reciprocity and mutual respect occur, but, as Loevinger observes, often only within a small group. Loyalty and justice are now conceived of in terms of the group, and individual advantage is balanced against group sanctions. Societal rules are at last seen as worthy in their own right, again with reference to group notions of what is right and acceptable. Status and favor within the group become important as the child is fully able to recognize the relative equality of others' points of view. Prior to this transformation, the child was only interested in the ascendancy of his own interests. Now he requires the legitimacy of group support of his point of view. He becomes able to change his attitudes and beliefs to make them conform to the prevailing consensus of his peers.

This phase lasts through late childhood and into early adolescence, but many children may remain in this stage for a much longer period of time. For most, however, entry into adolescence marks the beginnings of the transformation of affect that culminates in the psychological-personal, and sometimes in the autonomous, stage of affective development.

The Psychological-Personal Stage

In a way that is closely tied to the development of formal thought in adolescence, affectivity invested in ideals and values that are related to an evolving sense of personal identity begins to shape character and prepare the child for successful entry into the adult world. Several important processes aid in this development, but the ability to comprehend and to use abstract ideas and the structures of formal operations is central to them all.

The child's reflective power is, in a sense, matured by the constant adjustments, conflicts, and equilibrations of the interpersonal stage. The child has come to reflect or engage in a kind of semiconscious internal dialogue on his actions and intentions. Development of the role-taking perspective has strengthened this discussion with the self by adding new voices to the dialogue. The child can now take into account the actions and opinions of others and make accommodations to his social reality.

With the onset of the formal operations stage of cognitive development, the reflective skill takes on a new dimension. The child moves from semiconscious reflection to conscious introspection. He is now able to think about his thoughts and feelings. The implications of this new power are significant. The adolescent with introspection has reached another milestone in his conception of selfhood. In the earlier stages, the child is unaware of identity because he cannot reflect on his actions, thoughts, and feelings. Although he has a vague sense of self in action, being ego centered and unaware of the selfhood of others, he is oblivious to self as a distinct entity. In the interpersonal stage, the child becomes aware of other selves and begins to have a conception of his identity, but only in relation to his peers. He discovers the limits of his own self by comparing and contrasting it with others. "I am I to the extent that I am not they." This is, of course, not a self-conscious process. It is, indeed, only with the advent of self-conscious introspection and the ability to conceptualize in abstracts that the adolescent is able to evaluate himself and his relationships with peers from a detached psychological frame of reference, with the potential of considering many standards and points of view. He now sees himself as having an identity that is distinct from others and seeks to determine how it is unique. This is the beginning of the child's awareness of his psychological existence.

Self-examination is enhanced by experience in role taking. From their first social awareness, children classify and characterize other people. At first, characteristics such as sex, age, and size are significant. As the child becomes involved with his peers, more differentiated traits are noted, such as mean, fair, brave, or scary. All of these are affective traits, having large value and emotional content as well as referring to tendencies toward action. With the role-taking perspective, the child can bring the rich diversity and many dimensions of personality in his peer group into clear focus, and he becomes sharply aware of others as individuals with distinctive identities. Identity at this stage is defined, as we have seen, in terms of significant physical traits, action tendencies, and social relationships. With the advent of abstract reasoning the child increasingly augments his judgment of others with psychological constructs; he begins to recognize others' needs, motives, and feelings, and as being, for example, trustworthy, conniving, or loyal. He is able to keep all of these constructs and traits in balance, recognizing the circumstances under which they apply, and being aware of inconsistencies in these complex psychological portraits.

As it is important for the adolescent to know and predict the character of his peers, so is it important for him to know himself and mark off the boundaries of his own identity. As he has characterized others, so now does the newly introspective adolescent begin to characterize himself. Because the individual increasingly tends to use such abstractions as honesty, courage, loyalty, and independence of mind to define himself, it is necessary to look carefully at the adolescent's experience with the realm of abstract concepts in order to understand fully the dynamics of the stage of psychological-personal affectivity.

The transformation of affectivity to the psychological-personal stage is not automatic with the acquisition of introspection and abstract thought. All development is mediated by experience and interaction with the environment and builds on the previous stage of development. Thus, the adolescent encounters values, ideals, life-styles, social roles, codes of behavior, laws, theories, and speculations everywhere. These encounters can be attributed only to a small extent to formal instruction by teachers, parents, and religious leaders. A much greater stimulation is given by the adolescent's changing social environment. His growing physical maturity, with its attendant social expectations, his participation in such value-loaded activities as sports and dating, his increased mobility and financial resources, and his efforts to explore the limits of his independence, provide the kind of conflict and uncertainty that force the adolescent to consider what he values and to construct a system by which to guide the increasingly numerous and difficult choices he must make. Using his ability to abstract from the concrete and to generalize from specifics the adolescent elaborates the nascent ideas of reciprocity and loyalty formed within the peer group into fully developed systems of values. These values are usually concerned with universal justice, equality under a single law, patriotic conceptions of the nation or the world, and allegiance to an abstract code of ethics, laws, or religious doctrine.

The adolescent's concern with questions of value is related to his quest for self-knowledge. During this period of learning, the experientially evaluated concepts of value, life-style, and behavior lead to possible modes of action, or, in other words, they give personal meaning and validity to these schemata. The process of interpreting abstract concepts of value, using them as guides to personal behavior, creating some sort of systematic array for these new beliefs and modes of action, and arranging them in a value hierarchy is analogous to the earlier representational period of cognitive development in which the child assimilates action schemata and object relations as symbols.

Adolescents spend many hours with their peers discussing their ideals, their life-style, and their sense of personal identity. They contemplate hypothetical cases, they project into the future, and they construct utopian schemes of social reform. It is during these kinds of experiences that the adolescent moves from being aware of values and possible systems of belief and conduct to investing them with affect and claiming them as his own. The culmination of the period of representation comes when the individual realizes, perhaps in the course of resolving a conflict between a personal value and that of a peer group, the importance of his investment in things represented by abstract thought. He can now be said to have entered fully into the psychological-personal stage of affective development.

The process of constructing personal hierarchies of values, ideals, and interests does not end with psychological-personal affective development. It has been described by many observers as partaking of characteristics of development by stages. Loevinger's stages of ego development[28] and Kohlberg's stages of moral development[29] shed helpful light on this process. Probably most adolescents begin the task of building a value system while in the Conformist Stage of ego development and the good-boy-good-girl stage of moral development. While initially conforming to group standards because of group sanctions (an attitude that is an elaboration of the earlier heteronomous affects), the individual gradually shifts, as his ability to abstract develops, to adhering to group standards in their own right. Many individuals remain at this stage for a long time; some never get beyond it. For most, however, loyalty to group ideals becomes further differentiated to include allegiance to abstract conceptions of law, social order, and the higher authority of government or religion. Again, many do not progress beyond this step, which Kohlberg[30] calls the law and order stage of moral development. At some point within this stage of moral development, most people advance to the Conscientious Stage of ego development. Here, the rule of law has been internalized, and feelings of obligation and duty become important. External standards of conduct, achievement, and personal worth have become internal standards, usually coinciding with social norms, but with an inner power that the external standards lacked. Self-criticism is implicit in adherence to an internal standard, and the significant authority in the individual's life has been transferred to the self.

The Autonomous Stage

During the period of growth in ego and moral development in the psychological-personal stage, affect is invested largely in the self and in the ideals and values that delimit the person's identity. But these ideals and values are subject to change. Indeed, a large part of adolescence and young adulthood is spent in testing them against reality and in accommodating one's personal beliefs and life-style to an empirically determined view of the world as it is. A major factor is the multitude of social forces that apply conflicting pressures on the young person to conform. Family, peers, employers, government, and the ubiquitous commercial media all compete in the individual's search for self and shape his identity in a predetermined image. It is only after putting these contradictory value systems to the test and making choices among them that the individual is able to reach the Conscientious Stage of ego development, with its concomitant internalized standards of conduct and value.

A limited number of persons reach the Autonomous Stage of affective and ego development. An individual at this stage is increasingly aware of the extent to which he has become responsible to a self-generated standard. He begins to value the concept of his self as an autonomous human being controlling his own destiny. He is aware of and resistant to the many pressures to conform to external standards. The abstract parameters of self become invested with affect as the person brings them into focus and conscious awareness. Self-determinism is an important part of the individual's self-concept; efforts to limit or violate his autonomy are threatening in a new and powerful way.

The Integritous Stage

The highest stage of affective development is the integritous stage. At this level, the person has a fully developed philosophy of life, and integrity itself is invested with affect. Integrity refers not only to consistent conduct in accordance with principle, but also to a feeling of wholeness or completeness that the individual prizes greatly. Actions, or even thoughts, that threaten this feeling are abhorred. Integrity may become even more valued than life itself. Socrates, Jesus Christ, and Sir Thomas More are examples of those who have reached this level of development. It is fortunate that such devotion to integrity is only rarely put to the final test.

Implications for Education

The theory of affective development described in the preceding section shares many basic assumptions with all developmental stage theories. Indeed, as I have pointed out, affective development is an integral part of general mental development. Beginning with Dewey, advocates of development in education have argued that experience and interaction are the key to intellectual and personal growth.

An implication following from the interactional view of development is the peripheral role of language. Language is commonly held to be the medium of thought. Piaget's experiments have repeatedly shown that children's verbal conceptualizations lag behind their intellectual capabilities, which are developed through activity and environmental manipulation. Until the child reaches the stage of formal operations in adolescence, the development of thought and feeling structures is primarily a nonverbal process. Language does not, in fact, become accessible as a tool for understanding experience until the child has reached a level of intellectual development that enables him to comprehend and use abstract concepts.

To the extent to which this is true of cognitive processes, it is doubly true of affect. Affective structures are acquired without the aid of language. A verbal understanding of an affective structure of action and response is only possible after the structure itself is sufficiently well developed and integrated to provide a referent for the verbal concept.

The implications for educators are clear: educators seeking to stimulate mental development must provide activity-centered curricula, as the passivity required of students in traditional instructional methodology prevents the interactions and equilibrations necessary for developmental growth. One can tell a child about reciprocity, but the child will not understand it until he has experienced reciprocity. I see the role of language in developmental education to be the medium of consciously representing new operations. Discussion is used to generalize, consolidate, and integrate the feeling and thought structures gained via interaction and experience. The child's level of cognitive and affective development must be taken into consideration when educators are planning both the type of activities and the kind of language experiences to be included in the curriculum.

Notes

1. B. Russell, "The Expanding Mental Universe," in *Adventures of the Mind*, ed. R. Thruelson and J. Kobler (New York: Alfred A. Knopf, 1960), 278.

2. L. Kohlberg and R. Mayer, "Development as the Aim of Education," *Harvard Educational Review*, 42 (November 1972), 449-496.

182   Adolescent Development

3. L. Kohlberg, "Stage and Sequence: The Cognitive-Developmental Approach to Socialization," in *Handbook of Socialization Theory and Research*, ed. D. A. Goslin (Chicago: Rand McNally, 1969); L. Kohlberg, "The Concepts of Developmental Psychology as the Central Guide to Education: Examples from Cognitive, Moral, and Psychological Education," in *Psychology and the Process of Schooling in the Next Decade,* ed. M. C. Reynolds (Minneapolis: Department of Audio-Visual Extension, University of Minnesota, 1972).

4. L. Kohlberg and E. Turiel, "Moral Development and Moral Education," in *Collected Papers on Moral Development and Moral Education* (Cambridge, Mass.: Laboratory of Human Development, Harvard University, 1973).

5. J. Loevinger, "The Meaning and Measurement of Ego Development," *American Psychologist*, 21 (March 1966), 195-217; *id.*, "Issues in the Measure of Moral Development," in *Moral Development: Proceedings of the 1974 ETS Invitational Conference* (Princeton, N.J.: Educational Testing Service, 1974).

6. R. L. Mosher, "Funny Things Happen on the Way to Curriculum Development," *Focus on Guidance*, 7 (March 1975), 1-12.

7. N. A. Sprinthall, "A Cognitive Developmental Curriculum: The Adolescent as a Psychologist," *Counseling and Values*, 18 (Winter 1974), 94-101.

8. R. L. Mosher and N. A. Sprinthall, "Psychological Education in Secondary Schools," *American Psychologist*, 25 (No. 10, 1970), 911-924.

9. E. H. Erikson, *Childhood and Society*, 2d ed. (New York: W. W. Norton, 1963).

10. J. Kagan, *Understanding Children: Behavior, Motives, and Thought* (New York: Harcourt Brace Jovanovich, 1971).

11. J. Piaget, *The Moral Judgment of the Child* (New York: Free Press, 1965); *id.*, *Six Psychological Studies* (New York: Random House, 1968); *id., Psychology of Intelligence* (Totowa, N.J.: Littlefield Adams, 1972); *id.*, "The Relation of Affectivity to Intelligence in the Mental Development of the Child," in *Childhood Psychopathology*, ed. S. I. Harrison and J. F. McDermott (New York: International Universities Press, 1972); J. Piaget, "Development and Learning," in *Readings in Child Behavior and Development*, ed. C. S. Lavatelli and F. Stendler (New York: Harcourt Brace Jovanovich, 1972).

12. J. Piaget and B. Inhelder, *The Psychology of the Child* (New York: Basic Books, 1969).

13. Piaget, "The Relation of Affectivity to Intelligence in the Mental Development of the Child," 168, 169.

14. See L. Kohlberg, J. LaCrosse, and D. Ricks, "The Predictability of Adult Mental Health from Childhood Behavior," in *Manual of Child Psychopathology*, ed. B. B. Wolman (New York: McGraw-Hill, 1972).

15. Piaget and Inhelder, *The Psychology of the Child*, 22.

16. Loevinger, "The Meaning and Measurement of Ego Development."

17. Erikson, *Childhood and Society*.

18. Loevinger, "The Meaning and Measurement of Ego Development."

19. Kagan, *Understanding Children*.

20. Kohlberg, "The Concepts of Developmental Psychology as the Central Guide to Education."

21. Erikson, *Childhood and Society.*

22. J. H. Flavell *et al., The Development of Role-Taking and Communication Skills in Children* (New York: John Wiley and Sons, 1968); M. J. Chandler, "Egocentrism and Antisocial Behavior: The Assessment and Training of Social Perspective-Taking Skills," *Developmental Psychology,* 9 (No. 3, 1973), 326-332.

23. Piaget, *The Moral Judgment of the Child,* 61.

24. *Ibid.,* 62.

25. Loevinger, "The Meaning and Measurement of Ego Development."

26. Kohlberg, "The Concepts of Developmental Psychology as the Central Guide to Education."

27. Loevinger, "The Meaning and Measurement of Ego Development."

28. *Ibid.*

29. Kohlberg, "The Concepts of Developmental Psychology as the Central Guide to Education."

30. *Ibid.*

6

"Who, Me, Pay Taxes?"
or "$2.65 an Hour and
All the Big Macs You Can Eat"

In many ways, finding the excerpts for this section was the most difficult task in preparing Part I. The literature on the relationship of adolescent development to work and career is, frankly, passé. A decade ago Super, Tiedeman, Roe, and others were publishing sophisticated theoretical papers on the interactive effect of work and career on people's lives.[1] Erikson stated: "In general it is primarily the inability to settle on an occupational identity which disturbs young people."[2] But that line of speculation and research seems to be stalled. Super is emeritus, and Tiedeman is interested in adult development and careers. No one, to my knowledge, has applied a cognitive-developmental approach to adolescents' evolving conceptions of work and career; when that happens it will, I believe, move theory building in this area into a new generation. (Judith G. Touchton and her colleagues have articulated such an approach for youth of college age.[3])

There seems little value in including a number of examples of this earlier writing on career development. What I have chosen to do is to make some general remarks, based on a review of the literature, about the practical significance of work and of career education for the adolescent. These remarks are followed by one example from the literature: Charles Bujold's "Activation of Vocational and Personal Development." Finally, there is a discussion of the need for new theory and new education for work and careers.

Some Generalizations on Career and Employment in Adolescence

As a practical matter, work and career are not major influences in the lives of most adolescents. Schooling is their work.[4] Having a part-time job is a way to acquire a modest amount of money, a degree of autonomy

184

of parents, some work experience, and a number of possessions. Kalachek, an economist, has analyzed the economic status of teenagers in a refreshingly straightforward way. He reports that teenage unemployment is high (17 percent in 1971 as compared to an adult rate of 5 percent) and especially acute for black teenagers (running between 30 and 40 percent in 1971; in 1978 the figure was 47 percent). Because teenagers attend school longer, there is a growing demand for part-time and part-year jobs.

Work for in-school teenagers represents the acquisition of some experience, some discipline and some income rather than the origins of a career. The work done at age 16 normally has little to do with long-run job prospects. There is a youth labor market, where one earns income, rather than establishing oneself on the rungs of a career ladder. The youth labor market consists mainly of jobs in the trade and service sector, and mainly of jobs with smaller, non-unionized and low wage-paying firms. Even out-of-school youth 16-17 years of age are condemned to this youth labor market.[5]

Further, during the 1960's an explosion in the number of teenagers exacerbated their economic problems. There are simply more teenagers than part-time and part-year jobs. One effect of this is to depress the wages paid to adolescents (for example, in 1971 boys working part-time earned $82 a week, as compared to $162 for men; girls, who are in double jeopardy, earned $73, as compared to $100 for women).

The employment of low-cost, readily available youth has risen substantially. Between 1960 and 1971 teenage employment rose by 2.1 million, or 50 percent, while total employment was increasing by 13.3 million, or 20 percent. "The problem of the past decade is not an erosion of jobs. It is that jobs have not risen as rapidly as has the number of teenagers . . . . Hopefully, we have touched bottom. Teenage job prospects should improve dramatically over the next decade, primarily because the growth in supply is beginning to taper off. Teenagers now [1971] account for 10.5% of the population; in 1975 they will account for 10.7 and in 1980 for 10.1%."[6]

Kalachek finds no evidence to support the belief that today's adolescents are refusing to take low-status, low-wage jobs, that they are lazy, or that they are underage welfare chiselers. Turnover rates among the young are high, but that is an old story because youth are willing to take low-status jobs. Studies "indicate extremely high educational and occupational aspirations among high school students; job satisfaction among youth is high; the evidence indicates that in areas where unemployment is low, youth labor force participation is high . . . . It is hard to escape the impression that if there were more teenage jobs there would be more teenage workers."[7] (I am reminded of the enormous crush of black teenagers in New York City in April 1977 for relatively few federally funded summer jobs.)

Kalachek summarizes the economic facts concerning adolescent employment: "The shift to part-time work has reduced the real current earnings of teenagers. Suburbanization and elongated school attendance have increased the real cost of being a teenager. The net result is a reduction in economic autonomy. The period of economic adolescence has been lengthened."[8]

A Developmental Conception of Career and of Vocational Education

Bujold's piece argues both a developmental conception of career and of vocational education, but it is not a cognitive-developmental or Piagetian model.[9] Bujold bases his analysis of the essential developmental tasks the adolescent confronts concerning his vocation on the work of Super.[10] Further, Bujold employs a different psychology of cognition— Guilford's theory of intellect—to comprehend how we think about work and career.[11] This model of thinking is based on the idea of building blocks: learning one cognitive ability or operation permits the person to move to the second, more comprehensive one. The task of education is to teach people to think better or more logically. The adolescent may apply these intellectual abilities to his vocation, work, career, or his social or personal growth. Bujold's contribution concerns the former areas and anticipates the application of the same approach to the latter areas.

The argument is that adolescents face certain developmental tasks relative to their careers, for example, exploring the possibilities of various jobs or careers. These tasks seem to require specific intellectual abilities, such as "cognition of semantic transformation," or, more simply, "penetrating thinking" as well as fluidity, flexibility, perceiving implications, autonomy—elements of creative thinking in general. The aim of the counselor or vocational educator is to teach these abilities within the framework of a curriculum that provides experience, active thinking about the experience, and derivation of meaning from the experience. Certainly the pedagogy Bujold suggests is Deweyan.

Bujold's implicit view of career and vocation is pragmatic to some degree: students should be provided the "opportunity to realize that occupations exist to solve problems and that choosing an occupation is choosing the kind of problems that one is interested in working on." Further, "the more aspects of a situation (the student) can grasp (cognitively) the more he can increase his occupational knowledge."[12] This resembles the vocationalism criticized by Wirth.[13] People exist for work rather than vice versa. But, in Bujold's model, vocational education (if not vocation) can enhance human development. While its subject matter or content is jobs, work, and career, the development of penetrating and creative thinking cannot, by definition, be restricted to vocational matters. Bujold aims to enhance human intellect, and that may, incidentally, make people less happy with their work or a corporate and technological society.

Bujold's piece also raises some issues beyond that of its uncritical vocationalism. The effectiveness of the vocational education he proposes seems to depend on the adolescents' stage of cognitive development, in Piagetian terms. Bujold's model makes no stipulations concerning when or if an adolescent can learn "divergent production," "convergent production," "evaluation," "penetrating thinking," or "perceiving implications." And those abilities sound suspiciously like formal operations. His plan of vocational education provides for an alternation between concrete experience, active thinking about the experience, and the abstraction, or integration, of meaning. As noted, the pedagogy is long on Dewey but short on Piaget. Bujold could adopt a Piagetian approach in the development of cognitions of vocation. He is, however, more interested in applying Guilford's analysis and developing his own pedagogy to teach cognitive abilities functional to "the individual's socialization process or to his personal growth."[14]

The Need for New Theory and Education

This introduction concludes with a brief review of three articles that cannot be included because of space limitations. And yet they are directly concerned with the critical need for both new theory and education for work and career. Wirth describes "a widening contemporary tension between an economic technical order oriented to functional rationality and efficiency, organized on the simple principle of economizing—of least costs and optimization of production and profits; and counter-trends concerned with reaches for 'wholeness of persons' and self-realization." (This is reminiscent of Erikson's technological and humanist-universal ideologies.) Wirth sees the counter-trends as related to "the democratic ethos with its insistence on persons being treated as ends rather than as means only."[15] He relates this current tension and its implications for education to an early ideological split in the vocational education movement. Dewey argued that we must match jobs and education to men, and not men to jobs. For him, the measure of work and the industrial order was the degree to which they contribute to the individual's all-around development. According to the opposing ideology—social Darwinism— society and schooling were based on a model of job efficiency. The latter theory prevailed in vocational and contemporary career education.

Wirth's article provides particularly important background for understanding career education, its assumptions about work and the individual, and its critics.[16] An article by McGowen and Cohen, "Career Education—

Reforming School through Work," savages career education as a bubble inflated by professionals, the U.S.O.E., and the N.I.E. Business does not want it, labor does not want it, educators do not want it, and counselors do not want it. It is a field where "all the action is at the elementary level" and where "the social division of labor simply overwhelmed the reform."[17] Grubb and Lazerson are more scholarly, but are equally critical:

Despite its assertions to the contrary [career education] is primarily a renewal and expansion of vocational education, a movement that has previously proven itself ineffective . . . . Career education is not directed at resolving social problems, developing avenues of upward mobility or making school and work more satisfying experiences. It is aimed instead at reducing expectations, limiting aspirations and increasing commitments to the existing social structure. The replacement of hazy educational goals with "realistic" vocational goals, while appearing benevolent, actually strengthens the "cooling-out" function of schooling . . . . Accepting the economic system as just, it seeks to make people satisfied with their roles in a society that distributes social goods inequitably . . . . It claims that American society does not need all the "intellectual and developed capacities of its citizens in the work force" without asking whether such a waste of capabilities makes sense.[18]

Wirth makes a clear philosophical statement of the ultimate problem— whether work experience and career education should lead to human growth and wholeness.

Notes

1. D. E. Super, *The Psychology of Careers* (New York: Harper and Row, 1957); D. V. Tiedeman and R. P. O'Hara, *Career Development: Choice and Adjustment* (New York: College Entrance and Examination Board, 1963); A. Roe and Marvin Siegelman, *The Origins of Interests* (Washington, D.C.: American Personnel and Guidance Association, 1964).

2. E. Erikson, "Growth and Crises of the Healthy Personality," in *Identity and the Life Cycle* (New York: International Universities Press, 1959). Published by *Psychological Issues*, 1 (No. 1, 1959).

3. J. G. Touchton *et al.*, "Career Planning and Decision-Making: A Developmental Approach to the Classroom," *Counseling Psychologist*, 6 (No. 4, 1977), 42-47.

4. See T. S. Popkewitz and G. Wehlage, "Schooling as Work: An Approach to Research and Evaluation," *Teachers College Record*, 79 (No. 1, 1977), 69-85.

5. Edward Kalachek, "The Changing Economic Status of the Young," *Journal of Youth and Adolescence*, 2 (No. 2, 1973), 128.

6. *Ibid.*, 130.

7. *Ibid.*, 130-131.

8. *Ibid.*, 132.

9. Charles Bujold, "Activation of Vocational and Personal Development," in *Adolescents' Development and Education: A Janus Knot*, ed. Ralph L. Mosher (Berkeley, Calif.: McCutchan Publishing Corp., 1979), Chapter 6.

10. Super, *The Psychology of Careers.*

11. J. P. Guilford and Ralph Hoepfner, *The Analysis of Intelligence* (New York: McGraw-Hill, 1971).

12. Bujold, "Activation of Vocational and Personal Development."

13. A. G. Wirth, "Issues Affecting Education and Work in the Eighties," *Teachers College Record*, 79 (No. 1, 1977), 55-67.

14. Bujold, "Activation of Vocational and Personal Development."

15. Wirth, "Issues Affecting Education and Work in the Eighties," 55.

16. See, for example, W. N. Grubb and M. Lazerson, "Rally 'Round the Workplace: Continuities and Fallacies in Career Education," *Harvard Educational Review*, 45 (No. 4, 1975), 451-474; E. F. McGowan and D. F. Cohen, "Career Education—Reforming School through Work," *Public Interest*, 46 (Winter 1977), 28-47.

17. McGowan and Cohen, "Career Education," 40, 43.

18. Grubb and Lazerson, "Rally 'Round the Workplace," 473-474.

Activation of Vocational and Personal Development

Charles Bujold

It has been over a quarter of a century since Ginzberg criticized guidance workers for not basing their practices upon solid theory. For more than four decades, Parsons' successors had adhered closely to his idea[1] that vocational choice is the result of the individual's comparison of two sets of facts: those relating to himself and those relating to occupations. At the same time, they had drawn on related fields such as statistics, psychometry, and counseling in order to assist young people in solving vocational problems.

In spite of its insufficiencies, the approach to a general theory elaborated by Ginzberg and his colleagues[2] stimulated considerable

In this piece is presented an approach to career guidance that has been developed by Denis Pelletier, Gilles Noiseaux, and Charles Bujold. A more extensive presentation of the approach can be found in the book by the aforementioned authors: *Développement vocationnel et croissance personnelle: Approche opératoire* (Montreal: McGraw-Hill, 1974).

activity. This was directed toward identifying the variables affecting vocational behavior and its correlates, illustrating the sequential nature of this behavior, conceptualizing its underlying mechanisms, understanding its dynamics, and proposing types of procedures likely to facilitate its development.[3]

All of the conceptual frameworks that have been proposed suggest useful explanations and provide certain strategic elements. It is worth noting that while many concepts in science fall into disuse after a short time, the developmental approach to the problem of vocational behavior has withstood the test of time since it continues to stimulate interest among practitioners and researchers. Though this fact is in itself noteworthy, the developmental approach has importance beyond it. The approach provides our most complete and integrated view of vocational behavior. Further, it clears the path for more research on the way the individual interacts with his milieu and suggests to guidance counselors some methods that are distinctly different from the more traditional approaches.

The Functional Approach

It seems possible to proceed even further along this path. This in no way denies the value of the programs that have been proposed to date to facilitate vocational development. It is, nonetheless, absolutely necessary that we examine this phenomenon from a functional point of view, that is, consider what has to be done in each of the diverse developmental tasks, and, consequently, the abilities and cognitive attitudes that make these operations possible.

Vocational behavior can be analyzed in various ways. It can be viewed purely descriptively; thus, one simply defines the tasks that mark this behavior. By probing deeper, one can identify the conditions that make the accomplishment of these tasks possible. On another level one can examine the way the individual does his job, while attempting to understand and predict this behavior. This can be done by studying the way the individual's personality is organized and by observing the interaction of personal and situational factors that determine the behavior. In my opinion, however, the functional approach is preferable since it analyzes an individual's behavior in relation to the way he lives his experiences, the way in which his experiences are cognitively processed, the significance he draws from them, and the manner in which he integrates them.

This approach permits a significant advance in the study of vocational development and in the approach to its guidance. The developmental theorists[4] have made a worthy contribution. They have clarified, to varying degrees, thought concerning the periods and stages that an individual passes through during his vocational development, the tasks he must perform, the relationship between his career development and personal development, and the mechanisms involved not only in his decision-making process but also in his adjustment to school and work. In spite of its qualities, however, the developmental approach does not provide an interpretation of these phenomena in functional terms. The statements made by Havighurst, Ginzberg, or Super concerning developmental tasks fail to indicate which intellectual abilities and cognitive attitudes are necessary for the accomplishment of these tasks. Hershenson's system, which aims at relating the phases of vocational development to personality development, is highly descriptive. Both Super's extensive analysis of the role of self-concept in vocational development and Tiedeman's and O'Hara's concept of choice and adjustment take into account the cognitive and affective elements involved in the phenomena they study, but they do not account for the processes underlying these phenomena. On the practical level, then, a counselor who applies Super's theory is able to help an adolescent become aware of what he must do to perform his developmental tasks and can sensitize him to the attitudes necessary to facilitate their accomplishment. The theory does not, however, help the counselor provide the adolescent with the necessary psychological tools; it does not enable him to mobilize the adolescent's cognitive and affective resources to complete his developmental tasks.

The functional approach, when applied to the study of vocational development (as well as to social, personal, and family development), makes it possible to analyze the way a person functions by examining the inner processes of his thinking and his attitudes toward work. It allows a more adequate description, in functional terms, of the nature and complexity of vocational phenomena. In addition, it can serve as a guide in creating practices likely to influence vocational development.

This view of vocational development makes it possible to conceive a more varied and adequate methodology for use by guidance counselors. This methodology consists of learning situations that not only guide an individual's vocational development but also mobilize within him the cognitive and emotional resources necessary to accomplish developmental tasks. Thus, this method provides the individual with the psychological tools by which he can learn to learn.

I will attempt below to illustrate briefly, within the framework of the functional approach, the possible rapport between developmental tasks and the abilities and attitudes necessary for their realization. I will then discuss the basic principles of the model of activation that my colleagues and I are proposing. Finally, I will present an illustration of its methods of application.

Developmental Tasks: A Functional View

From the developmental perspective, educational and career choices can be seen as long-term problems, whose solutions involve a certain number of tasks. According to the rules of logic, a given task that has been successfully performed facilitates, in turn, the accomplishment of a following task; thus, a person is able to pass through the different phases of choosing a career without much difficulty. In order to conceptualize the relationships that exist between developmental tasks and the abilities and attitudes likely to influence them, we began to consider the tasks of exploration, crystallization, specification, and implementation in relation to Guilford's model of the intellect,[5] and we attempted both an inductive and deductive analysis of these relationships.

Guilford and his associates have elaborated and tested what they call a morphological model, in which intellectual abilities are classified in three different ways. The categories of one way intersect with those of the others. One way of classification involves operations (or ways of thinking), and it includes five categories (cognition; memory; divergent production, or production of new information; convergent production, or production of tightly logical conclusions; and, finally, evaluation, or the operation of judging the goodness of what is known or produced).

The second way of classification relates to contents (or areas of information about which we think). Within it, four categories are identified: figural, which pertains to information in concrete form, as perceived in images; symbolic, which involves signs, code elements such as numbers or letters; semantic, which concerns information in the form of conceptions or mental constructs; and behavioral, which relates to information involved in human interactions. Thus, all of these categories refer to basic, substantive kinds of information.

The third way of classification—products—refers to formal kinds of information. It consists of six categories, ranging from the simplest to the most complex: units, classes, relations, systems, transformations, and implications.

By combining the three classifications in one whole, we obtain a cubic model. Since there are five categories of operations, four of contents, and six of products, there is a total of 120 possible combinations, and so, in theory, we have 120 unique abilities. The ability represented by each cube within the model is unique since it represents one type of operation, which exerts itself on a certain type of content, in order to yield a particular kind of product.

The structure and functioning of the human intellect obviously is a question that remains largely open to research. It is remarkable, nonetheless, that Guilford and his associates, in a series of studies, have demonstrated the existence of ninety-eight out of 120 of the theoretically identified abilities.[6] In light of this model, therefore, one is led to ask not whether a person is intelligent, but, rather, for what kind of task or activity he demonstrates certain abilities. We are, in other words, far removed from a unitary conception of intelligence, which was in favor in the past.

What relationships exist between developmental tasks, on the one hand, and cognitive abilities and attitudes, on the other? Let us take, for example, the task of exploration. One who explores has to observe, to make trials; he must be capable of judging, or formulating inferences and interpreting information; he is also led to experiment, investigate, and formulate hypotheses concerning the object and the methods of investigation.[7] Novelty, complexity, and incongruity (perhaps because of the divergence they introduce into the perceptual field) are variables that are likely to provoke and stimulate exploration,[8] which, in turn, provides the individual with the means for satisfying his need for variety and stimulation.[9]

Many intellectual abilities and a certain number of attitudes play a role in the exploratory process. But observation and curiosity, the process of trial and error, the elaboration of hypotheses, and risk taking all seem to be components of exploration that require creative thinking. Consequently, it is interesting to ask whether the abilities related to creative thinking that Guilford has isolated, as well as a certain number of personal components, do not play a primary role in this task.

Guilford[10] makes a distinction between creative thinking and logical thinking. Whereas convergent production (or logical thinking) concerns what is logically necessary, divergent production (or creative thinking) concerns what is logically possible. The person exploring careers is, by definition, not obliged to make final decisions. Rather, in order to explore fully, he should be able to see all the possible aspects of a situation. Guilford and his colleagues have tested the hypothesis that creative thinking enables the individual to go beyond the superficial aspects of the things he observes and permits him to penetrate more deeply the meaning of his experiences. They determined the existence of an intellectual factor that fulfills this function and termed it "cognition of semantic transformations." According to them,[11] a person who possesses this form of "penetrating" thinking is capable of perceiving a greater number of characteristics pertinent to a given situation, because he can, in fact, perceive all possible transformations. The importance of this ability for the individual involved in vocational exploration is obvious: the more aspects of a situation he can grasp, the more he can increase his occupational knowledge through career conferences, industrial visits, internships, or meetings with workers.

Other components of creative thinking are likely to play an equally important role in career exploration. Sensitivity to problems, which Guilford and Hoepfner[12] define as the ability to perceive the implications arising from a given piece of information, appears to be closely related to exploratory behavior,[13] as are two other categories of abilities, fluidity and flexibility. Fluidity permits an individual to enrich the information he acquires with what he already knows.[14] Flexibility, on the other hand, refers to the person's adaptability in classifying the information he has acquired (about himself or the world of work) and his versatility in transposing the information he possesses.[15] One may assume again that a fruitful exploration depends upon a person's ability to avoid classifying his information into rigid classes and fixed organizations.

Thus, the research conducted by Guilford and his colleagues has identified several abilities relevant to creative thinking. Other researchers in the field of creativity have discovered a certain number of cognitive components and personal variables that may play a role in exploration, such as autonomy, tolerance of ambiguity, willingness to take risks, and originality.[16] The functional conception of vocational development suggests, therefore, that exploration depends upon the intellectual abilities and cognitive attitudes characteristic of creative thinking. It also suggests that the other developmental tasks are dependent upon different modes of thinking. Each of these tasks and the types of thinking hypothetically related to them will merely be mentioned here.

As a person accumulates numerous experiences through his exploration, he is likely to feel confused. This he translates into a need to clarify his situation, to establish order among the various pieces of information he possesses concerning himself. He also needs to organize his perceptions of professional roles, the world of work, and the educational structure. This is the task of "crystallization,"[17] during which the adolescent must eliminate certain possibilities, thereby reducing his field of preferences in order to arrive at a general preference that embraces a certain number of related activities. The categories of intellectual operations that appear to be particularly important during crystallization are cognition and convergent production.[18] In order to be able to crystallize his preference, a person must be aware of the elements involved in a problem and must be able to classify them according to certain logical principles. He must decide that certain fields of vocational activity correspond to his aptitudes, interests, and values, while others do not. He must discern the characteristics common to several occupations and must identify which of his own attributes correspond to the requirements of several occupations. In general, he must be able to think in terms of logically organized systems. All these operations are likely to call upon the abilities of cognition and logical thinking, in short, upon conceptual thinking.

Super[19] suggests that, following crystallization, the adolescent normally converts a general or provisional vocational preference into a specific one. Specification could be viewed as that point where a person's values intersect with the possibilities provided by his environment. Should the adolescent have an extensive list of requirements, one of his immediate difficulties would be to determine his priorities in regard to his expectations for the future. Thus, he must organize his values so that the most essential and important criteria serve as guidelines for comparing diverse projects. He must coordinate what is desirable with what is probable, a task that requires a tolerance of complexity and a capacity to take into account several variables at a time.

Referring back to Guilford's model, we find that, as is true for other tasks, there are many diverse abilities involved in the task of specification. One particular group of intellectual abilities seems, however, particularly important in specification: evaluative thinking. Guilford defines this type of thinking as the process by which one compares items of information, in terms of known specifications, on the basis of logical criteria, such as identity and consistency.[20]

The last task to be considered is implementation, which Super[21] in particular has defined. After an adolescent has explored all possible choices, has reduced the number of choices, and has finally specified one choice, he must commit himself by enrolling in a program of studies or by finding a job in his chosen occupation. The individual who is about to implement his preference will be preoccupied with the realization of his project. He will ask himself certain questions: What steps should he take in order to be admitted to a certain training school? How can he improve his work in the disciplines related to his choice? How can he guarantee his choice? What difficulties must he anticipate? Thus, in general, the individual becomes more involved and more motivated to commit himself concretely and efficiently. This indicates that implementation requires such abilities as anticipation, planning, and elaboration, which Guilford called implicative thinking.[22]

The functional conception of vocational development suggests, therefore, that relationships exist between what has to be done in choosing a vocation, on the one hand, and intellectual abilities and cognitive attitudes, on the other. Particularly with regard to the rapport between developmental tasks and abilities, we are led to link theoretically exploration and creative thinking, crystallization and categorical-conceptual thinking, specification and evaluative thinking, and implementation and implicative thinking. If these linkages are valid, then cognitive psychology could contribute greatly to the conceptualization of vocational behavior and to the elaboration of approaches likely to facilitate choice of career. In fact, the types of thinking to which we refer are actually groupings of the various factors found in Guilford's model of the intellect. If we focus our attention on the semantic and behavioral contents, then we find that creative thinking involves the operation of divergent production and the products are "transformations"; in categorical-conceptual thinking, the intellectual operations yield mainly classes and relations; in evaluative thinking, the operation of evaluation and the products called systems are prevalent; and implicative thinking refers primarily to the products called implications that are yielded by the five intellectual operations.

On the basis of this analysis, we can restate the developmental tasks in functional terms, that is, describe or transpose them in a language reflecting the internal processes underlying them. For example, "exploration" can be transposed into functional language. In the model we propose, exploration means discovering that there exists, within the immediate surroundings and in society in general, problems that need to be solved and tasks that must be accomplished. This sensitivity to problems is essential for a valid exploration. Exploration also means accumulating a wealth of information about one's environment and oneself, an ability known as "fluidity." In addition exploring entails having at one's disposal a rich repository of information, which implies the exercise of flexibility. Obtaining information that is unusual and not readily accessible in one's immediate surroundings is also involved in exploring. This formulation takes into account the components of creative thinking termed originality and penetration, as well as the attitude called autonomy. Exploring means, too, that one is able to recognize the fact that not only is it necessary to orient oneself to a vocational goal, but that it is of great importance to do so. This subtask implies sensitivity to problems. The ability to accept one's orientation as a complex matter, for which there is not necessarily a unique and definite answer, is part of exploring. This attitude, which is of the utmost importance in relation to one's exploration of occupations, demands that the individual be able to tolerate ambiguity. Finally, exploring involves testing professional or career roles in one's imagination, which requires the willingness to take risks.

These kinds of statements, or definitions, can also be proposed for the tasks of crystallization, specification, and implementation. Each task, in other words, can be divided into subtasks, and these subtasks can then be conceptually related to the abilities and attitudes that seem important for their achievement. Six statements have been formulated for the task of crystallization and specification, and five for implementation. Because of space limitations, it is possible to give but one illustration for each of the tasks. For instance, organizing one's knowledge of the world of work in relation to the understanding of oneself forms a part of the task of crystallizing a vocational choice. It requires a positive attitude toward doing so, convergent thinking, and the ability to evaluate and elaborate. Ordering one's needs and values according to their importance is a component of specification, and it is likely to call upon the ability to evaluate and a reflexive attitude. Anticipating possible difficulties is a component of the task of implementation; it depends upon the exercise of implicative thinking and upon a willingness to assume responsibilities.

Applications

Concerning the possible applications of this approach, we formulate the following question: is it possible to facilitate vocational development through stimulation of the development and exercise of intellectual abilities and cognitive attitudes? It has been suggested by Havighurst[23] and Super[24] that the successful performance of one task is a prerequisite to the performance of the following task. If such is the case, insufficient exploration could result in pseudocrystallization, which could itself make difficult or impossible the specification of a vocational preference. If individuals whose work life is characterized by a series of trials and errors could learn the sequence of vocational developmental tasks, many of their problems could be avoided. In other words, it would be possible to promote vocational maturity by mobilizing in the individual the requisite abilities and attitudes.

The implication that can be drawn from this analysis is that the individual can be helped in a number of ways to accomplish these diverse vocational developmental tasks. He would, therefore, have opportunities for growth. Such strategies could be useful to counselors in their attempts to help individuals develop and utilize the abilities and cognitive attitudes that are necessary for the satisfactory performance of given tasks.

Before discussing strategies, however, it is necessary to deal with two questions: Is it possible to influence the development and exercise of cognitive processes (that is, intellectual abilities and cognitive attitudes)? If so, what model would underlie the counselor's action?

The Training of Cognitive Processes

A body of theory and research has been concerned with the training of cognitive processes. Twenty years ago, Bartlett[25] argued that thinking abilities could be trained. Since then, as a review of research shows,[26] the processes of creative thinking can be improved by proper training, and such improvement persists over time. As Pelletier reports,[27] work pursued in the field of cognitive psychology has resulted in the use of numerous strategies (such as brainstorming and synectics) intended to foster creative, conceptual, and evaluative abilities. Research studies indicate that such cognitive attitudes as preference for complexity and tolerance of ambiguity can be developed by training.

Since cognitive processes can be trained, it thus appears possible to activate vocational development. Exploration would be facilitated by procedures involving divergence and analogy, crystallization by procedures conducive to the use of convergent thinking abilities, specification by experiences devised to stimulate activities of evaluation and comparison, and, finally, implementation by activities involving anticipation and planning. At the same time, some activities could stimulate the attitudes related to the intellectual processes just mentioned. Vocational maturity—the ultimate goal of all these activities—thus implies much more than merely acquiring knowledge. It is shaped by the individual's initiative and participation, by his intellectual and emotional involvement.

With these considerations in mind, we have elaborated a model of activation. In this model, three conditions are essential for the successful accomplishment of the individual's vocational developmental tasks: something that is experienced; something that is cognitively processed; and something that is logically and psychologically integrated. In other words, each learning situation involves an experiential, a cognitive, and an integrative dimension.

Experiential Dimension

A Chinese proverb says: "I hear, and I forget; I see, and I remember; I do, and I understand." Thus, it is not by reading about happiness that one becomes happy, and it is not by knowing what development implies that one starts growing. Whatever their theoretical background, most, if not all, vocational couselors agree with Gendlin[28] on the point that a client begins to make progress when his expression emerges from his impression, when the words he uses symbolize what he really feels, and when the concepts he has developed do not remain merely intellectual matter, but give direction to his actions.

For a person to develop, he must have experiences. The more the person involves himself, with all his cognitive, sensory, and emotional resources, in a situation, the more the situation is experiential. In Guilford's terminology, the contents he has identified[29] offer different levels of experiencing. Symbolic and semantic contents offer the lowest level; figural material, the intermediate; and behavioral content, the highest. For example, reading a play is a learning experience at the lowest level. Attending the play provides more experiential knowledge of it and is at the intermediate level. Acting in the play, however, with all the feelings and behaviors that involves, is the highest level. Words, figures, mental imagery, feelings, and behavior can be seen as representing different levels of experiencing. Thus, a learning stituation is fully experiential to the extent that it involves all such content.

Cognitive Dimension

A simple activity such as reading, for example, can involve many intellectual behaviors. These cognitive processes contribute to the individual's adjustment. He uses them to reach his objectives and to solve his problems. One person may read in order to understand an author's thought. If asked, he will be able to give a true account of his reading. A second person may read with the hope of stimulating his mind and then be able to synthesize the subject matter. He will consider what he has read in relation to the problem that interests him. A third person may read from a critical viewpoint, looking for contradictions, weak points, and ambiguities in the text. Still another person may be interested in drawing theoretical implications and practical applications from the principles discussed in the written material.

A large body of literature is concerned with problem solving.[30] In Guilford's view[31] most researchers agree on the major phases of this process. These phases are: first, there is an awareness of a problem, and there is a desire to reach a solution, with all the observations and analyses that are involved in this initial step; second, the situation is defined, and its various elements are conceptually organized; third, possibilities are considered and evaluated; fourth, a solution is chosen and checked.

This sequential model of problem solving resembles closely the vocational sequence of exploration, crystallization, specification, and implementation. It is, in fact, the connection between the two sequences that was the origin of the idea of analyzing vocational developmental tasks in terms of the cognitive processes that are likely to be involved in their realization. According to this principle, activating vocational development consists in helping the individual cognitively to organize his experience and information in relation to the vocational task that he is facing. This assumes that the counselor has an understanding of the various thinking abilities and a mastery of the techniques and strategies available for stimulating them.

Integrative Dimension

Educators agree that, in order for learning to occur, information must be presented sequentially, the simpler concepts being introduced before the more complex ones. The same requirement holds for the counselor who plans to help students in their vocational developmental tasks. He must foresee the logical sequence of the themes and activities that he proposes so that cumulative outcomes emerge from the experiences.

An important factor in the individual's development, however, might be the capacity to discard his usual way of interpreting reality, in order to build other schemes that could be more easily adapted to his experiences and to his personal observations. In other words, it might be his capacity to abandon his stereotypes and preconceptions and to allow himself to be impressed by reality as it is actually perceived and experienced. Psychological integration probably consists in relating actual events, as they are experienced, to what the individual has experienced before so that he can adjust more effectively.

The principle of integration seems fundamental in the sense that any learning supposes that the new be made familiar. If this familiarization is the result of an interaction between the experience and the individual's symbolizing processes, then psychological integration will be achieved, provided that the experience initially had a potential meaning for the individual. If this condition is met, there is a good chance that an explicit meaning will be the ultimate outcome of the experience.

Strategies Facilitating Vocational Development

These principles, along with a functional analysis of the vocational developmental tasks and the results of studies indicating that cognitive processes can be trained, led to the elaboration of a program of activities intended to facilitate vocational development through the use of a number of strategies. These strategies have been drawn primarily from the fields of psychotherapy and cognitive psychology.[32] Two kinds of strategies are used: the first are called experiential modes, which include content related to perception, imagery, emotion, and behavior; the second, called cognitive procedures, stimulate the exercise of the cognitive abilities by means of which the individual processes the data of his experiences. In this program, various themes and learning situations are presented in relation to the diverse vocational developmental tasks.

One Learning Situation Elaborated

Following is an example of an activity that is suggested in relation to the first subtask of exploration. This subtask is formulated as follows: discovering that there exist, within the immediate surroundings and in society in general, problems that need to be solved and tasks that must be accomplished. Thus, it is proposed to the participants that some problems are so complex that their solution requires the participation of various workers. The learning situation is entitled "Problems and Occupations."

In it the counselor refers to winter and invites the participants to list the problems, difficulties, and inconveniences associated with that season. Then the students are asked to imagine all the occupations that would be modified or would disappear if winter no longer existed and to determine the way this situation would change their way of life.

Next, the counselor asks the students to identify the possible causes of air and water pollution and proposes that they elaborate plans of action leading to the elimination of such problems and that they suggest occupations likely to help in this enterprise. The group is divided into subgroups, and the team whose plan is considered the best becomes the hiring committee. The other participants are invited to meet the members of the committee and to explain how the occupations they have proposed could contribute to the implementation of the plan that has been chosen.

The experiential modes called role playing and "esprit martien" (that is, making the familiar unusual) and the cognitive procedures called divergence are used. The resultant activity aims at three objectives: to provide an opportunity to realize that occupations exist to solve problems and that choosing an occupation means choosing the kind of problems that one is interested in working on; to stimulate the exercise of the intellectual abilities of fluidity, sensitivity to problems, and elaboration; to stimulate attitudes of curiosity and risk taking.

Space limitations preclude a discussion of the way this approach can be adapted to other kinds of tasks, such as the individual's socialization process or his personal growth. Such an adaptation might be possible, and research should be done on this question.

But with regard to testing the validity of the approach in relation to a vocational content, a program of fundamental and applied research was launched in 1971,[33] and the gathering of the data was completed in 1975. The major purposes of the study were to examine the relationships between certain intellectual abilities and cognitive attitudes, and the relation of such abilities and attitudes to vocational maturity. The study also aimed at studying the effects, over a three-year period, of a program of activation, with a sample of ninth, tenth, eleventh, and twelfth graders of both sexes.

The first report of this research will not be available before the fall of 1979. However, the clinical evidence that has resulted is encouraging, and so, too, are the empirical results that have been examined to date. On the clinical side, it has been observed, for example, that students with whom the approach had been used were seeing their problem of vocational choice more concretely, that they were more motivated, namely, to seek information relating to their choice, and that subsequent individual interviews with them were more fruitful.

As for the empirical data, some significant results suggest that creative thinking abilities contribute to vocational maturity at the beginning of secondary school, whereas vocational maturity is more strongly related, somewhat later, to conceptual thinking. At the eleventh-grade level, some data reveal relationships between vocational maturity and various measures of evaluative and implicative thinking.

Thus, there already seems to be evidence supporting the basic hypotheses underlying the approach. Forthcoming publications will present a detailed and critical report of these findings. It is hoped that a deeper analysis of the data will contribute to answering some important questions in the field of adolescent vocational development and career guidance.

Notes

1. Frank Parsons, *Choosing a Vocation* (Boston: Houghton Mifflin, 1909).

2. Eli Ginzberg *et al.*, *Occupational Choice: An Approach to a General Theory* (New York: Columbia University Press, 1951).

3. E. S. Bordin, Barbara Nachmann, and S. J. Segal, "An Articulated Framework for Vocational Development," *Journal of Counseling Psychology*, 10 (No. 2, 1963), 107-117; Anne Roe, "A Psychological Study of Eminent Psychologists and Anthropologists and a Comparison with Biological and Physical Scientists," *Psychological Monographs*, 67 (No. 352, 1953); *id.*, "Early Determinants of Vocational Choice," *Journal of Counseling Psychology*, 4 (No. 3, 1957), 212-217; *id.* and Marvin Siegelman, *The Origins of Interests* (Washington, D.C.: American Personnel and Guidance Association, 1964); P. M. Blau *et al.*, "Occupational Choice: A Conceptual Framework," *Industrial and Labor Relations Review*, 9 (No. 4, 1956), 531-543; H. B. Gelatt, "Decisionmaking: A Conceptual Frame of Reference for Counseling," *Journal of Counseling Psychology*, 9 (No. 3, 1962), 240-245; T. L. Hilton, "Career Decision-making," *ibid.*, 291-298; D. B. Herschenson and R. M. Roth, "A Decisional Process Model of Vocational Development," *ibid.*, 13 (No. 3, 1966), 368-370; J. L. Holland, "A Theory of Vocational Choice," *ibid.*, 6 (No. 1, 1959), 35-45; *id.*, "Major Programs of Research on Vocational Behavior," in *Man in a World at Work,* ed. Henry Borow (Boston: Houghton Mifflin, 1964), 259-284; *id.*, "A Psychological Classification Scheme for Vocations and Major Fields," *Journal of Counseling Psychology*, 13 (No. 3, 1966), 278-288; *id.*, *The Psychology of Vocational Choice: A Theory of Personality Types and Model Environments* (New York: Ginn, 1966); *id.*, *Making Vocational Choices: A Theory of Careers* (Englewood Cliffs, N.J.: Prentice-Hall, 1973); R. J. Havighurst, "Youth in Exploration and Man Emergent," in *Man in a World at Work,* ed. Borow, 215-236; D. E. Super, "A Theory of Vocational Development," *American Psychologist*, 8 (No. 5, 1953), 185-190; *id.*, *The Psychology of Careers* (New York: Harper and Row, 1957); *id.*, "Vocational Development Theory: Persons, Positions and Processes," *Counseling Psychologist*, 1 (No. 1, 1969), 2-14; *id.*, "The Natural History of a Study of Lives and Vocations," *Perspectives on Education*, 2 (1969), 13-22; *id.*, "Les Théories du choix professionnel: Leur évolution, leur condition

courante et leur utilité pour le conseiller," *L'Information scolaire et profession-nelle dans l'orientation: Approche multidisciplinaire*, ed. Claude Laflamme and André Petit (Sherbrooke: Centre de documentation scolaire et professionnelle, Faculté des Sciences de l'Éducation, Université de Sherbrooke, 1973), 45-64; D. E. Super *et al., Vocational Development: A Framework for Research* (New York: Bureau of Publications, Teachers College, Columbia University, 1957); *id. et al., Career Development: Self-Concept Theory* (New York: College Entrance Examination Board, 1963); D. V. Tiedeman and R. P. O'Hara, *Career Development: Choice and Adjustment* (New York: College Entrance Examination Board, 1963); D. B. Hershenson, "A Life Stage Vocational Development System," *Journal of Counseling Psychology*, 15 (No. 1, 1968), 23-30.

4. Havighurst, "Youth in Exploration and Man Emergent"; Hershenson, "A Life Stage Vocational Development System"; Ginzberg *et al., Occupational Choice;* Eli Ginzberg, "Toward a Theory of Occupational Choice: A Restatement," *Vocational Guidance Quarterly*, 20 (No. 3, 1972), 169-176; Tiedeman and O'Hara, *Career Development*; Super, "A Theory of Vocational Development"; *id., The Psychology of Careers*; *id.*, "Vocational Development Theory"; *id.*, "Les Théories du choix professionnel"; *id. et al., Vocational Development; id. et al., Career Development.*

5. J. P. Guilford, *The Nature of Human Intelligence* (New York: McGraw-Hill, 1967); *id.* and Ralph Hoepfner, *The Analysis of Intelligence* (New York: McGraw-Hill, 1971).

6. Guilford and Hoepfner, *The Analysis of Intelligence.*

7. J. P. Jordaan, "Exploratory Behavior: The Formation of Self and Occupational Concepts," in Super *et al., Career Development*, 42-78.

8. S. R. Maddi, "Exploratory Behavior and Variation Seeking in Man," in D. W. Fiske and S. R. Maddi, *Functions of Varied Experience* (Homewood, Ill.: Dorsey Press, 1961), 265.

9. David Lester, "The Effect of Fear and Anxiety on Exploration and Curiosity: Toward a Theory of Exploration," *Journal of General Psychology*, 79 (1968), 105-120.

10. Guilford, *The Nature of Human Intelligence*, 220.

11. *id.* and Hoepfner, *The Analysis of Intelligence*, 187.

12. *Ibid.*, 86.

13. D. E. Berlyne, *Conflict, Arousal and Curiosity* (New York: McGraw-Hill, 1960), 282.

14. Guilford and Hoepfner, *The Analysis of Intelligence*, 187.

15. *Ibid.*

16. F. Barron, "The Disposition toward Originality," *Journal of Abnormal and Social Psychology*, 51 (No. 3, 1955), 478-485; A. J. Cropley, *Creativity* (London: Longmans, Green, 1967); J. Kagan, *Creativity and Learning* (Boston: Beacon Press, 1967); D. W. Mackinnon, "The Nature and Nurture of Creative Talent," *American Psychologist*, 17 (No. 7, 1962), 484-495; P. E. Vernon, *Creativity* (London: Penguin Books, 1970).

17. D. E. Super, "Vocational Development in Adolescence and Early Adulthood," in Super et al., Career Development, 79-95.

18. Guilford and Hoepfner, The Analysis of Intelligence, 121-122.

19. Super, "Vocational Development in Adolescence and Early Adulthood," 87-88.

20. Guilford and Hoepfner, The Analysis of Intelligence, 288.

21. Super, "Vocational Development in Adolescence and Early Adulthood."

22. Guilford and Hoepfner, The Analysis of Intelligence, 142-150.

23. Havighurst, "Youth in Exploration and Man Emergent," 221.

24. Super, "Vocational Development in Adolescence and Early Adulthood," 87.

25. F. C. Bartlett, Thinking: An Experimental and Social Study (New York: Basic Books, 1958).

26. Denis Pelletier, Gilles Noiseux, and Charles Bujold, Développement vocationnel et croissance personnelle: Approche opératoire (Montreal: McGraw-Hill, 1974), Chapter 3.

27. Denis Pelletier, "Une methodologie radicalement nouvelle de l'orientation scolaire et professionnelle," paper presented at the Colloque en Information scolaire et professionnelle, Université de Sherbrooke, April 1973.

28. E. T. Gendlin, "A Theory of Personality Change," in Personality Change, ed. P. Worchel and D. Byrne (New York: John Wiley, 1964), translated as Une théorie du changement de la personne, by F. Roussel (Montreal: Centre interdisciplinaire de Montréal, 1970).

29. Guilford, The Nature of Human Intelligence; id. and Hoepfner, The Analysis of Intelligence.

30. J. Dewey, How We Think (Boston: D. C. Heath, 1910); G. Wallas, The Art of Thought (London: Watts, 1926); J. A. Rossman, "A Study of the Childhood, Education and Age of 710 Inventors," Journal of the Patent Office Society, 17 (1935), 411-421; G. Polya, How to Solve It (Princeton, N.J.: Princeton University Press, 1945); D. M. Johnson, G. R. Parrot, and R. P. Stratton, "Production and Judgment of Solutions to Five Problems," Journal of Educational Psychology, 59 (No. 6, Pt. 2, 1968), 1-21; C. E. Gregory, The Management of Intelligence: Scientific Problem Solving and Creativity (Toronto: McGraw-Hill, 1967); H. E. Gruber, G. Terrel, and M. Wertheimer, Contemporary Approaches to Creative Thinking (New York: Atherton Press, 1967); K. Duncker, "On Problem Solving," Psychological Monographs, 58, No. 5 (Washington, D.C.: American Psychological Association, 1945); C. P. Duncan, Thinking: Current Experimental Studies (Philadelphia: Lippincott, 1967).

31. Guilford, The Nature of Human Intelligence, Chapter 14.

32. See, for example, J. Moreno, The Theatre of Spontaneity (New York: Beacon House, 1947); W. C. Schutz, Joy (New York: Grove Press, 1967); J. S. Bruner, Toward a Theory of Instruction (New York: W. W. Norton, 1966); W. J. J. Gordon, Stimulation des facultés créatrices dans les groupes de recherche par la méthode synectique (Paris: Editions hommes et techniques, 1965).

33. Denis Pelletier, Gilles Noiseux, and Charles Bujold, *Activation du développement vocationnel et personnel* (Quebec: Université Laval, 1971). Research project No. DGES-FCAC-72-04, under a grant from Gouvernement du Québec (Programme de formation de chercheurs et d'action concertée).

7
To Think of Beauty

In introducing Dupont's chapter, I spoke of missing pieces in the puzzle of human growth. The contribution by Parsons, Johnston, and Durham on the development of aesthetic experience in children and adolescents is another such link.[1] It is included not because it posits definite stages in aesthetic judgment nor even suggests that they exist, but because of its heuristic value to both psychology and education. The chapter describes the evolution in our response to art, of the way in which our perception, understanding, feeling, and judgment of paintings progress. Beauty is not exclusively in the eye, the mind, or the heart of the beholder; it is in the interaction of all three with art. It is not surprising that we learn what is beautiful. That people understand art through common lenses, thoughts, and feelings and that aesthetic judgments evolve through predictable stages are quite different matters, however, to those who see the definition of beauty as ultimately personal, an expression of individual uniqueness or taste. If there is a stage behind every Picasso, what does that tell us? Parsons and his colleagues feel that human response to art is not random, idiosyncratic, or elusive. A science of aesthetic judgment is possible. A unitary development may underlie the arts as a whole, and that development would enable us to educate all people more intelligently and comprehensively for the aesthetic in life. We need not be so dependent on the notion of special artistic gifts, which, among other limitations, creates its own elitism.

The following piece is noteworthy in several other ways. First, the authors argue that the application of Piagetian stages of scientific thinking to aesthetic judgment would be an error. This is so because scientific and artistic thinking are really not alike and because the application is insufficiently radical: "it does not take seriously the autonomy of aesthetic experience."[2] Both our experience and our way of thinking about art have a different quality than our reasoning about physical reality. When one considers what has already been said in Part I by Dulit, Broughton, Dupont, and Erikson, as well as the book's general thesis concerning the complexity and wholeness with which human development progresses, he should not find the last statement surprising. In regard to the actual interaction of aesthetic judgment with other forms of thinking—cognitive, moral, social—Parsons and his colleagues can tell us little. But their model clearly points to such studies. For example, are students at the higher stages of aesthetic judgment also advanced in cognitive development, perspective taking, affective development? What are the necessary conditions of aesthetic development? Do students who study art systematically or students who produce it show higher stage development?

The second way in which the piece is noteworthy is that the authors clearly define what they mean by aesthetic development. It is not just the power of one's feelings or affect about art that develops. It is the ability to respond relevantly to a work of art as an aesthetic object that grows, and that requires thinking, which is a cognitive achievement. The authors argue against isolating and studying children's judgments of art. We need to look, rather, at their whole experience of, say, a painting—their perceptions, ideas, feelings, and judgment—and try to reconstruct the implicit way they think about art. To analyze that progressive construction of relevant aesthetic understanding is the task of the psychologist; to use such knowledge in the individualization of aesthetic education is the task of the teacher.

The third contribution of the authors is that they are not advancing a definitive theory of aesthetic development. "We are, therefore, unable to this point to speak of aesthetic stages in general, that is, stages across all topics."[3] Neither the most mature nor the least mature stage of aesthetic judgment is described or validated empirically. The former is, however, philosophically anticipated and described in the work of Monroe Beardsley.[4] Thus, we have a case for what ought to be but not what is. This we might call the philosopher's fallacy—of going from ought to is. And the samples from which Parsons and his colleagues derive their stages are preliminary. But they candidly admit this, and they invite replication studies.

The fourth contribution is the authors' terse and cautious comments concerning the educational applications of possible stages in the development of aesthetic judgment. If we assume the existence of such stages, can we aim educationally to stimulate children's progression to "higher" stages? The answer is that we do not really know. It seems likely that viewing art, discussing it in groups (especially where children can benefit from higher stage thinking), and doing it (painting, dancing, writing, performing) will stimulate development. This is particularly likely since, as the authors say, "in our culture individuals are exposed unevenly to the arts. Moreover, many people do not encounter the arts frequently; nor do they often debate questions concerning them."[5] Parsons and his colleagues make one other comment on the present state of our psychological knowledge of aesthetic development that is equally applicable to the way we should educate for it: "We are limited [only] by our ingenuity and our data."[6]

The fifth contribution is the authors' recognition that they do not yet know how their data fit together into aesthetic stages in general. But they believe that when stages of aesthetic development are validated they will apply "potentially to the arts." Such a unitary development underlying the arts as a whole will, however, require "a serious engagement with each art for its actualization."[7] Parsons and his colleagues have made a beginning. They have challenged psychology to describe a unitary development underlying the arts as a whole and education to actualize that human capacity.

Notes

1. Michael J. Parsons, Marilyn A. Johnston, and Robert F. Durham, "A Cognitive-Developmental Approach to Aesthetic Experience," in *Adolescents' Development and Education: A Janus Knot*, ed. Ralph L. Mosher (Berkeley, Calif.: McCutchan Publishing Corp., 1979), Chapter 7.

2. *Ibid.*

3. *Ibid.*

4. Monroe Beardsley, *Aesthetics: Problems in the Philosophy of Criticism* (New York: Harcourt, Brace and World, 1958).

5. Parsons, Johnston, and Durham, "A Cognitive-Developmental Approach to Aesthetic Experience."

6. *Ibid.*

7. *Ibid.*

A Cognitive-Developmental Approach to
Aesthetic Experience

Michael J. Parsons
Marilyn A. Johnston
Robert F. Durham

This contribution, devoted to a discussion of a cognitive-developmental approach to the aesthetic experience of children, presents some of the assumptions such a project requires, together with certain relevant findings in the literature. These assumptions are followed by a summary of the results of an initial empirical inquiry.

The focus is on the aesthetic experience of children, which includes judgments of and responses to works of art and is much broader than their creative abilities in the arts. A cognitive-developmental theory would undertake to trace the cognitive elements that underlie aesthetic experience, assuming that they determine, to some significant extent, the nature of that experience. The descriptions of these elements would have to be stated in terms that make clear both the way in which the aesthetic responses of children and of adults differ and the reasons for which these differences are relevant to their aesthetic character.

This is not a new idea. Although developmental psychologists as a group have not in the past been greatly interested in development in the arts, the question of aesthetic development has been approached in several different ways, and interest in the area has grown recently. The psychoanalytic school has studied the development of practicing individual artists.[1] Much work has been done on the developing abilities of the average child in making art, especially painting and drawing.[2] James Mark Baldwin's theory of development included an aesthetic stage,[3] and both Piaget and Werner and Kaplan have touched upon it in their studies of the development of the use of symbols.[4] Howard Gardner has made the most direct and recent approach.[5] He is interested not only in the use of symbols in general but particularly in those uses that constitute art, and not only in the child as a practitioner of art but also as a responder to it. His work also includes a useful review of the literature.

An early verson of the first two sections of this contribution appeared in the *Journal of Aesthetics and Art Criticism*, 34 (Spring 1976). Most of the third section appeared in the *Journal of Aesthetic Education*, 12 (January 1978). Both are reprinted with the publishers' permission.

In spite of the existence of the above studies, the cognitive-developmental approach has not been explored in any thoroughgoing way. There are a number of reasons for this situation, and Gardner discusses some of them.[6] For example, he is most concerned to warn against the temptation to import the Piagetian stages into the aesthetic realm and to apply them to the way children think about art objects. The work of Machotka,[7] which will be reviewed below, is the best example of an attempt to do this. This approach cannot, however, take one very far. It seems unlikely that the advent of concrete and formal operations (which determine the chief stages of the development of scientific thinking) will be of primary importance in developing aesthetic judgment. The approach is not sufficiently radical: it does not take seriously the autonomy of aesthetic experience. Its effect is to treat aesthetic objects as if they were any other object and aesthetic concepts as if they were similar to nonaesthetic concepts. But this seems wrongheaded. Concepts like art, form, and expression combine with each other ("make a structure"), and not with concepts like space, length, and volume because the latter are ingredients in a different normative experience. Aesthetic experience is not a kind of scientific experience; nor is aesthetic judgment a kind of scientific judgment. There is virtual unanimity on this among philosophers, and, unless they are all wrong, it seems there should be a correspondingly distinct developmental history to be investigated. If aesthetic judgments and experience are sui generis, a developmental account of them must have its own categories and definitions. The same can be said, of course, of moral judgments, and perhaps also of religious ones.

The above does not necessarily mean that aesthetic development is unrelated to development in terms of operational thinking. Whether it is or is not cannot be decided in advance of the facts. It may be that operational thinking is necessary for aesthetic development, but it cannot be sufficient because some experience with the arts (how much and of what kinds are not clearly known) is also necessary. But the important point is that the one cannot be used to define the other.

One problem with speaking of a distinctive aesthetic development in the child is that it ignores important distinctions within the arts. It implies that development in all arts is the same and can be described in the same terms, and it ignores the differences between the various art forms and media, the different kinds of skills they call for, and the uneven development of individuals with respect to them. These differences might suggest that there is unlikely to be some unitary development underlying the arts as a whole; perhaps, rather, there is a separate development with respect to each art form. At this point it can only be said that this is ultimately an empirical question, for which the evidence is not available. The empirical work for this essay consisted only of studying what children said of paintings. But it seems reasonable to speak of aesthetic experience and aesthetic judgments, and to do this is not to pick out any particular art form or medium. It can be assumed, therefore, that the development described applies potentially to all the arts, but also that it requires a serious engagement with each art for its actualization. Shortage of time alone would account for its unequal unfolding in individuals in all the arts. Also, in our culture individuals are exposed unequally to the arts. Moreover, many people do not encounter the arts frequently; nor do they often debate questions concerning them.

A further obstacle to a cognitive-developmental theory is based on the view that what is distinctive about the arts is their power to engage feeling, and, therefore, a cognitive theory is inappropriate. Such a view might hold that, if there is a development, it will be one of affective abilities, and cognitive elements or structures will miss this. This seems to be, in various forms, a commonly held view. Gardner's distinction between the "audience member" and the "critic" lends it credence, though his distinction is adopted for another purpose.[8] This objection is founded on a view of the relation between cognition and affect; it is with this view that a cognitive-developmental approach would have to take issue. We assume that cognition and affect interact to a significant degree in both children and adults. Affect is certainly important in aesthetic response, but what develops is not just the power of feeling, which the young child already has. It is the power of relevant feeling that develops. Thus, aesthetic development consists of the ability to respond relevantly to a work of art as an aesthetic object. This ability rests on a cognitive achievement, as the word "relevant" makes plain. And, for this reason, the development of both aesthetic judgment and aesthetic experience are considered parts of a single whole. It is not enough to study, as is sometimes done, judgments in isolation from whatever else people have to say about their experience of a work of art. When one tries to articulate that experience, he reveals (imperfectly, of course) what he thinks is relevant about the work. Thus, what one thinks is relevant will affect what he looks for in the work, and, hence, what he sees and what he responds affectively to. No doubt the reverse relation is also true: what affects one in a work will influence what he thinks is relevant to look for and will provide possible reasons for judgments.

There is no reason to believe that there is a direct relationship between what affects an individual and the reasons he gives for his judgments. The limits of self-awareness and the poverty of language make this unlikely, especially with children. Given also our capacities for stereotyping and overlooking, it is equally unlikely that there is no connection at all. Thus, if one thinks it relevant to say that a patch of color is his favorite color, he is not likely to examine it closely enough to notice variations of tone and hue. Or, if one's vocabulary for praise and disapproval is limited to "beautiful" and "ugly," how can he be anything but confused by, say, Beckett's plays, or Picasso's *Guernica*?

In fact, a cognitive-developmental theory requires a varying discrepancy between what affects a person and what he can articulate. As in the areas of moral and scientific development, such a discrepancy is the motive force behind development. When one begins to be affected by new kinds of things in works of art, he strains to revise what he thinks can relevantly be said about them; when affect and articulation are more in equilibrium, the person is at a relatively stable stage. "Relevant" here means aesthetically relevant, that is, relevant to a response or judgment concerned with the work as an aesthetic object. As has been said, this sense of relevance is the core of development in this area. One could, instead, speak of the development of a "theory" of aesthetic relevance, though not, of course, of a self-conscious or articulated theory. This formulation would stress the parallel developments of scientific and moral judgments in the theories of Piaget and Kohlberg.

One can arrive at such a "theory" in the same way that Piaget and Kohlberg have. He can look at children's judgments concerning particular works of art and the reasons given for them and try to reconstruct what lies behind the judgments and the reasons. This is not very different from what the philosophers of criticism have tried to do with the language of critics, though, of course, they work with a higher level of cognitive sophistication.

The final and perhaps the most important obstacle to constructing a cognitive theory of aesthetic development has been simply the difficulty of conceiving the terms in which to couch it. Before one can profitably discuss judgments and reasons with children, with an eye to reconstructing implicit cognitive structures, he needs some conception of what to look for. This conception, as has been said, must rest on a view of what is distinctive about aesthetic experience across the arts and of what is different about the experience of the child and the adult. What follows is meant to illustrate the possibility with data from a study concerned with painting. At this point the account should be considered plausible rather than conclusive and should suggest parallel inquiries that might be conducted in connection with music, literature, dance, or other art forms.

Aesthetic Judgment: What We Now Know

It is necessary to look briefly at some of the already known facts a theory of aesthetic development would have to explain.

A number of studies of the aesthetic judgments or preferences of children have been undertaken for various purposes, though most of them have not been guided by developmental considerations. Two important exceptions are the studies by Machotka and by Gardner, Winner, and Kircher.[9] Machotka deduced several hypotheses from the nature of the Piagetian stages of formal and concrete operations, all of which his findings tended to support. He reasoned that the interest in realism, and the use of criteria related to it, which is commonly observed in children, should appear with the advent of concrete operations (around the age of seven). He argued that to judge a painting in such terms requires a comparison of the painting as a picture with the appearance of the objects depicted in the real world. He found, in fact, that reasons related to realism did first appear at about seven years and that their number grew steadily until they peaked at about eleven years. He also reasoned that references to formal qualities, such as balance, harmony, and contrast, should first appear with the beginning of concrete operations and increase in frequency thereafter. This also seemed to be correct. Before age seven, the emphasis is on subject matter and color. The overwhelming importance to young children of subject matter in paintings is often commented on in the literature and is described in various ways, such as an interest in an abundance of detail and a failure to take note of the nature of the medium. Gardner, Winner, and Kircher, who questioned children closely about their conceptions of art, also found that their results "mirror Piagetian trends" in a general way, but with some limitations. They add at least two interesting facts about opinions during the adolescent years. Only at that time do they find the opinion that art requires native ability, talent, or genius, as opposed to simply hard work or skill. Also, there is a kind of relativism in judgments, which the authors interpret as a return to the relativism of the early years, which has been interrupted by a period of increasing respect for the criteria of realism and the authority of experts.

Child[10] discovered that, when college students make choices between pairs of works, they distinguish preference from judgments of aesthetic value, but that children in the first through the fifth grade do not. For the latter group there appears to be no difference between liking a work and judging it as good.

Finally, there are some suggestive findings concerning the expression of emotions. Bullough, studying the judgments of adults, and following him Myers and Valentine,[11] distinguished four common kinds of reasons for judgments:

Objective: remarks about the content of the work, the grouping, and so forth;

Subjective: remarks about the effect of the painting on oneself ("the picture makes me smell the sea and hear the waves");

Associative: remarks about what one is reminded of, or made to think of;

Character: remarks about the character or the emotional qualities seen in the work itself.

Bullough and Valentine tended to see these as types of judgment related to types of character in people, but clearly it is possible to look at these categories as potentially forming a developmental sequence. Moore[12] attempted to do this, hypothesizing that the fourth category ("character") would come last developmentally. His results showed, indeed, that the youngest children gave the most "objective" reasons (dominance of subject matter) and that the oldest gave the most "character" reasons. Both Child and Machotka made a distinction that seems related to that between the second and third categories and the fourth. Child tried to distinguish between what he called sentimental responses and emotional responses. He found that the first were most characteristic of elementary school children, but, unfortunately, there was poor interjudge reliability concerning the second. Machotka distinguished reasons relying on "empathetic identity" from those referring to the "global" character of the work; the latter appeared in his sample only after the age of twelve.

How might a developmental theory explain these and other facts? Below is an empirically based account of stages in the development of aesthetic experience that seems to encompass both these facts and additional data. The major thread running through these stages consists of two parts: one psychological and the other aesthetic. The first entails a progressive decrease in egocentricity of response; the second involves a progressive increase in relevance to the aesthetic object. The structure behind these stages consists essentially in the way the aesthetic qualities of an object are conceived. What varies is the location of these qualities as between the person and the object. At the beginning, children speak as if these qualities are very close to the self, as if there is no distance between the object and the self. Later, they are conceived of as residing in varying sets of rules, though the authority embodied in these rules shows a progressive decentering. Finally, though the data do not reach this far, aesthetic qualities are thought of as qualities of the object itself, as being in principle publicly accessible and based on the perceptual or intentional aspects of the object.[13] At the same time, the kinds of qualities thought to be relevant are progressively differentiated. Initially they include memories, private preferences, associations of all kinds; ultimately aesthetic matters are more clearly distinguished from moral and other considerations. If one focuses on judgment rather than aesthetic experience in general, he can conceive of these stages in terms of their relation to rules. First, there are no rules; next, there is a set of rather clear and rigid rules; then, in adolescence, there are many and conflicting sets of rules (a phase in this scheme that would cover the relativism spoken of by Gardner); and, finally, the multiplicity of competing rules is settled by principles of relevance, that is, any quality is relevant that is public and is based on the perceptual or intentional aspects of the object. Any developmental scheme implies a normative conception of the end state to which development leads. In this case it is necessary to give an account of the kinds of features of aesthetic objects found to be relevant in the aesthetic experience of sophisticated adults. This is, of course, primarily a matter for the philosophy of art, or at least of art criticism, and all that can be done here is to point to the tradition on which this scheme has relied. According to that tradition, what is finally found to be important about a painting (considered as an aesthetic object) is its appearance—whatever is phenomenally available to the perception of any qualified observer. Our understanding of the meaning of this has relied heavily on the work of Monroe Beardsley.[14] At the adult level it may sometimes be difficult to decide whether a particular quality meets this criterion (for example, the faint sadness of a line), but with the earlier stages it is usually not. For example, the following (when given as a sufficient reason for judgment) seem to be irrelevant according to almost anyone's theory: "It's my favorite color"; "It took a long time to paint"; "I disapprove of boxing and people hitting each other." Further examples abound in what follows.

The Development of Aesthetic Experience: An Empirical Study

Following are the results of a study that used the foregoing ideas. The account, written as descriptively as possible, begins with a brief explanation of the methodology.

Methodology

We showed three large reproductions of well-known paintings to students individually from the first through the twelfth grade (thirteen from each grade) and asked them questions relating to the topics discussed below. The usual precautions were taken to make the child feel at ease and to point out that the situation involved no right or wrong answers. The topics and questions were prepared and practiced in advance, but the discussions were loosely structured, to allow further exploration of points as it seemed desirable. For the first six grades the paintings were Klee's *Head of a Man*, Picasso's *Weeping Woman*, and Renoir's *Girl and a Dog*; for the last six grades they were Bellows' *Dempsey and Firpo*, Picasso's *Guernica*, and Chagall's *Circus*.

The transcripts were analyzed in two steps: identification of sense units (those passages, long or short, in which the respondent discussed some one identifiable idea relating to the painting) and their assignment to one of our topics; assignment of each unit within a topic to a stage. The second was done without knowledge of grade level. We began with descriptions of topics and stages, but the process of matching these with the data made it necessary for us to modify our descriptions and, in some cases, to scrap them and start over. It also caused us to see various inadequacies in the interviews themselves. By holding descriptions stable and taking random samples, however, we obtained an interjudge reliability of over 90 percent between the three of us on both operations—assigning units to topics and to stages.

Having assigned sense units to stages, we returned to the transcripts to match stages with grade levels. Where a student had several sense units on one topic and those units were not all scored at the same stage, we assigned the student to the highest stage reached within the topic. Table 7-1 gives the average stage level of the thirteen students in each grade for each topic and demonstrates a satisfactory directionality for the stages. The apparent regression in the topics "subject matter" and "color" between the sixth and seventh grade we attribute largely to the use of different reproductions, which elicited slightly different kinds of information. We should caution that we do not regard these figures as proof; only longitudinal studies could approach that status.

Table 7-1
Average stage score for each topic by grade level

Grade	Semblance	Subject matter	Feeling	Artist's properties	Color	Judgment
First	1.0	1.0	0.9	1.6	1.5	1.2
Second	1.0	1.1	0.9	2.0	1.5	1.7
Third	1.0	1.2	1.0	1.9	2.0	2.0
Fourth	1.0	1.2	1.0	2.0	1.9	1.8
Fifth	1.2	1.5	1.0	2.0	2.0	1.9
Sixth	1.7	1.8	1.0	2.1	2.0	2.0
Seventh	1.7	1.3	1.5	2.4	1.4	2.2
Eighth	2.0	1.3	1.2	2.3	1.8	2.0
Ninth	2.5	1.6	1.9	2.9	2.3	2.6
Tenth	2.8	1.8	2.1	2.8	2.5	3.3
Eleventh	2.4	2.2	2.1	3.2	2.4	3.0
Twelfth	2.9	2.5	2.3	3.6	2.8	3.1

Topics and Stages

We were able to identify six topics that revealed developmental levels. A "topic" is a coherent unit of discussion on which students were able to offer opinions and reasons for opinions. Although there appear to be logical relations between topics, we have not worked them out because our data did not seem sufficient to provide empirical support. We are, therefore, unable to this point to speak of aesthetic stages in general, that is, stages across all topics. A premature attempt to generalize in this way would tend to shut off further research rather than to stimulate it. Thus, we present the topics one by one, each followed by the stages within them.

We should emphasize that we do not think we have identified all the important topics or stages within topics. We are limited by our ingenuity and our data. It seems particularly evident that there must be both earlier and later stages than the ones described. Since we did not interview preschool children nor postsecondary students, we have no data for them, and so they are not included. In some cases it is quite clear that there must be an earlier stage than the ones we report; for example, in our first topic, all the children we interviewed already understood that paintings can refer to something by pictorially representing it. We assume that this is an idea that must be learned, though we have no data on how or when this learning takes place.

Topic I: Semblance. This topic is meant to cover the range of possible views concerning how and whether a painting refers, or what makes it a "picture." We were able to distinguish three stages within this topic.

Stage 1. Dominating this first stage is the idea of representation. It is presumably a new achievement, which distinguishes this from an earlier stage. We know from studies of children's drawing activities that for the very young a scribble is a scribble, a line is a line, and a color is a color. There are no pictures; paintings are not "about" something. In the first stage the idea of picturing by representing is taken for granted, and attention is concentrated far more on subject matter than on anything else.

Paintings depict objects by representing their important features, both what can be seen and what is known to be true about them. For instance, a person's head must have two eyes, a nose, and a mouth, and a hand must not have six fingers. Representation is considered item by item; the whole may or may not be distorted or out of proportion. Of primary importance is that the painting be comprehensible; one must be able to recognize what is represented. Often this is articulated as the demand that things look "real" or like they are "supposed to." We call this the stage of "schematic realism." Examples of it follow.

Boy, Second Grade [Picasso]

Q.: Is this the way you'd expect a painting of a weeping woman to be painted?
A.: No.
Q.: Why?
A.: When someone cries that's not how he looks. The other eye is supposed to be over here, not there.
Q.: What do you think the artist should have done differently?
A.: Put the eye over here, put another finger on that hand.

Girl, Fourth Grade [Picasso]

Q.: How can you tell a good painting from a bad painting?
A.: You can tell what it is if it's a good painting.

Stage 2. The new distinction achieved at this stage is that between schematic and visual realism. Paintings are still required to represent and to look "real," but what is to be represented is the visual appearance of objects, rather than simply what is known about them. "Real" means what objects look like, rather than what they are commonly known to be. This constitutes a more precise set of expectations, which we called "photographic realism." The change requires a further degree of de-centering because it takes account of what others know about the object— what can be seen by anyone. Discussions of Picasso's *Weeping Woman* best illustrate the shift. The youngest students objected to the placement of two eyes on one side of the face and to the fact that the eyes looked like "boats," and yet they usually did not object to the hands. While the hands are contorted, they do have five fingers and fingernails, as hands are "supposed to."

Boy, Second Grade [Picasso]

Q.: What about the eyes?
A.: They're weird, and they shouldn't both be on the same side.
Q.: What about the hands?
A.: They're OK.
Q.: Do you think the artist should have done them any differently?
A.: No, they're OK.

Older students objected to the hands also. Although the hands had five fingers and fingernails, they were not enough like "real" hands.

Girl, Sixth Grade [Picasso]

Q.: What about the hands?
A.: They're weird.
Q.: Is there anything he should have done differently?
A.: Made the hands look like real hands.

Girl, Sixth Grade [Picasso]

Q.: What about how he made the hands?

A.: The fingers are weird cause they don't go like a real hand.

Stage 3. The demand for "realism" is dropped, except in cases where the painting seems to require it. Otherwise, various styles and degrees of abstraction and distortion are accepted. There is increased awareness of, and tolerance for, a variety of kinds of painting, intentions of the artist, and responses by the viewer. The criterion for deciding how paintings should picture objects is usually inferred from the painting as a whole. For example, the artist's intention is often appealed to, or a genre, however vague (such as "modern art"), is considered. Again, this seems to require an advanced perspective since it acknowledges the possible multiplicity of intentions, points of view, or responses to an object.

Girl, Eighth Grade [Chagall]

Q.: What do you think the artist should have done differently?

A.: He could have made it more real, if he wanted to, but for this kind of painting, I think it's good.

Boy, Twelfth Grade [Picasso]

Q.: Would this be a better painting if it were more realistic?

A.: I think it is better the way it is, abstract, or even more so, in a way. This relates to the total confusion of the situation.

Girl, Tenth Grade [Chagall]

Q.: Would this be a better painting if it were more realistic?

A.: No, I don't think so. If he's trying to show his feelings, and if this is what his feelings are, then this is the way the painting should be.

Boy, Twelfth Grade [Chagall]

Q.: Would this be a better painting if it were more realistic?

A.: I don't think so, because photographs will capture action, but I think the artist tried to go inside of the action, and I think a simple photograph or reproducing it on a painting just reduces the effect of what this tries to do.

Topic II: Subject Matter. This topic includes all views on the kind of subject matter that is appropriate or acceptable in a painting, where "subject matter" means what is referred to or what is pictured. The first topic (semblance) concerned the way paintings refer; this topic concerns what is referred to. Though we found that we could make this distinction quite reliably, there is a close parallel between the stages in the two topics. In each we found three, and we conjecture that there is an earlier one for which we had no evidence.

Stage 1. At this stage the character of the subject matter dominates the response to a painting. The child thinks paintings should be about pleasant, interesting, and usual subjects. They should, for example, depict happy rather than sad things, and it is better if there is some action. There is an implication that appropriate subjects are a matter of common consensus: that it is obvious that people prefer pleasant to unpleasant subjects, and, also, that everyone will agree what is pleasant. We take this to be a sign of relative egocentricity.

Girl, Second Grade [Picasso]

Q.: What do you think painters should paint about?
A.: Happy things and pretty things.

Boy, Third Grade [Picasso]

Q.: Is this the kind of thing you'd expect an artist to paint about?
A.: No, 'cause I sometimes look at sad paintings, and I get tears in my eyes, and I just want things to come out all right. I don't like sad things.
Q.: Is it good to paint about things that are sad?
A.: No, I like paintings to be nice and not about sad things.

Stage 2. The range of suitable subjects expands to include much that was previously thought unsuitable, particularly sad, nostalgic, and unpleasant subjects. Violent, cruel, or tragic themes are, however, still rejected, often on moral grounds. The moral grounds are not always clear; "Most people wouldn't like that" is often given as a reason for rejecting a subject. There is also a more explicit appeal to what other people like and dislike.

Boy, Fifth Grade [Renoir]

Q.: Is this a good thing to paint about, a girl and a dog?
A.: Yeah.
Q.: Why:
A.: 'Cause . . . I like animals.
Q.: It's a good thing to paint about animals?
A.: Yeah.
Q.: What if this was a sad painting about an animal, like the dog was hurt or something bad had happened to him? Would that be a good thing to paint a painting about?
A.: Yeah, 'cause it would show that dogs get hurt . . . it would show that animals get hurt.
Q.: What if it were about something mean, like someone being mean to an animal?
A.: I wouldn't like that.
Q.: Would that be a good thing to paint about?
A.: I don't think so.

Girl, Tenth Grade [Bellows]

Q.: Is boxing the kind of subject that you would expect people to paint about?

A.: No, because it's portraying violence, and I don't think many people like that.

Boy, Tenth Grade [Picasso]

Q.: Is this the kind of thing you'd expect an artist to paint about?

A.: Sort of, but not this way, because people don't like to look at it. This is a sad picture, they look at it, not as something to relate to, but they look at the parts all mangled, and people don't want to look at that. When parts of the body are missing people don't like to keep that in their mind. Most war pictures are painted about people who have just been shot and are laying on the ground, but this picture has people all in different pieces, and it's not how most war paintings would be painted.

Stage 3. Good art can be made of any subject, including violence, cruelty, and tragedy. Moral objections are finally abandoned as irrelevant to art. Appropriateness of subject matter is determined by considering various criteria, such as the viewer's responses or the reality of the theme. There is a much greater awareness of the variety of possible attitudes toward any subject. In addition, what is referred to is often formulated as something more abstract than in previous stages, for example, "winning and losing" and "sadness at war."

Boy, Twelfth Grade [Chagall]

Q.: Is this the kind of thing you'd expect an artist to paint about?

A.: Yes, because I think that a circus has overtones on life. In a sense it represents life and is also a chance to get away from life. It offers the painter a wide range of possibilities; whatever meanings he's trying to get across, he can probably take a circus and find a place to use those ideas.

Boy, Eleventh Grade [Picasso]

Q.: Is this the kind of thing you'd expect an artist to paint about?

A.: Yeah, for someone who has lived through an experience. I wouldn't expect someone who has read about it, but for someone who was in the town and for him to come out and to paint something like this, I wouldn't think him off his rocker because in an abstract way it's captured all the feelings and expressions and things that went on in that time.

Girl, Twelfth Grade [Picasso]

Q.: Do you like this painting?

A.: I like it because wars are sometimes necessary. I think there are other ways to solve things; I think since I was born I can remember war going on with one country or another, and it is a fact, and I would buy it because it represents it and the people.

Topic III: Feelings. The key question in this topic is: what kinds and sources of feelings are influential in the aesthetic response? As already indicated, we assume that the aesthetic response includes affective components, but that affect may be more or less clearly based on the aesthetic object. Again, we were able to distinguish three stages.

Stage 1. Here the child focuses on particular characters in the painting one at a time and attributes feelings to them. In doing this he is guided as much, or more, by the overt subject matter as by the expressiveness of painting. He uses stereotypes and implies that others have motives and feelings similar to what his own would be. He does not see subtle, complex, or ambiguous feelings.

This is an advance on the stage that, we presume, precedes it. The child focuses on the painting itself and is guided by what he sees far more than previously. He is not a prey to arbitrary associations and distinguishes more clearly what he sees from what he is reminded of. Nor does he project so freely his own feeling into the painting. If asked how the painting makes him feel, he usually identifies the emotion attributed to a major character.

Girl, Eighth Grade [Bellows]
Q.: What kind of feeling would you say is in this painting:
A.: Hatred.
Q.: Why's that?
A.: Because they are fighting.
Q.: Is that the main feeling, or are there other feelings?
A.: I think that's the only one.
Q.: What feeling do you get when you look at this painting?
A.: The feeling of hatred, like out to kill.

Girl, Seventh Grade [Chagall]
Q.: What kind of feeling would you say is in this painting?
A.: Like someone at a circus.
Q.: Is it a happy feeling or a sad feeling?
A.: These people up here look like they are having a good time.
Q.: Is there one or many feelings in the painting?
A.: There can be more than one feeling.
Q.: What other feeling is there?
A.: You can see someone looking at someone else.
Q.: What feeling do you get when you look at this painting?
A.: They look like they are happy.

Stage 2. The distinction between one's own feeling and that attributed to characters in the painting is made explicit at this stage. One's own feelings often derive from prior views of subject matter—interest, moral disapproval, boredom, personal sympathy, and so forth. This rests on a new understanding that different people may respond in different ways to the same painting, and particularly that one's own feelings may not be shared by everyone. Although attention is still on individual characters considered one by one, rather than on the painting as a whole, there is greater tolerance of ambiguity of feeling both in oneself and in a painting.

Girl, Tenth Grade [Bellows]

Q.: What kind of feeling would you say is in this painting?

A.: Excitement, because all of the people around the ring are cheering him on.

Q.: Would you say there is one or many feelings?

A.: There's probably many.

Q.: What other feelings would you say are there?

A.: These other people here are afraid because they are scared something is going to happen to that guy. He might hurt himself.

Q.: What feeling do you get when you look at this painting?

A.: Emptiness really, like if I were to go to one of those fights, I'd probably be bored stiff.

Boy, Ninth Grade [Bellows]

Q.: What kind of feeling would you say is in the painting?

A.: Well, sadness and gloom on one side and roaring emotion on the other.

Q.: Which one do you think is the strongest?

A.: The roaring emotion, because everybody is cheering the guy that knocked the other guy down into the stands.

Q.: What kind of feeling do you get when you look at the painting, what emotion?

A.: I feel sorry for the guy that's falling over, and I feel sorry for the guy underneath too.

Girl, Eleventh Grade [Chagall]

Q.: Well, what kind of feeling comes across from the painting?

A.: Well, sort of a happy feeling if you like circuses, but I hate circuses.

Q.: What kind of feeling do you get when you look at the painting, what emotion?

A.: I don't get feelings out of the picture; I don't enjoy pictures like that.

Stage 3. This stage generalizes beyond the feelings of individual characters to the emotional impact of the painting as a whole. In order to do this, the person may or may not adopt the point of view of the artist, that is, he may speak of the artist's feelings or intentions. Or he may adopt the point of view of the "universal spectator." Again, this seems to require advanced perspective-taking abilities. The distinction between one's own and others' feelings is very clear, and the person can set aside his own feelings as prejudices, when they are not relevant. Feelings are seen as complex and particular.

Boy, Eleventh Grade [Chagall]

Q.: What kind of feeling would you say is in the painting?

A.: Well, I think he's sort of mocking the circus with this, and without the head, and a few of these things like that.

Girl, Twelfth Grade [Bellows]

Q.: What kind of feeling would you say is in the painting?

A.: Like I said, some would say violence, but I would say anticipation.

Q.: Anticipation of what exactly?

A.: Well, it's a battle of physical prowess, and you fight it out to the end, and one is beaten, and one has made the better showing. I'm not happy about it; I don't like to see people hurt. It's not that; it's just that if you're a boxing buff that's what you want to see, and that's what he's got down here.

Girl, Twelfth Grade [Picasso]

Q.: What kind of feeling would you say is in the painting?

A.: Confusion and fear.

Q.: Why do you get that?

A.: Because you don't know what it's about. You look at all of the mouths, and they are trying to scream; this person over here looks like she is looking for light and doesn't know where to go; and this guy here in the corner, he's screaming like let me out.

Q.: What feeling do you get when you look at this painting?

A.: In a way, it's very strange because I wish I could help. I wish something like that wouldn't happen. Maybe Picasso was trying to get his point across saying why do you do this? Look what it does to the people: look what happens. It makes you feel like you are guilty almost, like this is your doing.

Topic IV: Color. Here we looked more particularly at an element of the medium itself—color. The basic question shaping this topic is: what is it about color that is pleasing, or, what constitutes goodness of color in a painting? Children seem to find this the most readily intelligible and easily answered question of all ("Are these good colors?" "What makes them good colors?"), and the answers fall into three rather clear levels. We tried to do the same thing with other particular aspects of painting, especially with "form," but could not get worthwhile results. There is no doubt that more work with topics of this kind is merited.

Stage 1. Young children appear to respond very directly to color. They delight in color itself, relishing colorfulness and preferring bright, gay, distinct colors. They feel that any color is better than no color (black and white) and that many colors are better than few. They have strong preferences for some colors over others. Brightness is preferred to dullness. Their choices are egocentrically based. "It's a good color" means much the same as "I like the color"—a situation sometimes summed up by "It's my favorite color." The term "favorite" seems to indicate a relation between the color and the individual that does not acknowledge the presence of others. It names a quality of the color as most important ("being my favorite"), which is inaccessible to others and cannot be seen by them.

Young children do not look closely at particular patches of color; they seem content to recognize the color rather than to realize its particular qualities in the particular instance. In other words, red, not a particular patch of red, is the favorite. It is as if the general color word acts as a kind of prejudice that bypasses the need for closer scrutiny of individual patches. Thus, although children are very responsive to color at this stage, it is paradoxical that they do not individuate them very well.

When children were asked how they could tell "good colors," typical responses included: "I look at 'em," "They're bright, and they show up," and "They're my favorites."

Boy, First Grade [Klee]

Q.: Which painting do you like best?
A.: This one.
Q.: The Klee? Why?
A.: It has more colors. This one has more colors, too.
Q.: Which do you like best?
A.: This one [Renoir] has more colors, and this one [Klee] doesn't have green.

Boy, Second Grade [Picasso]

Q.: What do you think about the colors?
A.: I don't know; I don't like 'em.
Q.: How come?
A.: They're all dark, and they don't look good.
Q.: What would have been better?
A.: If they looked like this [Renoir]. It needs to have a lot of colors.

Stage 2. At this stage there is a new sense of the appropriateness of color. This is clearly dependent on the notion of realistic representation discussed under the topic "semblance." Colors are good if they are appropriate to the subject represented, that is, if they are "realistic." Vocabulary at this stage included "real," "right," "proper." Some typical responses to the question "What makes these good colors"? include: "'Cause there's dogs that color and dresses that color." "'Cause when you look at a real person like that you think that's what it would look like." "Well, you know, it's just like if it wasn't a painting it would really look like that."

There was little doubt about how one tells that a color is realistic, what things really look like, or who is to decide such matters. It was assumed that everyone thinks the same and that the colors of things are obvious and indisputable. This implies continued stereotyping and is similar to the assumptions in the first stage of "subject matter" and of "feelings."

One noticeable difference from the first stage is that a painting might have "too many" colors, as several children said of the one by Klee.

Girl, Sixth Grade [Klee]
A.: It's got weird colors, too.
Q.: What's weird about the colors?
A.: Too many colors on the face.

Stage 3. At the third stage there is a greater sense of the appropriateness of color: colors should be appropriate to the whole painting, to its mood and its theme. Appropriateness also includes realism, which is synonymous with the "intention of the artist." What is new is the view that colors can express emotion or mood directly, without the necessity for realism in every case. This view only emerged clearly among students in the last years of high school.

Girl, Twelfth Grade [Picasso]
Q.: What do you think about the choice of colors for this painting?
A.: I like them because, when you think of war, you think of everything being dark and gloomy, but if it had to be changed I think it would be darker because when you think of death, you think of darkness.

Boy, Twelfth Grade [Picasso]
Q.: What do you think of the colors that were used for this painting?
A.: I thought they were a good choice, not real sharp black and whites, mostly a gray, and it seems to bring out the darkness and the fury and panic and death.

Topic V: The Artist's Properties. This topic deals with children's views of what it takes to be a good artist. We asked what an artist would need to paint a good painting, and, in particular, what would be difficult about it. We use the label "The Artist's Properties" because the first stage is not concerned with personal qualities. Development through the four stages of this topic most obviously reveals an increasing ability to see a painting from the point of view of the painter and a growing awareness of the importance of the affective and emotional in art.

This topic is further removed from actual paintings than the others since it is overtly about artists. The artists involved are not usually particular people, however, but are generalized, as in "anyone who painted this painting . . . ." The topic is, moreover, clearly normative since it refers to qualities needed to paint a good painting.

Stage 1. Young children mentioned only physical items as necessary to paint a good painting. Characteristic responses include: "A brush and paint and some water to get the paint out of the brushes." "Lots of colors and a paintbrush." "Just a paper and paints to color it."

The implication seems to be that anyone who has the physical equipment could paint well. When children at this stage were asked which paintings would have been hardest to do, they chose the largest ones, those with most colors and objects represented in them, and those with small spaces to put colors.

Stage 2. At the second stage the artist's attributes were mentioned most. While these are personal qualities, they are not really individual. They include manual skill, perseverance, patience, hard work. Time is also frequently mentioned. It is assumed that the harder a painting is to do, the better it is. This amounts to admiration for craftsmanship, which has often been thought the beginning of aesthetic appreciation.

Girl, Fourth Grade [Renoir]
Q.: Why would this painting be hard?
A.: They'd have to try really hard to get the drawing right, and it might take a month to draw one thing.

Boy, Second Grade [Klee]
Q.: What does it take to paint a painting like this?
A.: It takes time, and you really have to work at it.

Girl, Sixth Grade [Klee, Renoir]
Q.: Which do you think would be the hardest painting to paint?
A.: The first [Renoir] because it would be hard to get the colors in it, and it has a lot of details.

Boy, Fifth Grade [Klee, Renoir]
Q.: Would the Renoir be harder or easier than the Klee?
A.: Harder because it has more things in it, and it's real.

Stage 3. Here, children become aware of mental abilities as being essential. An artist has to know what to do, to know what things look like, and to be able to think of things to paint. Often this means having seen the reality and noticed carefully how things look. At other times it means thinking carefully about the subject and how to represent it. There is a stress on the cognitive, rather than the experiential or affective, results of these activities.

Boy, Ninth Grade [Chagall]
Q.: What do you think it would take on the part of the artist to paint this picture?
A.: He had to study for a long time, I guess. He had to go to a lot of concerts, a lot of ballets to learn the forms, and he had to study the people who were doing it. Just things like that, he'd have to know a lot about it.

Girl, Eighth Grade [Chagall]

Q.: What do you think it would take on the part of the artist to paint this picture?

A.: Well, he probably went to a circus and sort of imagined from some of the things that were seen, and I think he probably saw a guitar and made an animal out of it, from the animal in the circus, and he sort of departed things like the body from her head, and made different things out of the original picture.

Boy, Ninth Grade [Picasso]

Q.: What do you think it would take on the part of the artist to paint this picture?

A.: I'd say a lot of thought and a lot of imagination, the way he doesn't paint all of the people realistic; they are just all distorted, their hands and faces, and I think that's a part of it which shows confusion.

Stage 4. In the final stage, affective qualities are considered more essential to the artist than cognitive ones. Experience is necessary more because it affected the artist than because it gave him ideas or knowledge. Creativity, meaningfulness, and talent are largely matters of feeling.

Boy, Eleventh Grade [Picasso]

Q.: What do you think it would take on the part of the artist to paint this picture?

A.: He'd have to experience almost everyone of those feelings that's represented by different animals and things, in order to capture it like he has, because he's done a good job as far as the animals and the woman, plus he would have to have been there. He probably would have been against the people who were bombing.

Q.: How do you get that?

A.: If he was for the bombers then he would have made the people look small and weak and very scared and showed it as them being the people in trouble, whereas I get the impression from this as being for them and relating to what they felt.

Girl, Twelfth Grade [Picasso]

Q.: What do you think it would take on the part of the artist to paint this picture?

A.: I think the person that painted it must have gone through a lot of suffering.

Q.: How can you tell?

A.: Just the expression on people's faces; they look helpless.

Girl, Twelfth Grade [Picasso]

Q.: What do you think it would take on the part of the artist to paint this picture?

A.: It seems like he can kind of remove himself from the whole situation, and he kind of sees the war in a way and shows the uselessness of it and the agony that people experience and the destruction, and, in a way, it gives the feeling of how useless it all is.

Girl, Twelfth Grade [Picasso]

Q.: What do you think it would take on the part of the artist to paint this picture?

A.: I think if he was there during the bombing I think he is a man that has a lot of fear and horror inside of him.

Boy, Eleventh Grade [Picasso]

Q.: What do you think it would take on the part of the artist to paint this picture?

A.: The artist probably had to have been there when it happened, and he might have lost somebody close to him, because it looks like it's all about death and destruction.

Topic VI: Judgment. This topic includes all of the kinds of reasons offered for an aesthetic judgment, that is, anything that is counted as a reason for claiming "this is a good painting." "Judgment" is different from the other topics in that it can provide a kind of synopsis of any of them. Any view classified in a previous topic can reappear here, reinterpreted as a reason for judgment. This topic is, therefore, at a different level than the others, and it is more comprehensive. We have hesitated to include it because of its nonparallel character, but retain it for two reasons.

The first reason is that it is the culmination of the others, rather than just a repetition; it is a focal point, not just another section. Aesthetic experience naturally leads to, includes, and rests upon aesthetic evaluations, though these are not always explicit. This is to say that it is a form of experience with its own normative structure, and it is the development of this structure, as filtered through the abilities of children, with which we are centrally concerned.

The second reason is that, as a separate topic, it contains some new distinctions. For instance, in no other topic is it clear, although it may be implicit, that the youngest children cannot tell the difference between judgment and preference; that is, they have not mastered the concepts necessary for making this distinction. In the first stage, the meanings of "I like this painting" and "I think this is a good painting" are indistinguishable. We interpret this again as early egocentricity. This is significantly different from the "relativism" of the fourth stage, where it may be claimed that, for example, "I think this is a good painting" *means* "I like this painting." In the first case the distinction at issue is overlooked or ignored. The second presumes that distinction, simply because it is a denial of its importance or meaningfulness. It is a reaction, perhaps, to the intermediate stages in which the distinction is first learned and taken for granted, but it is not a return to the first. We would argue that it is, rather, an advance over the previous stage in the same direction that previous movement

had pointed: diminished egocentricity and greater relevance to the aesthetic object. Hence the whole is better described as a development than
as a circular path.

Stage 1. In the first stage, reasons for judging a painting as good were
based directly on personal preferences. Hence they were often idiosyncratic, dogmatic, or both. Children could not distinguish preference from
judgment; they used "I like it" interchangeably with "It's good." There
were not, however, many cases of this.

Boy, First Grade [Renoir]
Q.: Do you think this is a good painting?
A.: Yeah.
Q.: Why?
A.: I just like it.

Boy, Fourth Grade [Klee, Picasso, Renoir]
Q.: Which do you like the best of the three paintings?
A.: Probably this one.
Q.: The Renoir? Why?
A.: 'Cause I like pets. I have one dog, one bird, two cats, and a horse.

Stage 2. The main criteria for judging a painting at this stage are:
the amount of time and effort it took; the manual skill involved; the
amount of detail; the degree of realism achieved. Criteria such as these
implicitly acknowledge the experience of others because they appeal to
features that are not idiosyncratic, but are thought to be there for anyone
to see. They constitute a lever by which to create the distinction between
judgment and preference and are a milestone of decentering in aesthetic
experience.

These criteria are taken for granted, not argued for; the similarity of
everyone's perceptions is also taken for granted. Characteristic reasons
for judging a painting good include the following: "The colors mainly
make it good." "It's done very carefully." "It has good colors, and things
look right." "He made the outlines just right." "It looks like the real thing."
"It has lots of good details." "It has a lot more things in it, and it would
be harder to draw and put everything in it."

Stage 3. The criteria for judgment expand and change at this stage; of
primary importance is whether a painting is expressive. This is sometimes
thought of as cognitive—"conveys a message"—and sometimes as affective—"expresses an emotion." The criteria of skill, effort, and realism
found in the second stage are retained only as instrumental to these effects.
What is expressed is often vaguely conceived, but it is assumed that the
message or emotion is unambiguous.

Boy, Twelfth Grade [Bellows]

Q.: Now this is more realistic, and you said you don't like it?

A.: I don't like the subject matter and feeling. That Dempsey painting may be doing what it's supposed to do; I mean it's a really popular painting; it's been around; and it's supposed to make you hurt. I mean a painter is supposed to arouse an emotion whether it's negative or positive, but I don't like it.

Girl, Tenth Grade [Picasso]

Q.: Would you say that you like this painting, or you don't like this painting?

A.: I don't like it.

Q.: Why?

A.: It's good for what he's feeling. It's a good painting for after war, but I just don't like it.

Q.: Can you tell me why?

A.: It's not something you'd like hanging in your room; it's not a very happy picture.

Q.: So you're saying you don't like it because it's not happy?

A.: Well, it is just ugh!

Q.: Would you say that this is a good painting, or it's not a good painting?

A.: I think it's a good painting because it shows all of his real feelings. If you look at it, you can tell what his real feelings are.

Stage 4. The distinguishing feature of this stage is that the criteria for judging are seen as depending on the circumstance: the artist's intention, the beholder's response, or the genre or style to which it belongs. The emphasis is still on expressiveness, but how, what, and whether something has been expressed is a matter for interpretation. Sometimes the criteria of the second stage (especially realism) apply, because of the artist's intention or because of considerations concerning genre. This seems to constitute an advance in perspective-taking ability in that it is no longer assumed that everyone interprets a painting in exactly the same way. The result is sometimes what can loosely be termed "relativism" with respect to aesthetic judgments—the view that "It is a good painting" means "I like it" or "The artist likes it." This is not always so. There is also the view, for instance, that a painting is good if it is exactly as the artist intended it to be. We do not suppose that this is the final stage of aesthetic judgment, but it is the last one we could distinguish.

Girl, Seventh Grade [Bellows]

Q.: Would you say that you like this painting, or you don't like this painting?

A.: Yeah, it's OK. It would be nice for a tourist to see, like Muhammad Ali, if he comes in, and he could picture what happened.

Q.: Would you say that this is a good painting, or it's not a good painting?

A.: In a way yes and in a way no. Like some older people might not enjoy it because it would take a violent act to do this, and why can't they just be nice?

And some younger people would say, it's all right and if you want to fight, then go fight, and they'd say this guy is strong because he won the crown.

Boy, Twelfth Grade [Chagall]

Q.: Would you say that this is a good painting, or it's not a good painting?

A.: Well, the artist has talent obviously. As far as talent goes I can say that it's good, but as far as—I can't say too much for his style.

Q.: You say he obviously has talent. What shows you that?

A.: Just some of these pictures, the heads, the details. It's just like music; you may not like country western music, but you can say he has talent. So he obviously has talent, but I don't like it.

Girl, Twelfth Grade [Picasso]

Q.: Would you say that you like this painting, or you don't like this painting?

A.: I don't think I like it because, I think—not because it scares me, I think that has a little to do with it—but I don't like the way it was done.

Q.: You just don't like it?

A.: Yeah. It could be because it bothers me.

Q.: Would you say that this is a good painting, or it's not a good painting?

A.: I think it's a good painting because he portrays emotion. It's like a poem; if you don't like it, it's just a bunch of jumbled words unless it has meaning to you. This would have meaning.

Boy, Tenth Grade [Picasso]

Q.: Would you say that you like this painting, or you don't like this painting?

A.: I really don't like it.

Q.: Why don't you like it?

A.: It's something that doesn't interest me, and it's sort of abstract. I wouldn't mind having it to sort of sit back and try and interpret it.

Q.: Would you say that this is a good painting, or it's not a good painting?

A.: I think that depends on the artist, like what point he was trying to get across. It's good if he accomplished that, and if he didn't, then it's bad.

Q.: So you'd say you would probably have to know what the artist intended?

A.: Yeah.

Educational Implications

We have presented our findings to date as descriptively as our admittedly interpretive framework allows. We think the right conclusion is that a cognitive-developmental approach along these lines is plausible. We do not think we have identified all of the topics and stages of the development of aesthetic response. We consider the foregoing account a stimulus to further research, and we hope that it will be so. It needs corroboration, and it suggests a great number of further questions. Any further program of inquiry would, of course, need to be a fairly long-term effort. It seems reasonable to ask in the meantime, however, what the "educational implications" of a scheme like this might be. We will address this question very briefly, recognizing that one can only speak tentatively.

It seems to us easy (and common) to overstate the importance of cognitive-developmental schemes for educators. We would not want to say that a scheme like the above, were it well founded, would define *the* aim of teaching art in the secondary schools. We might say that, insofar as there is already commitment to the aim of enhancing appreciative abilities in the education of the average student, then this aim might be clarified by such a scheme. And, as a matter of fact, there is a contemporary movement among art educators that does favor increased emphasis on such an aim—a movement for what is sometimes called "aesthetic education."[15] This is, of course, the normal thing to say about cognitive-developmental schemes. We think it might be particularly important in art education because of the unusual difficulties in clarifying what "appreciative abilities" are. Art educators probably have more trouble articulating their aims clearly than teachers in any other area. They must rely primarily on intuition and personal experience in the selection of materials or the choice of day-to-day objectives. Most art educators know that their principal goal is not to provide knowledge about art (either its history or techniques), to furnish a vocabulary in which to talk about it, nor to pass on conventional judgments of aesthetic merit. They realize, on the other hand, that they are obligated to do more than promote a kind of standard-free, free-association response in which everyone does his own thing. For this reason we think that a knowledge of the cognitive structures underlying our stages would be helpful to the profession.

An example may be helpful. The similarities between the attitudes of the very young and of adolescents have struck a number of observers. As we have seen, both groups are more disposed to accept abstraction and distortion than the intermediate group. Both are less conventional in their preferences, less rigid in their approach. Gardner, in the study cited earlier, sees adolescents' tendency toward relativism in judgment as a return to the freedom of the early years. Both groups seem to have more interest in the emotional and personal aspects of art. All this, combined with the unalloyed enjoyment of art by young children, and the frequent excellence of their products, has led at times to the view that the normal path of development in this area is at best circular, and at worst a decline. Our schools and the character of society at large have been variously blamed for this.[16]

This kind of romanticism can be paralyzing to educators since it gives them little to teach and much to worry about. The aim is to protect the "innocent eye" of the young child, but the deleterious effects of the late elementary school years are seen as more or less inevitable. Any cognitive-developmental scheme, on the other hand, will interpret these facts as progressively developmental: the adolescent differs from the late elementary school child in the same way and in the same direction as that child differs from the very young. It stresses the much greater reflectiveness of the adolescent; his increased awareness of the nature of art, and its expressivity; his sense of the multiple interpretations possible, and of the variety of possible criteria that might apply; his differentiation of kinds of experience and judgments; and so on. We think that the details supplied in this contribution have already made this view plausible. If then, in addition, it is true that the average level of attainment of adults, in cognitive-developmental terms, is lower in the arts than in other areas, art educators have a positive task ahead of them. The school is the only institution in American society where most people are likely to be exposed to a wide range of aesthetic objects, in a context of discussion, stimulation, and the kind of cognitive conflict that might help them develop further. We see this as an important aim for schools. A well-conceived account of development could provide suggestions for the necessary curriculum and instruction and for modes of ascertaining success in detail. In view of the present state of knowledge, it seems premature to say more than this. We hope we have said enough to encourage continuing inquiry in the field.

Notes

1. See, for example, Otto Rank, *Art and Artist: Creative Urge and Personality Development* (New York: Alfred A. Knopf, 1932).

2. See, for example, Victor Lowenfeld and W. Lambert Brittain, *Creative and Mental Growth*, 5th ed. (New York: Macmillan, 1970); and R. Kellogg, *Analyzing Children's Art* (Palo Alto, Calif.: National Press Books, 1969).

3. James Mark Baldwin, *Thought and Things*, Volume 3 (London: Swann Sonnenschein, 1911), esp. Parts 4 and 5.

4. Jean Piaget, mostly in *Play, Dreams and Imitation* (New York: W. W. Norton, 1962); and H. Werner and Bernard Kaplan, *Symbol Formation* (New York: John Wiley, 1963).

5. Howard Gardner, *The Arts and Human Development* (New York: John Wiley, 1973).

6. *Ibid.*, 304-310, 323-329.

7. Pavel Machotka, "The Development of Aesthetic Criteria in Childhood," doctoral dissertation, Harvard University, 1961; and *id.*, "Aesthetic Criteria in Childhood: Justifications of Preference," *Child Development*, 37 (December 1966), 877-885.

8. See Gardner, *The Arts and Human Development*, 323, 324.

9. Machotka, "The Development of Aesthetic Criteria in Childhood"; *id.*, "Aesthetic Criteria in Childhood"; Howard Gardner, Ellen Winner, and M. Kircher, "Children's Conceptions of the Arts," *Journal of Aesthetic Education*, 9 (July 1975), 60-77.

10. Irvin Child, *The Development of Sensitivity to Esthetic Values* (New Haven, Conn.: Yale University, 1964).

11. Summarized in C. W. Valentine, *The Experimental Psychology of Beauty* (London: Methuen, 1962), 53-57, 123-135, 203-208.

12. Barry Moore, "A Description of Children's Verbal Responses to Works of Art in Selected Grades," *Studies in Art Education*, 14 (Spring 1973), 27-34.

13. This view of the end state is based in particular on the work of Monroe Beardsley, especially his *Aesthetics: Problems in the Philosophy of Criticism* (New York: Harcourt, Brace and World, 1958), and this formulation is based in particular on his "Aesthetic Theory and Educational Theory," in *Aesthetic Concepts and Education*, ed. R. A. Smith (Urbana: University of Illinois Press, 1972); and, for music education, in Bennett Reimer, *A Philosophy of Music Education* (Englewood Cliffs, N.J.: Prentice-Hall, 1970).

16. See, for example, Herbert Read, *Education through Art* (New York: Pantheon Books, 1958).

II
Education for Adolescent Development

Part I of the book described adolescence as modern developmental psychology understands it. The special nature of teenagers' logical thinking, moral reasoning, affect, their development of identity and other broad interrelated paths along which they grow were discussed in detail. The aim was to present contemporary developmental theories that explain what is happening with our teenagers. Such knowledge and understanding obviously can be very important to any professional or parent who deals with them. A number of educators have already gone further and have begun to apply that knowledge in creating curricula and in initiating instruction to enhance adolescent growth. The estate labels on the educational bottles are somewhat confusing: "Psychological Education," "Developmental Education," "Toward Affective Development," "'Just Community' High School," "Education for Social Action"—to mention a few. All of them have as one aim to enhance the personal development of teenagers.

Part II describes some of these practical programs. It does not presume to tell the whole story of an education to enhance adolescents' growth, any more than Part I could be definitive on how they come of age. It is addressed to educators—administrators, teachers, counselors, curriculum directors, psychologists, other professionals, and parents interested in using developmental theory to advance development. The basic purpose is to justify, define, and make concrete what is meant by an education to stimulate teenage growth. There is an important shift here from the study, description, and analysis of how teenagers develop to ways education may enhance that development. That Part I came into being largely independent of a concern for educational application is clear; that Part II reports original educational development, informed by psychological knowledge of adolescents, will be apparent. A basic thesis is that both our theoretical understanding of teenagers and an education for their development now can be advanced to great advantage by a progressive interdependence.

Part II begins with a theoretical justification for development as the aim of education. Otherwise, we could commit the naturalistic fallacy— deciding that what is, in human development, is what should be. Many people in this country do not learn to read. That fact of arrested human development obviously does not mean that we should educate for illiteracy. Quite the contrary, we must educate to avoid arrested development. The theoretical case for education as a means of helping people grow is, thus, of prime importance. Not only do we argue that this is the vital concern of education, but we describe how to create the educational practices to implement it.

The major purpose of Part II is to present enough concrete, tested examples of developmental education so that readers can judge for themselves how a psychological understanding of teenagers can be translated into practical courses and more general changes in schools to enhance students' growth. There is also another message: there is no mystery here, and there are no practices hopelessly beyond the resources of teachers with the brains to read and the guts to try. What is required is a willingness to see adolescents in a fresh way, to consider their subjectivity to be at least as important as our subjects, and to sharpen our crafts of designing curricula and of teaching.

The examples of education to effect development are discussed along a continuum: from how growth may be brought about within the existing high school curriculum (for example, in the teaching of subject matter) to a more radical and comprehensive involvement with the community and the family in programs for adolescent development. The former is feasible now; the latter demands greater commitment to the development of youth and involves more people and programs working toward that goal. This will require additional time and effort by educators and many others, but the prototypes are clear and compelling. And a considerable body of data indicates that this kind of education does what it sets out to do: stimulate teenage growth. A separate section of Part II is devoted to the significant effects on adolescents' moral and social development of being involved in efforts to make their schooling more democratic or participatory. This means that students share in decisionmaking and responsibility in matters of the school's governance and their social and institutional life together and in the effort to individualize their teaching.

In summary, American history that teaches adolescents to reason about moral issues; courses that contribute to women's development; adolescents' participation in governing their school or classroom; social service and action to influence public affairs in the larger community and helping families make more democratic, shared decisions are concrete examples of what it is now possible to do in enhancing the personal development of adolescents by education. The examples are substantial but are only part of a vigorous, continuing effort in research and development; thus, they are subject to disproof, improvement, and obsolence. Indeed, if many of the practices described in Part II are not supplanted in five years by more substantial, and especially systematic, courses and curricula, the metaphor of development will not have been served. The point is that much of the story of how adolescents mature and how education can interact with that process remains to be understood. It is to be hoped that this book brings the essentials of what is presently known to the attention of the profession. If it fuels and excites the further elaboration of an education that recognizes and responds to the real complexity of adolescent growth, being, and coming of age and the need for more people and more institutions to be partners in that process, it will have served our young people well and truly.

8
Education for
Human Development:
The Theoretical Case

Chapter 8 makes the case for development as the aim of education. Before brief overviews of the three principal contributions in this section are presented, several questions about education for development need clarifying. Piaget talks about "the American question" or "How do we accelerate development?" The vision of our children being pushed prematurely to consider career goals, to become more self-reliant, to reason at Stage 3 ("good-boy-good-girl" morality), to score in the 600's on an achievement test of nonacademic attributes is *not* what this book is about. Stimulating human development by education could be misunderstood or misapplied in this way. Career education in elementary school may be an example. Part II propounds the idea that education can contribute to the normal all-around growth of each child. More particularly, that means trying to avoid arrested development, the problem of children lagging behind broad developmental averages. Selman has described the individual costs to such children fixated at low levels;[1] the fact that our prisons are full of adults at Kohlberg's Stages 1 and 2 has incalculable social costs. Put another way, this means we need education that can help all people achieve enhanced (potentially mature) competence, whether that be formal thought, conventional-postconventional morality, or the ability to exercise influence in public affairs. The objective is to effect all-around, mature competence for more people and to support appropriate progress toward full maturity in each developmental period—not to make children adults sooner.

For example, adolescents need educational opportunites to learn fully and to consolidate conventional morality. To learn to care for others—friends, children, the ill, the aged—to exercise a wider social responsibility; to understand the relationship of authority and laws to the maintenance and effective functioning of social groups; to see the tie between the benefits accorded to individuals by groups and the concomitant responsibility of the individual to the group constitute subtle, developmentally appropriate understanding for adolescents to be acquiring. That understanding cannot be hurried; neither should it be neglected. It is not fully mature moral thought, but it is a critical stage in the passage to maturity. And it carries with it obvious social benefits. Thus, it should be consolidated by education in its own right.

Whether development is sufficient has been questioned in several ways. Greenberger and Sorensen ask: "Are attributes of individuals which are useful to society also optimal from the perspective of the individual's growth in his own right? Are societal and psychological views of the person identical?"[2] Their answer is to construct a conception and a measure of students' personal and social growth—of psychosocial maturity—to cut through the welter of values, traits, attitudes, and nonacademic attributes that, it is argued, schools should promote.

Purpel, in a recent commentary on development as the aim of education, says: "The concept of growth as a goal by itself is troublesome to me since it begs the question of the value of a particular stage of growth. Do our responsibilities as educators end if a person is at Stage 5, has a strong ego, can deal with abstractions fluently, has a positive self-image, and plays a smooth, well-coordinated, graceful tennis game? Are we as pleased with educating a person to become an Alan Greenspan as a Ralph Nader? What purpose and what meaning does the struggle for maturity have? Can we as educators go beyond growth as a value in itself?"[3]

Dewey argued long ago that the basic environment in which we grow is social and that the ultimate purpose of our life is to improve the common good:

As the material of genuine development is that of human contacts and associations, so the end, the value that is the criterion and directing guide of educational work, is social . . . . Perhaps the greatest need for a philosophy of education . . . is the urgent need that exists for making clear in idea and effective in practice that its end is social, and that the criterion to be applied in estimating the value of the practices that exist in schools is also social. It is true that the aim of education is devlopment of individuals to the utmost of their potentialities. But this statement in isolation leaves unanswered the question as to what is the measure of the development. A society of free individuals in which all, through their own work, contribute to the liberation and enrichment of the lives of others, is the only environment in which any individual can really grow normally to his full stature. An environment in which some are practically enslaved, degraded, limited, will always react to create conditions that prevent the full development even of those who fancy they enjoy complete freedom for unhindered growth.[4]

The point is clear. Development, per se, as the aim of education can be seen to avoid the issue of social purpose. What is worse, it may be interpreted to mean privatism. Implicitly, it does not. An enlarged social and moral perspective and commitments are at the heart of modern conceptions of the individual's development. To grow as an individual means to consider the rights of others, to care about one's neighbors, to share responsibility for the common welfare. The most mature stages of cognition, morality, and ego enable the individual to think about the broadest possible implications; to comprehend the greatest good, justice, and human dignity as universal principles and requirements; to see the interdependence of one's own freedom to develop with that same opportunity for all other people. Mature and complex ways of thinking or principles such as these produce certain social arrangements. They do not, in themselves, specify the particular constitutional, legislative, or judicial content of these social contracts. Indeed, by definition, only complex social forms could embody or actualize such principles.

In America, for a combination of historical and cultural reasons (including the influence of English common law, parliamentary and constitutional democracy, the American Revolution, and the Judeo-Christian ethic), mature human competencies are expressed within social democracy and vice versa. Democracy in America has a historical, political, and social life of its own quite apart from its impact on psychological development. It is a remarkable evolutionary invention by which a society may govern itself, share power, rights, and responsibilities; rationalize its social life in terms of the common good, shared purposes, and mutual caring; accord dignity and justice to the individual. From the point of view of the need for an institution to ensure optimal human development, however, if democracy did not exist, we would have to invent it. Dewey said that the crucial test of any institution is the extent to which it contributes to the all-around growth of every member of the society. Democracy, then, because of its commitment to the general welfare, to social justice, to participation by citizens in deciding public policy as well as to the enhancement of individual development and dignity is the ideal form of governance and way of living together. Individual development and a democratic society are inextricably tied and are synergistic. Education thus must aim to promote both. The purpose of this book is to translate the broad aims of individual development and social democracy into consistent, valid educational practices. Newmann's article on citizenship education in Chapter 11 and Chapter 12, which deals with efforts to democratize schooling, make the general case for democracy as education.

Development as the Aim of Education: Theoretical Roots

Kohlberg and Mayer look to progressive education and John Dewey for the roots of this view of education and then examine the psychology and philosophy that underlie it. They argue that human development is the essential purpose of education and that growth is best understood as the person's progression through stages of understanding of himself and his world. Thus, we grow as our thinking is stretched to fit what we experience and do in our social world, and the "higher" stages of human development not only provide wider views and options but also produce more humane, ethical people.

Sprinthall and Mosher's review of Dewey is similarly central to the justification of human development as the aim of education. If classic statements of the bridge between psychology and educational practice to enhance development presently exist, this contribution is one of them. Its focus, which is both analytical and wide ranging, is on adolescence, the schools teenagers attend, and developmental education as it relates to adolescents—issues that are at the core of this book. Educators should find the essay particularly helpful because it identifies the kind of developmental education programs that are already available and presents findings about their effects on adolescents. The point is that education for human development is more than pie in the sky or an excited workshop at the National Council for the Social Studies; its programs have psychological and philosophical heft as well as a growing body of research data.

On the Making of Wine

It has already been said that Part II can include only a few exemplary programs for promoting growth in teenagers. Even though the climate for this model of education is somewhat clouded by, among other things, budget cuts, back to basics, and business as usual, a considerable amount of curriculum development and dissemination activity is ongoing nationally. And that is the way things must be if the development of all-around students is again to be a vital concern of the American high school. Finding successful ways to promote developmental psychology among administrators, teachers, and counselors, to introduce them to the means by which these theories are being translated into educational programs to aid adolescent growth, and, most importantly, to help them create developmental courses of their own are essential parts of the tasks of staff development and of dissemination.

Chapter 8 addresses some of these issues. In "Funny Things Happen on the Way to Curriculum Development" the steps in building curricula designed to help people grow are outlined in practical language. The connections between developmental psychology and education to promote human growth are also closely drawn and illustrated. The point of the essay is to demystify both developmental psychology and curriculum development and to assist teachers who want to do something in their own field or courses to enhance the growth of their students. To pursue our metaphor further, educators need recipes for homemade wines, which in many ways are more appropriate than expensive wines with incomprehensible labels and uncertain taste.

Notes

1. Robert L. Selman, "A Structural-Developmental Model of Social Cognition; Implications for Intervention Research," *Counseling Psychologist*, 6 (No. 4, 1977), 5-6.
2. Ellen Greenberger and Aage Sorenson, "Toward a Concept of Psychosocial Maturity," *Journal of Youth and Adolescence*, 3 (No. 4, 1974), 338.
3. David E. Purpel, "Reactions and Reflections," in *Humanistic Education: Visions and Realities*, ed. Richard H. Weller (Berkeley, Calif.: McCutchan Publishing Corp., 1977), 292.
4. John Dewey, "The Need for a Philosophy of Education," in *John Dewey on Education: Selected Writings*, ed. R. Archambault (New York: Random House, 1964), 12.

Development as the Aim of Education

Lawrence Kohlberg
Rochelle Mayer

Three Streams of Educational Ideology

There have been three broad streams in the development of Western educational ideology. While their detailed statements vary from generation to generation, each stream exhibits a continuity based upon particular assumptions of psychological development.

Reprinted from *Harvard Educational Review*, 42 (November 1972), 451-496.

Romanticism

The first stream of thought, the "romantic," commences with Rousseau and is currently represented by Freud's and Gesell's followers. A. S. Neill's Summerhill represents an example of a school based on these principles. Romantics hold that what comes from within the child is the most important aspect of development; therefore the pedagogical environment should be permissive enough to allow the inner "good" (abilities and social virtues) to unfold and the inner "bad" to come under control. Thus teaching the child the ideas and attitudes of others through rote or drill would result in meaningless learning and the suppression of inner spontaneous tendencies of positive value.

Romantics stress the biological metaphors of "health" and "growth" in equating optimal physical development with bodily health and optimal mental development with mental health. Accordingly, early education should allow the child to work through aspects of emotional development not allowed expression at home, such as the formation of social relations with peers and adults other than his parents. It should also allow the expression of intellectual questioning and curiosity. To label this ideology "romantic" is not to accuse it of being unscientific; rather it is to recognize that the nineteenth-century discovery of the natural development of the child was part of a larger romantic philosophy, an ethic and epistemology involving a discovery of the natural and the inner self.

With regard to childhood, this philosophy involved not only an awareness that the child possessed an inner self but also a valuing of childhood, to which the origins of the self could be traced. The adult, through taking the child's point of view, could experience otherwise inaccessible elements of truth, goodness, and reality.

As stated by G. H. Mead: "The romantic comes back to the existence of the self as the primary fact. That is what gives the standard to values. What the Romantic period revealed was not simply a past but a past as the point of view from which to come back at the self. . . . It is this self-conscious setting-up of the past again that constitutes the origin of romanticism."[1]

The work of G. Stanley Hall, the founder of American child psychology, contains the core ideas of modern romantic educational thought, including "deschooling."

The guardians of the young should strive first to keep out of nature's way and to prevent harm and should merit the proud title of the defenders of the happiness and rights of children. They should feel profoundly that childhood, as it comes from the hand of God, is not corrupt but illustrates the survival of the most consummate thing in the world; they should be convinced that there is nothing else so worthy of love, reverence and service as the body and soul of the growing child.

Before we let the pedagog loose upon childhood, we must overcome the fetishes of the alphabet, of the multiplication tables, and must reflect that but a few generations ago the ancestors of all of us were illiterate. There are many who ought not to be educated and who would be better in mind, body and morals if they knew no school. What shall it profit a child to gain the world of knowledge and lose his own health?[2]

Cultural Transmission

The origins of the cultural transmission ideology are rooted in the classical academic tradition of Western education. Traditional educators believe that their primary task is the transmission to the present generation of bodies of information and of rules or values collected in the past; they believe that the educator's job is the direct instruction of such information and rules. The important emphasis, however, is not on the sanctity of the past, but on the view that educating consists of transmitting knowledge, skills, and social and moral rules of the culture. Knowledge and rules of the culture may be rapidly changing, or they may be static. In either case, however, it is assumed that education is the transmission of the culturally given.

More modern or innovative variations of the cultural transmission view are represented by educational technology and behavior modification.[3] Like traditional education, these approaches assume that knowledge and values—first located in the culture—are afterward internalized by children through the imitation of adult behavior models, or through explicit instruction and reward and punishment. Accordingly, the educational technologist evaluates the individual's success in terms of his ability to incorporate the responses he has been taught and to respond favorably to the demands of the system. Although the technologist stresses the child as an individual learner, learning at his own pace, he, like the traditionalist, assumes that what is learned and what is valued in education is a culturally given body of knowledge and rules.

There are, of course, a number of contrasts between the traditional academic and the educational technology variations of the cultural transmission ideology. The traditional academic school has been humanistic in the sense that it has emphasized the transmission of knowledge considered central to the culture of Western man. The educational technology school, in contrast, has emphasized the transmission of skills and habits deemed necessary for adjustment to a technological society. With regard to early education, however, the two variations of the cultural transmission school find an easy rapprochement in stressing such goals as literacy and mathematical skills. The traditionalist sees literacy as the central avenue to the culture of Western man; the technologist sees it as a means to vocational adaptation to a society depending on impersonal information codes. Both approaches, however, emphasize definition of educational goals in terms of fixed knowledge or skills assessed by standards of cultural correctness. Both also stress internalization of basic moral rules of the culture. The clearest and most thoughtful contemporary elaboration of this view in relation to preschool education is to be found in the writing of Bereiter and Engelmann.[4]

In contrast to the child-centered romantic school, the cultural transmission school is society centered. It defines educational ends as the internalization of the values and knowledge of the culture. The cultural transmission school focuses on the child's need to learn the discipline of the social order, while the romantic stresses the child's freedom. The cultural transmission view emphasizes the common and the established; the romantic view stresses the unique, the novel, and the personal.

Progressivism

The third stream of educational ideology which is still best termed "progressive," following Dewey,[5] developed as part of the pragmatic functional-genetic philosophies of the late nineteenth and early twentieth centuries. As an educational ideology, progressivism holds that education should nourish the child's natural interaction with a developing society or environment. Unlike the romantics, the progressives do not assume that development is the unfolding of an innate pattern or that the primary aim of education is to create an unconflicted environment able to foster healthy development. Instead, they define development as a progression through invariant ordered sequential stages. The educational goal is the eventual attainment of a higher level or stage of development in adulthood, not merely the healthy functioning of the child at a present level. In 1895, Dewey and McLellan suggested the following notion of education for attainment of a higher stage: "Only knowledge of the order and connection of the stages in the development of the psychical functions can insure the full maturing of the psychical powers. Education is the work of supplying the conditions which will enable the psychical functions, as they successively arise, to mature and pass into higher functions in the freest and fullest manner."[6]

In the progressive view, this aim requires an educational environment that actively stimulates development through the presentation of resolvable but genuine problems or conflicts. For progressives, the organizing and developing force in the child's experience is the child's active thinking, and thinking is stimulated by the problematic, by cognitive conflict. Educative experience makes the child think—think in ways which organize both cognition and emotion. Although both the cultural transmission and the progressive views emphasize "knowledge," only the latter sees the acquisition of "knowledge" as *an active change in patterns of thinking* brought about by experiential problem-solving situations. Similarly, both views emphasize "morality," but the progressive sees the acquisition of morality as an active change in patterns of response to problematic social situations rather than the learning of culturally accepted rules.

The progressive educator stresses the essential links between cognitive and moral development; he assumes that moral development is not purely affective, and that cognitive development is a necessary though not sufficient condition for moral development. The development of logical and critical thought, central to cognitive education, finds its larger meaning in a broad set of moral values. The progressive also points out that moral development arises from social interaction in situations of social conflict. Morality is neither the internalization of established cultural values nor the unfolding of spontaneous impulses and emotions; it is justice, the reciprocity between the individual and others in his social environment.

Psychological Theories Underlying Educational Ideologies

We have described three schools of thought describing the general ends and means of education. Central to each of these educational ideologies is a distinctive educational psychology, a distinctive psychological theory of development.[7] Underlying the romantic ideology is a maturationist theory of development; underlying the cultural transmission ideology is an associationistic-learning or environmental-contingency theory of development; and underlying the progressive ideology is a cognitive-developmental or interactionist theory of development.

The three psychological theories described represent three basic metaphors of development.[8] The romantic model views the development of the mind through the metaphor of organic growth, the physical growth of a plant or animal. In this metaphor, the environment affects development by providing necessary nourishment for the naturally growing organism. Maturationist psychologists elaborating the romantic metaphor conceive of cognitive development as unfolding through prepatterned stages. They have usually assumed not only that cognitive development unfolds but that individual variations in rate of cognitive development are largely inborn. Emotional development is also believed to unfold through hereditary stages, such as the Freudian psychosexual stages, but is thought to be vulnerable to fixation and frustration by the environment. For the maturationist, although both cognitive and social-emotional development unfold, they are two different things. Since social-emotional development is an unfolding of something biologically given and is not based on knowledge of the social world, it does not depend upon cognitive growth.

The cultural transmission model views the development of the mind through the metaphor of the machine. The machine may be the wax on which the environment transcribes its markings, it may be the telephone switchboard through which environmental stimulus-energies are transmitted, or it may be the computer in which bits of information from the environment are stored, retrieved, and recombined. In any case, the environment is seen as "input," as information or energy more or less directly transmitted to, and accumulated in, the organism. The organism in turn emits "output" behavior. Underlying the mechanistic metaphor is the associationistic, stimulus-response, or environmentalist psychological theory, which can be traced from John Locke to Thorndike to B. F. Skinner. This psychology views both specific concepts and general cognitive structures as reflections of structures that exist outside the child in the physical and social world. The structure of the child's concepts or of his behavior is viewed as the result of the association of discrete stimuli with one another, with the child's responses, and with his experiences of pleasure and pain. Cognitive development is the result of guided learning and teaching. Consequently, cognitive education requires a careful statement of desirable behavior patterns described in terms of specific responses. Implied here is the idea that the child's behavior can be shaped by immediate repetition and elaboration of the correct response, and by association with feedback or reward.

The cognitive-developmental metaphor is not material; it is dialectical; it is a model of the progression of ideas in discourse and conversation. The dialectical metaphor was first elaborated by Plato, given new meaning by Hegel, and finally stripped of its metaphysical claims by John Dewey and Jean Piaget, to form a psychological method. In the dialectical metaphor, a core of universal ideas are redefined and reorganized as their implications are played out in experience and as they are confronted by their opposites in argument and discourse. These reorganizations define qualitative levels of thought, levels of increased epistemic adequacy. The child is not a plant or a machine; he is a philosopher or a scientist-poet. The dialectical metaphor of progressive education is supported by a cognitive-developmental or interactional psychological theory. Discarding the dichotomy between maturation and environmentally determined learning, Piaget and Dewey claim that mature thought emerges through a process of development that is neither direct biological maturation nor direct learning, but rather a reorganization of psychological structures resulting from organism-environment interactions. Basic mental structure is the product of the patterning of interaction between the organism and the environment, rather than a direct reflection of either innate neurological patterns or external environmental patterns.

To understand this Piaget-Dewey concept of the development of mental pattern, we must first understand its conception of cognition. Cognitions are assumed to be structures, internally organized wholes or systems of internal relations. These structures are *rules* for the processing of information or the connecting of events. Events in the child's experience are organized actively through these cognitive connecting processes, not passively through external association and repetition. Cognitive development, which is defined as change in cognitive structures, is assumed to depend on experience. But the effects of experience are not regarded as learning in the ordinary sense (training, instruction, modeling, or specific response practices). If two events which follow one another in time are cognitively connected in the child's mind, this implies that he relates them by means of a category such as causality; he perceives his operant behavior as causing the reinforcer to occur. A program of reinforcement, then, cannot directly change the child's causal structures since it is assimilated by the child in terms of his present mode of thinking. When a program of reinforcement cannot be assimilated to the child's causal structure, however, the child's structure may be reorganized to obtain a better fit between the two. Cognitive development is a dialogue between the child's cognitive structures and the structures of the environment. Further, the theory emphasizes that the core of development is not the unfolding of instincts, emotions, or sensorimotor patterns, but instead is cognitive change in distinctively human, general patterns of thinking about the self and the world. The child's relation to his social environment is cognitive; it involves thought and symbolic interaction.

Because of its emphasis on ways of perceiving and responding to experience, cognitive-developmental theory discards the traditional dichotomy of social versus intellectual development. Rather, cognitive and affective development are parallel aspects of the structural transformations which take place in development. At the core of this interactional or cognitive-developmental theory is the doctrine of cognitive stages. Stages have the following general characteristics:

1. Stages imply distinct or qualitative differences in children's modes of thinking or of solving the same problem.

2. These different modes of thought form an invariant sequence, order, or succession in individual development. While cultural factors may speed up, slow down, or stop development, they do not change its sequence.

3. Each of these different and sequential modes of thought forms a "structural whole." A given stage-response on a task does not just represent a specific response determined by knowledge and familiarity with that task or tasks similar to it; rather, it represents an underlying thought-organization.

4. Cognitive stages are hierarchical integrations. Stages form an order of increasingly differentiated and integrated *structures* to fulfill a common function.[9]

In other words, a series of stages form an invariant developmental sequence; the sequence is invariant because each stage stems from the previous one and prepares the way for the subsequent stage. Of course, children may move through these stages at varying speeds, and they may be found to be half in and half out of a particular stage. Individuals may stop at any given stage and at any age, but if they continue to progress they must move in accord with these steps.

The cognitive-developmental conception of stage has a number of features in common with maturational theory conceptions of stage. The maturational conception of stage, however, is "embryological," while the interactional conception is "structural-hierarchical." For maturational theory, a stage represents the total state of the organism at a given period of time; for example, Gesell's embryological concept of stage equates it with the typical behavior pattern of an age period; for example, there is a stage of "five-year-olders." While in the theories of Freud and Erikson stages are less directly equated with ages, psychoanalytic stages are still embryological in the sense that age leads to a new stage regardless of experience and regardless of reorganizations at previous stages. As a result, education and experience become valuable not for movement to a new stage but for healthy or successful integration of the concerns of the present stage. Onset of the next stage occurs regardless of experience; only healthy integration of a stage is contingent on experience.

By contrast, in cognitive-developmental theory a stage is a delimited structure of thought, fixed in a sequence of structures but theoretically independent of time and total organismic state.[10] Such stages are hierarchical reorganizations; attainment of a higher stage presupposes attainment of the prior stage and represents a reorganization or transformation of it. Accordingly, attainment of the next stage is a valid aim of educational experience.

For the interactionist, experience is essential to stage progression, and more or richer stimulation leads to faster advance through the series of stages. On the other hand, the maturational theory assumes that extreme deprivation will retard or fixate development, but that enrichment will not necessarily accelerate it. To understand the effects of experience in stimulating stage development, cognitive-developmental theory holds that one must analyze the relation of the structure of a child's specific experience to behavior structures. The analysis focuses upon discrepancies between the child's action system or expectancies and the events experienced. The hypothesis is that some moderate or optimal degree of conflict or discrepancy constitutes the most effective experience for structural change.

As applied to educational intervention, the theory holds that facilitating the child's movement to the next step of development involves exposure to the next higher level of thought and conflict requiring the active application of the current level of thought to problematic situations. This implies: (1) attention to the child's mode or styles of thought, that is, stage; (2) match of stimulation to that stage, for example, exposure to modes of reasoning one stage above the child's own; (3) arousal, among children, of genuine cognitive and social conflict and disagreement about problematic situations (in contrast to traditional education which has stressed adult "right answers" and has reinforced "behaving well"); and (4) exposure to stimuli toward which the child can be active, in which assimilatory response to the stimulus situation is associated with "natural" feedback.

In summary, the maturationist theory assumes that basic mental structure results from an innate patterning; the environmentalist learning theory assumes that basic mental structure results from the patterning or association of events in the outside world; the cognitive-developmental theory assumes that basic mental structure results from an interaction between organismic structuring tendencies and the structure of the outside world, not reflecting either one directly. This interaction leads to cognitive stages that represent the transformations of early cognitive structures as they are applied to the external world and as they accommodate to it.

Epistemological Components of Educational Ideologies

We have considered the various psychological theories as parts of educational ideologies. Associated with these theories are differing epistemologies or philosophies of science, specifying what is knowledge, that is, what are observable facts and how these facts can be interpreted. Differences in epistemology, just as differences in actual theory, generate different strategies for defining objectives.

Romantic educational ideology springs not only from a maturational psychology, but from an existentialist or phenomenological epistemology, defining knowledge and reality as referring to the immediate inner experience of the self. Knowledge or truth in the romantic epistemology is self-awareness or self-insight, a form of truth with emotional as well as intellectual components. As this form of truth extends beyond the self, it is through sympathetic understanding of humans and natural beings as other "selves."

In contrast, cultural transmission ideologies of education tend to involve epistemologies which stress knowledge as that which is repetitive and "objective," that which can be pointed to in sense experience and measurement and which can be culturally shared and tested.

The progressive ideology, in turn, derives from a functional or pragmatic epistemology which equates knowledge with neither inner experience nor outer sense-reality, but with an equilibrated or resolved relationship between an inquiring human actor and a problematic situation. For the progressive epistemology, the immediate or introspective experience of the child does not have ultimate truth or reality. The meaning and truth of the child's experience depend upon their relationship to the situations in which he is acting. At the same time, the progressive epistemology does not attempt to reduce psychological experience to observable responses in reaction to observable stimuli or situations. Rather, it attempts to functionally coordinate the external meaning of the child's experiences as *behavior* with its internal meaning as it appears to the observer.

With regard to educational objectives, these differences in epistemology generate differences with respect to three issues. The first issue concerns whether to focus objectives on internal states or external behavior. In this respect, cultural transmission and romantic ideologies represent opposite poles. The cultural transmission view evaluates educational change from children's performances, not from their feelings or thoughts. Social growth is defined by the conformity of behavior to particular cultural standards such as honesty and industriousness. These skill and trait terms are found in both common-sense evaluations of school grades and report cards, and in "objective" educational psychological measurement. Behaviorist ideologies systematize this focus by rigorously eliminating references to internal or subjective experience as "nonscientific." Skinner says: "We can follow the path taken by physics and biology by turning directly to the relation between behavior and the environment and neglecting . . . states of mind . . . . We do not need to try to discover what personalities, states of mind, feelings, . . . intentions—or other prerequisites of autonomous man really are in order to get on with a scientific analysis of behavior."[11]

In contrast, the romantic view emphasizes inner feelings and states. Supported by the field of psychotherapy, romantics maintain that skills, achievements, and performances are not satisfying in themselves, but are only a means to inner awareness, happiness, or mental health. They hold that an educator or therapist who ignores the child's inner states in the name of science does so at his peril, since it is these which are most real to the child.

The progressive or cognitive-developmental view attempts to integrate both behavior and internal states in a functional epistemology of mind.

It takes inner experience seriously by attempting to observe thought process rather than language behavior and by observing valuing processes rather than reinforced behavior. In doing so, however, it combines interviews, behavioral tests, and naturalistic observation methods in mental assessment. The cognitive-developmental approach stresses the need to examine mental competence or mental structure as opposed to examining only performance, but it employs a functional rather than an introspective approach to the observation of mental structure. An example is Piaget's systematic and reproducible observations of the preverbal infant's thought structure of space, time, and causality. In short, the cognitive-developmental approach does not select a focus on inner experience or on outer behavior objectives by epistemological fiat, but uses a functional methodology to coordinate the two through empirical study.

A second issue in the definition of educational objectives involves whether to emphasize immediate experience and behavior or long-term consequences in the child's development. The progressive ideology centers on education as it relates to the child's experience, but attempts to observe or assess experience in functional terms rather than by immediate self-projection into the child's place. As a result the progressive distinguishes between *humanitarian* criteria of the quality of the child's experience and *educative* criteria of quality of experience, in terms of long-term developmental consequences. According to Dewey:

Some experiences are miseducative. Any experience is miseducative that has the effect of arresting or distorting the growth of further experience . . . . An experience may be immediately enjoyable and yet promote the formation of a slack and careless attitude . . . [which] operates to modify the quality of subsequent experiences so as to prevent a person from getting out of them what they have to give . . . . Just as no man lives or dies to himself, so no experience lives or dies to itself. Wholly independent of desire or intent, every experience lives on in further experiences. Hence the central problem of an education based on experience is to select the kind of present experiences that live fruitfully and creatively in subsequent experience.[12]

Dewey maintains that an educational experience which stimulates development is one which arouses interest, enjoyment, and challenge in the immediate experience of the student. The reverse is not necessarily the case; immediate interest and enjoyment do not always indicate that an educational experience stimulates long-range development. Interest and involvement is a necessary but not sufficient condition for education as development. For romantics, expecially of the "humanistic psychology" variety, having a novel, intense, and complex experience is *self-development* or self-actualization. For progressives, a more objective test of the effects of the experience on later behavior is required before deciding that the experience is developmental. The progressive views the child's enjoyment and interest as a basic and legitimate criterion of education, but views it as a humanitarian rather than an educational criterion. The progressive holds that education must meet humanitarian criteria, but argues that a concern for the enjoyment and liberty of the child is not in itself equivalent to a concern for his development.

Psychologically, the distinction between humanitarian and developmental criteria is the distinction between the short-term value of the child's immediate experience and the long-term value of that experience as it relates to development. According to the progressive view, this question of the relation of the immediate to the long-term is an empirical rather than a philosophic question. As an example, a characteristic behaviorist strategy is to demonstrate the reversibility of learning by performing an experiment in which a preschooler is reinforced for interacting with other children rather than withdrawing in a corner. This is followed by a reversal of the experiment, demonstrating that when the reinforcement is removed the child again becomes withdrawn. From the progressive or cognitive-developmental perspective, if behavior changes are of this reversible character they cannot define genuine educational objectives. The progressive approach maintains that the worth of an educational effect is decided by its effects upon later behavior and development. Thus, in the progressive view, the basic problems of choosing and validating educational ends can only be solved by longitudinal studies of the effects of educational experience.

The third basic issue is whether the aims of education should be universal as opposed to unique or individual. This issue has an epistemological aspect because romantics have often defined educational goals in terms of the expression or development of a unique self or identity; "objectivist" epistemologies deny that such concepts are accessible to clear observation and definition. In contrast, cultural transmission approaches characteristically focus on measures of individual differences in general dimensions of achievement, or social behavior dimensions on which any individual can be ranked. The progressive, like the romantic, questions the significance of defining behavior relative to some population norm external to the individual. Searching for the "objective" in human experience, the progressive seeks universal qualitative states or sequences in development. Movement from one stage to the next is significant because it is a sequence in the individual's own development, not just a population average or norm. At the same time, insofar as the sequence is a universally observed development, it is not unique to the individual in question.

In summary, the cognitive-developmental approach derives from a functional or pragmatic epistemology which attempts to integrate the dichotomies of the inner versus the outer, the immediate versus the remote in time, the unique versus the general. The cognitive-developmental approach focuses on an empirical search for continuities between inner states and outer behavior and between immediate reaction and remote outcome. While focusing on the child's experience, the progressive ideology defines such experience in terms of universal and empirically observable sequences of development.

Ethical Value Positions Underlying Educational Ideologies

When psychologists like Dewey, Skinner, Neill, and Montessori actually engage in innovative education, they develop a theory which is not a mere statement of psychological principle; it is an ideology. This is not because of the dogmatic, nonscientific attitude they have as psychologists, but because prescription of educational practice cannot be derived from psychological theory or science alone. In addition to theoretical assumptions about how children learn or develop (the psychological theory component), educational ideologies include value assumptions about what is educationally good or worthwhile. To call a pattern of educational thought an ideology is to indicate it is a fairly systematic combination of a theory about psychological and social fact with a set of value principles.

The Fallacy of Value Neutrality

A "value-neutral" position, based only on facts about child development or about methods of education, cannot in itself directly contribute to educational practice. Factual statements about what the processes of learning and development *are* cannot be directly translated into statements about what children's learning and development *ought to be* without introduction of some value principles.

In "value-neutral" research, learning does not necessarily imply movement to a stage of greater cognitive or ethical adequacy. As an example, acquisition of a cognitively arbitrary or erroneous concept (for example, it is best to put a marble in the hole) is considered learning in the same general sense as is acquisition of a capacity for logical inference. Such studies do not relate learning to some justifiable notion of knowledge, truth, or cognitive adequacy. Values are defined relative to a particular culture. Thus, morality is equivalent to conformity to, or internalization of, the particular standards of the child's group or culture. As an example, Berkowitz writes: "Moral values are evaluations of actions generally believed by the members of a given society to be either 'right' or 'wrong'."[13]

Such "value-free" research cannot be translated into prescriptions for practice without importing a set of value assumptions having no relation to psychology itself. The effort to remain "value free" or "nonideological" and yet prescribe educational goals usually has followed the basic model of counseling or consulting. In the *value-free consulting model*, the client (whether student or school) defines educational ends, and the psychologist can then advise about means of education without losing his value neutrality or imposing his values. Outside education, the value-free consulting model not only provides the basic model for counseling and psychotherapy, where the client is an individual, but also for industrial psychology, where the client is a social system. In both therapy and industrial psychology the consultant is paid by the client, and the financial contract defines whose values are to be chosen. The educator or educational psychologist, however, has more than one client. What the child wants, what parents want, and what the larger community wants are often at odds with one another.

An even more fundamental problem for the value-free consulting model is the logical impossibility of making a dichotomy between value-free means and value-loaded ends. Skinner claims that "a behavior technology is ethically neutral. Both the villain and the saint can use it. There is nothing in a methodology that determines the values governing its use."[14] But consider the use of torture on the rack as a behavior technology for learning which could be used by saint and villain alike. On technological grounds Skinner advises against punishment, but this does not solve the ethical issue.

Dewey's logical analysis and our present historical awareness of the value consequences of adopting new technologies have made us realize that choices of means, in the last analysis, also imply choices of ends. Advice about means and methods involves value considerations and cannot be made purely on a basis of "facts." Concrete, positive reinforcement is not an ethically neutral means. To advise the use of concrete reinforcement is to advise that a certain kind of character, motivated by concrete reinforcement, is the end of education. Not only can advice about means not be separated from choice of ends, but there is no way for an educational consultant to avoid harboring his own criteria for choosing ends. The value-neutral consulting model equates value neutrality with acceptance of value relativity, that is, acceptance of whatever the values of the client are. But the educator or educational psychologist cannot be neutral in this sense either.

Values and the Cultural Transmission Ideology

In an effort to cope with the dilemmas inherent in value-neutral pre-scription, many psychologists tend to move to a cultural transmission ideology, based on the value premise of *social relativity*. Social relativity assumes some consistent set of values characteristic of the culture, nation, or system as a whole. While these values may be arbitrary and may vary from one social system to another, there is at least some consensus about them. This approach says, "Since values are relative and arbitrary, we might as well take the given values of the society as our starting point and advocate 'adjustment' to the culture or achievement in it as the educa-tional end." The social relativist basis of the Bereiter-Engelmann system, for example, is stated as follows: "In order to use the term cultural depriva-tion, it is necessary to assume some point of reference . . . . The standards of the American public schools represent one such point of reference . . . . There are standards of knowledge and ability which are consistently held to be valuable in the schools, and any child in the schools who falls short of these standards by reason of his particular cultural background may be said to be culturally deprived."[15]

The Bereiter-Engelmann preschool model takes as its standard of value "the standards of the American public schools." It recognizes that this standard is arbitrary and that the kinds of learning prized by the American public schools may not be the most worthy, but it accepts this arbitrariness because it assumes that "all values are relative," that there is no ultimate standard of worth for learning and development.

Unlike Bereiter and Engelmann, many social relativist educators do not simply accept the standards of the school and culture and attempt to maximize conformity to them. Rather, they are likely to elaborate or create standards for a school or society based on value premises derived from what we shall call "the psychologist's fallacy." According to many philosophical analysts, the effort to derive statements of *ought* (or value) directly from statements of *is* (or fact) is a logical fallacy termed the "naturalistic fallacy."[16] The psychologist's fallacy is a form of the natural-istic fallacy. As practiced by psychologists, the naturalistic fallacy is the direct derivation of statements about what human nature, human values, and human desires ought to be from psychological statements about what they are. Typically, this derivation slides over the distinction between what is desired and what is desirable.

The following statement from B. F. Skinner offers a good example of the psychologist's fallacy:

Good things are positive reinforcers. Physics and biology study things without reference to their values, but the reinforcing effects of things are the province of behavioral science, which, to the extent that it concerns itself with operant re-inforcement, is a science of values. Things are good (positively reinforcing) pre-sumably because of the contingencies of survival under which the species evolved. It is part of the genetic endowment called "human nature" to be reinforced in particular ways by particular things . . . . The effective reinforcers are matters of observation and no one can dispute them.[17]

In this statement, Skinner equates or derives a value word (good) from a fact word (positive reinforcement). This equation is questionable; we wonder whether obtaining positive reinforcement really is good. The psychologist's fallacy or the naturalistic fallacy is a fallacy because we can always ask the further question, "Why is that good?". or "By what standard is that good?" Skinner does not attempt to deal with this further question, called the "open question" by philosophers. He also defines good as "cul-tural survival." The postulation of cultural survival as an ultimate value raises the open question too. We may ask, "Why should the Nazi culture (or the American culture) survive?" The reason Skinner is not concerned with answering the open question about survival is because he is a cultural relativist, believing that any nonfactual reasoning about what is good or about the validity of moral principles is meaningless. He says: "What a given group of people calls good is a fact, it is what members of the group find reinforcing as a result of their genetic endowment and the natural and social contingencies to which they have been exposed. Each culture has its own set of goods, and what is good in one culture may not be good in another."[18]

The Fallacy of Value Relativism

Behind Skinner's value-relativism, then, lie the related notions that: 1) all valid inferences or principles are factual or scientific; 2) valid state-ments about values must be statements about facts of valuing; and 3) what people actually value differs. The fact that people do value different things only becomes an argument for the notion that values are relative if one accepts the first two assumptions listed. Both assumptions are believed by many philosophers to be mistaken because they represent forms of the fact-value confusion already described as the naturalistic fallacy. Confusing discourse about fact with discourse about values, the relativist believes that when ethical judgment is not empirical science, it is not rational. This equation of science with rationality arises because the relativist does not correctly understand philosophical modes of inquiry. In modern conceptions, philosophy is the clarification of concepts for the purpose of critical evaluation of beliefs and standards. The kinds of beliefs which primarily concern philosophy are normative beliefs or standards, beliefs about what ought to be rather than about what is. These include standards of the right or good (ethics), of the true (epistemology), and of the beautiful (aesthetics). In science, the critical evaluation of factual beliefs is limited to criteria of causal explanation and prediction; a "scientific" critical evaluation of normative beliefs is limited to treating them as a class of facts. Philosophy, by contrast, seeks rational justification and criticism of normative beliefs, based on considerations additional to their predictive or causal explanatory power. There is fairly widespread agreement among philosophers that criteria for the validity of ethical judgments can be established independent of "scientific" or predictive criteria. Since patterns for the rational statement and justification of normative beliefs, or "oughts," are not identical with patterns of scientific statement and justification, philosophers can reject both Skinner's notion of a strictly "scientific" ethics and Skinner's notion that whatever is not "scientific" is relative. The open question, "Why is reinforcement or cultural survival good?" is meaningful because there are patterns of ethical justification which are ignored by Skinner's relativistic science.

Distinguishing criteria of moral judgment from criteria of scientific judgment, most philosophers accept the "methodological nonrelativism" of moral judgment just as they accept the methodological nonrelativism of scientific judgment.[19] This ethical nonrelativism is based on appeal to principles for making moral judgments, just as scientific nonrelativism is based on appeal to principles of scientific method or of scientific judgment.

In summary, cultural transmission ideologies rest on the value premise of social relativism—the doctrine that values are relative to, and based upon, the standards of the particular culture and cannot be questioned or further justified. Cultural transmission ideologies of the "scientific" variety, like Skinner's, do not recognize moral principles since they equate what is desirable with what is observable by science, or with what is desired. Philosophers are not in agreement on the exact formulation of valid moral principles though they agree that such formulations center around notions like "the greatest welfare" or "justice as equity." They also do not agree on choice of priorities between principles such as "justice" and "the greatest welfare." Most philosophers do agree, however, that moral evaluations must be rooted in, or justified by, reference to such a realm of principles. Most also maintain that certain values or principles ought to be universal and that these principles are distinct from the rules of any given culture. A principle is a universalizable, impartial mode of deciding or judging, not a concrete cultural rule. "Thou shalt not commit adultery" is a rule for specific behavior in specific situations in a monogamous society. By contrast, Kant's Categorical Imperative—act only as you would be willing that everyone should act in the same situation—is a principle. It is a guide for choosing among behaviors, not a prescription for behavior. As such it is free from culturally defined content; it both transcends and subsumes particular social laws. Hence it has universal applicability.

In regard to values, Skinner's cultural transmission ideology is little different from other, older ideologies based on social relativism and on subjective forms of hedonism, for example, social Darwinism and Benthamite utilitarianism. As an educational ideology, however, Skinner's relativistic behavior technology has one feature which distinguishes it from older forms of social utilitarianism. This is its denial that rational concern for social utility is itself a matter of moral character or moral principle to be transmitted to the young. In Skinner's view, moral character concepts which go beyond responsiveness to social reinforcement and control rely on "prescientific" concepts of free will. Stated in different terms, the concept of moral education is irrelevant to Skinner; he is not concerned with teaching to the children of his society the value principles which he himself adopts. The culture designer is a *psychologist-king*, a value relativist, who somehow makes a free, rational decision to devote himself to controlling individual behavior more effectively in the service of cultural survival. In Skinner's scheme there is no plan to make the controlled controllers, or to educate psychologist-kings.

Values and the Romantic Ideology

At first sight the value premises of the romantic ideology appear to be the polar opposites of Skinner's cultural transmission ideology. Opposed to social control and survival is individual freedom, freedom for the child to be himself. For example, A. S. Neill says: "How can happiness be bestowed? My own answer is: Abolish authority. Let the child be himself. Don't push him around. Don't teach him. Don't lecture him. Don't elevate him. Don't force him to do anything."[20]

As we have pointed out, the romantic ideology rests on a psychology which conceives of the child as having a spontaneously growing mind. In addition, however, it rests on the ethical postulate that "the guardians of the young should merit the proud title of the defenders of the happiness and rights of children."[21] The current popularity of the romantic ideology in "free school," "deschool," and "open school" movements is related to increased adult respect for the rights of children. Bereiter carries this orientation to an extreme conclusion:

Teachers are looking for a way to get out of playing God . . . . The same humanistic ethos that tells them what qualities the next generation should have also tells them that they have no right to manipulate other people or impose their goals upon them. The fact is that there are no morally safe goals for teachers any more. Only processes are safe. When it comes to goals, everything is in doubt . . . . A common expression, often thrown at me, when I have argued for what I believed children should be taught, is "Who are we to say what this child should learn." The basic moral problem . . . is inherent in education itself. If you are engaged in education, you are engaged in an effort to influence the course of the child's development . . . it is to determine what kinds of people they turn out to be. It is to create human beings, it is, therefore, to play God.[22]

This line of thought leads Bereiter to conclude: "The Godlike role of teachers in setting goals for the development of children is no longer morally tenable. A shift to informal modes of education does not remove the difficulty. This paper, then, questions the assumption that education, itself, is a good undertaking and considers the possibilities of a world in which values other than educational ones, come to the fore."[23]

According to Bereiter, then, a humanistic ethical concern for the child's rights must go beyond romantic free schools, beyond deschooling, to the abandonment of an explicit concern for education. Bereiter contrasts the modern "humanistic ethic," and its concern for the child's rights, with the earlier "liberal" concern for human rights which held education and the common school as the foundation of a free society. This earlier concern Bereiter sees expressed most cogently in Dewey's progressivism.

Bereiter is led to question the moral legitimacy of education because he equates a regard for the child's liberty with a belief in ethical relativity, rather than recognizing that liberty and justice are universal ethical principles. "The teacher may try to play it safe by sticking to the middle of the road and only aiming to teach what is generally approved, but there are not enough universally endorsed values (if, indeed, there are any) to form the basis of an education."[24] Here, he confuses an ethical position of tolerance or respect for the child's freedom with a belief in ethical relativity, not recognizing that respect for the child's liberty derives from a principle of justice rather than from a belief that all moral values are arbitrary. Respect for the child's liberty means awarding him the maximum liberty compatible with the liberty of others (and of himself when older), not refusal to deal with his values and behavior. The assumption of individual relativity of values underlying modern romantic statements of the child's liberty is also reflected in the following quote from Neill: "Well, we set out to make a school in which we should allow children freedom to be themselves. In order to do this, we had to renounce all discipline, all direction, all suggestion, all moral training, all religious instruction. We have been called brave, but it did not require courage. All it required was what we had—a complete belief in the child as a good, not an evil, being. For almost forty years, this belief in the goodness of the child has never wavered; it rather has become a final faith."[25]

For Neill, as for many free school advocates, value relativity does not involve what it did for Bereiter—a questioning of all conceptions of what is good in children and good for them. Neill's statement that the child is "good" is a completely nonrelativist conception. It does not, however, refer to an ethical or moral principle or standard used to direct the child's education. Instead, just as in Skinner's cultural transmission ideology, the conception of the good is derived from what we have termed the psychologist's fallacy. Neill's faith in the "goodness of the child" is the belief that what children *do* want, when left to themselves, can be equated with what they *should* want from an ethical standpoint. In one way this faith is a belief that children are wired so as to act and develop compatibly with ethical norms. In another sense, however, it is an ethical postulation that decisions about what is right for children should be derived from what children do desire—that whatever children do is right.

This position begs the open question, "Why is freedom to be oneself good; by what standard is it a good thing?"

The question is raised by Dewey as follows: "The objection made [to identifying the educative process with growing or developing] is that growth might take many different directions: a man, for example, who starts out on a career of burglary may grow in that direction . . . into a highly expert burglar. Hence it is argued that 'growth' is not enough; we must also specify the direction in which growth takes place, the end toward which it tends."[26]

In Neill's view it is not clear whether there is a standard of development, that is, some standard of goodness which children who grow up freely all meet, or whether children who grow up freely are good only by their own standards, even if they are thieves or villains by some other ethical standards. To the extent that there is a nonrelativist criterion employed by Neill, it does not derive from, nor is it justified by, the ethical principles of philosophy. Rather, it is derived from matters of psychological fact about "mental health" and "happiness." "The merits of Summerhill are the merits of healthy free children whose lives are unspoiled by fear and hate."[27] "The aim of education, in fact, the aim of life is to work joyfully and to find happiness."[28]

Freedom, then, is not justified as an ethical principle but as a matter of psychological fact, leading to "mental health and happiness." These are ultimate terms, as are the terms "maximizing reinforcement" and "cultural survival" for Skinner. For other romantic educators the ultimate value terms are also psychological, for example, "self-realization," "self-actualization," and "spontaneity." These are defined as "basic human tendencies" and are taken as good in themselves rather than being subject to the scrutiny of moral philosophy.

We have attempted to show that romantic libertarian ideologies are grounded on value relativism and reliance on the psychologist's fallacy, just as are cultural transmission ideologies, which see education as behavior control in the service of cultural survival. As a result of these shared premises, both romantic and cultural transmission ideologies tend to generate a kind of elitism. In the case of Skinner, this elitism is reflected in the vision of the psychologist as a culture designer, who "educates others" to conform to culture and maintain it but not to develop the values and knowledge which would be required for culture designing. In the case of the romantic, the elitism is reflected in a refusal to impose intellectual and ethical values of libertarianism, equal justice, intellectual inquiry, and social reconstructionism on the child, even though these values are held to be the most important ones: ". . . Summerhill is a place in which people who have the innate ability and wish to be scholars will be scholars; while those who are only fit to sweep the streets will sweep the streets. But we have not produced a street cleaner so far. Nor do I write this snobbishly, for I would rather see a school produce a happy street cleaner than a neurotic scholar."[29]

In summary, in spite of their libertarian and nonindoctrinative emphases, romantic ideologies also have a tendency to be elitist or patronizing. Recalling the role of Dostoievsky's Grand Inquisitor, they see education as a process which only intends the child to be happy and adjusted rather than one which confronts the child with the ethical and intellectual problems and principles which the educator himself confronts. Skinner and Neill agree it is better for the child to be a happy pig than an unhappy Socrates. We may question, however, whether they have the right to withhold that choice.

Value Postulates of Progressivism

Progressive ideology, in turn, rests on the value postulates of ethical liberalism.[30] This position rejects traditional standards and value relativism in favor of ethical universals. Further, it recognizes that value universals are ethical principles formulated and justified by the method of philosophy, not simply by the method of psychology. The ethical liberal position favors the active stimulation of the development of these principles in children. These principles are presented through a process of critical questioning which creates an awareness of the ground and limits of rational assent; they also are seen as relevant to universal trends in the child's own social and moral development. The liberal recognition of principles as *principles* clears them from confusion with psychological facts. To be concerned about children's happiness is an ethical imperative for the educator without regard to "mental health," "positive reinforcement," or other psychological terms used by educators who commit the "psychologist's fallacy." Rational ethical principles, not the values of parents or culture, are the final value arbiters in defining educational aims. Such principles may call for consultation with parents, community, and children in formulating aims, but they do not warrant making them final judges of aims.

The liberal school recognizes that ethical principles determine the ends as well as the means of education. There is great concern not only to make schools more just, that is, to provide equality of educational opportunity and to allow freedom of belief, but also to educate so that free and just people emerge from the schools. Accordingly, liberals also conscientiously engage in moral education. It is here that the progressive and romantic diverge, in spite of a common concern for the liberty and rights of the child. For the romantic, liberty means noninterference. For the liberal, the principle of respect for liberty is itself defined as a moral aim of education. Not only are the rights of the child to be respected by the teacher, but the child's development is to be stimulated so that he may come to respect and defend his own rights and the rights of others.

Recognition of concern for liberty as a principle leads to an explicit, libertarian conception of moral education. According to Dewey and McLellan, "Summing up, we may say that every teacher requires a sound knowledge of ethical and psychological principles . . . . Only psychology and ethics can take education out of the rule-of-thumb stage and elevate the school to a vital, effective institution in the *greatest of all constructions—the building of a free and powerful character.*"[31]

In the liberal view, educational concern for the development of a "free character" is rooted in the principle of liberty. For the romantic or relativist libertarian this means that "everyone has his own bag," which may or may not include liberty; and to actively stimulate the development of regard for liberty or a free character in the child is as much an imposition on the child as any other educational intervention. The progressive libertarians differ on this point. They advocate a strong rather than a weak application of liberal principles to education. Consistent application of ethical principles to education means that education *should* stimulate the development of ethical principles in students.

In regard to ethical values, the progressive ideology adds the postulates of *development* and *democracy* to the postulates of liberalism. The notion of educational democracy is one in which justice between teacher and child means joining in a community in which value decisions are made on a shared and equitable basis, rather than non-interference with the child's value decisions. Because ethical principles function as principles, the progressive ideology is "democratic" in a sense that romantic and cultural transmission ideologies are not.

In discussing Skinner we pointed to a fundamental problem in the relation between the ideology of the relativist educator and that of the student. Traditional education did not find it a problem to reconcile the role of teacher and the role of student. Both were members of a common culture, and the task of the teacher was to transmit that culture and its values to the student. In contrast, modern psychologists advocating cultural transmission ideologies do not hold this position. As social relativists they do not really believe in a common culture; instead they are in the position of transmitting values which are different both from those they believe in and those believed in by the student. At the extreme, as we mentioned earlier, Skinner proposes an ideology for ethically relative psychologist-kings or culture designers who control others. Clearly there is a contradiction between the ideology for the psychologist-king and the ideology for the child.

Romantic or radical ideologies are also unable to solve this problem. The romantic adopts what he assumes are the child's values, or takes as his value premise what is "natural" in the child rather than endorsing the culture's values. But while the adult believes in the child's freedom and creativity and wants a free, more natural society, the child neither fully comprehends nor necessarily adheres to the adult's beliefs. In addition, the romantic must strive to give the child freedom to grow even though such freedom may lead the child to become a reactionary. Like the behavior modifier, then, the romantic has an ideology, but it is different from the one which the student is supposed to develop.

The progressive is nonelitist because he attempts to get all children to develop in the direction of recognizing the principles he holds. But is this not indoctrinative? Here we need to clarify the postulates of development and democracy as they guide education.

For the progressive, the problem of offering a nonindoctrinative education which is based on ethical and epistemological principles is partially resolved by a conception that these principles represent developmentally advanced or mature stages of reasoning, judgment, and action. Because there are culturally universal stages or sequences of moral development[32], stimulation of the child's development to the next step in a natural direction is equivalent to a long-range goal of teaching ethical principles.

Because the development of these principles is natural, they are not imposed on the child—he chooses them himself. A similar developmental approach is taken toward intellectual values. Intellectual education in the progressive view is not merely a transmission of information and intellectual skills; it is the communication of patterns and methods of "scientific" reflection and inquiry. These patterns correspond to higher stages of logical reasoning, Piaget's formal operations. According to the progressive, there is an important analogy between scientific and ethical patterns of judgment or problem solving, and there are overlapping rationales for intellectual and ethical education. In exposing the child to opportunities for reflective scientific inquiry, the teacher is guided by the principles of scientific method which the teacher himself accepts as the basis of rational reflection. Reference to such principles is nonindoctrinative if these principles are not presented as formulas to be learned ready-made or as rote patterns grounded in authority. Rather, they are part of a process of reflection by the student and teacher. A similar approach guides the process of reflection on ethical or value problems.

The problem of indoctrination is also resolved for the progressive by the concept of democracy. A concern for the child's freedom from indoctrination is part of a concern for the child's freedom to make decisions and act meaningfully. Freedom, in this context, means democracy, that is, power and participation in a social system which recognizes basic equal rights. It is impossible for teachers not to engage in value judgments and decisions. A concern for the liberty of the child does not create a school in which the teacher is value neutral, and any pretense of it creates "the hidden curriculum."[33] But it can create a school in which the teacher's value judgments and decisions involve the students democratically.

We turn, now, to the nature and justification of these universal and intrinsically worthy aims and principles. In the next sections we attempt to indicate the way in which the concept of development, rooted in psychological study, can aid in prescribing aims of education without commission of the psychologist's fallacy. We call this the developmental-philosophic strategy for defining educational aims . . . .

Development as the Aim of Education

We have attempted to clarify and justify the basic claim that developmental criteria are the best ones for defining educationally important behavior changes. We need now to clarify how the psychological study of development can concretely define educational goals. A common criticism is that the concept of development is too vague to genuinely clarify the choice of the curricular content and aims of education. A second, related criticism is that the concept of development, with its connotation of the "natural," is unsuited to determine actual educational policy.

With regard to the issue of vagueness, if the concept of development is to aid in selecting educational aims and content, this assumes that only

some behavior changes out of many can be labeled developmental. We
need to justify this assumption and to clarify the conditions for developmental change.

Our position has been challenged by Bereiter[34] who claims that determining whether or not a behavior change is development is a matter
of theory, not an empirical issue. For example, Piagetian research shows
that fundamental arithemetical reasoning (awareness of one-to-one correspondence, of inclusion of a larger class in a subclass, of addition and
subtraction as inverse operations) usually develops naturally, without
formal instruction or schooling, that is, it constitutes development. Such
reasoning can also be explicitly taught, however, following various nondevelopmental learning theories. Accordingly, says Bereiter, to call fundamental arithmetical reasoning developmental does not define it as a developmental educational objective distinct from nondevelopmental objectives like rote knowledge of the multiplication tables.

In answer, the cognitive-developmental position claims that developmental behavior change is irreversible, general over a field of responses,
sequential, and hierarchical.[35] When a set of behavior changes meets all
these criteria, changes are termed stages or structural reorganizations. A
specific area of behavioral change like fundamental arithmetical reasoning may or may not meet these criteria. Engelmann claims to have artificially taught children the "naturally developing" operation of conservation, but Kamii[36] found that the children so taught met Engelmann's
criteria of conservation without meeting the criteria of development, for
example, the response could be later forgotten or unlearned, it was not
generalized, and so forth.

When a set of responses taught artificially does not meet the criteria
of natural development, this is not because educational intervention is
generally incompatible with developmental change. It is because the
particular intervention is found to mimic development rather than to stimulate it. The issue of whether an educational change warrants the honorific
label "development" is a question for empirical examination, not simply
a matter of theory.

We have claimed that development can occur either naturally or as
the result of a planned educational program. As was discussed earlier,
development depends on experience. It is true, however, that the way in
which experience stimulates development (through discrepancy and match
between experienced events and information-processing structures) is
not the way experience is programmed in many forms of instruction and
educational intervention. It is also true that the kinds of experience leading to development must be viewed in terms of a stimulation which is
general rather than highly specific in its content or meaning.

Because the experiences necessary for structural development are believed to be *universal*, it is possible for the child to develop the behavior naturally, without planned instruction. But the fact that only about half of the adult American population fully reaches Piaget's stage of formal operational reasoning and only 5 percent reach the highest moral stage demonstrates that natural or universal forms of development are not inevitable, but depend on experience.[37]

If this argument is accepted, it not only answers the charge that development is a vague concept, but helps answer the charge that there are kinds of development (such as growth in skill at burglary) which are not valuable.

Such questionable types of "development" do not constitute development in the sense of a universal sequence or in the sense of growth of some general aspect of personality. As stated by Dewey: "That a man may grow in efficiency as a burglar . . . cannot be doubted. But from the standpoint of growth as education and education as growth the question is whether such growth promotes or retards growth in general."[38]

While a coherent argument has been made for why universal developmental sequences define something of educational value, we need to consider why such sequences comprise the ultimate criteria of educational value. We also need to consider how they relate to competing educational values. How does universal structural development as an educational aim relate to ordinary definitions of information and skills central to the educational curriculum? It seems obvious that many changes or forms of learning are of value which are not universals in development. As an example, while many unschooled persons have learned to read, the capacity and motivation to read does not define a developmental universal; nonetheless, it seems to us a basic educational objective. We cannot dispose of "growth in reading" as an educational objective, as we could "growth in burglary," simply because it is not a universal in development. But we argue that the ultimate importance of learning to read can only be understood in the context of more universal forms of development. Increased capacity to read is not itself a development, although it is an attainment reflecting various aspects of development. The value or importance of reading lies in its potential contribution to further cognitive, social, and aesthetic development. As stated by Dewey:

No one can estimate the benumbing and hardening effect of continued drill in reading as mere form. It should be obvious that what I have in mind is not a Philistine attack upon books and reading. The question is not how to get rid of them, but how to get their value—how to use them to their capacity as servants of the intellectual and moral life. To answer this question, we must consider what is the effect of growth in a special direction upon the attitudes and habits which alone open up avenues for development in other lines.[39]

A developmental definition of educational objectives must not only cope with competing objectives usually defined nondevelopmentally, but with the fact that the universal aspects of development are multiple. Here, as in the case of evaluating nondevelopmental objectives, the progressive educator must consider the relation of a particular development to development in general. As an example, Kamii[40] has defined a program of preschool intervention related to each of the chapter headings of Piaget's books: space, time, causality, number, classification, and so on. Kamii's intent in making use of all the areas of cognitive development discussed by Piaget is not to imply that each constitutes a separate, intrinsic educational objective. Rather, her interest is to make use of all aspects of the child's experience relevant to *general* Piagetian cognitive development. Such a concept of generalized cognitive stage development is meaningful because Kohlberg and DeVries[41] and others have shown that there is a general Piagetian cognitive level factor distinct from psychometric general intelligence.

In contrast to the psychometric concept of intelligence, the developmental level concept of intelligence does provide a standard or a set of aims for preschool education. It does not assume a concept of fixed capacity or "intelligence quotient" constant over development. In this sense, developmental level is more like "achievement" than like "capacity," but developmental level tests differ from achievement tests in several ways. While the developmental level concept does not distinguish between achievement and capacity, it distinguishes between cognitive achievement (performance) and cognitive process (or competence). Developmental tests measure level of thought process, not the difficulty or correctness of thought product. They measure not cognitive performance but cognitive competence, the basic possession of a core concept, not the speed and agility with which the concept is expressed or used under rigid test conditions.

Psychometric and developmental level concepts of intelligence are quite different. In practice, however, the two kinds of measures are highly correlated with one another, explaining why clear theoretical and operational distinctions between the two concepts of intelligence have not been made until recently. Factor-analytic findings now can provide an empirical basis for this distinction.[42] While psychometric measures of general intelligence and of "primary mental abilities" at mental age six correlate with Piagetian measures of cognitive level, there is also a common factor to all developmental level tests. This factor is independent of general intelligence or of any special psychometric ability. In other words, it is possible to distinguish between psychometric capacity and developmental level concepts or measures of intelligence. Given the empirical distinction, cognitive stage measures provide a rational standard for educational intervention where psychometric intelligence tests do not. This is true for the following reasons:

1. The core structure defined by stage tests is in theory and experiment more amenable to educational intervention—Piagetian theory is a theory of stage movement occurring through *experience* of structural disequilibrium.

2. Piagetian performance predicts later development independent of a fixed biological rate or capacity factor, as demonstrated by evidence for longitudinal stability or prediction independent of IQ. Because Piaget's items define invariant sequences, development to one stage facilitates development to the next.

3. Piagetian test content has cognitive value in its own right. If a child is able to think causally instead of magically about phenomena, for instance, his ability has a cognitive value apart from arbitrary cultural demands—it is not a mere indicator of brightness, like knowing the word "envelope" or "amanuensis." This is reflected in the fact that Piagetian test scores are qualitative; they are not arbitrary points on a curve. The capacity to engage in concrete logical reasoning is a definite attainment; being at mental age six is not. We can ask that all children reason in terms of logical operations; we cannot ask that all children have high IQ's.

4. This cognitive value is culturally universal; the sequence of development occurs in every culture and subculture.

The existence of a general level factor in cognitive development allows us to put particular universal sequences of cognitive development into perspective as educational aims. The worth of a development in any particular cognitive sequence is determined by its contribution to the whole of cognitive development.

We must now consider the relation of developmental aims of education to the notion of developmental acceleration as an educational objective. We indicated that a concept of stages as "natural" does not mean that they are inevitable; many individuals fail to attain the higher stages of logical and moral reasoning. Accordingly, the aim of the developmental educator is not the acceleration of development but the eventual adult attainment of the highest stage. In this sense, the developmentalist is not interested in *stage-acceleration*, but in avoiding *stage-retardation*. Moral development research reviewed elsewhere suggests that there is what approaches an optimal period for movement from one stage to the next.[43] When a child has just attained a given stage, he is unlikely to respond to stimulation toward movement to the next stage. In addition, after a long period of use of a given stage of thought, a child tends to "stabilize" at that stage and develops screening mechanisms for contradictory stimulation. Accordingly, it has been found that both very young and very old children at a given stage (compared to the age norm for that stage) are less responsive or less able to assimilate stimulation at the next higher stage than children at the age norm for that stage. The notion of an "open period" is not age specific; it is individual. A child late in reaching Stage 2 may be "open" to Stage 3 at an age beyond that of another child who reached Stage 2 earlier. Nevertheless, gross age periods may be defined which are "open periods" for movement from one stage to the next. Avoidance of retardation as an educational aim means presenting stimulation in these periods where the possibility for development is still open.

We need to consider a related distinction between *acceleration* and *decalage* as an aim of education. Piaget distinguishes between the appearance of a stage and its "horizontal *decalage*," its spread or generalization across the range of basic physical and social actions, concepts, and objects to which the stage potentially applies. As a simple example, concrete logic or conservation is first noted in the concept of mass and only later in weight and volume. Accordingly, acceleration of the stage of concrete operations is one educational enterprise and the encouragement of *decalage* of concrete reasoning to a new concept or phenomenon is another. It is the latter which is most relevant to education. Education is concerned not so much with age of onset of a child's capacity for concrete logical thought, but with the possession of a logical mind—the degree to which he has organized his experience or his world in a logical fashion.

It is likely that the occurrence of such horizontal *decalage*, rather than age of first appearance of concrete operations, predicts to later formal operational thought. Formal reasoning develops because concrete reasoning represents a poor, though partially successful, strategy for solving many problems. The child who has never explored the limits of concrete logical reasoning and lives in a world determined by arbitrary unexplained events and forces will see the limits of the partial solutions of concrete logic as set by intangible forces, rather than looking for a more adequate logic to deal with unexplained problems.

We have so far discussed development only as general cognitive development. According to cognitive-developmental theory there is always a cognitive component to development, even in social, moral, and aesthetic areas. Development, however, is broader than cognitive-logical development. One central area is moral development, as defined by invariant stages of moral reasoning.[44] On the one hand, these stages have a cognitive component; attainment of a given Piagetian cognitive stage is a necessary, though not sufficient, condition for the parallel moral stage. On the other hand, moral reasoning stages relate to action; principled moral reasoning has been found to be a precondition for principled moral action.[45] For reasons elaborated throughout this paper, the stimulation of moral development through the stages represents a rational and ethical focus of education related to, but broadening, an educational focus upon cognitive development as such.[46] Programs effective in stimulating moral development have been successfully demonstrated.[47]

While developmental moral education widens the focus of cognitive-developmental education beyond the purely cognitive, there is a still broader unity, called ego development, of which both cognitive and moral development are part.[48] Particularly in the earlier childhood years, it is difficult to distinguish moral development from ego development. Cognitive development, in the Piagetian sense, is also related to ego development, since both concern the child's core beliefs about the physical and social world. Much recent research demonstrates that the development of the ego, as attitudes and beliefs about the self, involves step-by-step parallel development of attitudes and beliefs about the physical and social world. Further, it indicates definite stages of ego development, defined by Loevinger, Wessler, and Redmore,[49] van den Daele[50] and others, which imply step-by-step parallels to Piaget's cognitive stages, although they include more social emotional content. In general, attainment of a Piagetian cognitive stage is a necessary but not sufficient condition for attainment of the parallel ego stage. All children at a given ego stage must have attained the parallel cognitive stage, but not all children at a cognitive stage will have organized their self-concept and social experience at the corresponding ego stage. Thus, a general concept of ego development as a universal sequential phenomenon is becoming an empirically meaningful guide to defining broad educational objectives. Furthermore, experimental educational programs to stimulate ego development have been piloted with some definite success at both the preschool and the high school levels.[51]

Thus, education for general cognitive development, and perhaps even education for moral development, must be judged by its contribution to a more general concept of ego development. In saying this, we must remember that "ego development" is the psychologist's term for a sequence which also must have a philosophic rationale. One pole of ego development is self-awareness; the parallel pole is awareness of the world. Increasing awareness is not only "cognitive"; it is moral, aesthetic, and metaphysical; it is the awareness of new meanings in life.

Finally, we need to note that in the realm of ego development, a focus upon "horizontal *decalage*," rather than acceleration, is especially salient.

The distinction reflects in a more precise and viable fashion the concern of maturational or romantic stage theorists for an educational focus upon "healthy" passage through stages, rather than their acceleration. In maturational theories of personality stages, age leads to a new stage regardless of experience and reorganizations at previous stages. As a result, education and experience become valuable not for movement to a new stage, but for healthy or *successful integration* of the concerns of a stage. Onset of the next stage occurs regardless of experience; it is only healthy integration of the stages which is contingent on experience and which should be the focus for education. Without accepting this contention, cognitive-developmental theory would agree that premature development to a higher ego stage without a corresponding *decalage* throughout the child's world and life presents problems. In psychoanalytic maturational terms, the dangers of uneven or premature ego development are expressed as defects in ego strength with consequent vulnerability to regression. In cognitive-developmental terms, inadequate "horizontal *decalage*" represents a somewhat similar phenomenon. While the relation of "ego strength" to logical and moral *decalage* is not well understood, there are many reasons to believe they are related. A child who continues to think in magical or egocentric terms in some areas of cognition and morality is likely to be vulnerable to something like "regression" under stress later in life.

In conclusion, if a broad concept of development, conceived in stage sequential terms, is still vague as a definer of educational ends, it is not due to the inherent narrowness or vagueness of the concept. Rather, it is due to the fact that researchers have only recently begun the kind of longitudinal and educational research needed to make the concept precise and usable. When Dewey advocated education as development at the turn of the century, most American educational psychologists turned instead to industrial psychology or to the mental health bag of virtues. If the results of the cognitive-developmental research of the last decades are still limited, they indicate real promise for finally translating Dewey's vision into a precise reality.

Summary and Conclusions

The present paper essentially recapitulates the progressive position first formulated by John Dewey. This position has been clarified psychologically by the work of Piaget and his followers; its philosophic premises have been advanced by the work of modern analytic philosophers like Hare, Rawls, and Peters. The progressive view of education makes the following claims:

1. That the aims of education may be identified with development, both intellectual and moral.

2. That education so conceived supplies the conditions for passing through an order of connected stages.

3. That such a developmental definition of educational aims and processes requires both the method of philosophy or ethics and the method of psychology or science. The justification of education as development requires a philosophic statement explaining why a higher stage is a better or a more adequate stage. In addition, before one can define a set of educational goals based on a philosophical statement of ethical, scientific, or logical principles, one must be able to translate it into a statement about psychological stages of development.

4. This, in turn, implies that the understanding of logical and ethical principles is a central aim of education. This understanding is the philosophic counterpart of the psychological statement that the aim of education is the development of the individual through cognitive and moral stages. It is characteristic of higher cognitive and moral stages that the child himself constructs logical and ethical principles; these, in turn, are elaborated by science and philosophy.

5. A notion of education as attainment of higher stages of development, involving an understanding of principles, was central to "aristocratic" Platonic doctrines of liberal education. This conception is also central to Dewey's notion of a democratic education. The democratic educational end for all humans must be "the development of a free and powerful character." Nothing less than democratic education will prepare free people for factual and moral choices which they will inevitably confront in society. The democratic educator must be guided by a set of psychological and ethical principles which he openly presents to his students, inviting criticism as well as understanding. The alternative is the "educator-king," such as the behavior modifier with an ideology of controlling behavior, or the teacher-psychiatrist with an ideology of "improving" students' mental health. Neither exposes his ideology to the students, allowing them to evaluate its merit for themselves.

6. A notion of education for development and education for principles is liberal, democratic, and nonindoctrinative. It relies on open methods of stimulation through a sequence of stages, in a direction of movement which is universal for all children. In this sense, it is natural.

The progressive position appears idealistic rather than pragmatic, industrial-vocational, or adjustment oriented, as is often charged by critics of progressivism who view it as ignoring "excellence." But Dewey's idealism is supported by Piagetian psychological findings which indicate that all children, not only well-born college students, are "philosophers" intent on organizing their lives into universal patterns of meaning. It is supported by findings that most students seem to move forward in developmentally oriented educational programs. Furthermore, the idealism of the developmental position is compatible with the notion that the child is involved in a process of both academic and vocational education. Dewey denied that educational experience stimulating intellectual and moral development could be equated with academic schooling. He claimed that practical or vocational education as well as academic education could contribute to cognitive and moral development; it should be for all children, not only for the poor or the "slow." Our educational system currently faces a choice between two forms of injustice, the first an imposition of an arbitrary academic education on all, the second a division into a superior academic track and an inferior vocational track. The developmental conception remains the only rationale for solving these injustices, and for providing the basis for a truly democratic educational process.

Notes

1. G. H. Mead, *Movements of Thought in the Nineteenth Century* (Chicago: University of Chicago Press, 1936), 61.

2. G. S. Hall, "The Ideal School Based on Child Study," *Forum and Century*, 32 (September 1901), 24.

3. The romantic-maturationist position also has "conservative" and "radical" wings. Emphasizing "adaptation to reality," psychoanalytic educators like A. Freud (*The Ego and the Mechanisms of Defense* [London: Hogarth Press, 1937]) and B. Bettelheim ("On Moral Education," in *Moral Education*, ed. T. Sizer [Cambridge, Mass.: Harvard University Press, 1970]) stress mental health as ego control, while radicals stress spontaneity, creativity, and so forth.

4. C. Bereiter and S. Engelmann, *Teaching Disadvantaged Children in the Preschool* (Englewood Cliffs, N.J.: Prentice-Hall, 1966).

5. J. Dewey, *Experience and Education* (New York: Collier, 1963 [originally written in 1938]).

6. *Id.* and J. McLellan, "The Psychology of Number," in *John Dewey on Education: Selected Writings*, ed. R. Archambault (New York: Random House, 1964), 207.

7. L. Kohlberg, "Early Education: A Cognitive-Developmental View," *Child Development*, 39 (December 1968), 1013-1062.

8. J. Langer, *Theories of Development* (New York: Holt, Rinehart and Winston, 1969).

9. J. Piaget, "The General Problem of the Psychobiological Development of the Child," in *Discussion on Child Development*, Volume 4, ed. J. M. Tanner and B. Inhelder (New York: International Universities Press, 1960), 13-15.

10. L. Kohlberg, "Stage and Sequence: The Cognitive-Developmental Approach to Socialization," in *Handbook of Socialization Theory and Research*, ed. D. Goslin (Chicago: Rand McNally, 1969); J. Loevinger, J. Wessler, and C. Redmore, *Measuring Ego Development* (San Francisco: Jossey-Bass, 1970).

11. B. F. Skinner, *Beyond Freedom and Dignity* (New York: Alfred A. Knopf, 1971), 15.

12. Dewey, *Experience and Education*, 25-28.

13. L. Berkowitz, *Development of Motives and Values in a Child* (New York: Basic Books, 1964), 44.

14. Skinner, *Beyond Freedom and Dignity*, 17.

15. Bereiter and Engelmann, *Teaching Disadvantaged Children in the Preschool*, 24.

16. L. Kohlberg, "From Is to Ought: How to Commit the Naturalistic Fallacy and Get Away with It in the Study of Moral Development," in *Cognitive Development and Epistemology*, ed. T. Mischel (New York: Academic Press, 1971).

17. Skinner, *Beyond Freedom and Dignity*, 104.

18. *Ibid.*, 128.

19. R. B. Brandt, *Ethical Theory* (Englewood Cliffs, N.J.: Prentice-Hall, 1956).

20. A. S. Neill, *Summerhill* (New York: Hart, 1960), 297.

21. Hall, "The Ideal School Based on Child Study," 24.

22. C. Bereiter, "Moral Alternatives to Education," *Interchange,* 3 (No. 1, 1972), 26-27.

23. *Ibid.,* 25.

24. *Ibid.,* 27.

25. Neill, *Summerhill,* 4.

26. Dewey, *Experience and Education*, 75.

27. Neill, *Summerhill,* 4.

28. *Ibid.,* 297.

29. *Ibid.,* 4-5.

30. There are two main schools of ethical liberalism. The more naturalistic or utilitarian one is represented in the works of J. S. Mill, Sidgewick, Dewey, and Tufts. The other is represented in the works of Locke, Kant, and Rawls. A modern statement of the liberal ethical tradition in relation to education is provided by R. S. Peters (*Ethics and Education* [Chicago: Scott, Foresman, 1968]).

31. Dewey and McLellan, "The Psychology of Number," 207.

32. L. Kohlberg and E. Turiel, "Moral Development and Moral Education," in *Psychology and Educational Practice*, ed. G. Lesser (Chicago: Scott, Foresman, 1971).

33. Kohlberg, "Stage and Sequence."

34. C. Bereiter, "Educational Implications of Kohlberg's Cognitive-Developmental View," *Interchange*, 1 (No. 2, 1970), 25-32.

35. L. Kohlberg, "Reply to Bereiter's Statement on Kohlberg's Cognitive-Developmental View," *ibid.*, 40-48.

36. C. Kamii, "Evaluating Pupil Learning in Preschool Education: Socio-Emotional, Perceptual-Motor, and Cognitive Objectives," in *Formative and Summative Evaluation of Student Learning*, ed. B. S. Bloom, J. T. Hastings, and G. Madaus (New York: McGraw-Hill, 1971).

37. D. Kuhn *et al.*, "The Development of Formal Operations in Logical and Moral Judgment," unpublished mimeo monograph, Columbia University, 1971.

38. Dewey, *Experience and Education*, 75.

39. *Id.,* "The Primary-Education Fetish," *The Forum* (May 1898), 29.

40. Kamii, "Evaluating Pupil Learning in Preschool Education."

41. L. Kohlberg and R. DeVries, "Relations between Piaget and Psychometric Assessments of Intelligence," in *The Natural Curriculum*, ed. C. Lavatelli (Urbana, Ill.: ERIC, 1971), revised version to be published in L. Kohlberg and R. Mayer, *Early Education: A Cognitive-Developmental View* (Chicago: Dryden Press, forthcoming).

42. *Ibid.*

43. *Recent Research in Moral Development*, ed. L. Kohlberg and E. Turiel (New York: Holt, Rinehart and Winston, 1973).

44. Kohlberg and Turiel, "Moral Development and Moral Education"; *Recent Research in Moral Development*, ed. *id.*

45. *Recent Research in Moral Development*, ed. *id.*

46. *Id.*, "Moral Development and Moral Education."

47. M. Blatt and L. Kohlberg, "Effects of Classroom Discussion upon Children's Level of Moral Judgment," in *Recent Research in Moral Development*, ed. Kohlberg and Turiel.

48. Loevinger, Wessler, and Redmore, *Measuring Ego Development*.

49. *Ibid.*

50. L. van den Daele, "Preschool Intervention with Social Learning," *Journal of Negro Education*, 39 (Fall 1970), 296-304.

51. *Ibid.*; R. L. Mosher and N. A. Sprinthall, "Psychological Education in Secondary Schools: A Program to Promote Individual and Human Development," *American Psychologist*, 25 (October 1970), 911-924.

A Developmental Curriculum for Secondary Schools: Need, Purpose, and Programs

Norman A. Sprinthall
Ralph L. Mosher

The Challenge of Adolescence as a Stage of Development

A few years ago, an eminent theorist on the nature of adolescence, Gisela Konopka, challenged adult society to develop effective educational programs for teenagers of the country. She noted that the extent to which adolescents participate responsibly in society determines and maximizes their human development. This does not suggest that adolescence is simply a transitory stage humans pass through. If such were the case, we could all survive the process through forbearance. Instead, adolescence presents a special opportunity to all adults who are concerned with maximizing effective human growth. "We believe adolescents are persons with specific qualities and characteristics who have a participatory and responsible role to play, tasks to perform, skills to develop . . . ."[1] Adolescents should not be viewed as preadults, preparents, or preworkers, but as growing, developing persons. The kind and quality of their development do not unfold automatically, romantically, or idealistically. Their development is seen as a function of their interaction with society at large. Erik Erikson has commented that society rebaptizes its youth during adolescence. The confirmation can be as active, psychologically healthy, mature, significant humans with a strong sense of personal identity or as passive, dependent, inferior, and other-directed humans with a confused and diffused identity. If we exploit, demean, order, and direct the growing adolescent, we can inflict permanent scars and inhibit healthy development. Such damage may not be as visible as a physical handicap, but the scars remain on the inside.

Adolescents in the American culture are thus, by any standards,

This paper was commissioned by Research for Better Schools (RBS), Philadelphia, Pa., for presentation at the National Conference on Moral/Citizenship Education, held in Philadelphia in June 1976. The project was funded by a grant from the National Institute of Education. The opinions expressed in the paper do not necessarily reflect the position or policy of the funding agency, and no official endorsement by it should be inferred. It is reprinted here with the permission of RBS.

confronted with major problems of personal development during the time they attend secondary schools. Almost any index confirms the existence of multiple difficulties in personal development for adolescents and young adults. High school dropout rates, low academic achievement, drug usage among teenagers, the matter of runaways, and personal alienation are examples of current and obvious problems. It must be noted, of course, that many of these problems are not new. Adolescence, by definition, has always been a somewhat turbulent era, especially in societies that deliberately make the adolescent a "marginal person" by denying him adult status and responsibility. In addition to the difficulties created by "coming of age," there are also the problems of adjustment caused by the pronounced rate of physiological change, with its inevitable psychological effect.

Some years ago we published an article entitled "Psychological Education in Secondary Schools: A Program to Promote Individual and Human Development" in *The American Psychologist.*[2] The response to that article was extraordinary: there were thousands of letters of inquiry. The basic argument was that personal development should be a central focus of education. Included was a sketchy outline of what education for personal development might be like. In retrospect the rationale was more persuasive than the alternate curriculum to stimulate personal development that was outlined. We wrote, essentially, as counseling psychologists, humanists, and teachers frustrated by the gap between what we taught and offered adolescents and what we knew our students' lives and concerns to be. And we were writing at a time (the end of the 1960's) of marked turmoil, which the universities and young people felt with particular intensity. We said then, and still believe: "Youth (both white and black) experience and are more deeply affected by such problems because they live, psychologically, in a more exposed and vulnerable position."[3] Adolescence, in the best of times, is not something one would choose for his children; exacerbated by the divisions over Vietnam, racism, drugs, and the generation gap, the 1960's seemed the worst of times to come of age. Perhaps we exaggerated the problems, as self-appointed tribunes of the young have been known to do. But we also remembered how John Kennedy and Martin Luther King had represented to the young what seemed best about America. The evidence that a tractableness has now replaced student militancy in suburbia, that a generation of poor adolescents, both black and white, will get, at best, an inferior education because of the short-term disaster of urban school desegregation, and that alcohol rather than barbiturates is the current teenage drug of choice is cold comfort for anyone who continues to care about humanizing education.

Similarly, a "school is dead" theology or pessimism for the sake of pessimism had nothing to do with a second point we made. We believed that public schools were in trouble—deeply so in the city, subtly so in the suburbs. Confronted by a peculiarly confused and anguished group of young people, they lacked appropriate programs.

Schools, either city, suburban or rural, have tended to define their role as the transmitters of academic ideas and skills. Recent efforts at reform have been directed at revitalizing the existing academic curriculum and its teaching. Very little intellectual energy or funding has been directed toward reformulating education—that is, the development of essentially new curricula and new forms of educating adolescents. In most schools and in most eras, the personal side of education has had a lower priority than the academic. The school has always had extensive *rhetoric* about individual growth, but de facto personal or psychological development has been largely the result of random (and often inimical) forces in the school.[4]

In short, we argued that psychology and education have no choice but to help adolescents and young adults as they attempt to mature in the face of unusual vicissitudes. The form of the difficulties has changed in the past six years but not the substance. As noted, alcohol has replaced acid, and privatism has replaced protest, but the generic problems of development remain. Cosmetic changes only mask, but do not fundamentally alter.

James Coleman presented the first detailed account of the result of society's failure to provide for effective psychological education for adults. In his classic study, *The Adolescent Society*, he clearly pointed out the negative effects of the oppressive peer group in promoting the values extolled by Madison Avenue: good looks, fast cars, and the advantages of being a part of the in crowd. He found the impact so broad as to appear almost endemic.[5] In a remarkably prophetic statement just prior to Coleman's study, Erikson noted, "Youth after youth, bewildered by some assumed role, a role forced on him by the inexorable standardization of American adolescence, runs away in one form or another; leaving schools and jobs, staying out all night, or withdrawing into bizarre and inaccessible moods."[6]

Thus, our society has not, in any general sense, responded effectively to the challenge posed by adolescence as a stage of development and to the opportunity it presents to maximize psychological growth during this period. The next section will consider the current impact of schooling and the need for new forms of education that involve elements of action learning and experience for growth.

Schooling Is Not Neutral

An examination of the impact of schooling upon teenagers demonstrates the urgent need for educational solutions—new forms, new programs, and new experiences designed to enhance rather than impede development. Paulo Friere has correctly pointed out that there is no such thing as a neutral educational process. By definition, education is not a value-free concept. Richard Shaull, in his foreword to Friere's work, notes, "Education either functions as an instrument which is used to facilitate the integration of the younger generation into the logic of the present system and bring about conformity to it, *or* it becomes the 'practice of freedom,' the means by which men and women deal critically and creatively with reality and discover how to participate in the transformation of their world."[7]

A series of recent extensive studies has researched the psychological impact of schooling upon adolescent pupils. Such studies provide a searching illustration of the extent to which schooling becomes the "practice of freedom" or something quite different. Many books and articles depict graphically what is really "learned" in school.[8] Research on teaching indicates that instruction still predominantly consists of telling and that pupils typically are intellectually passive and dependent on teachers.[9]

All of these studies raise profound questions about the basic objectives of schooling. Multiple failures of the institution of schooling are implied. The "common" school as the goal of public education, as Peter Schrag[10] and others point out, is simply a convenient myth. Schools tend to perpetuate, rather than reduce, social and educational differences among children.[11] Seeley and his colleagues indicated the extent to which the values of students in secondary schools reflect family backgrounds,[12] a result cross-validated through the massive study by Coleman on the equality of educational opportunity.[13] The explosive situation in slum schools heightens our awareness of the problems created by schooling that systematically avoids personal development and human growth as major educational objectives. It is now obvious that poor children, both black and white, have learned, and indelibly so, to regard themselves with self-contempt as a result of schooling.[14] What else they may have learned (reading, spelling, writing) may be "academic" and esoteric in the most literal sense. It is also obvious if we listen to the voices from the ghetto that adults want their children to have the opportunity to develop a strong and stable self-concept, a sense of personal identity.

The Role of the School in Psychological Education

Until recently, schools have generally assumed that their mission was to develop the intellect and the skills of their pupils. Personal and psychological growth was considered inappropriate for regular classroom experiences. It was hoped, of course, that subjects in the standard curriculum would positively influence the personal development of pupils, at least as a by-product. It is ironic that recent research on the impact of schooling indicates that just the reverse actually happens.[15] Schools are now providing a personal and psychological education, and yet the effect is not positive. The so-called hidden agenda or implicit curriculum of most schools produces negative results. Intrinsic interest in learning *declines* the longer a pupil remains in school. Negative self-concepts *increase* with time spent in school. Stereotyped "surface" and judgmental thinking *increases*. Self-confidence in the ability to solve problems *decreases*, as does personal autonomy in learning tasks. Personal alienation, inhibition, isolation, and interpersonal competition in a negative sense *increase*.[16] The conclusion is inescapable: the schools are psychological educators. For example, in various subject-matter areas it may be taught that teachers have power and that children are impotent, irresponsible, and should be intellectually and personally dependent. The emphasis on achievement and competitiveness (or cheating) and a belief that self-worth is tied to academic achievement are further examples. This is a harsh critique of the school, but evidence suggests that this hidden curriculum is typically more inimical and psychologically crippling than it is positive and developmental.

Who Is to Blame? The Culprit Theory

It is important to recognize that this critique of schooling is not based on any specific culprit theory that advocates the deliberate educational destruction of children. Such conspiracy theories do exist, however. For example, teachers themselves are only "near-adults" and, therefore, unconsciously punish any attempt by teenagers to develop independence, or educational administrators are only concerned about the exercise of power and manipulation as latter-day versions of Machiavelli's *Prince*. Obviously such thinking and assumptions are simple-minded stereotypes and clearly hinder the creation of more effective educational programs. In a paradoxical sense it is our contention that we are all victims of inadequate educational theory and practice. Teachers, counselors, administrators, and university professors, as well as children and their parents, are all caught in the same web. For too long we have accepted a series of educational myths and unexamined assumptions about teaching and learning. We have also avoided facing the implications as negative information emerged. Recently, for example, a massive systematic study by Flanagan on the impact of traditional methods of curricula has revealed less than positive outcomes.[17] Less than two-thirds of a huge sample of secondary pupils in English (250,000) could understand one-half of Robert Louis Stevenson's *Treasure Island*. Less than one-third understood Rudyard Kipling, and only 8 percent understood Jane Austen. In social studies the picture was no more optimistic. Scriven reported that less than one-quarter of the teenagers in this country can present a two-page outline with arguments for and against democracy as a form of government and that approximately two-thirds of the general public in this country resolutely opposes every practical instance of free speech.[18] And yet the "standard" curriculum remains intact.

The so-called standard curriculum, no matter how imaginatively taught, contains an intrinsic educational contradiction. The material and the teaching style tend to assume rather than promote development. They assume that pupils are capable of transferring and incorporating vicarious concepts to enhance their own psychological and intellectual development. The balance of real experience and reflection, process and content, emotions and thought, and affective and cognitive learning is significantly missing in most curricula. In other words, instructional theory and materials are inadequate to the task. John Dewey remarked to the effect that education is and always will be in the hands of "ordinary" men and women.[19] Because most educators are ordinary men and women, with inadequate tools, they cannot succeed. It is our view, based on our experience, that ordinary men and women can accomplish positive and extraordinary goals with appropriate educational techniques guided by theory. The problem, then, is to create new educational forms, practice, and theory to enhance classroom learning. We know that we cannot continue to view teaching and learning as the transmission of knowledge from books directly into pupils' minds.

William James perhaps best summarized the inadequacy of the rote memorization approach (thinking without experience) with the following example: "A friend of mine, visiting a school, was asked to examine a young class in geography. Glancing at the book she said, 'Suppose you should dig a hole in the ground, hundreds of feet deep, how should you find it at the bottom—warmer or colder than on top?' None of the class replying, the teacher said: 'I'm sure they know, but I think you don't ask the question quite rightly. Let me try.' So, taking the book, she said: 'In what condition is the interior of the globe?' and received the immediate answer from half the class at once: 'The interior of the globe is in a condition of igneous fusion.'"[20]

On the other hand, learning through experience alone is clearly not a viable alternative. Experience for its own sake will not necessarily stimulate growth to more complex stages. When a teacher candidate presented himself to John Dewey with the claim, "I've been teaching for ten years," Dewey's question was, "Ten years? Or one year ten times?"[21] Romantic educational critics have wrongly assumed that Dewey's dictum of learning by doing did not include the parallel component of hard thinking and disciplined inquiry. There are qualitative differences in what and how much learning can be drawn from a variety of experiences.

A Time for a Paradigm Shift

Thomas Kuhn has suggested that scientific and educational change does not occur as a result of sudden, dramatic breakthroughs. He points out that the process of real change follows, instead, a predictable but slow evolutionary sequence. As studies, findings, and discussions that increasingly cast doubt on our basic assumptions accrue over a number of years, the process of gradual change is set in motion. He terms this process a slow paradigm shift. The generally accepted assumptions that make up the current paradigm or theoretical model become increasingly more difficult to defend logically. The ground weakens upon which the common frame of reference stands. Most people, being creatures of habit and stability, have difficulty recognizing these gradual shifts.[22] As William James noted many years ago, we become perceptual "old fogies" at tender ages and use our intellectual mechanisms to make the "new" look like the "old."[23] At the same time the accrual of logic eventually causes us to accept the new assumptions or, in Kuhn's phrase, the new paradigm and frame of reference. Thus, in a specific sense, many of the assumptions of so-called traditional teaching methods and definitions of curricular materials have been undergoing examination over the past ten to fifteen years. This suggests the importance for all of us to catch up with the process of change and to understand the paradigm shift rather than to engage in recriminations or expend energy in seeking single causes for educational disasters.

We should recall that Freire posed the original question: "Do schools seek to induce conformity or can they stimulate the practice of freedom?"[24] The evidence strongly suggests that the general impact is negative. This does not mean that all schools fail or that all teaching is narrow, pedantic, and passive. It does mean that the common assumptions of vicarious learning, of the transmission of knowledge, and of the receptivity of pupils are no longer adequate. It also means that we must look further than new ways to teach about the Tigris and Euphrates, *Beowulf*, and the scientific equivalents of igneous fusion to accept the implications of the paradigm shift.

It is both interesting and disheartening that recent studies show that actual classroom interaction in most schools still consists predominantly of teachers' talking and pupils' listening. Studies in 1912 found that over 80 percent of all classroom talk consisted of the teacher's asking brief, direct, factual questions at the rate of about four per minute. In studies conducted in the 1960's, fully fifty years later, the results were astonishingly similar. The teacher's talk accounted for 70 percent of all classroom talk, and, again, it was mostly in the form of brief, direct, factual questions at the rate of two to three per minute. The study of Goodlad and Klein in 1974 of a national random cross section of classrooms indicated the same general pattern. "At all grade levels, the teacher-to-child pattern of interaction overwhelmingly prevailed. This was one of the most monotonously recurring pieces of data. The teacher asked questions and the children responded, usually in a few words and phrases . . . . It is fair to say that this teacher-to-child interaction was the mode in all but about 5 percent of the classes."[25]

It is time for a paradigm shift. Both form and content at the secondary school level require fundamental reexamination.

Coleman has suggested that the school must shift its function from such limited and classical objectives. The school's dependence on such goals must be reduced so that it can adopt new ones: "The new goal must be to integrate the young into functional community roles . . . since the school's function will no longer be to protect the child from society but rather to move him into it. The school must be integrated with service organizations, such as those providing medical services, so that the young can help in them."[26] In Coleman's view the critical goal of education is to shape responsible, productive human beings, ". . . who can *lead* in a task or follow, and who are able to live with the consequences of their actions."[27]

It is clear throughout this entire rationale that adolescents need and deserve responsible roles to play, and schools need and deserve new programs to meet such reciprocal needs. Dr. Harvey Scribner, the former head of the largest school system in the country, accurately perceived the problem as arising from the false dichotomy of intellectual versus personal learning. As a result, he has called for a redefinition to eliminate the distinctions between acquisition of skills and psychological development. The effective school, he suggests, is the one "which defines its curriculum as opportunities to grow simultaneously both in skills and psychologically."[28]

Ralph Tyler, an eminent educational psychologist, has called for similar changes in curricular experiences for adolescents. "Schools have failed to provide opportunities for young people to mature through assuming responsible social roles. The schools tend to serve children, to plan *for* them when the need is for the teenagers to serve and plan for others."[29]

If the school is to enhance the "practice of freedom" on the part of growing citizens in its charge, it is clear that new developmental learning programs are now essential. The assumptions of a new educational balance between action and reflection are, of course, critical. The following section presents a careful examination of the educational assumptions and objectives that form the framework for new educational programs as well as a new paradigm for basic assumptions and guiding constructs.

Educational Objectives and Developmental Theories

Archambault, in his preface to *John Dewey on Education*, has said: "It is a commonplace that everyone talks about Dewey and no one reads him."[30] A careful reading, however, reveals even now that his argument that "the aim of education is development of individuals to the utmost of their potentialities" is still the clearest philosophical rationale for the education we are creating. In a succinct essay, "The Need for a Philosophy of Education," published originally in 1934, Dewey made a series of telling points: "What then is education when we find actual satisfactory specimens of it in existence? In the first place it is a process of development, of growth. And it is the *process* and not merely the result that is important . . . an educated person is the person who has the power to go on and get more education."[31] Dewey then stated that Rousseau's notion of "natural" development (human beings, analogous to seeds, have latent powers that, if left to themselves, will ultimately flower and bear fruit) has at least two fallacies. First, people are vastly more complex in their development and potential than plants. Second, development is a matter of the kind of interaction that occurs between the organism and its environment. Nature and nurture, in interaction, produce development. And Dewey argued that development (or education) starts with the pupil. "Every mind, even of the youngest, is naturally or inherently seeking for those modes of active operation that are within the limits of its capacity.... The problem, a difficult and delicate one, is to discover what tendencies are especially seeking expression at a particular time and just what materials and methods will serve to evoke and direct a truly educative development."[32] What Dewey did not and could not know was what actually characterizes development, whether intellectual, moral, or social, at a particular stage or time in the person's life. A generation of research in genetic epistemology and developmental psychology—by such people as Piaget, Kohlberg, and Loevinger—now offers educators relatively clear blueprints of what people are like at various stages in their lives and what stimulates their intellectual, moral, and personal-social growth.[33] This information that is available to us and not to Dewey says much, in developmental "fact," about that remarkably prophetic phrase the "tendencies especially seeking expression at a particular time."[34] What developmental psychology does not concern itself with, but developmental education does, is "just what materials and methods will serve to evoke and direct a truly educative development."[35]

There is little need here to examine Dewey's critique of traditional education—the external and authoritative imposition of subject matter and skills that he compared quaintly to "inscribing records upon a passive phonographic disc to result in giving back what has been inscribed when the proper button is pressed in recitation or examination."[36] That system (and its more contemporary critique) is still too much with us, as we have noted, and needs no further comment. Criticism is, in the final analysis, easy; constructive reformulation of educational practice is much harder. But our critique of the schools discussed in the article in *The American Psychologist*[37] is absolutely fundamental to understanding our continuing odyssey in developmental education.

Dewey's more important point was that progressive education should not stop with the recognition of the importance of giving free scope to native capacities and interests. This is simply another way of saying that we should not fall into the Rousseauistic trap and merely get out of the child's way.[38] Much of the criticism of progressivism as a "country-club existentialism" or "directionless activity"[39] may have resulted from progressive educators and critics who genuinely misunderstood how much more than this Dewey was saying, both about the intricate characteristics of development in children and about how they have to be seen as potentialities and processes that are not enduring or end points but that, with experience and time, will themselves evolve profoundly.

The special obligation of the educator to understand, thoroughly, the psychology of cognitive, moral, and social development is part of the charge that Dewey was anticipating. The other part concerns the central task of developmental education: to devise and test curricula (the systematic educational experiences) that permit the person continuously to grow from experience. And Dewey foresaw something we are learning—that we have to pay more, not less, attention to the subject matter and pedagogy of developmental education. Devising and validating those experiences that, indeed, affect development are far more complex tasks than rewriting curricula in American history or literature. There are far more precedents and criteria for doing the latter.

The great problem of the adult who has to deal with the young is to see, and to feel deeply as well as merely to see intellectually, the forces that are moving in the young; but it is to see them as possibilities, as signs and promises; to interpret them, in short, in the light of what they may come to be. Nor does the task end there. It is bound up with the further problem of judging and devising the conditions, the materials, both physical, such as tools of work, and moral and social, which will, once more, so *interact* with existing powers and preferences as to bring about transformation in the desired direction.[40]

The point is that it would be nearly a generation before the first part of this metaphor—"to see intellectually, the forces that are moving in the young"—would be translated into comprehensive, empirical psychological data or knowledge. (More will be said about that knowledge of development in the next section.) And it is only in the past five years that the educational work of translating the second part of the metaphor—"devising the conditions . . . [which will] *interact* with existing powers . . . to bring about transformation"—into concrete curriculum with developmental effects has begun. And, again, how rigorously that must be done was anticipated by Dewey. "If we do not go on and go far in the positive direction of providing a body of subject matter much richer, more varied and flexible, and also in truth more definite . . . than traditional education supplied, we shall tend to leave an educational vacuum in which anything can happen."[41] A valid supposition is that this is what the progressive educators could not accomplish. Why this is so is a complex story, part of which Lawrence Cremin tells in *The Transformation of the School*.[42] Some of it had to do with the fact that the psychological knowledge of the stages, characteristics, and experiences contributing to human development available to them was grossly inadequate. In any event, the project method is a pretty lightweight translation of what Dewey was calling for. It may be that current or subsequent critics of developmental education will similarly damn our efforts with faint praise. The charge remains, however, as does the consequence of ineptitude.

The young live in some environment whether we intend it or not and this environment is constantly interacting with what children bring to it, and the result is the shaping of their interests—minds and character—either educatively or miseducatively. If the professed educator abdicates his responsibility for judging and selecting the kind of environment that his best understanding leads him to think will be conducive to growth, then the young are left at the mercy of all the unorganized and casual forces of the modern social environment that inevitably play upon them as long as they live.[43]

Dewey made two additional points in this essay that have profound meaning for contemporary developmental education. Development, he said, is a continuous process, which means that the experiences or action stimulating development will have a quality of consecutiveness—of planned order. He warned that "it is comparatively easy to improvise, to try a little of this today and this week and then something else tomorrow and next week . . . without care and thought [this] results all too readily, in a detached multiplicity of isolated short-time activities or projects and the continuity necessary for growth is lost."[44] The curriculum we outlined in the article in *The American Psychologist*[45] is vulnerable to this charge; our present curricula, as discussed below, are much less so. But we are still some distance from the curricula or the knowledge by which to order experiences to stimulate consecutive development. We perceive the need and the outline of how to get there, but much development and testing remain to be done. This is the essential justification for developmental education.

Programs in Developmental Education

And so we come, finally, to the genuinely original thing we have learned in six years of research on curriculum: "[some of] what materials and methods will serve to evoke and direct a truly educative development."[46] The most important point to be made in support of the theoretical argument for developmental education is that it is practicable. That is, we now have reasonable evidence that it is feasible through education to stimulate human development as modern psychology understands it. No one group of developmental educators can do it all, but the creation and the testing of the educational prototypes are feasible.

What is the evidence? First, there is a series of studies that document discrete effects on aspects of development, primarily moral and ego development. These studies, among many others, include those initiated at Harvard by Mosher and Sprinthall[47] and their students: Atkins,[48] Dowell,[49] Griffin,[50] Katz,[51] Mager,[52] Greenspan;[53] the research of Kohlberg[54] and his associates: Blatt,[55] Hickey,[56] Scharf;[57] Mosher and his students at Boston University: Grimes,[58] Lorish,[59] Mackie,[60] Felton,[61] Sullivan,[62] Paolitto,[63] Stanley,[64] DiStefano,[65] Wasserman;[66] Sprinthall and his students at Minnesota: Erickson,[67] Rustad,[68] Schaffer,[69] Hurt,[70] Brock;[71] and Beck, Sullivan, and Taylor at Toronto.[72]

The estimates or measures of development used have included: Kohlberg's moral dilemmas; Loevinger's ego development test; Rest's defining issues test; Harvey, Hunt, and Schroder's conceptual systems test; William Perry's measure of intellectual development; interviews with students; thematic and structural analyses of journals; and classroom climate inventories. On these measures of development the studies provide significant evidence of the effect of education on moral reasoning and ego development in children, adolescents, and young adults.

And there is replication of what has been found. For example, Dowell, Erickson, Rustad, and Sullivan all found significant effects on both moral reasoning and ego development of high school students taking various courses in psychological and moral education.[73] Dowell, Griffin, Sprinthall, and Felton taught adolescents to counsel and found the experience to have had a significant effect on their development.[74] Blatt, Grimes, and Paolitto established that it is practicable to stimulate the moral reasoning of elementary and junior high school students.[75] Somewhat less extensive curriculum development has been done with young adults. Hurt found significant increases in moral reasoning among juniors and seniors in college.[76] Kohlberg and Gilligan reported similar effects with undergraduates at Harvard.[77] Further studies include Whiteley's research at the University of California at Irvine on the effects of living and participating in a just university residence community and Santa Luca's work with women in junior colleges in Boston.[78]

As the data from these studies show, many of the classes stimulate similar shifts in moral-ethical and psychological-personal development. Scores on the Kohlberg test show a consistent shift from Stage 3 to Stage 4. Results on the Loevinger test also indicate a shift from Stage 3 to Stages 3-4 and Stage 4. The change was from wary and self-protective to more trust and open communication and greater self-respect and complexity. This is, essentially, a shift from other-directedness to the beginnings of a more integrated inner-reliant and less egocentric stage. The results on the Kohlberg test, while not as dramatic, statistically confirmed the trend: the pupils moved from Stage 3 toward Stage 4. The content of those stages is analogous to that in Loevinger's stages except that it is much more difficult to move through an entire stage in Kohlberg's system. There, it usually takes teenagers two or three years to move from Stage 3 to Stage 4, and, even then, a substantial minority never makes it past Stage 3. Thus, the smaller quantitative shift exhibited in Kohlberg's results may well be more significant theoretically. Certainly the changes are internally consistent across all these studies. In many of the courses referred to above, the pupils played various social roles—counselor, interviewer, and childcare helpers. Such participation would thus seem requisite for growth. In the regular or control classes the pupils remained merely pupils, and the learning was more traditional and passive. Thus, it seems that active social role taking by adolescents represents a promising method of stimulating their cognitive structural growth.[79]

As noted earlier, one of the basic assumptions from Dewey is the concept of qualitatively different stages, or systems of thinking. Growth and development then represent a series of milestones, or qualitatively distinct schemata, each more comprehensive and complex than the previous one. The structural changes in Stage 4 thinking by the teenagers on questions of social justice represent an important step toward greater complexity, especially in regard to empathy. The pupils were no longer as concerned over what the "leading crowd" might think or do. They gained, rather, an increasing ability genuinely to understand another person's perspective—to feel at an experiential level what another human may be confronting in his or her own life. Similar shifts in ego development represent structural change of a higher order that implies greater differentiation (seeing and understanding at a more complex level).

What developmental education has learned can be summarized as follows: First, the volume of research on the developmental effects of various curricula is expanding quickly. It is obvious that the research is far from complete or definitive, is overly dependent on doctoral dissertations, and is heuristic. Of the several strands of human development, we know most how to educate for moral and ego development in preadolescence, adolescence, and young adulthood. Stimulation of these two basic strands of development is practicable. The Biological Sciences Curriculum Study Project, *The Human Sciences: A Developmental Approach to Adolescent Education*,[80] may yield data on whether that three-year curriculum, at least, can stimulate movement from concrete to formal operations at the junior high school level. The variety of studies of moral education using Kohlberg's cognitive developmental measure are the only present indicators that it may be possible to "teach" people to think in more complex ways. Our intuition is that this will be the acid test of developmental education.[81] (We hasten to reiterate an earlier point: that the claims of existing curricula to be teaching children to think are equally vulnerable and questionable.) Groundbreaking research in the area of education for aesthetic, vocational, and physical development remains to be done. In some instances the requisite developmental theory is lacking. The need for hard thinking and hard educational development is very clear.

The further development of children, adolescents, and young adults is easiest (though no "pure" development is easy) to effect by education when it is time for that development to occur normally. The study by Grimes, in which all sixth-grade children in the experimental class moved from preconventional to conventional moral reasoning as a result of a course in moral education shared by their mothers, is an illustration. Age eleven to thirteen is the normal time for this transition to occur. Grimes's research (so, too, Felton's and Stanley's) also underscores the importance of providing knowledge of human development and how education can support it to parents, who are, obviously, the primary educators of their children.[82] By contrast, education is most difficult and requires the most intensive interaction with people whose development has been arrested.[83] But this is hardly surprising in light of the literature on therapy, corrections, and remedial education.

What we are able to learn about stimulating people's development by education is limited, in part, by what we can measure. There is, for example, a paucity of valid instruments that can register the emergence of more complex ways of thinking about logical propositions or one's moral obligations, about who one is, or about an enlarging social conscience. The complexity and cost of administering some of the available measures constitute a further handicap. Other outcomes of the variety of curricula being tested are, however, clearly significant. Thus, it has been discovered that adolescents can learn to counsel or teach as well as many professionals and, in the process, mature morally and socially and that they can create genuine self-government in their schools, become skillful in conducting and participating in democratic groups, and acquire higher stage moral reasoning in so doing.

Of special importance is that we are learning what educational experiences are particularly appropriate to produce decalage or consolidation in development at a given period in the individual's life and to ensure transition to higher stages of moral reasoning or ego development. We also are beginning to understand the necessary consecutiveness in these experiences. We know, for example, that moral development is caused by several factors: being exposed to and interacting intellectually with higher stage arguments; learning to understand the thinking and feeling of other people, which produces increased empathy for others and an enlarged social perspective and concern; and action on behalf of chosen moral and social goals. What educational experiences, then, may be expected to stimulate moral development? A first category is the discussion of moral dilemmas, of which current curricular examples include written dilemmas,[84] filmstrips,[85] and films.[86] A second kind of generic educational experience is in what Mead called role taking.[87] Among curricula providing this experience are learning to counsel,[88] adolescents as moral educators,[89] and role-taking curriculum for the junior high school.[90] A third kind of experience is that provided by social service and social action, the study of the justice structure of institutions (such as the school, the family, and the courts and government), and experiences in making rules, in creating fairer institutions, and in participating in democratic institutions. Experimental curricula providing these kinds of experience include Sullivan's, where adolescents taught moral education classes to younger children and formed a high school disciplinary appeals board,[91] B.S.C.S.'s *Human Sciences'* units on "Rules" and "What's Happening to Me?"[92] Newmann's curricula in social and political action,[93] democratic high school experiments in Brookline and Cambridge, Massachusetts, and in

Pittsburgh, Pennsylvania,[94] and Stanley's work on the justice structure of the family as a focus for the education of parents and adolescents.[95]

Further, it is now possible, on the basis of this growing body of research, to suggest what educational experiences are most appropriate to an individual's stage of moral development and how they may be sequenced for progressive growth. For example, to stimulate development from preconventional to conventional moral reasoning in the fifth and sixth grades Grimes suggests the discussion of moral dilemmas, creating and role playing original dilemmas, and training mothers to be moral educators.[96] Paolitto used a variety of imaginative role-taking experiences to the same end with junior high school students.[97] Both Dowell[98] (and many others), who taught adolescents to counsel, and Lorish,[99] who trained prisoners to be peer counselors for other inmates, argue that teaching people to counsel others may be the single most powerful educational experience presently available to stimulate conventional moral thinking, empathy, and role taking.

To consolidate conventional moral reasoning, the discussion of dilemmas and the study of law, constitutions, governance, and fairness of institutions, plus involvement in social service and social-political action, are appropriate to the various stages of educational experience. Two kinds of educational experience have been demonstrated to be critical in stimulating the development of principled moral reasoning. One is the systematic experience in rule making and the democratic governance of classrooms, alternative high schools, or undergraduate residences.[100] The other is participation in moral discussion[101] or the study of normative philosophy or topics in ethics and moral philosophy by high school seniors.[102]

Thus, the picture of what we know is a mixed one. Research is progressing on more extensive curricula, particularly on the "just community," or democracy as education, experiments at the high school level in Brookline and Cambridge, Massachusetts, in Pittsburgh, Pennsylvania, and at the University of California, Irvine. Teachers and counselors are being trained in developmental psychology and in the creating and teaching of developmental curricula in Brookline, Cambridge, Pittsburgh, Minneapolis, and Tacoma. In Brookline, this education of teachers is being extended to the elementary school level and, in moral development, through adult education.[103] In Tacoma, it will involve over three years of developing and testing moral education curricula for the elementary school through senior high; a large number of teachers will be trained, and these programs will be disseminated to other school districts in the state of Washington.

In summary, substantial educational development is under way. Though it is incomplete and fractionated, it is as promising and as vital a movement as currently exists anywhere in American public education. On the basis of this emergent picture, then, we can reach some tentative conclusions and make some recommendations.

Summary and Recommendations

Developmental education programs, as Mildred McCloskey of the National Commission on Resources for Youth has noted, have a number of similar characteristics. She had characterized the average teaching-learning experience for teenagers as "over-stimulated and under-used." In the variety of exemplary programs, however, she found singular exceptions. Such programs seemingly reversed the usual educational assumptions during adolescence and succeeded in promoting healthy psychological and personal growth. She was able to identify eight characteristics of these outstanding programs:

1. *They fill genuine needs* for both adolescents and society, involving students in a significant task—one that both young people and society recognize as important.

2. *They offer active learning* in an age of spectatorship. Learning through experience, through actual observation and involvement, is a natural way to learn and is especially suited to today's youth.

3. *They offer challenge*, providing youth a chance to do something not only meaningful, but also difficult. They demand from adolescents a full expenditure of mind and spirit.

4. *They promote maturity and responsibility*, stimulating growth on several levels—developmental, interpersonal, as well as cognitive. The youth involved in them learn to make decisions, share in governance, and perform leadership roles.

5. *They relate theory to practice* and demand more learning to guide further practice.

6. *They give adolescents a glimpse of the real options that are available* in the adult world. Youth find out about the world of work and about their own interests and potentials.

7. *The represent delicate working partnerships between youth and adult*, collaborative models in which each age group offers what it uniquely can.

8. *They offer a community experience*—a sense of belonging to an extended family and the exhilaration that comes from being associated with significant others.[104]

Another way to summarize the programs can be stated in the following manner.

1. *The adolescent as an "adult."* Adolescents can learn and perform effectively in significant "adult" roles such as in teaching, counseling, and child-care activities. Learning to perform these functions stimulates the intellectual, moral, ethical, and psychological development of the teenage tutors, counselors, and child-care workers. Significant social role taking stimulates moral maturity.

2. *The adolescent as a "philosopher."* Teenagers can learn to think through significant questions concerning values, to analyze critically clashes between general and personal values, and to discern the ethical implications from such analysis. The adolescent can be viewed as a moral philosopher. By learning to examine such questions regarding values, moral and cognitive growth is stimulated. Teenagers can also learn to lead and teach discussions on values.

3. *The adolescent as a "democrat and a citizen."* Teenagers can learn to participate in "just" communities, to create democratic systems of rules, and to distinguish between laws and principles. Such participation (genuine participatory democracy) stimulates psychological and ethical maturity.

4. *The adolescent as a "psychologist."* Teenagers can learn to analyze human behavior and to understand its multiple causes, to master the skills of caring, and to differentiate thoughts and feelings. Such experiences induce personal (ego), intellectual, and ethical growth.

One final point should be made. There is a single important quality that distinguishes all of the successful developmental education programs noted above: each provides students with a relatively continuous sequence of experiences. The programs, courses, and readings are not designed as a brief educational supplement or as a one-shot experience to liven up a class late on a Friday afternoon. Developmental education programs are sometimes confused with the so-called "human potential movement." The developmental programs are designed as regular one- or two-term classes, usually as a major component of humanities and social studies or even as an entire learning sequence. This is substantially different from and not to be confused with the large number of brief, episodic, and mostly one-shot psychological games and gimmicks currently available in the educational marketplace. So far as we can tell, no research evidence attests to the effectiveness of these tricks in the bags of psychological hucksters. Observation indicates that a specific simulation may indeed create momentary interest, turn some students on, and appear as a welcome change in the ordinary routine. Such versions of a psychological recess, however, should not become confused with sequenced educational programs designed to stimulate developmental growth. Experience has shown that significant change is immune to a momentary classroom psychological simulation. Certainly a basic manifestation of human complexity and strength is the ability to overlook the superficial. The reverse also seems to be true—that teenagers have the ability to engage in and learn from actual human experience.

The conclusions are, in a sense, obvious. The work in psychological, ethical, and ego development is indicative of the possible. Specific school programs, developed, tried, and evaluated in real world settings, provide consistent evidence of positive results. The programs of Sprinthall and Mosher to stimulate growth through adult role taking, the programs of Beck and Sullivan to promote ethical and cognitive development through an in-depth value curriculum, the programs of Kohlberg and others to promote discussions on moral dilemmas, and the program of Newmann to encourage participatory democracy are all working examples. They are not armchair theories, ephemeral paradigms, or esoteric abstractions waiting to be tested.

The goals of such programs also appear to be an important educational synthesis. In simplified terms, the 1950's could be considered the era of intellectual objectives for schooling. The so-called Brunerian revolution, combined with Conant's report on the nation's high schools,[105] created a climate for a major emphasis on conceptual development. The 1960's, on the other hand, represented almost a backlash. Personal learning, humane development, education for personal relevance, as represented by the so-called humanistic or third-force revolution, became a new focus. In our view, neither position can or should become the exclusive objective. Developmental education programs seek to stimulate the mind *and* the heart, the brain *and* the soul, thinking *and* feeling, the intellect *and* the character of each pupil. To promote and stimulate the development of such programs is the objective. In accord with this objective, a series of brief recommendations merits consideration.

The first recommendation concerns finances. Since the current programs are beyond the developmental stage, there is no need for huge amounts of funding. Relatively small supplemental grants are all that may be necessary to provide impetus for the further elaboration of developmental programs. Funding on the scale as that in the era of the Great Society would be a major mistake. There would be a temptation to expand the programs too quickly. The success of current programs has resulted largely from small-scale, carefully evaluated, closely monitored projects. The limited funds available should be used to continue the current promising projects in Brookline, Cambridge, Pittsburgh, Minneapolis, and Irvine. It is noteworthy that each represents an "odd" or atypical combination of university faculty, classroom teachers, graduate students experienced in classroom problems, and researchers all working at school sites. This team approach is fraught with problems, but it does seem to produce programs to be used in the real world.

The second recommendation relates to the education of teachers. New curricular materials designed for consecutive experience would bear no fruit unless requisite work is started in the education of teachers. It is an illusion to build teacherproof materials. The instructional strategies necessary to make any of the programs work must be systematically translated into a model system for educating teachers. Both in-service and preservice education require attention. The teacher as a developmental educator plays a complex instructional role.

The third recommendation involves needed programmatic development in educational administration. Even if we succeed in creating an effective curriculum and in educating teachers, there will be a need for the third component of change. For programs to take root, grow, and expand, principals and assistant principals (the on-line educational policy-makers) need not only understand but must also contribute to the programs. The "just high school," for example, fundamentally alters all the relationships in a school building—teacher, pupil, principal. So-called action-learning or adult role-taking programs affect all scheduling as well as relationships both within the school and in relation to the community. The educational administrator becomes a key figure in leadership, staff development, and new formulations. Such programs can also be implemented in institutions other than the school. For example, when Kohlberg's group worked so successfully within a prison system, the lives and activities of the guards and the warden were as fundamentally changed as were those of the prisoners.

The fourth recommendation relates to the necessity for further study and programmatic development of the community-school relationship. Some of the promising work in the education of parents and in educating teenagers for "parenting" is pertinent. It is obvious that parents can become significant, positive resources to promote the human, ethical, and psychological development of their children. It is also obvious that adolescents can learn techniques of child care and principles of child development.

The fifth recommendation concerns the continuing need for research on the exact nature of the relation of behavior and ethical stage as well as the consequences of these alternative developmental experiences. The context and impact of democracy as educative probably will always defy exact specification, and, yet, even within those limitations, our present successive approximations are still preliminary.

Notes

1. G. Konopka, "Requirements for Healthy Development of Adolescent Youth," *Adolescence*, 31 (No. 8, 1973), 292.

2. R. Mosher and N. A. Sprinthall, "Psychological Education in Secondary Schools: A Program to Promote Individual and Human Development," *American Psychologist*, 25 (October 1970), 911-924.

3. *Ibid.*, 912.

4. *Ibid.*, 913-914.

5. J. Coleman, *The Adolescent Society* (New York: Free Press, 1961).

6. E. H. Erikson, "Identity and the Life Cycle," *Psychological Issues,* 1 (No. 1, 1959), 91.

7. P. Friere, *The Pedagogy of the Oppressed* (New York: Herder and Herder, 1972), 15.

8. Coleman, *The Adolescent Society*; E. Z. Friedenberg, *The Vanishing Adolescent* (Boston: Beacon Press, 1959); P. Jackson, *Life in Classrooms* (New York: Holt, Rinehart and Winston, 1968); H. Kohl, *Thirty-six Children* (New York: New American Library, 1967); J. Kozol, *Death at an Early Age* (Boston: Houghton Mifflin, 1967).

9. J. Hoetker and W. P. Ahlbrand, "The Persistence of Recitation," *American Educational Research Journal*, 6 (No. 12, 1969), 145-167.

10. P. Schrag, *Voices in the Classroom* (Boston: Beacon Press, 1965).

11. J. E. Brophy and T. L. Good, *Teacher-Student Relationships: Causes and Consequences* (New York: Holt, Rinehart and Winston, 1974).

12. J. R. Seeley, R. A. Sim, and E. W. Loosley, *Crestwood Heights* (New York: Basic Books, 1956).

13. J. Coleman *et al.*, *Equality of Educational Opportunity* (Washington, D.C.: Department of Health, Education, and Welfare, 1966).

14. Kohl, *Thirty-six Children*; Kozol, *Death at an Early Age*; Coleman, *The Adolescent Society*; E. Leacock, *Teaching and Learning in City Schools* (New York: Basic Books, 1969).

15. Coleman, *The Adolescent Society*; Jackson, *Life in Classrooms*; P. Minuchin *et al., The Psychological Impact of School Experience* (New York: Basic Books, 1969); R. H. Ojemann, "Basic Approaches to Mental Health," *Personnel and Guidance Journal*, 37 (November 1958), 198-206; C. Silberman, *Crisis in the Classroom* (New York: Random House, 1970); N. A. Sprinthall and R. L. Mosher, "Voices from the Back of the Classroom," *Journal of Teacher Education*, 22 (No. 2, 1971), 166-175.

16. D. Johnson and R. Johnson, "Instructional Goal Structure: Cooperative, Competitive, or Individualistic," *Review of Educational Research*, 44 (No. 2, 1974), 213-240.

17. J. Flanagan, "Education: How and for What," *American Psychologist*, 28 (No. 7, 1973), 551-556.

18. M. Scriven, "Education for Survival," in *Curriculum and the Cultural Revolution,* ed. D. E. Purpel and M. Belanger (Berkeley, Calif.: McCutchan Publishing Corp., 1972), 166-204.

19. *John Dewey on Education: Selected Writings,* ed. R. Archambault (New York: Random House, 1964).

20. W. James, *Talks with Teachers* (New York: W. W. Norton, 1958), 106.

21. This has often been attributed to Dewey.

22. T. Kuhn, *The Structure of Scientific Revolutions* (Chicago: University of Chicago Press, 1965).

23. William James, *Psychology: Briefer Course* (New York: Collier, 1962), 332.

24. Friere, *The Pedagogy of the Oppressed,* Preface.

25. J. Goodlad and M. Klein, *Looking behind the Classroom Door* (Worthington, Ohio: Charles A. Jones, 1974).

26. J. Coleman, "The Children Have Outgrown the Schools," *Psychology Today,* 5 (February 1972), 75.

27. *Ibid.,* 82.

28. H. Scribner, "Responsibilities beyond the Curriculum," conference report to the Association of Orthodox Jewish Teachers, New York, March 1972.

29. R. Tyler, "Summary of Conference Proceedings on Youth-Counseling-Youth Programs," sponsored by the National Commission on Resources for Youth, Baltimore, June 1974.

30. *John Dewey on Education,* ed. Archambault, Preface.

31. *Ibid.,* 4.

32. *Ibid.,* 5-6.

33. J. Piaget, *The Language and Thought of the Child* (London: Routledge and Kegan Paul, 1952); L. Kohlberg, in *Collected Papers on Moral Development and Moral Education* (Cambridge, Mass.: Laboratory of Human Development, Harvard University, 1973); J. Loevinger and R. Wessler, *Measuring Ego Development,* Volumes 1 and 2 (San Francisco: Jossey-Bass, 1970).

34. *John Dewey on Education,* ed. Archambault, 6.

35. *Ibid.*

36. *Ibid.*

37. Mosher and Sprinthall, "Psychological Education in Secondary Schools."

38. *John Dewey on Education,* ed. Archambault, 7-9.

39. *Ibid.,* xxx.

40. *Ibid.,* 8.

41. *Ibid.,* 9.

42. L. Cremin, *The Transformation of the School: Progressivism in American Education, 1876-1957* (New York: Alfred A. Knopf, 1961).

43. *John Dewey on Education,* ed. Archambault, 9.

44. *Ibid.,* 10.

45. Mosher and Sprinthall, "Psychological Education in Secondary Schools."

46. *John Dewey on Education,* ed. Archambault, 6.

47. R. L. Mosher and N. A. Sprinthall, "Deliberate Psychological Education," *Counseling Psychologist,* 2 (No. 4, 1971), 3-82.

48. V. Atkins, "High School Students Who Teach: An Approach to Personal Learning," doctoral dissertation, Graduate School of Education, Harvard University, 1972.

49. R. C. Dowell, "Adolescents as Peer Counselors: A Program for Psychological Growth," doctoral dissertation, Graduate School of Education, Harvard University, 1971.

50. A. Griffin, "Teaching Counselor Education to Black Teenagers," doctoral dissertation, Graduate School of Education, Harvard University, 1972.

51. T. Katz, "The Arts as a Vehicle for the Exploration of Personal Concerns," doctoral dissertation, Graduate School of Education, Harvard University, 1972.

52. G. Mager, "Improvisation Drama as a Way to Learn about Oneself," doctoral dissertation, Graduate School of Education, Harvard University, 1972.

53. B. Greenspan, "Facilitating Psychological Growth in Adolescents through Child Development Curricula," doctoral dissertation, Graduate School of Education, Harvard University, 1974.

54. Kohlberg, in *Collected Papers on Moral Development and Moral Education*.

55. M. Blatt, "Studies on the Effects of Classroom Discussions upon Children's Moral Development," doctoral dissertation, University of Chicago, 1970.

56. J. Hickey, "The Effects of Guided Moral Discussion upon Youthful Offenders' Level of Moral Judgment," doctoral dissertation, School of Education, Boston University, 1972.

57. P. Scharf, "Moral Education in the Prison," doctoral dissertation, Graduate School of Education, Harvard University, 1973.

58. P. Grimes, "Teaching Moral Reasoning to Eleven Year Olds and Their Mothers: A Means of Promoting Moral Development," doctoral dissertation, School of Education, Boston University, 1974.

59. R. Lorish, "Teaching Counseling to Disadvantaged Young Adults," doctoral dissertation, School of Education, Boston University, 1974.

60. P. Mackie, "Teaching Counseling Skills to Low Achieving High School Students," doctoral dissertation, School of Education, Boston University, 1974.

61. L. Felton, "Teaching Counseling to Adolescents and Adults," doctoral dissertation, School of Education, Boston University, 1974.

62. P. Sullivan, "A Curriculum for Stimulating Moral Reasoning and Ego Development in Adolescents," doctoral dissertation, School of Education, Boston University, 1975.

63. D. Paolitto, "Role-Taking Opportunities for Early Adolescents: A Program in Moral Education," doctoral dissertation, School of Education, Boston University, 1975.

64. S. Stanley, "A Curriculum to Affect the Moral Atmosphere of the Family and the Moral Development of Adolescents," doctoral dissertation, School of Education, Boston University, 1976.

65. A. Di Stefano, "Adolescent Moral Reasoning after a Curriculum in Sexual and Interpersonal Dilemmas," doctoral dissertation, School of Education, Boston University, 1977.

66. E. Wasserman, "The Development of an Alternative High School Based

on Kohlberg's Just Community Approach to Education," doctoral dissertation, School of Education, Boston University, 1977.

67. V. L. Erickson, "Psychological Growth for Women: A Cognitive-Developmental Curriculum Intervention," doctoral dissertation, University of Minnesota, 1973.

68. K. Rustad, "Teaching Counseling Skills to Adolescents: A Cognitive-Developmental Approach to Psychological Education," doctoral dissertation, University of Minnesota, 1974.

69. P. A. Schaffer, "Moral Judgment: A Cognitive-Developmental Project in Psychological Education," doctoral dissertation, University of Minnesota, 1974.

70. B. L. Hurt, "Psychological Education of College Students," doctoral dissertation, University of Minnesota, 1974.

71. S. Brock, "Facilitating Psychological Growth in Postadolescents," doctoral dissertation, University of Minnesota, 1974.

72. C. Beck, E. Sullivan, and N. Taylor, "Stimulating Transition to Postconventional Morality: The Pickering High School Study," *Interchange*, 3 (1972), 28-37.

73. Dowell, "Adolescents as Peer Counselors"; Erickson, "Psychological Growth for Women"; Rustad, "Teaching Counseling Skills to Adolescents"; Sullivan, "A Curriculum for Stimulating Moral Reasoning and Ego Development in Adolescents."

74. Dowell, "Adolescents as Peer Counselors"; Griffin, "Teaching Counselor Education to Black Teenagers"; N. A. Sprinthall, "Learning Psychology by Doing Psychology: A High School Curriculum in the Psychology of Counseling," in *Developmental Education*, ed. G. Dean Miller (St. Paul: Minnesota Department of Education, 1976), 23-43; Felton, "Teaching Counseling to Adolescents and Adults."

75. Blatt, "Studies on the Effects of Classroom Discussions upon Children's Moral Development"; Grimes, "Teaching Moral Reasoning to Eleven Year Olds and Their Mothers"; Paolitto, "Role-Taking Opportunities for Early Adolescents."

76. Hurt, "Psychological Education of College Students."

77. L. Kohlberg and C. Gilligan, in *Collected Papers*.

78. J. M. Whiteley, "A Developmental Intervention in Higher Education," in *Developmental Counseling and Teaching*, ed. V. Erickson and J. M. Whiteley (Monterey, Calif.: Brooks/Cole, forthcoming); N. Santa Luca, "Psychological Education for Women in Junior College," doctoral dissertation, School of Education, Boston University, in process.

79. Erickson, "Psychological Growth for Women"; Sullivan, "A Curriculum for Stimulating Moral Reasoning and Ego Development in Adolescents."

80. *The Human Sciences: A Developmental Approach to Adolescent Education* (Boulder, Colo.: Biological Sciences Curriculum Study Group, 1975).

81. Experimental, although by no means *educationally* definitive, studies indicate that stimulating the development of formal operational thinking through systematic intervention is extremely difficult. (See Kuhn, *The Structure of Scientific Revolutions*; M. Schwebel, "Logical Thinking in College Freshmen," unpublished manuscript, Rutgers University, 1972.) It is interesting that similar

statements were made by developmental psychologists about both moral and ego development before the intensive educational interventions reported here were undertaken.

82. Grimes, "Teaching Moral Reasoning to Eleven Year Olds and Their Mothers"; Felton, "Teaching Counseling to Adolescents and Adults"; Stanley, "A Curriculum to Affect the Moral Atmosphere of the Family and the Moral Development of Adolescents."

83. Paolitto, "Role-Taking Opportunities for Early Adolescents"; Hickey, "The Effects of Guided Moral Discussion upon Youthful Offenders' Level of Moral Judgment"; Lorish, "Teaching Counseling to Disadvantaged Young Adults"; Scharf, "Moral Education in the Prison."

84. See, for example, Blatt, "Studies on the Effects of Classroom Discussions upon Children's Moral Development"; E. Speicher and A. Colby, *Hypothetical Moral Dilemmas for Use in the Classroom* (Cambridge, Mass.: Center for Moral Education, Harvard University, 1974).

85. See, for example, Guidance Associates, *First Things First* (New York: Harcourt Brace Jovanovich, 1977).

86. *Searching for Values: A Film Anthology* (New York: Learning Corporation of America, 1975).

87. G. Mead, *Mind, Self and Society* (Chicago: University of Chicago Press, 1934).

88. See, for example, Dowell, "Adolescents as Peer Counselors"; Lorish, "Teaching Counseling to Disadvantaged Young Adults"; Felton, "Teaching Counseling to Adolescents and Adults"; Rustad, "Teaching Counseling Skills to Adolescents."

89. Sullivan, "A Curriculum for Stimulating Moral Reasoning and Ego Development in Adolescents"; R. Alexander, "A Moral Education Curriculum in Prejudice," doctoral dissertation, School of Education, Boston University, 1977.

90. Paolitto, "Role-Taking Opportunities for Early Adolescents."

91. Sullivan, "A Curriculum for Stimulating Moral Reasoning and Ego Development in Adolescents."

92. *The Human Sciences.*

93. F. Newmann, T. A. Bertocci, and R. M. Lundsness, *Skills in Citizen Action* (Madison: University of Wisconsin Publications, 1977).

94. E. Fenton, Danforth Civic Education Project, Carnegie-Mellon University, Pittsburgh.

95. Stanley, "A Curriculum to Affect the Moral Atmosphere of the Family and the Moral Development of Adolescents."

96. Grimes, "Teaching Moral Reasoning to Eleven Year Olds and Their Mothers."

97. Paolitto, "Role-Taking Opportunities for Early Adolescents."

98. Dowell, "Adolescents as Peer Counselors."

99. Lorish, "Teaching Counseling to Disadvantaged Young Adults."

100. R. Mosher, "A Democratic High School: Damn It, Your Feet Are Always in the Water," *Character Potential: A Record of Research*, 8 (Spring 1978); Wasserman, "The Development of an Alternative High School Based on Kohlberg's Just Community Approach to Education."

101. Sullivan, "A Curriculum for Stimulating Moral Reasoning and Ego Development in Adolescents"; R. L. Mosher and P. Sullivan, "A Curriculum in Moral Education for Adolescents," *Journal of Moral Education*, 5 (February 1976), 159-172.

102. Beck, Sullivan, and Taylor, "Stimulating Transition to Postconventional Morality."

103. R. Mosher, "The Brookline Moral Education Project: A Report of Year 1," unpublished manuscript, Center for Moral Education, Harvard University, 1975.

104. M. McCloskey and P. Kleinbard, *Youth into Adult* (New York: National Commission on Resources for Youth, 1974).

105. J. Conant, *The American High School Today: A First Report to Interested Citizens* (New York: McGraw-Hill, 1959).

Funny Things Happen on the Way to Curriculum Development

Ralph L. Mosher

I have been asked to write about how one develops curriculum and to address that topic for a group of people—guidance counselors and school psychologists—who have little history or tendency to teach, let alone create curriculum. Apart from a temperamental disposition to losing causes (for example, I have spent the last twenty years in and out of the field of guidance and counseling psychology), why else try to make such a quixotic case? The answer is in several parts. First, the editors of *Guidance: Strategies and Techniques* have paid me to write about the process of curriculum development; apparently, they think it is a pertinent one for counselors. More fundamentally, I have argued for some time that guidance counselors and school psychologists need to get out of the little white clinic and back into the educational mainstream of the school—that is, the curriculum and teaching—where all of the students and the action are. I think counselors need to do that to escape from the labyrinth of performing low-order administrative tasks (for example, making schedule changes, arranging for college or job interviews), of spending 75 percent of their time with 15 percent of the kids in schools, of adjusting students to the rules and

Reprinted from *Guidance: Strategies and Techniques*, ed. Roger Aubrey and Herman Peters (Denver, Colo.: Love Publishing Co., 1975).

norms of the institution—in short, of working primarily for the school's administration instead of their professed clients, the students. Maybe guidance counselors will dispute that this is what they do or rationalize why it must be so. But I suspect that there are more positive objectives for their work on which we could agree . . . .

Curriculum and Teaching: The School's Mainstream

A social studies department chairman recently said about the interest of counselors in a moral education workshop, "The counselors are trying to get back into the school." While his comment was not entirely flattering, he stated a considerable part of the central argument of this paper. I, too, believe that counselors must get back into the school, more particularly into the curriculum and teaching. Survival or significance as an occupational group probably depends on their so doing. But there are more noble reasons than keeping one's job for so doing. Willie Sutton still makes the best statement of the fundamental raison d'être. The famous bandit, when asked why he robbed banks, replied very matter-of-factly, "Because that's where the money is." At the risk of repetition, the curriculum and teaching, the classroom, are where all students and much of their learning are to be found. So let us stipulate my belief that, if counselors are to get back into schooling, curriculum and teaching is the place for them to have their maximum impact.

But is there any room in the inn? At first glance things look pretty crowded. English teachers seek more time, courses, and effect on children's reading, literacy, and language skills. Social studies curricula increasingly include courses in areas such as psychology, moral reasoning, women's development, and so forth. Teachers really struggle very hard to offer students more and better education. Practically speaking, however, there is some room in the inn. Counselors, with a background in psychology and human development, can make a logical case for a voice in, if not control of, the emerging high school curriculum area of psychology. Some social studies and English teachers, at least, are open to sharing or coteaching classes with counselors. In many schools, independent studies programs are available to students and staff. Time is often scheduled for group guidance—whatever that is. If counselors choose to teach, a way can be found for them to do so. What may be harder is to free significant blocks of their time for instruction. Indeed, the change I advocate for counselors will require them to allocate their time differently than at present. But I assume that where there is a will there is a way into the classroom.

For now, I will pass over a second problem in getting counselors into classrooms. Many counselors are not trained to teach; they may, in fact, have gone into counseling to avoid teaching, evaluating, or working with large groups of children. Clearly, this is a major practical problem for someone arguing that counselors should get back into the school, but I have no patience with people who argue that one-to-one counseling is ideologically the purest way to deal with kids. Their ability to deny the evidence as to the lack of training[1] and effect[2] of counselors is equaled only by their tolerance for the injustices of providing services to one out of five students who have a right to them. Economically, I just do not see the one-on-one argument carrying weight with most taxpayers. Further, I am somewhat heartened by the number of students coming into counseling who want to extend their effect by teaching, who want to get into the school in this way.

The question of what counselors are to teach to further the new day is one which is to be addressed in this paper. At this point we return to the topic at hand—curriculum development. My argument here is fairly straightforward. If counselors are to get back into the school, then their teaching should have to do with personal development, values education and moral reasoning, social development, and vocational education. Clearly, these aspects of growing up are paid less attention in schooling than is the stimulation of the child's intellectual development. Yet few educators would argue against their inclusion in making the child's education whole. In short, there are real needs to help kids grow in these dimensions and a genuine opportunity for counselors and psychologists to contribute to this kind of education. As yet, there are not many ready-made curricula or programs on which the counselor can rely. Such curricula are coming rather rapidly.[3] But this paper has to do with how counselors and teachers can create their own materials of instruction. And because this process can contribute to the professional renewal of the counselor or teacher, I hope people will not wait for the publishing companies to do it for them. But how do busy practitioners develop programs suited to their own purposes? I am reminded of the Israeli general who reported his military situation as hopeless but not serious. Certainly curriculum development under the real conditions of the schools is not easy, but it can be done. One of the myths in education is that only research and development centers or university professors who receive large grants of money can create curriculum. I think this particular myth is created by those professors who want to go on getting large grants of money. Increasingly, my own view is that it does not mean a thing if we cannot give curriculum development skills away to a large number of teachers and counselors and, further, that we can do that. So what does it take to develop curriculum? Initially, let me outline what I see to be the steps involved and then illustrate this overview in a case study.

Curriculum Development: The Essential Steps

At the risk of sounding like a stuck record, let me say that a first condition is simply making up one's mind that it is important to develop curriculum—that is, commitment. I believe that people can think themselves into courses of action and should do so. A second condition is time in which to work. The assistance of a few colleagues is also important. So far we are talking about the prerequisites of will, time, and colleagues. Money is not necessary, except for coffee.

The first substantial step in curriculum development is some hard thinking about the "clients" (for example, elementary school children, high school adolescents) and what one wants them to become, do, or learn. This, in my experience, is a major part of curriculum development and one, I suspect, that teachers or counselors might tend to underestimate or shortchange. It may be too easy to say, "Well, our 'clients' are high school freshman, and the objective is to help them adjust more readily to high school by an eight-week orientation program. So we'll have them meet the principal, visit the library, and talk in group guidance classes about their feelings and apprehensions on beginning high school." But there are, I think, more basic questions to consider: What do we know about ninth graders developmentally? Where are they in terms of cognitive and intellectual development? At what stage of moral and ego development are they likely to be? What are their fundamental characteristics and concerns? Socially, might they be more affected by an orientation program designed and conducted by juniors and seniors in high school? And why an orientation program anyway? Why commit counselors' time and energy to this? Is not such a service simply another ad hoc crisis intervention, more dictated by the need to make the school operate smoothly than by any longer-range development needs of the students? How will an orientation program help ninth graders six to twelve months from now?

The point is not whether these are the precise questions that should be asked. Nor are the answers the issue. What is crucial, in my view, is that teachers or counselors ask hard questions (examine their basic assumptions) about the learners and the proposed educational curricula or experiences. First answers may not be the best ones, although they will serve to reduce everyone's anxiety. Further, the working answers a group arrives at should be seen as precisely that—working answers, subject to reexamination and reformulation on the basis of a tryout of the curriculum with the clients.

Relative to hard thinking about the clients and what we want them to learn, do, or become, all the theory one can get will not be too much. In the ubiquitous example of freshman orientation programs cited above, the reader will remember that the first questions suggested were these: What do we know about ninth graders developmentally? Where are they in terms of cognitive intellectual and development? (not What does Xville do in its freshman orientation program? Time for that one later.) These are questions concerning which knowledge exists in developmental psychology. I would want to extract from theory, from psychology and sociology, everything I could about fourteen-year-olds. I would begin by reading and discussing the *Daedalus* special issue on preadolescence (1972). From there I would go on to reread and discuss some of Piaget, Kohlberg, Elkind, Erikson, Coleman, and Sullivan. I am serious in saying this. First, I do not believe curriculum development (or anything else in education) should be done in half-measures. There now are available to practitioners some very useful blueprints of what is happening to kids at various stages of development, of how they characteristically think about academic problems or moral issues, of what preoccupies them and what kind of experiences may help them develop, and so on. This "theoretical" knowledge is far from complete, but to ignore it is a mistake. Eighty years ago John Dewey argued: "To the educator, therefore, the only solid ground of assurance that he is not setting up impossible or artificial aims . . . is a clear and definite knowledge of the normal end and the normal forms of mental action (i.e., the characteristic ways individuals think and how these develop in our time). To know these things is to be a true psychologist . . . and to have the essential qualifications of the true educationist."[4] What educators now have available to them is an extraordinary amount of psychological knowledge about development (for example, about what is happening to fourteen-year-olds in this culture) which was not "known" to Dewey. My own view is that this steadily increasing body of knowledge about the stage, sequence, and causes of individual development tied to Dewey's philosophical case for development as the aim of education can lead to a neo-progressivism, a renewed emphasis and substance for developmental education in this country. Whether neo-progressivism is a wave of the future in public education, any practitioner should get neck deep in developmental psychology as part of the ongoing process of developing curriculum for children or adolescents.

Defining Objectives

A next step is to make some tentative decisions as to what the students are to learn, do, or become. In simplest terms, what are the objectives or the aims of the proposed curriculum? What are we educating or teaching for? The answers to this central question, of course, will vary with the age of the student and with the aims of the people developing the curriculum. One may want to introduce real problem solving into the educational experience of children and adolescents; relate science more closely to human concerns; have teenagers discuss ethical issues in the context of an American history course; participate in programs of responsible social and political action in the community; study the scientific method as a form of intellectual inquiry; learn to write more clearly and effectively. While stated in simplified terms, these objectives are currently being pursued by curriculum development projects in this country.

The point is that any curriculum development work has to define, tentatively, its objectives. Objectives, characteristically, have been stated in terms of some content or body of knowledge (for example, the biology of animal and human reproduction, the U.S. Constitution); or "structure"— the essential ideas and method of inquiry of a discipline (for example, the logic of mathematical operations); or skills to be acquired (for example, being able to write and speak English clearly and effectively, play a trumpet in a school band, and so on). Curriculum writers may also want kids to value certain things—the U.S. Constitution, rational thought, academic achievement, winning in football, a Mozart symphony. Earlier, I argued that knowledge of how people grow can contribute to an educational-philosophical objective of stimulating human development. The curriculum developer's underlying assumptions about the purposes of education, of what the learner should know, do, become, or value, of what knowledge is of most worth will determine his choice of objectives. In the subsequent case study my own ideological position that stimulating human development is the proper aim of education will dictate my choice of objectives. In this paper, I cannot examine the relative philosophical and psychological merits of the several predominant ideologies (for example, the "cultural transmission," "romantic," and "progressive" models) into which most curricular objectives are likely to fit. Let me simply urge every person who is serious about curriculum development to read Kohlberg and Mayer[5] so as to be conscious of the profound philosophical choices we make in deciding what children should know, do, or become.

The discussion could further bog down for as long as it takes to read Bloom on the cognitive and affective domains on the issue of how specifically, or behaviorally, these curriculum objectives must be defined. For practical purposes they have to be specific enough that those developing the curriculum can have a common understanding of what the students are to know, do, or become as a result of the instruction. Further, there has to be a sufficient specificity of aim that the systematic educational experiences and materials can be developed to get the kids there (that is, to whatever they are to know, do, or become). Again, I would like to stress that these first objectives need not, however, be carved in stone, that they be seen as carefully thought through, yet tentative, to be revised in light of the effectiveness of the curriculum itself in realizing them.

Designing Experiences

We move now to the most interesting, creative phase—the actual development and "pilot teaching" of the curriculum. I am not sure that there is any way to teach people, in the abstract, how to develop curriculum. It is a classic example of what Dewey meant when he talked about learning by doing. Apart from saying that revising existing curriculum or creating it de novo is challenging, without any inherent mystery, and subject to clarification and improvement with practice, is there any more specific guidance for the beginner? Now may be a good time to look at the curricula which other people have created. Reinventing the wheel is not especially useful to anyone. Analyze the available curricula carefully and teach some materials to a "tryout" class of students like those you intend to work with. Check in your school or district to see if anyone is working on a similar project. (I continue to be amazed at how many people can be trying analogous curricula, pretty much unbeknown to one another.) A nearby university department of education may be able to offer useful references and advice on curriculum development, although you may have to take a course in order to . . . get their attention. Publishing houses are also aware of what is commercially available, but do not expect them to evaluate their own material for you—to say nothing of the competition's publications.

At some point, however, plunge in—create some curriculum of your own. Maybe it will be an adaptation of available material; maybe it will be "original." For example, the idea of using full-length feature films as the basis for classroom discussions of their ethical dilemmas first occurred to me when to fill an evening in Greensboro, North Carolina, I attended *The Godfather,* which among other things is a powerful, modern American morality play. Subsequently, it was easier to take high school classes to *Deliverance* which *they* suggested, *Serpico,* and so on. Meanwhile, and predictably, it turned out that other people had the same idea. Indeed, Learning Corporation of America had produced "Searching for Values: A Film Anthology," a series of feature motion pictures edited to focus on the moral issues at the center of the film. How one gets from a motion picture theater in Greensboro to a film curriculum in value education is somewhat idiosyncratic. But it takes no great talent or imagination. (One begins, tries things with students, and builds.) A complete curriculum is not necessary to begin. Two or three lessons probably are. Colleagues can help brainstorm ideas, materials, and experiences for these lessons. So can the students, as mentioned. And, sooner rather than later, it is time to try these first materials in the classroom.

Let me digress for a moment to state, in abstract terms, the basic thesis of this paper. Curriculum development, as I see it, is a process of concurrently thinking about problems in educating people and intervening or acting on those problems. The method is an alternating cycle of reflection and action, of hard thinking, careful practice, and evaluation designed to produce a more comprehensive understanding of how by systematic educational experience to effect specified knowledge, skill, or development in students.

Teaching, Recording

So we come to the "careful practice" phase. Essentially, I mean teaching the curriculum and studying, very carefully, the extent to which it affects students' knowledge, skills, or development in the way it is intended to. The previous paragraph errs if it suggests a split between reflection and practice in curriculum development. Any curriculum developer who is serious thinks while he practices. The cycle is not one of theorizing about students and what we want them to know, do, or become; mindless practice; then synthesis. The focus in evaluation is on the curriculum, the teaching, and their interactive effect on the students' learning. Generating knowledge of this kind is a much more rigorous aim and process than the usual test of classroom practice.

But before all of this sounds too formal let me reiterate that the curriculum (whether it be a few trial lessons and experiences for the students or a more comprehensive program) is taught to a pilot class. No mystery. Teach and record as carefully as possible what happens (perhaps using a tape recorder or notes you make to yourself afterward, perhaps designating a student to act as a participant observer . . .). No formal testing, "pre" and "post" measures yet—if ever. Concentrate on a careful journalistic recording and description of what happened when you visited the principal with the ninth graders, discussed an episode from "All in the Family," tried a values clarification activity, attended a juvenile court with your students, read and discussed Freud's theory of the id, ego, and superego, and so forth. The teacher's role in evaluting the curriculum is anticipated by a careful description of the students' reactions to the experience. What things seemed to interest them most? Least? Why? What aspects of the experience contributed most (least) to what you hoped the students would learn? Why? How would you revise the experience in light of both your objectives for it and the students' reactions? Also, what teaching problems were there with the materials, and what went better than expected? Capitalizing on productive surprises—on materials or ways of teaching that go unexpectedly well in practice—is a vital part of curriculum development. And serendipity does happen on the way to curriculum development. In general, share this kind of "stop-action" analysis and discussion with any colleagues who will listen or, better, with a group collaborating in developing curriculum. It need not be a large group—two or three colleagues can get a great deal accomplished. Feed the analysis back into the planning both of subsequent experiences as well as revision and a second classroom test of the original lessons. My opinion is that when you have pilot tested a particular educational experience and revised it in this way three times, ideally with different classes, you will feel a considerable intuitive confidence and command of what student knowledge, skills, or growth can come from that experience.

Now let me talk in less cookbook fashion. In summary, what does the practice or action phase in curriculum development involve? Practice is "real". The conditions under which a curriculum is taught can be designed to represent the typical classroom circumstances. In another sense, practice is the best measure of one's objectives, the curriculum, and the methods of teaching it. More generally, the opportunity for as comprehensive a test or evaluation as one wishes is presented by practice. Teaching is always hard work. Practice is particularly demanding where one is trying new materials and new ways of teaching and where there is a self-imposed expectation that important applied professional knowledge may result. In short, practice is the crucible for curriculum. I believe the kids' responses to curriculum more than any other evidence.

Evaluating Curriculum and Teaching

Some form of evaluation of the curriculum is the step that closes the developmental loop. I assume that most people who read this paper are practicing counselors or teachers who have not done much curriculum development. It seems to me that the tests for the effect of the curriculum developed can, for practitioners, be quite pragmatic ones. Do the students like the experience? Are they motivated by it? How would they suggest improving the course next time? Do they learn the knowledge, skills? Do they develop in ways consistent with the curricular objectives? Do they attend class regularly, complete readings and assignments, participate in class discussion and activities? Are their grades consistent with what they do in other curricula? . . . Simple teacher-constructed interviews or unsigned questionnaires can elicit the students' attitudes toward the curriculum; measures of knowledge or skills can be created by the teacher as for any course; attendance is easily recorded, as is the completion of assignments. A student can be trained to make a simple tally in every third class of who talks, how often, and so on. Coteachers' or colleagues' observations can be sources of important evaluation. The point of this kind of assessment is not primarily to grade students (that can be decided on the basis of assignments and in-class participation) but to evaluate the curriculum and, to some degree, the teaching. The basic purpose is to help in reformulating the course, the materials, or the educational experiences the second time around. Those counselors or teachers interested in a more rigorous evaluation of the curricula they are developing may wish to read the section "Evaluation Procedures: A Modified Formative Evaluation" in an article entitled "Knowledge from Practice: Clinical Research and Development in Education."[6]

So the cycle of thinking about the students, what we want them to know, do, or become, designing a systematic set of educational experiences to get them to those objectives, trying out those experiences (that is, the curriculum) in the classroom, and evaluating the effect of the curriculum and the teaching on the students' knowledge, skills, or growth—which, as an integral process, is what I mean by developing curriculum—comes full circle. In summary form, that is how it is done. There is one important stipulation— . . . in curriculum development you do not only go around once. This cycle, in my view, should be completed, at minimum, twice and preferably three times relative to any particular curriculum before I would feel it to be "developed" (that is, pretty much understood and polished). In the normal course of things that does not seem to place too stringent a requirement on a curriculum or its developer since if it is any good I assume the teacher or counselor will want to use it with a number of different classes. While I believe the process of curriculum development, or inquiry as I have described it, is a way for the teacher to stay alive, to renew himself professionally, I also see it as a very practical process resulting in improved curriculum, education, and learning for students. In a word, important "products" can come from it. I will return to this point at the end of the paper. But first, I want to flesh out this general overview of curriculum development by taking the reader through an extended case study based on some recent curriculum writing I have done.

Case Study in Curriculum Development

In the summer of 1974 I worked as a curriculum writer for the National Science Foundation on a project called "Human Sciences: A Developmental Approach to Adolescent Education." I was one of three writers (the others being a university professor of biology and science education and a junior high school teacher) assigned to work on a seventh-grade science module entitled "What's Happening to Me?" Other writing teams were creating analogous modules on topics such as "Reproduction," "Rules," "Future-self"—the whole to constitute a year's work in science for seventh graders. I now want to illustrate the process of curriculum development by reference to some of the issues encountered and some of the materials produced in the development of this particular curriculum.

Let me pass quickly over the stated prerequisites. We were committed to curriculum development by contract, as was the "Human Sciences" staff. That was our job; we were paid for it. We had time, two uninterrupted months, in fact, to get the first draft of the module done. There were colleagues—two other writers, a number of other writing teams, a "Human Sciences" staff. All of this may sound optimal to a teacher or counselor contemplating doing curriculum development economy class. Unquestionably, it was. But most of what we learned and produced was not dependent on traveling first class.

Hard Thinking

We come, then, to the first substantial step in curriculum development—some hard thinking about the students and what one wants them to become, do, or learn. Remember that we were to write curriculum for seventh-grade students to be used nationally as part of an innovative program in the human sciences. Our more "specific" concern was to help the seventh graders understand "What's Happening to Me?" while at the same time encouraging inferences and the making of abstract meaning about their own growing up. It was to be learning by doing in the best sense of Dewey.

Getting our objectives straight was hard thinking, and we went through several approximations in the process. We started (as though we had read this paper) with the question: "What is happening, developmentally, to seventh graders?" I had not taught the seventh grade since 1955, but did have a daughter who had just finished that grade. The professor of biology had a son just entering the seventh grade, and the junior high school teacher obviously had extensive experience with kids of this age. My only other qualification was that I knew where to look for the literature on preadolescence. So we all read the aforementioned special issue of *Daedalus* on preadolescence, Piaget on *The Language and Thought of the Child*, and so forth. After a week of intensive reading and discussion we were in agreement that at least four basic things are happening, developmentally, in early adolescence. These are rapid physical growth and sexual maturation, especially in girls; a gradual development of the capacity to think abstractly; a change in values from a primary concern with pleasing oneself to pleasing others; and the beginning of a social orientation dominated by conformity to friends and peers. The seventh grader obviously is growing in other essential ways . . . personally and emotionally, vocationally, and in terms of what he likes in music, art, and so on. His development does not proceed in a separate but equal way along these broad dimensions of human growth and functioning. Rather it is correlative or interdependent and based on certain large regularities or stages in the age development of personal and social attitudes. Nonetheless, a focus on the "Big 4" of early adolescent development, while arbitrary, is a useful framework from psychological theory in conceptualizing what is happening at this age and in devising curriculum to stimulate these aspects of the teenagers' growth.

Remember that all the theory one can get about the learner will not be too much. What, in somewhat more detail, is happening to the seventh graders cognitively, morally, socially? Piaget says the period from seven to eleven years of age is characterized by concrete thought. Reality-bound thinking takes over, and the child must test out problems in order to understand them. The difference between dreams and facts can be clearly distinguished but that between a hyposthesis and a fact cannot. The child becomes overly logical and concrete; and once his mind is made up, new facts will not change it. Fact and order become absolutes. From eleven to sixteen (our clients, seventh graders, are here) the shift to formal operations or thought occurs. At this stage the child enters adolescence, and the potential for developing full formal patterns of thinking emerges. The adolescent begins to be capable of logical, rational, and abstract thinking—of thinking about thinking. Symbolic meaning, metaphors, and similes can be understood. Implications and generalizations can be made. So seventh graders are in transition from thinking based on experience, activity, and doing to abstract thinking based on thinking. Obviously, the knowledge that seventh graders are at a transition point (to abstract thinking) of a significance equal to the young child's development of speech has clear implications for curriculum developers working with this age group. Cognitive development became an implicit objective of each activity we were to design. The activities required the seventh grader both to do and to think. The aim was to have him examine a variety of experiences which were in the physical, moral, and social domains. The assumption is that intellectual development is stimulated by the interaction between the adolescent's existing ways of thinking and real problems in his environment. What is "in" the kid's head (such as ideas, answers, rules for processing experience) is altered by disagreement or "poor fit" with real social, physical, ethical, or other problems. The dissonance generated calls for new rules, new answers, and more comprehensive and differentiated thinking. Basically, then, seventh graders have to rediscover the wheel; they have to reformulate in their own terms and thinking what adults know. This process cannot be speeded up by teaching adult answers, whether they be in the physical sciences, the social sciences, or moral philosophy. Most curriculum and teaching, of course, are still engaged in this kind of indoctrination. Movement toward abstract thinking occurs slowly but surely when the seventh grader both thinks and acts on real problems.

In moral development we know seventh graders are also at a critical transition point. In Kohlberg's terms, they are moving to conventional moral thinking where moral value resides in performing good or right roles, in supporting the conventions, rules, and expectations of others (for example, one's family, friends, the school, the church). More specifically their moral reasoning will tend to reflect either Kohlberg's Stage 2—in which what is right is what satisfies one's own needs or self-interest, where consideration of others is essentially instrumental or manipulative . . . ("You scratch my back, and I'll scratch yours")—or Kohlberg's Stage 3—often characterized as a "good boy-good girl" phase—in which the adolescent's orientation . . . is to social approval, to pleasing and helping others. The individual conforms to the stereotypes judged good or right by the majority (. . . his family, friends, teachers). Further, the person's intentions become very important as a basis for judging his behavior.

Defining Objectives

Before the reader cries "enough, already" with detailed theory of what is happening to seventh graders (remember, however, that we spent an intensive week and much subsequent time over two months discussing such theory), let me shift to the next step in curriculum development. This involved making tentative decisions about what the seventh graders were to become and do. I will then go on to illustrate how these were realized through actual classroom activities. We agreed that stimulating the development of seventh graders is a proper educational aim. To move from what is known about the characteristics of cognitive, moral, and social development in early adolescence to educational experiences which would stimulate these broad strands of development became a basic aim of the module. Some of the activities were intended to give seventh graders conventional understanding or insight into what is happening to them at this time of their lives; where the activities became more subtle was in their attempt to involve kids in doing and thinking about problems which, accumulatively, could be expected to produce measured gains in abstract thinking, conventional moral reasoning, and increased social perspective and competence.

Designing Activities

In terms of curriculum or activities, what does it mean to stimulate adolescent development? I will use curriculum materials from the module designed to stimulate moral and cognitive development for illustrative purposes. One final bridge (which I hope is not a bridge over what philosophers would call the naturalistic fallacy) from theory to educational practice then became important. Psychologists now believe that at least three kinds of experiences are associated with moral development at this age—debate about moral dilemmas and exposure to moral thinking a stage "higher" than one's own; systematic opportunities to "role-take" (that is, to learn to understand, more fully, how often other people think and feel); and the chance to help other people (. . . an opportunity for real social service or action). So it seemed that the activities in the module should include (1) a number of moral dilemmas to be discussed in class, (2) role-taking opportunities, and (3) activities in which the seventh grader teaches younger children, helps old people, and so on. I do not want to imply that ideas for appropriate educational experiences or activities to get the kids to do or develop in the desired direction sprang full bloom from a detailed consideration of moral development theory. It helped, however. So did prior experience with teaching moral dilemmas to high school students, brainstorming with my writing colleagues, using ideas stolen from classes, teachers, and doctoral students I have known, an occasional original idea in the shower, and sitting down and writing drafts of activities. And one does get better at all of this with practice.

Let me now include, for illustrative purposes, activities[7] I wrote under each of the above categories. They are presented not as definitive but, to demythologize curriculum writing, as examples of what I believe many teachers and counselors could produce and improve upon.

Activities Involving Class Discussion of Moral Dilemmas. The students encounter moral dilemmas in the module entitled "Right or Wrong: Who Decides?" Initially, they are instructed to read the incidents as described.

The Informer

Mr. Adams, a seventh grade science teacher is talking: It happened during class yesterday. I'd been out sick and a substitute had given the class their quarterly science test. Mary came to me during class. She was crying and said she wanted permission to see the counselor. She seemed really upset and said she wanted to talk with someone. I suggested that she see the counselor between classes, or we could talk about it now. I had the feeling, though, that she might run out of the room at any second. Finally, she blurted out that her best friend, Cathy, had cheated on the science test and had bragged to Mary about getting away with it. Mary had studied hard for the exam, but felt she hadn't done well on it. She was angry at herself for messing up and at Cathy who would get a much better grade because she cheated. "It just isn't fair, Mr. Adams. Cheating is wrong. That's one thing I really believe in. I feel sick telling bout this because it's Cathy and she's my best friend. Please don't ever let her know I was the one who told. But it's not fair to me or to the other kids who didn't cheat—even if it is your best friend who is the cheater."

Directions: Find three to five students and discuss the following questions.

1. What would you do in Mary's place?

2. What would you do about the cheating if you were the teacher? Why? What alternative do you have?

3. What would you say to Cathy if you were Mary?

4. Can you think of a situation *where you would tell on a friend* or someone you don't like?

My Brother, the Pusher

Karen, an eighth grade girl is talking: Two years ago my older brother, Bob, was busted for pushing dope. He got a suspended jail sentence and probation. It just about killed my parents, especially my father. He's got a heart condition anyway and worrying about my brother just makes things worse. Well, my brother swore he'd never do it again, and I guess for two years he didn't. But the other day I found a cache of dope hidden in my closet. My brother admitted he'd put it there, but said he was only keeping it for a friend. I know he's lying—he's pushing again. He begged me not to tell Dad. He said he'd get the dope out of the house, that he wouldn't pull a dumb stunt like that again. But it's obvious he's pushing and it's only a matter of time . . . . My father asked me to tell him if I found out Bob was getting into trouble again and I promised him I would. Nice dilemma, huh? Keep a promise to your father and rat on your brother. So what do I do?

1. What should Karen do? Keep her promise to her father or rat on her brother?
2. Is it right for Karen's father to ask her to spy on her brother?
3. What should the father do if Karen tells?
4. What should the father do if he finds out that Karen didn't keep her promise?
5. How would you feel in Bob's place?

Activities Involving Seventh Graders in Role Taking. In reading the next extended activity, remember that the basic purpose is to have the seventh grader take the role of another person. Being able to think in a nonselfish perspective, to understand and consider the thinking, feelings, and rights of another person, is central to the cognitive and social change involved in moving from Kohlberg's Stage 2 to Stage 3. In this case kids are asked to *be* someone else—a detective, a juror, a judge, and so forth. Admittedly it is role playing, but seventh graders can "de-center" and invest themselves powerfully in such roles. Obviously, this happens for a limited time. The assumption, however, is that systematic and cumulative experiences of getting outside themselves and into the shoes of others is what leads to development. Further, it merits noting that many of the roles the students take in this activity, the processes they engage in, and the knowledge they acquire are of the system of justice (that is, a Kohlberg Stage 4 structure of thinking, rules, conventions, and procedures for handling ethical and legal dilemmas).

Murder Incorporated and Trial by Jury

Attention: Calling all Godfathers, Detective Columbos, and Owen Marshalls, Counselors-at-law!

In this activity you and other teams of kids are going to plan a perfect crime, actually carry it out so that real clues and witnesses exist, investigate the crime, conduct a trial, and establish whether the suspects are guilty or innocent.

The activity is going to take time, imagination, study, and planning but can involve a lot of fun and a lot of learning.

Act I: Murder Incorporated

Find three to five kids and an interested teacher. You have two jobs:

1. Plan a (near) perfect crime. Be really clever! The crime actually is to take place in school. There should be real clues and witnesses (but not too many, so that the job of the team of student detectives will be a difficult one). Your group will plan and carry out the crime. Maybe the crime will be a make believe kidnapping of a student or the theft of a valuable object in the school. (Obviously, you will have to let a few key adults, for example, the principal, in on the fact that the crime is being planned. Here, the teacher can help.)

2. Your second job is to find other teams of three to five students who will be (a) police detectives investigating the crime, (b) "legal eagles"—students who will be the presiding judge, district attorney prosecuting the case, defense attorneys, jurors. (Here again, the teacher can help in getting these teams set up and operating.) Each of these teams will then have separate responsibility for planning and carrying out the investigation of the crime, the correct conduct of the trial, etc. You may want to add other teams—for example, reporters, television crews, private investigators, etc. Your committee will have to let the class, as a whole, know the general plan; that kids can select the team (e.g., detectives, legal eagles) they want to be on, and that the crime will happen when the cops and the legal eagles have had time to get organized. But there will be no advance warning of the time, place, or nature of the crime.

Act II: Detective Columbo or "Nothing But the Facts Ma'am!"

The police detectives investigating the crime should know as much in advance as possible about actual police procedures. One way to learn this would be to get the teacher to arrange for this team to talk with a real police detective. This team really has these jobs: (a) to learn in advance as much as possible about actual detective work, finding clues, finding and interviewing witnesses, collecting evidence, obtaining proper arrest warrants, advising suspects of their rights, etc., (b) to conduct a legally correct and, hopefully, successful investigation of the crime leading to an arrest of suspects, and (c) to cooperate with the District Attorney's office in preparing and presenting the case in court. Who plays which roles in the police investigation is for the team members to decide.

Act III: Trial by Jury

The legal eagles team has a *big* job. It must learn how proper court trials are conducted, how juries are selected, how and what evidence is introduced, what judges, prosecutors, and defense attorneys, in fact, do. Careful research will be necessary. In the module folder you will find materials to help you prepare for the mock trial. Other suggestions include attending several actual trials to observe their procedures, talking with actual District Attorneys and defense lawyers in your community (here, again, the teachers can help in making the necessary arrangements). Each person on the legal eagles team will also be preparing for a specific job (example, Judge, Defense Attorney) in the (mock) trial. The basic job of the legal eagles is to see that the trial is as fair and as true to life (and to law) as possible. Jurors can be selected from your own or another class.

You will probably want to rehearse for the trial. Use the teacher and interested lawyers or judges as coaches for your part in the trial. The teacher can also be the final judge when disputes come up during the trial as to what correct court procedure is.

Epilog: The Defense Rests

Some follow-up activities:

1. Study the reporters' account of the class trial (or a videotape of it if a student TV news team covered the trial). Criticize the class trial on the basis of what you have learned.

2. Attend an actual trial. Criticize it on the basis of what you have learned.

3. Write individual reports, for credit, on some part of what you have learned in this activity about our system of law and justice. (For example, you might want to concentrate on the job of the judge, the defense attorney, the rights of the defendant, etc.)

Activities in Which Seventh Graders Help Others

Help-a-Person #1

Directions: An important part of growing up involves learning to understand and help other people. In this activity you will tutor two kids in elementary school for at least two weeks. For example, find a child who is having trouble with reading or math and help him. Maybe you would rather coach younger children in sports (e.g., to hit a softball or to ride a bike better). Choose an activity you are interested in and make the arrangements to teach or coach. Ask the teacher for help only if necessary. After you get to know the children whom you are helping, answer the following questions:

Why do you think the child has trouble with reading or a physical skill like batting?

How does the child feel about needing and getting help?

What makes the child most discouraged?

What was the *most* helpful thing you did for the child? The *least* helpful?

What might the regular teacher do to really help the child? Share your ideas on this with the child's teacher.

Other things to do:

1. Get three to five other students involved in tutoring or coaching.

2. Discuss, with these students, what kids your age can do to help younger children learn.

3. Make videotapes of younger children learning physical skills or sports so they can see in replay what they are doing right or wrong.

Help-a-Person #2

Directions: Growing up involves learning to understand and help other people. In this activity you will visit an old person in a nursing home or in your neighborhood at least four times. You make the arrangements. Perhaps you will read to the old person, go for a walk or to a movie with him, play cards, or simply watch TV and talk. When you have gotten to know the old person, ask him about the following questions, then add your own questions to the interview.

What does he or she do all day?
What is he most interested in?
What are his favorite subjects to talk about?
What does he think about kids today?
How was he disciplined when he was young?
Other things to do:
1. Take other students with you to visit your friend.
2. Invite your friend to class.
3. Get a group of three to five kids together. Discuss what students your age really can do to help old people like your friend. Then organize such an activity or program for several of the old people at the nursing home.
4. Videotape a typical day in your friend's life at the nursing home to show to other kids in the class.

Space limitations do not permit the inclusion of other activities from the module aimed at stimulating moral and social development in seventh graders. Hopefully, the essential point has been made. It is that curriculum writing is not a mystical act. Rather it is a matter of a systematic approach such as that outlined in this paper coupled with time and practice. Imagination helps, and there is a lot of it in schools. So does a mind set that picks up and develops ideas being tried by colleagues. For example, the dilemma for "The Informer" was suggested by the junior high school teacher on our writing team, the incident actually having occurred in his class. "My Brother, the Pusher," similarly was based on a real case reported by a girl in one of my high school moral education classes. "Trial by Jury" was suggested by an eighth-grade class project conducted by one of my doctoral students ("stolen," I might add, with her knowledge and concurrence). "Help-a-Person #1" was prompted by the work several other doctoral students of mine had done with "cross-age" teaching programs. The only "original" activity was "Help-a-Person #2." In short, I believe that counselors and teachers can create similar teaching and learning materials—indeed, can improve on such activities by making them appropriate or indigenous to their students and communities.

The natural history of the "What's Happening to Me?" module is, at the time of writing, short on the careful practice and formative evaluation phases. That is because the pilot teaching and evaluation of the module was done in a number of test schools throughout the nation in 1975-1976, but has yet to be published. We did, however, test the dilemmas described above with a small pilot class in Boulder during the summer of 1974. The report from the teachers was that "the kids loved the dilemmas . . . stayed with them and recognized the issues as real." In our first draft of the activity we had had a teacher and a student record the particular dilemma on a cassette to avoid a written format and, we thought, to make the problem more real. The test teachers suggested that the written script was enough, that all dilemmas (there were six) be put in one booklet, that we might make a tape recording of all the dilemmas plus directions for those students who do not read well. They also recommended changes in the directions (for instance, how to appoint and rotate discussion leaders) so that the group would be clearer about beginning and conducting a discussion. In a similar way, the students were asked to rate each activity along a number of dimensions such as "the activity was interesting and fun to do," "the directions were clear," "I learned [complete the sentence] from this activity," "I would change the activity in the following ways _____." Hopefully, these illustrations of feedback and the revisions suggested will underscore the obvious importance of trying out new curricula with students. And this can be asked of any counselor or teacher. The more extensive pilot testing presently under way in experimental classrooms across the country, the major revisions and rewriting of modules based on that tryout, and the testing of large samples of students taking the curriculum on formal measures of cognitive and ego development are important to note. It is part of large national curriculum development projects. Clearly, however, this kind of evaluation and revision is neither feasible nor necessary for the average practitioner of "home brew" curriculum development I am addressing in this paper.

Epilogue

Let me offer some summary thoughts about curriculum development. Basically, I hope this paper will encourage counselors, school psychologists, and teachers to try curriculum development. You may like it. Until this activity is seen not as an exclusive, esoteric, heavily funded specialty of university professors, the National Science Foundation, and so forth, and until its particular knowledge and skills are given back to practitioners, I expect what is taught to children will change very slowly. Not that curriculum experimentation is any complete panacea. In education we too often seek or promulgate single variable solutions to multivariable problems. But I do think curriculum development by teachers and counselors may reasonably further some important education outcomes, including the following:

1. Experimenting with curriculum can introduce a new sense of creativity and effect into one's professional life—for those who want that. Put another way, curriculum development is an antidote to simply getting better at doing the same things (such as individual counseling or schedule changes) to a point of boredom and declining effect.

2. Curriculum development can also produce new professional knowledge—

for example, the new curriculum itself and knowledge about children and adolescents and what they can do, learn, or become when given appropriate education. I have elaborated this point elsewhere.

We have found that some adolescents can learn to counsel other adolescents as effectively as do practicing professionals. They can learn to teach in nursery and elementary schools; they can provide significant help to other people. The essential element for them to develop in these ways is that they have the opportunity to take "real" social and vocational roles and responsibility under adult supervision. Significant development, we believe, will follow from this juxtaposition of the adolescent with the performance of real tasks where what he does is subject both to careful intellectual scrutiny and to sensitive personal examination. We further believe it unlikely that these findings would have come from basic research in education. Yet such knowledge, if it is supported by replication studies, in our estimation, has profound implications both for developmental psychology and for education. This, then, is a further illustration of what we mean by knowledge generated from practice.[8]

For the practicing counselor or teacher neither the findings nor the rhetoric need to be this inflated for a solid sense of professional contribution to occur. And all of us need that.

3. Finally, curriculum development, especially when its aim is to stimulate personal, moral, social, and vocational development, offers the opportunity to deal with and affect large numbers of children or adolescents in the most vital aspects of their being and growing. And that really is what counseling and teaching are all about.

Notes

1. D. J. Armor, *The American School Counselor: A Case Study in the Sociology of Professions* (New York: Russell Sage Foundation, 1969).

2. T. Volsky *et al.*, *The Outcomes of Counseling and Psychotherapy* (Minneapolis: University of Minnesota Press, 1965); A. E. Bergin, "The Evaluation of Therapeutic Outcomes," in *Handbook of Psychotherapy and Behavior Change*, ed. *id.* and S. L. Garfield (New York: John Wiley, 1971).

3. R. F. Aubrey, "Understanding and Developing Programs of Guidance and Counseling for the Young Adolescent," *Focus on Guidance*, 7 (No. 3, 1974), 1-15.

4. J. Dewey and J. McLelland, "What Psychology Can Do for the Teacher," in *John Dewey on Education*, ed. R. Archambault (New York: Random House, 1964), 198.

5. L. Kohlberg and R. Mayer, "Development as the Aim of Education," *Harvard Educational Review*, 42 (November 1972), 449-496.

6. R. L. Mosher, "Knowledge from Practice: Clinical Research and Development in Education," *Counseling Psychologist*, 4 (No. 4, 1974), 73-82.

7. All the activities used for illustrative purposes in this section are copyrighted by the Biological Sciences Curriculum Study, *Human Science: A Developmental Approach to Adolescent Education*, and not to be reproduced.

8. Mosher, "Knowledge from Practice," 80.

9
The Disciplines and Development

One finding that will be reiterated in Part II is that development, in people or their institutions, does not happen overnight. Given the profound nature and complexity of the human capacities with which we are dealing— abstract thought; moral reasoning and an understanding of principles such as the common or greatest good, justice, the dignity of the individual; individuation in adolescence; the feelings associated with sexuality—it should not be surprising that growth on these dimensions and education to enhance it will not be easy. Educators looking for a quick method of development, a six-week course in Kohlberg's Stage 4 "law and order" morality to solve discipline problems in the high school, need not read Part II.

Newton's law that bodies at rest tend to remain at rest seems to apply peculiarly to education. Curricula, teaching, and ideologies related, for example, to the purposes or management of schools are subject to much inertia. In addition, schools are complex social institutions, difficult to understand, let alone change. Innovation has typically faltered before one or more of these hurdles. Blocher explains part of why this has been so and some of what developmental education must do differently if it is to be accepted. A first step is to "identify target groups and situations that . . . represent potential opportunity to facilitate constructive change in key elements of the organization."[1] Put another way, we need to pursue students' development in "all of the relevant sub-systems of the school."[2]

It is appropriate at this point to discuss the various disciplines—English, history, science, mathematics, foreign languages—that comprise the present high school curriculum. If developmental education is to be a serious objective in the American high school, it will be accomplished primarily through the existing curriculum. High school teachers will have to be convinced that it is possible to have both the disciplines and

327

development, that students can be taught traditional knowledge and skills and be trained to think in more rational or principled ways. The papers in this chapter present examples of how this has been accomplished in some disciplines. Before reading about them, however, the teacher might find some general remarks concerning the relationship of the disciplines and development helpful.

It has always been asserted that the academic subjects teach students to think more rationally, deeply, scientifically, to use knowledge and facts as a basis for logic plus some understanding, at least of the methods by which new knowledge is created in the disciplines. It is also frequently said or implied that the disciplines form character or good habits and assist students to know themselves as individuals. The evidence to support these contentions, however, seems extraordinarily thin. People learn a vast amount of content, much of which they forget within a short period of time. Something, however, enables 50 percent of American adolescents and adults to achieve formal operations and 20 percent to understand the morality of the Constitution. Schooling may be a part of that something, but it is not possible to determine what part of the relationship is the fiction of teachers and what part is real.

This is not intended to denigrate the disciplines. Part II is meant to show that higher levels of human competence, whether logical thought, moral reasoning, or aesthetic judgment, can be achieved by education, and they would affect people in a far more permanent and pervasive way than content per se. Two points must be made in relation to the above. First, we can now begin to test the ways the disciplines enhance adolescents' cognition, morality, and ego. It would be cause for celebration if academic subjects would teach students to think more rationally, rather than what to think, or if they would affect character, rather than moralize. Second, if the disciplines are not doing this, we should examine how they can be taught differently. Establishing the present effects of the disciplines or the ways to improve them will not be easy. But some of the most exciting and potentially significant future research on the enhancement of human competence can be done at this intersection of developmental psychology and the disciplines. It should be noted that the latter are not sacrosanct. They are, in fact, under considerable pressure to justify themselves in the face of students' declining achievement and interest. "Hard" developmental data concerning their effects on rationality and character would enormously strengthen the claim that they should occupy a central place in the high school curriculum. And adolescence may be the prime time for such an effect to take place.

Rowher, quoting Elkind, has argued that adolescence is, indeed, the prime time for development. ". . . *the longer we delay formal instruction* [at least until early adolescence], *the greater the period of plasticity and the higher the ultimate level of achievement.*"[3] Rowher arrived at that rather arresting conclusion by an interesting route. He wanted to substitute for a neoclassical philosophy of education, particularly the teaching of the content of the disciplines, an education in which objectives are explicitly defined in terms of cognitive skills ("Content proficiency at the secondary level is exemplified by stating Ohm's law: skill proficiency, by conducting experiments to test the law"). He believed that virtually any intellectual skill could be taught if it was specified in behavioral terms (which is reminiscent of Bruner and Bujold[4]). Rowher's research showed that intellectual skills characteristic of abstract thinking, such as the ability to link and remember pairs of nouns by putting them together in sentences, could be taught most advantageously in adolescence, when the transition to formal operations is occurring. Thus, he simply and provocatively proposes adolescence as the prime time for all formal education, which for him means stimulation of cognitive skills.

Without accepting Rowher's radical position that formal education be delayed to adolescence, one could argue that there may be no time more propitious for both the disciplines and development than adolescence. It is the prime time for the shift to abstract thought. Piaget has conceded that formal operations may be actualized in different areas of the adolescents' aptitude and functioning—the arts, literature, or cabinetmaking—rather than simply in mathematics or the physical sciences.[5] This provides another argument for seeking both formal operations and their development in diverse discipline and curricular areas. It also partially removes the sting of Broughton's critique of formal operations as old-fashioned and narrow scientific thinking.[6] One must also keep in mind that the disciplines have within their extraordinarily rich content the potential to effect many strands of adolescent development other than the cognitive: morality, ego identity, affect, the aesthetic. Developmental theories can help the disciplines realize those effects.

Chapter 9 confronts this issue of the disciplines and development and demonstrates that they can be successfully combined. Ladenburg, a practicing history teacher, shows how one can produce growth in students' moral reasoning with no loss in integrity to the discipline.[7] Renner and Lawson do the same for physical science.[8]

The potential of other disciplines to affect adolescent thinking, moral reasoning, and ego development has been little studied. That research has begun, however, in the Biological Sciences Curriculum Study group and in health education. The necessary psychological theory and skill in curriculum building certainly exist for that work to go forward. It awaits only the interest and initiative of teachers. But were we able to add to students' growth in all five of what Purpel terms the "sacred subjects" of the high school course of study,[9] we would still be short of an education for all-around adolescent growth. A discipline-based curriculum is intended, after all, to teach what is known by the disciplines and perhaps some of the methods by which it comes to be known; its major developmental aim at present is to teach students to think. How it may do that more conclusively and broaden its effect by an alliance with developmental psychology and education is what Chapter 9 is about.

Notes

1. D. H. Blocher, "Toward an Ecology of Student Development," *Personnel and Guidance Journal*, 52 (February 1974), 361-365.
2. *Ibid.*
3. D. Elkind, quoted in W. D. Rowher, "Prime Time for Education: Early Childhood or Adolescence," *Harvard Educational Review*, 41 (No. 3, 1971), 336.
4. J. Bruner, *The Process of Education* (Cambridge, Mass.: Harvard University Press, 1966); C. Bujold, "Activation of Vocational and Personal Development," in *Adolescents' Development and Education: A Janus Knot*, ed. R. L. Mosher (Berkeley, Calif.: McCutchan Publishing Corp., 1979), Chapter 6.
5. J. Piaget, "Intellectual Evolution from Adolescence to Adulthood," *Human Development*, 15 (No. 1, 1972), 1-12.
6. J. M. Broughton, "The Limits of Formal Thought," in *Adolescents' Development and Education*, ed. Mosher, Chapter 1.
7. T. J. Ladenburg, "Cognitive Development and Moral Reasoning in the Teaching of History," *The History Teacher*, 10 (February 1977), 183-198.
8. J. W. Renner and A. E. Lawson, "Piagetian Theory and Instruction in Physics," *The Physics Teacher*, 11 (No. 3, 1973), 165-169; *id.*, "Promoting Intellectual Development through Science Teaching," *ibid.* (No. 5, 1973), 273-276.
9. D. Purpel, public lecture at Harvard University, Master of Arts in Teaching Program, 1964.

Cognitive Development and
Moral Reasoning in the
Teaching of History

Thomas J. Ladenburg

The idea that human development should be the aim of education was first stated by John Dewey:

The aim of education is growth or development both intellectual and moral . . . . Only knowledge of the order and connection of the stages in psychological development can insure the maturing of psychic powers. Education is the work of supplying the conditions which will enable the psychological functions to mature and pass into higher functions in the freest and fullest manner.[1]

While Dewey envisioned the development of intellectual capacities as a goal, he did not have the "knowledge of the order and connection of the [various growth] stages" or the conceptual tools to measure them. The groundwork for that discovery was produced by Jean Piaget and his colleagues in the 1930's. Through their studies, they learned to distinguish different mental capacities which were involved in reasoning about concrete data and in the ability to think about thought or formal operations. Human development, Piaget informed us, is a process in which one acquires the means to progress from one kind of thinking to another. Building on Piaget's discoveries, Professor Lawrence Kohlberg identified six distinct stages of reasoning when dealing with moral issues differentiated by increasing complexity and inclusiveness at each stage. They begin with primitive obedience to authority and the avoidance of pain and move progressively on to the egocentric realization of reciprocal exchange, and from the recognition of the need for loyalty to family and peers to the incorporation of a societal perspective, and finally to a recognition of global or universal principles of human dignity and equality.

Professor Kohlberg found that progressing to different stages of reasoning requires the incorporation of previous stages; indeed, a stage cannot be omitted. Moreover, the process is not influenced by cultural factors. Kohlberg's great contribution to developmental education was his (and his colleagues Moshe Blatt, Ralph Mosher, and Norman Sprinthall's) revolutionary discovery that educational interventions could stimulate

Reprinted from *The History Teacher*, 10 (February 1977), 183-198.

the development of moral reasoning from lower to higher, more complete, and holistic stages. This discovery has made it possible to realize Dewey's dictum that the aim of education is the growth and development of both intellectual and moral faculties.

Courses designed to stimulate the ability to reason about moral issues typically include two components. First, they involve students in exploring moral dilemmas, generally short, hypothetical case studies in which choices must be made between equally compelling alternatives. Secondly, students are involved in an affective component such as leading moral dilemma discussions with younger students or counseling elementary school youngsters, By employing these rich and varied techniques over a period of but one academic year, developmental educators have been able to stimulate moral reasoning by as much as a full stage.

While this effort has served as the cutting edge of a new curriculum movement, it has failed to gain widespread acceptance in schools throughout the country. Most schools generally see their roles more in terms of intellectual rather than developmental education, if we are to define "intellectual" as mastering traditional subject matter and "developmental" as stimulating increased capacity for moral reasoning. However, there is no need to continue maintaining these artificial distinctions. Since Kohlberg and his colleagues have provided the tools and data which can enable us to realize the full potentials of Dewey's insights, developmental education can and should be integrated into the traditional curriculum in general and into the teaching of history and social studies in particular.

This work has already begun. Several school systems—Tacoma, Washington; Brookline and Cambridge, Massachusetts; Pittsburgh, Pennsylvania; and Minneapolis, Minnesota—are all in the process of producing and distributing experimental materials designed to stimulate development. Moshe Blatt and others have published a collection of hypothetical dilemmas for classroom use, and Edwin Fenton has produced a series of filmstrips for Guidance Associates. Thomas Jones and Ronald Galbraith and Barry Beyer have written carefully constructed guides to help teachers lead discussions of moral issues.

The work produced and made available by the social studies educators, however, has not been as rich in its conception or as varied in its execution as the course materials generated by developmental educators. In general, the social studies materials have been modeled after the dilemmas used by Kohlberg in his experiments to test and validate his theory of moral reasoning. Typically they involve contrived moral conflicts cast in hypothetical, ahistoric settings, in which individuals are left to choose between only two courses of action. Writing in *Social Education*, Barry Beyer gives the rationale for this design. He suggests that the moral dilemma "be as simple as possible," involving "only a few characters in a relatively uncomplicated situation."[2] However, Jack Fraenkel in the same issue of *Social Education* criticizes this approach. If students "are to find out about the nature of the world in which they live," he argues, "they must be exposed to a wide variety of different kinds of issues and dilemmas."[3] I heartily concur with Professor Fraenkel. Social studies educators must improve upon the techniques espoused by Jones, Galbraith, and Beyer. Otherwise, they run the risk of reducing the study of history, with its recurrent moral themes, to simplistic case studies devoid of the discipline's rich complexities.

In addition to the hypothetical dilemmas, the history curriculum can and should include dilemmas as rich and varied as those faced, for example, by the Founding Fathers in writing the Constitution, by Congress in ratifying the Jay Treaty, or by Franklin Roosevelt in proposing the Social Security system. Dilemmas of this character have the potential of developing into a new "new social studies" effort that can achieve the cognitive and affective goals of the developmentalists as well as the traditional intellectual objectives of education.

The central purpose of this paper is to present a model that will help teachers and curriculum writers begin this necessary task. In order for history teachers to reach this ambitious goal, it is essential that:

1. The high school teacher be provided with an acceptable definition of his subject area which also embraces developmental goals.

2. This definition be translated into a model for teaching history and developing social studies curriculum that combines subject matter with developmental education, and that allows cognitive development and moral reasoning to be used as a means of teaching the discipline as well as an end in itself.

3. The concept of a moral dilemma be so broadened as to include a continuum ranging from simple, hypothetical dilemmas on one end to complex, moral development units on the other.

4. Specific examples of units that bridge the gap between teaching subject matter and stimulating growth be provided to enable teachers to apply principles inherent in the model to their own curriculum.

A Definition of History That Embraces Developmental Goals

In his book, *The Aims of Education*, Alfred North Whitehead defines education as "the art of the utilization of knowledge." He reminds us that "ideas which are not utilized are positively harmful."[4] Unless they become more concerned with the reasons certain decisions are made rather than with the decisions themselves, it seems that history teachers are particularly open to the accusation of imparting information which is no longer usable. True, the new social studies have placed more emphasis on process and discovery than on isolated facts. Nonetheless, history does not become alive for most students unless they are somehow involved in the vicarious process of making or rethinking historic decisions. Indeed, it is this idea of process that provides a link between the past and present.

By taking part in the effort of making and evaluating decisions, students become participants in a continual drama. Through simulations, discussions, and debates, they learn to use facts and concepts in order to buttress an argument, support a point, or reason to a new conclusion. These dialogues with the past impart knowledge that can be applied to current problems or to analogous cases. As students become conversant with history in this manner, they incorporate new ideas and facts into their thought processes. If the subject matter is carefully chosen, they become active participants in the historical-political culture which has shaped our past and now defines our present.

Man operates within a time frame or context. He perceives problems and makes decisions from alternatives open to him. At some future moment he may look back and more clearly analyze the reasons for his decisions. The model of man as a decision maker operating within the context of time, and of man standing apart from the decision, reflecting back on it, helps us to understand the many and diverse activities of the historian, as well as the nature of the discipline and the four types of questions historians try to answer. These questions are: What was the historical context in which the dilemma occurred? What sequence of events preceded the decision? Was the decision that was reached a correct one? Why was the particular decision made at that time?

In posing the first question, historians are guided by their interest in the past as a unique and singular example of man as a universal entity. Their search into specific kinds of history, the social, economic, political, and intellectual, gives rise to specialties in these areas. In seeking answers to the second question, historians probe into events with the skill of trained detectives and attempt to learn exactly what transpired. Whether consciously or not, historians pass judgments on events, sometimes using standards which even they can or do not define, and thus in the role of moral philosophers answer the third question, on ethics. Finally, historians seek answers to the fourth question: why did it happen? Here they uncover the motives of men and women, wrestle with the problem of inevitability, and uncover causes in social, economic, and political-ideological circumstances.

A Model for Teaching That Combines
Subject Matter with Developmental Goals

In posing these questions and involving students in the search for their answers, the high school history instructor can impart a small but representative sampling of the total import of the discipline he teaches. But he can also encourage cognitive growth by stimulating the ability to reason at higher and more complex stages. This is possible because the questions posed in the classroom are both sequential and consequential; students learn about the general context of any period; this information allows them to understand the events; they then resolve the decision maker's dilemma by participating in a reconstruction of the decision-making process; and they reflect back on their own deliberations as they analyze why the decision was made. At each stage, the student seeks answers which he can understand only at his level of reasoning, and each set of conclusions is therefore tailor made (as Dewey would have it, with his own "hands") to his intellectual ability. As he progresses from one stage of questioning to the next, his level of understanding will grow and deepen, and his ability to master facts or comprehend concepts will be similarly expanded.

The four-stage model can be applied to the American Revolution. First, the teacher explores the first question by asking what the climate of the times was and leads his students through an examination of the social, economic, political, and ideological background to the Revolution. Youngsters study the class structure of colonial America, the mercantile policies of England, the relationship between colonial governments and the British Parliament, and the colonists' conceptions of "liberty" and "power." Secondly, classes inquire into the events that actually took place at the time, occasionally using the historian's inquiry tools in sifting through conflicting source materials. Here they learn of the French and Indian War, the problems of ruling an empire, the Stamp Act and the protest it aroused, the Boston Massacre, the Tea Party, the Battle of Lexington, and the Declaration of Independence. This is traditional fare. But interlaced with descriptions of these events, products of economic and social conditions, students are involved in the third level of questioning. They make moral judgments about decisions that were reached or were about to be made. They may be asked whether the Stamp Act riots were justified, whether British soldiers had the right to fire at colonists on King Street, and whether the British were justified in imposing the Intolerable Acts as punishment for the Tea Party. Finally, and only after completing the earlier stages of questioning, students are required to reflect on the series of events they had studied and are asked what caused the Revolution or, more simply, why disagreements were not resolved peacefully. Here they are forced to seek adequate explanations for events they have studied within the context of their own times and which they have measured against their own structures of moral reasoning.

This model—requiring sequential development of four different types of questions—can form the blueprint governing the construction of most history courses. The planning involved, of course, is extremely complex, and the ideal may not always be attained. But the payoff in terms of developmental and traditional intellectual education can hardly be exaggerated. Every question prepares the way for the next, and the final exercise allows the dilemmas built into the unit to provide evidence for the analysis required at the end.

A Broadened Definition of Moral Dilemmas

Besides linking the "what" and the "why" questions, moral dilemmas also have the unique quality of "turning students on." The query, What should_____ do? Was _____ justified? or Who was right? whether asked in the context of the Stamp Act, the Tea Party, or the Battle of Lexington, has always been in my experience the question that excited the most interest, discussion, and debate. The reasons for its power to elicit a response are partially a matter of speculation, but seem closely connected to Piagetian and Kohlbergian theories. Every student has formulated a mental construct, uniquely his own, concerning issues of justice, fairness, or right and wrong. A contrary opinion, or one argued at a higher stage that serves to jar this construct or attack the structure of the reasoning, is opposed as long as there are intellectually valid grounds to combat it. In defending their views against alien ideas, students are forced to dig deeply into their own resources and ultimately modify their own structure of moral thought. Facts become weapons that are used to reinforce their own ideas or eventually to batter down their citadels. As the mind is exposed to reasoning which it recognizes as more complex or complete, it alters or modifies its views, incorporating these newer and more adequate concepts. Thus dilemma discussions are the means by which we encourage students to deal with new ideas and to modify their own patterns of thought. Moral dilemmas have more power to accomplish this change than abstract discussions of causality because they summon immediate feelings of right and wrong which are always with us and which press uniquely on adolescents.

Since moral dilemmas necessarily play so central a role in cognitive development and moral reasoning, it is important to distinguish among several kinds of dilemmas that may be used. At one end of the scale are the cases involving hypothetical dilemmas. They deal with universal principles of right and wrong, devoid of considerations of either time or place. The classic in the Kohlberg literature is the case of Heinz whose wife will die of a rare disease because he cannot afford to pay the druggist's exorbitant price for the necessary medicine. "Should Heinz steal the medicine?" the subject is asked. This dilemma was a central one used by Kohlberg to discover and validate the character of the six stages of moral reasoning. The value of this and similar dilemmas involving fictionalized case studies is limited from the standpoint of the history teacher because the ethical questions they raise lack a historical context. Heinz's dilemma is equally perplexing whether he lived in Europe at the turn of the century or in America in the 1970's. It reveals nothing about the nature of any particular point in time and does not force students to come to a deeper understanding of any historical period.

The second mode is the historical dilemma. Like the former, it deals with a person caught in an ethical problem, but this time the situation contains another dimension because it includes consideration of the nature of the time period within which the decision must be made. An example of the historical dilemma is the case of Helga who is asked by her friend Rachael to hide her from the Nazis. This dilemma is similar to one involving a man who must decide whether he will hide a runaway slave and violate the Fugitive Slave Act. Both dilemmas can be reasoned at several different levels. The former involves conflicting claims of loyalty to friend or family, the danger to self (what if the Nazis discover Rachael?), and the morality of the German laws against the Jews. The latter involves a parallel conflict between duty to another human being and the morality of slavery and the laws protecting property rights.

In an article appearing in *Social Education*, Ronald Galbraith and Thomas Jones[5] clearly elucidate a strategy to teach this type of historical dilemma. It involves reviewing the facts of the case, clarifying alternatives for the decision maker, and eliciting reasons for each opposing course of action. Discussions are to focus on the reasoning employed. If the class does not divide naturally into opposing camps, the terms of the dilemma are changed somewhat by the teacher. What if Rachael were only an acquaintance instead of a good friend? What if the punishment for hiding Jews were imprisonment in a concentration camp? Once a clear division is found in the class, opposing arguments are presented, and student discussion is focused on reasons rather than solutions.

While these strategies may meet the needs of the developmental psychologists, it is doubtful whether they are equally useful in teaching history. If dilemmas are to serve as a means for teaching subject matter as well as developing moral reasoning, more complex examples must be used.

And with the wealth that historical events afford, there is ample reason to require that the dilemma be real rather than hypothetical. The case of the slave mother who kills her child rather than permit the master to sell it as he has the other three is one example. So, too, is the case of Johnathan Harrington who must choose between his loyalty to family and his allegiance to friends and the Revolution, when he decides whether or not to stand with the Lexington militia in the face of superior British forces. Both of these dilemmas are real and reveal something of the nature of the conditions surrounding them.

More complex historical dilemmas can be drawn from cases of actual decision makers faced with crucial decisions that affect the lives of others. Several examples easily come to mind: Abraham Lincoln agonizing over the Emancipation Proclamation, Harry Truman debating whether to drop the atomic bomb on Hiroshima, or a juror at the trial of the soldiers involved in the Boston Massacre. The reasoning needed to engage in these dilemmas must of necessity become interlaced with a consideration of the historical factors which played a role in the decision.

A single historical dilemma can easily be made the basis for a two- or three-day activity and involve many of the thinking and reasoning skills necessary to the learning of history. For example, students can be given the information to stage a mock trial of the British soldiers accused of murder in the Boston Massacre. During the trial, youngsters may act out the parts of witnesses, defendants, lawyers, judges, or "impartial" jurors. The decision rendered will most likely depend on the skill of opposing lawyers in presenting the case, and in the process of preparation, opening statements, cross-examination, and summation students will learn a great deal about our advocacy system of justice. Jurists and witnesses, too, can learn much about courtroom procedure and are required to think through some complex legal issues.

The enterprising teacher can build this lesson on the Boston Massacre into a dilemma miniunit, the third kind of moral dilemma useful to the history teacher. He could follow the mock trial with a reading on the Kent State incident and ask who were the people more clearly to blame, the British soldiers or the National Guardsmen. This discussion may be continued, using the Battle of Lexington as another example; students could add the militia's stand on the Green, the shot from an unknown source, and the subsequent killings of New England farmers as a parallel case to follow the Boston Massacre and Kent State discussions. These three lessons could form the basis of the miniunit and would undoubtedly evoke controversy, hard thinking, and a search for some general principles regarding dissent and protest. By this time, the students should be sufficiently immersed in history as process, making decisions they will later stand away from and try to analyze.

Historical miniunits can be built around a number of other events. One which works very well examines the issue of how to deal with a great wrong such as slavery. Rather than involve students in the hypothetical case of the runaway slave, teachers can have youngsters re-create the Lincoln-Douglas debate over how the nation should resolve the question of slavery in the territories, followed by a discussion of John Brown's dramatic raid on Harper's Ferry, and ending with an analysis of Lincoln's decision to put priority on saving the Union rather than ending slavery.

Units That Bridge the Gap
between Subject and Developmental Goals

It is hoped that teachers will not stop with the dilemma miniunits. They should construct entire units designed to stimulate cognitive development and history courses using moral issues to promote the desired development. The basic pattern for such units has already been described. It revolves around the four questions historians most frequently ask. A sample of such a unit on the writing of the United States Constitution was developed by the author and refined as part of the Brookline, Massachusetts, Moral Development Project. It has been taught to over 350 students and meets most of the established criteria for a moral development unit. This unit is described here in the hope that it will encourage other teachers to try similar enterprises.

The heart of the unit is a simulation requiring that youngsters assume the roles of the Founding Fathers and resolve five major issues before the Constitutional Convention. Each student delegate prepares for his role by analyzing the Articles of Confederation, debating the justification of Shays' Rebellion, and reading excerpts from Madison's *Federalist Paper* Number 10. Following this exposure to the social, economic, and political-ideological background to the Convention, he is given an explanation of the issues to be resolved and a political biography of the delegates, which includes their views on the issues.

The mock convention opens with delegates attempting to resolve the conflict between the large and small states over representation. Students spend roughly equal amounts of time hearing prepared speeches, debating the issues as a "committee of the whole," jawboning with students during "caucuses," and analyzing or voting on conflicting resolutions. On succeeding days, the mock convention considers how power should be divided between the national and state governments, what powers should be given the President, the Congress, and the people, what should be done about slavery and the slave trade, and whether to write a Bill of Rights. After each of these issues is resolved through simulation, students read

the Constitution and learn how these same questions were resolved in
1789. Now, aware that the solutions of 1789 were not necessarily perfect,
they debate ratification and read several historians' interpretations of the
Founders' motives. Thus prepared, they reflect back over the historical
context of the times, the problems faced by the Founders, their solutions
as embodied in the Constitution, and the experience of the simulation
itself in an attempt to determine why the Constitution was written.

On the surface, discussions focusing on such issues as dividing power
between the national and state governments may not appear to involve
moral dilemmas. Certainly, they involve questions far more complex than
those raised in the Heinz or Rachael cases. But behind all political decisions lies the fundamental question of justice, which is central to the
resolution of all moral dilemmas and at the very heart of the political
process. It is impossible to separate moral questions from political issues,
and, indeed, any attempt to do so would deny the latter their essential
character. In writing of Stephen Douglas' miscalculation in framing the
Kansas-Nebraska Act, historian Allan Nevins made essentially the same
point:

He did not remember that it is the essence of democratic government that a tempo-
rary majority shall not abuse its power, nor shall cardinal changes be forced in
national policy except after full and free discussion . . . . These were all at bottom
moral considerations, and his apprehension of them was cloudy and limited.[6]

The exercise of writing a constitution is really an experience in arriving
at a social contract. Students are required to go beyond simple obedience
to the law; they must decide what the fundamental arrangements governing our political institutions should be. This would obviously require some
application of what Professor Kohlberg labeled as Stage 5 reasoning, the
"official morality of the American government."[7] However, in arriving at
this stage many lower stage arguments are used. The following dialogue
was recorded during the mock convention and illustrates distinct stages
of reasoning used by students in discussing the issue of dividing power
between the national and state governments:

Luther Martin: The purpose of these United States was because we needed to
protect the state government from bigger powers. Before they were the United
States they had to be protected from the British Power and now you want to just
impose the power of the national government on each state. The state of Massachusetts should have the right to take care of any law itself . . . .
Gouverneur Morris: Do you realize what might have happened if Shays' Rebellion had occurred in another state? It might have been taken care of in a completely different way. They might all have been executed—maybe they would have

been tarred and feathered. We don't know. We can't have that type of disorder going around. We have to have a unified type of law that will affect everyone in every state; that they will get the same punishment no matter what state the rebellion took place in.

John Lansing: I really disagree with that statement. That is saying that each person's feelings and each person's ideas are the same throughout the whole country, and people in New Hampshire, say, are going to have different issues and are going to feel differently about things than people in Georgia which is about 900 miles away—so you can't say that in one country each person is going to feel the same way and going to want to react the same way; so you can't have one law govern all those people.

Charles Pinckney: What has been stated as an idea is that all men are equal. If all men are equal, they deserve to have the same rights, the same laws governing them . . . .

John Lansing: You are saying that all men are robots—that's what you're saying.

Charles Pinckney: I'm not saying that; I'm saying they deserve to have equal rights; they deserve to be treated equally; which means they must have equal laws.

Assumed in this author's definition of history is the premise that students must be involved in the process of making historic decisions and that there is no fundamental conflict between teaching subject matter conceived as decision making and stimulating cognitive development or moral reasoning. By playing the roles assigned them in the convention, students not only partake in their nation's political-historical culture; they gain the ability to see a situation from another point of view which is an essential factor in cognitive development. Perceiving problems from a responsible adult perspective also provides the adolescent with conditions that promote the confidence, self-esteem, and sense of mastery so important to psychological development. Thus, the young man who argues against the national government on the basis that its power may be excessive learns something for himself about the relationship between authority and freedom. So does the young woman who, as Gouverneur Morris, tells the convention that because of Shays' Rebellion "we obviously need a stronger federal government."

As Madison and Wilson could cite their Aristotle, Sidney, Locke, or Hobbes and make references to Greek city-states and European constitutional monarchies, so the veterans of the mock convention are able to refer to *Federalist* Number 10, the theory behind England's unwritten constitution, the ineffectiveness of the Articles of Confederation, and Hobbes's concept of the state of nature. In becoming conversant about the problems confronting the Constitution makers, students begin to incorporate into their own thought processes the political science concepts and factual information necessary to understand the complexities of framing the Constitution. They are prepared not only to discuss the Constitution intelligently, but to participate in discussions of analogous problems confronting the nation today. Thus, the convention, in Whitehead's words, teaches utilizable knowledge.

It is possible to design an entire history course which continues the dialogue begun at the convention and to use many of the same techniques. The Federalist era, for instance, can be seen as the working out, through concrete policy decisions, of the broad and general conceptions of government discussed at the convention. Debates over funding the national debt, establishing the Bank, suppressing the Whiskey Rebellion, supporting the Alien and Sedition Acts, and the Virginia and Kentucky Resolutions, after all, raise issues and problems very similar to those decided at the Convention. The issues raised by the Tariff of Abominations, the Bank veto, the compromises of Henry Clay, the Dred Scott decision, and secession continue the dialogue, involving students in reasoning through the underlying dilemmas posed by our conceptions of majority rule and minority rights. Resolving the problem of justice for black Americans may start with debates over the extension of slavery and continue in arguments over balancing the need to preserve the Union against the moral necessity of ending slavery. Related issues can be raised in a unit on Reconstruction, debating the relative merits of Lincoln's and Stevens' plans for dealing with the South, simulating the trial of Andrew Johnson, examining the opposing arguments in the *Plessy* decision, and considering current manifestations such as the cases for and against compensatory treatment and bussing.

The rise of industrial America raises other perplexing dilemmas, pitting the freedom of businessmen against the needs of consumers, the rights of workers against the prerogatives of employers, and the plight of immigrants against the obligations of society. Foreign policy is similarly laced with fundamental moral concerns regarding true national interests and obligations, the moral restraints on pursuing those interests, and the necessity of foreign involvements. Finally, the 1920's and the Depression raise issues concerning the obligation of the national government to the plight of the unemployed and disabled within the context of fiscal and monetary policies geared toward encouraging economic expansion or combating inflation.

In all of the units outlined briefly above, it is possible and desirable to continue involving students in the dialogue initiated at the convention, to teach the economic and sociological concepts that make the present understandable, and, finally, to involve students in the process of making decisions as well as requiring them to analyze the reason they were made. Knowledge thus obtained will never be inert, but will create citizens competent to take part in the political process which is, after all, the out-growth of our historical experience. Students thus equipped will un-doubtedly reason at higher moral and cognitive levels and will, in Dewey's words, "mature and pass into higher functions in the freest and fullest manner."

Involving students of low academic ability in discussing moral issues is more difficult than working with honors students. Nevertheless, the same principles that govern the successful use of hypothetical dilemmas, histor-ical dilemmas, mini- and full dilemma units for the talented will work in teaching the less talented. With students who are not motivated dilemmas often induce discussion where other more traditional methods fail. The challenge is to develop or find material at the correct reading and con-ceptual level. The Constitution unit described here has been rewritten for low ability students, and a sample version has been developed for fifth graders. Since youngsters cannot discuss ideas they do not under-stand, it is important to translate problems into familiar terms. The fifth-grade class discussed the issue of secession rather than the question of power between national and state governments. One student translated the issue into his own words: "If you join a club, you can't quit and take the clubhouse with you."

Other units described here also work well with less able students by employing reasoning at lower stages. The mock trial of the soldiers in-volved in the Boston Massacre was a great success. In debating the Kent State incident, several youngsters argued that the dead students deserved their fate because "they would not have been shot if they had not done something wrong." Several viewed the situation from the Guardsmen's point of view, claiming that they were shooting in self-defense. Others adopted the victim's perspective and asked, "How would you like to be shot (like Sandy Sheuer) for looking for a lost dog?" Taking a more philosophical outlook, others argued "it all depends on who you were."

Although the level of discussion seldom reaches Stage 4, teachers should avoid despair. Instead, they should realize that the best way to raise the level of reasoning is by continued exposure to arguments at higher levels that will eventually cause the more complete and developed senti-ments to become incorporated into the youngster's reasoning structure, thus advancing his capacity for logical, structured thought. The field studies by Professors Kohlberg [and] Mosher and their students have clearly demonstrated this point.

In general, units used with students of low academic ability seem to work well in proportion to the extent that the material presented is about "people" rather than "things." A unit on slavery can be particularly suc-cessful because cases like that of the woman who killed her child, a girl severely beaten for avoiding work, and Frederick Douglass besting his master are real dilemmas and illustrative of a society which systematically repressed human rights and dignity. Other successful units revolve around the plight of Indians and immigrants, areas equally rich in human interest stories and illustrative of fundamental issues involving the conflict between individuals and society.

This is not to say that moral dilemmas that pose significant political problems cannot be raised within the context of an American history course designed for the nonacademic student. A unit on the "limits of war" is generally successful. It employs the *Lusitania* case, the "final solution," Hiroshima, and the My Lai massacre. Similarly, the New Deal raises important political and economic issues in an ethical context. Students of all ability levels can and should be involved in discussions of postwar foreign policy questions such as the Truman-MacArthur controversy, the Cuban missile crisis, the Berlin blockade, and the Marshall Plan. Nor should the curriculum avoid discussions of civil rights, feminism, the counterculture, and so forth.

Teachers should not be discouraged if some youngsters are not facile with sophisticated concepts. Too many of us have tried and failed to teach the distinction between the protective and revenue tariff, learning the lesson that we cannot teach what the student is unwilling or intellectually unable to absorb. Rather than be defeated by this experience, teachers should concentrate on understandable concepts and design historical materials and miniunits that involve their classes in the process of confronting the dilemmas of history. One must rely on the reasoning processes revealed in the classroom to stimulate cognitive and moral growth. History can be taught in significant ways to students of all ability groups; the limiting factors are not the youngsters themselves, but the time and the imagination of the teacher and the availability of materials.

The time has arrived for social studies educators to apply the developmental educators' knowledge, insights, and techniques to their own disciplines. Unfortunately, the work done to date, although a necessary beginning, has been too simplistic to encompass or exploit the rich and varied cloth of historical experience. Social studies people must develop moral dilemma units which present man as a decision maker operating within a context of time. Students can then experience historical dilemmas by participating in the decision-making process and then analyzing the reasons those decisions were made. Only after this difficult but necessary challenge to create a new "new social studies" is accepted, can the social studies teacher claim his rightful and central role in stimulating both cognitive development and moral reasoning.

Notes

1. Quoted by Lawrence Kohlberg in "Moral Development and the New Social Studies," lecture given to annual meeting of the National Council for the Social Studies, Boston, November 23, 1972, reprinted in *Collected Papers on Moral Development and Moral Education,* ed. *id.* (Cambridge, Mass.: Center for Moral Education, Harvard University, 1973), 1.

2. Barry K. Beyer, "Conducting Moral Discussions in the Classroom," *Social Education,* 40 (April 1976), 196.

3. Jack R. Fraenkel, "The Kohlberg Bandwagon: Some Reservations," *ibid.,* 221.

4. Alfred North Whitehead, *The Aims of Education* (New York: Mentor Books, 1956), 15-16.

5. Ronald E. Galbraith and Thomas M. Jones, "Teaching Strategies for Moral Dilemmas: An Application of Kohlberg's Theory to the Social Studies Classroom," *Social Education,* 39 (January 1975), 16-22.

6. Allan Nevins, *The Ordeal of the Union,* Volume 2 (New York: Charles Scribner's Sons, 1947), 108-109.

7. Kenneth L. Woodward with Mary Lord, "Moral Education," *Newsweek,* March 1, 1975, 74.

Piagetian Theory and Instruction in Physics

John W. Renner
Anton E. Lawson

Jean Piaget and his associates have been gathering data and formulating important theoretical observations about the intellectual development of children since 1927. Although it has taken American psychologists and educators a relatively long time to become acquainted with his work, it is becoming apparent that we can gain much by a careful evaluation of his efforts and their educational implications.

Numerous texts[1] have become available in recent years attempting to explain Piaget's theory and its educational significance. The primary purpose of this paper is similarly to explain his ideas, and further to expand a scheme of instruction and classroom procedures that arise as a consequence of that theory.[2] When possible these ideas will be put forth using examples in physics context in an effort to elucidate difficult ideas.

Reprinted from *The Physics Teacher,* 11 (No. 3, 1973), 165-169. ©1973 by The American Association of Physics Teachers.

Mental Structures

A central idea in Piaget's work and fundamental in understanding his theory is the concept of mental structure. It would be satisfying to be able to indicate the physiological and chemical nature of these structures, but at this point in the study of human mental functioning that is not possible.[3] Instead their existence in the brain is hypothesized from observable behavior; determination of their exact nature awaits further research. These hypothesized mental structures function to organize the environment so that the organism can function effectively. In this sense the construction of these structures carries adaptive value for the individual. An analogous situation is found in the genetic adaptation of evolving species. Basically, then, mental structures represent a more or less tightly organized mental system to guide behavior.

During development of the human infant to adulthood, these structures must be built within the brain. A complete developmental sequence of the structures is not genetically given to the child; they must be learned. According to Piaget, the building and rebuilding of these mental structures is what underlies the process of intellectual development. These structures control how and what we think and guide behavior. In other words, structures actually represent our knowledge.

Since science educators are deeply concerned with intellectual development and the building of mental structures about everything from the metric system to the theory of relativity, two questions need to be asked: (1) How are structures built? (2) Once the structure is built, is it static or can it be altered?

These two questions are not mutually exclusive, and we will answer the second one first. Structures can be altered, and that may be a more than adequate definition of education— the building and rebuilding of structures. The answer to the first question should then give us good insights into how learning takes place and how instruction should be planned.

The Building of Mental Structures—A Problem

An important point must be made before examining the process by which mental structures are formed according to Piaget. Structures do not come from simply making a mental record of the world by keeping eyes and ears open. Unfortunately, it would appear that many teachers subscribe to this view. Work done by Van Senden with congenitally blind persons provides an interesting example of this point.[4] These persons, who had gained sight after surgery, could not identify objects without handling them. They were unable to distinguish a key from a book, when both lay on a table. Also they were unable to report seeing any difference between a square and a circle. The important idea to note is this: Whether the task is to simply distinguish objects in the environment or complex relationships such as $F = ma$, acceleration, or velocity, the ability to develop the understandings requires much more than a simple photographing of the environment.

According to Piaget a person is unable to perceive things until his mind has a structure which enables its perception. Without the development of a mental structure things which seem obvious to an adult, such as the difference between a key and a book, a square and a circle, are simply not perceived by beginners. But this leads us to a fundamental problem. If learning is the building or rebuilding of mental structures, and if structures are needed in order to perceive and learn and are not derived from simply copying the external world, then where do they come from?

Plato's answer to this question was simple. The structures were innate and developed through the passage of time and the growth of the brain. Of course at the other end of the spectrum is the belief that these structures derived directly from the environment. This is the classical empiricist's view; but we have already seen that this view is untenable.

Piaget rejects the Platonic view, except to admit that certain very primary structures must be present at birth. Piaget's view is that the development of structures derives from a dynamic interaction of the organism and the environment which he calls equilibration.

The Building of Mental Structures—Equilibration

From birth, basic structures enable the child to begin interacting with his surroundings. As long as that interaction is successful the basic structures continue to guide behavior. However, owing to the child's inborn drive to interact with his environment, he meets contradictions, that is, things which do not fit his present mental structures. These contradictions produce a state of disequilibrium. In other words, his present mental structures are disrupted and must be replaced. Through continued investigation and guidance from others, the child alters or accommodates his disrupted mental structure. Once this is accomplished he is then able to assimilate the new situation. The new structure that is developed is then tried. If the structure guides behavior so that the child's efforts are rewarded (reinforced), the structure is also reinforced. In this manner the child builds new mental structures and adapts to new situations.

The above-described process underlies all development according to theory. The entire process of development of mental structures is viewed as a process of *equilibration* or self-regulation. This process results in the development of progressively more complex and useful mental structures.

The Building of Mental Structures—Contributing Factors

The role of three main factors, *experience, social transmission,* and *maturation,* can be isolated in the process of equilibration. It is apparent that experience is a necessary part of learning. With no contact with the environment, no contradictions of present structures arise, and no possibility for further exploration into the situation that produced the contradiction is possible.

There are basically two kinds of experience—physical and logical-mathematical. This distinction is important because the different experiences lead to different kinds of mental structures.

Physical experience is exactly what the phrase connotes—actual physical action on the objects in the world. This physical experience leads to the development of structures about objects. At some point, however, the learner begins to see more in his interaction with the world than just objects. He sees that his actions with objects produce some kind of order themselves. An example of this is when a learner discovers that ten objects, when counted left to right provide the same result as when counted right to left. In other words, the action itself has properties. The learner now can make the generalization that the sum of any set of objects is independent of their order. Now the student has a mental structure that he can utilize in many situations, and that is a logical-mathematical structure. The structures then enable the learner to operate logically within his environment. The basic behavioral patterns directed by the mental structure are called operations. In the early structure-building stages the opportunity for the learner to interact with concrete material is mandatory.

Piaget has not projected to what academic level the necessity for interaction with material exists; he says, "coordination of actions before the stage of operations needs to be supported by concrete material."[5] A literal interpretation of that statement would be that, regardless of age, the student must have materials to perform actions with until he can begin to utilize logical-mathematical operations. Our research with kindergarten and elementary school children,[6] junior high school students,[7] and college freshmen,[8] all studying science, supports our interpretation of the foregoing quotation.

The factor of experience, then, helps students to build operational structures which can ultimately lead them to think abstractly about the world around them. In other words, it is experience with the materials of the discipline that produces the person who can understand abstract content and *not* studying abstract content which produces students who can interact with the materials and invent abstract generalizations. This says to science teachers that the laboratory *must precede* the introduction of an abstract generalization.

Piaget's second factor, *social transmission*, also provides a basis for structure building. The very young child—and some not so young—operate from a very egocentric frame of reference. He cannot see things objectively because he always looks at them as related to himself. Such a thinker cannot objectively view and/or evaluate anything. In order to shake the learner from an egocentric view of anything, he must experience the viewpoints and thoughts of others. He must, in other words, interact with other people. If he does not, he has no reason to alter the mental structures which he gained from an egocentric frame of reference. Social interaction can lead to conflict, debate, shared data, and the clear delineation and expression of ideas. All of these require that the student carefully examine his present beliefs which will, according to the Piagetian model, develop and change structures. In order to have all of this happen, however, students must be encouraged to talk with each other and their teachers. Data from an experiment must be shared, discussed, retaken, and rediscussed. Students "should converse, share experience, and argue."[9] The factor of social interaction is valuable in building and rebuilding structures, but it is insufficient because the learner can receive valuable information via language or via education directed by an adult only if he is in a state where he can understand this information. That is, to receive this information he must have a set of experiences that enables him to assimilate this information.

Maturation, the third factor, must also be considered. Evidence indicates that these structures require time to develop. Old structures cannot be accommodated to new experiences all at once. The process of development is slow, as any teacher can attest.

Perhaps this personal example will help clarify how these three factors interact in the process of equilibration to change structures. Our first contact with $V = IR$ was a rather traumatic experience. We vaguely understood that it involved the conservation of energy, but concentrated upon memorizing what the symbols meant and how to juggle the formula. In short, an advanced state of disequilibrium was our lot! When meter readings were substituted for the very abstract terms of potential difference and current, the symbols began to have meaning, and after a good deal of thinking equilibrium was achieved. Then a series circuit with one source and more than one resistor and parallel circuit was introduced. The notion that in a series circuit the total potential difference, V_t, of the source equaled the sum of all voltage drops, V_i, $i = 1,2,3,....n$, around the circuit brought on another disequilibration. Once again meter reading (objects) were salvation; we began to really understand that

$$V_t = \sum_{i=1}^{n} V_i, \, i = 1,2,3,....,n,$$

really was a conservation of energy statement. Now $V = IR$ was a concept which was available for use and once again equilibrium was achieved. Parallel circuits presented no problem, and Kirchhoff's laws were nearly obvious.

This example demonstrates that the science laboratory clearly has a place in promoting equilibration and disequilibration. Data from an experiment can be very threatening, because they too often produce disequilibrium. But to the sensitive, concerned science teacher, disequilibrium is an opportunity; he can now introduce the student to the major conceptualizations of the discipline which will produce equilibrium. This sequence of events suggests that perhaps the principal role of the teacher is to promote disequilibrium and equilibrium, because through the process of equilibration structures are built and rebuilt. Equilibration proceeds through experience with the materials worked with and the social interaction of those around us.

The Learning Cycle

An instructional technique incorporating much of Piagetian theory has been developed and refined by the Science Curriculum Improvement Study, University of California, Berkeley. Their procedure is basically a three-phase process: (1) exploration, (2) invention, and (3) discovery.

Exploration involves the students in concrete experience with materials. As a consequence of these initial explorations, which sometimes may be highly structured by the teacher or on other occasions relatively free, the learner encounters new information which does not fit his existing structures. This produces disequilibrium. At the appropriate time, determined by the teacher, he suggests a way of ordering the experiences. In essence, the teacher invents a new structure which often involves a new concept. This phase, termed *invention*, is analogous to Piaget's structure building and promotes a new state of understanding or equilibrium. The question now is: can the new situation be applied in other situations? During phase three, *discovery*, further application of the inventions are discovered by the students. Discovery experiences serve to reinforce, refine, and enlarge the content of the invention.[10]

Again an example from physics may help to clarify these points. Experience in the laboratory with voltage and resistance, seeing the effect these have on current, and recording all these data is exploration. These exploratory experiences, if provided at the appropriate time, will promote disequilibrium and lead students to question relationships. Since it would take a brilliant student to invent the notion that $V = IR$, the formal statement of that relationship is left up to the teacher. The teacher, having explained the relationship, has in effect provided a way of ordering the student's experience. This is invention. Now the student is in a position to make discovery with this new concept. He can apply it to various types of circuits, magnitudes of voltage, current, and resistance, practically any type of situation he can design. That is the true notion of discovery. Exploration, invention, and discovery are the three phases of the learning cycle and represent a process which will lead the learner to move from physical action to abstract mental operations. Science in general—and in our opinion physics in particular—has a unique opportunity to lead students to build structures. Are we utilizing it? There is much evidence to suggest we are not.[11]

Levels of Thinking

Piaget's theory has gone further than describing how mental structures are formed. He has outlined the basic structures that dictate behavior from birth to adulthood. The structures fall roughly into four categories. Each category or stage incorporates and adds to the structure of the previous stages. If Piaget is correct, it becomes imperative for educators to understand these stages of development. They provide a possible key for adapting instruction to the learner's capabilities. They further suggest types of activities which could promote intellectual development.

The child at birth is in a state Piaget calls *sensory-motor*. During this period, which lasts until about eighteen months, the child acquires such practical knowledge as the fact that objects are permanent. The name of the second stage describes the characteristics of the child—*preoperational*, the stage of intellectual development before mental operations appear. In this stage, which persists until around seven years of age, the child does not, for example, reverse his thinking; he exhibits extreme egocentricism, centers his attention upon a particular aspect of a given object, event, or situation, reasons transductively, and does not demonstrate conservation[12] reasoning. In other words, the child's thinking is very rigid.

At about seven years of age the thinking stages of children begin to "thaw out"—they show less rigidity. The stage the child has entered is called *concrete operational*. Those structures which permit the reversal of thinking and so on, which are denied a preoperational thinker, begin to show themselves as the child moves more and more deeply into the concrete operational stage. The child can now perform what Piaget calls mental experiments—he can assimilate data from a concrete experience and arrange and rearrange them in his head. In other words, the concrete operational child has a much greater mobility of thought than when he was younger.

The name of this stage of development—concrete operational—is representative of the type of thinking of this type of learner. As Piaget explains this stage: "The operations involved . . . are called 'concrete' because they related directly to objects and not yet to verbally stated hypotheses."[13] In other words, the mental operations performed at this stage are "object bound"—operations are tied to objects. This point must be firmly entrenched in the minds of teachers, because when working with students who are moving through this stage they must focus their teaching on the object—the actuality—and not on the abstract. Density, for example, is an abstraction; lenses are concrete.

As the child begins to emerge from the concrete operational stage of thought, according to the Piagetian model, he enters the last stage called *formal operational.* According to Piaget, this occurs between eleven and fifteen years of age. A person who has entered that stage of formal thought "is an individual who thinks beyond the present and forms theories about everything, delighting especially in considerations of that which is not."[14] Formal operational thought is capable of reasoning with propositions only and has no need for objects. It should be pointed out, however, that for this type of thought to occur it must be developed through the use of objects. For that reason this type of thought can be described as propositional logic. An analysis of formal operations reveals that they "consist, essentially of 'implication' . . . and 'contradiction' established between propositions which themselves express classifications, seriatations, etc."[15] The formal thinker can form hypotheses and test them. To do this, he must isolate and control variables and exclude irrelevant ones. This type of thought can truly be described as abstract.

The maximum educational gain that comes from the study of science is derived from the isolation and investigation of a problem. Quite obviously this involves the formulation and stating of hypotheses and using a form of thinking which can be described as, if . . . , therefore . . . . That is, of course, propositional logic. In other words, science teaching should promote formal thought. But it cannot do so if concrete operational thinkers are asked to interact with science on a formal operational level and their teacher teaches them as though they think formally. Concrete operational learners must interact with science at that level; they *cannot* do otherwise. Only then will they build the structures that promote their intellectual development toward formal thought.

Where are today's science students in the development of formal thought? If the programs of study available for high school physics are examined, for example, the fact that they require the use of abstract thinking is immediately apparent. The same can be said for most of the new curriculum developments in science. As Kohlberg and Gilligan recently said: "Clearly the new curricula assumed formal operational thought rather than attempting to develop it."[16] Is such a statement justified? Can science taught at the precollegiate and college levels promote formal thought? What can teachers do, if anything, as they select and arrange curricula and interact with students to promote formal thought? . . .

Notes

1. Examples of these texts are: Herbert Ginsburg and Sylvia Opper, *Piaget's Theory of Intellectual Development* (Englewood Cliffs, N.J.: Prentice-Hall, 1969); Richard Gorman, *Discovering Piaget* (Columbus, Ohio: Charles E. Merrill, 1972); John L. Phillips, Jr., *The Origins of Intellect: Piaget's Theory* (San Francisco: W. H. Freeman, 1969); John G. Flavell, *The Developmental Psychology of Jean Piaget* (Princeton, N.J.: D. Van Nostrand, 1963).
2. This scheme of instruction also incorporates theoretical observations detailed in Chester A. Lawson, *Brain Mechanisms and Human Learning* (Boston: Houghton Mifflin, 1967).
3. For hypothesized neural mechanisms, see *ibid.,* 9-16.
4. D. O. Hebb, *The Organization of Behavior* (New York: John Wiley, 1949), 31-36.
5. Jean Piaget, "Development and Learning," *Journal of Research in Science Teaching*, 2 (No. 3, 1964), 180.
6. Don G. Stafford and John W. Renner, "SCIS Helps the First Grader to the Logic in Problem Solving," *School Science and Mathematics*, 70 (February 1970), 159.
7. Faith Elizabeth Friot, "The Relationships between an Inquiry Teaching Approach and Intellectual Development," doctoral dissertation, University of Oklahoma, 1970.
8. Joe W. McKinnon and John W. Renner, "Are Colleges Concerned with Intellectual Development?" *American Journal of Physics*, 39 (No. 9, 1971), 1047.
9. Ginsburg and Opper, *Piaget's Theory of Intellectual Development*, 228.
10. Chester A. Lawson, *So Little Done: So Much to Do* (Berkeley: Regents of the University of California, 1966), 7.
11. Robert J. Whitaker, "Teaching Practices in Introductory Physics Courses in Selected Oklahoma Colleges," doctoral dissertation, University of Oklahoma, 1972.
12. Ginsburg and Opper, *Piaget's Theory of Intellectual Development*, 164.
13. Jean Piaget and Bärbell Inhelder, *The Psychology of the Child* (New York: Basic Books, 1969), 100.
14. Jean Piaget, *Psychology of Intelligence* (Totowa, N.J.: Littlefield, Adams, 1966), 148.
15. *Ibid.*, 149.
16. Lawrence Kohlberg and Carol Gilligan, "The Adolescent as a Philosopher: The Discovery of the Self in a Postconventional World," *Daedalus*, 100 (No. 4, 1971), 1051.

Promoting Intellectual Development through Science Teaching

John W. Renner
Anton E. Lawson

In the previous paper, we discussed the process of intellectual development and the intellectual level concepts of Jean Piaget and briefly commented upon the relation of those ideas to teaching and learning physics.
The purpose of this paper is to comment upon the thought patterns of
secondary school and first-year college students and to suggest types of
experiences students need to have to enable them to move toward acquiring formal thought.

We start with the assumption that all students deserve the opportunity
to develop the capacity to think with the "if . . . , then . . . , therefore . . ."
form—in other words, to develop formal thought. Three questions immediately arise:

1. What type(s) of thought do secondary school and first-year college
students use?

2. How can the student's level of thought be assessed?

3. What can educational institutions do to change the type(s) of thinking students do?

Levels of Thought, Students, and Content

If you reflect back to the previous paper on the topic of learning, you
will recall that we pointed out that learners begin to leave the preoperational stage at around seven years of age. At this point, they enter the
concrete operational stage of thought and, according to Piaget, move
more and more deeply into that stage until somewhere between eleven
and fifteen years of age. That is the time when they begin to move into
the last stage of intellectual development—formal operational thought.

Now the transition from concrete to formal thought is of the utmost
importance to teachers who work with students in grades ten to twelve
in the secondary schools and in their first years of college. *If* students
have achieved the ability to think formally, the teacher can proceed to
lead them to deal in the great abstractions of science because they can
think with form, "if . . . , then . . . , therefore . . .," or

Reprinted from *The Physics Teacher*, 11 (No. 5, 1973), 273-276. © 1973 by The
American Association of Physics Teachers.

propositional logic. These teachers need not be as concerned with providing students direct experience with the materials of the discipline as those teaching concrete operational thinkers. But if students are concrete operational, they cannot think with propositional logic, and *all* they learn will come from interacting with the materials of the discipline. These statements carry with them serious implications for science teaching, indeed for all types of teaching which deal with abstractions. Therefore, the validity of these statements must be carefully evaluated. At this particular time such an evaluation has not been carried out to any satisfactory extent. However, to any teacher who has had the experience of having his students simply not comprehend what to him seemed eminently clear, Piaget's hypothesis becomes extremely compelling.

Basically, one can grasp why Piaget asserts that "if . . . , then . . . , therefore . . . ," thinking is required to understand the nature of the abstract concepts themselves. The abstractions in physics, as well as in biology and chemistry, are in actuality models created by scientists to explain observable data. These models do not arise directly from the observations; rather, they simply represent attempts to construct an explanation or model which implies what is observed. The scientist creates the model (we do not know how) and reasons *if* his model is true, *then* consequences should be found. If the predicted consequences are indeed found, he has *therefore* supported his model. The process is hypothetico-deductive or in the if . . . , then . . . , therefore . . . , form. For a student to fully grasp the meaning of the abstract models he, too, must be able to think in the if . . . , then . . . , therefore . . . , form. The inertia principle, for example, has to be deduced and verified from its implied consequences. Strictly speaking, it does not give rise to observable empirical evidence.

Consider Newton's second law, $F = ma$. That law is always stated (and properly so) in terms of the mass of a body. Now mass is not a concrete concept—it is an abstraction. All matter that students have *experienced* exists in a gravitational field. Therefore what students have experienced is not mass but weight. This point is of little consequence to a formal operational thinker; mass is an abstract concept he can comprehend and do mental experiments with. To succeed in understanding $F = ma$ (particularly when identifying its units), however, the learner must be able to do mental experiments with abstract concepts. Now look at acceleration— a rate of change of a rate of change. A rate of change is a concrete concept; miles/hour, cents/pound, and pounds/foot are all situations with which a learner can have concrete experiences. But when you change that rate of change so that you are referring to miles/hour/second, providing experience which will lead a student to that is nearly impossible. (To make acceleration even more abstract, it is usually written, for example, as ft/sec.^{2}.) About the best that can be done is to let the student experience the fact that as an object slows down, the time intervals required to travel equal distances get progressively longer. Now consider the experience students have had with forces. Those experiences have no doubt been pushes and pulls and have probably been measured in pounds. Now a student takes an abstract quantity (mass) which he has not experienced and multiplies it by a second very abstract quantity (acceleration) and produces a third quantity called force. But here the force is not measured in pounds but in kilogram-meters/second^2 and is called a newton. *There is nothing concrete about that entire process. It is a complete abstraction.* Now if a student is a formal thinker, he can probably handle that abstraction—*he can't if he is concrete operational.* Do not misread *can't* to mean "doesn't want to"; it means exactly what it says, *can't.*

Couple Newton's second law with the calorie, transverse waves, the particle theory of light, and the gauss and maxwell, and the second law of thermodynamics and you have a pretty good sampling of a first-year physics course. You also have a fair list of abstractions. Those are abstract topics for which formal operations are a necessity. How does a teacher determine whether or not his class can handle such abstract topics?

Assessing Student Level of Thought

What we have done in the area of determining student success with tasks which reflect formal operational thought has been greatly influenced by four sources:

1. Bärbel Inhelder and Jean Piaget, *The Growth of Logical Thinking from Childhood to Adolescence* (New York: Basic Books, 1958), Chapters 1-7.

2. *The Developmental Theory of Piaget: Conservation* (San Francisco: John Davidson Film Producers, 1969).

3. Elizabeth F. Karplus and Robert Karplus, "Intellectual Development beyond the Elementary School: I. Deductive Logic," *School Science and Mathematics*, 70 (May 1970), 398.

4. Robert Karplus and Rita W. Peterson, "Intellectual Development beyond Elementary School: II. Ratio A Survey," *School Science and Mathematics,* 70 (December 1970) 813.

The foregoing sources contain many more tasks than will be described here, and you are urged to try them. Here are two tasks which we have used quite extensively.[1]

1. *The conservation of volume* (source 2, above). This task requires two cylinders of exactly the same size but having different weight (we have used one made of brass and the other of aluminum); those properties

of the cylinders are pointed out to the student. He is next presented with two identical tubes partially filled with water and allowed to adjust the water levels until he is convinced that each tube contains exactly the same amount. The student is then asked if when the cylinders are put in the tubes, the heavy cylinder will push the water up more, if the lighter cylinder will push the level up more, or if the cylinders will push the levels up the same. The examiner requires the student to explain his answer, and often it is the explanations and not the initial responses that are most revealing of thought patterns. If the student completes the task successfully, he has provided evidence of beginning formal operational thought.

2. *The exclusion of irrelevant variables*[2] (source 1, above). The student is presented with a pendulum whose length can be easily changed and three different sized weights which can be used for the pendulum bob. He is told to do as many experiments as he needs to, using many different lengths of string and all the various sized weights until he can explain what he needs to do to make the pendulum go fast or slow. Again, note that the examiner bases his evaluation on the student's explanations. The variables of string length, angle, and push are also pointed out to the student. If the examinee recognizes that length is the only relevant variable, he is about to enter into the formal operational thought period. If he not only excludes the irrelevant variables but hypothesizes a solution to the problem and demonstrates his solution, he has entered the formal period. If the student can state a general rule about pendula in such a way that it can be tested, he is probably capable of working with propositional logic. Although the concept of an oscillating pendulum and its period is not an abstract concept itself (its discovery and construction related directly to a concrete physical experiment), solution of the pendulum problem does indicate the use of propositional logic, and that is a prerequisite to the understanding of abstractions.[3]

Student Performance on the Tasks

Physics is normally taught in the high schools to students in grades eleven and twelve. We administered these tasks, therefore, to ninety-nine eleventh graders and ninety-seven twelfth graders from Oklahoma public schools. The schools were randomly selected, and students in each selected school were also randomly selected. Table 9-1 shows what we found.

The data in Table 9-1 suggest that out of the population from which physics students are drawn, not many are formal operational. You are urged to administer these tasks to your students. If you are interested in doing some group evaluations of your students, study sources three and four listed earlier. Source three deals with determining student ability

Table 9-1

Performance of formal operational tasks by a random sample of high school students

Population	Conservation of volume	Exclusion
Eleventh grade (N= 99)		
Females (N= 54)	19	14
Males (N= 45)	26	23
Twelfth grade (N= 97)		
Females (N=47)	18	16
Males (N=50)	34	20

to reason abstractly by presenting a problem and then providing one clue at a time. The clues and the original statement of the problem must then be analyzed and used to draw conclusions. Source four assesses student ability to apply the concept of ratio. When using ratios, the student is utilizing proportional thinking which is an essential component of formal thought. Please do not make the assumption that by the time students get to physics in high school only those who think formally enroll. Our high school data from those enrolling in high school physics, though not extensive enough to make a definite statement, suggest that such is not the case. Data will be presented later which show that many concrete operational thinkers are found at the first-year college level.

Kohlberg and Gilligan[4] report that in a study of the ability of 265 persons to perform successfully on the pendulum task (exclusion), these results were obtained:

> age 10-15 — 45%;   age 21-30 — 65%;
> age 16-20 — 53%;   age 45-50 — 57%.

If you assume that performance on the pendulum task is an indication that formal operational thought is present, the foregoing data suggest what our data do—a large percentage of the adolescent population is not formal operational. Unfortunately, our age ranges and those of Kohlberg and Gilligan do not coincide exactly, and so no more definite statement can be made from those two groups of data.

The conservation of volume and the pendulum tasks were taken by college freshmen. The results shown in Table 9-2 were obtained.

The data shown in Table 9-2 clearly reflect that the majority of college freshmen have not moved deeply into the formal operational stage of thought—77 of 185 experiencing success on the exclusion task is not too impressive. We do not mean to infer that performance on the pendulum

Table 9-2

Performance of college freshmen for formal operational tasks

Number of college freshmen	Conservation of volume	Exclusion
185	133	77

task is an absolute measure of the achievement of formal operational thought. We *do* mean to infer that performance on these tasks is a strong indication of student ability to use propositional logic. We tested our inference that these two tasks do help isolate formal thinkers—those that use thought patterns which are "the stock in trade of the logician, the scientist, or the abstract thinker."[5] In searching for a test population we ruled out all quantitative fields because the tasks are quantitative in nature. We were reminded that the if . . . , then . . . , therefore . . . , construct is also the stock-in-trade of the lawyer. In order to survive in the study of law, students have to think mainly on the abstract level. We asked several groups of second- and third-year law students to react to the two tasks we just described. Table 9-3 reflects our results. A total of sixty-six students reacted to the tasks, and fifty of them demonstrated formal operational thought. We feel, therefore, that these two tasks have a good probability of identifying formal thought.

What Educational Institutions Can Do to Foster Formal Thought

Our research has shown us that the level of thought of junior high school students[6] and college freshmen[7] can be changed by providing them inquiry-centered experiences in science. We believe that the principal

Table 9-3

Performance of second- and third-year law students on two formal operational tasks

Tasks	Concrete operational	Formal operational
Conservation of volume ($N=22$)	3	19
Exclusion of irrelevant variables ($N=44$)	13	31

reason our research has shown an increase in the thought levels of students is because *we accepted that most of them participating in the experiments were concrete operational.* That put squarely upon us the responsibility for providing concrete experiences with the objects and ideas of the discipline. These students were involved in actually creating some knowledge of their very own. We know that this was the first time some of them had been given that opportunity. We believe that actual involvement with the materials and ideas of science and being allowed to find out something for themselves account for the movement toward and into formal thought which we found.

Science teachers in general and physics teachers in particular have a vehicle at their command that makes active student involvement convenient. That vehicle is the laboratory. Both of our research studies had the laboratory at its nerve center. In the case of the college study that laboratory did not too frequently involve hardware and chemicals, but it was a place where data were gathered, ideas were honed, hypotheses were made and tested, and verifications were carried out. That is the true laboratory.

In teaching the majority of physics courses (both college and high school) the laboratory can be used to lead students, through inquiry,[8] to develop understandings of the concepts to be learned. The teacher, then, has three responsibilities to discharge before ever meeting a class:

1. Isolate those concepts which, when learned, will provide students with an accurate and adequate understanding of the discipline. The teacher must use his understanding of the structure of the discipline in order to select the concepts, and his goal is to provide the learner with *his own* understanding of the discipline's structure. Textbooks are of little help here.

2. Find those laboratory investigations which when cast in an inquiry framework will, upon completion, allow the student to develop an understanding of the concept being considered. Textbooks are of no help here.

3. Make sure the investigations are cast into an inquiry framework, and be sure the necessary materials are available.

Now classes start.[9] The teacher becomes an asker of questions, a provider of materials, a laboratory participant, and a class chairman and secretary. Perhaps most importantly, he is a discussion leader. He gathers the class together (chairman) and solicits the data they have gathered (secretary). He then leads a discussion on what the data mean (discussion leader). He also makes the necessary conceptual inventions at the proper time [and] decides when discovery can take place and when the present concept needs to be related to the next one by exploration. He must also decide when exploration of a completely new concept must begin. This teacher is not a teller; he is a director of learning. Traditional teaching methods embrace the notions that (a) teaching is telling, (b) memorization is learning, and (c) being able to repeat something on an examination is evidence of understanding—those points are the antithesis of inquiry.

The development of formal thought must become the focus of attention of every teacher in the country. The Educational Policies Commission said, in 1961, that the *central* purpose of the school must be to teach students to think, and they operationally defined thinking.[10] Such good advice! We would add that the central role of the school must be to teach children to think with form not objects—in other words, to move students into the stage of formal operational thought. Science has the structure to enhance greatly the achievement of this objective. We must not blow our chances to make a maximum contribution to education in general and education in science in particular. Let us establish an environment in our classrooms that encourages and promotes formal thought.

Notes

1. For a nearly complete picture of one research with formal operations, see John W. Renner and Don G. Stafford, *Teaching Science in the Secondary School* (New York: Harper and Row, 1972), Appendix A; and Joe W. McKinnon and John W. Renner, "Are Colleges·Concerned with Intellectual Development?" *American Journal of Physics*, 39 (No. 9, 1971), 1047.

2. Renner and Stafford, *Teaching Science in the Secondary School*, 294.

3. Bärbel Inhelder and Jean Piaget, *The Growth of Logical Thinking from Childhood to Adolescence* (New York: Basic Books, 1958), Chapters 1-7, 309.

4. Lawrence Kohlberg and Carol Gilligan, "The Adolescent as a Philosopher: The Discovery of the Self in a Postconventional World," *Daedalus*, 100 (No. 4, 1971), 1051.

5. Jerome S. Bruner, *The Process of Education* (New York: Vintage Books, 1960), 37.

6. Faith Elizabeth Friot, "The Relationship between an Inquiry Teaching Approach and Intellectual Development," doctoral dissertation, University of Oklahoma, 1970.

7. McKinnon and Renner, "Are Colleges Concerned with Intellectual Development?" 1047.

8. See John W. Renner and Anton E. Lawson, "Piagetian Theory and Instruction in Physics," *Physics Teacher*, 11 (No. 3, 1973), section on "Learning Cycle," 165, for an explanation of this term and its phases of explanation, invention, and discovery.

9. Renner and Stafford, *Teaching Science in the Secondary School*, contains suggestions that will be helpful in classroom implementation of inquiry.

10. Educational Policies Commission, *The Central Purpose of American Education* (Washington, D.C.: National Education Association, 1961).

10
New Curricula for Students' Development

As students' development is taken seriously as an educational aim, new courses and curricula are required. Chapter 8 outlined how they are created. Their most distinguishing characteristic is a clear-cut commitment to students' development as a primary objective. Enhancing teenagers' growth is the hard part of the equation. Content is seen as a means and may be as diverse as classical literature, John Stuart Mill, and the methods of client-centered counseling. Such courses may be taught by practitioners, such as high school counselors, who are trying to get back into the curriculum or by classroom teachers. The ways to students may be as diverse as through social studies, English electives, high school psychology, or independent study. But the means to personal development is a high school course and is recognizable as such. How such new courses may find their rightful place in the high school curriculum is a real but separate issue. The primary concern of Part II is to illustrate and establish the practicability of affecting students' growth by education, both within and without the existing curriculum. For this reason we talk about such courses as creating new bottles and new wines. Three such courses are described in this chapter.

Developmental Guidance

The first contribution, by Sprinthall, describes a course in which high school students are taught to counsel.[1] The purpose is not vocationalism nor to create a cohort of future counselors of America. It is to impart to adolescents what counseling has learned about the subtleties of human communication, to help them hear and respond to more of the ideas and feelings people express, and to have greater empathy and respect for others. To understand and communicate sensitively with another person is a profound adolescent (and human) need; an enhanced ability to do so is a necessary strand in adolescent social and moral development. It is at the heart of the shift from thinking of oneself first to a sensitivity and an ability to respond to other people. That is critical in the passage toward adulthood. While to teachers and parents it may seem to be an obvious convention or expectation, to adolescents it is new and risky. They have not learned, in Gordon Allport's phrase, to be "half-sure and whole-hearted."[2] What if one gives himself or herself to the wrong other person, ideal, or career? The possibility of making such a mistake can be frighteningly real for the adolescent and his parents. Consider the threat (rejection, for example) or the reward (acceptance, perhaps) to an adolescent with a still uncertain sense of self, of affiliation, and of obligation to others.

To accomplish both socialization and individuation is a central problem for the teenager. The shift from me to we is, nonetheless, an absolute building block in the life of the individual and in the institutionalizing of norms in any society. Thus, its enhancement by education has direct individual and social benefits. And, if the contemporary movement in moral education began with Blatt's discussion of moral dilemmas in a Chicago Sunday school,[3] deliberate education for personal and social development may be said to have begun with Dowell's pioneering work in teaching counseling at Newton High School.[4]

Moral Education

The second contribution illustrating developmental education, by Mosher and Sullivan, describes a moral education course for high school students.[5] It involves teenagers in a series of experiences: counseling, discussing moral dilemmas with younger children, and creating a students' appeal board for a high school. Such experiences were not suggested by a discipline or a professional training course. They were, rather, chosen because it was assumed that they produce growth, that is, affect teenagers' moral reasoning and ego development. And, as it turns out, such experiences do produce growth, and to a significant degree.

Women's Development and Education

The final contribution in Chapter 10 is Erickson's "Deliberate Psychological Education for Women: From Iphigenia to Antigone."[6] It addresses two central preoccupations of developmental education: "A current major omission [in education] has been a sound theoretical perspective of women's development . . . [plus] a lack of serious proposals for curriculum programs that promote growth in women."[7] Erickson has been the major figure in focusing developmental education on studies of women's growth and their education. The number, variety, and data on these developmental effects are extensive. Thus, this particular paper represents many programs promoting comprehensive personal growth in young women. The individual and social case for education for women's development, as part of the case for human development in general, seems incontrovertible. That does not mean that women will automatically achieve equal opportunities for all-around growth in high schools or state legislatures. But, in addition to the moral imperative of such rights for women, there is preliminary but challenging educational evidence that adolescent women, on no dimension of the helix of human development, need be weaker or more like men.

Notes

1. N. A. Sprinthall, "Learning Psychology by Doing Psychology: A High School Curriculum in the Psychology of Counseling," in *Developmental Education*, ed. G. Dean Miller (St. Paul: Minnesota Department of Education, 1976), 23-43.

2. Gordon Allport, "Psychological Models for Guidance," in *Guidance: An Examination*, ed. R. L. Mosher *et al.* (New York: Harcourt, Brace and World, 1965), 19.

3. M. Blatt, "Studies of the Effects of Classroom Discussion upon Children's Moral Development," doctoral dissertation, University of Chicago, 1969.

4. R. C. Dowell, "Adolescents as Peer Counselors," doctoral dissertation, Graduate School of Education, Harvard University, 1971.

5. R. L. Mosher and P. J. Sullivan, "A Curriculum in Moral Education for Adolescents," *Journal of Moral Education*, 5 (No. 2, 1976), 159-172.

6. V. L. Erickson, "Deliberate Psychological Education for Women: From Iphigenia to Antigone," *Counselor Education and Supervision*, 14 (June 1975), 297-309.

7. *Ibid.*, 297.

Learning Psychology by Doing Psychology: A High School Curriculum in the Psychology of Counseling

Norman A. Sprinthall

Experience is not what happens to you; it is what you do with what happens to you.

— Aldous Huxley

Introduction

The program in psychological education represents an attempt to create *new forms, new content, and new ways to educate youth* and to train school personnel. We believe there are manifest needs for reformulating the forms, the content, and the methods of education. It is easier to provide evidence for this contention than it is to develop alternatives. This is a principal reason why educational intervention has been left in many instances at a piecemeal and craft level. We consider that the most pressing need in school guidance is for various alternative concepts of how to educate for psychological maturity and how to translate these ideas into working examples.

One example of what we mean by reformulating education is a curriculum in *personal* and *human development*; a comprehensive set of educational experiences designed to affect personal, ethical, aesthetic, and philosophical development in children, adolescents, and adults. We believe that a powerful intellectual, social, and psychological argument can be made for such education and that the need is neither age nor social class specific. The development of morally and emotionally sensitive human beings is by no means an exhaustive education, but it is usually missing in our present institutions and curricula. The beginnings of the conceptual framework and of the educational experiences facilitating such development are present in the program to be described. Also we will include a description of the current status of our work and the plans for development and implementation.

Reprinted from *Developmental Education*, ed. G. Dean Miller (St. Paul: Minnesota Department of Education, 1976), 23-43. This piece, part of the Deliberate Psychological Curriculum Program, was funded under the Experimental Schools Program, U.S.O.E., Minneapolis Public Schools.

Rationale for the Approach

The current need and demand for effective educational programs have been extensively and exhaustively described and documented. We will not plan to add one more educational autopsy in support of the need for new and more powerful ways to educate children and teenagers. It is obvious that schools, communities, or, indeed, nations cannot afford to leave the process of psychological development to the mercy of random forces as is now the case in so many instances.

In addition to the need for personal development, our rationale also includes the necessity to develop a substantive basis for a curriculum in psychological education. Thus our approach is oriented to the creation of "knowledge" about children and adolescence as a stage of psychological development and the implication of that view for intervention strategies. Too often school programs pay only lip service to the concept of psychological development and then immediately create curriculum materials that bear small relation to a developmental framework. We are convinced that an effective program can be based upon solid psychological theory. Precise definitions from developmental psychology at present seem to us as the most promising theoretical framework. Some of the most critical issues in this regard have been enumerated in a recent article.[1] For example, if adolescence represents a stage of development *qualitatively* distinct from childhood, the concepts of the shifts to "formal operations" (Piaget), a higher level of "moral judgments" (Kohlberg), and an accompanying shift to egocentric schemata (Elkind) have major theoretical implications for programs that seek to nurture psychological growth and ego development (Loevinger). Such a theoretical framework also prevents programs in psychological education from a philosophical "cul de sac" of simply offering "a new bag of virtues."[2]

Other important aspects of the rationale for our approach concern the physical location for the research, the pedagogy of the seminar *and* practicum approach, and the emphasis on simultaneously training teachers and developing curriculum materials. We have found that the best place for an educational research and development project is in the natural setting of the school. Willie Sutton, when asked why he robbed banks, replied, "That's where the money is!" Our view is analogous. Curriculum reformulation should take place in the school because that is where the teachers and pupils are. More elegant and eloquent is the view suggested by Dean Shaefer of Columbia when he called for the school systems themselves to become "centers for inquiry."[3] Such inquiry, in our view, can create needed programs for change.

In a parallel sense, our view is that in-service training of counselors and teachers should take place in sequence with the development of new materials. The shared development of new ideas and new teaching modes seems a natural alliance of people and programs (as opposed to sending teachers to a sensitivity training marathon on one hand and importing a package of new curriculum materials on the other). Training teachers and counselors through direct involvement with the formative process of curriculum development avoids the problems of expecting teachers to use alien material and helps them acquire the needed experience base to reorient their own practice. There is enough negative evidence from the long history of efforts in teacher and counselor training to indicate that, in general, teachers and counselors do not change their practice as a result of exhortations, directives from the "central office," or brief in-service workshops. The shiny new curriculum packages that appear from the assembly lines of educational laboratories often meet a similarly negative fate—badly damaged in transit!

In sum, our rationale for educating pupils psychologically/personally is to provide significant experience (counseling peers, cross-age teaching, early childhood work, and so on) and a systematic analysis of that experience in natural settings. The seminar and practicum pedagogy provides for educating under conditions that are *real*, with genuine *responsibility* and include *rigorous* analysis. The training of teachers and counselors follows a similar format. Perhaps the most significant summary of both the need and the rationale for this program comes from the recent statements of James Coleman:

In attacking the problems of modern society, the most critical step is to reduce the school's dependence on its classical functions so that it can take on new ones. This requires policies that explicitly move the classical activities out of the school . . . . The new goal must be to integrate the young into functional community roles that move them into adulthood . . . . The school must be integrated with service organizations . . . so that the young can help in them. Since the school's function will no longer be to protect the child from society but rather to move him into it, the school must be integrated with these other organizations of society and not insulated from them."[4]

Objectives: *Psychological Growth and Psychology Skills*

The objectives of the classes in the project are really twofold: (1) to increase [the] level of psychological maturity of the pupils and (2) to teach particular psychological skills. In each class the first objective is always the same while the second always depends upon the particular aspects of psychology under deliberate instruction. Using a cognitive-developmental approach as we noted in the rationale, we attempt to maximally facilitate psychological development as a major objective. We employ an array of assessment procedures as proximate measures of psychological change such as the Kohlberg test of moral maturity, the Loevinger test of ego development, interviews, clinical assessments of writing assignments, and student journals. For the assessment of skill development, we employ measures specific to each class. For example, in the counseling class skills are assessed through ratings of their counseling responses. In the psychology of women's growth class their interviewing skills are rated. In the psychology of child development class their performance with nursery age children is rated as well as their abilities to observe the array of individual differences in children. It is our view that effective skill learning in these areas essentially provides means . . . or methods to teenagers so they experience the world differently. Theoretically we see the technique training as a procedure for broadening the experience table of each pupil, . . . thus producing a higher level of psychological maturity.

In this report we will not discuss a third set of objectives, namely, teacher training. We do wish to point out, though, that staff development is a critical domain and will be under development in programmatic terms . . . . Also we consider that such teacher training can occur simultaneously with the instructor of the teenage pupils. A more comprehensive report on the teacher training [and] staff development issues will appear in the future.

The Setting

During the school year 1972-73, we . . . tried out a series of courses, largely as electives in a social studies department. This represents a second trial and an initial replication of previous findings reported from the program developed in a Massachusetts school system.[5] It is not an exact replication, however, because curriculum development done in the natural setting of regular high school classes does not permit the same degree of controlled experimentation as in a laboratory setting.

The setting of our current program is a local public high school population. The school, with an enrollment of approximately 1,200 students in grades seven to twelve, of which 17 percent are minority, serves a wide population—a public school for the southeast district [of Minneapolis], approximately one-quarter of the school's students are from out of district including about one hundred racial transfers; and the school services about seventy orthopedic, hearing, and mentally handicapped students drawn from throughout the metropolitan area. This is a wide range of abilities throughout the entire student body. The plans of recent graduating classes indicate that about 60 percent plan to go to college, 15 percent plan to go directly to work, and about 15 percent plan to attend a vocational or business school. The remaining 10 percent are undecided.

The Psychology of Counseling Class

This course is designed as a practicum and seminar experience to promote the learning of listening skills and the development of empathic responses through actual peer counseling experience. The practicum sessions consist of sequential training in role-play exercises, examinations of counseling tapes, and counseling of high school peers. The seminar sessions include readings on communication, discussions of counseling films and tapes, and an integration of this with the practicum units to encourage reflection and cognitive restructuring of the total learning experience. This class, like others in the overall program, was offered on a pass-fail basis and was an elective. In this particular school almost one-half of all the academic classes are offered as electives. The instructional approach represents an attempt to balance and integrate the process and content of counseling psychology. Thus actual process experiences in learning counseling techniques, active listening skills, and learning to rate appropriate versus inappropriate responses are balanced by content experiences through readings, writing assignments, and discussions of counseling films.

Introductions

The first phase of the class begins with personal introductions by each participant. In previous classes we tried out a series of procedures for these introductions including structured exercises, games, and simulations. We found that the development of listening skills, building the class as a group, and the creation of a collegial atmosphere between the pupils and the instructional staff could best occur without the use of such so-called simulation techniques. Instead we asked each person to take about five to ten minutes to introduce him/herself, say something that would help us get acquainted, and mention some significant learning experience in the past week or so. The class coteachers would then respond to the introduction in a manner designed to indicate that they heard and understood both the content and some of the feelings that the person introducing him/herself was experiencing. There are some moments of awkwardness and self-consciousness in this procedure which the coteachers acknowledge as well as a sense of relief when a person gets through his/her turn. To speak about "self" in front of twenty-five to thirty-five classmates and staff is a significant and difficult experience, yet the procedure is designed to provide a common experience base for the initial stages of the class as well as a demonstration of difficulties of both sending and receiving communication messages. At the conclusion of this phase we ask everyone to fill out a two-page question guide on the introductions:

Please describe your *thoughts* and *feelings* as you introduced yourself.
How uncomfortable were you just prior to your turn?
Did you prepare something to say in your mind?
What were your feelings while you were talking?
Can you describe how you felt afterwards?
Did you have a sense that the class was listening to you? Were any specific individuals helpful with their questions?
Did you have difficulty at times listening to others?
Did you learn new ideas, more about your classmates, teachers, during the introductions? Any new thoughts and ideas about yourself?

We then summarize the comments for the pupils as a means of helping them understand that everyone in the class including the staff is somewhat uncomfortable, would like to say more about themselves, felt they were slightly incoherent, had difficulty in really listening to others, and so forth. Such information gleaned from their reflections upon the experience helps to promote an equalization and democraticizing of the classroom process. Also it is noteworthy how many times pupils comment that it is the first time they knew anything about many of their colleagues more than a name. The procedure also helps to begin to break down some of the previously formed teenage cliques.

Teaching Active Listening Scales

Immediately following the introductions we start direct teaching of the active listening scale [see Table 10-1]. We found that by modifying the original Rogerian Empathy Scale into two components, response to content and response to feeling, we could teach the skills more effectively. We could more easily focus on the particular domain that the pupils were having difficulty mastering by separating the dimensions. We described the scales briefly and handed out one-page copies to each pupil.

Practicing Listening Skills

Through practice such as writing down single responses to stated role-play or actual concerns, the pupils gradually develop skill and comfort with the scales. It is a slow process to move from the artificial and

Table 10-1

Active listening scale

Response to feelings—emotions	Response to content—ideas
5. Goes well beyond the person's expressed feelings. Provides the person with a major new view of the emotions he/she is experiencing.	5. Goes well beyond the stated meaning. Provides new insight.
4. Goes to a slightly deeper feeling than expressed. Helps person understand his/her own feelings in more depth. Goes just beyond the emotions expressed.	4. Goes slightly beyond the meaning stated. Provides some new insight. More concise. Helps the person understand his/her own ideas better.
3. An accurate understanding of feelings and/or emotions, expressed in your own words. An accurate reading of feelings.	3. An accurate understanding of the content—a restatement in your own words of what the person said.
2. A slight distortion of the feelings expressed—a near miss.	2. A slight distortion of meaning—just misses what the person said.
1. No awareness of feelings expressed, the wrong feelings—or a genuine put-down.	1. Dead wrong—the opposite of what was said. A complete miss as to meaning or an active disinterest.

somewhat "plastic" experience of writing single responses to the point of maintaining verbal dialogue with a role-play counselee and requires patience and support. The students' initial resistance to practicing the scales tends to be somewhat high. We found, however, that this structured approach seems to yield positive outcomes in skill learning. Also, we usually play audiotapes from some actual initial counseling interviews made by graduate students. By showing some of these first awkward interviews between real clients and graduate counselors in training, the high school pupils see firsthand the difficulty in accurately identifying and responding to content and feelings. We emphasize the two-stage nature of these learnings, (a) to accurately pick up, hear, and identify content and feelings, and (b) to frame a response, "using your own words which communicate to the role-play client that you do accurately understand the message." The pupils then learn to score responses both on the audiotapes and on the single-response, in-class practice sessions. By teaching the pupils to "judge" their own as well as others' responses, learning the scale is hastened. The pupils become conscious of the dual process of identifying on one hand and responding on the other to understand and experience the process itself.

We have also used practice role-play responses to videotaped excerpts as one further aspect of this skill training phase. We play an excerpt on video to the class, stop the tape, and ask them to write a response which captures both content and feeling. These excerpts can be "homemade" simply by asking pupils in a drama class to make up a problem that teenagers often experience and then tape a series of statements describing the problem. After showing the taped excerpts we then go over the responses in class, usually listing on the blackboard all the content responses and then all the feeling responses to each excerpt. This particularly teaches a language for identifying emotions, as we as a group then pick out from the list on the board the responses that seem most accurate. The pupils then rate their own responses on the two five-point scales. Thus the process teaches judging or rating skills and a language system for identifying emotions simultaneously.

Adding Nonverbal Skills

After the first three or four weeks on the active listening scales we introduce a third aspect of counseling and communication training—the nonverbal components. The summary [in Table 10-2] represents a framework around which we focus the questions of body language. In the same way as the content feeling dimensions are presented, we have the students learn to *identify* nonverbal messages and then after some practice sessions in class we routinely assign a pupil the task of process observation of role-play counseling sessions. Thus with the one-page handout as a guide a pupil will jot down examples of body language "talk" observing the class practicing active listening responses. At the end of each exercise the process observer will make a short presentation of his/her findings. This helps to illustrate the three major aspects of communication, content, feelings, and the nonverbal aspects.

These three dimensions provide us with information on the *content* of what is being said, the *feelings* behind the content, and the *body* language. Sometimes the feelings and the nonverbal language are referred to as the "hidden agenda"—the messages just below the surface. If we learn to "see" and respond to these dimensions, we will tend to increase our own understanding of the complexities of "where the other person is coming from" or we will become more accurate in "reading" . . . another person. Often when we say the "medium is the message," we mean, *how* a message is communicated (the feelings and the body language) is more important than the content itself. Actions speak louder than words [and] feelings are more significant than rhetoric . . . are other ways of saying this same concept.

Table 10-2
The psychology of counseling

1. *Nonverbal cues: Body language signs*

	Quality	
Voice	Harsh/overly sweet	Genuine
Facial expression	Stone-face or distinterested	Interested
Posture	Leans away Tense, rigid, or too casual	Leans toward—relaxed
Eye contact	Avoidance of eye contact or excessive staring	Maintains reasonable eye contact
Touching	Avoids all contact or smothers (backslapper)	Contact appropriate to situation
Gestures	Closed: guarded or overly jovial	Open, flexible
Spatial distance	Too far or too close	About "right" comfortable

2. *General congruence*
Similarity of verbal and nonverbal cues—how "together" are the talk and the body language?
Examples: "Oh, I'm not embarrassed." (Face reddens.)
"I really enjoy lecturing to students." (Knuckles white.)
"It's so nice to see you." (Voice tight.)
"The test you gave us was a useful learning experience."
(Eyes like black darts.)

3. *Three areas of communication: A summary*

Verbal content (5-pt. scale)	Feelings (5-pt scale)	Nonverbal cues Congruent/dissonant

Writing Assignments

Following these process learnings, we then handed out short reading assignments such as "Barriers and Gateways to Communication" by Cari Rogers[6] and "Parent-Child Communication Skills" by the National Education Association.[7] We also showed the Gloria films ("Three Approaches to Psychotherapy") with counseling segments by Rogers, Ellis, and Perls. We asked the students to prepare papers examining the communication issues. The format for one such writing assignment was as follows:

Writing Assignment (Sample A)

1. Read . . . Rogers' article, "Barriers and Gateways to Communication."

2. Write a reaction paper, two to three pages, due next week. Hand in to your small group leader.

3. Almost any format will do since the purpose is for us to see how understandable and significant his comments are for you. If you wish, you can (1) *describe his basic idea:* (How clearly does he state his position? Is his language too "academic?" Does he explain his view adequately or is it too vague, too trivial, too utopian?). (2) *Put his ideas in your own words*, for example, this is like a level three response. How would you say what he says if you were talking with him? (3) Without being too judgmental, *how do you evaluate the significance* of his view for everyday life? (4) *Other comments:* Did he seem much different on "paper" than in the film? Does he make more sense in action with Gloria than in the paragraphs? Are his nonverbal behavior and body language congruent (all together) with his words?

After completing the film of Perls and Ellis, including Gloria's addendum, we hand out another writing assignment seeking to synthesize or integrate the three appraoches to our overall goal of effective communication in all three modes. The writing format follows:

Writing Assignment (Sample B)

Write a reaction paper (two to three pages) comparing Rogers, Perls, and Ellis. Again, your paper may take almost any format that best fits your method of description and examination of the issues.

1. Gloria summed it up that Rogers responded to her emotions, Ellis to her mind, and Perls to her as a person. You might start by explaining in your own words what she meant by this.

2. Also, you could comment on your own reactions to her choice at the end— surprise, disbelief, dismay— that she chose Perls!

3. You also might comment on how complete are any of the single communication systems depicted in the films. For example, is it complete just to focus on content (Ellis), feelings (Rogers), or body language (Perls)?

Is it possible to consider a "super-gestalt" of communicating in all three basic modes? Can a person learn to accurately identify content, feelings, and body language simultaneously (or is it like a three-ring circus)? And further, can a person learn not only to *identify* in the three areas but also to respond accurately?

The Shift from Role Plays

As we proceeded through the term we would follow the same overall format employing part of the class time on process skills and part on intellectual discussion and writing assignments. As the class proceeded the skill training aspect of the process work declined. Instead the pupils began to bring in their own "real life" concerns. The role-play counseling shifted to actual problems, and the pupils started using their newly learned active listening skills on these genuine issues. The range of issues was substantial from one student expressing anger over being falsely accused by a teacher of stealing a book, another concerned over the loss of her dog, to yet another who had an overprotective mother and felt suffocated. Students had the opportunity to both counsel their peers and be counseled in turn by these same peers.

Reciprocal Helping

At an experiential level, we were stressing the reciprocal nature of counseling and communication. We were not interested in creating a professional cadre of teenager counselors as one class of helpers with the balance of the school population as helpees. Instead we wanted the concepts of helping, caring, active listening to remain an essentially democratic responsibility. Pupils were asked to note the difference between this approach to counseling and communication and the regular professional approach with its univocal focus.

Transfer of Training Issues

As the class neared the end of the term, we then stressed the transfer of training problem. We examined the issues involved in moving from the context of the particular class into the "outside" world. We asked the pupils to make brief communication audiotapes with friends as a means of trying out their skills with nonclassmates—this provided for a significant discussion when the pupils realized both how much they had learned as well as how difficult it was to transfer such learning to different situations. As a final test of transfer we administered counseling skill tests to the class as a whole and reported those results at the final class.

Continuing issues that we stressed throughout this transfer of training phase concerned the questions of choice and the meaning of behavior in general. In the first instance we would focus on the responsibility that accompanies the use of active listening and helping others. As pupils learned to use these skills in the real world they often found themselves confronted with such difficult choice questions—"Should I respond to my friend now that I can hear the pain?" or "I'm not really sure that I like this at all. I was happier not listening to others" or "I was really surprised to find out how complicated the problem was, but now what?" We try to help the pupils understand that they can become effective helpers to each other, are genuine resources, and can themselves be helped by their peers.

Also we point out that the process of active listening as helping provides all of us with an understanding of how complicated and multifaceted are problems of human behavior. In a sense the communication training becomes a means of teaching pupils that behavior is not the result of a single cause and effect sequence (we call that view the billiard ball theory of human behavior). Instead the process becomes the road to multiple causation and what it means to say that human behavior is overdetermined. Learning to explore and examine for meaning and the series of factors that are involved in almost any aspect of human behavior becomes our way of teaching for nonstereotyped thinking about human behavior and its causes. The process of developing psychological and personal maturity on the part of teenagers is aided, in our view, by these learnings. To understand the complexities of behavior in ourselves and others is certainly a step toward the development of genuine empathy.

Counseling Class Results

Since the objectives or dependent variables of the classes were twofold, we shall report the results in two categories: (1) the effects upon skill development and (2) the effects upon overall stages of psychological growth.

Skill Development

We assessed their preclass counseling skill level using the Porter scales, ten situations with multiple-choice responses. Their original scores were $\overline{X} = 1.17$ ($N=30$, range 1-3 on a five-point empathy scale). These pretest scores compare almost exactly to the average empathy scores of college freshmen reported in the literature, $\overline{X} = 1.20$.[8] Since these scores were so close we did not do further pretest assessments of counseling skills. The baseline appears well established at a level slightly above level one, defined as a response pattern that misses both the content and feeling of a communication message.

On a series of posttest communication skill measures, the results were encouraging. In the fall term we read ten excerpts from a transcript of an actual therapy session, "A Study in Claustrophobia" by Finesinger and Powdermaker.[9] The high school pupils scored $\overline{X} = 2.76$ ($N=23$, range 2.3-3.5). The actual therapist responses were rated 2.1!

In the winter term class with a new set of pupils we employed the affective sensitivity scale developed by Norman Kagan[10] as the posttest. Their scores were $\overline{X} = 30$ ($N=24$, range 17-48). It is difficult to interpret the exact meaning of this as a post score since there are no norms for high school pupils. The high school scores, however, are not appreciably lower than undergraduate and graduate students. For example, with a small sample of doctorate and masters students currently enrolled at the University of Minnesota, the scores on the same scale were $\overline{X} = 36$ ($N=12$, range 28-48). Since the entire scale contains sixty-six items the overall range on the test runs from zero to sixty-six. The reported scores tend to stand about in the middle of this distribution.

In the spring term with a third set of new pupils, we employed role-play videotapes developed by Tom Skovholt at the University of Missouri. The tape depicted ten client statements with a pause after each for a written response. The posttest scores on a five-point empathy scale for the spring class were $\overline{X} = 2.61$ ($N=21$, range 1.9-3.5). We found that this procedure was far superior to either reading excerpts, or employing the multiple-choice format of the affective sensitivity scale, at least for high school pupils. Their attention, interest, and motivation were highest on the Skovholt coached client videotapes. It appears to us that it would be appropriate to develop a series of such tapes depicting both high school and college students presenting "problem" responses.[11]

The posttest skill level attained was similar to the levels of responses the pupils were making at the end of each term in the actual classwork counseling sessions, lending credence to the overall effectiveness of their skill development. All students in the class demonstrated substantial improvement in these skills, and their writing assignments demonstrated good abilities to reflect upon the specific issues.

Psychological Growth

Since a major objective of the program was to affect the developmental level of the teenager, we used a series of proximate measures as estimates of developmental change—the Loevinger scales of ego development[12] and the Kohlberg scales of moral maturity.[13] In the counseling seminar and practicum we found that a major change occurred on the Loevinger scales. As a general indicator of ego development in a sequence of stages, the teenagers in one counseling class moved from Level 3 to Level 4 ($\overline{X}_1 = 5.21$, $X_2 = 6.42$, $p<.001$). The shift was from wary, self-protective to more trust and open communication and higher self-respect and complexity. Essentially, this is a shift from other-directedness to the beginnings of a more integrated inner-reliant and less egocentric stage. The Kohlberg results, while not as dramatic, statistically confirmed the trend shift. The pupils moved from Stage 3 toward 4 $\overline{X}_1 = 3.22$, $\overline{X}_2 = 3.56$, $p<.08$). The content of those stages is analogous to the Loevinger, except that it is much more difficult to move through an entire stage in the Kohlberg system. It usually takes teenagers two or three years to move from Stage 3 to 4, and even then a substantial minority never make it past Stage 3. Thus the smaller quantitative shift in the Kohlberg results may well be more significant theoretically.[14]

In a second study of the counseling seminar and practicum we found the same shifts in both the Kohlberg scores ($\overline{X}_1 = 3.70$, $\overline{X}_2 = 4.01$, $p < .05$) and the Loevinger scales ($\overline{X}_1 = 4.70$, $\overline{X}_2 = 6.04$, $p < .05$). The movement was from Kohlberg Stage 3 to 4 and Loevinger Stage Delta 3/3-4. The changes on both scales suggest that learning through genuine experience (the practicum), which includes structured examination of that experience (the seminar), becomes a means of promoting rather than assuming development.[15] The skills learned in the counseling class, for example, become the means that teenagers can then employ to hear and understand each other. The excessive personal uniqueness and romantic personal fable to which Elkind[16] refers loses some of its transcendental quality when the wary self-protectiveness in the class fades in the face of emerging "real" problems of teenagers. The learning of active listening skills helps the teenagers develop a language and a repertoire of responses. Such procedures appear as a first step toward empathy in communication. By teaching focused reflection and the meaning of non-verbal responses, each pupil can become more perceptive toward others and less self-centered. The activity of employing these new skills seemingly promotes what Piaget might call a "decalage" of a decentering process through which the teenager becomes less egocentric. Through the use of formal operations to understand and experience the subjective nature of their own world and the world of others, the teenagers' growth process toward maturity may be facilitated. Growth within the stage of formal operations leading to higher levels on both the Kohlberg and Loevinger measures appears theoretically consistent with the content of those stages and with the instructional process as well.

In addition to these measures, the students on questionnaires indicated that they "learned" the following activities or concepts from the class— "to express myself more clearly," "to evaluate myself," "to talk freely," "to be aware of other people," "to understand people different from myself," "to listen to others," "to see the effects others have upon me," and "to help other people." These responses were selected from a list of twelve possible activities and were noted by at least half of the students in the class. Perhaps most significant was one further item. In one class ($N=27$) all students listed "students learn from each other, not just from the teacher," as their major perception of what they had learned in class.

Open-ended written assessments from pupils included comments like:

It was easy to listen to and learn from others in the class, teachers and students. My group seemed together and powerful working toward a common goal, we achieved a lot.

A weird class but I think I learned a lot without the usual books, and just from other people. Also it's useful outside of school too and in the future.

The class was very helpful to me. In our small group we dealt with the real feelings and not *just* practicing the things we learned (empathy scale, Rogers' article, etc.). Maybe that's why it was so good—because it was real and not *just* a learning experience. I enjoyed it. P.S. There should be a follow up course to this.

The project staff of clinically oriented counselors and teachers felt without question that the statistical results confirmed their own subjective impressions of growth and maturity. The levels of responsiveness, helping, caring, and responsibility in the classes themselves subjectively attested to behavior change at a psychological level. Certainly the students in their own "talk" and in postclass interviews indicated that their experiences had been of positive growth and development. Similar positive effects were found in the other seminar and practicum classes while the control or comparison classes showed no change. As a result we may conclude that such a program apparently is a step in the direction of significant educational change rather than just another version of, "the more things change . . . ."[17]

Adolescence as a Stage of Development

The program for curriculum reformulation described here is being created to serve as an operational translation of cognitive developmental theory. Our objective is to build a series of learning experiences for regular classroom pupils at the secondary level designed to deliberately acknowledge concepts from developmental stage theory. Instead of ignoring stages or assuming that the stage of development of the individual is irrelevant (as was the case with many "new" curricula), we are attempting to create a program based on stage concepts. We seek to *match* an intervention system with the psychological development of the secondary pupils.

Essentially we started with the concepts of adolescence as a developmental stage in both the Kohlberg and Piagetian sense. Given the onset of formal operations as a potential (not necessarily realized by all teenagers), and the possibility of higher levels of moral maturity, we explored ideas for teaching and learning experiences that would connect to such psychological issues, namely, to promote the emergence of new cognitive structures or, more generally, psychological growth. Piaget[18] had provided a theoretical breakthrough with the idea of a child as a moral philosopher. Following the same reasoning, Kohlberg was able to document and extend such a view.[19] Both the child and the teenager, in a Piaget-Kohlberg sense, are moral philosophers. Thus it made educational sense to create intervention schemes that would facilitate and develop the capacity to reflect and examine the generic moral questions—the dilemmas of living, the difficult questions of choosing without easy solutions, and so on. The . . . work of Blatt is a clear example of an intervention system tied directly to such a developmental framework.[20]

If the adolescent was a moral philosopher, was he not also a psychologist? That was the question Piaget and Kohlberg posed to us. The developmental shift from the concrete operations of the seven- to eleven-year-old to the beginning of formal abstract and metaphorical thought during adolescence dramatically changes the individual. No longer is the external world viewed as a given or permanent and unchanging. Instead the teenager begins to perceive the subjective, the phenomenological, the relative, and above all the "self." As we have noted, Elkind calls this the shift to a subjective but highly egocentric thinking process in which the teenager genuinely views himself as the center of the universe.[21] This Ptolemaic view is perhaps best exemplified by the following interview excerpt—"I asked a fifteen-year girl: 'What is the most real thing to you?' Her unhesitating reply was 'myself.'"[22]

Without belaboring the point, then, the interaction question became: what strategies might be most appropriate to educate teenagers vis-à-vis questions of the subjective nature of perception, the differentiation of self and others, and the inevitable (and ubiquitous) questions of identity? While considering an array of curriculum experiences for the teenager as a "psychologist," we also wanted to avoid the problems inherent in a preoccupation with the teenage "self." In a recent article the implied curriculum design problem was denoted, "In particular we would need to create conditions that do not foster or necessarily encourage further movement to ego-centric thinking especially about self."[23]

In this regard Elkind has noted that a major intervention question concerns the need to provide experience and reality testing to move the adolescent away from particular aspects of formal but highly egocentric thought. These well-known aspects include the personal fable, preoccupation with appearance, playing to an imaginary audience, lack of genuine empathy, and excessive criticism of adult shortcomings. "Perhaps it is because the adolescent is relatively uninvolved with serious issues of justice, integrity . . . that he feels so superior to adults in these regards."[24] The adolescent's lack of significant experience may promote an easy hypocrisy rather than genuine development in formal operations.

Learning Psychology by Doing Psychology: A Summary

After a number of trials in which we deliberately employed a series of different teaching strategies, we have realized that the most successful classroom procedures involved a deliberate reversal of the usual methods and objectives of teaching. Instead of either transmitting knowledge about psychology as an academic course, or teaching the structure of psychology as a discipline, we found the most effective procedure to be the practicum-seminar format usually employed in graduate schools. Indeed we are now teaching a series of high school courses using the same practicum and seminar outline, for example, a class in peer counseling, in cross-age teaching, in early childhood education, in psychological growth for women, and so forth.[25] This approach had particular immediate advantages. First, as noted, we wanted to teach deliberately toward the objective of psychological development. We sought to avoid passive, rote, and impersonal learning. The practicum format required by definition that the high school pupils become directly involved in the learning process. Also they had the responsibility for their own performance in the various practice settings. When a teenager knows he will teach a class of elementary age pupils, or run part of a nursery school program, or counsel another teenager, the immediate motivation for learning is high— active responsibility versus passive observation is one way to describe the difference.

A second major component was the seminar. We attached a weekly seminar to each practicum class. Each is designed as an intensive examination on the meaning of the experience for the teenagers as well as a discussion on the development of requisite skills. Thus the seminar for the counseling class practicum would focus on learning the skills of communication *and* a reflection on the personal issues involved in such a process. In a similar manner the seminars in the cross-age teaching and nursery school work maintained the dual focus on information and skill development and the impact of the ongoing experience. For example, the seminar in nursery school work might focus on some questions of how three-year-old children learn and how they perceive adults. This could be followed by a discussion on what happens to the teenagers when the small children perceive them as adults. In the cross-age teaching similar questions were generated in the seminar. Teenage "teachers" would discuss how to handle emotional problems of elementary pupils, for instance, the effect of a death of a second grader on the children. This also quite naturally could lead to their own examination of how they handle such problems themselves. In the peer counseling seminar, when teenagers learned to listen and respond to an age-mate, they often would see some of their own "problems" being portrayed. These are just a few examples of the educational/psychological learnings that could occur in the seminar discussions. They learn to act and to reflect upon volunteer efforts which were not prevocational in objective. The objective is to promote and acknowledge the development of the teenager as a "psychologist." As Kohlberg has noted, "The program was an attempt to make the concept of development real to adolescents in order to enable them to see their own life careers in development terms, including general observational experiences about human development, such as work with younger children and adolescent self-reflection."[26]

Instructional Issues

The pedagogical approach raises a series of questions and issues. For example, to manage a weekly seminar discussion is more akin to supervision as a process, or what has sometimes been called clinical teaching, than the usual mode. The teenagers need help in examining the practicum experiences and developing meaning from these reflections. The actual curriculum in this sense emerges from the experience. We have followed the format that usual academic inputs (readings, films, writing assignments) are concurrent with or follow the actual experience. Experience preceding discussions is an important element in the process. Thus the rationale for active listening skills is not presented in advance of the experience but rather follows after the pupils have had direct experience. The seminar discussion pedagogy becomes the method of making meaning of practicum experience. If the adolescent is a natural psychologist, then clinical teaching in the seminar enhances that process.

A second teaching issue in this format comes from the personal issues discussed in the seminar. The usual teacher (and, for that matter, counselor) constraints on personal or emotional questions in regular classrooms obviously would inhibit the development of a perspective toward self and others. The development of genuine empathy depends upon learning to identify the subjective nature of emotions, to label them, and to accurately respond both in self and in others. Teaching that avoids, sidesteps, or homogenizes such issues would inhibit rather than enhance development. To get beyond the stereotypes in human interaction becomes one of the important teaching tasks. Again from developmental theory we find the concept of disequilibrium helpful to comprehend the process. By forcing an adolescent out of a preoccupation with his or her own "self," we create a dissonance or disequilibrium. By reversing counselor and counselee roles in the practicum experiences, it is necessary for the pupils to change set and perspective. Pointedly, this is often a painful process. A fast talking, advice-giving, dominating teenager hears himself on tape and sees the adverse reaction upon a fellow teenage "client." There is resistance to such personal glimpses and awkward insights. This is also the opportunity for important learning. In our view the teaching ability to supervise the pupils in such a manner is a major ingredient in the success of such a program. Obviously there is a series of important factors such as the curriculum itself, the instructional method, and the teaching/supervision competency. These are the necessary and sufficient conditions for effectiveness. Through preservice and in-service programs we hope to further specify such teacher-training procedures.

Summary

The program described has been an attempt to create regular classroom learning experiences for teenagers that would promote psychological (ego) development. Based on concepts from stage theory, namely, Kohlberg, Piaget, and Loevinger, the program contains a series of high school classes in psychology designed deliberately toward the developmental objective, that is, higher stage attainment. By employing real experience through a practicum and extensive examination of issues through a seminar, a powerful and necessary conflict situation was created. The classes focused both on the meaning of "self" and understanding others. To a large degree, in fact, the teenager, at times, had to learn to deliberately set aside some of his own preoccupations with self to perceive and understand others. The deliberate expansion of social role participation and broadened experience "table" appears as a major ingredient resulting in personal and psychological growth as outcome. The beginning of the so-called Copernican revolution may start here.

The most significant general implication for schooling and the practice of psychology would be a new framework for intervention. Instead of the special remedial, adjustive, placement, and referral scope for psychology, we could move directly toward the educational-developmental function. Programs and classes in psychological and moral education could then become part of an overall school curriculum. Primary prevention, education, and development would then become synonymous. Further reports will be forthcoming presenting other examples of the curriculum under development and examining in detail important issues of educational change.

A Final Note

The program in deliberate psychological education is contained in a larger frame of reference as part of the Southeast Alternatives District Project. The educational objectives of the larger project are to promote the development of an array of approaches toward a goal of effective educational intervention. Since students, like all other human beings, learn through a variety of modes, the project has been designed to test out some alternative educational experiences and to evaluate the resulting impact. Schools in general, as we noted in the introduction, have been somewhat slow to recognize that the psychology of the individual differences between pupils and stages of psychological and cognitive growth at different ages both strongly suggest that need to create a broader curriculum. Thus the program described here, as well as future descriptions, is based on the assumption that school curriculum should be defined more broadly in content and process and employ alternative teaching strategies. A series of complementary (rather than supplementary or add-on experiences) classes, courses, and programs could then expand and enrich the standard academic subject-oriented teaching at the secondary level. It is our contention that such a relationship must be genuine. We do not suggest throwing out the proverbial baby of regular concept teaching with the bath water of effective learning. Similarly we do not suggest that all school curricula model our experience base practicum-seminar format. We do see the possibility of alternative educational traditions existing within the same school, enriching each other to the benefit of the pupils.

Notes

1. N. A. Sprinthall, "A Program for Psychological Education: Some Preliminary Issues," *Journal of School Psychology*, 9 (No. 4, 1971), 373-382.

2. *Id.*, "Humanism: A New Bag of Virtues for Guidance?" *Personnel and Guidance Journal*, 50 (No. 5, 1972), 349-356.

3. R. Shafer, *The School as a Center of Inquiry* (New York: Harper and Row, 1967).

4. J. S. Coleman, "The Children Have Outgrown the Schools," *Psychology Today*, 5 (February 1972), 72-82.

5. R. L. Mosher and N. A. Sprinthall, "Deliberate Psychological Education," *Counseling Psychologist*, 2 (No. 4, 1971), 3-82.

6. Carl Rogers, "Barriers and Gateways to Communication," *Harvard Business Review*, 30 (July-August 1952), 46-52.

7. National Education Association, "Parent-Child Communication Skills," *Today's Education*, 60 (April 1971), 33-48.

8. R. R. Carkhuff, *The Development of Human Resources* (New York: Holt, Rinehart and Winston, 1971).

9. J. Finesinger and F. Powdermaker, *A Clinical Picture of Claustrophobia* (Washington, D.C.: Veterans Administration, 1951).

10. Norman Kagan, personal communication, 1973.

11. The responses were scored by a single judge after scoring reliability had been established. The judge reliability was nine of ten "hits" with the Carkhuff protocols and eight of ten "hits" with the Skovholt ratings.

12. J. Loevinger and R. Wessler, *Measuring Ego Development*, Volumes 1 and 2 (San Francisco: Jossey-Bass, 1970).

13. L. Kohlberg, "A Concept of Developmental Psychology as the Central Guide to Education," in *Psychology and the Process of Schooling in the Next Decade*, ed. M. Reynolds ([Minneapolis:] University of Minnesota Department of Audio-Visual Extension, 1972), 1-55.

14. R. C. Dowell, "Adolescents as Peer Counselors," doctoral dissertation, Graduate School of Education, Harvard University, 1971. The control groups of regular high school classes in psychology showed no change in either scale pre-post. They remained at the 13 on Loevinger and Stage 3 on Kohlberg. In replication, the same finding reappeared, namely, that regular high school classes remain unchanged on pre-post measures of psychological growth.

15. K. R. Rustad and C. Rogers, "Promoting Psychological Growth in a High School Class," *Counselor Education and Supervision*, 14 (No. 4, 1975), 277-285.

16. D. Elkind, *Children and Adolescents* (New York: Oxford University Press, 1970).

17. N. A. Sprinthall and V. L. Erickson, "The Systems Approach: Plus ça change, plus c'est la même chose," *Counseling Psychologist*, 4 (No. 1, 1973), 120-122.

18. J. Piaget, *The Science of Education and the Psychology of the Child* (New York: Viking, 1970).

19. L. Kohlberg and R. DeVries, "Relation between Piaget and Psychometric Assessments of Intelligence," in *The Natural Curriculum*, ed. C. Lavatelli (Urbana: University of Illinois, 1971).

20. M. Blatt, "Studies of the Effects of Classroom Discussion upon Children's Moral Development," doctoral dissertation, University of Chicago, 1969.

21. Elkind, *Children and Adolescents.*

22. L. Kohlberg and C. Gilligan, "The Adolescent as a Philosopher," *Daedalus*, 100 (No. 4, 1971), 1064.

23. Sprinthall, "A Program for Psychological Education," 379.

24. Elkind, *Children and Adolescents*, 80.

25. Reports will be forthcoming describing these classes. The psychological growth for women report starts on page 44.

26. Kohlberg, "A Concept of Developmental Psychology as the Central Guide to Education," 48.

A Curriculum in Moral Education
for Adolescents

Ralph L. Mosher
Paul J. Sullivan

Guidance has had a long adolescence or search for its identity. Historically, counselors began by matching man and job. Assessment, in the form of the testing of intelligence, academic achievement, job aptitude, vocational interest, and personality, followed. Most recently, the field has been preoccupied with providing psychotherapy or psychological counseling to troubled children, adolescents, and adults. Here counseling combines the industrial psychology objective of "making it" in the system with terminology and methods from mental health and psychiatry. Throughout, guidance has had important influence, both real and symbolic, on education. It has consistently argued the importance of emotional, social, and vocational development in an educational system giving priority to intellect; it has valued the individual against the institution and believed in his potential. Guidance has promised much and delivered too little, yet it remains as an important ideology in public education.

But as the little red school house recently has come under increasing criticism so, too, has the little white clinic. Fewer than half the counselors in the United States have had training to do psychological counseling. "Longitudinal studies indicate that these fields [counseling, guidance, and school psychology] failed to successfully prognose, much less cure, mental illness partly because they confused mental illnes with deviance from the middle class norms of the schools."[1]

Guidance has been a stepchild. It has derived its theory from other sources: industrial psychology, educational psychology, clinical psychology, and psychiatry. Counselors often do what others choose not to do (for example, college advising and academic scheduling) meanwhile coveting what other professionals, especially psychiatrists and clinical psychologists, do. We believe that counseling must transcend its derivative status and overcome a passivity and inefficacy in the face of great human pain, confusion, and need. The time is opportune both for a rigorous accounting and for a reformulation of counseling's objectives. New initiatives are essential. They should come from an honest appraisal of what guidance has and has not done, a comprehensive view of the many factors which

---

Reprinted from *Journal of Moral Education*, 5 (No. 2, 1976), 159-172. © Pemberton Publishing Company Ltd.

affect growth and learning in this culture and an acknowledgment that the
problems we face are larger than the survival of counselors per se.

A New Rationale for Guidance

A basic need in counseling is for theory which will enable the field to
move beyond a primary concern with the treatment or rehabilitation of
atypical individuals or subpopulations (such as school underachievers,
the emotionally disturbed, drug-dependent adolescents). John Dewey
argued that the stimulation of human development is the basic objective
of education. And Lawrence Cremin[2] has said that guidance is the most
characteristic child of the progressive movement in American education.
Our ideology is that the education of the person must be whole: that is,
it must stimulate cognitive or intellectual growth, moral sensibilities and
reasoning, emotional growth, social skills, vocational competencies,
aesthetic development, and physical maturation. Within a concern for
overall ego or personal development then, we believe that guidance
uniquely should provide educational experiences which help every individual grow as a person—more specifically in terms of moral, emotional,
social, and vocational development. Obviously, these are major and
crucial aspects of human development. They are the dimensions which
have historically concerned and at least implicitly unified the fields of
counseling, guidance, and school psychology. Thus we both reassert and
reformulate generic objectives in arguing that the stimulation of personal,
emotional, ethical, social, and vocational development for all is the basic
justification for the professional specialty of guidance.

We believe further that counseling should *provide leadership* in educational and psychological programs to stimulate human development on
these dimensions. Counselors, as we see it, will work where crucial educational effects on ego, emotional, and moral development occur: in schools,
with teachers and students; in the community, with parents and the numerous educational resources which exist there. Functionally, this means
the counselor must have the ability to analyze, prescribe, and . . . act for
psychological growth on individual, organizational, and community levels.
He will cooperate with others in stimulating development in individuals
and in the organizations or social systems which affect their growth.

It is essential to be specific about the means by which the counselor
is to accomplish these very ambitious objectives. Obviously, it is presumptuous to suggest that counselors can realize these aims by themselves.
But we envisage a guidance counselor who knows more, does more, and
has different priorities than at present. In this paper, we suggest that the
requisite theory and educational programs already exist to make it possible

for counselors to be moral educators. We have at least three reasons for
focusing counselors' attention on moral education. A first reason has
already been set out: . . . that the basic purpose of education, and of
guidance, is the stimulation of individual development. In this case, we
refer to the major aspect of morality. The course in moral education we
will describe is *one* further example of educational programs designed to
stimulate overall ego development in adolescence.[3] Secondly, we believe
that counselors generally should be knowledgeable concerning the substantial theory and educational experimentation now going on in moral
education. In our opinion, this is likely to be one of the major areas of
educational innovation in the 1970's. Thirdly, we believe that counselors
are uniquely confronted by the moral dilemmas with which children and
adolescents struggle developmentally and that they have skills and contributions essential to effective programs of moral education.

For these reasons we suggest that counselors act as moral educators.
Rather than claiming to be "value neutral" (a claim debunked a decade
ago by Shoben's argument that counselors are, in fact, "smugglers" of
school and adult values), we believe that counselors should join teachers,
administrators, and parents in the development of systematic programs of
moral education in the school. Our thesis, very simply, is that counselors
should both study the process of moral development in children and
adolescents and take an active role in stimulating moral development by
education . . . .

Moral Education for Adolescents

The course we will describe is intended primarily for juniors and seniors
in high school. . . . The course presently is taken for credit as a social
studies elective. It could as logically be offered in a guidance, human
development, psychology, or philosophy curriculum. The course can be
taught both within a regular four-period per week schedule or as an after-
school course for three hours once per week. It is designed to be taught
for one term or during a full year.

The course is introduced to the students in a relatively simple and
straightforward way. They are told that they will be taking a course in
ethical or moral reasoning; that the fundamental purpose of the experience is to have them think deeply and at length about a variety of complex
social and personal moral dilemmas or issues. We suggest certain general
synonyms for the term "moral"—for example, that we will be talking about
questions of "right" and "wrong"—value issues—both social and personal,
questions of the individual's rights, his obligations to others and to his
family, and so forth. We emphasize that our purpose is not to teach a set

of right and wrong answers—that issues and choices of what is right and wrong involve much that is personal and situational. The point is to allay for the adolescent or his parent any concern that the course will involve him in indoctrination or the preaching of some catechism of morally right arguments or behavior.

Units in the Course

"Phase" terminology has been made popular relative to the economy. We will use it to describe distinctive and sequential stages in the course. However, we would not argue at this point that the educational experiences characteristic of these several phases need to be offered in the order we use in introducing them to the students. They are best seen as units or components in an overall course which involves high school students in systematic intellectual analysis of moral dilemmas and in a variety of role-taking experiences, such as "ethical" counseling with other adolescents or acting as moral educators with peers or younger children. The basic learning paradigm is to involve the adolescents' ways of thinking about moral questions and issues with the perspectives and thought of other adolescents and the teacher. The student is then put in "real" situations or experiences where he must apply moral thought to the ethical problems or dilemmas of other people and see such dilemmas and their resolution as others would choose that resolution. The point is to personalize the course—that is, to involve and stimulate the student's own moral thinking and action.

Personal Introductions

Phase 1 of the course involves personal introductions. The student is asked to introduce himself and, if he chooses, to talk about some recent experience which involved special significance or learning. Students make extended introductions in which they talk about adverse experiences with drugs, learning to fly, Outward Bound "solo" experiences, disciplinary problems with housemasters at school or with parents, problems with boyfriends, and so on. Other students (those less verbal, less secure in a new group) introduce themselves briefly and with some embarrassment. The teacher supports the student in this introduction and often in a subtle way focuses on the personal moral issues mentioned by the student.

Dilemma Discussions

Phase 2 of the course involves discussion and analysis of moral dilemmas through the case study method. We use two kinds of case study materials. The first is films, either full-length or edited segments of feature films which depict ethical dilemmas. The second is written case study

material presenting moral dilemmas. Since we prefer to use films to introduce actual systematic discussion of moral issues with the high school
students we will talk about that medium first.

The use of films as a stimulus for classroom discussion is hardly a new
educational technology. Nonetheless, using films specifically to stimulate
moral discussion was suggested originally by seeing *The Godfather*.
Among other things, it is a modern American morality play. We subsequently used the films *Deliverance, Serpico, Judgment at Nuremburg,
On the Waterfront*, and the television dramatization of the Andersonville trial, in the same way. A number of films from the Learning Corporation of America series, "Searching for Values," also were used. The latter
series is made up of edited versions of fourteen feature-length films. They
are edited in terms of length and a focus on salient moral dilemmas so as
to be suitable for regular classroom use. We have tested these films sufficiently to feel that at least two-thirds of them are probably very useful in
generating moral discussions with adolescents.

Our experience is that appropriately selected films are very powerful
stimuli to moral discussion and reasoning with high school students. There
are several reasons for this. We happily misquote McLuhan as saying that
film is the medium of this generation. Second, film, in very subtle and
potent ways, can personalize moral issues in the lives and actions of the
protagonists. Michael Corleone, the young don in *The Godfather*, is a
very compelling figure for adolescents—one with whom they can and do
identify. Further, one does not have to be a good reader to be able to
understand issues in a film. Finally, film in our classes has simply *worked*.
We did find it important to ensure that everyone in the class had *recently*
seen the film to be discussed. Arguments about facts are not moral discussion; arguments about value or ethical positions are. The problem that
a particular feature film may not be available when the teacher wants a
class to see it will be solved as film series such as that projected by Guidance Associates and those produced by Learning Corporation of America
and Encyclopaedia Britannica become more extensively available. We
also encourage teachers to experiment with moral discussion of other,
new feature films and not to rely exclusively on canned series.

There is also a distinct place in this aspect of the course for written
case materials. *Moral Reasoning: The Value of Life* by Alan Lockwood[4]
is an excellent example. We used this inexpensive paperback unit book
as a text for the course. It contains a series of brief, well-written, and arresting case studies on the issue of life and its value. Some of the case titles
suggest the nature of the situations dealt with: "Should the Baby Live?"
"Hitler Must Be Killed," "The 'Wasting' of a Village" (Lieutenant Calley
and the massacre at My Lai). Discussion questions are suggested for the

students; there is also a treatment of the psychology of moral development, which is of significant interest to many of the students. Coupled with
a film such as *The Right to Live: Who Decides?* in the Learning Corporation of America series and with the television film "The Andersonville
Trial," they permit an in-depth discussion of a central moral dilemma: the
value of a human life. Our experience, however, is that a class can reach a
point of saturation or redundancy in the discussion of any moral issue,
no matter how basic it is (for example, the value of human life and the
extent to which it supersedes all other considerations). When that occurs
we tend to move on to other case materials or issues and perhaps, at a
later point, return.

Teaching Counseling Skills

Phase 3 of the course involves teaching counseling skills to the students.
Why do we do this in a course designed to stimulate moral development?
In part, because of a serendipity. Some years ago we used the Kohlberg
moral development scale as one *developmental* measure to assess the
effect of teaching counseling to high school students.[5] We selected the
instrument because it was designed to measure growth-developmental
change and not because of any postulated relationship between learning
to counsel and moral development. What we found, to our surprise, was
that students studying counseling for a term developed on average about a
third to a half stage in terms of measured moral reasoning. This was a
change roughly equivalent to that achieved by Blatt in courses designed
specifically and directly to analyze and discuss moral dilemmas and,
thereby, to effect moral development.

On reflection, it became apparent to us that adolescents, in learning to
counsel, at first (and quite typically) responded to personal dilemmas in
the lives of people they were attempting to help by either judging behavior
as appropriate or inappropriate, "good" or "bad," or by writing the other
person a prescription—that is, by telling him what to do. The cumulative
effect of the experience of counseling under supervision was that the
adolescent came to see that human problems are very complex and different and that judging another person's behavior or simple prescription
of what to do is not really very helpful—in terms either of his better understanding of that dilemma or of his ability to resolve it. In short, we were
training adolescents to understand a person's ideas, feelings, and dilemmas
in more complex, comprehensive, and subtle ways and to respond to them
on their own terms and with more options.

There are, we now see, further theoretical reasons to assume that
training in counseling may contribute to moral reasoning. Kohlberg suggests that at least two central things are happening in the process of moral

development. One of these is that the individual's capacity for empathy develops; the other has to do with the emergence of a more comprehensive understanding of the principle of justice in human relationships and human social units. Clearly, in teaching adolescents to counsel, we are offering them *systematic* theoretical and, especially, *applied* training in empathy. By that we mean, very simply, to accurately identify and sensitively respond to the feelings and ideas of another person. In a general sense, training in counseling really is intended to give the adolescent greater understanding and skill in exactly this process. The training in empathy can be, of course, very explicit, indeed behavioristic, as in the case of the Carkhuff methodology in training for empathy. The essential point is that a method of training and a function heretofore seen as the specialty of counselors or therapists (that is, the offering of an empathic relationship to another human being) coincide almost exactly with a major component in the development of greater moral sensitivity. The effect of counseling is also due to the role taking which occurs in responding empathically. Role taking and empathy have much in common. In a larger sense, we are talking about a generic strand in ego development. In short, there is a solid basis in Kohlberg's theory to support what we stumbled upon—but found to work—in an earlier phase of curriculum development.

Theoretically, counselors are in the best position, experientially, to teach counseling to adolescents. That is one of the reasons that we argue for the inclusion of guidance counselors in moral education programs. But, in fact, counselors, too, will be somewhat less than secure in approaching the teaching of counseling to high school students.

The way in which we teach counseling has been described at length elsewhere and will not be extensively recapitulated here.[6] Nonetheless, a brief overview of the procedures we employ may be useful. A unit on counseling probably should not take less than six weeks of the course time (eighteen to twenty hours) and could be expanded to occupy a large part of one semester. It will be recalled that during the students' personal introductions the teachers tend to "model" some counseling responses. They listen and respond to the central feelings, personal concerns, or ethical issues raised by the students in a supportive and, at that point, nonconfronting way. The phase of the course which teaches counseling moves through a general sequence of experiences for the students. We first involve them in exercises adapted from Carkhuff in which they are asked as helpers to respond to brief "role plays" of "client" personal problems done by other students. They are taught to rate their responses for degree of empathy, specificity, and related counseling behavior, argued by Rogers, Carkhuff, and others as essential to effectiveness. We then ask them to prepare a longer case problem or ethical issue to be discussed with a counselor, divide the students into pairs, and have them alternate in the roles of helper or counselor and client. These discussions are taped. One or more of them will be analyzed and discussed before the group as a whole. The supervision is quite specific and intensive. The tapes are then individually supervised with the two students present, and the feedback of the student who has been the "client" is used as the final criterion of the perceptiveness and sensitivity of the "counselor" in helping. Students make a number of these tapes in both roles; they work with different students and are supervised in so doing.

The issues which the students introduce are almost always personal issues although there is no formal pressure that their role-play cases be so. It simply happens that way. And many of these cases, as was true of the introductions, clearly involve subtle ethical dilemmas. For example, one girl talked in her first tape about a problem in her own family. An older brother, already convicted of one charge of pushing or selling drugs, had left a cache of dope in the home, where she found it. It was evident to her that he was again selling drugs, a fact he admitted when confronted. The ethical issue was whether she should tell her father about her brother's pushing or keep silent: to honor her father and "rat" on her brother. The dilemma was further complicated by the fact that her father was not well and that the older brother had been for some years a source of disappointment and very real worry for both parents. In addition, she had been throughout (or saw herself as) a dutiful daughter—essentially straight, a nondrug user. Yet the older brother, by acting out, got a disproportionate amount of the parents' attention, concern, and time whereas she felt herself somewhat taken for granted as a steady and reliable daughter. Not surprisingly she had real feelings of anger toward the brother for the way he treated both his parents and her. She saw this as an opportunity to get back at the brother, but had concomitant feelings of guilt about so doing. It is worth mentioning that this kind of complex, very real ethical issue was introduced by the girl in the first session in which students were asked to present role plays or problems. In a sense, her dilemma is a classic Stage 3 dilemma in Kohlberg's terms: a good girl and daughter who really wants to do the right thing for others in her family caught in a contradiction. If she tells her father, as she feels she must, she tells on (and prejudices) her brother—which he has asked her not to do.

Another girl talked about the problem of a friend, the oldest child in a family of six in which the parents were divorced. Late in the evening she picked up an extension phone to hear her mother planning an assignation with the husband of one of the mother's best friends. The obvious question is what she should do with that kind of information. These cases are dramatic illustrations of the kinds of personal ethical issues which are raised in counseling. But both were introduced in the same evening with no particular prompting. They also raise another question relative to a course in moral reasoning. Put rhetorically, the question is to what extent does the teacher deal with the ethical issues and their analysis in somewhat abstract terms or does the instructor deal directly (for example, counsel or give advice) about the very real moral dilemma that the adolescent is experiencing? Our position is that the teacher should attempt to do both things. That is, he should help the student (and the peer counselor) to probe the student's perceptions and analysis of the dilemma, to think about the options open to her, to introduce and weigh alternative plans of action, *and* to try to assist the student to decide on some resolution with which she is comfortable. It is a delicate matter for the teacher in such a situation to avoid either being wishy-washy or trying directly (or subtly) to persuade an adolescent of the "rightness" of a particular course of action. But a thorough examination or analysis of the problem, the courses of action open to the individual and their consequences, plus support for the individual's reasoned decision about the dilemma seem to us the responsible and defensible path for the teacher.

Teaching Teaching Skills

The next phase in the course involves training high school students to be moral educators with younger children. The purposes in having them teach moral reasoning are several. A first is to give them systematic experience in role taking. We put them in a real role—as a teacher—where they can apply or use, under supervision, what they have learned about moral development and moral reasoning. Our experience in related courses, where high school students have taught in elementary schools or counseled on community "hot lines" or in peer counseling programs at the high school level, suggests to us that these kinds of role-taking experiences are, in fact, growth producing. Our belief is that, by being involved in teaching moral reasoning to younger children or peers, the adolescent's own moral development will be stimulated. One learns by doing. (Parenthetically, the writers' own understanding of moral development theory and ethical analysis has become much more comprehensive under the stimulus of creating this curriculum and teaching it to adolescents. We expect this will be true for most teachers and not simply adolescents who teach.) In a larger sense, the opportunities to see how younger children reason about moral dilemmas in testing, to teach moral reasoning, and so forth offer to adolescents a broader understanding of aspects of human growth. They also give adolescents who teach some enhanced sense of personal competency. But the basic raison d'être is to deepen, to make more comprehensive, their own understanding of moral issues.

This phase of the course consists of a weekly seminar and a practicum for the adolescents lasting most of a term. The practicum opportunities include teaching in religious schools (where adolescents typically act as student aides) and in regular elementary classrooms. Guidance Associates now has available filmstrip case material for use in the elementary classroom especially adapted to the concerns and attention span of younger children.

An important aspect of this phase is the ongoing seminar and supervision of the adolescents. We help the students prepare for the moral discussions and then allow them to analyze what occurred. On-the-spot supervision of the actual teaching is provided as often as possible; classroom discussions are tape-recorded for future review. Our plan has the adolescent coteach with at least one other teenager. This affords mutual support; it is also invaluable to have more than one person leading a discussion, since each sees the discussion in somewhat different terms or perspectives and can respond to things the other does not see—both during the discussion and when analyzing it afterward.

The weekly seminar serves several functions. Cases, materials, and teaching strategies are prepared, including learning more about Kohlberg and related theories, how to frame specific stage arguments, how to ask probe questions that elicit an individual's reasoning about moral issues, and so on. Also, the seminar is a place to examine how well particular discussions went, which arguments or tactics were effective, which were not, what ways of reasoning were used . . . . In analyzing the discussions, the high school students themselves become involved in moral discussions, which prove to be developmental. Finally, the group can provide support for one another as well as share their successes and happy experiences during seminar sessions.

Evaluation

Employing a series of measures of psychological growth as estimates of the dependent variable, we found a clear indication that the combination of dilemma discussions, counseling skills, and actual cross-age teaching by the teenagers induced significant and positive psychological development. Using the Kohlberg test of moral maturity and the Loevinger test of ego development as estimates of stage growth, we compared the results on a pre-post basis for the experimental class and across two "control" groups, that is, two regular high school classes. The pupils in all three classes were in the last two years of secondary school with an average age of sixteen years. There were no subgroup differences between males and females on the pretest scores so each class was treated statistically as a single unit.

Table 10-3

Summary of pretest and posttest means and standard deviations for the Kohlberg moral judgment interview

Group	N	Test	Score	Test	Score
Experimental	14	Pre	$\overline{X}$ 301.07	Post	$\overline{X}$ 344.93
Class			SD 47.91		SD 46.71
1. Control	14	Pre	$\overline{X}$ 263.57	Post	$\overline{X}$ 272.36
Class			SD 24.35		SD 36.54
2. Control	14	Pre	$\overline{X}$ 234.64	Post	$\overline{X}$ 239.14
Class			SD 31.26		SD 36.34
All	42	Pre	$\overline{X}$ 266.43	Post	$\overline{X}$ 285.48
			SD 44.23		SD 59.44

Table 10-4

Analysis of covariance for Kohlberg moral judgment interview

Source	df	SS'	MS'
Between	2	10258.40	5129.20
Within	38	20213.92	531.94
Total	40	30472.32	XXXXX

Note: $f = 9.6411$; $p < .001$

The Kohlberg test results are presented in Table 10-3.

The Scheffe test was used to make multiple comparisons of the adjusted group means. These data are summarized in Table 10-5.

There was a highly significant difference between the experimental class and control class 1 and between the experimental class and control class 2 but no differences between the control classes.

Figure 10-1 is a graph representing the movement of pretest to posttest means for each of the groups.

The Loevinger test results are presented in Table 10-6. The pretests and posttests on the Loevinger sentence completion test were subjected to an analysis of covariance with the pretest scores being the covariate. Table 10-6 is a summary of pretest and posttest means and standard deviations for this measure.

Table 10-7 summarizes the data from the analysis of covariance. There was a highly significant difference between the groups as indicated by the f score.

Table 10-5
Scheffe multiple comparisons test

	Means	Group A	Group B	Group C
		312.64	275.02	268.76
Control class 1	275.02	37.62**		
Control class 2	268.76	43.88**	6.25	

Note: $df = 2.39$; ** indicates $p < .001$

Table 10-8 presents the data from the Scheffe test of the adjusted group means. There was a highly significant difference between the experimental class and the control classes and, once again, no difference between the two control classes.

Figure 10-2 is a graph of the movement from pretest to posttest for each of the groups.

The overall results, then, indicate that the high school pupils enrolled

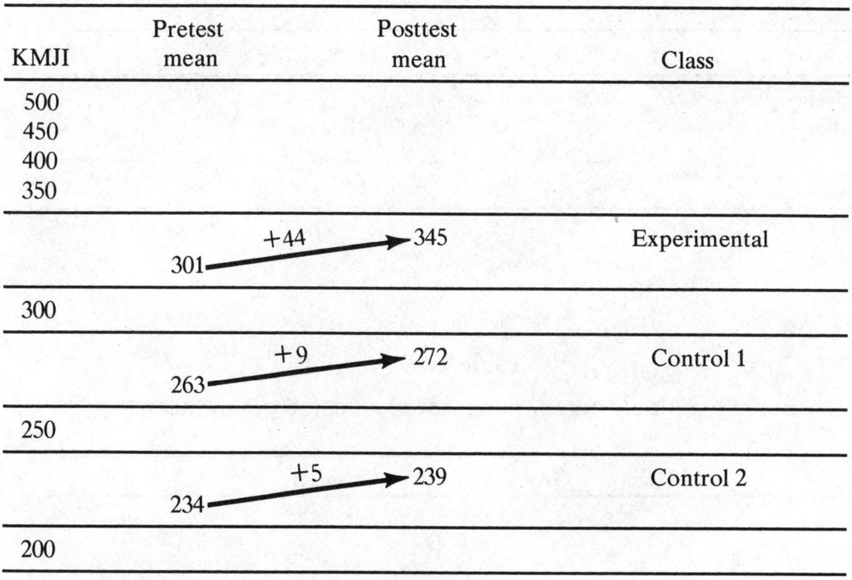

KMJI	Pretest mean	Posttest mean	Class
500			
450			
400			
350			
	301 +44 →	345	Experimental
300			
	263 +9 →	272	Control 1
250			
	234 +5 →	239	Control 2
200			

Figure 10-1
Graph of group pretest and posttest means for Kohlberg's moral judgment interviews

Table 10-6

Summary of pretest and posttest means and standard deviations for the Loevinger sentence completion test

Group	N	Test	Score	Test	Score
Experimental Class	14	Pre	$\overline{X}$ 5.43 SD 1.09	Post	$\overline{X}$ 7.21 SD 1.18
Experimental Class	14	Pre	$\overline{X}$ 5.78 SD 1.25	Post	$\overline{X}$ 5.57 SD 1.40
Experimental Class	14	Pre	$\overline{X}$ 5.07 SD 1.14	Post	$\overline{X}$ 4.57 SD 1.09
All	42	Pre	$\overline{X}$ 5.43 SD 1.17	Post	$\overline{X}$ 5.79 SD 1.63

Table 10-7

Analysis of covariance for Loevinger sentence completion test

Source	df	SS'	MS'
Between	2	43.73	21.86
Within	38	17.56	.46
Total	40	61.29	XXXXX

Note: $f = 47.30$; $p < .001$

Table 10-8

Scheffe multiple comparison test of adjusted group means

	Means	Group A	Group B	Group C
		7.21	5.25	4.89
Control class 1	5.25	1.96**		
Control class 2	4.89	2.33**	0.37	

Note: $df = 2.39$; ** indicates $p < .001$

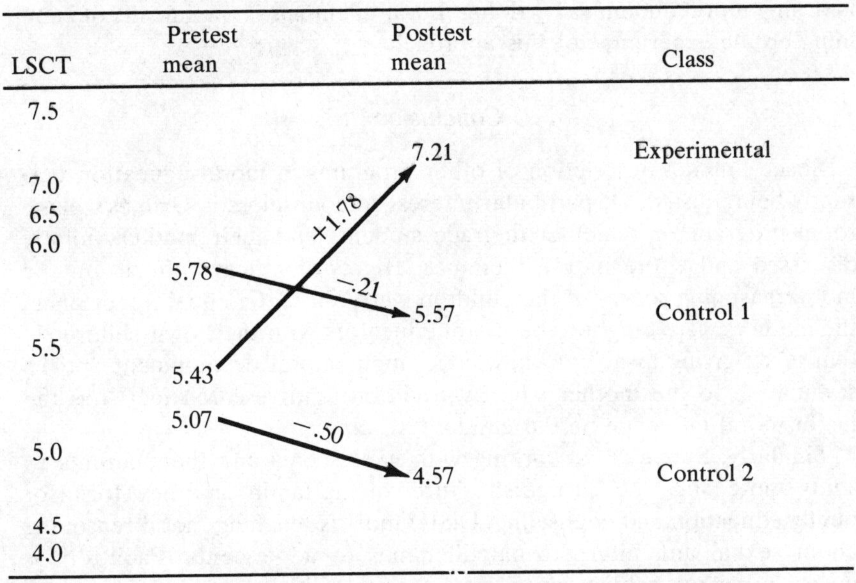

LSCT	Pretest mean	Posttest mean	Class
7.5			
		7.21	Experimental
7.0			
6.5			
6.0			
	5.78		
		5.57	Control 1
5.5			
	5.43		
	5.07		
5.0			
		4.57	Control 2
4.5			
4.0			

+1.78   −.21   −.50

Figure 10-2

**Graph of group pretest and posttest means for
Loevinger sentence completion test**

in a class designed to have them discuss and analyze moral dilemmas and then teach and/or lead dilemma discussions with other pupils exhibited significant developmental shifts. The combined experience of learning about dilemmas and teaching others formed an active curriculum for the teenagers. An earlier attempt at Minnesota yielded negative results in one class. In that class, high school pupils discussed and analyzed moral dilemmas, but did not actively participate in teaching other pupils. The results indicated that there was no change on pre- to posttests with the Kohlberg and the Loevinger tests. In other words, when high school pupils discussed dilemmas for an entire term yet did not apply their learning to a real situation there was no significant shift in their own cognitive structures. The systems or schemata as to how such pupils thought about issues of social justice and the level of complexity in their definitions of developmental ego stage remained essentially unchanged.[7] However, when the moral dilemma format was combined with actual active teaching by the teenagers, then cognitive developmental shifts occurred. In this manner the results are parallel to a series of other high school classes developed at Harvard and at the University of Minnesota.[8] Significant cognitive development changes appear to be definitely associated with curriculum materials which involve active social role taking by teenagers.

Learning moral dilemmas by doing moral dilemmas is one means of summing up the experience of this approach.

Conclusion

Space limits a description of other programs in moral education currently being tested. Of particular interest to counselors is Grimes's classroom program[9] in which sixth-grade students and their mothers jointly discussed and wrote moral dilemmas. Highly significant effects on the moral reasoning scores of the children were found. Of equal importance, the mothers were taught to be moral educators with their own children—that is, a "giving away" of knowledge about moral development and its stimulation to the mother who by tradition (and research fact) has the major moral influence on the child.

Similarly, Stanley[10] is working with adolescents and their parents to study and change the "justice structure" of the family as a new form for family education and counseling, DiStefano[11] is teaching moral reasoning about sexual and interpersonal dilemmas to adolescents. Paolitto[12] is investigating role-taking experiences for junior high school children and their effects on the preadolescent's moral development. A project to train counselors and social studies teachers to teach moral education as part of high school psychology and American history is under way in Brookline, Massachusetts. Experiments in creating just high school units are beginning in Cambridge and Brookline, Massachusetts, and Irvine, California.

The essential point is that the creation of ways for counselors and psychologists actively to educate for moral development in children and adolescents (and to empower parents as moral educators) is proceeding apace. Whether counselors and school psychologists will join such programs of developmental education is moot. Sometimes it seems that the leadership in this profession beats a dead horse in issuing new charges to marginal men who really would rather make schedule changes. But the very creation of programs such as those described here is an augury of professional health. Further, these programs bode well, potentially, for our children. And the latter outcome, in the ultimate sense, is what is most important.

Notes

1. L. Kohlberg, "Humanistic and Cognitive-Developmental Perspectives on Psychological Education," in *Curriculum and the Cultural Revolution*, ed. D. E. Purpel and M. Belanger (Berkeley, Calif.: McCutchan Publishing Corp., 1972),396.

2. L. Cremin, "The Progressive Heritage of the Guidance Movement," in *Guidance: An Examination*, ed. R. L. Mosher *et al.* (New York: Harcourt, Brace and World, 1965), 3-12.

3. R. Mosher and N. A. Sprinthall, "Psychological Education: A Means to Promote Personal Development During Adolescence," *Counseling Psychologist*, 2 (No. 41, 1971), 3-82.

4. A. Lockwood, *Moral Reasoning: The Value of Life*, Harvard Project Social Studies (Middletown, Conn.: American Educational Publications, 1972).

5. Mosher and Sprinthall, "Psychological Education."

6. *Ibid.*; R. C. Dowell, "Adolescents as Peer Counselors," doctoral dissertation, Graduate School of Education, Harvard University, 1971; A. Griffin, "Teaching Counselor Education to Black Teenagers," doctoral dissertation, Graduate School of Education, Harvard University, 1971. N. A. Sprinthall, "A Curriculum for Secondary Schools: Counselors as Teachers for Psychological Growth," *School Counselor*, 5 (No. 3, 1973), 361-369; P. Mackie, "Teaching Counseling Skills to Low Achieving High School Students," doctoral dissertation, School of Education, Boston University, 1974.

7. P. Schaeffer, "Moral Judgment: A Cognitive Developmental Project," doctoral dissertation, University of Minnesota, 1974.

8. Dowell, "Adolescents as Peer Counselors"; V. L. Erickson, "Psychological Growth for Women," *Counseling and Values*, 18 (No. 2, 1974),. 102-116; *id.*, "Deliberate Psychological Education for Women: From Iphigenia to Antigone," *Counselor Education and Supervision*, 14 (No. 4, 1975), 297-309; K. Rustad and C. Rogers, "Promoting Psychological Growth in a High School Class," *ibid.*, 277-285.

9. P. Grimes, "Teaching Moral Reasoning to Eleven Year Olds and Their Mothers: A Means of Promoting Moral Development," doctoral dissertation, School of Education, Boston University, 1974.

10. S. Stanley, "The Justice Structure of the Family: A Focus for Education and Counseling," doctoral dissertation, School of Education, Boston University, 1975; see also *Adolescents' Development and Education: A Janus Knot*, ed. R. L. Mosher (Berkeley, Calif.: McCutchan Publishing Corp., 1979), Chapter 11.

11. A. DiStefano, "Teaching Moral Reasoning about Sexual Interpersonal Dilemmas," doctoral dissertation, School of Education, Boston University, 1975.

12. D. Paolitti, "Role-Taking Opportunities for Early Adolescents: A Program in Moral Education," doctoral dissertation, School of Education, Boston University, 1975.

Deliberate Psychological Education for Women: From Iphigenia to Antigone

V. Lois Erickson

The need to focus on development as the aim of education has been clearly set forth by Kohlberg and Kuriloff . . . . Sprinthall[1] has stressed that counselors need to become psychological educators who use their skills and knowledge to promote personal growth in the mainstream of the school through the school curriculum. Within this framework, it is my view that we need to acknowledge the importance of the counselor's role. The specific point set forth in this paper is that counselors are transmitters of expectations with respect to women's roles and, most important, that we are in a position to positively intervene, enhancing the process of personal growth and competence in women. A current major omission in counseling and guidance has been a sound theoretical perspective of women's development. There has also been a lack of serious proposals for curriculum programs that promote growth in women. If counselors are to promote equal growth opportunities for women in our schools, they must examine theories of growth and development and then propose, test out, and teach related classroom curricula. In this paper the assumptions of cognitive-developmental theories will be integrated into the curriculum materials, the instructional process, and the evaluation of a growth class for women.

From a developmental view the problem of sex role assignment is that it requires one to go through the lower stage of conformity and stereotyped thinking before reaching the higher stages of conceptual thought . . . , and many people never do achieve complex, differentiated levels of thinking.[2] Block,[3] in an excellent research article on cross-cultural and longitudinal perspectives of sex roles, presents a developmental sex role acquisition model derived from the work of Loevinger[4] and Wessler,[5] and Bakan.[6] Block suggests that during the impulse-ridden and self-protective stages of ego growth both sexes are concerned with self-assertion, self-expression, and self-extension—the characteristics Bakan describes as "unmitigated agency." Kohlberg[7] also discusses agency as an aspect of stages of ego development. He notes that the first critical period for

Reprinted, with permission, from *Counselor Education and Supervision*, 14 (June 1975), 297-309. © 1975 American Personnel and Guidance Association. Funding for this paper was from the U.S.O.E. Experimental Schools Program and the University of Minnesota.

intervention is during the years six to nine when the developmental focus is on cognitive orientation, interest, style, and attention.

Block hypothesizes that it is not until the conformity level of ego development (Loevinger's Stage 3) that a critical branching occurs and both sexes develop a set of sex role stereotypes conforming to the cultural definitions of appropriate girl or boy roles. In our society this means an exaggerated focus on communion, or interpersonal concern, for females and an agency-oriented focus for males. Kohlberg and Turiel[8] in a discussion of the relations of structural moral stages to functional ego stages also draw a parallel between accepting an ascribed identity and the theory of conventional morality.

During the next, or conscientious, stage, one's own values are weighed against those set forth by society. Kohlberg[9] indicates that this stage of development presents a third critical period for intervention in which the discovery of the self and the inner life occurs. It is at this stage that the balancing of agency with communion can begin, a process associated with developmental growth. If true integration of agency and communion at the highest developmental level is to occur, it in all probability requires different considerations for men and women given the differential socialization process, according to Block. She states that for men such an integration would require that:

... self-assertion, self-interest, and self-extension be tempered by considerations of mutuality, interdependence, and joint welfare. For women, integration of communion with agency requires that the concern for harmonious functioning of the group, the submersion of self, and the importance of consensus characteristics of communion be amended to include aspects of agentic self-assertion and self-expression—aspects that are essential for personal integration and self-actualization.[10]

Block presents impressive data that support this model. Personal maturity was found to be associated with greater integration of agency and communion within the personality.

The Damage: The Erosion of Female Competence

Dewey[11] stated that true education *is* development. In this sense women are receiving the smallest piece of the educational pie. A smaller percentage of women than men reach the highest stages of developmental maturity.[12] It is more difficult in our society for women than for men to integrate agency with communion.[13]

Extensive studies in human development areas using measures of IQ

gain, achievement motivation, career aspirations, self-concept independence, emotional stability, and moral maturity indicate that males
and females score equally well on these measures at an early age but that
females' scores tend to plateau or stabilize prematurely during the adolescent period.[14] The timing is likely to be developmentally and philosophically significant. Differential socialization of children in the public schools
has been clearly documented in studies by Saario, Tittle, and Jacklin.[15]
They indicate that textbooks, testing, and curriculum patterns portray
males and females in rigid, idealized, and nonoverlapping roles. Yet the
struggle for agency, by both sexes, seems to prevail during the early elementary years, and it is not until conventional character development
appears to crystallize, when social approval becomes a mode of orientation, that sex appropriate socialization takes hold.

The differential effects of socialization for males and females is clearly
set forth by Block in longitudinal findings of the University of California,
Berkeley, Institute of Human Development:

To summarize, the socialization process—the internalization of values—appears to
have differential effects on the personality development of males and females. For
males, socialization tends to enhance experiential options and to encourage more
androgynous sex role definitions since some traditionally feminine concerns (conscientiousness, conservation, interdependency) are emphasized along with the
press to renounce negative aspects of the masculine role, opportunism, restless-
ness, and self-centeredness. For women, the socialization process tends to reinforce the nurturant, docile, submissive, and conservative aspects of the traditionally defined female role and discourages personal qualities conventionally defined
as masculine; self-assertiveness, achievement orientation, and independence. The
sex role definitions and behavioral options for women, then, are narrowed by the
socialization process, whereas, for men, the sex role definitions and behavioral
options are broadened by socialization. The achievement of higher levels of ego
functioning for women is more difficult because individuation involves conflict
with our prevailing cultural norms.[16]

The direction of change in young women during the conformity stage
of development is thus toward the traditional communion-oriented role.
In a society in which even mental health practitioners describe a well-
adjusted woman as more submissive, less independent, less adventurous,
more easily influenced, less aggressive, less competitive, more emotional,
excitable, and vain than the well-adjusted man,[17] it is not surprising that
this "sellout" of the agentic potentials occurs.

Let us examine in greater detail an example of this functional sellout.
The cognitive-developmental position presented by Kohlberg would not
posit sex differences in moral orientation. A structural view of moral

development implies that the same stages appear in the thinking process of both girls and boys.[18] However, several other studies using the Kohlberg scales indicate trends showing parallel gains in moral development between males and females until the adolescent period after which time a higher percentage of boys than girls moves on to principal levels. One recent study by Keasey[19] involving eighty boys and seventy-five girls, preadolescents of average intelligence from working- and middle-class families, indicates that the mean moral judgment quotient for girls is slightly but not significantly higher than that for boys. Keasey concludes that preadolescent males and females do not employ different underlying principles in making moral judgments.

In an excellent discussion, Turiel[20] concludes that although boys and girls pass through the same stages of moral maturity, there appear to be differences in the rate of development through the stages. In his study of 104 boys and 106 girls, on the average at ages ten and thirteen the girls are more advanced than the boys. By age sixteen, the boys are more advanced than the girls. The age by sex interaction is statistically significant ($f = 3.30$; $p < .05$), indicating that sex role and stage of development are significantly related. This finding also supports the critical branching hypothesis previously suggested by Block.

In samples of college students, Haan[21] found that more men than women attain Stages 4, 5, and 6, whereas twice as many college women as men stay at Stage 3, the stage of social conformity. Holstein,[22] from a sample of upper-middle-class parents, found four times as many women at Stage 3 as men. Stage 3 appears to be a stable adult stage of moral development for most women. Kohlberg hypothesizes that this is due to the limitations imposed on women's growth in our society. He indicates that men play roles entailing more participation and responsibility which stimulate their maturity. When these factors are equalized between the sexes so are the indexes of moral growth. In support of this position, the results of the Turiel study cited above can be examined by types of school (progressive, traditional, and parochial), and it becomes evident that environmental differences in treatment and expectations for males and females may be important variables for determining rate of stage attainment.

Within the progressive school no differences were evident between the sexes at the ages of thirteen and sixteen, whereas at age ten the girls are more advanced than the boys. Within the traditional school there is little difference between the sexes of ages ten and thirteen, but by age sixteen, the boys are more advanced than the girls in moral judgment thinking. Within the parochial schools the girls are more advanced at ages ten and thirteen, but by age sixteen their development has leveled off, and both groups have equivalent scores. Subjects from the progressive school were generally more advanced than those from the traditional school, who in turn were more advanced than those in the parochial school (f = 20.33; $p < .001$). Turiel asserts that in environments in which males and females have experiences of similar nature, as in the progressive school, no sex differences in moral judgment are apparent. In support of this position, Weisbrodt[23] found that professional women or those attending graduate school attain the higher stages with the same frequency as men with similar backgrounds. However, the development of women toward achieving their own potentials has barely begun.

The reality of the limited social role participation and responsibility of women in this society can best be recognized by looking at recent statistics. As yet, only 7 percent of the doctors, 3 percent of the lawyers, and 4 percent of the architects in the U.S. are women. There are only sixteen women in the House of Representatives, and not a single woman in the Senate. There are one woman governor and only four women ambassadors. A mere 6 percent of state legislators are women. In business, a 1972 *Fortune* survey indicated men outnumbered women six hundred to one in top-officer-level and board-level positions. In our higher education institutions less than 10 percent of the full professors on all U.S. campuses are women.[24]

Françoise Giroud, the newly appointed State Secretary for la Condition Feminine, has the job assignment of "overseeing the integration of women into contemporary French society." She sees the dimensions of women's growth clearly. What really counts, she says, is to be able to point with pride not to "ten bright, visible women, but to the average level of women in a country . . . ."[25] How do we intervene to raise the stage of development for the average woman in a country? How do we prevent the erosion of competency in half of the human race? What do we propose as educational programs for the great silent majority of women? It is clear, based on the review of developmental research, that young girls develop at rates equivalent to boys in all areas researched. Our culture, through its many socializing institutions, including schools, promotes a premature plateauing of the process of growth in women. Thus, a major injustice is before us. Women are being denied an equal opportunity for their human potentials.

Psychological Growth for Women: A Curriculum Model

David Riesman, in a response to women seeking equality of choices, replied: "Yes, when you're as far along as men."[26] Dr. Riesman is correct; however women will not automatically develop toward higher stages of growth without the requisite interactions. Surely, the injustice calls for action. The following curriculum, developed under a joint sponsorship of the Minneapolis Public School System (Southeast Alternatives Project) and the University of Minnesota, is a beginning approach to such a deliberate intervention. It represents an attempt to promote psychological growth in young women through the mainstream of the school—the school curriculum.

The experimental curriculum described in this section was taught by an English teacher, a counselor, and myself to a group of twenty-three sophomore women who registered for a one quarter class, "A Study of Women through Literature," at a Minneapolis public school, spring 1973. The follow-up data were collected one year later on twenty-one of the twenty-three students. For a more comprehensive review of the sample, rationale, curriculum, and analysis, see [my article in *Counseling and Values*].[27]

The Curriculum: Process and Content

Dewey[28] maintained that development occurs through a combination of active thinking and active doing, on both the cognitive and the emotional levels. The psychological education project under development at Minnesota reflects this theoretical position.[29] The purpose of the instructional model was to build a curriculum for women's growth with an experience component that is deeply significant and to actually teach for an active reflection of this experience.

Thus the curriculum in the women's growth class followed our deliberate psychological education format of a seminar-practicum model. Field interviewing of girls and women across the life span provided the significant experience of actually viewing the process of women's development through different ages, stages, and tasks. This practicum experience was coupled with seminar sessions to further examine, reflect upon, and integrate the experience on a personal level. The initial practicum sessions involved teaching communication and interviewing skills to the high school class. The pupils practiced listening and responding skills until they could hit at least Level 3, accurate content and feeling responses on an empathy scale. In-class role-play interviews followed, and then pairing off for actual interviewing sessions with classmates. Through this process the women students learned the skills of asking Piaget-type questions and value clarification procedures. They learned to recognize important content areas that would give information on the nature of women's development at different stages, and they began to build relationships and communications with other women in the class.

After learning the basic skills, the pupils conducted a series of field interviews with girls and women across the generational span. Content areas chosen for interviewing included general value questions and social role questions related to vocational, educational, intellectual, and marital roles of women. The objective of the student interviewers was to characterize the major motivational and value position of the female interviewees. In the process, the pupils were able to examine the content of the interview data and began to discern differences by ages and stages of development. Thus, to the general value question, "What is one thing in life that you really value?" responses reported by the women interviewing elementary school girls were typically in the range of "my pet dog" or "my bicycle." Responses to this question from young women in the secondary school tended to be in content areas such as: "my friends," "myself," "freedom," "my family," or "knowledge." Older women responded in a more varied range: "good health," "the safety and happiness of my husband and children," "my work," or "personal integrity."

The students had firsthand experience identifying many of the major issues related to the renaissance of the women's movement. They also learned to use the Piaget-type questions to get at reasons for positions held by the female interviewees. In the seminar sessions they carefully examined elaboration and complexity of thinking, awareness of feelings, empathy for others, awareness of psychological causes of behavior, and perceptions of choices in life situations as expressed in their interviewees' responses. These themes were used to develop a structural organization for sorting the interview data into a rough but helpful framework for examining stages of female development. "The thinking gets more abstract, . . . not so concrete, in the older women's answers," was an actual observation by a sophomore pupil. Toward the end of the quarter an interviewing instrument was developed by the pupils, and they then used the stage concepts they had learned to examine this series of questions with data from females over the generation span. The field interviewing experience and the coordinated seminar seemed to be an excellent format for promoting the "stretching and searching" process that restructures cognitions. The personal levels of the issues examined contributed to intense, deeply reflective small group discussions.

The seminar sessions were thus invaluable for examining, restructuring, and integrating the field interviewing experiences. However, they were also used to reflect on current articles on sexual stereotypes, language and inequality, the equal rights amendment, and selected roles of women portrayed in literary works. The attempt was made to provide a historical as well as a developmental perspective of women's rights and roles. Play readings and short stories were selected to get a representative view of stages of ego and moral maturity. Katherine in *The Taming of the Shrew*, Laura in *The Glass Menagerie*, Elisa in Steinbeck's *The Chrysanthemum*, Nora in *A Doll's House*, and finally the sixteen-year-old Grecian princess, Sophocles' Antigone, were examined by the students in their perspective of developmental stage theory.

To promote a structural organization for the students in examining the dilemmas of each of the women character's role, we focused on possible feelings experienced in the dilemma, the pupils' own feelings of empathy as they read the selection, possible multiple causes for the behavior of the literary character, the level of complexity of the reasoning of the character, the choices the pupils perceived as possible in the situation, and how they would choose given the alternatives. In the class sessions, they also examined the similarities of the process and content of the stages found in the selected literature to those found in the field data. Having evidence from the real world, the pupils seemed highly motivated to look for the relevance in the literature. But most important, throughout this process the pupils continually explored the implications of their own emerging choices and personal growth. In this way, there was a continuous, ongoing, three-way connection between interview data, works of literature, and an examination of the self.

A Formative Evaluation Model with Multiple Assessments

This study was one of a series of curriculum attempts employing a formative evaluation model in a psychological education research and development program.[30] The design chosen for this study meets the specific purpose of probing new curriculum directions within the natural setting. Over a series of intervention-evaluation cycles, specific elements that promote psychological development in the pupils are being identified. In the process, an ongoing assessment of effects will lead to continual modification of the curriculum materials and procedures. Multiple assessments for this women's course included psychological growth measures as developed by Kohlberg[31] and Loevinger and Wessler,[32] attitudes toward women as measured by the Spence and Helmreich[33] instrument, and clinical measures of personal growth as recorded in journals, questionnairs, class climate checks, student interviews, audiotapes of classes, and attendance. Comparison group data were available for interpretation of the results.

Kohlberg Moral Judgment Scores

The results on the Kohlberg instrument for the women's class indicate that the average amount of pre/post change on the moral maturity score represented a one-third stage increase over the one quarter intervention (see Table 10-9). The movement is from Stage 3 (other-directed conformity as a basis for moral judgment) partway to a Stage 4 (judgment based on general rules, rights, and duties).

In the interpretation of the results of the Kohlberg data it should be noted that a change in a full stage, from Stage 3 to Stage 4, is a major developmental shift that almost half the general population of adolescents never accomplishes. The work of Blatt and Kohlberg has indicated that, in high school control samples, there was no significant change in mean moral judgment scores during the intervention periods.[34] Regular classes of high school students have also been used as control groups in deliberate psychological education research,[35] and no change in the level of moral judgment in these control classes was evident (pretest $\overline{X} = 2.95$, posttest $\overline{X} = 2.85$, $t =$ N.S.). However, the experimental classes in the above studies and also the Rustad and Rogers study[36] show moral maturity gains of about one-third of a stage during deliberate interventions. It is also important for comparison data that in longitudinal studies on both the experimental and control groups, Blatt and Kohlberg[37] report that all of the groups increased about one-third of a stage during a one-year follow-up period. Rustad and Rogers, like Kohlberg,[38] report a ceiling is reached at Stage 4 for their late adolescent subjects. For adolescents at this stage in our society additional learning would probably promote horizontal decalage.

Thus, the results on the Kohlberg moral maturity scales for the women's curriculum line up directly with the above findings. The forty-two-point increase over the one quarter intervention is within range of the one-third stage movement trends reported in the above intervention studies. The thirty-seven-point change during the one-year follow-up phase is also in line with the follow-up data reported above.

Table 10-9

Selected statistics on the Kohlberg moral maturity scores of the women's class ($N=21$)

Study	M	SD	t	df
Pre	304.24	68.72	2.07*	20
Post	346.00	75.91	3.59**	20
One year follow-up	382.71	69.22		

Note: Twenty-one of the twenty-three students in the original study completed the follow-up testing.

*$p < .026$.

**$p < .001$.

Kohlberg, in this book, indicates that the third critical period of intervention is during adolescence when the discovery of the self, the inner life, and abstract values become possible This Stage 3-4 mode of thinking of the young women students and the curriculum that promoted introspection, contingent thinking, possibility of choices, weighing of consequences, and concern for justice seemed to combine to create a constructive mismatching, such that developmental growth was promoted. The holding of the gain score over the post-to-longitudinal period plus the one-third stage developmental increase during the year gives strong evidence that the curriculum for women's growth promoted a structural change toward a higher, more adequate mode of thought. It is important according to this study that Stage 3 as a stable adult stage of development for women need not hold.

Loevinger and Wessler Ego Maturity Scores

Ego development was a major psychological growth goal in this research. Using a ten-point scale, the data from the experimental classes are summarized in Table 10-10. (The Loevinger stage scores were transformed into a ten-point scale. This assumes that developmental scores represent interval data, an assumption usually followed in the Kohlberg scales.) A significant shift from Stage 3 (conformist) and Stage 3-4 (transition from conformist to conscientious) toward Stage 4 (conscientious) and Stage 4-5 (transition from conscientious to autonomous) occurred during the one quarter curriculum intervention.

Loevinger indicates that the Stage 4 subject not only displays complex thinking but also perceives complexity. Absolute standards and rules are often replaced at this stage with ones in comparative and contingent form. The Stage 4 subject sees life as presenting choices. She is not a pawn of fate but holds the reins of her own destiny. The

Table 10-10

Selected statistics on the Loevinger scores of the experimental class ($N=21$)

Study	M	SD	t	df
Pre	6.29	0.78	1.79*	20
Post	6.67	1.07	4.56**	20
One-year follow-up	7.38	0.97		

Note: Twenty-one of the twenty-three students in the original study completed the follow-up testing.

*$p < .05$.

**$p < .001$.

achievement motive is at its height at this stage, as is a strong sense of responsibility, a conception of privileges, rights, justice, and fairness. Self-evaluated standards, differentiated feelings, and concern for communication are all manifested in the Stage 4 ego level. The Stage 4-5 subject shows greater complexity in conception of interpersonal interaction, in psychological causality, and in the concept of individuality.

The results of the Loevinger ego maturity scales indicate about a one-third stage increase toward greater ego integration during the one quarter women's curriculum. Comparison of findings on ego maturity gain scores with the Rustad and Rogers data[39] is difficult given the number of delta subjects in their pretesting which lowered their pretest mean score. It is important, however, that the post to follow-up data on both studies show similar movement (about two-fifths of a stage during the one-year period). Research on the Loevinger instrument to date appears to be done with cross-sectional data, not with pre-post or longitudinal studies. Findings at the Ontario Institute for Studies in Education[40] report scores for a sample of forty fourteen-year-olds ($\overline{X}$ ego score = 5.1) and a sample of forty seventeen-year-olds ($\overline{X}$ ego score = 6.5). Comparisons are made using a ten-point ego maturity scale. The $\overline{X}$ pretest ego score of the fifteen-year-olds in this women's curriculum study ($\overline{X}$ = 6.28) seems to be within a probable developmental range of these findings.

In addition to these developmental procedures, several other clinical measures of change were also gathered: data on student journals, classroom tapes, affective learning questionnaires, attendance, and an attitudinal assessment on the rights and roles of women[41] are described in detail in Erickson.[42]

Considered together, the results of the multiple assessments in this study indicate that the experimental curriculum was successful as a start in the promotion of movement on the natural stages of growth in the women students.

Conclusions and Implications

The conclusions and implications of this study extend into three major areas. First, the investigation provided additional evidence that it is possible to promote positive psychological growth in a regular school class. The focus on affective as well as intellectual learning in the experimental course provided new directions for the standard curriculum so that psychological growth became a planned outcome. The integration of content and process in the curriculum in ways that promoted both aspects of cognitive growth, psychological as well as intellectual, became a new focus for the teacher and the counselor. Thus, the implication on a professional level is that counselor educators can train psychological educators who can then use their clinical skills to develop, teach, and test out curricula for personal growth, teaming up with regular teachers in the school classrooms.

Second, this study lends additional evidence to the position that it is possible for counselor educators to link instructional and counseling models to a given theoretical position, in this study the concepts of cognitive-developmental stage theory. The data on the psychological growth of the subjects in this study support the descriptive stages of growth as set forth by developmental theorists.

A third major implication involves the specific curriculum goal of promoting psychological growth in young women. Will young women forever be Iphigenias whose lives are sacrificed to the prevailing belief systems, or can they be Antigones—young women who make choices in their own lives based on principles of justice.

Research findings indicate that women stabilize in personal growth areas earlier than men, and yet no studies have been published that set forth a theory, intervention, and evaluation of a curriculum model for women for promoting movement on the stages of developmental growth. This study, then, sheds some light on an intervention mode that will promote movement from conventional toward principled morality and from external toward internal sources of ego in adolescent females.

This curriculum is the first of a series of classes being designed to promote growth in women through the psychological education program at the University of Minnesota and the Minneapolis Public Schools. Curriculum models to promote growth for women across the generation span are now under development in this program, and sequential classes in two-person relationships and child development, with males, have been developed and are under evaluation.

We are now in a social transition or equalization period, in which a deliberate educational focus needs to be on a press for agency in the lives of women. If we are successful, then the next task will be to merge agency with communion to promote the highest levels of integrated growth for all human beings.

Notes

1. N. A. Sprinthall, "A Curriculum for Secondary Schools: Counselors as Teachers for Psychological Growth," *School Counselor*, 20 (No. 5, 1973), 361-369.

2. L. Kohlberg and C. Gilligan, "The Adolescent as a Philosopher: The Discovery of the Self in a Postconventional World," *Daedalus*, 100 (No. 4, 1971), 1051-1086.

3. J. H. Block, "Conceptions of Sex Role: Some Cross-Cultural and Longitudinal Perspectives," *American Psychologist*, 28 (No. 6, 1973), 512-526.

4. J. Loevinger, "The Meaning and Measurement of Ego Development," *ibid.*, 21 (No. 3, 1966), 195-206.

5. *Id.* and R. Wessler, *Measuring Ego Development*, Volumes 1 and 2 (San Francisco: Jossey-Bass, 1970).

6. D. Bakan, *The Duality of Human Existence* (Chicago: Rand McNally, 1966).

7. L. Kohlberg, "Counseling and Counselor Education: A Developmental Approach," *Counselor Education and Supervision*, 14 (No. 4, 1975), 250-255.

8. *Id.* and E. Turiel, *Moralization: The Cognitive Developmental Approach* (New York: Holt, Rinehart and Winston, forthcoming).

9. Kohlberg, "Counseling and Counselor Education."

10. Block, "Conceptions of Sex Role," 515.

11. J. Dewey, *Experience and Education* (New York: Collier, 1963 [originally written in 1938]).

12. V. L. Erickson, "Psychological Growth for Women: A Cognitive-Developmental Curriculum Intervention," doctoral dissertation, University of Minnesota, 1973.

13. Block, "Conceptions of Sex Role."

14. Erickson, "Psychological Growth for Women."

15. T. N. Saario, C. K. Tittle, and C. N. Jacklin, "Sex Role Stereotyping in the Public Schools," *Harvard Educational Review,* 43 (No. 3, 1973), 386-416.

16. Block, "Conceptions of Sex Role," 525-526.

17. I. K. Broverman *et al.*, "Sex Role Stereotypes and Clinical Judgments of Mental Health," *Journal of Consulting Psychology*, 34 (No. 1, 1970), 1-7.

18. C. B. Keasey, "The Lack of Sex Differences in the Moral Judgments of Preadolescents," *Journal of Social Psychology,* 86 (February 1972), 157-158.

19. *Ibid.*

20. Kohlberg and Turiel, *Moralization.*

21. *Ibid.*

22. C. Holstein, "Moral Judgment in Early Adolescence and Middle Ages: A Longitudinal Study," paper presented at the biennial meeting of the Society for Research in Child Development, March 29-April 1, 1973, Philadelphia.

23. S. Weisbrodt, "Moral Judgment, Sex, and Parental Identification in Adults," *Developmental Psychology*, 2 (No. 1, 1970), 396-402.

24. *Time,* 104 (No. 5, 1974), 61.

25. *Ibid.* (No. 3, 1974), 33.

26. D. Riesman, "Dilemmas for Women in Higher Education," *Harvard Today,* 17 (No. 4, 1974), 8-9.

27. V. L. Erickson, "Psychological Growth for Women: A Cognitive-Developmental Curriculum Intervention," *Counseling and Values,* 18 (No. 2, 1974), 102-116.

28. Dewey, *Experience and Education.*

29. N. Sprinthall and V. L. Erickson, "Learning Psychology by Doing Psychology: Guidance through the Curriculum," *Personnel and Guidance Journal,* 52 (No. 6, 1974), 396-405.

30. N. Sprinthall, "Fantasy and Reality in Research: How to Move Beyond the Unproductive Paradox," *Counselor Education and Supervision*, 14 (No. 4, 1975), 310-321.

31. L. Kohlberg, "The Development of Children's Orientation toward a Moral Order. I: Sequence in the Development of Moral Thought," *Vita Humana*, 6 (1963), 11-33.

32. Loevinger and Wessler, *Measuring Ego Development.*

33. J. Spence and R. Helmreich, *The Attitudes toward the Rights and Roles of Women in Contemporary Society* (Washington, D.C.: Journal Supplement Abstract Service, American Psychological Association, 1973).

34. Kohlberg and Turiel, *Moralization.*

35. R. L. Mosher and N. A. Sprinthall, "Deliberate Psychological Education," *Counseling Psychologist,* 2 (No. 4, 1971), 3-82.

36. K. Rustad and C. Rogers, "Promoting Psychological Growth in a High School Class," *Counselor Education and Supervision*, 14 (No. 4, 1975), 277-285.

37. Kohlberg and Turiel, *Moralization.*

38. *Ibid.*

39. Rustad and Rogers, "Promoting Psychological Growth in a High School Class."

40. E. Sullivan, G. McCullough, and M. A. Stager, "A Developmental Study of the Relationship between Conceptual, Ego, and Moral Development," *Child Development,* 41 (No. 2, 1970), 399-411.

41. Spence and Helmreich, *The Attitudes toward the Rights and Roles of Women in Contemporary Society.*

42. Erickson, "Psychological Growth for Women."

11
Education for Adolescent Growth
in the Community

Passow, in a recent essay on "The Future of the High School," reviews criticisms of the high school and many proposed remedies. One theme is that less is best, that is, the high school should limit itself, perhaps to focusing on intellectual development. Providing youth a genuinely comprehensive education is to be done through a variety of resources in the community. A second theme is that "the objectives of youth education are broad and encompassing . . . aims more like those in the *Cardinal Principles of Secondary Education* than statements limited to the acquisition of cognitive skills and knowledge."[1] Intellectual, vocational, citizenship, aesthetic, personal, and social development must be attended to through a comprehensive education that draws on many resources of the community. If gown cannot be comprehensive, it is hoped that town and gown can be.

Cultivating the Vineyard

A central emphasis in Passow's article is the dispersion of this comprehensive education throughout the community. The isolation of our high schools from other agencies that serve, educate, and socialize youth and the need to lessen the segregation of adolescents through work-study programs and citizenship and social action education in the community are basic to the recommendations that Passow reviews. It may be easy in the late 1970's to think of education in the community as another splendid dream of the 1960's or an earlier progressive era that did not materialize. But the idea lives in the recommendations of virtually every major commission that has studied the American high school in the decade, in the practice of developmental education, and in Newmann's work in citizenship education.[2]

416

An underlying concern for all-around adolescent development has moved the programs in developmental education in this direction. Deweyan ideas of how teenagers learn—by feeling a need to learn, by doing, by experiencing true responsibility, by thinking about and acting on real social problems—have shaped the curriculum and teaching of developmental education. It has been, in a substantial way, education in the community. The primary purpose of this education is to enhance adolescent development. But, when teenagers teach in a nursery or elementary school, counsel on hot lines, establish a home for adolescents who are no longer able or willing to live with their parents, and work in mental hospitals, they contribute direct social services. In a small way they improve society. The purpose is not a children's crusade. It is, rather, a way of having an effect, of testing concretely the ideas about who they may become. Along with contributing social services to the community, teenagers should gain greater maturity and skill. What is obvious is that adolescents could do much more, if society wanted or permitted that, as it does in time of war.

Citizenship Education

The three papers that comprise this chapter illustrate how and where a more comprehensive education for teenage growth may occur. Newmann argues for education in the community—a social action curriculum. Education for social action includes rational reflection and ethical deliberation about a proposed action and should lead to greater skill in influencing public affairs. Newmann contends that competence in social action is not only a justifiable educational objective, but can contribute as well to the adolescent's development as a competent and moral person. He argues further that the individual's ability to exert influence in public affairs contributes directly to strengthening representative democracy and fostering social justice.[3]

Work and Students' Development

Scharf and Wilson, in "Work Experience: A Redefinition," use cognitive-developmental psychology as the basis for redesigning both the objective of "real" work experience for all teenagers and a curriculum in which such experiences are integrated. Their paper is intended primarily to illustrate the way in which conceptions and thinking about work and career might develop.[4]

The Family and Adolescent Growth

Finally, Stanley describes ground-breaking education with parents and their teenagers.[5] Focusing on the "justice structure" of the family, she teaches parents and teenagers to talk about and share the family's decisions concerning rules, responsibilities, and rights. Parents' authoritarianism is decreased, while teenagers' moral reasoning increases, and their behavior as family members improves. Though Stanley's work may be most directly pertinent to counselors, psychologists, or school social workers (to say nothing of the many community agencies dealing with parents and their disaffected children), it also completes the circle. It is another effort of developmental education to provide parents with a knowledge of adolescent growth, its determinants, and the way to support their teenagers' coming of age. In practice, this has proved difficult, but, in any comprehensive program for the all-around development and education of youth, parents (as well as other adults in the community, such as clergy and police) will have to be knowledgeable partners.

Notes

1. A. H. Passow, "The Future of the High School," *Teachers College Record*, 79 (No. 1, 1977), 23.
2. F. M. Newmann, *Education for Citizen Action: Challenge for the Secondary Curriculum* (Berkeley, Calif.: McCutchan Publishing Corp., 1975).
3. *Id.*, "Rationale and Program Overview," in *Skills in Citizen Action: An English-Social Studies Program for Secondary Schools* (Skokie, Ill.: National Textbook Co., 1977).
4. P. Scharf and T. C. Wilson, "Work Experience: A Redefinition," *Theory Into Practice,* 15 (June 1976), 205-212.
5. S. F. Stanley, "Family Education: A Means of Enhancing the Moral Atmosphere of the Family and the Moral Development of Adolescents," *Journal of Counseling Psychology*, 25 (No. 2, 1978), 110-118.

Skills in Citizen Action: An English-Social Studies Program for Secondary Schools

Fred M. Newmann

In spite of incessant rhetoric about the need to educate youth for responsible citizenship, civic education in the United States receives

From *Skills in Citizen Action: An English-Social Studies Program for Secondary Schools,* Chapter 1. © 1977 by National Textbook Company. Reprinted by permission of National Textbook Company, Skokie, Illinois 60077.

low priority, is approached unsystematically, and is fraught with crippling contradictions. Our troubles are due in part to an *intellectual* problem, the lack of a coherent conception of education for civic competence. In part we also face *institutional* obstacles—particular structures, programs, and requirements in public education that make it difficult to place central priority upon civic education. Here we speak to each problem.

Conceptual Difficulties

What is the difference between a competent, responsible, well-educated citizen and an incompetent, irresponsible or poorly educated one? What do those adjectives mean in a society such as ours? We are innundated with diverse conceptions of civic education, some or which are logically contradictory, and others, while not necessarily inconsistent, reflect different priorities. Some conceptions stress obedience to the law, respect for and allegiance to existing institutions, while others stress critical questioning of the existing social order and independent moral reasoning. Some approaches see knowledge of history and social science as the intellectual foundation of citizenship, others stress knowledge of particular social problems (such as racism, environmental issues, global interdependence). Still others stress specific knowledge of the functioning of the political-legal system. Some approaches seem less concerned with content or substantive knowledge, more concerned with intellectual skills such as critical thinking, problem solving, or communication skills in reading, writing, speaking, and listening. Some stress the importance of participation skills over academic preparation, but the "participation" position itself divides on different points of emphasis; for example, student governance and decision making in school versus volunteer service to help others in the community versus social-political action for institutional change.

Different philosophies manifest themselves in several curriculum movements: the academic disciplines, social problems, law-related education, values clarification, moral development, critical thinking, community involvement. In a sense these approaches compete with each other for a place in the school curriculum as teachers and administrators are bombarded with requests to give all of these top priority. A particular approach is not usually derived from an explicit conception of civic competence, or when it is, the conception is woefully incomplete.[1] Thus, the approaches are not usually proposed with reference to civic competence, but on other grounds (for example, "academic disciplines are important for college and have inherent value as well," or "community involvement is good, because it facilitates the transition to adulthood"). As proponents argue for specific curricula, the "cause" in question becomes values clarification, moral development, law-related education, and so forth, rather than civic competence. When educators are continually preoccupied with accepting or rejecting particular proposals, they can be seduced into defining the problem in terms that the proposals initiate, before they have worked out a coherent answer to the more basic question, what is civic competence? It would make more sense to *begin* with a conception of civic competence and to derive from that the kind of curriculum which might teach it.

Institutional Difficulties

Once a conception of civic competence is articulated, certain factors make it difficult to launch comprehensive civic education programs in schools as they now exist.

1. It is generally accepted that public education should serve several legitimate purposes (vocational preparation, general literacy, management of certain aspects of personal life: health, consumption, use of leisure time), and that civic education—dealing primarily with the relationship of the person to the state—should, therefore, consume only a small part of the total effort. The assumption that students should have the opportunity to study and grow in a variety of areas, rather than paying exclusive attention to any single one, results in a supermarket conception of curriculum, a fragmented school schedule that divides the student's instructional life into many subjects (and extracurricular activities), rather than concentrating on a few. One consequence of the multiple-purpose assumption is a set of requirements for graduation from secondary school and admission to higher education. Students must earn particular credits and learn certain proficiencies in such subjects as English, mathematics, science, social studies, foreign language, and vocational areas in order to proceed to the next step in the societal reward system. Regardless of the relevance of such subjects to civic education, students must have time to pursue them, for civic education cannot dominate the curriculum.

2. So that education is offered efficiently, systematically, in an organized fashion, it has come under the exclusive control of professionals, who, presumably, have special competence to teach. Many professionals assume that learning must occur in specially designed places (schools) that must be insulated from interruption or interference by incidental, noninstructional activity or "normal life." Thus schools are segregated, allowing little contact (for teachers or students) with adults in their daily occupational work, with persons caring for others in families or other relationships, or with persons active in trying to influence the political-

legal system. This protective, almost possessive, attitude makes it difficult
to send students to learn in places other than schools or from people who
are not credentialed educators.

3. As publicly supported institutions, schools must be "accountable"
to the taxpaying public. This creates pressure to demonstrate "school
effectiveness," which in turn generates pressure to conceptualize curriculum and learning only in those terms that lead to immediately quanti-
fiable, objective measurement of student achievement. By restricting
ways in which educational goals can be conceived and phrased, the pressure for accountability poses additional constraints, especially when
criteria stress goals other than civic competence.

These problems might be seen as symptoms of more fundamental
obstacles to social change: the undemocratic nature of bureaucracies
and their tendency to centralize and expand into structures unresponsive
to purposeful action; systemic forces in the economy, especially profit
motives for publishers and others economically dependent upon school
expenditures from teamsters to teachers; the political conservatism of
adults who control socialization. All are formidable roadblocks to meaningful curriculum change. In offering a curriculum proposal we imply
the belief that the power of such obstacles has not been sufficiently demonstrated to warrant surrender. But our main task here is not to verify this,
not to give a social analysis on how to bring curriculum change in schools.
Rather, our purpose is to offer a curriculum that is at least minimally
responsive to institutional constraints. The structure we suggest attempts
to address the three institutional difficulties first mentioned.

A Conception of Civic Competence

Ability to Exert Influence in Public Affairs

We begin with a few assumptions. First, that the purpose of civic education, as opposed, for example, to aesthetic, economic, or psychological
education, is to teach students to function in a particular relationship
with the state. Second, that the most desirable type of relationship between the citizen and the state is outlined in the structure of constitutional representative democracy. Third, that the major way in which this
political arrangement differs from others is that the state "belongs" to the
citizens, and the citizens have certain unalienable rights to influence what
the state shall do. The primary educational mission, therefore, is to teach
citizens to exert influence in public affairs, for without the competence to
influence the state, the unalienable right to do so (that is, the key feature
of representative democracy) cannot be exercised.

According to these assumptions the most fundamental civic competence is the ability to exert influence in public affairs. The phrase needs clarification. Public affairs are those issues of concern to groups of people to which, it is generally agreed, institutions of government should respond—through legislation, administrative action, judicial opinion, selection of office-holders, and other activities. There may be a tendency to recognize as public affairs only those issues with widespread impact, reported in the mass media (wars, elections, inflation, pollution). Our definition, however, also calls attention to countless issues at the local level and less publicized: cyclists trying to establish or regulate bike trails; volunteers trying to influence visitation policies in a mental hospital; students trying to increase the budget for women's sports in their school; black students trying to gain official school recognition of their "union." These are all "public affairs," and the citizens' ability to exert influence on such matters is as important to the functioning of democracy as a sense of involvement in issues with more global consequences.

The attempt to exert influence can be viewed as a process, diagramed [in Figure 11-1], in which the individual develops goals or desired outcomes (for instance, closing a juvenile detention center, electing a candidate). One then works for support of the goals through organizing, bargaining—various methods of persuasion. In building support it is often necessary to modify goals (such as hiring a new director instead of closing the center, or publicizing crucial issues instead of actually winning the election). Revised goals serve as a new basis for action that might

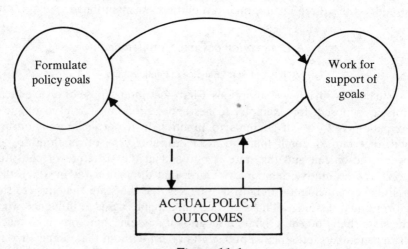

Figure 11-1

Exerting influence in public affairs

eventually call for even further revision as an action effort evolves. According to this dynamic, ability to exert influence should not be equated with the ability always to "win," but rather the ability to produce outcomes in public affairs in directions consistent with one's goals.

This view of civic competence may imply that each student should learn how to impose all his or her views on the world, but that would be both unethical and logically impossible. It would be ethically irresponsible to endorse unconditionally any view on public affairs that a student might profess. If a student wishes to provoke violence to protest racism, the teacher is not obligated to help, even though the student may believe this will increase his or her ability to win support. In some cases the teacher may, instead, be obligated to make it impossible for the student to succeed. Rather than assuming that students have a blank check to exercise their will as they see fit, students and staff have a moral responsibility to study and discuss the ethics of proposed policies and actions. While it is certainly possible to exert influence without offering moral justification, our definition assumes that attempts to exert influence in a constitutional representative democracy must be ethically justified. In this sense the ability to exert influence requires ability in moral reasoning (discussed below . . .).

No social system could function on the premise that each person has a right to implement all preferences, for this would require the logical impossibility that persons with contradictory views could each have his way. Genuine controversy over public affairs inevitably spawns "winners," "losers," and people who see themselves as somewhere in between; it is impossible to have only winners. Thus, a conception of ability to exercise influence should recognize (a) the impossibility of all citizens winning all of the time, but the desirability of all having the competence to win some of the time; (b) the fact that, in the process of "losing," even "losers" can exert influence on policy (for example, by demonstrating a power base that will have to be contended with in the future); and (c) that the decision to modify one's ideals in order to exert influence in a particular situation is not necessarily an indication of one's lack of ability to exert influence. Having one's way is surely implied in the concept of influence, but it cannot be taken to the extreme. The goal is to assist students in having some impact in public affairs, consistent with intentions which they develop through a process of rational moral deliberation.

As another point of clarification, note that the objective is not to make all students into adults obsessed with public affairs who participate intensively and continuously on every conceivable issue. Rather than prescribing for all students a standard style or expected frequency of actual involvement, the objective is concerned mainly with increasing the ability to exert influence. Each individual must retain choice as to where, when, and how he or she wishes to use competence, and some may choose to use it only sparingly. Without appropriate skills, however, the individual does not have the option to exert influence. An incompetent person has only two options: not to participate or to participate without effect. The school should create for all students a third option: to participate in a way that makes an impact. Even if this objective were achieved for most citizens, however, we would expect wide variation in rates and types of actual participation.

Specific Competencies

If people are to formulate goals, win support for them, and thereby exert influence, we suggest they must have the more specific competencies to

1. communicate effectively in spoken and written language;
2. collect and logically interpret information on problems of public concern;
3. describe political-legal decision-making processes;
4. rationally justify personal decisions on controversial public issues and strategies for action with reference to principles of justice and constitutional democracy;
5. work cooperatively with others;
6. discuss concrete personal experiences of self and others in ways that contribute to resolution of personal dilemmas encountered in civic action and that relate these experiences to more general human issues;
7. use selected technical skills as they are required for exercise of influence on specific issues.

As we elaborate on each, we shall see how the competencies suggest some concrete directions for curriculum.

1. Communicate effectively in spoken and written language. Skills in reading, writing, speaking, and listening are obviously required in order to learn about issues, to develop one's views, and to win support. To receive and send messages effectively one needs technical skills of literacy, sensitivity, and analytic ability to identify what one "really" wants to say, what others may be "trying to say," what kinds of messages may be most effective, given some knowledge of one's audience. This view of communication acknowledges the significance of both verbal and nonverbal cues, of personal dynamics within groups, of ways in which the medium affects the message.

2. Collect and logically interpret information on problems of public concern. To have impact, citizens must defend their views with persuasive evidence. They will need information on the history surrounding specific

people and events, on social trends, on existing law. Relevant data are often difficult to find and to interpret. The skills needed might be considered analogous to investigative skills of the journalist or private detective, the disciplined skills of the social scientist, the research skills of a legislative assistant. In short this refers to digging for the facts and making warranted inferences from them.

3. Describe political-legal decision-making processes. To formulate goals and to work for their support, one must know something about the formal and informal structures through which public decisions are made, and about strategies that seem appropriate for affecting different people and agencies. This calls for knowledge of realities in the dynamics of power wherever it relates to public affairs. Only a portion of this knowledge comes from formal descriptions of the political-legal system (such as the Constitution or a chart on how a bill becomes a law). In addition students need to view the system from the perspectives of actual participants and analysts who try to "tell it like it is." The intent here is to overcome myths or political naiveté, to look closely at ways in which political-legal decision making is and is not susceptible to deliberate citizen action efforts.

4. Rationally justify personal decisions on controversial public issues (including justification of strategies for action) with reference to principles of justice and constitutional democracy. In recommending courses of action, the citizen expresses value preferences that affect the lives of others. To develop support for value claims, students need instruction both in the format or style of argument and on the substantive values on which to defend their positions. In matters of style, this calls for a sincere attempt to be "rational" in the sense of providing reasons for one's preferences, grounding the reasons in some underlying principles, striving for consistency among the principles, and modifying one's views to eliminate serious logical contradictions. These can be seen as criteria for "rational" argument.

In the realm of substantive values, citizens must show that proposed actions help to advance, or at least do not violate, unalienable rights which the community is entrusted to protect. These rights are grounded in the principle of human dignity, or equal respect for every human life. From this basic premise a number of other values or principles can be derived: the right to certain liberties, to due process of law, to participation in the consent process, and more generally the value of organizing society according to principles of representative constitutional democracy. There are two general reasons why value judgments ought to be defended rationally and with reference to these particular principles. First, an ethical, philosophical argument can be made that this is required in order to have any reasonable moral system.[2] Second is the pragmatic argument that those persons skilled in such discourse will actually be more persuasive and act with more influence than those unskilled.

The commitment to rationality and the values of constitutional representative democracy, however, cannot justify moralistic preaching or blind faith in particular regimes, laws, values, or the U.S.A. as a nation. Now, as in the past, legitimate controversy rages over what the "best" values may be, the extent to which representative democracy might serve them, and the extent to which representative democracy actually exists or can conceivably ever exist. Students should not be insulated from such controversy but encouraged to pursue it in a studious, uncensored fashion. The essential educational task is not to indoctrinate, but to remain intellectually honest and at the same time to help students justify the belief that principles of representative constitutional democracy offer the most promise for organizing community to serve the value of human dignity.

5. Work cooperatively with others. A prevailing image of the responsible citizen is the "intelligent voter" or the person who writes a letter to a congressional representative. Most individuals, however, can exert influence only to the extent that they are backed by united group effort, and this requires far greater attention to collective process as the foundation for citizen action. Individuals need to learn to work within groups in selecting and attacking issues. Groups must develop internal mechanisms for governance and division of labor, along with approaches for eliciting cooperative alliance with other groups. Solidarity and commitment to a group must be generated, but it must also remain receptive to criticism and fulfill genuine individual needs of group members. All of this suggests the need to teach skills in group work and community organization.

6. Discuss concrete experiences of self and others in ways that contribute to resolution of personal dilemmas encountered in civic action and that relate these experiences to more general human issues. The effective citizen must be able to see relationships between specific happenings and issues phrased in general terms. If one feels frustrated at being apparently ignored by a public official, one should be able to talk about the incident in ways that help to explain why it occurred and what might be done in the future to avoid it. If students observe a leader trying to justify dishonesty on the grounds that it was necessary to gain enough power to "do good," they should be able to discuss this as the more general problem of means and ends. The point here is to try to transcend the immediacy, specificity, or concreteness of personal incidents to search for meanings that have some generalizability, and can, therefore, make personal action more informed in the future.

7. Use selected technical skills as required for exercise of influence on specific issues. Here we refer to the "nuts and bolts" of civic action, "tricks of the trade," or skills in such areas as political canvassing, fund raising, record keeping, bargaining and negotiating, preparing public testimony, gaining endorsements, use of the mass media, or parliamentary procedure. Such skills should not be taught to all students as general preparation, but learned as needed with regard to students' pursuit of specific issues. This last competence differs from the first six by calling attention to specific technical training in an ad hoc or issue-related fashion.

Curriculum Overview

To teach the civic competencies, we propose a voluntary yearlong program in the eleventh or twelfth grade, where students would spend almost full time in the citizen action program (for example, 9:30 a.m. to 2:00 p.m.). They would earn the equivalent of two academic credits in English and two in social studies, would have time to take one additional course, such as mathematics, science, or foreign language, and could participate as time permits in music, athletics, or other activities. Initially we recommend a pilot program of sixty student volunteers and a teaching team with the equivalent of two full-time teachers, one in English, one in social studies. Aiming toward a balance among systematic classroom instruction, field observation, and active student participation, the program includes six main components:

1. *Political-Legal Process Course,* three mornings per week for fourteen weeks, first semester, including one morning per week of firsthand observation in the field. This course would teach the "realities" of influence and power in the political-legal system. In addition to information on the formal structure of the system, including constitutional rights, emphasis would be placed on informal and "behind-the-scene" processes, especially at local levels of decision making. Classroom instruction would relate to field assignments in which students conduct interviews, attend meetings, observe aspects of the political-legal process in the community at large. Skills in gathering data and drawing valid conclusions would be emphasized. Empirical observation and conceptual teaching would provide background for ethical analysis and moral deliberation on problems of justice. Students would develop positions on controversial aspects of public policy and political-legal process.

2. *Communication Course*, four afternoons per week for sixteen weeks, first semester. The course would focus on the use of written, spoken, and nonverbal language in four contexts: intrapersonal, interpersonal, group, and public. Listening, speaking, reading, and writing would be

emphasized in receiving and sending messages accurately and effectively. Students would have extensive practice in different communication styles and techniques appropriate for interpersonal helping, problem solving in groups, developing rational justifications, building group cohesion, and addressing public audiences. To improve skills in such areas, students would learn to analyze the dynamics of communication in different settings according to communication and group theory.

3. *Community Service Internship,* two full mornings per week for fourteen weeks, first semester. Students would be placed in volunteer service positions in social agencies, government bodies, public interest groups, and so on. They would have responsibility for working for the host organization and would be supervised by agency and school personnel. As they become involved in public service work, they would analyze aspects of institutional process in the political-legal process course, and in the communication course they would work on language skills relevant to the internship. One afternoon per week, students would share their volunteer experiences, discuss common problems, and begin to explore issues that might develop into the citizen action project for the second semester.

4. *Citizen Action Project,* four mornings per week for ten weeks, second semester. Students would work in small groups in attempts to influence public policy. Projects could involve working for political candidates, establishment of special youth institutions, revision of administrative regulations, lobbying for legislation, and so forth. The issues could concern national, state, or local agencies, including the schools; for example, student rights within a school, zoning provisions to protect the environment, consumer protection, interracial cooperation, improved social services for youth in trouble. The projects would hopefully grow out of the first semester internship and field studies in the political-legal process course. During the project students would take selected "skill clinics" on such matters as techniques of canvassing, bargaining and negotiation skills, fund raising, how to run a meeting, press releases. They would also participate in "project counseling sessions" where peers and faculty discuss issues arising from the action work. The counseling sessions would give psychological support and deal with confusion, stress, uncertainty likely to arise in active participation.

5. *Action in Literature Course,* two afternoons per week for ten weeks, second semester. The aim would be to examine persisting issues of citizenship, rather than to focus on specific problems of students' projects, and to pursue this through diverse literature: fiction, biography, poetry, drama, and nonfiction social analysis. Students might read a biography of Ghandi, Thoreau on civil disobedience, a novel such as *All the King's Men,* the

work of James Baldwin. They might study such questions as, "What is meaningful social change?" "Can an individual make a difference?" "How should humans govern themselves?" The course would offer a special opportunity for the teacher to introduce the work of previous thinkers whose distinguished writing illuminates universal problems of citizenship.

6. *Public Message,* periodically through second semester. Each citizen action group would develop a final "message" which communicated the meaning of its work to peers and the public at large. The message could take the form of a written report, a radio or TV program, a play, a film or photo essay. The point would be to tell the public what has been accomplished and to interpret the students' experience. A unit on critical analysis of the mass media would precede the creation of student messages. Producing the message would further refine communication skills and offer a creative opportunity for students to synthesize previous coursework.

The program is not advocated as a verified model. To our knowledge no such program has ever been tried, although many schools seem to offer in some form one or more of its parts. We propose it only as a suggestion for how schools which take citizen participation seriously might create an alternative program at the eleventh or twelfth grade. The design is responsive, we think, to certain institutional givens; for example, the need to assign formal credit based on disciplinary categories (English and social studies), the fact that schools have other missions besides civic education, and the conventional work loads of teachers. . . .

Note that no component is aimed exclusively at any one of the seven competencies. Communication skills, for example, would not be restricted to the communication course; they would be taught in all parts of the program. The nature of political-legal decision making would be taught most directly in the political-legal process course, but to function successfully in the program, students would have to develop political knowledge continuously beyond that, especially in the internship, action project, and public message. While some components would stress certain competencies more than others . . . , our intent is that all competencies would be reinforced in all components. The decision not to develop a specialized instructional module for each competency reflects our assumption that educational programs must aim toward more than expedient individual mastery. Students have a right not only to become individually competent, but also to a sense of personal dignity in the learning process. That dignity can often be violated by curricula that increasingly separate and dissect human competence. Instead, the instructional environment must encourage a holistic, interactive view of learning. Its own activities must nourish interpersonal sharing and a just system of governance, as well as individual achievement.

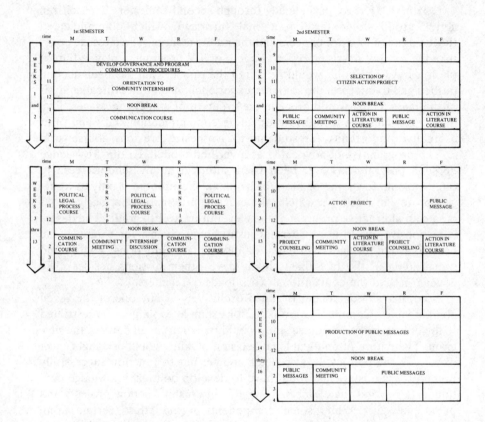

Figure 11-2

Sample program schedule

Table 11-1

Educational movements related to the citizen action curriculum

Related program	CA consistency	CA difference
Kohlberg moral development	Systematic discussion of moral issues, aiming toward ethical justification through principled reasoning.	Focus on moral issues related to public affairs. Not aimed primarily at stage development in individual students, but more at general participation skills.
Values clarification	Emphasizes clarification of personal values related to public issues in non-threatening atmosphere.	Preparation to face challenges and strong opposition to one's values.
Communication skills	Major emphasis on use of spoken and written language to receive and send messages.	Focus on use of language in the role of citizen. Adds to technical literacy skills the role of interpersonal dynamics and mass media.
Law-related education	Major emphasis on dynamics of political-legal system.	Focus on problems related to citizens exerting influence, rather than abstract understanding of topics in political science or law.
Media education	Emphasis on analysis of and production of media.	Orientation to how the citizen is influenced by and can use the media to exert influence, rather than only aesthetic dimensions.
Psychological awareness	Examines students' sense of self and emotional stress.	Focus on sense of efficacy and anxiety related especially to citizen participation.

Table 11-1 (continued)

Related program	CA consistency	CA difference
Volunteerism	Students placed in responsible roles of participation in the community beyond the school.	An integrated set of courses surrounds the experience. Volunteer service is seen as a first step toward action for some institutional change.

Relationship to Other Innovative Programs

The program integrates a variety of innovative themes currently advocated in secondary education: communication skills, media analysis, moral development, values clarification, volunteerism, law-related education, psychological awareness. The program can be considered an alternative "school-within-a-school," where, for a full year, students take major responsibility for their actions and can develop a sense of community among themselves. By providing intensive opportunities for learning with adults in the community at large and integrating this experience with school-based instruction, it implements recommendations from reports of recent commissions on youth and secondary education.[3] . . . the program also incorporates much of the experience of the alternative school movement (for example, use of out of school resources, combined role of teacher and counselor, project-and advocacy-oriented course work).

While it synthesizes many efforts, the citizen action curriculum in no sense tries to offer all things to all people; nor does it pursue objectives precisely as intended by other programs. To illustrate consistencies and differences between the citizen action (CA) program and other approaches, consider [Table 11-1]. Our entries give an incomplete picture of related movements, for we identify only those aspects that seem particularly pertinent to the citizen action programs. We do not pretend to list all differences between our program and theirs, but highlight only one or a few of the most significant.

When each of the related approaches is considered in isolation, we may quibble with aspects of its philosophy, yet each has something to offer civic education. We have tried to structure a program that builds on strengths that these otherwise disparate movements might contribute toward enhancing student ability to exert influence in public affairs . . . .

Notes

1. Fred M. Newmann, "Building a Rationale for Civic Education," in *Building Rationales for Citizenship Education*, ed. James Shaver (Arlington, Va.: Bulletin 52, National Council for the Social Studies, 1977), 1-33, discusses criteria for a comprehensive rationale for civic education.

2. For an elaboration on this point, see Lawrence Kohlberg, "From Is to Ought: How to Commit the Naturalistic Fallacy and Get Away with It in the Study of Moral Development," in *Cognitive and Developmental Epistemology*, ed. T. Mischel (New York: Academic Press, 1971); and John Rawls, *A Theory of Justice* (Cambridge, Mass.: Harvard University Press, 1971).

3. See, e.g., National Association of Secondary-School Principals, National Committee on Secondary Education, *American Youth in the Mid-Seventies* (Washington, D.C.: the Association, 1972); National Commission on the Reform of Secondary Education, *The Reform of Secondary Education: A Report to the Public and the Profession* (New York: McGraw-Hill, 1972); and James Coleman *et al.*, *Youth: Transition to Adulthood* (Chicago: University of Chicago Press, 1974).

Work Experience: A Redefinition

Peter Scharf
Thomas C. Wilson

Work Experience/Study Programs have been historically associated with the ritual of "training" lower-class students in public high schools to perform the more menial tasks of an industrial society. The assumptions underlying such programs included such notions as:

lower-class students were destined for labor-oriented careers and would not profit from academic instruction;

middle-class (typically academically able) students had no time available from their academic studies to explore work experiences;

instruction related to work-study students had to be presented in a rote fashion. Work-study students could not profit from intellectual stimulation and that instruction should be geared to the: a) "practical" techniques of work, and b) the inculcation of the accepted work ideology (Protestant ethic).

Reprinted from *Theory Into Practice*, 15 (June 1976), 205-212. Published by College of Education, Ohio State University. Research for this paper was funded by Title III of the Elementary and Secondary Education Act in cooperation with the University of California and the Newport-Mesa Unified School District.

This paper offers that such notions are misleading in two respects. First, they are clearly inconsistent with a democratic creed. Certain students end up being "sorted" into a social caste of undereducated "laborers." Second, "rote" learning techniques fail to provide the kinds of experiences likely to facilitate necessary developmental growth. We offer instead that work experience programs:

should rework the class ideology and be redefined in terms of experiences that might be applicable to students other than the traditional marginal students (academic and economic) who have until now constituted the major target population of work experience programs;

should be reconceptualized in terms of psychological assumptions underlying work experience instruction and instead of operant habitual training, an interactional-cognitive developmental model be utilized to provide for students' cognitive moral growth through meaningful work experiences.

Our approach, then, is to examine these two reconceptualized notions in some detail and then offer a concrete, functioning program designed to implement the two redefinitions.

Reworking the Class Ideology of Work Experience Programs

Perhaps the most critical flaw of traditional work experience programs is that they have existed mainly for economically deprived youth rather than for all students. The problems with this assumption are manifestly obvious for they lead to channeling "economically" deprived youth into lower-status, lower-security, lower-paid vocations and already economically advantaged youth into prestigious professional careers. This is damaging in several respects. Capable working-class youth tend to overlook careers which might require college training. As well, middle-class youth of average ability ignore skilled labor careers which might be more economically viable than are current marginal professional careers (for example, a career as a tool die maker versus a career as a high school teacher). In addition to stratifying the interests of youth prematurely and often inappropriately, the overall social consequence of such programs is to create a fixed undereducated working class with anachronistic skills and a white-collar, social advantaged elite with overpopulation and insecurity.

The implication of the broad critique implies that *all* students should be given access to experiences in the work-business world. Coleman[1] argues that such experiences are more meaningful to students than are traditional programs and, as well, prepare students for available work roles (which purely academic programs clearly do not). While it is true that many jobs require specific intellectual and/or technological skills that only advanced academic training (probably college level) can provide, early immersion in the work world gives students a chance to identify which skills are needed for particular work roles. Then the student can realistically define a personal strategy for acquiring needed skills. This type of experience makes as much sense for white-collar (computer operator), semiprofessional (teacher), or professional (lawyer) roles as it does for blue-collar jobs (auto mechanic).

This strategy implies that all students might become more aware of the vocational options available in American society through interaction with a broad range of work settings. For example, a student who now would be blithely channeled into "going to college" would, in the new context, become aware of alternative valid, meaningful noncollege vocations. Similarly, a student heading toward a trade-oriented career would become aware of college as a viable option through interaction with more academically oriented students as well as with college educated professionals. This approach to work experience, we believe, is ultimately more consistent with the democratic creed than is the class-defined work experience program. Students are offered a range of options to choose from with a reasonable reality context for each choice. With suitable counseling on the requirements for each career option, the student is given a reasonable opportunity to match his values, needs, and abilities with a tentative career choice.

Beyond the skill level, such work experiences for *all* youth would have monumental effect in terms of social growth. In presenting a case for an alternative of school and work. Coleman states it well: "The proposal here, however, is for school work alternation for college preparatory programs as well as vocational programs. The aim of such programs should not be primarily to "learn a skill," but to gain experience in responsible interdependent activity—and the importance of such experience is not limited to youth with manual labor destinations."[2]

This ideology is not totally new in American educational thought. Dewey's *Schools for Tomorrow*[3] documented cases of well-defined and executed educational experiments which linked in a meaningful way the work of the school and the world of work such as the Gary School experiment. Founded in the new town of Gary, the school was transformed into a microwork environment. Custodial, food, and maintenance functions were shared by the students, but in such a way that students had to resolve policy issues as well as perform the concrete work involved. Nutrition, resource allocation, systematic accounting, and futuristic planning were all the tasks of student managers. Many "academic" lessons were derived from conflicts from the task of physically and economically maintaining the school.

A more modern example is Richmond's *The Micro-Society School.*[4] Richmond advocates a microeconomy school which parallels the economic world at large. Students create banks, tutoring services, protection services, restaurants, employ others, and even stage revolutions. In both the Micro-Economy School and the Gary interventions, there is the idea that exposure to work be neither demeaning nor simply manual application. Such examples of successfully uniting work experience with sound academic content (as well as opening experience in the work world to all students) provide models with which to help us design contemporary programs. Coleman[5] suggests similarly that youth are overschooled and underexperienced. Rather than channeling students into dead-end vocational careers, properly reflective work experiences can provide students with both practical expertise as well as a reality context for classroom intellectual experiences. Even in conventional terms, contact with real life institutions give traditional subjects greater meaning. For example, a youth who has worked in a factory might find a book like Sinclair's *The Jungle* a powerful educational experience. In contrast, for a youth who has no contact with institutions outside the school, peer group, and family, the same book might not have value. So, too, jobs involving arithmetical operations might stimulate an interest in mathematics as might a job involving interpersonal contact (sales, counseling, and so forth), stimulate an interest in psychology or sociology. The overall thrust of all these innovations is providing experience in the work world which makes sense only if it is common for all students, and not merely a means for segregating the youth community into a preworking-class and preprofessional elite.

Reconceptualizing the Psychological Assumptions Underlying Work Instruction

Most traditional approaches to work study assume a behaviorist orientation toward student learning: specifically, students are taught to perform specific job skills and develop work-oriented attitudes.

In terms of job requirements, students are taught skills tied to specific technologies. The skills are taught usually in a rote manner (for example, "press green button to lift drive shaft, then lower blue lever . . ."). Often advanced behavioral techniques, such as computer guided instruction or programmed learning, are used, but still within this general behavioristic pattern of learning.

Work values are taught in a similar fashion. Teachers repeat clichés about "cleanliness in the job interview," "the importance of being on time," or "the value of diligence." Often, successful lower-class models (either black or poor) who "made it" are eulogized. In some programs there have been efforts through token economies or similar strategies to reward particular work behaviors and attitudes. Students who show particular Protestant ethic virtues (punctuality, diligence, or cleanliness) are rewarded through use of tokens or other rewards. Such a learning strategy raises three critical issues.

1. There are some powerful indications that the skills approach even where effective is not functional due to a rapidly changing technology. Often students trained to operate with particular technologies find that the technology has shifted even before they graduate from the skills program. The high unemployment rate among "successful" job corps graduates is an indication of this problem. Training students in concrete skills may not make much sense for a time of rapid technological change.

2. The training of attitudes is apparently ineffective. Few of the studies reviewed indicate any long-term success with any of the models attempted. Such efforts as those of Hartshorne and May[6] found that the attitudes reinforced two years before were not retained, and, even where they were retained over a short period of time, they did not correlate with any known measure of behavior. Rokeach[7] reports essentially the same: attitude change cannot theoretically be expected to lead to behavioral change. Particular value contents are short lived and cannot be trained through rote, associationist training.[8]

3. Finally, there is a serious ethical issue raised in the training of work attitudes. The attitudes chosen characteristically represent those of the teachers and school administrators rather than those of the students. To students, they often appear as impositions from without, reminding us of the efforts to teach "proper toothbrush use" to immigrant children at the turn of the century. Most generally, the work attitude approach involves efforts to impose one cultural "bag of virtues" on a particular group of children. Since these values are arbitrary and not chosen by the students, it represents a highly questionable educational act by the school.

Both the training in skills and proper definitions of moral responsibility can be viewed from a quite different psychological perspective. This is from the cognitive developmental orientation—that tradition beginning with John Dewey[9] and George Herbert Mead[10] and including Piaget[11] and Kohlberg.[12] Where the behaviorist position is that specific skills and attitudes should be taught by reward, modeling, and punishment, the cognitive-developmental school offers that only by students interacting with a broad range of technical and moral problems can they develop the necessary capacities to solve a variety of complex tasks in more adequate, comprehensive ways. Thus, skills should not be taught as isolated capacities by rote. Rather, the focus should be on allowing the student to develop the necessary mental structures to solve a range of practical problems. Similarly, it is futile to teach specific positive work attitudes such as hard work or punctuality. Rather, the school should focus on the student's capacity to solve adequately a range of moral problems and dilemmas.

The developmental approach has been well documented in terms of formal research. Piaget[13] has documented an invariant sequence of logical stages which have been found to describe a universal order of learning mental operations. Children move through the stages sequentially, and each higher stage represents a more adequate mode of thinking about physical and social problems.

The stages:

1. (Birth-two years) *Sensorimotor*: Learning here is based primarily on immediate experience through the five senses. The child has perceptions and movements as his only tools for learning. Lacking language, the child has neither the ability to represent or symbolize thinking, and thus no way to categorize experiences. One of the first sensorimotor abilities to develop is that of visual pursuit—the ability to perceive and hold a visual object with the eyes. Later, the capacity of object permanence—the ability to understand that an object can still exist even though it cannot be seen— develops. Lacking vision during this period prevents the growth of mental structures.

2. (Two-seven years) *Preoperational or intuitive mode:* During this period, the child is no longer bound to the immediate sensory environ- ment, and it builds upon abilities such as object permanence from the sensorimotor stage. The ability to store mental images, symbols (words and language as a structure for words), increases dramatically. The mode of learning is a freely experimenting intuitive approach—one that is generally unconcerned with reality. Communication occurs in collective monologues in which children talk to themselves more than to each other. Use of language during this period, then, is both egocentric and spontaneous. Though use of language is the major learning focus at this age, many other environmental discoveries are made—each using the free- wheeling, intuitive approach.

3. (Seven-eleven years) *Concrete operations:* This period sees the dramatic shift in learning strategy from intuition to concrete thought. Reality-bound thinking takes over, and the child must test out problems in order to understand them. The difference between dreams and facts can be clearly distinguished, but that between a hypothesis and a fact cannot. The child becomes overly logical and concrete so that once his or her mind is made up, new facts will not change it. Facts and order become absolutes.

4. (Eleven-sixteen years) *Formal operations:* At this stage, the child

enters adolescence, and the potential for developing full formal patterns of thinking emerges. The adolescent is capable of attaining logical-rational or abstract strategies. Symbolic meanings, metaphors, and similes can be understood. Implications and generalizations can be made.

In terms of the problems of work-study programs, the focus has to be on the transition between concrete and formal operations. Junior high school and high school students will be divided between concrete operational and formal operational youth. The ways that skills are learned according to this model directly conflicts with the associationist model described earlier. Where the associationist-conditioning model focused on the acquisition of particular skills, this model offers that the overall capacity of the student to think through practical problems is critical. For example, a concrete operational student, when faced with a problem at work—for example, fixing a radio—will focus on the simple rules for fixing the machine, such as,

1. Disconnect wire.
2. Look for blown out tube.
3. Find new tube.
4. Reinsert in #3 socket.

A formal operative student will begin to discover the dynamics and logical principles governing the functioning of the radio. Why do tubes blow out? What are better ways to build a radio? Also, when there is doubt about the causes of malfunction, the formally operational student is able to reason through which of a number of possible causes is the real cause for the malfunction.

This formally operational capacity clearly has an advantage over the concrete operational approach. When technologies shift, the formally operative student is able to adapt to them. The student can move from being a radio repairer to possibly an engineer or designer as he or she is able to conceive of the radio as an abstract electronic system and think of ways to redesign it to give it new capacities. The concrete operational worker is more or less stuck in the role of a rote technician.

Key to Piaget's approach is the notion of *assimilation* and *accommodation*. Piaget defines assimilation as the taking in of impressions into one's own available cognitive structures. Accommodation is defined as the testing of such structures against the world. In terms of creating a meaningful and effective work experience for students, it is assumed that there be a balance between assimilation and accommodation. Work cannot be simply a totally theoretical (assimilatory) experience . . . . (reading about work environments); nor can it be pure accommodation (simply working without any external input). Rather, work experience should involve both opportunities for the student to explore practically the world of work, as well as a means to stimulate the intellect of the adolescent.

Another compatible way of thinking about the same problem is to use Dewey's Reflection-Experience paradigm. Dewey argued that educational experience could be thought of as a continuum, with optimum effectiveness being at the midpoint between purely experiential and purely reflective educational experiences.[14] The diagram below represents Dewey's model:

Pure experience		Pure reflection
(Working at McDonald's)	Optimum effectiveness	(Reading about work)

Experiences that are purely reflection are meaningless, as are experiences which are purely experiential. The goal is to give students valid, existentially powerful work experiences and at the same time provide opportunity (1) in which they can actively reflect about those experiences, and (2) in such a way that does not violate the power and immediacy of those experiences. Such reflective and experiential educational moments should stimulate the student toward more mature thinking about both technical and social worlds.

The experience reflection model is also most appropriate for moral education. Kohlberg[15] describes a realm of social development and attempts to define the conditions which might stimulate development in the aspect of moral thought. The theory (guided by eighteen years of observations by Kohlberg and his colleagues) argues that moral thinking develops sequentially through six stages of moral thinking. In a variety of cultural contexts, individuals have been found to move through the stages in the same order though the speed of development and final stage achieved vary.

These studies likewise indicate certain conditions associated with rapid and complete moral development. One condition is that individuals are provided opportunities for resolving moral conflict. A second postulate offers that moral change is associated with active role taking and participation in the maintenance functions of "secondary institutions." Finally it has been found that moral change occurs where individuals accept an institution's moral climate as being legitimate and just as understood at the person's stage of moral maturity.

The implication of Kohlberg's theory is that simply teaching students "good work attitudes" is totally inadequate. As we indicated earlier, while it is possible to condition attitudes for a short period of time, we cannot expect that these attitudes will endure; nor will they correlate with behavior. Additionally, particular attitudes are culture bound and will appear imposed by students and will be rejected. The alternative we pose is a reflective work-study experience setting wherein the students face real life moral and social conflicts and attempt to resolve them in a group context with a general goal of developing a more mature moral and social consciousness on the part of the student. Instead of seeing work study as a means for facilitating "good work habits," it becomes a means of presenting new opportunities for interaction and conflict to stimulate positive moral development.

A Concrete Program to Create a New Work Experience Program at Newport Harbor High School, Newport Beach, California

Given our argument that an effective work-study program requires a new sociological and psychological base, we are in the process of creating a work-study program which would:

1. Involve a new population of work-study students, not drawn from class distinctions but from (1) those identified as alienated, and (2) those who volunteer.

2. Try to match students with role models and environments suited to their needs.

3. Create a model of related instruction geared to stimulating students' thinking in a reflective manner about, first, their own characteristic way of "learning," and, second, their experiences at work, the nature of work in American society, and their futures in the work world in the society.

As indicated earlier, the typical work experience class is comprised of the bottom of the academic barrel. The model here assumes that work experience should be a valuable component of *all* efforts at general education in the high school. The experience of real life involvement, we believe, has particular importance for students whom the school has not reached with traditional programs and/or who demonstrate symptoms of alienation. This grouping is distinguishable from students who are socially and economically destined for lower-class careers. Such groups of alienated youth might be bright underachievers, those bored with academic experiences, or genuine low achievers in traditional realms.

While we have developed a model of alienation and means to measure it, its presentation here is beyond the scope of this introductory paper. It suffices to say that our rather comprehensive model attempts to combine the work of Maslow, Rokeach, Rotter, Keniston, Schwartz and Stryker, and Stokols.[16]

Though there should be a primary focus on students we define as alienated and who are not maximally benefiting from traditional programs, clearly the work experience program should be open to all students, and a broader range of students should be encouraged. Our arguments for this mix of students is that it will foster a more democratic open class structure and that the mix of life-styles and talents will enrich all students involved.

Perhaps even more essential to the program is the identification of types of work settings which might provide an appropriate context for a meaningful work experience. The primary goal is to get students in roles where they interact with older possible work role models, involve them in interesting, challenging work tasks and which, in some way, yield insight and information about a possible future career. For example, such settings as McDonald's where the "counter kids" are all of high school age is less preferable than say a setting where through informal apprenticeships the student is able to role test and interact with significant older individuals in an intensive manner. The "old" nonregimented craft shop with masters working with apprentices is a prototype of such a psychologically advantageous setting.

In addition, the nature of the work involved is critical to the meaningfulness of the work experience. Settings where students are provided a variety of operations—say repairing machinery or even sales—are preferable to an assembly line or mechanical (impersonal) counter job. Work which is intellectually stimulating is preferable to routine work.

Finally, settings where students interact with professionals or master craftsmen are preferable to things which stratify older and younger workers. These relationships might be called "natural projective apprenticeships" and are obviously desirable. For example, the student interested in education might be an apprentice to a day-care teacher. Likewise, the student interested in engineering or architecture might apprentice himself or herself to an architect. The student interested in being a mechanic may find a suitable [master mechanic] in the garage. The dynamics of such relationships are not simply informational but involve what Erikson[17] calls the process of "adolescent future projection and identity formation." The adolescent tries to project himself or herself in a future orientation and decides on a career to create the self he or she wants to be. This contact with an older person is critical in forming a vocational identity choice. The adolescent in such a relationship is fundamentally asking himself, "Do I want to be like this older person?" The answer to this question may provide a significant event in the adolescent's choosing of a future career.

In addition to providing rich work experiences for all students, we will strive to match students according to the students' vocational interests, personal style, and level of moral expectation. The basic model to be proposed involves measuring the work setting in terms of moral atmosphere, alienation environment, and organizational climate and then matching the student in such a way that the setting provides upward moral/social conflicts for the student.

The related instruction consists of groups of about fifteen students who meet weekly for four hours with a faculty member to (a) reflect upon their own learning styles, and (b) reflect upon their work experiences.

Reflection upon Learning Styles

This occurs through the utilization of REAL (Relevant Experiences in Active Learning) "minipacs" developed by the Northwest Regional Education Laboratory, Portland, Oregon. The packages come in pairs and focus upon a basic issue experienced by all learners such as, "Why Learn Anything?" or "Letting Someone Teach You." One version of each pair has a format and illustrations appropriate to youth, and the other is appropriate to adults.

Below is a description of the materials which may be found in each minipac.

Directions. The direction papers contain the methods for using the materials and specify which materials are to be used with which method.

Key Ideas Booklet. This booklet gives a brief discussion of the minipac topic in terms of a set of important psychosocial ideas. For example, the Key Ideas Booklet for the "Being Helped" package contains a brief explanation of what being helped means and eight key ideas discussed in the Key Ideas Booklet.

Audio Cassette. The tape contains examples of the key ideas as they appear in human experiences. These human experiences are illustrated by interviews, confrontations, and music. There may be different cassettes for students and for adults.

Search Booklets. There are two search booklets in each Set I Minipac. One introduces the learners to completing needs assessments, problem identification, dilemma clarification, and values clarification through recalling specific information that is relevant to the learners' past experiences. The other booklet includes directions for performing various activities that call for behavioral outcomes rather than just knowledge. Set II Minipacs have one Search Booklet that combines these focuses. The learners may be involved in some writing, drawing, manipulating, and simulation situations as they respond to the search directions.

Self-Assessment Booklet. This booklet (called "Where Are You Now?") invites learners to evaluate their behaviors in working with the ideas of each minipac. The evaluation includes open-ended questions, fill-in statements, checklists, and a card sort. Each is designed to provide self-checks regarding cognitive-affective learnings, attitude changes, and the degree of increased self-awareness relative to the key ideas.

Use of the package is completely self-directed and is accomplished either individually or in a leaderless small group. A package explains the dynamics of the issue it focuses on and suggests ways that the user can have experiences to learn. The materials do not tell the user what a person should do in any way. They are, rather, intended to enable the user to recognize the human dynamics of issues so as to better determine ways to cope with them in his or her own style and according to his or her own desires. Such recognition is intended to make the issue of responsibility for the factor of choice in behavior an explicit one. The idea and design of these self-directed minipackages derive directly from a theoretical model of social-psychological self-evolution based upon the work of Erikson, Piaget, Kohlberg, and Maslow.[18]

Reflection upon Work Experience

This involves the creation of a discussion climate in which students feel free to bring up problem issues which occur in the work setting. Such problems are then dealt with within the group, and resolution is sought after collective effort.

The issues which might result are obviously many. One example might be labeled an ethical conflict which might occur. In one pilot session, a student working in a mental hospital offered the group the following: "I was working with the little mentally disturbed girl, Francis. The nurse was ignoring her so I went to talk to her. The nurse bawled me out because she said that the girl was being punished, and everyone was supposed to ignore her. I went and talked to her, even though I might get fired for it . . . ."

The goal of the leader is to get the group to help the student deal with the moral conflict posed (doing what one considers right for the patient versus conforming to the norms for the institution). The leader in this discussion raised several issues to the group: Why did the nurse want the students to ignore the girl? Were these reasons justified? What would happen to the girl patient if the student got fired? Who would relate to her then? When is it right to violate the rules of the institution? What are the responsibilities for a person who violates such rules?

The goals are not to preach a particular answer, but to get the students to reflect on the issues posed. The leaders will be trained in using the models reflection/experience and moral education[19] and will try and encourage better reasoned responses, rather than the "right response." The goal is to encourage students to better think about their responsibilities in a work setting, rather than to rebel or conform to the system. The group, after a resolution of such a conflict, will attempt to assist the student involved to better deal with his or her work role.

Another type of issue might involve the context of work. Students working in fast-food chains (such as McDonald's) might reflect upon the effect of such institutions upon the nation's nutrition and local ecology. Leaders might suggest surveys of customer opinions or other such observations.

Another type of issue involves students choosing a vocation. Students might project as to what kinds of work they would find meaningful in the future. Through role plays and projective exercises the leaders could involve the students in defining potential career options while encouraging them to plan realistically for such careers.

Other issues which might arise are: "personal conflicts at work; the nature of the organization of work; power in the work world; effects of capitalism on work; ways to make work more interesting . . . ."

Such issues would be dealt with in an open, nonindoctrinative manner where students and leaders would reflect in an intellectually stimulating and supportive manner about the issue being discussed. There would be a focus upon resolving the conflict on the intellectual level as well as contracting with the students solutions to be applied in the work setting. Thus, if a student brought to the group a dilemma dealing with a disagreement with a supervisor over a particular matter, and the group concluded that the student was in the wrong, he or she might be reasonably expected to apologize to the boss as compliance with the contract made with the group. The related instruction then serves as a moral basis for relating to the job as well as an intellectual forum to air problems occurring in the work world.

Conclusions

This paper has attempted to formulate a new conceptual outline for work experience programs. It offers a new sociological principle for selecting work experience students as well as suggests a new psychological strategy with which to formulate supplementary educational training. The program suggested by this paper is now being implemented at Newport Harbor High School, Newport-Mesa Unified School District, Newport Beach, California. We are conducting a careful evaluation of the program to determine the project's impact upon reduction of student alienation and increased maturity of moral thinking. We hope the results of this research are in the anticipated directions and that it is possible to create work experience programs which will have moral and intellectual impact upon a broad range of students.

Notes

1. J. Coleman *et al.*, *Youth: Transition to Adulthood* (Chicago: University of Chicago Press, 1974).

2. *Ibid.*, 158.

3. J. Dewey, *Schools for Tomorrow* (Boston: Heath, 1906).

4. G. Richmond, *The Micro-Society School* (New York: Harper and Row, 1975).

5. Coleman *et al., Youth.*

6. H. Hartshorne and M. A. May, *Studies in the Nature of Character.* Volume 1, *Studies in Deceit*; Volume 2, *Studies in Service and Self-Control*; Volume 3, *Studies in Organization of Character* (New York: Macmillan, 1928-1930).

7. M. Rokeach, *The Nature of Human Values* (New York: Free Press, 1973).

8. L. Kohlberg, "Stage and Sequence: The Cognitive-Developmental Approach to Socialization," in *Handbook of Socialization Theory and Research*, ed. D. Goslin (Chicago: Rand McNally, 1969).

9. J. Dewey, *Democracy and Education* (New York: Free Press, 1916).

10. G. Mead, *Mind, Self, and Society* (Chicago: University of Chicago Press, 1934).

11. J. Piaget, "The General Problem of the Psychobiological Development of the Child," in *Discussions on Child Development.* Volume 4. Ed. J. M. Tanner and B. Inhelder (New York: International Universities Press, 1960).

12. Kohlberg, "Stage and Sequence."

13. J. Piaget, "Cognitive Development in Children," in *Piaget Rediscovered: A Report on Cognitive Studies in Curriculum Development*, ed. R. Ripple and V. Rockcastle (Ithaca, N.Y.: Cornell University School of Education, 1966).

14. Dewey, *Democracy and Education.*

15. Kohlberg, "Stage and Sequence."

16. A. Maslow, *Toward a Psychology of Being* (New York: Van Nostrand Reinhold, 1968); Rokeach, *The Nature of Human Values*; J. Rotter, "General Expectancies for Internal versus External Control of Development," *Psychological Monographs*, 80 (No. 1, 1966), 1-28; K. Keniston, *The Uncommitted: Alienated Youth in American Society* (New York: Harcourt Brace Jovanovich, 1965); M. Schwartz and S. Stryker, *Deviance, Selves, and Others* (Washington, D.C.: American Sociological Association, 1970), cited in A. McCord, "Happiness as Educational Equality," *Society*, 12 (No. 1, 1974), 65-71; D. Stokols, "Toward a Psychological Theory of Alienation," *Psychological Review*, 82 (No. 1, 1975), 26-44.

17. E. Erikson, *Childhood and Society* (New York: W. W. Norton, 1950).

18. C. Jung, *Improving Teaching Competencies Program: Basic Program Plans* (Portland: Northwest Regional Education Laboratory, 1972).

19. Kohlberg, "Stage and Sequence."

The Family and Moral Education

Sheila F. Stanley

American society is experiencing deep problems. The Vietnam war, political corruption, increasing violence, epidemics of drug abuse, the decay of our cities, and the isolation of suburban life clearly reflect the extensive confusion that exists in our time. If society is in trouble, so is the American family. No longer supported by an extended family and the community, the modern family struggles uneasily and often unsuccessfully to cope with the breakneck pace of change and the moral crises of contemporary society.

Rather than see the family as a reflection of something awry in our society, social analysts often blame the family for what is wrong. Using the family as a scapegoat occurs because historically it has had the primary responsibility for the socialization of our children. As Ned Gaylin cogently points out, however, by focusing so intensely on the family, which admittedly is disorganized, we fail to explore the basic problem: the values and priorities of the society at large.

When things go amiss, rather than condemn, should we not, instead, question whether the family is adjusting perhaps *too* well, whether it is performing its functions too efficiently in grooming its children for society, the values of which may be somewhat askew? The basic question being raised is whether the social sciences any longer can afford the luxury of taking a stance of "scientific neutrality," of social relativism with regard to the society of which they are a part, while examining the institutions of that society. The answer seems apparent that social science must face its responsibilities as change agent and advocate, and therefore it must be prepared to examine and evaluate the values of that society in which it operates.[1]

Some social scientists, among them Urie Bronfenbrenner, Philip Slater, and Alan Toffler, agree with Gaylin and have critically scrutinized contemporary American values and their consequences. They charge that America's obsession with efficiency and the profit motive seriously interferes with the development of democratic values such as cooperation and concern for others. Productivity is given top priority in American society, and this compulsive need to "make it" has led to alienation and isolation in a variety of forms. We are a people segregated by age, race, class, and ability. The elderly are isolated because they are "unproductive." Children have little contact with adults other than their own parents and are segregated in school from others of different ages and abilities. Families play hopscotch from one community to another, thus aggravating the lack of commitment of suburban life. Shopping centers, large impersonal high schools, reliance upon the automobile, and pressure to conform, which characterize suburbia, breed anonymity and loneliness. We have lost the spirit of the democratic community, substituting instead the unrealistic fantasies of TV, competition rather than cooperation, and a preoccupation with privacy.

The lack of the emotional support formerly provided by an extended family and a neighborhood places added stress upon the already overburdened nuclear family. When the family fails at the impossible task of meeting all our needs for belonging, we condemn it as "a faultily constructed piece of social engineering."[2] We do not recognize that conditions of life have changed and that the actual responsibility for childrearing has shifted away from the family to other sectors of the society.

The family has lost much of its power and influence, partly because parents and children spend so little time together. And yet the family, as Bronfenbrenner[3] reminds us, still has the primary moral and legal responsibility for developing character in children. What can be done? It seems to me that we need to do two things: first, find ways to strengthen and support the family rather than gradually replace it with more education, more therapy, and more reliance upon television, the peer group, and drugs; second, provide family members with the skills to examine critically and to evaluate society's moral values and priorities.

The program described below grew out of my interest in family education and a conviction that the family plays a decisive role in the moral development of our young. Because of the moral crises of our times, finding ways to stimulate the development of moral thought and action in children is a crucial task. The study presented here demonstrates that parents can be helped in their role as primary moral educators of children.

The Family as a Moral Educator

Certain experiences have been found to enhance moral reasoning in children and adolescents. Among these are situations that encourage new ways of thinking about morality, such as role-taking opportunities, participation in groups perceived as fair or just, and exposure to cognitive conflict (to contradictions in one's own moral views and in their relation to the views of others). As one becomes increasingly aware that there are points of view and feelings other than his own, and as the capacity to look at his own behavior from these other perspectives develops, so too does his level of moral reasoning.[4]

The family is a crucial source of such role-taking opportunities for the growing child. But, as yet, there has been little research on strategies for moral education in the family. Research on learning theory provides some tentative support for the notion that parental styles influence the child's moral development.[5] To be more specific, the use of inductive discipline by parents appears to be correlated with more advanced moral reasoning and behavior than either the use of coercive power or threats of withdrawing love.[6] Inductive discipline refers to techniques that appeal to the child's rationality and responsibility, to his sense of right and wrong. By encouraging the child to consider carefully his obligations and the rights of others as well as his own, inductive discipline may furnish the child with important role-taking opportunities. In a similar vein, Holstein and Peck and Havighurst[7] found that moral maturity in children is related to active participation in family discussions and decision making.

The project described here was based on the assumption that, if a child perceives his family as being fair, and if conflicts involving members of the family are resolved equitably, he will have experienced significant role-taking opportunities and discussion of the right, wrong, or fair thing to do. Further, these experiences should stimulate the moral development of the child. No one has yet attempted to teach families methods of inductive discipline and problem solving with the purpose of evaluating the consequences for the moral development of the children. This study did that.

The purpose was twofold: to investigate whether a course that taught families democratic methods of resolving conflicts and establishing rules would affect the moral atmosphere of the family itself; to investigate whether such a course would stimulate the moral reasoning of the adolescent participants. Following Rawls[8] and Kohlberg, Scharf, and Hickey,[9] the moral atmosphere or justice structure of the family was defined as "the principles which govern the assignment of rights and duties and define the proper distribution of the benefits and burdens of social cooperation."[10]

The Course

The course was taught in a high school of a small city on the East Coast. The participants were volunteer ninth- and tenth-grade students and their parents; only families in which husband, wife, and adolescent all agreed to participate in the project were accepted. The families were divided into three groups. The first group (A) consisted of ten parents and seven adolescents (five families). The second (B) had twelve parents (six families) with their six adolescents participating in the evaluation only. This group was included to assess whether or not it made a difference to include adolescents in the course. The third group (C) was a control that was assessed, but did not attend the experimental course. The participants in all groups were predominantly lower middle class with occupations of the parents ranging from skilled labor to nonmanagerial white-collar jobs. All families were white and either Protestant or Catholic.

The course met for two and one-half hours a week for ten weeks. Both groups were led by me and a high school counselor whom I had trained to teach the course during the previous semester.

The course was influenced by two models of parental education: the Adlerian approach to family education[11] and Thomas Gordon's Parent Effectiveness Training. The Adlerian concept of the family meeting and Gordon's problem-solving method were, in particular, seen as potentially effective ways of helping families develop and live by more just rules and agreements. As will be seen, both are based on democratic procedures for resolving family conflicts.

The course had four phases. Although the phases could not be neatly separated from each other by sessions, blocks of time were allotted for each. The following is a description of the curriculum of the parent-adolescent group and the group that included only parents.

Phase One: Communication Skills

This phase involved discussions of how family members talked with one another, particularly about rules and conflicts; and the teaching and practicing of the skills of empathic listening and of confrontation.

Theoretical considerations, as well as my own experience in working with families, led me to include these communication skills in the course. To solve problems productively, parents and children must learn how to talk to each other in nonauthoritarian ways. The inclusion of listening and confrontation skills also fits with the developmental perspective of the course. Moral development theory states that, if individuals have the ability to take the role of the other and if they can understand another person and convey that understanding, they are more likely to consider other positions and reach an equitable decision when faced with a conflict. Dowell[13] had found that learning to listen and respond empathically has a significant impact on the moral reasoning of adolescents. Furthermore, it is possible that effective confrontation skills may also enhance moral development. Clear, nondestructive statements about a person's behavior help that individual understand the effects of his behavior. Practicing this skill would give parents and teenagers experience in accepting responsibility for the welfare of others. In addition, being able to empathize with and understand the claims of another can be expected to result in greater fairness toward that person.

The first class began with personal introductions and discussion of the goals of the workshop. Next, parents as a group were asked to reflect upon their own adolescence and to share with each other what communication and discipline were like in their families of origin. This was a powerful experience for all. Almost without exception, these parents grew up in families characterized by economic hardship, lack of communication, and much tension.

> L: There was a lot of arguing in my family. My father was an alcoholic. My parents didn't listen to me. I was the youngest, and they were too tired to care.
> J: I was very bitter about my own adolescence. There was no communication in my family. I felt very hurt and angry at my father for ignoring me, so I left home at an early age.
> M: I was an only child. Instead of asking me, "Do you like this?" they said, "You *will* like this." I never dared to disagree. I had never gone shopping for my own clothes until after I was married.

Many of the adolescents were visibly moved by what they had heard. Several said they had not realized what their parents had gone through. When they took their turn, the most emotionally charged responses were those concerning decision making. "I don't like how rules are made. My father makes most of them." "My mother orders me around and never listens to my side of things. It's not fair." This discussion led naturally into the last part of the class, which focused on rules and typical conflicts in families. The participants were asked to write down their family rules and how these were decided (an activity that will be described more thoroughly below).

The second class was devoted to the teaching of listening skills,[14] through modeling by the leaders and the role playing of both imaginary and real problems. The participants began by learning to distinguish between words and feelings and to focus on the feelings being expressed. They practiced, first, identifying feelings and, then, reflecting them by using the forms "You feel ____" and "You feel ____ because ____," filling in the blanks with the appropriate responses. They practiced in groups of three and were instructed to continue practicing these skills at home for the duration of the workshop. This was the case with all of the subsequent skills they were taught. Several participants found empathic listening artificial and difficult at first. As the weeks went by, however, most of the group members began to comment favorably on the positive results of their improved listening ability.

The third class focused on effective confrontations, that is, on some of the skills needed when one person's behavior interferes with another's. Complaints included: "My tools were left out in the rain" and "My dad borrowed some money and didn't return it." Participants examined the consequences (usually negative) of their typical responses to another's disturbing behavior. They were then taught "I messages,"[15] which communicate the feeling experienced by the person who is upset. The form used, at least initially, is: "I feel [feeling] when [description of behavior] because [effects upon me]." For example, "I'm really annoyed when you don't return the car at the agreed upon time because now I'm late for my doctor's appointment."

Peterson[16] found "I messages" to be effective because they are less apt to provoke resistance and because they make the other person accountable for modifying his behavior, thus helping him assume responsibility for his own actions. Furthermore, because "I messages" are honest, they are apt to influence the other person to send similar honest messages whenever he is upset. This may avoid the snowballing effect of mutual name calling and of assigning blame that so often happens in families. Finally, as mentioned earlier, being able to understand the claims and perspectives of another can result in more fairness toward that person. The focus on the "because ___" part of the "I message" is thus important. In attempting to determine why another person's behavior was upsetting, participants often brought up issues of fairness. "I get annoyed when you leave the kitchen in a mess because I've just cleaned it up, and it's unfair." "It makes me mad when you turn on the light after I've gone to sleep because that's not thinking of *my* rights."

Participants were given an "I message practice sheet" to complete at home. They were also urged to send "I messages" to each other during the week and to report the results to the group. Most tried this method of confrontation and were generally pleased with the results.

Even though the phase on communication skills was brief, it did encourage participants to put themselves in the place of others, to see the world through another person's perspective. It was intended to provide them with some of the skills necessary to resolve conflicts equitably—the focus of the third phase of the course.

Phase Two: The Family Meeting

This phase of the course centered on the discussion of family rules and the family meeting as a way of promoting more democracy in the family and providing participation, particularly for adolescents.

During the first class, both adolescents and parents were asked to write down the rules in their families and how they were decided. Then they were grouped by family and shared what each had written. This exercise was repeated at the last session to aid both participants and leaders in evaluating any changes in the process of decision making over the course of the workshop. In discussing this exercise, some fascinating observations were made. The parents believed, in general, that many of the rules were made by joint decision with their children. In these same families, however, the adolescents disagreed vehemently, maintaining that the decisions were handed down by parents, or, as one boy put it, "decided by God: parents, not kids, have the last word." Many parents who initially thought they were making joint decisions came to realize that one or both parents pushed through a decision without general agreement in the family. It became apparent that most families experienced much dissension in making decisions. Parents struggled to keep the upper hand, and adolescents resisted. The parents seemed to regard continuous family warfare as unpleasant but normal; it was considered a usual and expected condition. They did not like the ways conflicts were resolved, but saw no alternative.

As a possible solution to the friction common to all the families, we suggested a weekly family meeting.[17] The fourth class focused on discussion of such a meeting. It was described as a regular opportunity for family members to communicate with each other, to share information, and to make plans and decisions around such issues as chores and use of the TV and family car. It would provide a way of dealing with recurring problems and conflicts away from the heat of the moment. It would be a move toward participatory democracy in which each individual has a full and equal role. We explained that there would be less need for punishment because people are more likely to carry out jointly made decisions.

We urged that the weekly meetings be held at regularly scheduled times so that they would avoid being seen as the parents' meeting—to be called only when a parent had a gripe. We also recommended that each meeting have a leader and that the leadership be rotated and include all children in school. Finally, it was stressed that the way decisions are made is critical to successful meetings. Decisions can only be binding if every member present agrees. If a unanimous decision is not reached, further problem solving will be necessary, perhaps at another time. Majority decisions lead to grievances by the minority and impede cooperation. We advised, therefore, against voting in the family meeting.

The reactions to the concept of the family meeting ran the gamut from enthusiasm to strong resistance.

L (parent): [with a raised, trembling voice] The ultimate responsibility for the family is with the *parents*. I can't let a twelve-year-old tell me how to run my life.

M (parent): I'm not sure young kids can come up with intelligent alternatives to conflicts. Parents know best.

D (adolescent): You're not giving us much credit. We're not *that* ignorant. I want to do more on my own.

L (parent): Well, I really do wish they would do more on their own. They need to be reminded *all* the time. But I get the feeling I'd be losing my job if I let them help decide things.

B (parent): That's part of it, L. Letting go of some of the control isn't easy to do. It's hard for us mothers at first to think that anyone else could do what we do. But no one else will start assuming responsibility unless you let go of some.

D (parent): I agree. I used to make all the decisions for my girls. I finally realized they couldn't make any decisions for themselves. So I'm beginning to let up. Maybe these meetings would help us even more.

To demonstrate a family meeting and to provide an opportunity to practice, we asked for volunteers to role play a meeting in front of the group. Three adolescents volunteered, one to play mother, while two parents volunteered, one to play a child. They got into a discussion of chores prompted by complaints from the "son" that he always had to do the dishes, a job he detested. With a little coaching from the coleader, the "family" struggled through to a fair decision concerning the division and rotation of chores.

The families were instructed to conduct weekly meetings at home for the remainder of the workshop. Tape recorders and tapes were distributed to each family, as was a book entitled *The Family Council*, by Dreikurs, Gould, and Corsini.[18] The first and last meetings were tape-recorded, and the tapes were turned into the leaders for the purposes of supervision and assessment.

All participants were willing to tape-record the meetings, although a few seemed anxious and reluctant at first. The initial meeting of the M family illustrates a typical first meeting. They discussed summer curfews and mutually agreed upon times for all four children. The mother was a calm, rational chairperson in contrast to the father who was provocative and dictatorial at times. For example, when one boy began hitting his younger brother, the father blurted out, "No hitting J, or I'll belt you!" Despite some difficulties, the four family members present at the workshop session expressed delight at their first attempt at a family meeting.

Part of the following classes was devoted to the continued examination of the participants' family meetings. It was apparent that it took a lot of courage for many of the parents to share their power with children who formerly had very little. The meetings focused on a wide variety of issues ranging from conflicts between individuals, to infractions of family rules, to negotiations of new privileges. Problems were increasingly perceived not only as management issues ("How do we get the job done?") but also as moral conflicts ("What is the fair way to resolve this for everyone involved?"). There was slow but gradual progress toward democratic participation in the meetings, as evidenced by the tapes as well as the verbal reports of participants.

Phase Three: A Democratic Approach to Conflict Resolution

This phase of the course was designed to provide the families additional help in solving conflicts equitably. My experience had been that, without such help, family meetings did not work very well. Consequently, the participants were taught a democratic approach to problem solving that is based primarily on the work of Gordon.[19] Before the approach was explained to them, we discussed typical methods used by participants to resolve conflicts. Families shared personal examples of the "authoritarian parent" and the "tyrannical child" as methods of resolving conflicts. Parents and adolescents alike expressed feelings of resentment and anger at these methods of solving problems as well as their ways of "getting even."

As an alternative, the leaders presented a democratic approach to conflict resolution. The six steps in this approach, as adapted from Gordon, were described to the group.

1. *Defining the Problem:* This is the most critical phase of effective problem solving. Each person defines his perception of the problem, letting the others know what is problematic to him and how it is making him feel. Each needs to listen to the other's perceptions and feelings of the problem. Several attempts at clarifying both one's own and the other's definition may be necessary, with the aim to come to an agreement that *this* is the problem which we are going to solve, with a solution that is *mutually* acceptable. This phase also includes trying to understand why the conflict exists, what the factors are that are maintaining the problem in its present state.

2. *Brainstorming:* Everyone involved raises possible solutions, strictly avoiding any evaluation of solutions at this time. As many solutions as possible are generated.

3. *Evaluating:* At this stage, each person must be honest about which solutions he really and truly does find acceptable, and which will not meet his needs. Children will frequently need to be encouraged to share their evaluations and will need to be listened to with honest respect for their feelings about the possible solution. New solutions may be generated at this point, building on the acceptable parts of several earlier solutions.

4. *Deciding:* If problem solving is to result in *all* feeling that their needs are met by the solution, the decision must be by consensus. As one solution begins to emerge as superior, it helps to clearly restate it, and check again whether it satisfies each person's need, or can be modified to do so.

5. *Establishing Procedures:* Having agreed on a solution, the details of who will do what and when need to be spelled out, so no misunderstanding occurs. Having each member state what he will do to carry out the solution is helpful.

6. *Follow-up:* It is easier to reach a decision and carry it out when some agreement about when and how its effectiveness will be evaluated is agreed upon. Not all solutions will work, and a return to problem solving is needed when any party to the solution has further problems with it. Knowing that modifications can and will be made as new problems develop is an important part of the process, one which needs to be emphasized, and for which time must be set aside.

We explained to the group that this approach to problem solving could be used by two people at any time or by the entire family at family meetings. It was suggested as a means of making family meetings fairer. Because the participants had already begun to look for more equitable ways of resolving conflicts as a result of their experience with family meetings, there was less resistance to this method than I have found in my previous work with families. It should be noted that learning this method of problem solving was tied to the first two phases of the course. The first step toward solving problems democratically—defining the problem—relies heavily on listening and sending clear messages of confrontation, which is the focus of the first phase of the course.

In small groups the participants practiced resolving conflicts supplied by the leaders and, later, examples from their own lives. Sometimes positions were reversed, with the adolescent playing the parent and vice versa, in an attempt to enhance empathy. Over the next few weeks this approach to conflict resolution was incorporated into the family meetings. The more family members were able to trust each other to be considerate of their needs, the more comfortable they became with the method. Participants began reporting a decrease in the number of angry conflicts and unresolved battles at home, accompanied by an increased willingness to cooperate.

Phase Four: Dissension over Differences in Values

Although conflicts over values between parents and children had come up repeatedly throughout the workshop, they were the main subject of the last three classes. Friction in this area affected patterns of family communications, the rules that were made, and the way conflicts were resolved—in other words, the focus of the first three phases of the workshop. Consequently, it was critical that the course address the issue of values. Furthermore, as Kohlberg stated, "values clarification is a very useful component of moral education."[20] Discussions involving disagreements over values can help to stimulate moral thinking. If such discussions are sustained over a significant period of time and range of issues, they can provide cognitive conflict and opportunities for role taking, two of the most powerful ways of stimulating moral development.

As a beginning, each participant was asked to rank a list of values both for himself and for the other members of his family. Participants were then grouped by family and asked to share their perceptions of each other's values. In the resulting discussion, most parents were surprised (some were horrified) to learn what values their children imagined were most important to them. For example, many of the adolescents believed that their parents placed the highest value on such traits as politeness, obedience, and cleanliness. The parents, however, ranked broad-mindedness, love, and forgiveness as being most important to them. What might be responsible for this discrepancy was discussed. This exercise led to much interaction at home with family members disagreeing over the relative importance of certain values.

This segment of the course also included discussions of ways of handling conflicting values in the family and of moral dilemmas involving individual family members. Among the conflicting values were boys' long hair, girls' short skirts, drugs, choice of friends, political beliefs, and church attendance. We pointed out that the six-step method of resolving conflict would not be applicable here because people are usually unwilling to negotiate behaviors based on firmly held personal beliefs. We shared with the group the following ways suggested by Gordon[21] for parents to handle conflicting values: practice the desired behavior (if you value saving money, save money); encourage open discussions between parent and child concerning their differences and the reasons for them; and modify your own beliefs or personal tastes. The discussion that followed was emotionally charged. The notion that it may be risky or inadvisable to attempt to maintain control in the area of values came as a shock to some parents and a relief to others.

The group had a lively discussion of personal moral dilemmas. The following examples show the kinds of moral issues that were raised.

B (adolescent): One day in class I discovered that a good friend of mine was cheating on his math test. I confronted him about it after class, and he just laughed. He says that everyone does it. Well, I haven't so far, but math is real hard for me. And I sure need higher grades if I'm going to get into college.

K (parent): M's situation reminds me of the time I found out my boss was fudging on the business accounts. It didn't affect me directly, but it really bothered me. I had just gotten this job and was afraid of losing it. I just didn't know what to do.

D (adolescent): My best friend, G, is having this huge fight with her parents. They told her she can't date M anymore. They're really in love, and her parents are worried that something will happen. Besides, they don't like him anyway—he's not from the right family. She's seriously thinking of running away with him. What really gets her is they don't say anything to her brother who is going with someone.

The leaders focused the debate on the moral issues and encouraged interaction between the participants. For example, in the last dilemma, we raised such questions as: Do G's parents have the right to forbid her from dating M? Should G obey or disobey her parents? Why do you think the parents are reacting differently to her brother's going steady, and is that fair? Should G run away from home or not? What should G's friend do in this situation? What kind of authority, if any, do parents have over their children's lives? We asked participants why they thought the way they did about moral issues, requiring them to examine their own thinking. The teenagers, in particular, were encouraged to put themselves in the place of participants in the dilemma and to examine the way they would react. Members of the group seemed to feel free to challenge each other's perspectives.

Several members had a heated discussion of drinking while under age. The daughter in the M family faced a double dilemma: whether or not to drink at parties and what to tell her parents. Her friends pressured her to "join in," and she personally felt she could handle the amount of liquor she would drink. She knew her parents were terrified of her drinking, however, because alcoholism had been and still was a serious problem in their own families.

B (adolescent): I think you should do what you think is best for you. You can handle the liquor; besides, other kids make fun if you don't.

M (adolescent): I think you should do what your parents say unless you can convince them to change their minds. After all, they expect you not to drink and you have to realize what they've been through.

D (adolescent): I disagree. Kids are growing up faster today than ever before. Respecting oneself and one's own decisions is emphasized more than parents or others. Some kids are more mature.

L (parent): This thing has gotten away from the fact that it's against the law to drink under eighteen. Where does respect start if not with respecting the law? It was nice that D asked permission of her parents to drink at the prom, but if she had full respect for the law she wouldn't need to ask.

It was difficult at times to keep the discussion focused on the moral issues involved. The levels of moral reasoning present in the adolescents seemed to range from Kohlberg's Stage 2 to Stage 4½. All in all, this class was one of the liveliest of the entire workshop. Families were interested during this phase, as they were throughout the course, to continue at home this kind of open discussion about moral conflicts.

Evaluation of the Course

Three effects of the course were evaluated: the parents' attitudes toward family decision making and child raising; the families' actual decision making; and the adolescents' moral reasoning.

According to an inventory developed by me, parents in both groups significantly increased their egalitarian attitudes toward family decision making. A modified version of the Parental Attitude Research Instrument indicated that parents in both of the experimental groups became less authoritarian in their child-raising attitudes, but the changes were significant for parents in the class for parents only.

The second effect—actual family decision making—was studied by the Ferreira and Winter Questionnaire for Unrevealed Differences. Families in both groups substantially improved their effectiveness in democratic decision making. In other words, there was a significant increase in their ability to make decisions based on considerations of the greatest good for the greatest number. An analysis of the tape recordings of the family meetings led to the same conclusion. By the end of the course, parents in both groups had measurably decreased the amount of time they spent talking in proportion to the total time of the meeting, thus allowing more participation by the children. Parents in both experimental groups showed a marked improvement in eliciting feelings and opinions from their children. Only among parents in the class for parents and adolescents was there a significant decrease in the number of authoritarian statements they made. At the same time, these parents increased their reflective and summarizing responses during family meetings. Journals kept by the participants throughout the course provided further support for these results. They revealed enhanced communication, greater effectiveness in solving problems, and increasingly egalitarian family relationships.

The third effect of the course was upon the moral development of the adolescent participants as measured by the Kohlberg moral judgment interview. The gain in levels of moral reasoning by the adolescents who participated with their parents in the course (Group A) was significant. This was not the case for those in Group B whose parents participated alone in the training. The Kohlberg measure was given a year later as a follow-up. The moral reasoning scores of Group A continued to rise while Group B showed no significant change.[22]

Conclusion

The results of this study indicate that the course was effective in teaching families ways of becoming more just in their methods of establishing rules and resolving conflicts. Participants made real progress, as evidenced by significant changes in both attitudes and behavior, toward making contracts or agreements that involved equal consideration of all points of view.

Why did these changes occur? The most obvious answer is that the curriculum stimulated their learning. A more difficult question centers on which aspects of the course account for the changes. Careful reflection suggests some tentative answers.

Most families came to the workshop with some dissatisfaction with their previous methods of discipline and the quality of the family interaction, and yet they were skeptical that things could really be different. All but one family were willing to try a new approach. The experience of creating rules for the family and solving conflicts collectively gave the children the opportunity to be responsible, respected, and competent individuals with significant contributions to make. Once this process began to occur, most of the parents saw that the children were not going to abuse their increased power. This enabled the parents gradually to relinquish their tight control and to begin to share the decision making. The family meetings allowed the children to assert themselves as responsible members and both parents and children to work to revise the rules of the system to make it more just. Thus it would seem that the teaching of the family meeting and the model for conflict resolution were most crucial to change.

Not only is the content of the curriculum significant when one is considering the findings of this study, but its method is as well. The curriculum was experiential and interactive; furthermore, it dealt with the real problems of the participants. In contrast to many education programs for parents, which are basically lecture and discussion in format, this curriculum focused on the development of skills. The "supervised practicum" nature of the course seemed to be vital to the participants' growth. As Carkhuff[23] has suggested, people learn best what they practice most. Many families learned from practicing at home and listening to the tape recordings of their family meetings as well as from practicing new skills during the workshop sessions.

A major finding was that the course significantly affected both experimental groups, but in different ways. The class that included both parents and adolescents was more effective in changing parental behavior while the class of parents alone had more of an impact on parental attitudes. The first group of parents were more successful than the second in modifying their ways of responding to their children. This group had opportunities to practice with their adolescents the family meeting and skills of conflict resolution under direct supervision. The second group had no such opportunity; interacting with other adults who were playing the roles of adolescents was apparently not the same as attempting to solve conflicts directly with one's own children. The actual parent-adolescent interaction and supervised practice of skills may have been essential to bring about certain changes in the family's behavior.

There are several possible explanations for the finding that only the second group of parents changed significantly in their authoritarian attitudes. First, there was more time for them to discuss concerns since their group was smaller in size. Second, these parents were perhaps more willing and able to look honestly and critically at their own attitudes and behavior because their children were not present in the workshop. Finally, the socioeconomic background of the two groups was different. Those in the second group were better educated and thus may have been quicker to answer the questionnaire in the socially desirable manner.

The results also indicated that the course affected the moral development of the adolescents who participated directly in it. Despite the short duration of the curriculum and its lack of direct focus on moral dilemmas, four of the seven adolescents in Group A had made substantial gains in their levels of moral reasoning by the end of the ten weeks. We hypothesized that if the families continued to practice what they had learned during the course, the adolescents would show further change by the time of follow-up testing. This is in fact what happened. In Group A, all but one subject (whose score remained the same) showed gains in their moral reasoning scores. All five of these families were still holding family meetings by the time of the follow-up whereas only two families in Group B continued to conduct regular meetings throughout the year. Thus, the family meeting and the increased use of democratic problem solving may have provided the children with open discussions of conflicts and a greater sharing in the family's decision-making process.

Several limitations of the study need to be mentioned. All participants were volunteers who opted for the experience and therefore may have been predisposed to change. In addition, the size of the sample and the lack of randomization hinder the degree to which the results of the study can be generalized. Also, since the experimenter was also one of the group leaders, there was no control over possible bias on the part of the experimenter. The ideal situation is for the investigator to train others to conduct the groups. Finally, the democratic model of conflict resolution may not be a culturally fair technique for resolving family problems.

That is, the procedure may need to be modified when used with particular socioeconomic and ethnic groups.

Despite these limitations, the implications of the study for counselors and workers in mental health are clear. Educational programs for parents can have a powerful effect on both the attitudes and behavior of parents. Furthermore, more effective communication and resolution of conflicts in families may result if parents and adolescents participate jointly in a group experience. In addition, these families may be more likely to continue using the skills they have learned than those families where parents alone participate in the training. Finally, such family education programs can provide vital opportunities for stimulating the moral development of adolescents.

Notes

1. N. Gaylin, "The Family Is Dead—Long Live the Family," *Youth and Society,* 3 (September 1971), 66-67.

2. A. S. Skolnick and J. H. Skolnick, *Family in Transition* (Boston: Little, Brown, 1971), 29.

3. U. Bronfenbrenner, "The Split-Level American Family," *Saturday Review,* October 7, 1967, 60-66.

4. L. Kohlberg and E. Turiel, "Moral Development and Moral Education," in *Psychology and Educational Practice,* ed. G. S. Lesser (Glenview, Ill.: Scott, Foresman, 1971).

5. M. L. Hoffman, "Childrearing Practices and Moral Development: Generalization from Empirical Research," *Child Development,* 34 (No. 2, 1963), 295-318; A. Bandura and R. H. Walters, *Social Learning and Personality Development* (New York: Holt, Rinehart and Winston, 1963).

6. M. L. Hoffman and H. D. Saltzstein, "Parent Discipline and the Child's Moral Development," *Journal of Personality and Social Psychology,* 5 (No. 1, 1967), 45-57; P. G. Shoffeitt, "The Moral Development of Children as a Function of Parental Moral Judgments and Childrearing Practices," doctoral dissertation, George Peabody College for Teachers, 1971.

7. C. Holstein, "Parental Determinants of the Development of Moral Judgment," doctoral dissertation, University of California, Berkeley, 1969; R. Peck and R. Havighurst, *The Psychology of Character Development* (New York: John Wiley, 1960).

8. J. Rawls, *A Theory of Justice* (Cambridge, Mass.: Harvard University Press, 1971).

9. L. Kohlberg, P. Scharf, and J. Hickey, "The Justice Structure of the Prison: A Theory and Intervention," *Prison Journal,* 51 (No. 1, 1972), 3-14.

10. *Ibid.,* 4.

11. R. Dreikurs *et al., Adlerian Family Counseling* (Eugene: University of Oregon Press, 1959).

12. T. Gordon, *Parent Effectiveness Training* (New York: Peter Wyden, 1970).

13. R. C. Dowell, "Adolescents as Peer Counselors: A Program for Psychological Growth," doctoral dissertation, Harvard University, 1971.

14. R. Carkhuff, "Training as a Preferred Mode of Treatment," *Journal of Counseling Psychology*, 18 (March 1971), 123-131; Gordon, *Parent Effectiveness Training*.

15. Gordon, *Parent Effectiveness Training*.

16. B. Peterson, "Parent Effectiveness Training," *School Counselor*, 16 (No. 5, 1969), 367-369.

17. D. Dinkmeyer and G. D. McKay, *Raising a Responsible Child* (New York: Simon and Schuster, 1973).

18. R. Dreikurs, S. Gould, and R. Corsini, *The Family Council* (Chicago: Henry Regnery, 1974).

19. Gordon, *Parent Effectiveness Training*.

20. L. Kohlberg, in F. Gray, "Doing Something about Values," *Learning*, 1 (December 1972), 19.

21. Gordon, *Parent Effectiveness Training*.

22. A more thorough discussion of the instruments and results can be found in S. Stanley, "Family Education: A Means of Enhancing the Moral Atmosphere of the Family and the Moral Development of Adolescents," *Journal of Counseling Psychology*, 25 (March 1978), 110-118.

23. Carkhuff, "Training as a Preferred Mode of Treatment."

12
The School and Its Effect
on Students' Development

Improving the Winery

It is my belief that a serious concern for the all-around development of students in the American high school would lead to substantially more than development through the disciplines and the addition of new courses to the curriculum. The high school itself, as an institution, profoundly influences the professional development of its staff and the personal development of its students. It does that in countless direct and covert ways—by its very size; by its management, which may be bureaucratic, authoritarian, or simply "businesslike"; by its rules and discipline; by its standardization of, or success in, individualizing the curriculum and teaching; by its "hidden" curriculum; by its schedules; by its examination and evaluation of students; by the way it treats athletes, girls, minority students, those who do well academically; and, more than anything else, by its assertion of what is most important for students to know and to be.

John Dewey long ago stated that the acid test of social institutions in a democracy is "the contribution they make to the all-around growth of every member of society."[1] The point is clear: the schools educate both for and against development. Perhaps their effects on students' growth are more negative than positive, certainly far more so than they need be. It is necessary to understand how the ecology of schools produces or inhibits growth and then to determine practicable ways to change the school as an institution.

Chapter 12 contains three pieces that address the issue of the school as an organization, the way it affects students' development, and the means by which it might be changed. Sarason, in "The Teacher: Constitutional Issues in the Classroom," contends that an unwritten constitution determines what students may and should do in the class and the disciplinary

464

code.[2] This constitution is decided by teachers without any consultation with students. It typically reflects unexamined assumptions the teacher has about what children are capable of doing and learning. For example, "teacher knows best [and] children cannot participate constructively in the development of a classroom constitution."[3] These are only one set of assumptions and classroom practices from among a number of possible alternatives. And yet they are surprisingly unyielding. To change the teacher's behavior, one has to change these assumptions. Blocher, in "Toward an Ecology of Student Development," argues that we need to understand the characteristics of classrooms as learning environments that contribute to students' growth and that, further, specially trained developmental educators will be necessary to implement such a total environmental approach to students' growth.[4] Mosher's contribution, "A Democratic High School: Damn It, Your Feet Are Always in the Water," describes an alternative high school where the students have a significant voice and vote in the school's governance.[5] The effects of that experience on their moral, social, and political development are considered.

Funny Things Happen on the Way to Stage Five

It may be helpful to consider two related questions by way of introduction: What is school democracy? Why is it desirable? If students' development is a complex process to understand and promote, school democracy may be even more so. In the introduction to Chapter 8 we said that democracy is necessary for an institution to ensure optimal human development, and, if it did not exist, we would have to invent it. Among the reasons why democracy is essential for development are its commitment to promoting the common good, utilitarianism, social justice, and the individual's participation in deciding the policies under which he will live and a moral obligation to enhance human rights, dignity, and self-fulfillment. But what is meant by school democracy?

In one sense, the term is a cliché, considered as American as apple pie. But when democracy is seriously regarded as an idea or as part of the organization and practice of schooling, it assumes remarkable complexity. Interest in school and classroom democracy is experiencing a modest contemporary revival, often as a part of moral or citizenship education. Newmann's piece in Chapter 11 and three excerpts in this chapter describe some of that renaissance. It is difficult, incidentally, to imagine a more challenging or central question than how the schools can educate for democracy by themselves being democratic institutions.

To what extent can schools be democratic, and what are their inherent limits? Peters[6] discusses some factors that limit the democratization of the school. They include the particular purpose of educational institutions, which, he believes, is the development in people of specialized forms of knowledge on which there are provisional authorities—teachers, and the principle of academic freedom by which teachers pursue teaching, research, and the truth subject only to canons of evidence and argument. In concrete terms that means teachers should have the major say concerning the issues on which they are specialists: the type of research to be done, what should be taught, the selection of faculty, and the evaluation of students. Other limits to be discussed in this chapter are the students' different levels of understanding of democracy, governance, rights, rules, and obligations and their ability to act on these understandings; analogous limits in teachers' and administrators' understanding and practice of school democracy; the direct and hidden constitution and governance of the high school, already alluded to at the beginning of this introduction; the kind of democracy practiced by the adult community in which the school is located (for example, South Boston, Massachusetts, Grosse Pointe, Michigan, and San Clemente, California) are not alike in their understanding of democracy.

Peters also discusses issues included in school democracy, and the list is heartening: for example, teaching methods, budgets, school buildings, general policy, subjects to be taught, the question of whether the school should be comprehensive, the hiring of additional counselors, athletic budgets, clubs, out-of-school recreational programs and facilities, discipline and school rules. "The teacher of physics is little more qualified than a senior on the ethics of punishment or sexual relationships."[7] There is, then, significant philosophical scope for rationalizing authority in schools and for dispersing power and responsibility to those affected by it—the faculty and the students. But how, beyond this criterion, would we recognize a democratic school? What characteristics would convince us to let our children attend one?

This most critical issue of defining a democratic classroom or school can begin with a discussion of what school democracy is not. It is not student government in the colloquial sense, that is, the election of student council representatives to what is too often a company union. Nor is the political notion of democracy the primary idea; it is not anticipated that a children's parliament will run the school. Permissiveness—the abdication by teachers of the responsibility to argue the true, the good, the right, the obligatory, and the consequences of one's choices and actions as they understand these verities—is, most emphatically, not what is. meant. An adolescent, the editor of his high school newspaper, was recently overheard to say on the telephone: "Democracy? Democracy is anarchy!" That is another possible misunderstanding of democracy.

What then do we mean by school democracy? The contributions in this chapter suggest at least three distinguishing characteristics. First, there is a systematic effort to make more rational, considered, and fair the governance of our classrooms and schools. Governance refers to how decisions are made in school; how the authority of educators and teachers is thought through and explained to students, if at all; with whom it is shared—other teachers, the good, achieving students, the socially privileged students, poor students, "bad" students, all students—and with what degree of openness. Sarason[8] and Reimer[9] have called this the unwritten constitution of the classroom, a formidable phrase. And yet it refers, in practice, to decisions as pedestrian and vital as how rules about cheating or stealing become established; who gets called on in reading groups and who does not; who is confronted and punished for cutting class; to what extent students are held responsible for lost personal or school property and for making changes in their schedules. These are the tacit rules that make a classroom work on a minute-to-minute basis. Reimer argues that "the closer the teacher gets to this nitty-gritty the closer she gets to the heart of what classroom democracy is."[10]

I recall a vociferous dispute between two colleagues over office space. One claimed both authority and the space in question on the basis of external funding and prior understandings with an administrator; the other claimed equity in space as a faculty peer. The department chairman called for a thorough airing of all the relevant claims in this classic example of academic nitty-gritty. (Because of the propensities of professors, the debate may still be going on.) The point is that, however petty the issue, it is possible to make any process immediately more democratic. One brings the problem to the surface, discusses it fully and openly with the affected parties, and tries to resolve it fairly. School or classroom democracy does not have to wait for George III, the Intolerable Acts, Philadelphia, and the Founding Fathers to appear in sixth- or eleventh-grade American history. It can begin with the most trivial and mundane events in the classroom, the school, or the family. To understand democracy in this way may not make its practice or realization any easier, but, at least, it makes an essential part of the democratic process commonplace and immediately accessible to teachers and children rather than its being the remote imperial drama of London or Washington. Thus, a school's governance may be considered democratic to the extent that it is rationalized and thought about openly by teachers and students and that the reasoning that determines whether the teachers' authority is shared or retained is debated by all those affected.

The second characteristic of democracy is that it is popularly understood to be the American way of life. In schools or classrooms this means that students must live their institutional and social lives together in distinctive ways. In the first place, they need to share many common purposes and activities, both academic and extracurricular. By so doing they learn to cooperate with one another. Developing social skills and commitment requires a long apprenticeship. Selman has stressed that children behave themselves into more complex social understanding and that practice in social relations contributes to the growth of what he and Mead call the core of human intelligence[11] —that is, understanding other people. By sharing diverse activities—a seminar in peer counseling, social action in the community, mountain climbing, a school musical, basketball, jogging, a literature class, membership on a school hiring committee—adolescents hear and begin to understand the feelings and point of view of others, friends and especially strangers. They learn how and why others think differently and come to consider their claims and rights as individuals. The danger is social exclusiveness—that they will share only with peers and friends. Good fences do not good democrats make. Close friendships and cliques are typical of adolescent society; the educator's task is to open the doors to free intercourse with people of other races, religions, ages, and classes.

A closely related objective of democracy as a way of living together in schools or classrooms is a slow increase in adolescents' understanding of the meaning of "the common good," what it takes to effect it, and a realization of who is included in that democracy. Many adults know from experience in cooperation and in working together that the social whole can be greater than the sum of its individual parts. The individual's purpose and often his advantage are realized through a group, which carries with it certain obligations. The side of democracy that concerns freedom and advantages for the individual is popular, while the obligation to give to others is not. But the participation in power, rights, and responsibility by all members is essential in democracy. And democratic schools have to provide both the model and the opportunities for students to learn this.

The American dilemma, particularly for its adolescents, is not that the Constitution and the republic were born with a congenital defect—slavery. It is, rather, that our birthright commits us both to responsibility to our neighbors and a communitarian ethic and also to rugged individualism, competition, getting ahead, and making a success of oneself. These compelling cultural values are often in conflict, whether in a third-grade classroom or an alternative high school where decisions on college admissions are imminent. Does and should self come before society, should society come before self, or should it be self and society? In a democratic society such as the United States the answer is "yes" to both self and society. They are mutually interdependent. Dewey has been quoted several times on this point: "A society of free individuals in which all through their own work, contribute to the liberation and enrichment of the lives of others, is the only environment in which any individual can really grow normally to his full stature."[12] The need for schools that emphasize both cooperation and the institutionalization of norms as well as self-development is especially important for adolescents. Individuation is the basic psychological and cultural expectation of American teenagers.

A further complication for the adolescent is that the process of becoming both an individual and social democrat has to be accomplished against the pull of a strong preconscious undertow. Erikson has described how hard it is for adolescents to live on both horns of the American dilemma:

they become remarkably clannish, intolerant, and cruel in their exclusion of others who are "different," in skin color or cultural background, in tastes and gifts . . . . It is important to understand (which does not mean condone or participate in) such intolerance as the necessary *defense against a sense of identity diffusion*, which is unavoidable at [this] time of life . . . . Adolescents help one another temporarily through such discomfort by forming cliques and by stereotyping themselves, their ideals, and their enemies . . . . this . . . makes clear the appeal which simple and cruel totalitarian doctrines have on the minds of youth of [other] countries and classes as have lost . . . their group identities . . . .[13]

Further, "Democracy in a country like America poses special problems in that it insists on *self-made identities* ready to grasp many chances . . . . Our democracy, furthermore, must present the adolescent with ideals which can be shared by youths of many backgrounds and which emphasize autonomy in the form of independence and initiative in the form of enterprise . . . . This is hard on many young Americans because their whole upbringing, and therefore the development of a healthy personality, depends on a certain degree of *choice*, a certain hope for an individual *chance*, and a certain conviction in freedom of *self-determination*."[14][1]

Erikson's point is clear, important but not preemptive. Adolescents exhibit undemocratic behavior—prejudice, intolerance, and stereotyping based on color, religion, ethnicity, and social class—because of the reassurance such characteristics of totalitarianism offer an insecure, partly formed sense of self. And this militates against the school's efforts to democratize its social relations. Educators simply have to try harder, to be more conscious and systematic in creating the social conditions of democracy. For there is no question of the profoundly educative effects of the social institutions in which we live. Rather than permit the curriculum in our schools to be hidden and inimical to both the development and the promotion of democracy, we must create classrooms that teach democracy by being democratic.

A related objective of a democratic classroom is that it should provide opportunities for students to learn to care about each other. If adolescents are given the opportunities, whether they be clubs, advisory groups, peer counseling courses, a telephone, or a school yard and a Frisbee, they will respond. Adolescents are probably the most naturally tribal people in our society, and even if their horizon is too frequently the clique, they are impelled, however awkwardly and self-consciously, to identify with and care for their friends. This is a conscious counterbalance to the preconscious undertow discussed above. They are engaged in more important activities than discussion of rock groups, boys, and athletics. Enhanced perspective taking, empathy, social cognition, and progress toward and understanding of social cooperation and interconnectedness underlie the surface content. Their natural community is their peer group. If the schools deny the opportunity to learn to care for others in such groups—by authority, repression, the size of classes or the school itself, or idolatry of the academic—they deny democracy itself.

A final criterion of a democratic classroom or school is the extent to which it individualizes its students' instruction. Much of the argument here has already been anticipated. Students in democratic schools must have, as much as is humanly possible, equal opportunities for all-around development. That does not mean that all students are considered to have equal capacity or that their achievement must be equal. Morality and education cannot alter variability in and among people. But a democratic school understands that children are ends, not means, and that they have an inalienable right to an equal chance for full development. That means, in practice, that there must be a careful assessment of where the individual student is relative to the various contents and skills that are to be learned and that his instruction should begin there. Curriculum and teaching are adapted to the individual: the learner is the hard factor in the equation; the subject matter is the soft factor. Individualizing assessment, curricula, and teaching is extended to all aspects of the students' academic and nonacademic growth. The reader will recognize this as but another restatement of a central educational philosophy of this book. Thus, the model for the organization of curriculum and teaching and the governance and the social character of the democratic classroom and school is based on the belief that democratic institutions have as one of their central purposes and effects the all-around development of their members. Education that is impersonal, authoritarian, and bureaucratized and does not disperse educational opportunities and resources equitably is untrue to this final democratic criterion.

One point should be made in conclusion. It is not coincidental that Newmann's curriculum for teaching civic and democratic competence by the actual exercise of influence on public affairs and Stanley's efforts to "democratize" the adolescent's family are presented in concert with Chapter 11. They illustrate in how many ways and institutions the twin cause of strengthening democracy and individual development must be advanced.

Notes

1. J. Dewey, *Reconstruction in Philosophy* (New York: New American Library, 1950), 147.

2. Seymour B. Sarason, *The Culture of the School and the Problem of Change* (Boston: Allyn and Bacon, 1971).

3. *Ibid.,* 176.

4. D. H. Blocher, "Toward an Ecology of Student Development," *Personnel and Guidance Journal,* 52 (February 1974), 361-365.

5. R. L. Mosher, "A Democratic High School: Damn It, Your Feet Are Always in the Water," *Character Potential: A Record of Research,* 8 (No. 4, 1978), 196-217, reprinted in *Value Development as the Aim of Education*, ed. N. A. Sprinthall and R. L. Mosher (Schenectady, N. Y.: Character Research Press, 1978), 69-116.

6. R. S. Peters, *Authority, Responsibility and Education*, rev. ed. (London: George Allen and Unwin, 1973).

7. *Ibid.,* 51.

8. Sarason, *The Culture of the School and the Problem of Change.*

9. Joseph Reimer, "Democratic Schools I Have Known," in *Moral Education: Three Years Before the Mast*, ed. R. L. Mosher (Brookline, Mass.: Brookline Dissemination Center, forthcoming).

10. J. Reimer, "School Democracy," unpublished lecture, Brookline, Massachusetts, Teacher Center, February 1978.

11. R. Selman, "A Structural-Developmental Model of Social Cognition; Implications for Intervention Research," *Counseling Psychologist*, 6 (No. 4, 1977); and G. H. Mead, *Mind, Self and Society* (Chicago: University of Chicago Press, 1934).

12. J. Dewey, "The Need for a Philosophy of Education," in *John Dewey on Education: Selected Writings*, ed. D. Archambault (New York: Random House, 1964), 12.

13. E. Erikson, "Growth and Crises of the Healthy Personality," in *Identity and the Life Cycle* (New York: Psychological Issues, Vol. 1, No. 1, Monograph 1, International Universities Press, 1959), 92.

14. *Ibid.,* 93.

The Teacher: Constitutional Issues in the Classroom

Seymour B. Sarason

[Previously] our primary aim was to convey how in the modal school certain internal and external forces, extending over time, are experienced by and influence the modal teacher. [Here] our focus will shift to what teachers think and do in regard to a number of specific and predictable events or issues that arise in any classroom. We can consider only a few of these events or issues, and they have been deliberately chosen to illustrate the general and obvious point that life in the classroom is a function of what and how teachers think about children, and how such thinking reflects the teacher's conception of his role. In a real sense this [piece] is concerned with the teacher's "theories" of human behavior and group living. As we shall see, it is only when these theories are made explicit, and are seen in contrast to alternative conceptions, that we get a deeper understanding of certain behavioral regularities in the culture of the school. Let us not forget that the existence and pervasiveness of a behavioral regularity are two of the best indicators of a covert regularity involving the relationships between thinking and conceptualization, on the one hand, and a scale of values (what is good and what is bad), on the other hand.

Constitutional Issues

Almost all teachers meet a new group of pupils on the first day of school. The beginning phase of the school year certainly extends beyond the first day, but by the third or fourth week a routine is established, and teacher and pupils have, so to speak, sized up each other; the rules of the game by which everyone will be governed are fairly well known. How does this come about? How do teachers present and explain these rules of group living? Are these rules discussed? Are they for children only? What role do pupils play, if any, in the formation of rules? These questions and others comprise what I like to call the constitutional question because in each classroom there is a constitution, verbalized or unverbalized, consistent or inconsistent, capable or incapable of amendment, that governs behavior. Constitutions tell us a good deal about history, tradition, and conceptions of human behavior.

From Seymour B. Sarason, *The Culture of the School and the Problem of Change.*
© 1971 by Allyn and Bacon, Inc., Boston. Reprinted with permission.

We did an informal observation study of six classrooms, two each in grades three, four, and five in a suburban school system. In each of these six classrooms we had an observer who sat in the classroom for the first month of school beginning the first day. The task of the observer was to record any statement by teacher and child that was relevant to "constitutional issues." The results were quite clear:

1. The constitution was invariably determined by the teacher. No teacher ever discussed why a constitution was necessary.

2. The teacher never solicited the opinions and feelings of any pupil about a constitutional question.

3. In three of the classrooms the rules of the game were verbalized by the end of the first week of school. In two others the rules were clear by the end of the month. In one it was never clear what the constitution was.

4. Except for the one chaotic classroom neither children nor teachers evidenced any discomfort with the content of constitutions—it was as if everyone agreed that this is the way things are and should be.

5. In all instances constitutional issues involved what *children* could or could not, should or should not, do. The issue of what a *teacher* could or could not, should or should not do, never arose.

On a number of occasions I have presented these findings to groups of teachers with the question: How do we explain them? In every group the question produced silence. In one group a teacher responded in a way that I think verbalized what most teachers were thinking: *What* is there to explain? I would then follow my initial question with another question: What do we have to assume to be true about children and teachers in order to justify these findings? These discussions were by no means easy or pleasant, and understandably so, if only because the teachers had never been called upon to make explicit the conceptions and values upon which these practices were based. But what were some of the assumptions that teachers could, after prolonged discussion, recognize and state?

1. Teacher knows best.

2. Children cannot participate constructively in the development of a classroom constitution.

3. Children want and expect the teacher to determine the rules of the game.

4. Children are not interested in constitutional issues.

5. Children should be governed by what a teacher thinks is right or wrong, but a teacher should not be governed by what children think is right or wrong.

6. The ethics of adults are obviously different from and superior to the ethics of children.

7. Children should not be given responsibility for something they cannot handle or for which they are not accountable.

8. If constitutional issues were handled differently, chaos might result.

If one does not make these assumptions, which is to say that one thinks differently about what children are and can do, one is very likely to think differently about what the role of the teacher might be. In this connection it is instructive to note that as I pursued the issues with the groups of teachers, and the assumptions could be clearly verbalized, *many of the teachers found themselves disagreeing with assumptions they themselves recognized as underlying their classroom behavior.* Equally as instructive was the awareness on the part of a few that if one changed one's assumptions one would have to change the character of one's role, and this was strange and upsetting, as indeed it should be because they realized that life in the classroom for them and the children would become different.

The problem we are discussing goes beyond the classroom and its generality hit me with full force during one of these discussions with teachers. That it hit me with such force in this particular group was in part due to the fact that several of the teachers were quite adamant in maintaining that young children had to have their lives structured for them by adults because they were too immature to participate in and take responsibility for important decisions governing classroom life. *What I became aware of during the discussion was that these teachers thought about children in precisely the same way that teachers say that school administrators think about teachers, that is, administrators do not discuss matters with teachers, they do not act as if the opinions of teachers were important, they treat teachers like a bunch of children, and so on.* The rise and militancy of teacher organizations have a complex history, but one of the important factors was the unwillingness of teachers to be governed by a tradition in which they had no part in decisions and plans that affected them. We are witnessing the same development on the part of students in our high schools, junior high schools, and, needless to say, in our colleges. The amending of constitutions has been and will be accompanied by strong conflict for two reasons: there are differences in conception of what people (teachers, students) are, and it is recognized that what is at issue is what life in a school is and could be.

It is not the purpose of this [piece], except in a very secondary way, to say how things should be. The primary purpose is to describe some of the important regularities in the culture of the school and to relate them to the conceptions and theories that "justify" these regularities. In order to do this I have tried, wherever possible, to contrast these existing relationships with the ever-present but neglected universe of alternatives of conceptions from which derives a universe of alternative actions. This tactic not only serves to make one aware how the weight of habit and tradition can obscure the difference between what is and what could be, but it also helps force those who want to introduce changes to be more precise about what it is they want to change. The "constitutional problem" is a case in point. I have known many teachers, principals, and school administrators who pride themselves on their adherence to democratic principles and feel strongly that the needs and rights of children have to be taken into account. In addition, these same people can point to colleagues whom they label as authoritarian or restrictive, with the implication that these characteristics are antieducational in spirit and effect. Without denying in the slightest that these differences exist, I have also to say that, constitutionally speaking, the differences are not all that great; in terms of how and on what basis the classroom constitution is determined, the "democratic" and "authoritarian" teacher are not as far apart as one might think.[1] In both cases I have been impressed by three things: constitutions are for children and not teachers, complete power is retained by the teacher, and children passively accept the constitution developed for them. Those who wish to change life in the classroom are dealing with constitutional issues and not, as is too frequently the case, with high-sounding slogans whose conceptual underpinnings remain unexamined with the usual result that there is a discrepancy between what is said and what is done.[2]

I should remind the reader that in this [piece] we are attempting to understand the relationship between what teachers do (or do not do) and how they think about children and themselves, to understand the "theories" of teachers —not their feelings or values but their conceptions of what people are. And teachers, like the rest of us, have such conceptions, which, again like for the rest of us, are usually implicit rather than explicit. In this connection we now turn to another issue that was the major reason we did our little observational study.

The Student's and Teacher's Conception of Learning

Prior to the observational study, I had, in connection with numerous studies on anxiety in elementary school children,[3] sat in scores of classrooms. It took quite some time for me to become aware that something was missing, and that was discussion in class of why and how people learned. It is obvious enough that however one defines such words as learning, schooling, and education they refer to things or processes that take place in a school. They can and do take place outside of a school, but they are involved in what goes on in a classroom. What do children in a classroom think about the business of learning? Do children have their own theories (as indeed they do) about how and why one learns? Are there discrepancies between the theories children think about and the theories they are asked or required to adopt? Would children like to talk about these matters? Are they able to talk about them? How do teachers explain and discuss their theories of learning and thinking with their students? In short, to what extent were the whys and hows of learning and thinking an explicit focus and subject of discussion in the classroom? My observations left no doubt that how children thought about the processes of learning and thinking rarely came up for scrutiny in the classroom, but I was not as certain that the teacher's theories were as rarely presented and discussed. Therefore, we placed observers in classrooms to study this, and we chose the first month of school on the assumption that it would be during this interval that a teacher was most likely to make her own thinking explicit to the students. The most general instruction given to the observers was to note anything that a teacher said bearing on the whys and hows of learning and thinking. More specifically, they were asked to record anything relevant to the following questions:

1. When a child did not know or could not do something, did the teacher's response in any way attempt to find out how the child had been thinking or how he might think — in contrast, for example, to telling and showing *a* correct procedure?

2. How frequently did a teacher say, "I don't know," and go on to discuss how he would think about going about *knowing*.

3. How frequently and in what ways does a teacher take up and discuss the role of question asking in intellectual inquiry or problem solving?

There were other questions, but I expect from those above that the reader will understand that we were interested in the degree to which such topics as thinking and problem solving were discussed in the classroom. The results were quite clear: such discussions did not take place. Although unverbalized, the ground rules were not difficult to discern. First, the task of the student was to get the right answer and this was more important than how he arrived at the answer. By "more important" I mean simply that the right answer was what teacher and student obviously treasured. Second, for any one problem or question there was a correct way of thinking about and answering it. Third, *thinking was really not a complicated affair.*

There is nothing new or surprising in this. For example, Wertheimer[4] well described, in the case of a geometry class, how the students were taught by their teacher to solve the parallelogram problem. When Wertheimer then tried to get the students to consider alternative ways of solving the problem they were hardly able to grasp the idea that there was more than one way one could think about the problem. When he demonstrated alternative proofs, the students said he was wrong because he did not do it "the right way."[5]

What happens when I take up these observations with teachers? One of the most frequent reactions is similar to what Susskind[6] reports when he presented to his teachers the discrepancy between the number of questions they asked of students and the number students asked of them: distress signifying that perhaps something was wrong. Another reaction is again similar to what only one of Susskind's teachers said, although I obtained it more frequently: "that is the way things should be." In a real sense these teachers were responding in a manner identical to that of Wertheimer's students, who could not accept the idea that there were other ways of thinking. But most instructive of all were those occasions when I could raise these issues with teachers *after* a discussion in which they had critcally examined their experiences as students in their college courses. *What I confronted them with was the startling identity between their complaints as students in college and what their own students might complain about if they could but talk.* Some teachers could immediately see the possible connection. Other teachers could not accept the idea that how they felt could bear resemblance to how their students felt, that is, children did not think about thinking or learning the way teachers did. Leaving aside these reactions, there were two reservations that teachers verbalized. First, there was little or nothing in their training that would enable them to handle the issues in the classrooms. Second, even if they wanted to or could handle them, the demands of curriculum coverage leave little time for such matters.

Life in the classroom can be viewed and understood from different vantage points, but in my opinion, one of the most important ones is that which looks at the implicit theories teachers have about thinking and learning. What I have tried to suggest in this section is that many teachers have two theories: *one that applies to them and one that applies to children.* Put in another way: many teachers are quite aware from their own experiences of the differences in characteristics between dull and exciting conditions of intellectual activity. But their inability to see or assume some kind of identity between their pupils and themselves leads them unwittingly to create those conditions that they would personally find boring. Classroom learning is primarily determined by teachers' perceived differences between children and adults, a fact that makes recognition of communalities almost impossible.

Classroom Seating

In asking how teachers think about and what they do with children in relation to predictable issues or events, we started with what are obviously two important issues: the constitutional question and the teacher's conception of the role of discussion of the whys and hows of inquiry.[7] A recent study by A. Schwebel . . . allows us to pursue the discussion in terms of a question that, on the surface at least, would not seem to be for our present purposes very important or productive. But complex questions tend on examination to remain complex at the same time that simple questions on examination tend to become complex.

Schwebel's study started with his observation, stemming from his work with teachers in their classroom, that children in the back of the room tended to behave differently than those in the front of the room. He did a small preliminary study (using independent observers who did not know the purposes of the study) and found confirmation for his own observations. He then developed a more elaborate study around the question: How are the seating arrangements in a classroom determined and what are their effects? Schwebel summarizes teacher descriptions of their procedures as follows:

From the post-experimental interviews with the participating teachers it was learned that seat assignment procedures as a social-psychological problem is not included in teacher training programs or discussed by elementary school teachers. Nonetheless, the procedures the teachers described using were highly similar, suggesting that they were reacting to common psychological and/or environmental demands. The one demand they spoke of in particular was that of *achieving classroom control.* . . .

The procedure which teachers typically reported using to prevent disruption was to separate those children they had judged as "disruptive" and to assign them to seats in various parts of the room. Most teachers stated that they could identify the "disruptive" children in the first day or two of school. "Good" children were typically seated by the teacher next to those judged as "disruptive." While this suggests that teachers use physical proximity to certain types of children as a control mechanism, it raises the question of why the teachers do not assign several or all of those they judge as disruptive to seats in the front of the room where they as teacher could act as the control agent.[8]

Among his major findings were: "(1) although individual teachers were consistent, as a group they varied with respect to the location in which they assigned pupils whom they judged as attentive, shy or likeable; (2) those children assigned by teachers to the front row are more attentive to classroom activities than their classmates in the middle and back rows; and (3) occupancy of seats in the front, in contrast to those in the middle and back, affects in a positive manner, the way in which pupils are perceived by their teacher and peers, the way in which pupils evaluate themselves, and the way in which they behave." Schwebel also points out, on the basis of his interviews, that "seat assignment procedures as a social psychological problem are not included in teacher training programs or discussed by elementary school teachers." Furthermore, although teachers were aware that they had assigned some "good" and some "bad" pupils to the front, and others to the back, the teachers could not verbalize their reasons. "Either they were less aware of the considerations which they had taken into account in making these decisions or, for one reason or another, they were hesitant to report them."[9]

Why were teachers rather unclear about how they consider seating procedures? Or was it that they were clear in that discipline and control were the primary considerations that governed their thinking and decisions? What complicates answering these questions is what may be Schwebel's most intriguing finding: teachers with a high need to please other people (according to the Marlowe-Crowne Social Desirability Scale) rated pupils who sat in the front of the room more positively than those who sat in the back; teachers with a low need to please others rated pupils in the front of the room less positively than those in the back. These findings suggest that characteristics of teachers may be as important in determining seating (and, therefore, behavior) as characteristics of children.

That a classroom is a social organization is a glimpse of the obvious. What is not so obvious and is suggested by Schwebel's other data from the children is that children seem to be more aware of, or attach more significances to, the social aspects of classroom organization than do teachers. To the extent that the teacher's thinking about seating is oversimple (that is, oriented almost exclusively toward control of disruptive behavior) or determined by his personal needs, *it is almost impossible for him ever to recognize that his pupils view seating differently.* That seating may not be high in the hierarchy of important problems facing a teacher requires no discussion, but this should not obscure the fact that in small as well as large problems two things are decisive: how one formulates the problem and, equally important, how one structures the situation so that the problem can be reformulated on the basis of new information provided by others. The relatively unimportant problem of seating contains within it all the constitutional issues raised earlier.

The Teacher as a Thinking Model

Thus far in this [piece] I have been, in one or another way, raising a descriptive type of question: what and how much do children know about what a teacher thinks? It is inevitable that children will know something about how a teacher thinks, how much depending on the teacher. I have never heard anyone argue that a teacher is not a model for children of how one should think and act. It is not a matter of *should* a teacher be a model but rather that he *is* a model. But the fact that he is a model of a particular kind and degree very definitely involves a variety of "shoulds," such as what children should learn, what a teacher should do, and so on.

The point I wish to emphasize is that it appears that children know relatively little about how a teacher thinks about the classroom, that is, what he takes into account, the alternatives he thinks about, the things that puzzle him about children and about learning, what he does when he is not sure of what he should do, how he feels when he does something wrong—there is quite a bit that goes on in a teacher's head that is never made public to children. Well, someone can ask, are you advocating that teachers act like patients on an analyst's couch and give forth with all that is inside them? Obviously not, in addition to which I am not advocating *anything*. I am merely pointing out that whatever the degree to which teachers make their thinking public inevitably reflects the kind of "thinking model" to which they adhere. Put in another way, it reflects a conception of what is helpful to children. How does one decide what is helpful? For example, if it were true that how a teacher thinks about the classroom is something about which children are curious, is it helpful *not* to satisfy this curiosity? Is there any reason to believe that it is helpful to children to know how a teacher thinks? Unfortunately, we do not have a truly firm foundation for answering the question. However, there is a good deal of anecdotal evidence strongly indicating that the more a teacher can make his own thinking public and subject for discussion—in the same way one expects of children—the more interesting and stimulating does the classroom become for students, and I assume that is a helpful state of affairs. Phillip Booth put it beautifully in a review of a book by the teacher and poet, Mark Van Doren: "His unique genius as a teacher was to speculate publicly; in opening the play of his mind to students, he gave each student a self-assigned role in resolving these questions his teaching dramatized."[10] I would be quite surprised if Professor Van Doren's "unique genius" was not in some measure a reflection of a clear conception of what would be helpful to his students.

The issue I am raising is well illustrated in the research endeavor. If one reads professional research journals, it is easy to gain the impression that research is conducted by rational people in rational, planned ways. In the modal research paper one finds hypotheses that are related to or stem from a theory, defined procedures, results, and then a discussion section in which one explains why things happened as they did. As often as not (probably more often than not) the discussion section is an implicit tribute to the researcher's ability to predict. It is hard for the reader, particularly if he himself is not a researcher, to avoid concluding that research is a cold, cut-and-dried set of logically related cognitive processes in which the personal and subjective are not allowed to intrude. That this is a partially true but horribly misleading model of how a researcher thinks and acts is something that researchers themselves well

know. Graduate students who are being introduced to the research endeavor frequently suffer trauma when it dawns on them that published
research is a most inadequate and incomplete representation of how the
researcher thinks. The public and private model are far from congruent.
*What I have tried to indicate in this section is that the modal teacher in
the modal classroom presents a "model of thinking" to students that is
as unrepresentative of his thinking as a published piece of research is of
its author's thinking.* It may be that the similarity does not end there. I
would venture the opinion that the similarity between teacher and researcher rests, among other factors, on their implicit belief that their audience would not be interested in or would not comprehend a more realistic presentation of their thinking. If my experience with schoolchildren—
in fact, with all levels of students, from elementary through graduate
school—is any guide, that large part of a teacher's "thinking about thinking," which is never made public, is precisely what the children are interested in and excited by on those rare occasions when it becomes public.

The Prepotent Response
to Misbehavior

No discussion of how teachers think can long avoid the problem of
discipline. Particularly in the case of the new teacher, nothing rivals
discipline as a problem[12] Is is interesting to note that in our observational
study of the first month of six classrooms, discipline as a problem in group
living was never discussed. Most teachers made clear what was good and
bad behavior—what the characteristics were of crime in the classroom—
but these were not discussions.

We might begin by asking the following question: what is a teacher's
prepotent response to a child's misbehavior? The answer is rather clear: the
teacher reprimands the child in one way or another, that is she tells him
(many times gently and nonpunitively) that what he is doing is wrong. The
more serious the infraction, or if it involves a child with a notable classroom criminal record, the stronger the teacher's response and the harsher
the punishment. This is all very obvious. What is not so obvious is the
content of the thinking that gives rise to this type of prepotent response.
I say this because when on scores of occasions I have asked teachers to
explain to me the justification for the prepotent response, they have been
puzzled by the question. From their standpoint the answer is obvious and
not necessary to justify: if a child does something wrong, you tell him so
that he will then do the right thing. If I then ask why it does not always
work, the answer is almost always in terms of characteristics of the child.[13]
(The "theory" is correct but the child does not know that!)

One teacher (in a suburban school) had been discussing with me a particularly troublesome boy. I said that I would be back in three days to see how things were going. When I returned the teacher gleefully said, "I am not superstitious but I don't want to say anything. He has been absolutely no problem for the last two days." I then said to the teacher, "Have you told *him* how pleased you are at how well he is doing?" His facial expression was sufficient to tell me that it did not occur to him to reward the child. His theory was explicit about when one punishes, but not about when one rewards. One might say that the principle underlying his thinking was: you let well enough alone until well enough becomes bad enough.

Wherein was the approach to this troublesome boy different from that of the teacher's? Let me paraphrase what I said to this teacher, although this summary should not be viewed as a cookbook recipe:

What you are doing with this boy is not working. We do not know why it is not working and we really don't have the time to find out why. The longer this continues the worse for you and the boy. What about trying this: tomorrow morning before school opens get this kid alone and tell him that you are quite aware that your way of trying to help him in regard to misbehavior is not working. He knows it and you know it. What he may not know is that you are puzzled and bothered. You do not enjoy punishing him, although that may be hard for him to believe. You have two questions to put to him. The first is what ideas does he have about how you can help him. The second is what does he think about this: from this point on when he misbehaves the two of you are going to leave the room and the two of you are going to discuss what had just happened and why, and how it could have been avoided. This does not mean that you are throwing punishment out of the window. You will have to punish, much as you, the two of you, may not like it, but that is less important than figuring out ways in which you can help him avoid trouble and that is what you are most interested in.[14]

It is not easy, nor is it our present task, to explicate the thinking from which the above is or can be derived. That it is different than what underlies the prepotent response is obvious. The reader may have noted that one of the differences reflects the content of the discussion in the previous section, that is, *the teacher makes public what and how he thinks about a problem.* A related difference, of course, is that *one assumes that children are really interested in what goes on in a teacher's head, particularly as that does or will affect children.* There is much more to it than these differences. The important point is that the prepotent response, which is so typical an aspect of life in the classroom, reflects only one way one could think about the problem.[15]

Let me now turn to two related questions I have asked teachers: is there something about children that makes them *completely* unable to participate in discussion and formulation of crime and punishment in the classroom? Please note that I italicized "completely" because I have never seen a classroom (although I am sure they exist) in which children participated in such discussion and formulation—and we are back, of course, to the constitutional issue. The second question: assuming that they are incapable, is it also true that they do not think about or are not concerned about crime and punishment in the classroom? To say they are completely unable is at least unjustified and at worst sheer ignorance of what children do outside of school in their spontaneous play groups. One does not need the support of formal research to assert that children in their relationships to each other have some concept of fairness—one needs only good eyes and ears.

The fact of the matter is that the great bulk of teachers assert (1) that children are not completely unable and (2) that children do think about crime and punishment in the classroom. *Whatever thinking allows teachers to make these positive assertions is not reflected in what they do, or, more specifically, in the justification of the prepotent response.*

There is another way of looking at the prepotent response, and the thinking surrounding it, and that is that it reflects an individual psychology. That is to say, when a teacher thinks about misbehavior he thinks primarily in terms of individual children. When he thinks about action he also tends to think about action in relation to individual children. Although the teacher is quite aware that there is a group of children, this plays far less of a role in his thinking and action than one might think. When we discussed Schwebel's study of seating we saw that teachers arrange seating patterns primarily for purposes of "control," patterns based explicitly on the assumption that one kind of child can influence another kind of child, that is, interrelationships within the group are presumed to be important. By and large, however, teachers do not think in terms of how a group can be organized and utilized so that as a group it plays a role in relation to the issues and problems that confront the group. Since this statement may be misinterpreted, I should be blatantly clear that I am not suggesting that children should run a classroom. All that I intend by that statement is what teachers themselves have asserted to the two questions I put to them. If these assertions were to be taken seriously, it would mean that one would have to think in terms of theories of groups, group processes, the relation of the leader (teacher) to the group, and the role of, as well as the phenomenology of, leadership. This is not to say that one scraps one type of psychology for another. They both have their places. It is the case, however, that in their training teachers have been exposed, almost exclusively, to a psychology of learning that has one past and one present characteristic: the latter is its emphasis on how an individual organism learns, and the former is that the major learning theories were based on studies of the individual Norway rat. If instead of putting one rat in the maze they had put two or more in the maze, the history of American psychology would have been quite different. Conceivably, the social nature of learning might not need to be rediscovered.

To illustrate further what I mean let us take the following problem which a number of first- and second-grade teachers have presented to me. The problem involves what to do about the dependent, crying, anxious, clinging child.[16] In a number of instances and on the basis of my observations in the classroom, I suggested to the teacher that when the child acts in this way she pick him up, cuddle and soothe, reassure him that she would do whatever she could to help, and try to find out about what he was afraid or thinking. A number of teachers responded by saying that they had thought of doing that but *if they did it with one child other children would want similar treatment.*

SBS: It is my impression that the rest of the class recognizes that Jimmy is different than they are. They seem fully to recognize that he is the only one who behaves in this way. What is your impression?

Teacher: I am sure that's true. In fact some of them have asked why Jimmy cries. And some of them try to soothe him.

SBS: But what if you were to do as I suggest and other children then ask for the same treatment—and I have no doubt that many of them would like the same treatment from you. How might you handle it?

Teacher: That's what I am afraid of—I don't know.

SBS: Well, one thing you could do is to tell the class that when anybody feels and acts like Jimmy, and that means they are unhappy and need help, you would do for them what you do for Jimmy. Do you think that if you took this up with the class, they would not understand what you were saying or how you expect them to cooperate? You seem to feel that they would take—they want to take—advantage of you.

Teacher: That's not true. I am sure they would understand. Maybe there's one who would put on an act!

SBS: You mean that you think the children are perceptive, that they would understand, and they would abide by the responsibility you are implicitly placing on them?

Teacher: I guess so.

SBS: But that means, doesn't it, that you have to present the problem to them, your way of thinking about it, your questions and hesitations, and solicit their thoughts both about what ought to be and what their responsibility should be?

The point is that when one begins to think in this way one is involved in problems of group process; one is not only involved with a Jimmy, or untested assumptions about what a group of children are and can become, or imagined consequences, but with a process that is deliberately public, involves obligations and responsibilities, and deals with issues of interest and concern to all. It is not a simple process and requires a way of thinking to which teachers are not exposed. It requires one other thing that was well put by one teacher who, with a glint in her eyes, said: "You mean we should treat children the way *we* like to be treated?"

A final word about the prepotent responses to misbehavior. I have by now asked hundreds of teachers the following two questions. "How many times in the last month have you, aside from the report card, made it your business to communicate to parents that their child was not doing well, or he was misbehaving, or one or another kind of problem?" I never kept an accurate count but I would guess that 25 percent of the teachers indicated that they had gone out of their way to contact parents about a child's problem. The second question was, "How many times in the last month have you, aside from the report card, made it your business to communicate to parents that their child was doing well, or very well, or very much better than previously?" At most, 1 percent of the teachers indicated that they had initiated such a contact.

The Goals of Change in the Classroom

One does not have to document the statement that there are many people, both from within and without schools, who feel that the quality of life and learning in the classroom needs to be changed. The goals of change vary in their scope and phraseology, for example, the classroom should be more child centered, it should be more democratically organized and run, it should be more relevant to the world that children do and will live in, teachers should be more creative, and so on. A basic assumption in these statements of virtue is that the teacher will be the agent of change; the teacher will possess that way of thinking, as well as appropriately derived procedures and tactics, that will bring about the desired kind of classroom life. It is rare, indeed, to find in these discussions serious consideration of the consequences of this basic assumption for the change process. That is to say, there is a remarkable blindness to the fact that one is confronted with the extremely difficult problem of how one changes how people think. This is all the more strange when one recognizes that underlying the different criticisms of classroom life is the more basic criticism that one does not agree with how the modal teacher thinks.

The more I have read about and personally observed efforts to introduce change in the classroom the more clear several things have become. First, those who attempt to introduce a change rarely, if ever, begin the process by being clear as to where the teachers *are*, that is, how and why they think as they do. In short, they are guilty of the very criticism they make of teachers: *not being sensitive to what and how and why children think as they do.* As a result, teachers react in much the same way that many children do and that is with the feeling they are both wrong and stupid.[17] Second, those who attempt to introduce a change seem unaware that they are asking teachers to unlearn and learn. Third, if there is any one principle common to efforts at change, it is that one effects change by *telling* people what is the "right" way to act and think. *Here, too, those who want change do exactly that for which they criticize teachers.*

The main purpose of this [piece] has been to obtain glimpses of how the modal teacher thinks and how this determines, in large part, life in the classroom. Put in another way: the overt regularities that can be discerned in the classroom reflect covert principles and theories. If we wish to change the overt regularities, we have as our first task to become clear about the covert principles and theories: those assumptions and conceptions that are so overlearned that one no longer questions or thinks about them. They are "second nature," so to speak. If these assumptions and conceptions remain unverbalized and unquestioned, which is to say that thinking does not change, the likelihood that any of the overt regularities one wants to change will in fact change is drastically reduced. It would all be so simple if one could legislate changes in thinking.

It is likely that some readers will use the contents of this [piece] as grist for their internal mill of prejudice and snobbery. It is not difficult, if one is so disposed, to feel superior to teachers—and many university critics (and others) are so disposed. This would not be worthy of comment were it not for two facts: many university critics spearhead the change process, and, as anyone familiar with the history of anthropology knows, the feeling of superiority ("bringing culture to the primitives") is lethal for the process of understanding and change.

My former colleague, Dr. Murray Levine, developed a concept on the basis of his intensive work with teachers in inner-city schools.

THE CHILD COMES BY HIS PROBLEM HONESTLY

From the point of view of the teacher who is concerned about teaching a large group of children any child who presents special difficulties is a nuisance. As long as education is defined in terms of the preparation and presentation of material to children, the teacher's first inclination, when faced with a difficult child, is to experience the child as trouble. Finding her own efforts frustrated or finding that she must divide her attention in more ways than she feels capable of doing, the teacher frequently feels angered and resentful of a child who demands something different by virtue of his behavior. She may also feel anxious because her image of herself as a competent professional person is threatened. Although we are taught that human behavior stems from sufficient causes, in the classroom situation the teacher is not always able or prepared to seek causes. Understandably, from her viewpoint, the child is at fault for acting as he does, and it is her feeling that both she and the child would be better off if the child were away from her. Sometimes the consultant can serve an important function by helping the teacher to see that the problem has a background. When the teacher sees that a child does come by his problems honestly, so to speak, her tolerance for the problem and her willingness to make the effort to work with the child are sometimes increased.[18]

Dr. Levine gives case examples of how the thinking and actions of teachers changed in relation to certain children once they understood that indeed they come by their problems honestly, which is another way of saying that the teacher understood the child in *his* terms and life experience. If we believe teachers have problems, and they do, we will not get very far in helping them if we do not understand that they come by their problems quite honestly.

Notes

1. This conclusion is similar to that made by Jules Henry, *Culture against Man* (New York: Random House, 1963), based on his observations of life in the suburban classroom. Henry is one of the very few anthropologists who has directly studied the classroom. His description and discussion of life in the classroom are illuminating and provocative. Given emphasis in anthropology on foreign and so-called primitive cultures, it is not surprising that this important discipline has not focused on the classroom in our society (e.g., *Education and Culture,* ed. G. D. Spindler (New York: Holt, Rinehart and Winston, 1963).

2. The constitutional issues, as well as others to be raised in this [piece] , could be regarded as relevant to, or subsumed under, a theory of instruction. This would be a matter of indifference to me were it not that theories of instruction do not deal with constitutional issues but rather focus on the cognitive characteristics of the individual child, and on how these characteristics develop and could be taken account of in curriculum building. As often as not the theory talks about *a* child, and not a child in a group of children. Any theory of instruction that does not confront the reality that the teacher does not instruct *a* child but a group of children is not worth very much, to teachers at least. Even where the teacher intends to instruct a particular child, it takes place psychologically (for the child, teacher, and the other children) in the context of being part of a larger group and set of relationships. I quite agree with R. M. Jones's critique in *Fantasy and Feeling in Education* (New York: New York University Press, 1968) of J. S. Bruner's theory of instruction *(Toward a Theory of Instruction* [Cambridge, Mass.: Harvard University Press, 1966]), that is, his overemphasis on cognitive skills and

curricular skills and underemphasis on the affective. Jones comes close to including the constitutional question in his theory of instruction but it is far from as explicit as I think will be found to be necessary. This may be because Jones, in reacting to Bruner's overemphasis on the cognitive side, gets riveted on the expression of the affective side, and what tends to get sidetracked are the constitutional arrangements between teacher and class that maximize such expression. Depending as Jones does on Freud's and Erikson's conceptions about individual development, he cannot develop what is needed: a truly social psychological theory of instruction. These objections aside, I consider Jones's book a distinct contribution.

3. S. Sarason *et al.*, *Anxiety in Elementary School Children* (New York: John Wiley, 1960).

4. M. Wertheimer, *Productive Thinking* (New York: Harper and Row, 1945).

5. One of the several justifications for the development of the new math was to counteract the kinds of things Wertheimer and others have described. That is to say, one wanted children to grasp the idea that there were different ways one could use and think about the world of numbers. As we pointed out [previously]. the new math is taught in much the same ways as the old math. It could not be otherwise if for no other reason than those who pushed for the change seemed unaware that the theories of learning and thinking that guide teachers, in addition to the constitutional issues discussed earlier, do not permit the processes of thinking to be an object of inquiry in the classroom.

6. E. C. Susskind, "Questioning and Curiosity in the Elementary School Classroom," doctoral dissertation, Yale University, 1969.

7. Following the completion of this [piece], Fuchs's *Teachers Talk* (Garden City, N. Y.: Anchor Books, 1969) was published. Most of Dr. Fuchs's book consists of excerpts from journals kept by fourteen new teachers during the first semester of the classroom in city schools. These excerpts constitute compelling confirmation of many points I have made [here]. My favorite excerpt (because of the importance I place on constitutional issues) is from a teacher's report of the first day of school: "Then I established class routines: how we would put away our clothing; how we would get our clothing; raising your hand when you have something to say, not calling out; not talking when I'm talking; not talking when I haven't given permission to talk; not talking when you are doing something. I told them that we would have free time for talking. Then we discussed fire drills. what we would do and how we would line up, and our behavior in the hall and in the yard. I also covered supplies, the things that I requested that they bring in, and any problems. I complimented them on how they were dressed and how I would like them to come to school from now on, dressed neatly and clean; we discussed routines at home, the time we go to bed at night, how we take our bath, what happens when you get up in the morning. We discussed why breakfast is called breakfast and why we eat breakfast. Before we knew it the whole morning had gone and it had been a very good morning." The book is a storehouse of accounts of life in the classroom and school.

8. A. Schwebel, "Physical and Social Distancing in Teacher-Pupil Relationship," doctoral dissertation, Yale University, 1969.

9. *Ibid.*

10. Phillip Booth, *New York Times Book Review*, June 22, 1969.

11. D. W. Taylor, "Education for Research in Psychology," *American Psychologist,* 14 (April 1959), 167-179; J. D. Watson, *The Double Helix* (New York: Atheneum Publishers, 1968).

12. S. Sarason, K. Davidson, and B. Blatt, *The Preparation of Teachers: An Unstudied Problem in Education* (New York: John Wiley, 1962).

13. The experiences I shall be relating here are based on those contacts with teachers who asked to see me about a misbehaving child. In almost all classrooms there is at least one child who is a chronic misbehaver, although teachers vary markedly in seeking help with these children. The frequency of such children is quite high in inner-city schools where I have spent most of my time, and it was my experiences in these schools that forcibly brought to my attention the significance of the prepotent response to misbehavior.

14. I must emphasize to the reader that this is a paraphrase and has to be viewed in the context of a relationship of weeks with this teacher in his classroom. What I presented [here] was not for the purposes of describing a procedure but, simply, a way of thinking.

15. The work of Kounin, Gump, and their colleagues (P. V. Gump and J. S. Kounin, "Issues Raised by Ecological and 'Classical' Research Efforts," paper read at the meeting of the Society for Research in Child Development, 1959; J. S. Kounin, P. V. Gump, and J. J. Ryan, "Explorations in Classroom Management," *Journal of Teacher Education*, 12 [No. 4, 1961], 235-246; J. S. Kounin, W. V. Friesen, and A. E. Norton, "Managing Emotionally Disturbed Children in Regular Classrooms," *Journal of Educational Psychology*, 57 [No. 1, 1966], 1-13; J. S. Kounin, "Observation and Analysis of Classroom Management," paper read at meeting of the American Educational Research Association, 1967), based on their research on the classroom management of deviant behavior, represents what I consider to be a productive and relevant approach to a theory of instruction more so than the efforts of Bruner and Jones [see n. 2, above]. Kounin ("Observation and Analysis of Classroom Management") has put it well: "the management of behavior in classrooms is not a function of the techniques of directly controlling behavior as such—that is, discipline or desist style. Rather, it is a function of the techniques of creating an effective classroom ecology. Nor is it a simple issue of admonishing teachers that 'prevention is better than cure,' or 'create rapport,' or 'make it interesting.' Nor is it an evasive preoccupation with 'personality' or the listing of boy scout type characteristics. Nor is it a simple extrapolation from other adult-child relationships—whether these be parents or professional psychotherapists. Nor is it solely a matter of understanding and knowing how to handle an individual child to the exclusion of the group. Rather, the business of running a classroom is a complicated technology having to do with developing a nonsatiating learning program, initiating and maintaining group and individual movement, aiming teacher actions at appropriate targets, and still others yet to be determined. And may I add my belief in the potential value of receptive, naturalistic ecological researches in arriving at a knowledge of what these dimensions are or might be."

16. This problem rarely was presented to me in suburban schools. It was a very frequent problem in inner-city schools.

17. J. Holt, *How Children Fail* (New York: Pitman Publishing Corp., 1964).

18. S. B. Sarason *et al.*, *Psychology in Community Settings* (New York: John Wiley, 1966).

Toward an Ecology of Student Development

Donald H. Blocher

The term *developmental* in regard to psychological services such as counseling and psychotherapy has become very prominent in recent years.[1] One probable reason for this emerging view is the relative disenchantment of the helping professions with models of diagnosis, treatment, and delivery of services based on psychopathology and medicine.

Several basic concerns underlie this disenchantment. For many years we have been aware of the notorious unreliability of traditional psychiatric diagnoses[2] and their uselessness in prescribing differential treatments.[3] We have also slowly come to recognize that much of what we call "abnormal behavior" or "mental illness" is an artifact of our imperfect social organization.[4] Indeed, we have become aware that abnormal behavior is in some senses merely a social role that conforms to a set of expectations imposed on its victims.[5]

In the face of these concerns, our psychology and the professions that it undergirds have steadily moved away from their traditional preoccupation with the abnormal and the bizarre and toward a greater interest in human effectiveness.[6] White[7] perhaps best described this newer focus of psychology when he called it "the study of lives."

Education has rather obviously been a principal beneficiary of this newer approach. In education we necessarily talk a great deal about human development, indeed, educational institutions are established by the society to help ensure that its children and youth will grow and develop in valued directions and reach full adulthood and humanity.

As educators, we need to use developmental concepts as more than mere rallying cries and slogans. Very often we are decidedly unclear about the basic relationships between a science of human development and our educational practices. Developmental psychology itself has traditionally been much more descriptive than prescriptive. It has primarily offered its students methods of observation instead of goals or

Reprinted, with permission, from *Personnel and Guidance Journal,* 52 (No. 6, 1974), 361-365. © 1974 American Personnel and Guidance Association.

techniques of intervention. Indeed, many people who are rather super-ficially enamored with the developmental language have tended to assume a kind of naive Rousseauian stance that implies that developmental processes simply unfold like some exotic flower and that our principal function as educators is to stand aside in some posture of benign non-interference while appreciating the marvels of human growth potentials.

Actually, of course, we are accumulating more evidence each day that developmental processes do not just happen but rather must be purpose-fully triggered and carefully nurtured by the environment if full potential for growth is to be reached.

Two rather striking illustrations of this premise can be found in the de-velopmental literature. Kohlberg's line of research on moral development[8] indicates that the majority of our population suffers permanent develop-mental arrest at Level Three of his six-stage developmental hierarchy. This fact undoubtedly has major negative consequences for individuals as well as society. The Berkeley longitudinal growth studies similarly suggested that only a small percentage of human beings maintain intel-lectual growth or stability throughout the life span, while the majority suffer developmental arrest in the midteens, a life span of intellectual de-terioration looming ahead of them from that point.[9]

In light of our present knowledge it seems clear that, as educators, we must be concerned with an ecology of human development. That is, we must not only appreciate the growth potentials that reside in our students, but we must actively study and nurture an optimal interaction between the growing child or adolescent and his or her learning environments, rep-resented by family, school, and community.

Developmental Frameworks

Two kinds of traditional developmental frameworks offer us the con-ceptual foundations on which to build an ecological approach to education. The frameworks can provide us with sets of guidelines for defining healthy and relevant educational processes and provide direction for eventually evaluating the effects of learning environments on the growth of students.

The first kind of general framework is chronological. This type is well represented by Erikson's "Eight Stages of Man."[10] Erikson has traced normal human development from infancy to old age through eight well-defined life stages. At each stage he has posited a central developmental task that must be accomplished if the growing person is to continue suc-cessfully to the next stage, with its correspondingly more complex and dif-ficult demands. The author has elaborated elsewhere[11] on Erikson's schema to formulate a developmental chronology that not only outlines a sequence of life stages and developmental tasks but also specifies a corresponding set of social roles and coping behaviors that assist in defining levels of effectiveness in present development to help prepare for development in subsequent stages.

Chronological frameworks themselves, however, are insufficient to conceptualize many developmental problems. In order to focus sharply on an ecological approach, we must also utilize hierarchical frameworks. The best known of these is Maslow's steps toward self-actualization.[12] Others include Kohlberg's moral development schema cited earlier and Loevinger's ego development model.[13]

Hierarchical fromeworks are essential because they are directional and define outcomes or goals around which interventions can be evaluated. Through these frameworks we can examine critically the quality of transactions that represent the individual's interaction with his or her learning environments. Through examining this interaction we can assess the kind of ecological balance that exists for any growing individual in a learning environment. Here Heisler's concept of "dynamic equilibrium"[14] is extremely useful. She conceptualized growth as a function of a dynamic equilibrium between the needs and capacities of the individual and the levels of stress and stimulation in the environment. When these levels are far above the individual's capacity, or "readiness," to cope, the individual withdraws—and precious opportunities for learning and growth are lost. When the levels of stimulation in the environment are below the individual's capacity, the rate of development is slowed because of the lack of challenge and opportunity. One of the primary responsibilities of the educational system, then, is to create the dynamic equilibrium, or "ecological balance," between the student and his or her environment that will allow maximum growth to occur.

An Ecological Model

Let us now take these frameworks and combine them to develop a concrete example. The elementary school years are, according to Erikson, the life stage in which the central developmental task is what Erikson terms "Industry vs. Inferiority." This is the period in which the child wants and needs to learn how to do and make things with others. In learning to accept instruction and to win recognition by producing, the child opens the way for the development of work enjoyment. The prime danger to development in this period is the formation of a sense of inadequacy and inferiority in a child who does not receive recognition for his or her efforts.

Let us now superimpose on the Erikson framework Maslow's hierarchy of needs. Maslow points out that in order to move toward the highest level of human growth and development, which he chooses to call "self-actualization," the individual must first satisfy a set of lower level needs. These needs, which he classified as physiological, safety, love, and esteem needs, give rise to "deficit" motivations; that is, they must be satisfied before positive motivations toward self-fulfillment or self-actualization are released.

In terms of our elementary school child seeking to develop industry and to avoid inferiority, we can check off the list of psychological nutrients that must exist in the environment in order to permit the kind of ecological balance, or dynamic equilibrium, that will be most conducive to growth. Obviously, the child must be able to satisfy basic physiological and safety needs. The child's environment must be dependable and stable enough to provide for these. The really problematical elements in the environment of most middle-class children are those that deal with the needs for love and esteem.

It is at this point that the Erikson and Maslow frameworks so neatly coincide to suggest a complete ecological system. The basic transaction through which growth and development occur in the elementary school years is the interaction between the child's industry, or what White[15] calls "competence," and the environment's capacity to provide love and, by providing love, foster the growth of self-esteem.

In the light of this dual framework, let us examine the ecological system represented by the elementary school classroom. This classroom represents an environment in which the growing child will spend about one-third of his or her waking hours for the formative periods or life stages that we call middle and later childhood. For about a thousand hours a year for more than six years this environment will determine the transactions that govern the development of the child.

In analyzing this ecological system we can look at three basic subsystems. The first we may call the "opportunity structure" of the classroom. The opportunity structure is represented essentially by the set of tasks, problems, or situations through which the child is able to attempt to exert mastery or control. An arithmetic problem, a puzzle, a spelling word, or a class office (such as president) all represent parts of the opportunity structure. The nature of the opportunity structure largely determines the level of stimulation in the environments. That level of stimulation is measurable largely in terms of four elements: novelty, intensity, complexity, and ambiguity. As these elements increase in magnitude, they raise the level of stimulation to the point where it may become stressful to particular individuals in the environment. As such individuals experience stress, they tend to reduce it by physical or psychological withdrawal from the environment. For a classroom environment to offer an ecological balance, or dynamic equilibrium, to twenty or thirty children differing considerably in their readiness to cope with stimulation, the classroom environment will obviously need to offer what can be termed a *broad-band opportunity structure.*

The second classroom subsystem can be termed the "support structure." The support structure is essentially the set of environmental resources available to students for coping with stress. Basically, the support structure determines the degree to which the student can manage the stress-producing elements of novelty, intensity, complexity, and ambiguity. Two kinds of resources are built into the support structure. These are the affective, or relationship, resources and the cognitive structures available. Relationship networks that touch the student allow stress reduction to occur through the operation of factors of warmth, empathy, acceptance, and involvement of others. In the presence of these relationship conditions, students are better able to manage and tolerate stressful situations. In addition to relationships, there are important cognitive structures that allow for improved coping with stress. These involve understanding, assessing, predicting, and labeling stress and stimulation factors. Such cognitive structures particularly help to reduce ambiguity and complexity. The elementary classroom, then, to maintain an ecological balance, must offer an affective and cognitive support structure to all youngsters.

The third and final classroom subsystem is the "reward structure." The reward structure determines the contingencies that intervene between effort expended and needs satisfied. The development of "industry," or "competence," is particularly dependent on a set of beliefs or attitudes that can be termed "effort-optimism." This is essentially a set or approach to a learning experience or opportunity for growth that yields a prediction that the expenditure of effort will in fact yield important need satisfactions. The key in the elementary school in terms of the reward system is to ensure the highest probability that effort expended will lead to increase in self-esteem. Any aspect of the environment that systematically interferes with that connection, whether it is an arbitrary grading system, a racist teacher, a destructively competitive peer group, or a random system of rewards, destroys the growth-sustaining ecological balance in the classroom learning environment.

Implications for Practice and Training

We have briefly examined a set of principles, propositions, and frameworks out of which a genuinely useful developmental approach to

education may emerge. We have restricted our illustration of this ecological approach to only one level and one setting: the elementary classroom.

For an ecology of student development to become fully viable as an
approach to education, a tremendous amount of research and conceptualization remains to be accomplished. Many of the promising approaches
to the accomplishment of this work are described [elsewhere]. Out of
these efforts may eventually come a new direction and a new focus for
student personnel work.

Perhaps our most immediate problem in beginning to implement
ecological models in education relates to training. If we are to create
learning environments of the kind described earlier—those which can
genuinely facilitate the development of students—our schools and colleges and the teachers, counselors, and administrators who operate them
will have to change significantly. The long-term answer to this challenge
is undoubtedly based in dramatic changes in the preparation of teachers
at all levels.

Most immediately, however, we need to prepare a nucleus of people
who can move directly into our schools as they now exist and operate
in training and consulting roles to facilitate constructive changes in school
learning environments. The most productive immediate approach seems
to be that of offering advanced graduate preparation to people who are
already in or who are about to enter leadership roles in schools and colleges. Such people may be functioning presently in teaching, administrative, counseling, or curriculum development positions.

Several basic assumptions can be specified at this time about training
programs for this purpose.

These programs should be at the doctoral level. They should prepare
people for key leadership positions.

Selections should be based heavily on demonstrated leadership ability
and practical competence as well as academic ability. Many of the traditional admissions criteria such as undergraduate grades and scholastic
aptitude test scores are useful only at the most preliminary screening
levels.

Traditional undergraduate psychology programs are not the major
sources of potential students in these programs. Students may come from
a wide variety of academic and professional backgrounds.

Programs should be competence based rather than content based.
Instructional systems need to be built that will integrate didactic, simulation, and practical experiences to produce a *thinking, feeling,* and
acting professional person.

Programs must be devised to prepare graduates within the same kinds of humane, growth-producing learning environments that they are expected to help create in their own professional practice.

Approaches to intervention must be devised that apply across wide ranges of populations and situations. We must move to a kind of systematic eclectic stance to draw on all sources of gain demonstrated to be effective in facilitating human development. We can no longer afford our academic tribalism, with its almost mystical commitment theories that claim much and prove little.[16]

The assumptions listed above imply tremendous challenges to our existing programs of teacher and counselor preparation. To meet these challenges new programs must be created and old ones modified or discarded. Probably the most urgent need for effective change agents now is in the training programs themselves.

We know that, on the whole, future educators will teach as they have been taught—not as they have been taught to teach. Our preparation programs need to do more than deplore present educational practices and piously exhort future educators to do better. Reform must begin with the people and the programs that prepare our educational leaders.

Notes

1. D. H. Blocher, *Developmental Counseling,* 2d ed. (New York: Ronald Press, 1974); B. I. Kell and J. M. Burow, *Developmental Counseling and Therapy* (Boston: Houghton Mifflin, 1970).

2. E. Zigler and L. Phillips, "Psychiatric Diagnosis and Symptomology," *Journal of Abnormal Social Psychology*, 63 (No. 1, 1961), 69-75.

3. H. J. Eysenck, "Classification and the Problem of Diagnosis," in *Handbook of Abnormal Psychology*, ed. *id.* (New York: Basic Books, 1961), 1-32.

4. T. Szasz, "The Myth of Mental Illness," *American Psychologist*, 15 (No. 2, 1960), 113-118.

5. E. Goffman, *Asylums* (New York: Doubleday, 1961).

6. D. H. Blocher, "Wanted: A Science of Human Effectiveness," *Personnel and Guidance Journal*, 44 (No. 7, 1966), 729-733.

7. *The Study of Lives*, ed. R. W. White (New York: Atherton Press, 1963).

8. L. Kohlberg, "Stage and Sequence: The Cognitive-Developmental Approach to Socialization," in *Handbook of Socialization Theory*, ed. D. Goslin (Chicago: Rand McNally, 1969), 347-480.

9. M. Bayley and M. Oden, "The Maintenance of Intellectual Ability in Gifted Adults," *Journal of Gerontology*, 10 (No. 1, 1955), 91-107.

10. E. H. Erikson, *Childhood and Society* (New York: W. W. Norton, 1950).

11. Blocher, *Developmental Counseling.*

12. A. Maslow, *Toward a Psychology of Being* (New York: Van Nostrand Reinhold, 1962).

13. J. Loevinger, *The Meaning and Measurement of Ego Development* (San Francisco: Jossey-Bass, 1970).

14. V. Heisler, "Toward a Process Model of Psychological Health," *Journal of Counseling Psychology*, 11 (No. 1, 1964), 59-62.

15. *The Study of Lives*, ed. White.

16. Blocher, *Developmental Counseling*; *id.* and R. S. Rapoza, "A Systematic Eclectic Model for Counseling-Consulting," *Elementary School Guidance and Counseling*, 7 (No. 2, 1972), 106-112.

A Democratic High School: Damn It, Your Feet Are Always in the Water

Ralph L. Mosher

[Nondemocratic government] is like a splendid ship, with all its sails set; it moves majestically on, then it hits a rock and sinks forever. Democracy is like a raft. It never sinks, but damn it, your feet are always in the water.
— D. W. Brogan

For the past two years I have been involved, as a consultant, in an experiment in student self-government in a small alternative high school in Brookline, Massachusetts. This is, essentially, an impressionistic account of the funny things that happen on the way to school democracy, or what Kohlberg terms Stage 5. I think that we also have enough experience now to make some considered, tempered statements about democracy in school. For example, like every constructive, substantial school reform, democratic governance is very hard to vitalize and sustain, and translating powerful political, educational, and psychological theory about democracy into human or institutional behavior and commitments is difficult, often frustrating, work. The Founding Fathers might very well reply: did anyone ever promise it would be otherwise? Everyone underestimates the difficulty of mobilizing people on behalf of higher ideals. But it is important to do so, on both ideological and evidentiary grounds.

This account of school democracy is presented in two parts. The first deals with the origins of our applied research and the critical issue

Reprinted, in a slightly different form, from Ralph L. Mosher, "A Democratic High School: Damn It, Your Feet Are Always in the Water," *Character Potential: A Record of Research*, 8 (No. 4, 1978), 196-217.

of defining school democracy. Kohlberg's conception of the "just community" school and, in particular, Dewey's ideas on democracy in education are examined carefully as definitional sources. The second section draws general conclusions regarding school democracy, in terms of both its promises and paradoxes, from our experience to date. Our applied study of school democracy, which is still in progress, continues to be rich in meaning.

Origins of School Democracy

Intoxicating and persuasive rhetoric has moved us to study ways in which high school students can learn about democracy directly by governing themselves. It is important to note that democracy in a school means more than self-government. Robert Hutchins contributed to our interest in the subject when he wrote:

Democracy is a system of government by which people rule and are ruled in turn for the good life of the whole. It is a system of self-government by the consent of the governed, who have consented, among other things, to majority rule . . . . The aim of any democracy must be the common good, which is that good which no member of the community would enjoy if he did not belong to the community . . . . The people of the United States are in fact defaulted citizens, with an indifference and even a hostility to government, politics and law that would have astounded . . . the Founding Fathers. Instead of being a citizen the American individual is a consumer, an object of propaganda and a statistical unit. In view of the condition of our education, our mass media and our political parties, the outlook for democracy, the free society and the political community seems dim . . . . The founding fathers meant us to learn . . . how to form a more perfect union, to establish justice, to insure domestic tranquility, to provide for the common defense, to promote the general welfare and to secure the blessings of liberty to ourselves and our posterity. They founded a political community; a community learning together to discover and achieve the common good, the elements of which they set forth, but did not elucidate, in the Preamble . . . . The Constitution is to be interpreted, therefore, as a charter of learning. We are to learn how to develop the seeds the fathers planted under the conditions of our own time . . . . What would be unconstitutional would be limitations or inhibitions on learning. Today freedom and justice demand that equality be applied to opportunities for each citizen to achieve his fullest possible development. This means equal educational opportunity. It also means access to the legal system, to the health system, to housing. The political community cannot be restored or maintained unless minorities and the poor are given that equality to which this community was originally dedicated . . . . We must revive, reconstruct and learn to operate the political community in the United States because the task we confront on our 200th anniversary is nothing less than the organization of the world political community.[1]

The gap between Hutchins' vision and my modest effort to assist one school to become democratic is sobering. Nonetheless, his imperatives make the case for learning democracy unequivocal. They cut like a January wind in New England to the political, constitutional, and moral case for revitalizing in each generation the "truths in which America was conceived." Powerful ideas, after all, are the only ones worth holding to.

Democratic Schooling and Students' Moral Development

A second impetus to my study of democracy in schools has been joint research with Lawrence Kohlberg on moral education. Kohlberg is best known for a theory of moral development that describes how our thinking concerning right and wrong evolves, what we ought to do, questions of value, and what our rights and obligations are. He has found that our moral reasoning becomes both intellectually more complex and morally more principled; that is, it "develops." There are, in this process, identifiable stages or characteristic ways of thinking morally; experience, not the calendar, causes this evolution to occur. One whole stage in Kohlberg's theory, Stage 5, describes the moral ideology underlying the Constitution and the democratic process: that all people are created equal; that they have certain inalienable rights—to be free, to own property, to achieve their fullest possible development; that people create community to secure these rights and to effect the greatest good for the greatest number; that they make and apply fair laws to extend these rights to all; that government is accountable to the people; that every citizen has an equal vote, voice, and mutual obligation in defining and managing the community. (It merits mentioning how critical a term "mutual obligation" is to the hard, frustrating work of sustaining the polis.)

Kohlberg's data suggest that Stage 5 moral reasoning is employed by only 20 percent of adult Americans and by few adolescents, although it can be understood, intuitively, by a larger proportion of people. If this is true, it may explain why the Equal Rights Amendment has yet to pass; why equality of opportunity or access to education, justice, medical care, and jobs is denied to so many people; why democracy is so difficult to establish and sustain; why the American revolution is unfinished. Kohlberg sees the problem partly in psychological terms: the moral and rational capacity for full democracy and justice is latent in human thought and must be stimulated by experience (by education and, in particular, by living in a community that is democratic and just). It is clear also that Kohlberg's essential preoccupation (and moral principle) is justice and that constitutional democracy is one procedural means by which it can be brought about. Kohlberg argues that the central objective of moral education is to promote justice in individuals and in human institutions. To do that requires a community where real moral issues of justice, rights, and obligations are decided by all. His own applied research has involved creating and studying such "just" communities in prison and school. The democratic school project described below is broadly influenced by Kohlberg's psychology. By intention, however, it does not conform to Kohlberg's exact method, organizational structure, or ideology of justice. There is no one definition or form of democracy or justice. It is especially important for people to be democratic according to self-selected general principles, rather than specific practices.

John Dewey: The Philosopher of Democracy

The philosophical roots of my efforts to democratize education lie in the writings of John Dewey. The discussion that follows is organized around two objectives. First, it is intended to help clarify what I mean by school or classroom democracy. My bias is that it is very difficult to innovate in schools (for example, to effect "moral education," "school democracy," or a "just community") without clear definitions of what is intended. Over time, however, an alternating cycle of hard thinking and carefully examined practice helps us understand something like school democracy in its full, applied complexity. But, to me, definitional clarity is critical, and for this I turned to Dewey. I looked also for the most profound definitions.

Second, the aspects of Dewey's thinking cited here were selected partly because they relate to problems in the realization of school democracy at the School-Within-A-School. Thus, our efforts have encountered at least the following hard questions: Is school democracy essentially student self-government? Is that all there is? Can self-government, in fact, be a substantial enough process to affect students? If school democracy is more than self-government, what more can it be? Is it possible for a group of students that is relatively homogeneous in terms of race, social class, or ethnicity to be democratic? To what extent is the individual in a democratic school free to ignore his school community, its rules, its governance, or its development? What claims may a democratic school fairly make on its members, and what obligations has a student in a democratic school? What purposes and processes uniquely characterize a democratic alternative school? It was with these very thorny and practical issues in mind that I read Dewey.

Democracy as Self-Government

In contrast to some of Dewey's other ideas, his conceptions of democracy are complex, but not obscure. He considered democracy, first, a political process. Most people would probably so construe it. Hutchins, for example, sees democracy as a system of self-government, while Dewey states: "Democracy is . . . a special political form, a method of conducting government, of making laws and carrying on governmental administration by means of popular suffrage and elected officers."[2] Dewey described political democracy in familiar terms: as a way to effect the will and the interests of the majority of the people where consent is freely given to the purposes and the rules by which the individual or the institution is to live. Agreement concerning the common purposes, rights, and obligations is embodied in a social contract; political procedures guarantee the individual a voice and a vote.

The Democratic Way of Life

Dewey was quick to stress that political procedures were means for realizing democracy as the truly human way of living. Democracy, he argued, is more than a form of government; it is primarily a way of living together. And the democratic community has two essential characteristics: its members consciously share numerous and varied interests, and the community has full and free interaction with other forms of social association, an "open door" to strangers. Thus, a democratic community (whether a classroom, a school, a New England village, or a nation-state) shares many common interests that require the individual member to consider the views, wishes, and claims of others relative to these common concerns. When the individual identifies and pursues such common interests with others, at least he hears conflicting opinions and claims and may come to consider them against some criterion such as the preferences of his friends, the interests of the neighborhood, the law, the interest and will of the majority, or a principle such as fairness. Taking the perspective of others into account begins to break down the barriers of class, ethnicity, race, or stereotyped points of view—things that obviously are antithetical to viewing individuals as equal in either a constitutional or a moral sense. The greater the diversity of people pursuing common interests, the more encompassing the individual's viewpoint may become.

Dewey, too, was interested in the relationship between the society (or the political process in which the individual lives) and what he learned from it. Thus, he recognized that we learn from novelty and that, the greater the differences among people we meet to achieve common ends, the more we are likely to learn. Nothing is so profoundly educative as to live in another culture. Democracy, ideally, would have us live with different people and cultures (the Irish Catholics of South Boston, the Jews of Skokie, the Chicanos of Los Angeles) within our broader community, but with whom we must work out tasks in common.

For the same reasons (such as role-taking opportunities and the decrease in stereotypes), Dewey argued that a democratic group will be characterized by full and free interactions with other social groups in the community-at-large (for example, young people, workers, blacks, and women).

The two points . . . by which to measure the worth of a form of social life are the extent in which the interests of a group are shared by all its members, and the fullness and freeness with which it interacts with other groups. An undesirable society . . . is one which internally and externally sets up barriers to free intercourse and communication of experience. A society which makes provision for participation in its good of all its members on equal terms and which secures flexible readjustment of its institutions through interaction of the different forms of associated life is in so far democratic.[3]

Two contemporary educators, Newmann and Oliver, have argued that

the most fundamental objective of education is the development of individual human dignity, or self-realization within community. The broadly stated objective can be specified in many ways, emphasizing either individualism or social association. However one defines dignity or fulfillment, the nature of the society within which it develops is critical . . . . Every educator . . . should be able, therefore, to explicate and clarify the particular conception of society or community upon which he justifies educational recommendations.[4]

For Dewey the answer is clear: democracy, with the characteristics identified above, is an ideal form of social association and, as well, an ideal education for self-realization. The evidence for this remarkable claim is interesting. Dewey simply said it was so and, then, offered moral and psychological arguments to support his contention. Scharf points to the lineage of support for the claim. "It has long been established that participation in democratically organized institutions is associated with rapid social development. Both Cooley (1916) and Mead (1933) suggested that democratic groups offer possibilities for interdependence and mutual sharing not found in authoritarian groups. Lewin (1954) suggests likewise that ideological change occurs more rapidly in democratic groups allowing for a shared sense of control and for the opportunities for dissent."[5]

For Dewey the individual and society are inextricable. The process of the individual's development is an enlargement of his social perspective and his social and moral commitments—a fundamental progression empirically validated by all contemporary psychological theories of development (such as those of Piaget, Kohlberg, and Loevinger). Kateb has argued the same point: "the process of self-realization is a process of continuous involvement with society."[6] Dewey's earlier and quainter statement was that "The cause of education . . . is one of development, focussing indeed in the growth of students, but to be conceived even in this connection as part of the larger development of society."[7]

Individual Freedom in a Democracy

Dewey was concerned that democracy, with its belief in legal and constitutional equality and the maximizing of individual liberty, might be understood as unbridled individualism: a hunting license and a twelve-month open season for doing one's own thing. Tocqueville had remarked much earlier that democracy fosters individualism and that individualism first saps the virtues of public life and ends in pure selfishness. Americans would be forced, he predicted, by the necessity of cooperating in the management of their free institutions and by their desire to exercise political rights into the habit of attending to the interests of the public. Unfettered freedom to be oneself and to do one's thing continues to have much appeal, however. And that is true not only for radical educators, whose passionate desire is to liberate mankind from culture with its patterns and authority, but also for certain faculty or students in the alternative high school in question, who do not see community as prior to the individual. But Dewey was clear that democracy is an interaction between society and selves:

The democratic idea of freedom is not the right of each individual to *do* as he pleases, even if it be qualified by adding "provided he does not interfere with the same freedom on the part of others" . . . the basic freedom is that of freedom of *mind* and of whatever degree of freedom of action and experience is necessary to produce freedom of intelligence. The modes of freedom guaranteed in the Bill of Rights are all of this nature: Freedom of belief and conscience, of expression of opinion, of assembly for discussion and conference, of the press as an organ of communication. They are guaranteed because without them individuals are not free to develop and society is deprived of what they might contribute.[8]

Democracy as an Acquired Taste

Dewey also knew that democracy, unlike the wheel, must be continually rediscovered in people's understanding and in the institutions they create. It is an idea and a process which, by definition, has to be reinvented through the hard thinking, practice, and majority consent of each group of people trying to be democratic. Thus a democratic school will be what its members decide is a democratic school, according to self-selected general principles. It is interesting to note the parallels between Dewey's thinking and Hutchins' observations, cited earlier, that "The Constitution is to be interpreted, therefore, as a charter of learning."

Dewey argued further that the reinvention of democracy in the individual's understanding and in our institutions must go beyond knowledge or information about "the anatomy of the government" (such as the federal and state constitutions and the names and duties of all of the officers) to understanding the "things that are done, that need to be done and how to do them."[9] Here he is saying that people need an understanding of democracy that permits them to *be* democratic. "If the classes in our schools asked, 'What would have to be done to give us genuine democratic government in our states, local communities and nation?' I think it is certainly true that a great many things had to be looked into and a great deal more knowledge obtained than is acquired as long as we simply take our democratic government as a fact and don't ask either how it is actively run or how it might be run."[10] Elsewhere Dewey says: "Schools in a democracy . . . must be willing to undertake whatever reorganization of studies, of methods of teaching, of administration, including that larger organization which concerns the relation of pupils and teachers to each other, and to the life of the community."[11] From this it seems evident that Dewey was prepared to go whatever distance was necessary to educate people both to understand democracy and to be democratic.

Given his recognition of the profoundly educative effect of the social groups and institutions in which the individual participates, it is not surprising that Dewey argued that democracy cannot be taught or understood in institutions (such as schools or families) that are nondemocratic. Neither old-fashioned civics classes, newer political science methodologies and theories (for example, systems analysis as propounded by Gillespie and Patrick[12]), nor student government can do more than caricature democracy in repressive institutions, such as that portrayed in Fredrick Wiseman's documentary, "High School." As Dewey said so pointedly, "Whether this educative process is carried on in a predominantly democratic or non-democratic way becomes, therefore, a question of transcendent importance not only for education itself but for its final effect upon all the interests and activities of a society that is committed to the democratic way of life."[13] The point is that, if we are serious about educating for democracy, we will have to begin to democratize classroom management, school governance, and the relations among administrators, teachers, and students—a task whose complexity may be exceeded only by its enduring significance.

Elements in the Democratic Creed

Dewey talked about two articles of faith that are fundamental for any democrat or democratic educator. They are also notably American in their optimism and their confidence in the further progress or evolution of the human personality. The first is that democracy requires a basic commitment to the reasonableness, the potential fairness, and the human frailties of each group trying to be democratic. "The foundation of democracy is faith in the capacities of human nature; faith in human intelligence and in the power of pooled and cooperative experience. It is not belief that these things are complete but that, if given a show, they will grow and be able to generate progressively the knowledge and wisdom needed to guide collective action."[14] The second is a belief in the equality of human beings. Dewey is careful to point out that this does not mean that all people are psychologically equal (in terms of intelligence, judgment, or character). They are, rather, legally, constitutionally, and morally equal. As individuals they are, as a matter of fact, markedly different in capacity and achievement, but, in terms of their rights and claims, they are equal. Their legal and constitutional rights are fundamental and uncompromisable in a democratic society, as is "the opportunity of every individual to develop to his full capacity."[15] It is significant that Hutchins, in analyzing the unfinished American revolution a generation later, makes the same point. "Today freedom and justice demand that equality be applied to opportunities for each citizen to achieve his fullest possible development."

Good Fences Do Not Make Good Democrats

Dewey made at least one other observation about democracy that is important for educators: if we are deprived, for whatever reason, of significant interaction with classes or groups of people different from ourselves (blacks, Chicanos, Jews, Orientals, Catholics, homosexuals), our opportunities for understanding them are minimized by that separation. Those who live in expensive homes in the planned, amenity-rich communities of Southern California are deprived in the same way that their Chicano gardeners are deprived. Neither realizes that talent, intelligence, character, and strength (as well as frailty) exist in all of us and are as common and characteristic as our blackness, our Jewishness, and our Protestant ethic. Thus, it is precisely our experiences with strangers that help us to see our common aspirations, goodness, and humanity and the essential respect that all of us, as individuals, deserve. In this sense, Dewey was saying that good fences do not make good neighbors, that unfamiliarity, not familiarity, breeds and sustains contempt between people.

Democratic Institutions and All-Around Growth

Dewey's most encompassing definition of school democracy is stated indelibly in the following excerpt:

All social institutions have a meaning, a purpose. That purpose is to set free and to develop the capacities of human individuals, without respect to race, sex, class or economic status . . . . The test of their value is the extent to which they educate every individual into the full stature of his possibility. Democracy has many meanings, but if it has a moral meaning, it is found in resolving that the supreme test of all political institutions and industrial arrangements shall be the contribution they make to the all-around growth of every member of society.[16]

It is important to stress what Dewey was saying: that schools are democratic to the extent that they contribute to the all-around growth of every student. Elsewhere Sprinthall and I have discussed Dewey's correlative and fundamental belief that the aim of education is the development of individuals to the utmost of their potentialities.[17] In arguing for the democratic administration of schools, he says: "All schools that pride themselves upon being up-to-date utilize methods of instruction that draw upon and utilize the life-experience of students and strive to individualize treatment of pupils. Whatever reasons hold for adopting this course with respect to the young certainly more strongly hold for teachers, since the latter are more mature and have more experience."[18] The reader will recall what Dewey said about teaching students the way to be democratic; his arguments concerning democracy as an ideal form for human relationships and as the optimal means for developing the human personality while living in a group; and the diminishing effects on all groups when one group is excluded from full participation in the democracy. The conclusion is inescapable: Dewey meant to create in schools the governance and the social, curricular, and instructional conditions that support children's full development. That is the ultimate criterion of a fully democratic school.

One can presume that Dewey felt, though he did not explicitly state, that children are at different points in their understanding and skill in democracy, just as their schools are at different stages of becoming democratic. Our present studies of the effects of democracy on children show, however, that students' understanding of democracy depends on their stage of cognitive, moral, and personal and social development. Students at Kohlberg's Stages 2 or 3 understand and appropriate the experience of democracy in their schools very differently from students at Stages 4, 4½, or 5. Further, it appears that schools or groups of teachers, students, and administrators trying to be democratic collectively understand and represent democracy in qualitatively different ways, and we should expect this to be so.

The evolution of democratic schools, from titular student government (the present norm), to self-governance, to communities offering equality

of access to the social, political, and educative conditions for every individual to develop to his full capacity, presumably will take as long to
realize as it will in the larger American community. Lipset and Schneider
have discussed how long the latter may take in an article entitled "America's Schizophrenia on Achieving Equality."[19] But it is important to recognize, as Dewey did (and for which modern developmental psychology
can offer certain plausible explanations), that this progression will not
occur in a day, a year, or a decade; that it will occur in individuals or
institutions in stages; and that Stage 2 and Stage 3 democratic schools
(and students) have integrity.

It is appropriate to conclude this section on the critical task of defining
school democracy by reiterating that much of what one needs to know
about democracy and education is to be found in Dewey's writings. In
addition, I suspect that teachers, administrators, students, and parents,
in trying to democratize their schools, or parts of them, will have to rediscover, through such experience, what Dewey, Kohlberg, or I may have
learned. As Dewey wrote forty years ago,

I can think of nothing so important in this country at present as a rethinking of . . .
democracy and its implications. Neither the rethinking nor the action it should
produce can be brought into being in a day or a year. The democratic idea itself
demands that the thinking and the activity proceed cooperatively. My utmost
hope will be fulfilled if anything I have said plays any part, however small, in
promoting cooperative inquiry and experimentation in this field of democratic
administration of our schools.[20]

Stage 5 Is Not Sufficient

This section provides a general summary of what was learned from a
modest effort during the years 1975-1977 about developing self-governance
in one alternative school, the School-Within-A-School in Brookline,
Massachusetts. A description of the very substantial progress of school
democracy in S.W.S. during 1977-78 is available elsewhere.[21]

Positive Aspects of the School-Within-A-School

First, it was discovered that these high school students can learn to
govern themselves. They can establish their own rules of order, make
reasoned arguments and proposals, and deliberate and legislate school
policy on a variety of complex and sensitive issues such as grading students, research on moral development, the appointment of new staff
members and a school coordinator, and the voting of mandatory town
meetings (student governance). Nor do they avoid difficult issues, although

they find it easier to deal with what they consider arbitrary school authority than to apply sanctions against irresponsibility by their peers. After two years of observing their weekly town meetings, I find it hard to say they govern themselves any less responsibly or democratically than do teachers, school committees, town meetings, or university faculties I have known. Though that may sound cynical, it is not intended to be so. These students practice self-government with more good humor, forgiveness of frailties (One student, rather generously, said to me: "I'm only fifteen; you're forty-five."), and lightheartedness than their elders. That may have something to do with the fact that they display little covetousness or abuse of authority. Self-government, it must be noted, is not a compelling interest to the majority of these students; its effects on their development, discussed below, are therefore restricted. The fact that many students are defaulted or indifferent citizens makes them no different, of course, from their parents. Hutchins has said precisely this: the average American is not an active citizen. To help rectify the situation, S.W.S. voted mandatory participation in town meetings for all its members in 1977-1978. But the disinterest of many students, over the first two years, in school democracy defined as self-government must be acknowledged.

Second, it seems valid to say that those students who participate in school democracy learn important parliamentary skills—chairing meetings, speaking to the point, taking other students' views into account—that they should be able to generalize in their later lives. We do not know, in fact, whether this happens. One can only hope that an appetite for democratic decision making and an attitude and understanding of its importance still persist. I strongly believe, however, that a case can be made that these students are learning, in Dewey's terms, to understand about self-government "the things that are done, that need to be done, and how to do them." And I think most objective observers would agree that the students not only become skillful parliamentarians but that they can apply the practical utility of such training to becoming effective citizens.

Third, there is preliminary evidence that children and adolescents who participate in democratic (self-governing) classrooms or alternative schools show significant gains in their measured moral reasoning.[22] Such gains approach a half-stage increase in moral reasoning, roughly double the gain achieved in most moral education courses within the existing curriculum. (See Table 12-1.) Much more comprehensive data to be collected longitudinally over the next two years on students at the School-Within-A-School, the Cluster School in Cambridge, Massachusetts, and the Civic Education units in Pittsburgh, Pennsylvania, will clarify these

Table 12-1

Change data across one year for ten students in the School-Within-A-School in Brookline, Massachusetts, 1977-78

Student grade level	Year in School-Within-A-School	1977 Data		1978 Data		Changes (1977-78)	
		Stage score	MMS	Stage score	MMS	Stage score	MMS
Tenth	1st(new)	3(2)	280	3(4)	325	+ ½	+45
Tenth	1st	3	300	3(4)	345	+ ⅓	+45
Eleventh	1st	3	300	4(3)	367	+ ⅔	+67
Eleventh	2nd	3(2)	262	3(4)	336	+ ½	+74
Eleventh	1st(new)	4(3)	379	3(4)	333	− ⅓	−46
Eleventh	2nd	4(3)	350	4(3)	369	000	+19
Eleventh	1st	3	300	4(3)	371	+ ⅔	+71
Eleventh	2nd	3	300	3(4)	320	+ ⅓	+20
Eleventh	1st(new)	3(4)	328	4	383	+ ½	+55
Eleventh	2nd	4	413	4	381	000	−32
COLUMN MEANS:			321		353	+ ⅓	+32
						Stage	MMS

Note: Stage Score = Measure of Moral Development (Kohlberg)
MMS = Moral Maturity Score (Kohlberg)

highly preliminary, but promising, data on the effects of a more democratic or just environment on moral and ego development. And the data will cover divergent groups of adolescents. An extension of development and research in Brookline into the effects of democratic classrooms on younger children similarly will help to clarify Rundle's pioneering study with fifth-grade students. There is, in addition, clinical evidence from the Cluster School that the incidence of stealing within the school has decreased significantly—to the point where students no longer steal from one another or from students in the larger school. This tangible change in their moral behavior has not extended to the street, however. The issue of whether changes in students' moral reasoning has consequences for their behavior in school and out is obviously of great theoretical and practical importance. Barrett states the issue well in relation to the School-Within-A-School.

From my observations of Town Meeting, I do believe those students who participate are benefiting from the discussions and will, in fact, progress in moral stage development . . . . However, what distresses me is that in their social interactions,

I'm not at all sure there is carry-over with regard to justice and fairness. There is a clique problem, a problem of exclusivity. I have not observed a great amount of cohesion, sensitivity, support and warmth exhibited in student relationships.[23]

Paradoxes of the School-Within-A-School

It should be stated at the outset that we need to avoid certain definitional mistakes in our research on school democracy. For example, it would be easy to equate studies of school democracy with those concerning the effects on students participating in the governance of alternative schools or classrooms. That may be as much or more than it is realistic, in the short run, to accomplish in most projects in school democracy. But all of us need to do our homework on John Dewey. If our understanding of the truly democratic school is that it is a community providing the political, social, and educative conditions supportive of the full development of every student, then we will need to conceptualize and create such schools. Self-government will be but one aspect of such schools. Moral development will be another aspect of these schools. It would be a mistake, however, to reduce school democracy to a means (albeit a sophisticated one) to stimulate the moral development of students. It is obvious that moral reasoning and behavior are critically missing in our present education of children and adolescents, but morality is not all there is to being human. It may not be that politics is character, as Pericles believed. Our "best" education has promoted idolatry of intellect.[24] Idolatry of character or an obsession with justice, "a creeping moral developmentalism," would be similarly reductionistic. We must hold a conception of a psychology and an education that promotes whole and full human development. There is also a danger that we may focus too exclusively on efforts to democratize the school and pay insufficient attention to opportunities for learning about and promoting democracy in other institutions in the community. While I accept the fact that educators should democratize schools first, Newmann's argument for education in democracy and social action in the community[25] is incontrovertible, as is Stanley's pioneering study of educating families to be democratic.[26]

The second paradox concerns what I believe are real constraints operating on democracy in schools. One constraint is that students understand and are democratic in qualitatively different ways, depending on their stage of development. If stage theories have any validity at all, it follows that these points of view (whether moral or personal) significantly affect one's understanding of self-government, democracy, school rules, students' rights and obligations, community, justice, and so forth. Further, most high school students tend to be somewhere between Stages 2 and 3 in Kohlberg's typology. Scharf[27] has illustrated the point in regard to students' different understanding of school rules and why they are essential. It is interesting that his illustration of Stage 4 reasoning ("rare in the schools we have observed") was drawn from an S.W.S. sophomore who was very active in the governance of the school: "In here it's important to enforce the rules so that everyone sees that they are respected. It's important to get everyone to come to town meeting so that the rules are seen as having real power. If people don't come they won't mean anything and it's better not to have them." This illustration underscores several points. In the first two years of the study, approximately one-quarter to one-third of the students at S.W.S. have given continuous leadership and commitment to school governance and the standing committees. They may be the students best able to understand and to state arguments about the complex moral and policy issues in governing the school and to see the importance of majority will and to tolerate the routine of management. Another one-quarter to one-third of the students were reasonably dutiful citizens (attended town meeting with some regularity, but spoke infrequently). Nearly half the students, as noted, were marginal or nonparticipants. The relationship between participation in school governance and the student's stage of development is obviously a real issue in the vitality and the general applicability of such projects (as well as an empirical question on which we are now gathering data). And even when participation is mandatory, as it now is, we would expect the students' stage to delimit their ability both to understand democracy and to be democratic.

The second paradox regards the limitations of teachers. Most teachers are assumed to be at the conventional level of moral reasoning (Stages 3 and 4)—approximately a stage higher than high school students. This means that some of their thinking incorporates Stage 5; thus, they see, for example, the need for the will of the majority and for consent freely given by all members of a community to the policies that govern their institutional life. Many teachers are, of course, genuinely attracted to the rhetoric and practice of democracy. But a significant part of their thinking concerns authority, maintaining rules, discipline, the order of the classroom (even if the issue becomes jealousness in defense of a new order or disagreements as to who possesses the true gospel of the just community). The concept of a school where teachers know and care about one another, where the emphasis is on the quality of their relationships, may also figure prominently in the thinking of many teachers and counselors, for whom community is more important than democracy or justice. I do not disagree with this conception of community. I simply suggest its immanence, predictability, and appropriateness because of the stage of the teachers in relation to that of the students. Finally, "the free schoolers"—those teachers whose thinking reflects the passionate desire to liberate mankind from culture with its patterns and authority and who celebrate the individual and his freedom from the school and from any community obligations—are ambivalent about the obligations a democratic school requires of students for the common good.

The foregoing means that not all, perhaps not even a majority, of teachers will be comfortable with school democracy or that they will have differing conceptions of it. All projects to date have encountered this issue: "Two of the teachers had marked trouble dealing with a more democratic classroom than they were accustomed to. Hence, they vacillated between permitting too much freedom and reverting to directive teaching and strict, teacher-enforced discipline. Both of these teachers had decided by the end of the first semester that they did not wish to return to the project the following year.[28] This observation underscores the importance of the selection and training of teachers for projects in school democracy.

An extension of the first two paradoxes is that groups of students and teachers will create qualitatively different democratic schools or just communities, depending on the predominant stage of moral and ego development. Some of the possible differences have already been alluded to. For example, I would expect a predominantly Stage 3 school to be much preoccupied with the students' social relationships with some, but by no means all, peers and with the teachers. Having and being with close friends and knowing teachers intimately—"a more personal education"—are important reasons for belonging. I would expect such students to be little troubled by the school's rules and the authority of teachers, both of which are seen as well intentioned and personalized. Students work very hard, academically or otherwise, to please and to be liked by teachers who know and care about them. Such students might be more likely to create a caring community and to expand the friendship group by increasing the number of students and faculty "who know and care about me" than to build a legislative, rule-maintaining, self-governing community. The other aspect of this predominant viewpoint is that the school might be divided into cliques that are, perhaps, allied with particular teachers and are to some degree exclusive of one another and certainly of outsiders. Self and peer group take precedence over the community as a whole; they constitute, in fact, one's community. Further, a student's popularity or attitude, rather than the rightness of his arguments or the objective "wrongness" of his behavior in school, become critical in the community's decision making. A student is loath to discipline friends or to bind them to obligations of the broader community because his social perspective and bond only extend to his immediate social group.

By contrast, students predominantly at Stage 4 understand that policy and rules are necessary for the school to exist as a community, that they protect the students' rights and freedoms and impartiality in discipline, that they have moral force and should be obeyed even if their friends, teachers, or parents never know. There is a recognition that if the school, through the town meeting, makes policy, it has to be respected. Otherwise both the rules and the process of making them are subverted. Thus, deliberating and making school policy and rules is a serious business, even when the content is insignificant. It is a critical process in identifying and legislating the common interests that bind the community. Students realize that it is better to have authority over themselves than to leave it to teachers (even trustworthy ones), and they know intuitively that being in authority (for example, as chairman of the town meeting or as a member of a standing committee) can be rewarding. The obverse side of this may be excessive debate, speechmaking, procedural rules, or legislation. This kind of procedural orgy can bore or frustrate many students or faculty. Peters has argued that the repetitiveness, tediousness, and inefficiency of such exercises in self-government are an inevitable and worthwhile price to pay because of the overall contribution they make to the students' education for democracy.[29]

It is to be hoped that these brief sketches of the ideological and practical differences in school democracy associated with two predominant stages make the desired point. Both ways of understanding and practicing democracy are likely to exist in experimental democratic high schools and classrooms; their relationship will be dialectical and will lead to development. Each ideology is an authentic expression of a complex idea. In interaction and common cause they move a school one step closer to democracy.

The fourth paradox—or problem—is the fact that schools are not now democratically organized or governed. This is a major and clear impediment to our efforts. Scharf states the problem effectively:

The increase in "comprehensive" schools over the past thirty years implies a size and organization which makes meaningful democracy improbable. Schools of 2,000 or more are simply too large to have effective student participation. The division of the academic day by periods and subjects prohibits the development of a sense of community likely to make democracy plausible or desirable. Similarly, the hierarchial model or management found in comprehensive schools makes student participation likely to appear as a threat to the principal's political control of the school[30]

This piece is not an anthology of all the constraints operating on school democracy. I have no doubt, however, what the major and most formidable obstacle is to all that this essay presages. It is the way in which public schools are presently managed—by professional "administrators" who set budgets, appoint and reward faculty, establish school regulations, administer discipline, and adjudicate students' rights. My sense, which is perhaps unfair, is that the rhetoric of school administration is Stage 4, while the actual management of schools is more characteristic of Stages 3, 2, and 1 in Kohlberg's typology[31] To identify a problem is always easier than to find its solution, but to recognize it is a crucial first step. And it has consistently been my experience that there are many people in schools (including headmasters, assistant superintendents, and superintendents) who are just as professionally prescient as I and are willing to try substantial, systematic changes.

From the practical viewpoint, we have a long way to go before we understand the complex consequences of and the constraints on experiments in school democracy, even on their present scale. Nor do we know how to vitalize representative school government, which is the predominant form of student government in the American high school. The question of the effective operational unit (the classroom, the alternative school, the house, the student council) within the existing school in which to experiment with democracy is open. My intuition is that the classroom is the most likely and practical place to promote democracy. That intuition is based on a number of facts: the size of the classroom permits individual participation and genuine common purposes; the classroom is the basic organizational unit of the school; and much of what happens in the classroom goes on behind closed doors and is thus protected from management. Further, there is encouraging information on elementary classrooms that are democratic.[32] Much work remains to be done, however, on the promise and the problems of democracy in the classroom.

Epilogue

Two points must be made in conclusion. The first is concerned with generating knowledge. I do not know whether the promise of school democracy, however it is defined, outweighs its problems. I do know that significant development in either individuals or institutions is not accomplished easily and that we need much more educational research before the answers become clear. I am unaware of any way to generate that knowledge except by more hard thinking and hard practice. Though experimental studies may be costly, their importance for democracy and their implications for education are incontrovertible. Our glass is sufficiently half full, in contrast to half empty, to warrant vigorous continuing study.

The last point is, for me, the most important. The aim of a democratic education is the full development of every individual's potential. It produces whole people. It is unfortunate that that term has become clichéd. Rationality, character, ego, social contribution, the aesthetic, a sound body, emotion, work, and soul are integral parts of the human being and his potential; they constitute the ninefold helix that is everyone's birthright. For a variety of reasons—a sufficiency or insufficiency of psychological theory about one or another of these interrelated strands of development, a division of labor, or the inability to keep a multivariable model of human growth in mind—we may choose to practice a reductionism in either our psychological research or our educational development. But I can see no moral justification for limiting our conception of, or educational provision for, human potential. We must persist in the effort to create the educational, social, and political conditions within and without our schools to support the full development of every person. Nor can we deny equal access to such an education, once it is practicable. That is the ultimate meaning of a democratic education.

Notes

1. Robert M. Hutchins, "The Unfinished Revolution: Is Democracy Possible?" *Boston Globe*, February 16, 1976.

2. John Dewey, *Problems of Men* (New York: Greenwood Press, 1968), 57.

3. *Id.*, *Democracy and Education* (New York: Free Press, 1968), 99.

4. Fred M. Newmann and Donald W. Oliver, "Education and Community," reprinted in *Curriculum and the Cultural Revolution*, ed. David E. Purpel and Maurice Belanger (Berkeley, Calif.: McCutchan Publishing Corp., 1972), 205.

5. Peter Scharf, "School Democracy: Promise and Paradox," in *Readings in Moral Education*, ed. *id.* (Minneapolis: Winston Press, 1977).

6. G. Kateb, "Utopia and the Good Life," *Daedalus*, 94 (Spring 1965), 456.

7. Dewey, *Problems of Men*, 69.

8. *Ibid.*, 61.

9. *Ibid.*, 50.

10. Ibid., 52.

11. *Ibid.*, 48.

12. Judith A. Gillespie and John J. Patrick, *Comparing Political Experiences* (Washington, D.C.: American Political Science Association, 1974).

13. Dewey, *Problems of Men*, 62-63.

14. *Ibid.*, 59.

15. *Ibid.*, 53.

16. John Dewey, *Reconstruction in Philosophy* (New York: New American Library, 1950), 147.

17. N. A. Sprinthall and R. L. Mosher, "A Developmental Curriculum for Secondary Schools: Need, Purpose, and Programs," in *Adolescents' Development and*

Education: A Janus Knot, ed. R. L. Mosher (Berkeley, Calif.: McCutchan Publishing Corp., 1979), Chapter 8.

18. Dewey, *Problems of Men*, 63-64.

19. Seymour Martin Lipset and William Schneider, "America's Schizophrenia on Achieving Equality," *Los Angeles Times*, July 31, 1977.

20. Dewey, *Problems of Men*, 66.

21. R. L. Mosher, *Democratic School and Classroom Research: A Report to the Danforth Foundation*, 1977-78 (Boston: Boston University, 1978).

22. Louis Rundle, "The Stimulation of Moral Development in the Elementary School . . .: A Fifth Grade Study," doctoral dissertation, Boston University, 1977; Elsa Wasserman, "The Development of an Alternative High School Based on Kohlberg's Just Community Approach to Education," doctoral dissertation, Boston University, 1977.

23. Diane Barnett, "The Just Community School Interaction Program: The School-Within-A-School, Brookline High School," unpublished paper, Boston University, 1977.

24. McGeorge Bundy, the former dean of Harvard College, writing in *Daedalus*, said: "I will assert that we were right on one absolutely vital point: we know what education was for, learning. The university is for learning—not for politics, not for growing up, not even for virtue . . . ." "Were Those the Days?" *Daedalus*, 99 (Summer 1970), 555.

25. Fred M. Newmann, *Education for Citizen Action: Challenge for Secondary Curriculum* (Berkeley, Calif.: McCutchan Publishing Corp., 1975).

26. Sheila Stanley, "A Curriculum to Affect the Moral Atmosphere of the Family and the Moral Development of Adolescents," doctoral dissertation, Boston University, 1976.

27. Scharf, "School Democracy."

28. Edwin Fenton, *The Pittsburgh Area Civic Education Project: A Report to the Danforth Foundation for the 1976-77 Fiscal Year* (Pittsburgh: Carnegie-Mellon University, 1977), 4.

29. Richard S. Peters, *Authority, Responsibility and Education* (London: George Allen and Unwin, 1973).

30. Scharf, "School Democracy."

31. For example, a handbook on students' rights distributed by the California State Board of Education identifies students' rights in the areas of corporal punishment, prayer in the classroom, sexual discrimination, and search and seizure of students' property. It is significant, however, that the handbook tells students they "must comply with the regulations, pursue the required course of study and submit to the authority of the teachers of the school." *Students' Rights and Responsibilities Handbook* (Sacramento: California State Department of Education, 1978), 2.

32. See Rundle, "The Stimulation of Moral Development in the Elementary School . . ."; D. Stuhr, "Moral Education with Children: An Examination of Related Studies," in *Value Development as the Aim of Education*, ed. N. A. Sprinthall and R. L. Mosher (Schenectady, N. Y.: Character Research Press, 1978), 41-52; Thomas Lickona, "Creating the Just Community with Children," *Theory Into Practice*, 16 (No. 2, 1977), 97-104.

13
The Last Word

The Bible allots each man threescore and ten years; books must end at 200,000 words. We will do that by attempting to answer three questions: Why is the concept of development so important in education and psychology? What are the key principles of developmental education? What do the critics say about this kind of education and its prospects?

Why Is Development Important?

First, why does the book argue so strongly that development is the most important aim of education? The reason is not simply that John Dewey said it was so. Nor is it nostalgia for a view that once had great force in American education. Like climate, the progressive ideology may go through cycles. Whether the author projects a developmental stage of his own onto the profession is moot. Loevinger says of the Autonomous person: "[He] sees himself and others as having motives that have developed as a result of past experiences. The interest in development thus represents a further complication of psychological causation. Self-fulfillment becomes a frequent goal, partly supplanting achievement."[1] Turning our psychology on our own motives can be informative rather than presumptuous.

At least five objective arguments may be made for development as the key aim of education. The first argument is a moral one. The development of individual human dignity and self-fulfillment is a moral principle basic in America. Any one of us, able to choose life's rules, almost certainly would select the opportunity for personal development as a condition and a right for ourselves and our children and, one would hope, for everyone else. Education for all-around adolescent growth is morally justified and required. It is the right of students and the obligation of teachers.

517

Second, development is a value for individuation in a democratic society because democracy respects and enhances the individual. It must be justified in contrast to other possible values of education: socialization in the knowledge, norms, and technology of American culture; literacy; learning to think like professional historians; vocationalism; citizenship. People, in the final analysis, are what matters; they are our most precious resource. Their well-being is the real measure of our political and social processes and our institutions. Thus, education must value, fundamentally, individuals and their realization.

The third argument relates to the second; development is a value, whether implicit or explicit, in many educational ideologies. Kohlberg and Mayer have suggested that cultural transmission and romantic and progressive schools are all metaphors for development.[2] Most teachers feel that education should contribute to the students' rationality, competence, and character, and they want to help adolescents come of age, acquire skills, get a better job, go to college, understand themselves, and think more deeply. Regardless of the fact that these are clichés, they all aim to benefit people. Educators obviously assert many other values. The purpose here is not to engage in oversimplification or reductionism of real differences between the teaching of Mendelian genetics, for example, and the moral analysis of DNA research. The concept that educators encourage individual growth, among other things, however, is not novel. A problem arises when greater priority is assigned to other objectives.

The fourth argument relates to the idea that the all-around development of the individual is a powerful prerequisite of and guarantor of a democratic society. Davidson found that the best antidote to racial and ethnic prejudice is the presence of Kohlberg's Stage 5 moral reasoning.[3] Chapter 12 suggested the difficulties in understanding and practicing school democracy experienced by adolescents at low stages of moral development. It seems logical, though it has not been empirically proven, that people at higher stages of development will be both more competent and more likely to contribute to a democratic, just, and humane society.

According to the fifth argument, we now have the psychology to understand and the education to enhance adolescent growth. In short, development as the aim of education is increasingly practicable.

Second, why does the book argue that modern developmental psychology presages so much for education? Rest has said that three ideas characterize developmental psychology.[4] One is structural organization. Development occurs primarily in our heads: our understanding of logical, physical, and social problems; our rights and obligations; our identity in the world; our bodies; our feelings; the meaning to us of work or career. Our insight into these things grows in complexity through experience with new problems, ways of thinking, and people. The change is orderly, and the key is in the increasingly comprehensive rules, criteria, and meanings we apply to these events in our lives. Thus, a common problem facing both psychologists and educators is to enhance the individual's ability to make decisions, to solve problems, and to think in more complex and principled ways, all of which have a cumulative effect on enriching the person's life.

Rest's second idea is developmental sequence; that is, our thinking grows through stages. Just as there are age and developmental periods in our lives (such as adolescence and old age) so, too, are there qualitatively different and evolving stages in our thinking. The developmental psychologist is engaged in analyzing human competence and its growth. For example, Piaget's stage of formal operations tells us what it means to be logical; Kohlberg's Stages 5 and 6 describe mature moral judgement. These step-by-step analyses of human development permit much more specific definitions of educational objectives than to be "self-actualized" or "a good citizen." They also enable educators to know which learnings contribute to development; to locate adolescents along a continuum of development; and to plan experiences to which the student will respond. Individualized instruction can be relatively precise if the course of development is defined and the student's level can be assessed.

Rest's third idea regarding developmental psychology is that the essential condition for the elaboration of human thinking is the presentation of experiences that stretch the individual's existing thought and set into motion a process of search and discovery for more adequate ways to organize his experience and actions. Much importance is attached to thoughtful interaction with things, problems, and people: with learning by doing; with changing our understanding by direct and examined experience of new problems and points of view. If that is not a theory for educational practice, it is difficult to imagine what would be.

Two other characteristics of developmental psychology make it especially pertinent for educators. First, it is a psychology that is totally concerned with the student. Its analyses of the growth of human competencies such as logic and morality and its description of stages result in an increasingly comprehensive map of adolescence. It describes comprehensively, and straightforwardly what is happening to teenagers and, in part, why they are as they are. The teenage phenomena reported by developmental psychologists fit with what teachers and parents experience day to day; their interpretations of adolescence make sense and can lead to more patience and sympathy for what adolescents are growing through (as should any genuine understanding).

Second, developmental psychology does not invoke demons. Adolescence is directly accessible in what teenagers think, say, and do; it is not described as Oedipus revisited or the shadow of an unconscious personality. Any holistic psychology of adolescence must include a description of its dark side—its times of turmoil and irrationality. For this reason Erikson was included in Part I, but so was Dupont. Developmental psychology sees adolescents as growing and mutable; as progressing to adult intellectuality, morality, and identity; and as capable of a higher order of human thought, affect, and action as of barbarism.

Human development is not a birthright. It can be slowed or stopped, and it is for many people. Experience and, therefore, education make a critical difference to growth. Developmental psychology, as much as any psychology (in contrast to psychoanalysis, which has had a major influence in interpreting this stage of life), contends that the human condition can be ameliorated; that schools, teachers, and education can add to human rationality, character, and competence. And the preliminary evidence of Part II of this book is that that psychological assumption can be realized— not easily, not definitively, but significantly. In short, developmental psychology accords to systematic experience a major influence in the construction of human personality and actively seeks a common cause with educators toward achieving that goal.

Caveats are clearly necessary. Some developmental psychologists (Rest and Loevinger among them) have argued that there is insufficient developmental knowledge for educational application. In an epistemological sense that will always be true. It is also a view that is partly purist, partly cautionary, and partly the luxury of the scholar who has no professional responsibility to educate children and no imperative of practice.

The concept of development is, of course, very broad, and it is difficult, in general, to oppose. It may not be as specific as teachers would like even when it is reduced to the cognitive, moral, ego, affective, and vocational dimensions presented in this book. There is also the problem of whether the pathways of development are so biased by culture as to be reliable. For example, if educators blindly assume that adolescents' patterns of development in *Captains Courageous*, in a Philadelphia street gang, or in Laguna Beach, California, are all the same, they could make profound mistakes. But Kohlberg has warned against the psychologist's fallacy. Further, educators have deep intuitive knowledge of adolescents; their crap detectors discover theories that do not fit that knowledge. And they are the ones who teach American adolescents. An uncritical acceptance or application of developmental psychology in education is unlikely under these conditions. The assertion of this book is that developmental psychology not only will stand the test of practice; it will strengthen it.

What Are the Principles of Developmental Education?

Developmental education is a new and fluid field. The extent to which it may transcend being simply another educational prefix ("confluent," "humanistic," "psychological," "open," "basic," and so forth) will depend in part on the enduring substance of its philosophical and psychological bases, in part on the curricular and teaching principles that follow.

The first principle is to know adolescents. We must know where they are developmentally, both as individuals and classes. For example, how concrete or how morally conventional is their thinking? Recognizing where a teenager is in terms of the particular things he needs to know, do, or value and adapting his education accordingly is the essence of individualizing learning and instruction. The second principle is to understand teenagers' growth and education in as complete and whole terms as psychology and practice can provide. They have no choice but to come of age on many dimensions at once. Our psychology and our education have to be as complex and as multidimensional as the reality of their lives. The third principle is to stimulate their growth. The aim of education is to promote maturity and to avoid arrested growth. Neither Rome nor maturity is conquered in a day or a year. Every person's journey toward maturity happens in steps; education helps the individual to keep trekking. Adolescence is not a time when the young person should delay his progress since it is a prime time for education. The fourth principle is not to define education for development as privatism or selfishness. It requires broad social participation, experiences, and commitments,

The fifth principle is to educate for all-around adolescent development. Adolescents should be challenged; they should encounter points of view, thinking, and experience that stretch their existing assumptions and ways of being and doing. Literature, films, history, and science, discussion, debate, and study of problems; diverse real life experiences, such as work, social service, community action, and participation in the governance of their schools—all are means to stimulate adolescent thinking and action. And the unexamined experience really is not worth having. Progressive education was criticized for providing so little for the mind. Developmental psychology and education argue for just the opposite: adolescent thinking, morality, identity, and experience need to be stimulated both Socratically and compassionately. At times, teachers should be a stage beyond their students. They should treat them as adults—as moral philosophers, as democrats and citizens, as psychologists, in short, as competent beings. People climb by looking and reaching above themselves.

Stimulating adolescents cognitively, morally, and personally should not be interpreted as simply teaching them more English, mathematics, history, science, and modern languages. The disciplines can contribute significantly to development. But the potential experiences to stimulate development are limited only by educators' creativeness and the evidence of their actual effect. The test of any experience involves asking how a course, a discipline, or a program of social service or action contributes to cognitive, moral, social, or ego development. The measurement tools of developmental psychology permit us to establish that with increasing confidence.

What ultimately counts are an enhanced ability to think about logical, moral, social, and personal problems, a growth of understanding and a greater competence to understand other people's thinking and feeling, to help children, to influence public affairs, to be democratic in their own schools, and so on. For example, education that helps the adolescent develop more complex intellectual and moral understandings of compromise and the ability to compromise in school or the family is more personally and socially enhancing than education that requires him to remember that Roger Sherman was principally responsible for the Great Compromise at Philadelphia. The former adds to human rationality, and character, and social competence; the latter fact leads nowhere.

Further, we need to provide adolescents a relatively continuous set of growth experiences. Morality cannot be taught in the second semester of the junior year. Some growth experiences, however, are better than none; indeed, the impact of the curricula described in Part II is impressive, given their brevity and their competition. The "delayed" developmental consequences of these experiences can be surprisingly potent. But provision for all-around adolescent growth is not a part-time vocation.

The principle is to create an educational program to advance adolescent development. This can be done in four steps: by hard thinking about adolescents and what one wants them to learn, do, and become; by making tentative decisions as to what the adolescents are to learn, do, and become (that is, by defining objectives); by developing and pilot teaching the curriculum or course (that is, by designing the experiences and carefully teaching and recording them); fourth, by evaluating the curriculum and teaching on the basis of actual tryouts with adolescents and modifying them accordingly.

What Do the Critics Say?

Our final comments have to do with what the critics of developmental education are saying. As a matter of fact, there have been few critics to date. That is our loss. It is not that the field has no shortcomings; rather, it is just now achieving visibility and impact. One should cherish a good critic with the same mixed feelings that one has about a good dentist. In this regard, Rest's critique[5] has been particularly valuable. He first comments that the extent to which these programs are based on developmental psychology is a complicated issue. The relationship is most evident in abstract discussions of the general aims of the program, of the appropriateness of the stages in regard to certain experiences, and of the rationale for the seminar and practice format in some of the courses.

In response, it is true that developmental psychology has been used in this field primarily as a topographical map of adolescence and as a justification for the general educational aims of growth and personal enhancement—which is not, by the way, an inconsequential use of developmental psychology. Developmental education has produced great interest throughout the country in curriculum design; this has occurred, for example, in Boston, Minneapolis, Pittsburgh, and Tacoma. Among these efforts have been studies on the developmental effects of counseling, courses in women's development, programs in moral education, and research on the impact of school and classroom democracy on adolescents' moral reasoning and social and political development. This is, in part, evidence of the remarkable energy that can be produced as a result of a paradigm shift, in this case, to developmental psychology and its educational application. It has also achieved the practical objective of getting the attention of educators and teachers through working examples whose relevance they are able to see. Another result is that developmental education has not been sufficiently tidied up. Replication studies, follow-up data, and detailed research studies of step-by-step curricula and teaching have not yet been generated. Newmann, by contrast, has been both less all encompassing in his statement of educational objectives and more rigorous in thinking them through fully in advance of applications. He is now beginning to test a coordinate practice for citizenship education. The point is that practice can take several epistemological and tactical roads. As courses in developmental education have become more systematic and consecutive, there has been an increasing articulation between what experiences are tried with adolescents and what the various theories suggest both about the developmental tasks of the stage and what experiences might contribute to growth.

Rest's second criticism is that the kind of developmental psychology necessary for these programs does not exist and that developmental psychology can at best be related to them in a piecemeal fashion. This is probably true—in a relative sense. One of the purposes of Part I of this book was to put together a more comprehensive anthology of developmental psychologies than has yet been available for psychologists and educators interested in professional applications. Educators may tend to press ahead where developmental psychologists fear to tread or are appropriately circumspect about the limits of what they know. There can be little doubt that educational application and practice, if not running ahead of developmental psychology, are at least running neck and neck with it. This is the reverse of the oft-heard complaint about how little use we make of what we know. New psychological knowledge about human development is not likely to be ignored as it emerges. Indeed, such knowledge is likely to be advanced more rapidly by pressure for educational use and common cause.

A third criticism made by Rest is that developmental educators do not derive guidance for the specific day-to-day activities of their programs from the developmental theories. This, too, is true. It is also the case that we should not expect to derive such specific day-to-day guidance as Rest, rather touchingly, suggests. The imagination and the craft of education, curriculum development, and teaching are important here. Identifying the curriculum and pedagogy optimally to enhance all-around adolescent growth is central to what we mean by developmental education. Developmental education is more than an identical twin to developmental psychology. But certainly the applied field will benefit greatly when theory approaches what Rest has suggested: "Potentially, however, the contribution that developmental research can make to program development would include the following: (1) psychological analysis of competence in a given domain; (2) step by step description of the development of the competencies; (3) assessment instruments for locating individuals on the courses of development; (4) characterization of the conditions for progressive structural change; and (5) models and instruments for analyzing the flow of events and interactions in an educational program."[6]

Conclusion

It should be clear from Part II of the book that substantial research on education for human development is under way. Though it is incomplete and fractionated, it is as promising and vital a movement as currently exists in American public education. It is true that such education puts a greater burden on our theory and measures of development than they currently can bear. Anything as profound as human intellectual, moral, and personal development should not be expected to yield to simple or immediate formulation, measurement, or stimulation. And the correlates of development in individual behavior and social outcomes have to be clarified. I believe, incidentally, that developmental education will contribute to our psychological understanding of the stages and characteristics of the human life cycle. But our most important contribution is that we are discovering ways to create an education for human development. My primary concern is further elaboration and validation of that education, and I believe that it will require, at minimum, a decade of work.

There is, of course, no guarantee that essential constituencies—teachers committed to their disciplines, school boards concerned with zero growth budgets, parents, or other policymaking groups—will agree that human development is the priority or proper aim of education. Indeed, there is probably less social support for this idea than was available to Dewey and the progressives. Are we, then, arguing an idea whose time has passed and whose "technology" has arrived? I do not presume to know. A common cause, rather than doctrinal dispute, between psychologists and those educators committed to individual self-realization within a democratic society is essential if we are serious about our constituency. Education for human actualization has no coherent lobby; it is ironic that dyslexia and other learning disabilities do. But I am optimistic that education to enhance human rationality and character is practicable. Further, it represents a way to move beyond Descartes's dictum to doubt everything.

Notes

1. J. Loevinger, *Ego Development* (San Francisco: Jossey-Bass, 1977), 23.

2. L. Kohlberg and R. Mayer, "Development as the Aim of Education," *Harvard Educational Review*, 42 (No. 4, 1972), 449-496.

3. F. H. Davidson, "Ability to Respect Persons Compared to Childhood Ethnic Prejudice," unpublished paper, Center for Moral Education and Research, Harvard Graduate School of Education, July 1975.

4. J. Rest, "Developmental Psychology as a Guide to Value Education: A Review of 'Kohlbergian' Programs," *Review of Educational Research*, 44 (No. 2, 1974), 241-259.

5. *Ibid.*, 246-257.

6. *Ibid.*, 256.